THE LIFE OF WILLIAM BLAKE

THE LIFE OF
WILLIAM BLAKE

BY

MONA WILSON

*Because he kept the Divine Vision
in time of trouble*

A NEW EDITION
EDITED BY

GEOFFREY KEYNES

OXFORD UNIVERSITY PRESS

LONDON   OXFORD   NEW YORK

1971

Oxford University Press

LONDON OXFORD NEW YORK

GLASGOW TORONTO MELBOURNE WELLINGTON CAPE TOWN

SALISBURY IBADAN NAIROBI DAR ES SALAAM LUSAKA ADDIS ABABA

BOMBAY CALCUTTA MADRAS KARACHI LAHORE DACCA

KUALA LUMPUR SINGAPORE HONG KONG TOKYO

Clothbound edition SBN 19 211707 6
Paperback edition SBN 19 281091 X

© *Oxford University Press* 1971

First published by the Nonesuch Press 1927; second
edition, with revisions and additional notes,
published by Rupert Hart-Davis Ltd 1948

This third edition, edited by Sir Geoffrey Keynes, published
simultaneously in clothbound form and as an Oxford
University Press paperback, by Oxford University Press,
London, 1971

*Printed in Great Britain by
Richard Clay (The Chaucer Press), Ltd
Bungay, Suffolk*

TO THE MEMORY OF

M.S.T. · H.S.W.

CONTENTS

EDITOR'S PREFACE

Mona Wilson's *Life of William Blake* was originally published by Sir Francis Meynell's Nonesuch Press in 1927 to range with my text of *Blake's Writings* which had appeared in 1925. A second edition with some revisions and additional notes by the author was published by Rupert Hart-Davis in a less sumptuous format in 1948. This has been out of print for many years and the Oxford University Press, wishing to preserve the book from extinction, have commissioned me to make the further revisions that have become necessary without changing its general character. Miss Wilson, a long-standing friend, though much older than I, had been stimulated to write her book, as she stated in her Preface, by the publication of my *Bibliography of Blake* in 1921 and of the approximately complete *Writings* four years later. I was delighted to give her every encouragement to do this and have always regarded her book as the most important biographical account of Blake to have appeared since the second edition of Gilchrist's *Life* in 1880. The new *Life* did not supersede Gilchrist's book, which will always be indispensable owing to the numerous primary sources available to him when he began to collect his material, but it did provide the improvements claimed by the author in her Preface. After a distinguished career as a civil servant, she was already a practised writer on literary matters and brought a highly cultivated mind to bear on Blake's life and writings.

Gilchrist had made little attempt to elucidate or summarize the symbolic works, and he was only just drawing clear of the general view that Blake was more than a little mad, finding it necessary to include a chapter headed, 'Mad or not Mad?'. Mona Wilson made quite clear from the start her belief that Blake, though having the eccentricities of genius, was perfectly sane and never wrote anything that did not make sense to himself. She provided a factually correct biography, as it seemed then, together with an intelligible account of his poetry and prose correlated with his output as an artist. A further revision of her text has necessitated some alteration of facts, but I have never, as editor, interfered with any expression of opinion or justifiable conjecture.

By far the most extensive alterations made in this edition are those affecting the presentation of notes and references. The notes, indicated in the text by signs, have been brought forward from the end of the book to the actual pages to which they refer, together with many additional notes, the authorship of which is denoted by the termination [Ed.]. The great majority of the references, numbered through each chapter and printed at the end of the book, are now keyed to recent authorities, the chief of which are my text of Blake's *Complete Writings* in the Oxford Standard Authors series (1966; reprinted with corrections 1969, 1971), and *Blake Records* (Oxford, 1969), accurately compiled by Professor G. E. Bentley, Jr., which largely eliminates the need to use a number of different primary sources. All the quotations from Blake's writings have been checked, and other references have, with very few exceptions, been verified and made more precise. This separation of substantive notes from over 700 references makes each category more accessible and more easily assimilated. Referring to one category by signs and the other by numbers seems better than the clumsy system previously used of keying them all, in an indigestible mass, to page numbers and non-existent line numbers.

Of the six appendixes included in the previous editions three have been omitted, leaving only the 'Extracts from Varley's *Zodiacal Physiognomy* and *Urania*' with Blake's horoscope, the one on 'Blake's Calligraphy', and the 'Extract from *Revue Britannique*', relating a false story of Blake's supposed insanity.

My task as editor has been a somewhat heavy one, though my method has, I trust, left the book unchanged in its general impact on the reader's consciousness. The author's sympathy with her subject and her understanding of his mind seem to me to take the presentation of Blake's life some way beyond the point at which Gilchrist left it. Much of the background has been admirably filled in more recently by books such as David Erdman's *Blake: Prophet against Empire*, and the new Blake scholarship has added enormously to the general understanding of his poetics and philosophy. Yet Mona Wilson's book as a biography for the general reader has, in my opinion, not yet been superseded.

1970   GEOFFREY KEYNES

PREFACE TO THE NONESUCH EDITION

The publication of Mr. Geoffrey Keynes's complete edition of *The Writings of William Blake* (Nonesuch Press, 1925) and the appearance of his *Bibliography*, printed by the Grolier Club of New York, have put at the disposal of a biographer material which was not available when Alexander Gilchrist wrote his *Life of William Blake*. The attempt has been made in this book to embody additional information and to examine by its light such of Gilchrist's statements as appear to be of doubtful accuracy. It would be impossible to give a true picture of Blake without some account of his symbolic writings, and equally impossible to deal with them adequately within the limits of a biography. The brief summaries of the symbolic books are intended not for students of Blake, but for the general reader who has no notion of their contents: they may serve also as a first aid to new readers of these books. Mr. S. Foster Damon's *William Blake: His Philosophy and Symbols* appeared soon after I began to write this book, and I have availed myself so freely of his interpretations that the references in the notes are by no means a sufficient acknowledgement of my debt to him. I have relied the more on his lucid exposition because the treatment of Blake's symbolism by Messrs. Ellis and Yeats in *The Works of William Blake, Poetic, Symbolic, and Critical*, which had hitherto held the field and may still be preferred by some readers, was often more obscure to me than Blake's own text. *William Blake's Prophetic Writings*, edited by D. J. Sloss and J. P. R. Wallis, appeared just as I was completing my book, and I was therefore unable to make as much use as I might otherwise have done of the valuable notes and of the Index of Symbols. My account of the inventions to the Book of Job is little other than a summary of the illuminating interpretations in the second edition of Mr. Joseph Wicksteed's *Blake's Vision of the Book of Job*. I have made no attempt to read all the numerous monographs on Blake, but among those by which I have benefited is Dr. P. Berger's brilliant *William Blake: Mysticisme et Poésie*. The list of abbreviations [now at p. 389. Ed.] shows the books mainly consulted, and reference has been made in the notes to others and to magazine articles which are, with few exceptions, included in Mr. Keynes's *Bibliography*. The six volumes of *The Farington Diary* now published contain several references to Blake and his friends. I have also read Flaxman's letters to Hayley and such of Hayley's own correspondence as appeared likely to contain references to Blake in the Fairfax Murray Collection at the Fitzwilliam Museum, Cambridge. I have been specially indebted to Mr. Arthur Symons's *William Blake*, in which he has supplemented and criticized Gilchrist's *Life* by bringing together original sources of information. The references to Crabb Robinson's *Diary* and *Reminiscences* are mainly to Professor Edith J. Morley's *Henry Crabb Robinson: Blake, Coleridge, Wordsworth, Lamb, etc.* No complete *catalogue raisonné* of Blake's paintings and drawings as yet exists, although this has been long promised by Mr. A. G. B. Russell, author of the admirable *Engravings of William Blake*, and editor of Frederick Tatham's *Life of William Blake*. In the absence of such a catalogue it is impossible to deal adequately with Blake's work as an artist.

The notes contain, in addition to references, information and discussion of controversial points which, if given in the text, would have blurred the 'firm and determined outline' which a biographer of Blake is in duty bound to make his aim.

Were I to thank individually all those who have given me information and suggestions the list would be too long. But I am specially indebted to Mr. Geoffrey Keynes for constant help and encouragement and for expert assistance in deciphering the drawings in the *Rossetti MS.*,* and to Mr. G. M. Young for many suggestions throughout the book. These two friends were good enough to read both the manuscript and the proofs. Mrs. Colville-Hyde, widow of Captain Butts, the grandson of Blake's friend and chief patron, Thomas Butts, has generously put at my disposal all her information with regard to Blake's relations with Thomas Butts. My thanks are due to Professor Selwyn Image, Mr. Graily Hewitt, and Mr. Charles Ricketts, for allowing me to quote their expert though diverse opinions upon the merits of Blake's calligraphy. I have also to thank Messrs. Macmillan, Messrs. Methuen, and Messrs. Heinemann for allowing me to quote at some length from the *Life of William Blake* by Alexander Gilchrist, from *The Letters of William Blake*, together with a Life by Frederick Tatham, and from *William Blake, A Critical Essay*, by Algernon Charles Swinburne, respectively.

Mona Wilson

The Old Oxyard,
Oare,
Marlborough
1927

* This appendix is now omitted. [Ed.]

PREFACE TO THE NEW EDITION (1948)

Since the centenary of his death both the writings and the art of Blake have been more accessible. The Everyman Edition of Gilchrist's *Life* has been ably edited by Mr. Ruthven Todd, and contains not merely corrections of Gilchrist's facts, but an excellent bibliography and up-to-date information about the paintings, drawings, and engravings both in the possession of private owners and of public galleries, which have recently been greatly enriched by gifts and bequests. Many new books have been published about Blake, among them Mr. W. P. Witcutt's *Blake: A Psychological Study*. He revives the legend of Blake's Irish ancestry with dogmatic fervour, basing it on the O'Neill family tradition and Blake's red hair. Has anyone, by the way, claimed Irish birth for Keats? This legend is undocumented, like the alternative fancy that he was descended from Admiral Blake, though this must have affected an American publisher who, on the strength of my *Life of William Blake*, invited me to write a life of Nelson. Mr. Wittcutt is undeterred by Blake's calling himself the 'English Blake', though he weakens his case by suggesting that his Irish origin may have been carefully concealed from him, though presumably known to his father. Mary Butts in her autobiography, *The Crystal Cabinet*, mentions that her great-grandfather was a Swedenborgian. This fact, which has not, so far as I am aware, been recognized hitherto, explains his patronage of Blake and also the congenial intimacy of their correspondence.

The Nonesuch Edition contained new matter—for example, Blake's first visit to Hayley, which had escaped attention—all of which has been assimilated, with or without acknowledgement, by later writers. My additional notes are restricted to points touched on in my own text, and many of them consist of references to Mr. Geoffrey Keynes's invaluable work on Blake since 1927.

My most important addition is that to Appendix III, which shows the origin of the legend that Blake was mad, and had been actually incarcerated in Bedlam, a legend which has had persistent effect, in spite of the unanimous assurances of his intimates and acquaintances that they had never seen the least trace of insanity. A friend, brilliant and scholarly, who suffered at times from mental instability, rising, as she said of herself, like a phoenix from its ashes, once asked me indignantly: 'But why are you so anxious to prove that Blake was not mad? What difference does it make?' My answer is that the supposition of madness has been made an excuse for not studying the Prophetic Books intelligently and thoroughly. Anyone who does so will be convinced that, though there are allusions and obscurities now impenetrable, Blake never wrote a word which had not a perfectly definite meaning for himself. The contrast between the Prophetic Books and Smart's *Jubilate Agno*, 'like sweet bells jangled out of tune and harsh', proves my contention.

My thanks are due to Messrs. Dent and Mr. Ruthven Todd for permission to quote from the Everyman Edition of Gilchrist's *Life*.

1948   M. W.

I
YOUTH

Whether on Ida's shady brow,
　　Or in the chambers of the East,
The chambers of the sun, that now
　　From antient melody have ceas'd;

Whether in Heav'n ye wander fair,
　　Or the green corners of the earth,
Or the blue regions of the air,
　　Where the melodious winds have birth;

Whether on chrystal rocks ye rove,
　　Beneath the bosom of the sea
Wand'ring in many a coral grove,
　　Fair Nine, forsaking Poetry!

How have you left the antient love
　　That bards of old enjoy'd in you!
The languid strings do scarcely move!
　　The sound is forc'd, the notes are few![1]

'In those lines,' it has been said, 'the eighteenth century dies to music.'[2] The singer of the dirge, William Blake, was born on 28 November 1757. We know nothing of his father's family, or even the maiden name of his mother,* and it is idle to speculate on the hereditary sources of his genius. Many years after his death two

---

[1] References, indicated by superior figures, will be found at p. 389.

* James Blake, William's father, was probably the son of another James Blake of Rotherhithe and was bound apprentice to a draper in July 1737. It is now believed that he married Catherine Harmitage of St. James's, Westminster, at St. George's, Hanover Square, on 15 October 1752, their ages being respectively twenty-nine and thirty. They lived first in the young man's house in Glasshouse Street and a year later moved to Catherine's family home in Broad Street, Golden Square. (See Bentley, *Blake Records*, 1969, p. 2.) [Ed.]

ladies of the name claimed him as second cousin, and Admiral Blake as a common ancestor.[3] Ellis and Yeats say that he was an Irish O'Neill whose grandfather had adopted his wife's name of Blake.[4] Neither statement rests on any documentary evidence,* and we should require an unassailable pedigree before we should believe that a man who described himself as 'English Blake'[5] was in fact Irish. Arthur Symons discovered the inconclusive but suggestive fact that eight other families of Blake were living in the parish of St. James's, Westminster, within forty years.[6] At the time of William's birth his father, James Blake, was a hosier in a fair way of business, living at 28 Broad Street, Golden Square; although he was a Nonconformist[7] (probably a Baptist) the child was christened on 11 December at St. James's Church, Piccadilly. William, it would appear, was the third son. (A second son, born 12 May 1755 and christened John, died in infancy.) James, the eldest (born 10 July 1753), practical like his father, inherited the business, and took upon himself to proffer advice to William.† 'My brother John, the evil one,' the fourth and favourite son, lived to beg bread from William, thereby reversing their parents' prophecy: he died young after a life of dissipation.‡ Catherine, the only daughter and the youngest member of the family, usually made her home with James, but was sufficiently adaptable to join William's household for a time, though there is a tradition that she was not acceptable to Mrs. Blake:[8] otherwise nothing is known of her except that she was distinguished in appearance and outlived her brothers. Robert, nearly ten years younger than William, the

* Nevertheless W. P. Witcutt in *Blake: A Psychological Study* (1946), accepted Blake's Irish origin as a fact, though without any further evidence. No credence is now given to this legend. [Ed.]

† According to Gilchrist, *Life of William Blake* (1880), i, p. 5, James was also attracted by the teaching of Swedenborg and saw visions. His relations with his brother were evidently friendly while Blake was at Felpham and at the time of his exhibition (see pp. 248–61), but Gilchrist, i, p. 275, says that after James's retirement they were not on speaking terms. The date of James's death is uncertain.

‡ According to Tatham, John Blake worked for a gingerbread baker. 'He lived a few reckless days, enlisted as a soldier and died.' (*Blake Records*, p. 509.) [Ed.]

only one of the family who was spiritually akin to him, died at nineteen.*

Blake's father seems to have become a symbol for that authority against which the poet and mystic, with his twofold hostility to reason, instinctively rebelled, whether in literature, art, religion, or morality; at least we may guess as much from his poems and from the little we know of his early life. Neither does any close sympathy with his mother seem to have survived the tenderness of early childhood recalled in the *Songs of Innocence*. But we need not insult her memory, as one biographer has done, by assigning to her as funeral oration the obviously symbolical poem, 'To Tirzah.'[9] Blake, according to his disciple Tatham, was wont in old age to speak in a kindly way of both father and mother. Clearly they had done their best to bridge the gulf not only of age but of temperament between themselves and their son. But the boy's visionary faculty was perplexing to his truth-loving parents. When he was only four years old God 'put his head to the window' and set him a-screaming:[10] angels walked among the hay-makers one summer morning,† and Mrs. Blake saved him from his father's wrath when, at the age of eight or so, he spoke of seeing a tree on Peckham Rye starred with angels, though she was less lenient to a later vision of Ezekiel. His father recognized that so strange and stormy a child must be spared the discipline of school. He learnt to read and write, probably with his mother's help, and showed such a passion for drawing that at the age of ten he was sent to Pars's drawing school in the Strand.[11] James Blake the elder encouraged this taste by giving him casts of the Gladiator, the Hercules, and the Venus de Medici, and pocket money to spend on his studies.

* Robert has hitherto been confused with Richard, born 19 June 1762, who died in infancy. Robert was almost certainly the youth who was admitted to the school at the Royal Academy on 2 April 1782 at the age of fourteen to study as an engraver. If this record is correct, he was born on 14 August 1768. (*Blake Records*, pp. 7, 20.) [Ed.]

† Gilchrist, i, p. 7. Another story told by Gilchrist, ibid., shows that the child lived in the world of imagination. A traveller, telling of some foreign city, was interrupted by the protest, 'Do you call *that* splendid? I should call a city splendid in which the houses were of gold, the pavement of silver, the gates ornamented with precious stones.'

His imagination was inflamed by prints after Raphael, Michelangelo, Albrecht Dürer, and others: he sought originals, genuine or spurious, in the sale-rooms and in private collections, and the auctioneer, Langford, favoured his small bids, calling the child, even then dogmatic in his predilections, his 'little connoisseur'. There was a talk of sending him to the studio of some well-known painter, but he thought the high premium an injustice to the rest of the family, and asked to be apprenticed to an engraver instead. Ryland, afterwards hanged for forgery, was chosen by his father, but the boy had an intuition of Ryland's fate, not repeated later in the case of his admirer Wainewright, the journalist and murderer. James Blake may be credited with a certain imaginativeness since he was attracted by the doctrines of Emanuel Swedenborg, and the fact that on this occasion he listened to William shows that he could be a sympathetic and reasonable parent. Basire was substituted for Ryland, receiving a premium of fifty guineas.* While Blake was with Basire Goldsmith called one day, and the boy envied his finely shaped head.[12] A later remark shows that Blake singled out Goldsmith from among his associates for admiration. 'Such Men as Goldsmith ought not to have been Acquainted with such Men as Reynolds.'[13] At Basire's he also came across Woollet and Strange, the engravers, whose work he afterwards criticized with vehemence in the *Public Address*.[14]

Blake worked at his craft under Basire for two years. Then new apprentices joined the establishment. The fortunate result of friction—'he was too simple and they too cunning'—was that Basire sent him to make drawings in Westminster Abbey for engravings required by the Society of Antiquaries. 'There'—as Blake himself told Malkin[15]—

he found a treasure, which he knew how to value. He saw the simple and plain road to the style of art at which he aimed, unentangled in the intricate windings of modern practice. The monuments of Kings and Queens in Westminster Abbey, which

* James Basire, master engraver, carried on his business at 31 Great Queen Street, Lincoln's Inn Fields, and it is assumed that Blake, as apprentice, lived there from 1772 to 1779. [Ed.]

surround the chapel of Edward the Confessor, particularly that of King Henry the Third, the beautiful monument and figure of Queen Elinor, Queen Philippa, King Edward the Third, King Richard the Second and his Queen, were among his first studies. All these he drew in every point he could catch, frequently standing on the monument, and viewing the figures from the top. The heads he considered as portraits; and all the ornaments appeared as miracles of art, to his Gothicised imagination.

And he saw them for himself as they had been, clothed in the glory of colour. This close study of Gothic—always for him the 'living form'—left indelible traces on his style. 'Everything connected with Gothic art and churches, and their builders, was a passion with him.'[16] He saw Christ and his Apostles among the tombs,[17] and he both saw a great procession of monks and priests, choristers and censer-bearers, and heard their chant.* Less congenial visitants were the Westminster School boys, then allowed to romp at will in the Abbey.[18] They naturally teased the queer, industrious apprentice with the snub nose and flames of golden hair. One climbed a pinnacle on a level with his scaffold. Blake, in a rage, threw him violently to the ground and complained to the Dean, who withdrew the schoolboys' privilege. Part of the last five years of his apprenticeship were spent thus in the Abbey and other churches.

Gough's *Sepulchral Monuments in Great Britain* contains six portraits from the Monuments of Kings and Queens which were both drawn and engraved by Blake:† that from the head of Queen Philippa was praised by Stothard as 'a remarkably correct and fine drawing.'[19] The engravings of the monuments which precede the portraits were probably also from drawings by Blake. Malkin speaks of a drawing of the monument of Aylmer de Valence, and of innumerable other drawings by Blake both in the Abbey and in other churches. It is therefore likely that other engravings in

* According to Oswald Crawfurd, 'William Blake: Artist, Poet, and Painter', *The New Quarterly Magazine*, ii (1874). Blake's letter, on which the writer bases his information, has not been traced.

† The story that Blake had been employed on heraldic painting in his youth was contradicted by Linnell. (*Rossetti Papers 1862 to 1870*, 1903, p. 22.)

Gough's book were from drawings by him, and possible that some of the prints signed by Basire in other architectural works published at this time were actually executed by Blake.* His earliest original engraving is 'Joseph of Arimathea among the Rocks of Albion.'† Below the engraving is 'Michael Angelo Pinxit. Engraved by W. Blake 1773 from an old Italian Drawing.'‡ The drawing has not been identified, but the figure is derived from one in Michelangelo's *Crucifixion of St. Peter* in the Vatican, and the landscape is probably Blake's own. The description of the engraving is as interesting as the work itself, remarkable enough for a boy of sixteen:

This is One of the Gothic Artists who Built the Cathedrals in what we call the Dark Ages, Wandering about in sheep skins & goat skins, of whom the World was not Worthy; such were the Christians in all Ages.[20]

A drawing of 'Moses and the Tablets of Stone', in black and white with touches of colour, is also extant. It is signed 'W.B. 1774', and resembles the engraving of Joseph of Arimathea.

But the home atmosphere was tolerant rather than sympathetic. Many years later Blake wrote to Cumberland: 'We remember when a Print shop was a rare bird in London & I myself remember when I thought my pursuits of Art a kind of criminal dissipation & neglect of the main chance, which I hid my face for not being able to abandon as a Passion which is forbidden by Law &

---

* In the Bodleian Library, Oxford, among Gough's collections, and in the library of the Society of Antiquaries at Burlington House there are numerous other drawings in pencil, sepia wash, and water colours attributable to Blake. Among the drawings is evidence that Blake was present at the opening of the tomb of King Edward I in 1774. (See Keynes, *Blake Studies*, 2nd ed., 1971, pp. 19–25.) [Ed.]

† The reference is to the tradition connecting Joseph of Arimathea with Glastonbury.

‡ A unique proof of the first state of the plate is inscribed by Blake, 'Engraved when I was a beginner at Basire's from a drawing by Salviati after Michael Angelo'. Salviati's drawing has not been identified. The title and the engraved inscriptions were added when Blake reworked the plate, probably after 1800. (See Keynes, *Engravings by William Blake: The Separate Plates*, 1956, pp. 3–5.) [Ed.]

Religion, but now it appears to be Law & Gospel too. . . .'²¹

The prose he read at this time did not serve to diminish this sense of isolation:

I read Burke's Treatise when very Young; at the same time I read Locke on Human Understanding & Bacon's Advancement of Learning; on Every one of these Books I wrote my Opinions, & on looking them over find that my Notes on Reynolds in this Book are exactly Similar. I felt the Same Contempt & Abhorrence then that I do now. They mock Inspiration & Vision. Inspiration & Vision was then, & now is, & I hope will always Remain, my Element, my Eternal Dwelling place; how can I then hear it Contemned without returning Scorn for Scorn?²²

A more congenial book, Fuseli's translation of Winckelmann's *Reflections on the Painting and Sculpture of the Greeks*, is known to have been in his possession during his apprenticeship.²³

But, happily, in the region of poetry Blake wandered further afield, finding pastime and good company. Drawing in the Abbey he had, in Malkin's phrase, 'himself almost become a Gothic monument.' At home he was seeking another living form, a form for verse. A small volume, printed, but thrown aside, in 1783, shows where he searched, and how he used what he had found. The *Poetical Sketches*, said to have been written between his twelfth and twentieth years, fall into two groups: the first for the most part imitative of works written or published in his own day, the second largely inspired by those treasures he had delved into the past to find. The first are the restless cries of a bird disturbed in the darkness, the second his songs at dawn. In the first another voice joins an ineffectual choir vaguely striving for they know not what; in the second a new voice sings, though it be sometimes to an old tune.

In the first group the rhythmical prose pieces* exhibit the disastrous influence of Ossian. The Scandinavian cult appears in

* Two more of these ('Then she bore Pale desire' and 'Woe, cried the muse'), written before 1777, are included in the *Complete Writings*, ed. Keynes (Oxford Standard Authors, 1966), pp. 40-3.

'Gwin, King of Norway.'* 'Blind Man's Buff' follows an eighteenth-century fashion. In 'Fair Elenor', a Strawberry of Otranto, only a few lines reveal his explorations among the Elizabethans.

> My lord was like a flower upon the brows
> Of lusty May! Ah, life as frail as flower!
>
> .   .   .   .
>
> My lord was like the opening eyes of day,
> When western winds creep softly o'er the flowers:
>
> But he is darken'd; like the summer's noon,
>   Clouded; fall'n like the stately tree, cut down;
> The breath of heaven dwelt among his leaves.

'King Edward the Third'—an interesting exercise—shows familiarity with Shakespeare's historical plays, but no dramatic power.

Yet even in their weakness the poems of this group are remarkable as the work of a boy when the foundations of the Augustan faith were not visibly shaken, a boy whose reading depended on his own initiative. It is clear that he had gone for his vocabulary not only to Spenser, Milton, and Shakespeare's plays, but to Shakespeare's poems, then little known, to Jonson, Fletcher, and the Carolines. Of his own time he had read, it may be guessed, Gray, Collins, and Thomson, certainly Percy's *Reliques*, and demonstrably Ossian. Later he became an admirer of Chatterton, whose poems were not published till 1777, but whether some likeness of form shows only kinship of genius or indicates additions made to the Sketches after 1777—his twentieth year—remains uncertain.†

* Damon, *William Blake, His Philosophy and Symbols* (1924), p. 31, thinks that 'Gwin, King of Norway' is derived from Chatterton's prose poem 'Godred Crovan', which was not published till June 1778, and that the *Poetical Sketches* were not, therefore, all written before 1777 as stated in the Mathew advertisement. In spite of the resemblances, it does not, however, seem out of the question that Blake should have taken the story from some other source.

† Blake possessed a copy of the third edition of Chatterton's *Poems*, 1778, but he did not annotate its pages. In 1826 he wrote among his annotations to Wordsworth's *Poems*, 'I believe both Macpherson & Chatterton, that what

The poems of the second group mark a moment of departure in English literature. The change which they announce is in essence a return from the ideal of Excellence to that of Ecstasy as the aim and justification of poetic enterprise. To the Augustans, as to the French classical poets, and to their Latin models before them, the poetic objective was the level and lucid statement, in a style sustained at the due height of dignity, clarity, and beauty, and warmed, coloured, and decorated with the appropriate graces of diction and rhythm. The new age, with the Elizabethans, the Greek lyrists, and the folk-singers of all lands on its side, was to aim at more intense and instantaneous effects, at the capture in their last subtlety of those moments of heightened capacity wherein it believed the secret of poetic experience to lie. And as the aim was different so the approach was different. The large and regular movement of epic, drama, and ode was left for swifter, more impulsive forms. The set phrasing of the classicists and their established metres were broken up. The poets went in quest of new words, new combinations, new rhythms, in short, of a new medium capable of rendering the gradations and refinements of the richer and more elusive moods which had now to be set down in verse.

This was the revolution which poetry was to achieve in the last years of the eighteenth century and the beginning of the nineteenth, and which Blake carried through in his own work, unknowing and unknown. He was not borne on the tide of new ideas which came setting in a few years later: painter and musician as he was, neither landscape nor folk-songs furnished him with inspiration; he had no time for waterfalls or ruins, and London could provide little or none of that popular poetry out of which the art of Burns arose. The poetry of Blake is self-begotten: it lived to itself without influence on the world; it might have perished without record. And yet it promises—and often realizes

---

they say is Ancient Is so. I own myself an admirer of Ossian equally with any other Poet whatever, Rowley & Chatterton also.' (*Complete Writings*, p. 783.) [Ed.]

—whatever is new and significant in the poetry which was to
declare itself twenty years later and to reign unchallenged from
that time onward.

At the head of this second group stands 'To the Muses.' Next
to it comes the lyric of which Malkin makes the amazing statement
that 'It was written before the age of fourteen, in the heat of
youthful fancy, unchastised by judgement.'

> How sweet I roam'd from field to field
>   And tasted all the summer's pride,
> 'Till I the prince of love beheld,
>   Who in the sunny beams did glide!
>
> He shew'd me lilies for my hair,
>   And blushing roses for my brow;
> He led me through his gardens fair,
>   Where all his golden pleasures grow.
>
> With sweet May dews my wings were wet,
>   And Phœbus fir'd my vocal rage;
> He caught me in his silken net,
>   And shut me in his golden cage.
>
> He loves to sit and hear me sing,
>   Then, laughing, sports and plays with me;
> Then stretches out my golden wing,
>   And mocks my loss of liberty.[24]

Here, in spite of Phoebus and the 'vocal rage', the boy has
wandered off the gravel walk and is gazing up into one of Marvell's
trees:

> My soul into the boughs does glide;
> There, like a bird, it sits and sings,
> Then whets and combs its silver wings
> And till prepared for longer flight
> Waves in its plumes the various light.

It is characteristic of Blake that whether from indifference, impatience, or lack of scholarship he could make nothing of the
prevalent Augustan metres: his couplets and his blank verse are
equally bad, and his six attempts at a Spenserian stanza have been

fairly dismissed with the criticism 'all different and all wrong'. The sonnet he appears never to have attempted, although his contemporaries were turning them out by the hundred. May it not be that the fourteenth Proverb of Hell—'Bring out number, weight & measure in a year of dearth'[25]—usually read as a jibe at the heroic couplet, is really a criticism of that dubious tribute to Milton, the fashionable sonnet, before Wordsworth gave new substance to the form? But in lyric metres he is revolutionary and a master. It was a principle of eighteenth-century lyric poetry that with rare variations each poem should be confined to one type of foot, generally iambic, occasionally, and for special purposes, anapaestic. Blake goes back to the freer handling of the Carolines; the quickening of iambic form by means of anapaests—and conversely the steadying of an anapaestic line by means of iambs and spondees—remained his metrical signature:

> And there the lion's ruddy eyes
> Shall flow with tears of gold,
> And pitying the tender cries,
> And walking round the fold,
> Saying 'Wrath, by his meekness,
> And by his health, sickness
> Is driven away
> From our immortal day.'[26]

> Ah, Sun-flower, weary of time,
> Who countest the steps of the Sun, . . .[27]

> The days of my youth rise fresh in my mind,
> My face turns green and pale.[28]

In the 'Mad Song' the new prosody is heard in its most daring form: the last traces of the eighteenth century have disappeared: in freedom of phrasing and diction it is wholly Blake and wholly of the new age:

> The wild winds weep,
>   And the night is a-cold;
> Come hither, Sleep,
>   And my griefs infold:

But lo! the morning peeps
  Over the eastern steeps,
And the rustling birds of dawn*
  The earth do scorn.

Lo! to the vault
  Of paved heaven
With sorrow fraught
  My notes are driven:
They strike the ear of night,
  Make weep the eyes of day;
They make mad the roaring winds,
  And with tempests play.

Like a fiend in a cloud,
  With howling woe,
After night I do croud,
  And with night will go;
I turn my back to the east,
  From whence comforts have increas'd;
For light doth seize my brain
  With frantic pain.[29]

Like his metre, his diction anticipates the freedom discovered a generation later by Coleridge and made over by him to the use of all future poets. Analysed, the phrasing of the *Poetical Sketches* reveals an eighteenth-century stratum of 'yawning deeps', 'modest eves', 'charming nests', and 'pleasing woes', but it also discloses that liberty of combination which is the note of the developed romantic style, where any epithet may be linked with any noun provided it gives the right picture: 'holy feet', 'rustling birds', 'feather'd clouds', 'flourishing hair', are so many essays in direct vision, once completely caught and rendered in those lines which Collins might have dreamt and forgotten on waking:

Let thy west wind sleep on
The lake; speak silence with thy glimmering eyes,
And wash the dusk with silver.[30]

---

* The correction 'birds' for 'beds' was made by Blake in at least two copies of *Poetical Sketches* and must therefore be accepted. Cf. 'The Couch of Death', '. . . the birds of day were heard in their nests, rustling in brakes and thickets. . . .' (*Complete Writings*, p. 35.)

Even the secret of the Parnassians is not unknown to this London apprentice—the use of antique imagery for romantic ends:

> We lack not songs, nor instruments of joy,
> Nor echoes sweet, nor waters clear as heaven,
> Nor laurel wreaths against the sultry heat.[31]

Blake, having completed his apprenticeship as an engraver under Basire, became, at the age of twenty-two, a student at the Royal Academy, of which the Swiss decorative artist, George Michael Moser, was Keeper. There he drew both from the antique and from the living model. But, according to Malkin, 'he professes drawing from life always to have been hateful to him; and speaks of it as looking more like death, or smelling of mortality.'[32] This impatience with the model, which brought him back from visions of beauty to a set pose and a set task, may be held accountable for some of Blake's shortcomings as an artist. It would seem likely that in later life he worked little from models, save for studies from himself and Mrs. Blake. This was probably due partly to distaste, and partly to economy. As a pupil he was rebellious in another matter also; he insisted on being left to form his own opinions. One of his notes on Reynolds's *Discourses* shows him, as usual, defying the powers that be:

I was once looking over the Prints from Rafael & Michael Angelo in the Library of the Royal Academy. Moser came to me & said: 'You should not Study these old Hard, Stiff & Dry, Unfinish'd Works of Art—Stay a little & I will shew you what you should Study.' He then went & took down Le Brun's and Rubens's Galleries. How I did secretly Rage! I also spoke my Mind. . . . [*A line cut away by the binder.*] I said to Moser, 'These things that you call Finish'd are not Even Begun; how can they then be Finish'd? The Man who does not know The Beginning never can know the End of Art.'[33]

His first interview with Reynolds may belong also to this period. Gilchrist quotes a letter from an unnamed friend of Blake: 'Once I remember his talking to me of Reynolds, he became furious at what the latter had dared to say of his early works. When a very young man he had called on Reynolds to show him some designs, and had been recommended to work with less extravagance and more simplicity, and to correct his drawing. This Blake seemed to regard as an affront never to be forgotten. He was very indignant when he spoke of it.'[34]

Rebels are not apt to repress the defects of their qualities, and Blake's lifelong antipathy to Reynolds may be partly accounted for by anger at this just criticism, although he used to describe a later and more friendly conversation: 'Well, Mr. Blake, I hear you despise our art of oil-painting.' 'No, Sir Joshua, I don't despise it; but I like fresco better.'[35]

Meanwhile Blake was not only drawing out of school for his own delight, but was earning his living as an engraver. He was well supplied with commissions both for book illustrations and for engravings from pictures. His principal employers were the booksellers Johnson and Harrison, and most of the illustrations were engraved from drawings by Stothard for novels and magazines. Malkin mentions two historical engravings from Blake's own designs, but these have not been identified. A drawing of 'Edward and Elinor', presumably for the engraving mentioned in Blake's *Prospectus* of 1793,[36] is assigned to *circa* 1779, which is also the approximate date of the drawing of 'The Penance of Jane Shore' exhibited thirty years later. The latter shows the influence of Mortimer, the historical painter, whom Blake admired, and 'The Ordeal of Queen Emma', painted about the same time, resembles it in treatment. 'Glad Day', engraved in 1780, gives the first promise of what was to come. It was perhaps inspired by the lines in *Romeo and Juliet*:[37]

> Night's candles are burnt out, and jocund day
> Stands tiptoe on the misty mountain tops.

The likeness to Mrs. Blake's drawing of her husband as a young man suggests that 'Day' is in some sort a portrait of the young Blake. The design must have been a favourite with Blake himself, as about 1794 he made two fine colour prints from the plate.

Below an early impression are engraved the lines:

Albion rose from where he labour'd at the Mill with Slaves:
Giving himself for the Nations he danc'd the dance of
Eternal Death.[38]

thus identifying Day with Blake's symbolical conception of
Albion, the Eternal Man.* The only original book illustration of
this period is the charming frontispiece of *An Elegy*, *Set to Music*
by Thos. Commins, Organist of Penzance, Cornwall (1786).[39]

Engraving brought him into contact with other artists, Stothard
and Flaxman, Fuseli and Barry. Stothard was two years older than
Blake and already acquiring reputation as a graceful illustrator.
Some time between 1780 and 1782 they sailed up the Medway
sketching with Stothard's friend Ogleby. An etching of Stothard's
survives, depicting an absurd interruption to their tour when they
were arrested as spies of the French Government, and detained in
a tent composed of their own sails until they could obtain certifi-
cates of their good faith from some members of the Royal
Academy.† This friendship was unfortunately shattered some years
afterwards by Cromek's Canterbury Pilgrims plot.

Blake was introduced by Stothard to Flaxman, who was a
Swedenborgian. He became an enthusiastic admirer of Blake's
genius both as poet and painter, and gave him considerable
professional assistance. Blake returned the affection of Flaxman,
his 'dear Sculptor of Eternity', although at a later time the friendship was clouded by suspicions. Both Flaxman and Stothard were
pilloried in some of those bitter epigrams, offspring of a mood
and not intended for publication.

* The title 'Glad Day' is conjectural, supplied by Gilchrist in the erroneous
belief that the lines embodying the name of Albion were added later. It
seems preferable to call the print 'The Dance of Albion', on the authority
of Blake's lines. (See Keynes, *The Separate Plates*, pp. 7–8.) [Ed.]
† The story is related in Mrs. Bray's *Life of Stothard* (1851), pp. 20–1, with
a small reproduction of the etching. A full-size reproduction is in Keynes,
A Bibliography of William Blake (1921), pl. 38. According to Gilchrist, i, p. 33,
Blake was introduced to Stothard by another engraver, Trotter. [Ed.]

> I found them blind: I taught them how to see;
> And now they know neither themselves nor me.
> 'Tis Excellent to turn a thorn to a pin,
> A Fool to a bolt, a Knave to a glass of gin.[40]

Henry Fuseli, the son of a Swiss painter, had received marked encouragement from Sir Joshua when he first came to England in 1764, as a youth, with a portfolio full of drawings. He returned in 1780 after a stay of some years in Italy, and lodged in Broad Street. With him Blake formed an enduring though chequered friendship, commemorated in the grotesquely affectionate epigram:

> The only Man that e'er I knew
> Who did not make me almost spew
> Was Fuseli: he was both Turk & Jew—
> And so, dear Christian Friends, how do you do?[41]

Tatham also says that 'Blake was more fond of Fuseli than any other man on earth.' Fuseli, although so much Blake's senior, found him 'damned good to steal from.' Reader, writer, and wit, as well as an artist of considerable power, he had no doubt in his turn a stimulating effect on the younger man. Which of the two first declared that nature put him out? Their literary tastes were congenial. Fuseli was a worshipper of Shakespeare and Milton: he it was who applied to Pope's 'Eloisa to Abelard' the phrase 'hot ice'.

The Irishman, Barry, was also an older man than Blake.* Dis-

---

* Barry was made Professor of Painting in 1782, but was deprived of his office and expelled from the Academy in 1799. He died in great poverty in 1806, just before the first payment of the annuity purchased for him by the Royal Society was due. He was buried in St. Paul's near Sir Joshua. (*The Farington Diary*, 1922–8, iii, pp. 153, 161, 24 February, 14 March 1806.) Farington gives a further account of Barry, iv, p. 84, stating that he had really saved a large sum of money although he allowed a subscription to be opened for his benefit. Johnson (Boswell's *Life*, 26 May 1783) said of Barry's paintings at the Royal Society: 'Whatever the hand may have done, the mind has done its part. There is a grasp of mind, there, which you find no where else.' Blake had a copy of Barry's *An Account of a Series of Pictures in the Great Room of the Society of Arts* (1783) in which he inserted his pencil sketch of Barry in old age (Keynes, *Bibliography*, p. 418; Gilchrist, i, p. 48). Blake would also have had some sympathy with Barry's rambling *Inquiry into the Real and Imaginary Obstructions to the Acquisition of the Arts in England* (1775).

appointed in a scheme for decorating St. Paul's, in which Sir Joshua and other artists were also concerned, he went with sixteen shillings in his pocket to offer his services free to the Royal Society of Arts. The result, his vast pictures on 'Human Improvement', completed in 1783, may be seen any day in the large room at the Adelphi—a parlous example of the grand style which won Dr. Johnson's approval. Barry may have inspired Blake to see what he had meant to do and what he declared in his descriptive pamphlet that he had sublimely accomplished, rather than the muddled and somewhat ridiculous performance he actually achieved. At any rate, Blake became a strong adherent of Barry's:

Who will Dare to Say that Polite Art is Encouraged or Either Wished or Tolerated in a Nation where The Society for the Encouragement of Art Suffer'd Barry to Give them his Labour for Nothing, A Society Composed of the Flower of the English Nobility & Gentry?—Suffering an Artist to Starve while he Supported Really what They, under Pretence of Encouraging, were Endeavouring to Depress.—Barry told me that while he Did that Work, he Lived on Bread & Apples.[42]

Blake's poem on Barry has disappeared, and nothing is known of its contents except that the verses beginning 'I ask'd my dear Friend, Orator Prigg' were marked by Blake 'to come in Barry, a Poem.'[43] And the lines 'To Venetian Artists',[44] also in the Notebook, may have been intended as a continuation of these. Barry quarrelled with most people, including his patron Edmund Burke, but his enthusiasm and sincerity would have endeared him to Blake, and he was also a seer of visions.

Even as it was [says his biographer] people soon forgot his rough language and his oaths in the strength of his mind: we have witnessed many instances of this, and once saw a devout old lady entering the room where he was, hold him for some time in a sort of horror. The conversation, however, happened to turn on the nature of Christian meekness, which gave him the opportunity of opening on the character of our Saviour—with that power of heart and mind, and energy of words, that in spite of the oaths which fell abundantly, the old lady remarked that she never heard so divine a man in her life, and desired to know who he was.[45]

At the Royal Academy in 1780 Blake exhibited 'The Death of Earl Goodwin', a water-colour drawing, and two drawings, 'War Unchained by an Angel—Fire, Pestilence and Famine following' and a 'Breach in a City—The Morning after a Battle,' in 1784.[46] These or other works of his attracted the attention of Romney, who declared that his historical drawings ranked with those of Michelangelo.[47] Blake also admired Romney, and the two artists probably had some influence upon each other's style. John Hawkins,* a Cornishman, who had ordered several drawings from Blake, tried at this time to raise a subscription that he might be sent to study in Rome. It may be left to those with more right to dogmatize on the probable effect on his genius, to deplore, or to be grateful for, the failure of this scheme.

Besides his development as an artist his life was an eventful one. The Lord George Gordon No-Popery Riots took place in June 1780, and Blake, chancing to meet the rioters, was swept down to Newgate in the front rank. There he saw the prison burnt, and the prisoners released. If his hatred of prisons, 'built with stones of Law', dates back from his youth, so, too, does his hatred of jealousy. Courting a 'lively little girl' called Polly Wood he found that she was encouraging another admirer. Blake expostulated. 'Are you a fool?' she scornfully asked. 'That cured me of jealousy,' said Blake, but his vehemence against the vice suggests that it was not entirely uprooted, but required the periodic application of a weedkiller.

Polly's behaviour had upset him and he went for a change of scene to stay at the home of a Battersea market-gardener named Boucher, to whose daughter, Catherine, he told his woes. 'Do you pity me?' he suddenly asked. 'Yes, indeed I do.' 'Then I love you.' Catherine was ready: her pity was the child of love. Mrs. Blake was wont to relate that when her mother spoke of marriage she

* John Hawkins, F.R.S., was the younger brother of Sir Christopher Hawkins of Trewithen, and lived at Bignor Place, near Petworth. He wrote several treatises on methods of mining, ancient and modern, and was also a traveller and archaeologist. Hayley in a letter to Flaxman of 14 September 1809 refers to him as 'the Attic Master of Bignor Park'. (Fairfax Murray Collection.)

used to answer that she had not yet seen the man, but when she first saw William Blake the conviction that this was he so over-whelmed her that she nearly fainted. Cunningham records a tra-dition that Blake's marriage was not acceptable to his father;[48] it was, perhaps, for this reason that he did not see Catherine again until he was making enough money to support her. A year later, 18 August 1782, they were married at Battersea Church,* and went to lodge at 23 Green Street, Leicester Fields.†

Catherine Blake, who was four years younger than her husband, had, to judge from vague descriptions and more reliable drawings, a face full of beauty and character, with large dark eyes. A woman who 'is like a flame of many colours of precious jewels'[49] when she thinks of exchanging London for the country, cannot have lacked expression. If we assume that she is portrayed in the draw-ing of a young woman sitting on the edge of a bed in which a man resembling Blake is lying,[50] she must have had also a graceful and well-proportioned figure. Testimony that she was a perfect wife comes both from their friends and from Blake himself. She was a competent and frugal housewife, avoiding fuss by the silent reminder of the empty plates when it was time for her husband to return from the other world to the provision of daily bread, though she held a secret precautionary guinea in reserve. She accepted his visions with the wonder and faith of a child. He taught her to write, and to help him in printing and colouring his engravings. He also taught her to draw; a sketch by her of him is still extant.‡ She was 'my Shadow of Delight,'[51] the complement, the manifes-tation of Blake's theory that sex is part of the 'division' from which the visible world has its being, and that the 'Eternal Man' unites in a single perfection the attributes of both sexes.

---

* The bride's name is written 'Butcher' in the marriage register. (*Blake Records*, p. 23.)

† The entries in the Rate Books suggest that the Blakes were lodgers in a house occupied by a Thomas Taylor (not the Platonist). Blake gave the Green Street address when exhibiting at the Royal Academy in 1784. They moved to 27 Broad Street later that year. (*Blake Records*, p. 557.) [Ed.]

‡ The drawing, probably made for Frederick Tatham after Blake's death, is now in the Fitzwilliam Museum, Cambridge. [Ed.]

The Blakes had no children; speculation as to the influence of this deprivation may be left to those who deem it worth their pains. In spite of, or because of it, the only indication of friction in their married life which does not rest on vague tradition or assumptions of autobiographical intention in the poems, is the account of a dispute between Mrs. Blake and Robert when he formed part of their household. 'Kneel down and beg Robert's pardon, directly,' said William, 'or you never see my face again!' She knelt and murmured, 'Robert, I beg your pardon, I am in the wrong.' The incident was closed by Robert's magnanimous 'Young woman, you lie! *I* am in the wrong.'[52] Is there a reminiscence of this in *Jerusalem*?

She who adores not your frowns will only loathe your smiles.[53]

What such partial and desultory reading cannot afford may be supplied by the conversation of learned and ingenious men, which is the best of all substitutes for those who have not the means or opportunities of deep study. There are many such men in this age, and they will be pleased with communicating their ideas to artists, when they see them curious and docile, if they are treated with that respect and deference which is so justly their due. Into such society, young artists, if they make it the point of their ambition, will by degrees be admitted. There, without formal teaching, they will insensibly come to feel and reason like those they live with, and find a rational and systematic taste imperceptibly formed in their minds, which they will know how to reduce to a standard, by applying general truth to their own purposes, better perhaps than those to whom they owed the original sentiment.[54]

Such was the advice of Sir Joshua Reynolds and such the behaviour of the modest young Flaxman. The Revd. Anthony Stephen Mathew,* incumbent of Percy Chapel, Charlotte Street, and afternoon preacher at St. Martin-in-the-Fields, had found the sickly child sitting behind the counter of his father's shop, trying

---

* The Revd. Anthony Stephen Mathew was erroneously named as 'the Revd. Henry Mathew' by Blake's early biographer, J. T. Smith, in his *Nollekens and his Times* (1828). The mistake was corrected by H. M. Margoliouth in 1951 (*Notes & Queries*, cxcvi, pp. 162–3). For Flaxman's portrait drawings of Mathew and his wife, see *Blake Records*, pl. iv and v. [Ed.]

to teach himself Latin.[55] He lent him books, and later Mrs. Mathew, a charming and well-educated woman, read Homer aloud while Flaxman drew subjects so suggested. Their drawing-room, with its putty-and-sand statuettes by Flaxman, painted glass window, and furniture in keeping with these adornments,[56] was a stronghold of culture, where struggling artists were welcomed and patronized. Their circle included such eminent persons as Mrs. Montagu, student of Shakespeare and patroness of chimney-sweeps, Mrs. Elizabeth Carter, linguist, poetess, and pudding-maker, Mrs. Chapone, impulsive and entertaining despite her improving books, Mrs. Brooke, the novelist, Mrs. Barbauld, and Mrs. Hannah More. They represented what was best in the cultured middle class which had grown up during the eighteenth century, intelligent, industrious, philanthropic, superbly didactic, pleased with themselves and their productions, but not wholly impervious to other influences. Mrs. Montagu,* for example, greatly as she admired Mr. Pope, felt that he lacked 'that something which makes a poet divine, that lifts him "above the visible diurnal sphere," that gives him visions of worlds unknown, makes him sing like a seraphim, tune his harp to the musick of the spheres, and raise enchantments around him.' Mrs. Chapone was emphatic in her dissatisfaction with modern writers. 'It is only from the ignorant that we can now have any thing original; every master copies from those that are of established authority, and does not look at the natural object.'[57]

To this company, then, Flaxman hopefully introduced his fellow-struggler Blake with the *Poetical Sketches* in his pocket, Blake who said of himself, 'I never made friends but by spiritual gifts, By severe contentions of friendship & the burning fire of thought.'[58] 'Opposition is true Friendship.'[59]

At first all went well. Blake read some of his poems, or sang them to his own tunes, which were so beautiful that professional musicians noted them down. The manuscript was produced, and Mrs. Mathew persuaded her husband to share the expense of

* See her letter to Mrs. Vesey of 12 August 1777, in Reginald Blunt, *Mrs. Montagu, 'The Queen of the Blues'*.

printing the *Poetical Sketches* with the generous Flaxman.[60] The
copies were given to Blake, but the book was neither published
nor offered for sale. Mr. Mathew contributed the Preface:

The following sketches were the production of an untutored
youth, commenced in his twelfth, and occasionally resumed by the
author till his twentieth year; since which time, his talents having
been wholly directed to the attainment of excellence in his profession, he has been deprived of the leisure requisite to such a
revisal of these sheets, as might have rendered them less unfit to
meet the public eye.

Conscious of the irregularities and defects to be found in almost
every page, his friends have still believed that they possessed a
poetic originality, which merited some respite from oblivion.
These their opinions remain, however, to be now reproved or
confirmed by a less partial public.

Broad-minded, kind-hearted orthodoxy, desirous to help and
instruct, is often more exasperating to the young and rebellious
than frank hostility. Bearing Mr. Mathew's preface in mind, it is
not surprising to learn from J. T. Smith, who also frequented the
salon, that 'it happened, unfortunately, soon after this period, that
in consequence of his unbending deportment, or what his adherents
are pleased to call his manly firmness of opinion, which certainly
was not at all times considered pleasing by every one, his visits
were not so frequent.'[61] A remark of Blake's own may be applied
to summarize the situation from his point of view. 'The Enquiry
in England is not whether a Man has Talents & Genius, But
whether he is Passive & Polite & a Virtuous Ass & obedient to
Noblemen's Opinions in Art & Science. If he is, he is a Good
Man. If Not, he must be Starved.'[62]

An Island in the Moon, the manuscript of which is now in the
Fitzwilliam Museum, was written after Blake's rupture with the
Mathew set, probably about 1787.* It is, epigrams apart, his one

* Doubt has been thrown on Gilchrist's authority for his description of
the Mathews' circle, as later on Blake's relations with that of Johnson, the
bookseller, but *An Island in the Moon* suggests that he is likely to have had
some basis for his caricatures. Mary Anne Galton, afterwards Mrs.
Schimmelpennick, says that their butler always referred to the learned Lunar
Society, of which her father was a member, as the Lunatics. Is it not probable

attempt at satire, and can never have been intended for publication. Coarse with the combined coarseness of youth and of the age to which he belonged, it is, despite the compressed nostrils of some of his critics, quite innocuous: entertaining enough to those of adaptable humour, interesting as autobiography, though unfinished and immature as literature. The victims pilloried as each intent on their own particular form of learned nonsense, and the pretentious and frivolous women, have not been identified with members of the Mathew circle, but the pages ring with Blake's irritation at contemporary culture. Mr. Foster Damon conjectures that 'Sipsop the Pythagorean' is a skit on Thomas Taylor,* the Platonist, who gave twelve lectures on the 'Platonic Philosophy' to a distinguished audience at Flaxman's house, and 'Inflammable Gass the Wind-Finder' on Dr. Priestley, scientist and revolutionist. Mrs. Gimblet suggests descriptions of Mrs. Charlotte Lennox, author of *The Female Quixote*, who may well have been a friend of Mrs. Mathew. Dr. Johnson did not, so far as we know, honour Mrs. Mathew's gatherings with his presence, but his opinions were doubtless quoted *ad nauseam*. Hence perhaps the ribald song beginning

> 'Lo the Bat with Leathern wing,
> Winking & blinking,
> Winking & blinking,
> Winking & blinking,
> Like Doctor Johnson.'[63]

---

that Blake knew of the existence of this Birmingham society, and that it suggested his title? Mrs. Schimmelpennick mentions the names of some of the members—Dr. Priestley, Dr. Parr, Richard Lovell Edgeworth, Day of *Sandford and Morton*, Sir William Herschell, Sir Joseph Banks, Watt of the steam engine, Joseph Berrington, the historian, and an absent-minded Dr. Stokes, from whose pocket there escaped during dinner a large yellow-and-black snake.

    * Taylor also figures as the half-crazy enthusiast in Isaac D'Israeli's *Vaurien*, and as 'the modern Pletho' in his *Curiosities of Literature*. Damon's conjecture would make it improbable that *An Island in the Moon* could have been written as early as 1784, the date formerly ascribed to it. (Damon, *Blake*, pp. 32–3.)

Towards the end of the manuscript a page or more is unfortunately missing, containing a discussion between the Cynic, Quid, who appears to be Blake himself, and his wife, on a new method of printing, foreshadowing the *Songs of Innocence*. They are just quitting this subject for a plot *pour épater les bourgeois* at the house of one Mr. Femality, and it should be noted that Blake's treatment of himself is fully as crude and cruel as that of his patrons and critics.

One or two extracts from this boyish performance, selected with due consideration for the reader's delicacy, will sufficiently indicate its quality:

The three Philosophers sat together thinking of nothing. In comes Etruscan Column the Antiquarian, & after an abundance of Enquiries to no purpose, sat himself down & described something that nobody listen'd to. So they were employ'd when Mrs. Gimblet came in. The corners of her mouth seem'd—I don't know how, but very odd, as if she hoped you had not an ill opinion of her,—to be sure, we are all poor creatures! Well, she seated [herself] & seem'd to listen with great attention while the Antiquarian seem'd to be talking of virtuous cats. But it was not so; she was thinking of the shape of her eyes & mouth, & he was thinking of his eternal fame. . . .[64]

Then Suction Ask'd if Pindar was not a better Poet than Ghiotto was a Painter.

'Plutarch has not the life of Ghiotto,' said Sipsop.

'No,' said Quid, 'to be sure, he was an Italian.'

'Well,' said Suction, 'that is not any proof.'

'Plutarch was a nasty ignorant Puppy,' said Quid. . . . Then said Quid, 'I think that Homer is bombast, & Shakespeare is too wild, & Milton has no feelings: they might be easily outdone. Chatterton never writ those poems! A parcel of fools, going to Bristol! If I was to go, I'd find it out in a minute, but I've found it out already.'[65]

Blake, as satirist, has been compared with Peacock. There is also some affinity with *Alice in Wonderland*, as, for instance, in the following scrap of conversation:

Obtuse Angle, Scopprell, Aradobo, & Tilly Lally are all met in Obtuse Angle's study.

'Pray' said Aradobo, 'is Chatterton a Mathematician?'

'No,' said Obtuse Angle. 'How can you be so foolish as to think he was?'

'Oh, I did not think he was—I only ask'd,' said Aradobo.

'How could you think he was not, & ask if he was?' said Obtuse Angle.

'Oh no, Sir. I did think he was, before you told me, but afterwards I thought he was not.'

Obtuse Angle said, 'In the first place you thought he was, & then afterwards when I said he was not, you thought he was not. Why, I know that——'

'Oh no, sir, I thought that he was not, but I ask'd to know whether he was.'

'How can that be?' said Obtuse Angle. 'How could you ask & think that he was not?'

'Why,' said he, 'it came into my head that he was not.'

'Why then,' said Obtuse Angle, 'you said that he was.'

'Did I say so? Law! I did not think I said that.'

'Did not he?' said Obtuse Angle.

'Yes,' said Scopprell.

'But I meant—' said Aradobo, 'I—I—I can't think. Law! Sir, I wish you'd tell me how it is.'

Then Obtuse Angle put his chin in his hand & said, 'Whenever you think, you must always think for yourself.'

'How, sir?' said Aradobo. 'Whenever I think, I must think myself? I think I do. In the first place——' said he with a grin.

'Poo! Poo!' said Obtuse Angle. 'Don't be a fool.'[66]

An Island in the Moon is a fresh and genuine essay in a genre to which Blake never returned. From a satirical criticism of society he passed at once to a mystical criticism of the universe, and the three Songs of Innocence which flower on his island show that the whole ebullition was but a part of the process by which the poet was arriving at full possession of his powers, the artist devising a new form of beauty, the mystic preparing for the first stage of the Way.*

* The first lines of the last verse of the song 'Phebe and Jellicoe',

    Happy people, who can be
    In happiness compar'd with ye?

seem a reminiscence of Cowley's 'Grasshopper', quoted in Bysshe's *Art of Poetry*, which Blake possessed:

    Happy Insect what can be
    In happiness compar'd to Thee?

After the death of his father in 1784 Blake, with help from Mrs. Mathew, started a print shop at 27 Broad Street, next door to the family business which was carried on by James Blake the younger. Parker, who had been a fellow apprentice at Basire's, became Blake's partner. The firm of Parker & Blake published only two prints engraved by Blake, namely 'Zephyrus and Flora' and 'Calypso', after Stothard, and there is little information about this unsuccessful venture. Meanwhile Blake continued his work for other publishers, and in 1785 again exhibited four drawings at the Academy. Three of these illustrate the story of Joseph: 'Joseph's Brethren bowing before him'; 'Joseph making himself known to them'; 'Joseph ordering Simeon to be bound.'[67] The fourth, 'The Bard, from Gray', was in Blake's own exhibition of 1809, and forms one of the subjects of his *Descriptive Catalogue*:

King Edward and his Queen Elenor are prostrated, with their horses, at the foot of a rock on which the Bard stands; prostrated by the terrors of his harp on the margin of the river Conway, whose waves bear up a corse of a slaughtered bard at the foot of the rock. The armies of Edward are seen winding among the Mountains.

"He wound with toilsome march his long array."

Mortimer and Gloucester lie spell bound behind their king.

The execution of this picture is also in Water Colours, or Fresco.[68]

Robert, now a pupil,* lived with William and Catherine. A drawing of Robert's, reminiscent of Blake both in style and subject, is in the Print Room at the British Museum, and Blake made an engraving after it. Robert, gifted and lovable, was, according to Tatham's account, consumptive, and early in 1787 he became

* In the Huntington Library and Art Galley, San Marino, California, is preserved a drawing book which had belonged to Robert. It contains drawings made by William for Robert to copy as best he could. For a description see Keynes, *Blake Studies*, pp. 4–6, where other drawings by Robert are also described and located. Blake's Notebook (formerly known as the 'Rossetti MS.') had been used by Robert and contains, among other drawings by him, 'The King and Queen of the Fairies'; this used to be ascribed to William and was reproduced as his on the cover of Gilchrist's *Life of Blake* (1880). [Ed.]

seriously ill. Blake nursed him without taking any rest for a fortnight till the end came, and then he slept for three days and nights.
At the last he saw Robert's soul rise through the ceiling 'clapping
its hands for joy.' But he had always the sense of Robert's presence.
In 1800 he wrote to Hayley: 'Thirteen years ago I lost a brother
& with his spirit I converse daily & hourly in the Spirit & See him
in my remembrance in the regions of my Imagination. I hear his
advice & even now write from his Dictate.'[69]

J. T. Smith says in his *Biographical Sketch* of Blake that Robert
revealed in a vision the secret of illuminated printing. The fragment from *An Island in the Moon*, referred to above, shows that the
matter was occupying Blake's attention.

'—them Illuminating the Manuscript.'
'Ay,' said she, 'that would be excellent.'
'Then,' said he, 'I would have all the writing Engraved instead
of Printed, & at every other leaf a high finish'd print—all in
three Volumes folio—& sell them a hundred pounds apiece. They
would print off two thousand.'
'Then,' said she, 'whoever will not have them will be ignorant
fools & will not deserve to live.'[70]

Smith's account is that

Blake, after deeply perplexing himself as to the mode of accom-
plishing the publication of his illustrated songs, without their
being subject to the expense of letter-press, his brother Robert
stood before him in one of his visionary imaginations, and so
decidedly directed him in the way in which he ought to proceed,
that he immediately followed his advice, by writing his poetry,
and drawing his marginal subjects of embellishments in outline
upon the copper-plate with an impervious liquid, and then eating
the plain parts or lights away with aquafortis considerably below
them, so that the outlines were left as a stereotype.* The plates in
this state were then printed in any tint that he wished, to enable
him or Mrs. Blake to colour the marginal figures up by hand in
imitation of drawings. . . . That Blake had many secret modes of

* The term 'stereotype' is properly used only for a cast of movable types,
but Blake and J. T. Smith employ it for etched copper blocks since the
resultant flat surface from which to print is similar. [Ed.]

working, both as a colourist and an engraver, I have no doubt.* His method of eating away the plain copper, and leaving his drawn lines of his subjects and his words as stereotype, is in my mind perfectly original.† Mrs. Blake is in possession of the secret, and she ought to receive something considerable for its communication, as I am quite certain it may be used to the greatest advantage both to artists and literary characters in general.[71]

It has been pointed out that the first idea of employing this process for book printing may have been suggested to Blake by George Cumberland, who was at work on a similar process, as appears from a letter to his brother, early in 1784.[72] In a later letter of 10 November 1784 he says, 'I sent my mode of Printing to M——'s last Review & they have copied it into all the Papers, but not quite correct.' This account is to be found in *A New Review with Literary Curiosities and Literary Intelligence*, edited by Henry Maty, A.M., Under-Librarian at the British Museum, and late Secretary to the Royal Society.

The first extant letter from Blake to Cumberland‡ is dated 6 December 1795, and implies some previous acquaintance. §

* Smith says that he used carpenter's glue instead of gum to mix with his colours, and Gilchrist, i, p. 70, says that St. Joseph had given him this hint in a vision. Gilchrist states, but without giving his authority, that Mrs. Blake next day spent 1s. 10d. of their last half-crown on the necessary materials.

† Blake's correspondence with his friend, George Cumberland, in 1808 shows that he was intending to publish an account of his 'Inventions in Art' (*Letters of William Blake*, ed. Keynes, 1968, p. 134), but the project was abandoned and no record of his techniques remains. (See Keynes, *Blake Studies*, p. 242.) [Ed.]

‡ At the time of his first extant correspondence with Blake, Cumberland was employed in the victualling department of the War Office. ('Letters of William Blake to George Cumberland', edited by Richard Garnett, *The Hampstead Annual*, 1903.) He was employed during his earlier years at the Royal Exchange Assurance Office. (Laurence Binyon, *The Engraved Designs of William Blake*, 1926, p. 12.)

§ A note by Cumberland proves that he was helping Blake to obtain work in 1791 by recommending his name as engraver of plates for Stuart and Revett's *Antiquities of Athens* (1794). (See *Letters*, p. 25, and *Blake Records*, p. 189.) In May 1780 he praised a design by Blake in an article on an exhibition at the Royal Academy, and it is quite possible that they were already friends at that date. See *Blake Records*, p. 17, n. 3. [Ed.]

Cumberland had helped Thomas Taylor to obtain literary work after he had set fire to the Freemasons' Tavern in his endeavour to invent a perpetual lamp,[73] and this led to Taylor's lectures on the Platonic Philosophy at Flaxman's house. It is therefore probable that Cumberland had met Blake some years before 1795. In any case Blake could hardly have failed to see the account published in the *New Review* and thence copied into the newspapers. If, as seems likely, Blake derived from Cumberland the idea of printing his own books, he may still have been inspired by Robert's spirit with the notion of colouring them by hand, and with the converse of Cumberland's process, which he jestingly describes in *The Marriage of Heaven and Hell*: 'But first the notion that man has a body distinct from his soul is to be expunged; this I shall do by printing in the infernal method, by corrosives, which in Hell are salutary and medicinal, melting apparent surfaces away, and displaying the infinite which was hid.'[74]

However this may be, it is clear that after Robert's death Blake found the door into the visionary world through which as a child he had strayed from time to time, as it were by accident. The *Songs of Innocence* is his twofold expression, as poet and artist, of his happiness during this, the first stage of the Mystic Way.

The first experiments in the new process were two tiny tractates: *There is No Natural Religion* and *All Religions are One*, to be described in a later chapter, which are less elaborate and less technically successful than the *Songs of Innocence*. The beauty of these songs—printed in coloured letters, the little pictures and decorations which intermingle with the text painted with a delicate brilliance by Blake's own hand—is at once too obvious and too subtle to describe; the Macgeorge copy in the Print Room at the British Museum, or another of the best examples, must be seen in order that it may be realized.*

---

* Readers will find a full and authoritative account of Blake's illuminated printing in Binyon's *Engraved Designs of William Blake*, and in Keynes, *Blake: Poet, Printer, Prophet* (Trianon Press, 1965).

II

THE CONTRARY STATES

Without Contraries is no progression.[1]

Piping down the valleys wild,
Piping songs of pleasant glee,
On a cloud I saw a child,
And he laughing said to me:

'Pipe a song about a Lamb!'
So I piped with merry chear.
'Piper, pipe that song again;'
So I piped: he wept to hear.

'Drop thy pipe, thy happy pipe;
Sing thy songs of happy chear:'
So I sung the same again,
While he wept with joy to hear.

'Piper, sit thee down and write
In a book, that all may read.'
So he vanish'd from my sight,
And I pluck'd a hollow reed,

And I made a rural pen,
And I stain'd the water clear,
And I wrote my happy songs
Every child may joy to hear.[2]

Such is the origin of the *Songs of Innocence* as told by Blake himself. Since the day of imitation and of experiment is past, the characteristics of ecstatic poetry are even more marked in these *Songs* than in the best of the *Poetical Sketches*. The poet who partakes of what has been called the 'sacramental perception' of nature[3] will try to render his experience in all its freshness and immediacy. Still more surely will the mystic's aim be ecstasy rather than excellence, since he not only knows that the veil, so beautiful and so luminous, is only a veil, but has caught glimpses of the mysteries which it protects from profane eyes. Throughout the *Songs of*

Innocence the world of nature and the world of humanity are seen through the eyes of imagination, and through the eyes of a child. The Songs are all such that 'every child may joy to hear', their primary meaning such that every child can understand. They are free not only from puerility, but from that equally common and deplorable quality, false *naïveté*: 'How wide the Gulf & Unpassable between Simplicity & Insipidity.'[4] They are written by a man who was also a child because his visionary powers enabled him to live for a time in the Age of Innocence. The children for whom he writes are in a sense ideal children, since no child is completely immune from the effects of his own experience or completely protected from the shadow cast upon him by the experience of others. But this does not make the songs unreal because every child—even the little chimney sweeper—has some stake in the Golden Age, some unreasoning, and, it may seem, unreasonable gleams of happiness.

It has been suggested that Blake in composing the *Songs of Innocence* may have acted on the hint in Dr. Watts's preface to his *Divine and Moral Songs for Children*, which he describes as 'a slight specimen, such as I could wish some happy and condescending genius would undertake for the use of children and perform much better.' There is no doubt that Blake had read the works of Watts. The resemblance between the lines from the *Horae Lyricae*,

> Nor is my soul refin'd enough
> To bear the Beaming of his Love,
>   And feel his warmer Smiles.
> When shall I rest this drooping Head?
> I love, I love the Sun, and yet I want the Shade.[5]

and the imagery of 'The Little Black Boy' is too close for coincidence.*

'Moral songs' were not needed in the age of innocence, and there is little that is didactic in these Songs of Blake's, but although

* J. H. Wicksteed suggested a connection with Salzmann's *Elements of Morality* (translated by Mary Wollstonecraft, 1791), for 'The Little Boy Lost' and 'Nurse's Song', reversing the moral. (*Times Literary Supplement*, 18 February 1932.)

the *contrary state* is not yet patent and the contrast between Innocence and Experience has not yet been made, except in so far as 'The Little Boy Lost' is a link between the two, some of them bear a secondary mystical meaning. There is, however, a tendency among students of Blake's symbolic books, especially among such as value the mystic above the poet, to impose too systematic and definite a meaning upon the lyrics in the light of their own interpretations of the details of his other works.

It is true that Blake always saw 'a Heaven in a Wild Flower',[6] but he did not carry about with him a plan of that heaven the details of which can be identified in every vision. As an example of this tendency a commentary on the Introduction to the *Songs of Innocence* may be cited: 'In this poem he declared his divine appointment to write, for the child is at once Jesus and the Spirit of Poetry—a daring identification, which later became the core of his metaphysics.'[7] 'Yet there is one hint that Innocence is not everything. In the introductory poem, the Piper pipes his song about the Lamb twice, and the second time the Poetic Genius "wept to hear". Blake meant to indicate that Innocence had its "Contrary State", which later he was to call "Experience." '[8]

The first sentence overburdens the poem with an idea which Blake has, it is true, expressed elsewhere; the second ignores the fact that the child, whose 'again' is the convincing note of childish approval, 'wept *with* joy to hear.' It is possible that critics of this school do not realize the strength of Blake's visual imagination, and therefore when he describes what he saw in a flash as a picture they give too definite an interpretation of the details, and so involve the reader in needless obscurities. For instance, the little Black Boy, whose 'soul is white', wants to say two things: that release from the body, whether black or white, will come when the beams of God's love can be borne, and that then he himself will be able to show his love and win that of the other child now estranged from him by the race barrier. This is how he says them:

> And thus I say to little English boy.
> When I from black and he from white cloud free,
> And round the tent of God like lambs we joy,

> I'll shade him from the heat, till he can bear
> To lean in joy upon our father's knee;
> And then I'll stand and stroke his silver hair,
> And be like him, and he will then love me.[9]

The picture is clear enough, but a critic[10] detects an ambiguity in the grammar which enables him to suggest that the little black boy may wish to stroke God's hair, not that of the other child, which would fit in with Blake's dictum in *There is No Natural Religion:* 'God becomes as we are, that we may be as he is.'[11] But this destroys the picture because while the little black boy is stroking God's hair the little white boy disappears. This critic also suggests that the last stanza shows that Blake did not believe in the equality of the races. Are we to infer that he thought the black or white superior? Either inference can be forced out of the details of the picture. Is the black boy able to protect the other till he is strong enough to bear the joy of God's love because he himself learnt his lesson better while in the body, or is he continuing to wait on him in a slavish capacity? The picture as Blake saw it and as we can see it forbids both interpretations.

Equally destructive of the picture is the suggestion that the fourteen-year-old Blake symbolized marriage by the golden cage in the Song 'How sweet I roamed.'[12] This would mean the superfluous insertion of a second little bird sulking in a corner of the cage or trilling unheeded songs from an importunate throat.

These criticisms of critics shall cease: we shall be grateful enough for their guidance when we come to the symbolic books, though it may sometimes seem to be but companionship in the darkness. And even among the *Songs of Innocence* there are some which only give up their full meaning if the symbolic reference be kept in mind.

'Night', for instance, is an anticipation of that later vision at Felpham described in a poetic letter to Butts,[13] which is more intense in its ecstasy and more difficult for the non-mystical reader to understand. It is, perhaps, not only the loveliest of the *Songs of Innocence*, but the most perfect poem Blake ever wrote. Even in the night of this life the moon is shining with the sun's reflected

light. Nature is beautiful, and there is care and deliverance for
those who sorrow or are in danger, but it is only when wrath
and sickness have been wholly destroyed that the universal day
can dawn.

> The sun descending in the west,
> The evening star does shine;
> The birds are silent in their nest,
> And I must seek for mine.
> The moon like a flower
> In heaven's high bower,
> With silent delight
> Sits and smiles on the night.
>
> Farewell, green fields and happy groves,
> Where flocks have took delight.
> Where lambs have nibbled, silent moves
> The feet of angels bright;
> Unseen they pour blessing
> And joy without ceasing,
> On each bud and blossom,
> And each sleeping bosom.
>
> They look in every thoughtless nest,
> Where birds are cover'd warm;
> They visit caves of every beast,
> To keep them all from harm.
> If they see any weeping
> That should have been sleeping,
> They pour sleep on their head,
> And sit down by their bed.
>
> When wolves and tygers howl for prey,
> They pitying stand and weep;
> Seeking to drive their thirst away,
> And keep them from the sheep;
> But if they rush dreadful,
> The angels, most heedful,
> Receive each mild spirit,
> New worlds to inherit.
>
> And there the lion's ruddy eyes
> Shall flow with tears of gold,
> And pitying the tender cries,
> And walking round the fold,

Saying 'Wrath, by his meekness,
And by his health, sickness
Is driven away
From our immortal day.

'And now beside thee, bleating lamb,
I can lie down and sleep;
Or think on him who bore thy name,
Graze after thee and weep.
For, wash'd in life's river,
My bright mane for ever
Shall shine like the gold
As I guard o'er the fold.'[14]

But Blake could not dwell for long in the Golden Age of
Innocence. While yet a boy he had realized that convention ruled
the world of art and letters, and that inspiration was little better
than dead. As man and mystic he gave another expression to the
same conviction. The first of his symbolic books is the 'Muses' of
the early *Poetical Sketches* writ large, but in a cryptic hieroglyph.
Tiriel is easier to read than most of these books because it is full
of movement and incident, but the symbolism is difficult to follow
in detail. Blind Tiriel, a creed outworn but still tyrannous, has lost
his wife, Myratana, Inspiration. He tries to console himself with
Har, Poetry, in his cage of conventional verse, and Heva, complacent, senile art, who are protected in their weakness by their
Mother, Mnetha,* goddess of reason. Tiriel pretends to be the
ruler of the North, the Spiritual, whereas he is, in fact, only
capable of ruling the West, the material. He deceives Reason, but
his imposition is detected by Poetry and Art, degenerate though
they be. Leaving them he encounters his mighty brother, Ijim,
Superstition, who refuses to recognize his power and returns to
his 'secret forests'. His sons, ways of thought generated by him,
refuse to help him in withstanding Superstition: he therefore
slays them, and his daughters, the Senses, who no longer have
any outlook beyond the material world, save the youngest, Hela,

* Damon, *Blake*, p. 307, notes that 'Mnetha is almost an anagram of
Athena.'

the fifth sense, Touch. She, still alive, though degraded, guides him back to the dwelling of Har and Heva, meeting on the way his 'foolish brother', Zazel, representing older creeds which have been subjected by him, who now jeers at his age and blindness. Tiriel at last admits that he is only the ruler of the material region, but dies when he realizes his error in substituting the restriction of law for the freedom of imagination.

> . . . when Tiriel felt the ankles of aged Har,
> He said: 'O weak mistaken father of a lawless race,
> Thy laws, O Har, & Tiriel's wisdom, end together in a curse.
> Why is one law given to the lion & the patient Ox?'[15]
>
> .   .   .   .   .
>
> 'And why men bound beneath the heavens in a reptile form,
> A worm of sixty winters creeping on the dusky ground?
> The child springs from the womb; the father ready stands to form
> The infant head, while the mother idle plays with the dog on her
>   couch:
> The young bosom is cold for lack of mother's nourishment, &
>   milk
> Is cut off from the weeping mouth: with difficulty & pain
> The little lids are lifted & the little nostrils open'd:
> The father forms a whip to rouze the sluggish senses to act
> And scourges off all youthful fancies from the new-born man.
> Then walks the weak infant in sorrow, compell'd to number
>   footsteps
> Upon the sand &c.
> And when the drone has reach'd his crawling length,
> Black berries appear that poison all around him. Such was Tiriel,
> Compell'd to pray repugnant & to humble the immortal spirit
> Till I am subtil as a serpent in a paradise,
> Consuming all, both flowers & fruits, insects & warbling birds.
> And now my paradise is fall'n & a drear sandy plain
> Returns my thirsty hissings in a curse on thee, O Har,
> Mistaken father of a lawless race, my voice is past.'

He ceast, outstretch'd at Har & Heva's feet in awful death.[16]

The text gives no promise of redemption, but there is a signifi-cant hint in the last illustration where the young vines of ecstasy are springing up round the dead body of Tiriel.

The metaphysic of *Tiriel* is developed in the later *Book of Urizen*, and the significance of the survival of Hela, the sense of touch, is explained in the Introduction to *Europe*. The poem was written about 1789, but was not printed till 1874, when W. M. Rossetti included it in his Aldine edition. Twelve drawings intended to illustrate it are described by him in his annotated catalogue.*

The mood of the *Songs of Innocence* more nearly recurs in *Thel*, 1789, the second of the symbolic books, and the next lovely example of illuminated printing. It is a link between the contrary states of the *Songs of Innocence* and the *Songs of Experience*, and, but for the malevolent influence of Ossian, it might have been similar in form; a lyric seems entangled in its ambling septenaries. Nevertheless *Thel* is the most perfect poem among the symbolic books; it contains indeed none of those intense passages of magnificent rhetoric which glorify some of the later books, but it never drops into an obscurity lacking beauty for a guide. Blake had been exploring Greek thought, perhaps in the company of Thomas Taylor: he now adopted the doctrine of pre-existence, and began to make use of symbolism obviously Greek in origin. The virgin, Thel, fears her death into this life: 'A land of sorrows & of tears where never smile was seen.'[17]

The Clod of Clay, as later in a Song of Experience, tells her how to build a Heaven in Hell's despair:

'O beauty of the vales of Har! we live not for ourselves.
Thou seest me the meanest thing, and so I am indeed.
My bosom of itself is cold, and of itself is dark;
But he, that loves the lowly, pours his oil upon my head,
And kisses me, and binds his nuptial bands around my breast,
And says: "Thou mother of my children, I have loved thee
And I have given thee a crown that none can take away."
But how this is, sweet maid, I know not, and I cannot know;
I ponder, and I cannot ponder; yet I live and love.'[18]

She invites her to enter the world of experience through the gate

---

* Nine of these are known at the present time, and they are reproduced in *Tiriel*, ed. G. E. Bentley, Jr. (1967). [Ed.]

of Imagination. There she is terrified when she sees 'her own grave-plot', the body in which she will be buried, and hears of the dangers to which the five senses will expose her. She flies back into eternity: her time for experience had not yet come. There is a hint in the last illustration that Thel fears death into the body over-much. Children, symbolic of Innocence, are guiding the serpent of the senses gaily through the sea of time and space.

The *Songs of Experience* are the record of the second stage of the the Mystic Way. Despite Blake's Ossianic excursions in *Tiriel* and *The Book of Thel* the lyric gift had not failed him. The *Songs of Innocence* were issued alone in 1789, but there is no authentic copy of the *Songs of Experience* as a separate publication. In 1794 *Songs of Innocence and of Experience Shewing the Two Contrary States of the Human Soul* appeared as one volume.

Most mystics during the second or Purgative stage—the inevitable reaction after the first ecstasy—are overwhelmed with self-disgust and feel an imperative need for self-mortification that they may escape from the snares of the senses, and so fit themselves for union with the absolute, the great reality of which they have just become dimly aware. But Blake suffered a more general disillusionment: his first ecstatic vision could not be recovered by purification of himself alone. He had looked on the world through the eyes of a child: he must now see it through the eyes of a man who perceives all the evil and misery, and rebels against the errors which cause them. In the Introduction he appeals to man, the 'lapsed soul', no longer typified by the innocent child but by Earth itself, imprisoned by the starry floor which symbolizes the discrete, and therefore misleading, light of reason, and the watery shore of time and space, to listen to the Holy Word of Imagination, that the sun of day may break again on his darkness. Earth answers with a despairing cry on which the Songs that follow are a commentary. Some of them are direct antitheses to *Songs of Innocence*. It is so with 'The Tyger', and Blake does not answer the question, 'Did he who made the Lamb make thee?' 'The roaring of lions, the howling of wolves, the raging of the stormy sea, and the destructive sword, are portions of eternity, too great for the eye of man,' he says in the 'Proverbs of Hell', but there he knows at least that 'the wrath of the lion is the wisdom of God', and that 'the tygers of wrath are wiser than the horses of instruction.' The Nurse will not let the children play any longer as she can see no light; she denies the reality of their innocent joys: 'Your spring & your day are wasted in play.' The sight of the children on Holy Thursday is painful because their poverty is itself a wrong which no belated charity can right. The infant is born into a dangerous world where no joy can befall him. The chimney sweeper knows that those who allow him to toil in misery are callous and hypocritical. 'A Little Boy Lost,' showing the cruel fate of Truth and Innocence in the World of Experience, has no happy ending like 'The Little Boy Lost' and 'The Little Boy Found' of the *Songs of Innocence*. There would have been a similar contrast between 'A Little Girl Lost' and 'The Little Girl Lost' with its sequel 'The Little Girl Found' if the two latter poems, originally included in the *Songs of Innocence*, had not been transferred by Blake to the *Songs of Experience*. The distribution of the songs between Innocence and Experience varies somewhat in different copies, a sign of the close relation between the Contrary States of the Soul. 'A Dream', for example, appears among the *Songs of Experience* in two of the later copies, and 'The Voice of the Ancient Bard', which is the utterance of one who has found his way towards the light through the tangled roots of experience, was more fitly placed there. 'The School Boy', originally also a Song of Innocence, was likewise moved; the plate contains its own contrast as, though the boy in the text complains of forced instruction at school, the boy in the picture is reading a book in the vine because he enjoys it. Some critics are surprised that 'The Lilly', which opposes innocence and experience in a single quatrain, was not included among the *Songs of Innocence*, but the irony of the adjectives 'modest' and 'humble' seems to have escaped them.

The other *Songs of Experience* all bear the clear impress of the *contrary state*. The ears of man are deaf to the Holy Word of Imagination, and therefore he fears love and is incapable of forgiveness.

'To Tirzah,' the only Song of Experience which is really obscure, although the full and subtler meanings of some of the others may not reveal themselves till they have been read again and again, bears evidence of having been written at a later date, and does not appear in the earlier issues of *Songs of Innocence and of Experience*. Its symbolism cannot be understood without reference to Blake's later books. Two other lyrics might fitly have been included among the *Songs of Experience*. 'A Divine Image' is antithetic to 'The Divine Image' of the *Songs of Innocence*, said to have been composed by Blake in the New Jerusalem Church.[19] It was not, however, included by Blake himself among the Songs, nor was it printed till some years after his death. It may have been rejected by him in favour of that other antithesis 'The Human Abstract', which gives the pseudo-religious version of the Divine Image. The tree of Mystery symbolizes such religions, and the caterpillar and fly their priests who defile the truth. 'As the catterpiller chooses the fairest leaves to lay her eggs on, so the priest lays his curse on the fairest joys.'[20] 'A Cradle Song', again, with its exquisite

> Sleep, Sleep: in thy sleep
> Little sorrows sit & weep.[21]

was obviously written as a contrast to 'A Cradle Song' of the *Songs of Innocence*, but was never included in the *Songs of Experience*.*

Some of the Songs of Experience appear in rough draft, or as fair copies from earlier drafts, in the MS. Notebook, formerly known as the Rossetti MS.† A note on the back of the fly-leaf, signed D. G. C. R., gives the history of the MS. book so far as it

---

* Blake himself wrote out an index for the *Songs* about 1818 (see *The Writings of William Blake*, ed. Keynes, Nonesuch Press, 1925, iii, p. 350), but this is not a final authority for the distribution, as he altered it in later copies of the book and in fact followed it in only a single copy. [Ed.]

† The Rossetti MS., now known as 'Blake's Notebook', having belonged first to Robert and then to William, is in the Manuscript Department of the British Museum, given by Mrs. William Emerson, daughter of W. A. White, the American collector. (See Keynes, *Blake Studies*, pp. 8–13.) [Ed.]

was known to Rossetti. 'I purchased this original MS. of Palmer, an attendant in the Antique Gallery at the British Museum, on the 30th April, '47. Palmer knew Blake personally, and it was from the artist's wife that he had the present MS. which he sold me for 10*s.* Among the sketches there are one or two profiles of Blake himself.'

It has been sometimes assumed that the Palmer referred to is Samuel Palmer, the well-known artist, and one of the group known as 'The Ancients', with whom Blake became acquainted toward the end of his life. But this is obviously an error, as Samuel Palmer was never on the staff of the British Museum; his brother, William Palmer, was appointed as attendant in the Antique Gallery in 1848, and it may therefore be concluded that it was he who sold the MS. Rossetti copied all that he considered of value in the book, both verse and prose. He apparently contemplated the separate publication of a part of the contents of the MS. book, as he wrote on 1 November 1860 to his friend, William Allingham:

A man (one Gilchrist, who lives next door to Carlyle, and is as near him in other respects as he can manage) wrote to me the other day, saying he was writing a life of Blake, and wanted to see my manuscript by that genius. Was there not some talk of *your* doing something in the way of publishing the contents? I know William thought of doing so, but fancy it might wait long for his efforts, and I have no time, but really think its contents ought to be edited, especially if a new Life gives a 'shove to the concern' (as Spurgeon expressed himself in thanking a liberal subscriber to his Tabernacle). I have not yet engaged myself any way to said Gilchrist on the subject, though I have told him he can see it here if he will give me a day's notice.[22]

Abandoning his first idea, Rossetti lent the MS. to Gilchrist in 1861, and after the death of Gilchrist he himself prepared a selection of both poems and prose for publication in the second volume of the *Life*, emending the text and sometimes adding titles of his own. In 1868 Swinburne had access to the MS. and made further extracts for his *Critical Essay*, especially from 'The Everlasting Gospel', of which he gave a long and enthusiastic exposition. He also copied from a loose scrap of paper the fragment of verse, 'A fairy leapt upon my knee.'* W. M. Rossetti made some further use of the MS. book in the Aldine edition of 1874. In 1887 the book became the property of Mr. W. A. White, and Messrs. Ellis and Yeats were enabled to print a few poems which had not appeared before. The first thorough and accurate account of the MS. was given by Dr. Sampson in his edition of 1905, from scholarly transcripts made by Mr. White, the owner. Geoffrey Keynes revised the text for the 1925 Nonesuch edition from a photographic reproduction, and corrected Dr. Sampson's reading in a, few particulars. Their careful researches have established the order and dates of the various sections.

The earliest section contains eighteen of the *Songs of Experience*, eight of which are evidently fair copies. They are distinguished from the lyrics which were not included in the *Songs of Innocence and of Experience* or ever published by Blake himself, by a vertical line drawn through them. These earlier versions differ in various particulars from the etched Songs. The other lyrics include 'Never pain to tell thy love'[23] and 'Silent, Silent Night'.[24] Here, too, is 'I asked a thief to steal me a peach',[25] that triumph of the devil-angel over the explanatory prig, of which Swinburne wrote 'a light of laughter shines and sounds through the words'; that plaint of the rebel artist-poet, uncertain where revolt should begin or end, 'Thou hast a lap full of seed',[26] and the verses 'To Nobodaddy',[27] one of the first suggestions of Urizen, the false god of this world.†

* This fragment was lost for a time and was not known to the author. It was found later, and is now in the Lessing J. Rosenwald Collection, Library of Congress, Washington, D.C. On the reverse side Blake made a pencil drawing of 'The Infant Hercules throttling the Serpents'. [Ed.]

† Max Plowman (*Times Literary Supplement*, 18 November 1926) concluded after examining the photographic reproduction of the Notebook that Blake intended the stanza entitled 'In a Mirtle Shade' (*Complete Writings*, p. 169) as the end of 'Infant Sorrow'. The two poems would then read as one, the last stanzas being in the order given by Keynes in the margin. It has been suggested that the lines

My mother groan'd! my father wept
Into the dangerous world I leapt:

The little picture book *For Children: The Gates of Paradise*,* designs for which are in the Notebook, was engraved in 1793, but the plates were reissued about 1818, with verses written after the later symbolic books, as *For the Sexes: The Gates of Paradise*. On page 116 of the Notebook is a list of twenty-two subjects for a history of England. The *History of England* is, like *The Gates of Paradise*, described in Blake's Prospectus of 10 October 1793 as 'a small book of Engravings, Price 3s.' It was therefore, presumably, also intended to be a children's picture book, but no copy of it is known.†

---

may have been a reminiscence of Robert Greene's

The wanton smiled, father wept,
Mother cried, baby leapt.   (Sephestia's Lullaby)

In this case there is no corroborating quotation in Bysshe's *Art of Poetry*, but the resemblance between the two passages is striking.

* A drawing with the inscription *For Children: The Gates of Hell*, now in the possession of Sir Geoffrey Keynes, appears to have been intended for the title-page of a companion volume, but if a work with this title ever existed it has been lost.

† Three small water-colour designs formerly in the collection of Graham Robertson were probably intended for it. For a list of 22 subjects see *Complete Writings*, pp. 208–9.

III

REVOLUTIONARY AND MYSTIC

Energy is the only life, and is from the Body; and Reason
is the bound or outward circumference of Energy.[1]

After his brother Robert's death, Blake gave up the print shop,
which apparently was not a financial success, and moved to 28
Poland Street, where he lived for five years. Gilchrist ascribed the
dissolution of the partnership to disagreements with Parker,[2] but
does not adduce any authority for his assertion. During this
period Blake exchanged the prosperous culture of the Mathew
circle for the company of politicians and social reformers, Friends
of Liberty and members of the London Corresponding Society.
He used to tell his Tory friends in jest that by the shape of his
forehead he was a predestined republican. 'I can't help being one,
any more than you can help being a Tory: your forehead is larger
above; mine, on the contrary, over the eyes.'[3] Neither did the eyes
with their look of exaltation, the 'little clenched nostril',[4] the large
sensitive mouth with tremulous lips, suggest a readiness to accept
as ultimate and necessary the evil of this best of all possible worlds.
The red cap was so natural a covering for the fiery aureole of hair
that he alone of the Liberty Boys would wear it serenely in the
London streets till the Days of Terror changed the symbolism of
its colour. Blake's employer, Joseph Johnson, publisher of Wordsworth's *Descriptive Sketches* (1793) and famous for his encouragement of Cowper and for his generous payment of an uncovenanted
thousand pounds for the *Task*, was also the friend of enthusiasts
for American Independence, and of those who were hopefully
watching the Revolution in France and planning a democratic but
bloodless programme for England. He gave weekly dinners to his
intimates above the shop in St. Paul's Churchyard, continuing
them in the Marshal's house when he was imprisoned for selling
seditious literature. At Johnson's Blake may have met old Dr.

Price, the preacher who provoked Burke's *Reflections on the French Revolution*, the advocate of international peace and religious toleration, the inventor of the doctrine of human perfectibility which was to become the basis of Godwin's philosophic system, and an inspiration to Shelley.

Another client of Johnson's was Dr. Price's friend and successor, Joseph Priestley, discoverer of oxygen and possibly the original of Blake's 'Inflammable Gass the Wind-Finder'.* His house, library, and laboratory were wrecked during the Birmingham Riots in 1791, on the occasion of a dinner in honour of the anniversary of the French Revolution, at which he was not even present. He was offered, but declined, a seat in the National Convention, and emigrated to America in 1794. Jeremy Bentham said that he owed to Priestley his phrase 'the greatest happiness of the greatest number', and Coleridge has celebrated him as

> . . . Patriot, and Saint, and Sage
> Whom that my fleshly eye hath never seen
> A childish pang of impotent regret
> Hath thrill'd my heart. Him from his native land
> Statesmen bloodstain'd and priests idolatrous
> By dark lies madd'ning the blind multitude,
> Drove with vain hate. Calm, pitying he retir'd,
> And mus'd expectant on these promis'd years.[5]

To Johnson's came also Thomas Paine, whose writings had inspired the American struggle for liberty. Paine was saved from the gallows by Blake's common sense and foresight. Already threatened with a Government prosecution for his *Rights of Man*, he was recapitulating one evening an inflammatory speech of the night before; Blake told him that he was a dead man if he went home, where, in fact, arrest awaited him.† He was hustled off to France and took his seat in the National Convention as member

---

* Priestley addressed a series of letters to the Swedenborgians in 1791 attacking their tenets, to which J. Proud and John Bellamy replied.

† The story of Paine's narrow escape was derived by Gilchrist from Frederick Tatham and from J. Cheetham's *Life of Paine* (1817), p. 85, but it is now regarded as apocryphal. See D. V. Erdman's *Blake: Prophet against Empire* (2nd ed., 1969), pp. 154–5, and *Blake Records*, pp. 530–1. [Ed.]

for the Department of Calais. In Paris he again escaped a violent death when a muddled gaoler chalked the guillotine mark on the inside of the door.

The most attractive member of the group, and the one likely to have been most sympathetic to Blake, was Mary Wollstonecraft, to whom Johnson was more of a father than the wastrel Wollstonecraft had ever been. He published her *Original Stories from Real Life* in 1791 with six illustrations by Blake,* and later in the same year *A Vindication of the Rights of Women*, which gained for her Walpole's soubriquet of 'hyena in petticoats'. Mary Wollstonecraft's later story is well known; her desertion by the American, Imlay, her strange alliance with Godwin, which perhaps gave her as full a happiness as her nature and bitter past experience allowed, and her death after the birth of the child who was to become Mary Shelley. To the period of the Johnson dinners belongs her passion for another of the guests, the flirtatious Fuseli.[6] According to his biographer she wished to join the Fuseli household as a spiritual concubine without interfering with Mrs. Fuseli's conjugal rights, and it has been suggested that Blake's poem 'Mary' is a sympathetic reminiscence of Mary Wollstonecraft's candour.[7] After Fuseli had rejected her love she went to France, where further unhappiness was in store for her.

Godwin, whose cold intellect and lucid style exercised an unparalleled influence on the young men of his own and the succeeding generation, is said to have been antipathetic to Blake.† He

---

* Blake made ten drawings, of which only six were used. These were formerly in the collection of A. E. Newton. One of the unpublished illustrations is reproduced in Gilchrist's *Life*, i, p. 90, two in Keynes, *Bibliography*, and all of them in W. Clark Durant's *Memoirs of Mary Wollstonecraft* (1927). Blake engraved about 16 of the 51 plates after Chodowiecki, in Mary Wollstonecraft's translation of Salzmann's *Elements of Morality, for the use of children; with an Introductory Address to Parents* (1791). See Keynes, *Bibliography*, pp. 235–6. In 1791 Blake also engraved five plates for *The Botanic Garden*, by Erasmus Darwin, which was published by Johnson. The engraving of the 'Fertilization of Egypt', after Fuseli, is signed by Blake, but the four of Wedgwood's Portland vase are unsigned though certainly by him. See Keynes, *Blake Studies*, pp. 59–61.

† Gilchrist (i, p. 92) does not give his authority for the statement, and no allusion to Blake by Godwin or Mary Wollstonecraft has been found.

preached the progress of human perfectibility by means of the improvement of external conditions, and the inducement of rational opinions by education and argument: error must be exterminated by expostulation, not by punishment. His ideal, modified towards the end of his life, was a universal benevolence based on reason in which there was place neither for affection nor for gratitude. Blake's philanthropy was more impulsive. To one free-thinker and treatise-writer, who complained that his children were dinnerless, he lent forty pounds, a part of which was exhibited by his wife to the thrifty Catherine Blake in the shape of a very gorgeous dress. The name of this plunderer has not survived.

Holcroft, who had once been a stable-boy, and whose fragment of autobiography is better remembered than his plays or his labours as a reformer, was an associate with whom Blake must have been more in sympathy. And Holcroft's stories of his ill treatment at Ascot, as a boy, may have had something to do with the vehemence of Blake's onslaught on the proprietor of Astley's circus.* Tatham tells how

Blake was standing at one of his Windows, which looked into Astleys premises (the Man who established the Theatre still called by his name) & saw a Boy hobbling along with a log to his foot such an one as is put on a Horse or Ass to prevent their straying. Blake called his Wife & asked her for what reason the log could be placed upon the boys foot: she answered that it must be for a punishment, for some inadvertency. Blakes blood boiled & his

---

H. L. Bruce ('William Blake and Gilchrist's Remarkable Coterie of Advanced Thinkers,' *Modern Philology*, February 1926) throws doubt on Blake's connection with the Johnson set. It is, however, likely that Gilchrist's reconstruction is not far out. Tatham, from whom he probably obtained information derived from Mrs. Blake, places the Paine episode at Johnson's, and says: 'He was intimate with a great many of the most learned and eminent men of his time, whom he generally met at Johnson's, the bookseller of St. Paul's Churchyard' (*Letters of William Blake*, ed. Russell, 1906, pp. 39–40). Palmer also wrote: 'Thrown early among the authors who resorted to Johnson, the bookseller, he rebuked the profanity of Paine, and was no disciple of Priestley' (Gilchrist, i, p. 347).

* This incident occurred when Blake was living in Lambeth.

indignation surpassed his forbearance, he sallied forth, & demanded in no very quiescent terms that the Boy should be loosed & that no Englishman should be subjected to those miseries, which he thought were inexcusable even towards a Slave. After having succeeded in obtaining the Boys release in some way or other he returned home. Astley by this time having heard of Blakes interference, came to his House & demanded in an equally peremptory manner, by what authority he dare come athwart his method of jurisdiction; to which Blake replied with such warmth, that blows were very nearly the consequence. The debate lasted long, but like all wise men whose anger is unavoidably raised, they ended in mutual forgiveness & mutual respect. Astley saw that his punishment was too degrading & admired Blake for his humane sensibility & Blake desisted from wrath when Astley was pacified.[8]

There is no record of Blake's conversation at Johnson's social gatherings, but the opinions which he held at this time can be gathered from his annotations to Bishop Watson's *An Apology for the Bible in a Series of Letters addressed to Thomas Paine*. He did not publish these notes. 'I have been commanded from Hell not to print this, as it is what our Enemies wish.'[9] He falls foul of the Bishop's 'Surpentine Dissimulation'. 'I believe that the Bishop laught at the Bible in his slieve & so did Locke.'[10] Paine, Deist though he was, had done good service by attacking the perversions of Christ's words and acts and also the perversions of the Bible:

Christ died as an Unbeliever & if the Bishops had their will so would Paine:* see page 1: but he who speaks a word against the Son of man shall be forgiven. Let the Bishop prove that he has not spoken against the Holy Ghost, who in Paine strives with Christendom as in Christ he strove with the Jews.[11]

The Bishop, according to Blake, gives up the case for the historical authenticity of the Bible by being ready to admit that Moses, Joshua, and Samuel may not have written the books ascribed to them:

* The Bishop intimates that it would have been better for the Christian world had Paine died before the publication of his book.

If Moses did not write the history of his acts, it takes away the authority altogether; it ceases to be history & becomes a Poem of probable impossibilities, fabricated for pleasure, as moderns say, but I say by Inspiration. . . .[12]

I cannot concieve the Divinity of the books in the Bible to consist either in who they were written by, or at what time, or in the historical evidence which may be all false in the eyes of one man & true in the eyes of another, but in the Sentiments & Examples, which, whether true or Parabolic, are Equally useful as Examples given to us of the perverseness of some & its consequent evil & the honesty of others & its consequent good. This sense of the Bible is equally true to all & equally plain to all. None can doubt the impression which he recieves from a book of Examples. If he is good he will abhor wickedness in David or Abraham; if he is wicked he will make their wickedness an excuse for his & so he would do by any other book.[13]

Paine is, of course, one of the 'moderns'. He had said in *The Age of Reason*, ch. vii, that:

There is not throughout the whole book called the Bible, any word that describes to us what we call a poet, or any word that describes what we call poetry. The case is that the word *prophet*, to which later times affixed a new idea, was the Bible word for poet, and the word *prophesying* meant the art of *making poetry*.

For the Bishop this is tantamount to describing all prophets as 'lying rascals'. Blake's comment is:

Prophets, in the modern sense of the word, have never existed. Jonah was no prophet in the modern sense, for his prophecy of Nineveh failed. Every honest man is a Prophet; he utters his opinion both of private & public matters. Thus: If you go on So, the result is So. He never says, such a thing shall happen let you do what you will. A Prophet is a Seer, not an Arbitrary Dictator. It is man's fault if God is not able to do him good, for he gives to the just & to the unjust, but the unjust reject his gift.[14]

Paine also understood the true nature of miracles better than the Bishop:

Jesus could not do miracles where unbelief hindered, hence we must conclude that the man who holds miracles to be ceased puts it out of his own power to ever witness one. The manner of a miracle being performed is in modern times considered as an arbitrary command of the agent upon the patient, but this is an impossibility, not a miracle, neither did Jesus ever do such a miracle. Is it a greater miracle to feed five thousand men with five loaves than to overthrow all the armies of Europe with a small pamphlet? Look over the events of your own life & if you do not find that you have both done such miracles & lived by such you do not see as I do. True, I cannot do a miracle thro' experiment & to domineer over & prove to others my superior power, as neither could Christ. But I can & do work such as both astonish & comfort me & mine. How can Paine, the worker of miracles, ever doubt Christ's in the above sense of the word miracle? But how can Watson ever believe the above sense of a miracle, who considers it as an arbitrary act of the agent upon an unbelieving patient, whereas the Gospel says that Christ could not do a miracle because of Unbelief?*

If Christ could not do miracles because of Unbelief, the reason alledged by Priests for miracles is false; for those who believe want not to be confounded by miracles. Christ & his Prophets & Apostles were not Ambitious miracle mongers.[15]

Here, as so often, Blake declares 'the Gospel is Forgiveness of Sins & has No Moral Precepts.' He asserts that 'the Bishops never saw the Everlasting Gospel† any more than Tom Paine', and concludes: 'It appears to me Now that Tom Paine is a better Christian that the Bishop. I have read this Book with attention & find that the Bishop has only hurt Paine's heel while Paine has broken his head. The Bishop has not answer'd one of Paine's grand objections.'[16]

With these annotations may be compared those from Blake's copy of Bacon's *Essays*, written about the same time (1798),‡

* Cf.

> 'Can you have greater Miracles than these? Men who devote
> Their life's whole comfort to intire scorn & injury & death?'
>   (*Milton, Complete Writings*, p. 506.)

† Blake's first known reference to the 'Everlasting Gospel', a phrase which he took from Revelation 14. 6.

‡ When the author was writing, Blake's annotated copy of Bacon's *Essays*, 1798, had been lost to sight and she could comment on only a few sentences quoted by Gilchrist. The book was, however, lying in an American collector's strong-room and it was brought back to this country in 1947. The annotations are printed in full in *Complete Writings*, pp. 396–410; and see Keynes, *Blake Studies*, pp. 90–7. [Ed.]

treating the philosopher with as little tenderness as the Bishop. The title-page was inscribed 'Good Advice for Satan's Kingdom'. The most noteworthy of Gilchrist's quotations are the comment on Bacon's 'Good thoughts are little better than good dreams,' 'Thought is Act. Christ's Acts were Nothing to Caesar's if this is not so,'[17] and that on 'The increase of any estate must be upon the foreigner,' 'The Increase of a State as of a Man is from Internal Improvement or Intellectual Acquirement. Man is not Improved by the hurt of another. States are not Improved at the Expense of Foreigners.'[18]

Two of Blake's later references to Bacon may be associated with these:

Meer Enthusiasm is the All in All! Bacon's Philosophy has Ruin'd England. Bacon is only Epicurus over again.[19]

Bacon's Philosophy has Destroy'd [word cut away] Art & Science, The Man who says that the Genius is not Born, but Taught—Is a Knave.
O Reader, behold the Philosopher's Grave!
He was born quite a Fool, but he died quite a Knave.[20]

But it would appear from Blake's *America: A Prophecy* that he read Bacon's *New Atlantis* to some purpose.*

Blake was in sympathy with the reformers in their revolt against priest and king, against the oppression of the poor, slavery, and the merely legal sanctity of marriage. But all these good people were concerned with external liberty only and were seeking to reinforce the tyranny of reason destructive of inner spiritual liberty. They taught the fatal doctrine of repression, not perceiving that energy, passion, even excess, lead to wisdom, and that error cannot be corrected, but must be cast out. Their criticisms of Christianity were negative, and based on a literal interpretation of the scriptures, meaningless to the student of Swedenborg. It is useful and sometimes amusing in reading Blake's later books to look back upon his association with the Johnson set; many of his

---

* See Damon, *Blake*, p. 337. Blake also quoted Bacon with approbation in a letter to Trusler (see p. 93).

bugbears, or shall we say his Angels, obviously took shape at that hospitable table. 'I have always found that Angels have the vanity to speak of themselves as the only wise; this they do with a confident insolence sprouting from systematic reasoning.'[21] He embodied their error in Urizen, the false god of Reason, and cast it out fiercely with his pen.

But his sympathy with France was as genuine as theirs, nor was it limited to a red cap and prudent advice to the Calais member of the National Convention. Only one book remains of the poem on the French Revolution which Blake probably began to write in the latter half of 1789. A page-proof of this, prepared for anonymous publication in 1791, was either withheld by Johnson's caution or withdrawn by Blake himself. It was not published till 1913.* Swinburne, who read these proof-sheets, pronounced it 'the only original work of its author worth little, or even nothing; consisting mainly of mere wind and splutter.'[22] This verdict from Blake's great champion is an aberration of criticism. Tremendous voices are audible above the tumult of Ossianic metaphor, voices whose speech is inspired by that imaginative sympathy which will not blame the individual, be he king or noble. Even the serpent-priest, the Archbishop of Paris, is vigorous and moving, while the eloquence of Orleans, 'generous as mountains', as Blake supposed in selecting him as his own mouthpiece, is surpassed by that of the Duke of Burgundy, an imaginary figure who represents the drunkenness of battle.

'Shall this marble built heaven become a clay cottage, this earth an
    oak stool, and these mowers
From the Atlantic mountains mow down all this great starry
    harvest of six thousand years?

---

* The First Book was prepared for publication by Johnson as a quarto pamphlet of ten leaves entitled: *The French Revolution. A Poem, in Seven Books. Book the First. London: Printed for J. Johnson, no. 72, St. Paul's Church-yard. MDCCXCI. [Price One Shilling]*. A proof copy was preserved in the Linnell collection and is now in the Huntington Library and Art Gallery. The poem was first reprinted in Dr. John Sampson's *The Poetical Works of William Blake* (1913), pp. 263–80. [Ed.]

And shall Necker, the hind of Geneva, stretch out his crook'd
   sickle o'er fertile France
Till our purple and crimson is faded to russet, and the kingdoms
   of earth bound in sheaves,
And the ancient forests of chivalry hewn, and the joys of the
   combat burnt for fuel;
Till the power and dominion is rent from the pole, sword and
   scepter from sun and moon,
The law and gospel from fire and air, and eternal reason and
   science
From the deep and the solid, and man lay his faded head down on
   the rock
Of eternity, where the eternal lion and eagle remain to devour?
This to prevent—urg'd by cries in day, and prophetic dreams
   hovering in night,
To enrich the lean earth that craves, furrow'd with plows, whose
   seed is departing from her—
Thy Nobles have gather'd thy starry hosts round this rebellious
   city,
To rouze up the ancient forests of Europe, with clarions of cloud
   breathing war,
To hear the horse neigh to the drum and trumpet, and the trumpet
   and war shout reply.
Stretch the hand that beckons the eagles of heaven: they cry over
   Paris, and wait
Till Fayette points his finger to Versailles; the eagles of heaven
   must have their prey!'[23]

Did Blake, finding that he had been too generous a prophet,
destroy the remaining six books of his only prophetic work, in
the accepted sense, after the September massacres? No trace of
them has been found.

Whatever may have been the contents of the lost books of *The
French Revolution*, or their scheme in Blake's mind if they were
never written, he was not content to be merely a political revolutionary, but was feeling his way towards a subversive metaphysical doctrine. There are no letters for this period to aid in
tracing his mental progress, but, fortunately, marginal notes on

Lavater's *Aphorisms** and on two of Swedenborg's books take their place.

A translation of Lavater's *Aphorisms* was published in 1788 by Lavater's friend, Fuseli, with a frontispiece designed by Fuseli and engraved by Blake, whose annotations show that at the time when he was writing the *Songs of Innocence* he was using the work of the worthy Swiss as a springboard for thought. Blake has written his name below that of Lavater, and has drawn the outline of a heart round the two names. He acted on the advice of the last Aphorism: 'If you mean to know yourself, interline such of these aphorisms as affected you agreeably in reading, and set a mark to such as left a sense of uneasiness with you; and then show your copy to whom you please.'

We have the authority of Fuseli, to whom he showed his notes, for saying that Blake, as a young man, may be known from them. Their autobiographical significance can only be fully appreciated by reading the *Aphorisms*, which today have lost their savour, and noting his comments and the passages which he has underlined.[24] The picture revealed is that of a man who prefers passion to cool villainy, active evil to passive good, a lover of laughter and downright speech, hating alike the sanctimonious and the sneerer. He venerates what is great and good in others, but cannot bear to be ignored, and so suspects himself both of egotism and of jealousy. Impulsive and emotional, he finds it difficult to form a calm and dispassionate judgement. This last defect shows itself in his relations with others: a good lover and a sound hater, he yet cannot afford to be judged by his friendships and his enmities because he errs in both, and it goes against the grain to forgive injuries. He thinks—and this is, perhaps, the

---

* In 1800 Johnson published a portrait of Lavater engraved by Blake after an unknown artist. (See Keynes, *The Separate Plates,* p. 79.) Tatham said that Blake, dissatisfied with his work, threw the plate across the room in a passion. When someone asked whether he had not injured it, he replied with his usual fun: 'Oh! I took good care of that!' (*Blake Records*, p. 526.) Blake had also engraved some plates for Lavater's *Physiognomy*, 1787. His copy of the *Aphorisms* belonged formerly to Samuel Palmer; it is now in the Huntington Library. [Ed.]

explanation of those outrageous speeches in uncongenial company to which his friends bear witness—that a man may lie for his own pleasure, provided he does not by so doing harm another or betray a sacred trust. The indirect criticism of his own genius shows that he is beset by doubts about the truth of his intuitions, and realizes that his difficulty in perfecting his work is a grave fault: at the same time he is convinced that genius manifests itself in devotion to a task which none other can achieve.* His final comment is the most precise statement which Blake anywhere makes of the philosophy from which he developed his myths and his symbolic books:

There is a strong objection to Lavater's principles (as I understand them) & that is He makes every thing originate in its accident; he makes the vicious propensity not only a leading feature of the man, but the stamina on which all his virtues grow. But as I understand Vice it is a Negative. It does not signify what the laws of Kings & Priests have call'd Vice; we who are philosophers ought not to call the Staminal Virtues of Humanity by the same name that we call the omissions of intellect springing from poverty.

Every man's leading propensity ought to be call'd his leading Virtue & his good Angel. But the Philosophy of Causes & Consequences misled Lavater as it has all his Cotemporaries. Each thing is its own cause & its own effect. Accident is the omission of act in self & the hindering of act in another; This is Vice, but all Act is Virtue. To hinder another is not an act; it is the contrary; it is a restraint on action both in ourselves & in the person hinder'd, for he who hinders another omits his own duty at the same time.

Murder is Hindering Another.

Theft is Hindering Another.

Backbiting, Undermining, Circumventing, & whatever is Negative is Vice. But the origin of this mistake in Lavater & his cotemporaries is, They suppose that Woman's Love is Sin; in consequence all the Loves & Graces with them are Sin.[25]

* Cf. Blake's annotations to Reynolds's *Discourses*: 'He who can be bound down is No Genius. Genius cannot be Bound; it may be Render'd Indignant & Outrageous.

'Oppression makes the Wise Man Mad.'
                                        SOLOMON.

(*Complete Writings*, p. 472.)

Blake, following the family tradition, was still a follower of Emanuel Swedenborg: in 1789, the year in which the *Songs of Innocence* were engraved, the names of William and Catherine Blake appear in the minute book of the Great Eastcheap Swedenborgian Society.* He may even have seen the picturesque old Baron in the flesh as he spent his eighty-fourth year in London, dying there in 1772. Swedenborg's accounts of his own visions, his belief in the spiritual symbolism of the material world and interpretation of the Bible in accordance with this belief, and his doctrine that Christ is the only God, had a lasting effect upon Blake's thought. Moreover, both point and support were given to Blake's rebellion against the old order by Swedenborg's announcement that 1757, the year of Blake's own birth, was, in consequence of a Spiritual Last Judgment, the first year of a New Age in which mankind would regain moral freedom.

His annotations to Swedenborg's *Wisdom of Angels concerning Divine Love and Divine Wisdom*, which were also written about 1789, show his sympathy in such phrases as 'The Whole of the New Church is in the Active Life & not in Ceremonies at all.'[26] He explains as against those who have misrepresented Swedenborg's meaning, that such may participate in Spiritual Wisdom 'while in the Body', and the comment 'He who Loves feels love descend into him & if he has wisdom may percieve it is from the Poetic Genius, which is the Lord,'[27] affirms the doctrine of his own tractate *All Religions are One*.

But the writings of Swedenborg's master, Jacob Boehme, the sixteenth-century German cobbler, which Blake read in Law's translation, contained a treasure of profounder thought, and induced a critical examination of Swedenborg's doctrines. From Boehme Blake derived his belief that the creation of the material world was an Act of Mercy, because by its means complete

---

* *Minutes of the First Seven Sessions* of the General Conference of the New Church, p. xx. Crabb Robinson, in his article in *Vaterländisches Museum*, 1811, says: 'He was invited to join the Swedenborgians under Proud, but declined. . . .' Joseph Proud (1745–1826) was minister of the New Church. Robinson's statement is apparently erroneous according to Mrs. K. M. Esdaile (*The Library*, 1914, p. 247).

destruction was intercepted and redemption became possible, that
union with the Eternal can be attained only by annihilation of the
selfhood, and that man is himself infinite. Two quotations from
Boehme's writings will at least suggest how stimulating and congenial they must have been to the young Blake:

If thou conceivest a small minute circle, as small as a grain of
mustard seed, yet the Heart of God is wholly and perfectly therein:
and if thou art born in God, then there is in thyself (in the circle
of thy life) the whole Heart of God undivided.

And again:

The Son of God, the Eternal Word in the Father, who is the glance,
or brightness, and the power of the light eternity, must become
man and be born in you, if you will know God: otherwise you are
in the dark stable and go about groping.[28]

Unfortunately no copy of Law's translation annotated by Blake
has yet come to light, but the two tiny tractates, *There is No
Natural Religion* and *All Religions are One*, etched about 1788,
show the impress of Boehme, their form being probably suggested
by Lavater's *Aphorisms*. Blake was quite sure that, whatever the
failings of the Established Church, the noisy rationalism of his
Deistic friends and acquaintances, Paine, Priestley, Godwin, and
the rest, was not the promised path to moral freedom. Accordingly
he exposes their limitations in the two series of *There is No Natural
Religion*, concluding that 'If it were not for the Poetic or Prophetic
character the Philosophic & Experimental would soon be at the
ratio of all things, & stand still, unable to do other than repeat the
same dull round over again.'[29] But since man's perceptions are not,
as the Deists wrongly held, limited by Sense, and his Desire is
Infinite, 'God becomes as we are, that we may be as he is.'[30]

The second tractate sets forth that *All Religions are One* inasmuch as they have one source, the True Man, who is the Poetic
Genius. This doctrine stands out against the obscure and crowded
background of his later myths.

Blake's second set of notes on Swedenborg, the annotations to
his *Wisdom of Angels Concerning Divine Providence*, written about
1790, show that he was realizing the limitations of his former

master, whom he now condemns as a predestinarian: 'Predestination after this Life is more Abominable than Calvin's, & Swedenborg is Such a Spiritual Predestinarian. . . . Cursed Folly!'[31]

The founder of the New Jerusalem Church followed other churches in appraising good and evil, in assigning reward and punishment.

'O Swedenborg! strongest of men, the Samson shorn by the Churches,
Shewing the Transgressors in Hell, the proud Warriors in Heaven,
Heaven as a Punisher, & Hell as One under Punishment.'[32]

Swedenborg, the man of science, had not been fully emancipated by his visionary enlightenment late in life; he was still ensnared by logic and reason;* as Blake put it, he had only conversed with angels, reasonable men, never with Devils, those inspired by Imagination. Moreover, his writings were not only conventional in spirit but a little ridiculous in form. So Blake began to scribble *The Marriage of Heaven and Hell* in a notebook; he had found his way through the dark, tangled wood of experience, and with a chuckle he entered upon the third stage of the Mystic Way.

This metaphor of the Mystic Way has been accepted as a useful graphic method of describing the spiritual history of those who reach the goal of their desire, union with the Eternal. Their absorption in this one aim, and their ultimate certainty that it has been fulfilled, sets them apart from others, and a study of their lives and writings shows that it is possible to recognize more or less well-defined psychological crises common to them all. Illumination, that is the renewal and increase of the first visionary intuition of the Eternal at 'Conversion', did not come to Blake as a merely personal revelation, a peaceful reassurance after the suffering of Purgation, but in the guise of a subversive rebellion against established religion, morality, and art. Illumination banished doubt, but spelt revolution.

* Blake said to Crabb Robinson that 'Swedenborg was wrong in endeavouring to explain to the *rational* faculty what the reason cannot comprehend'. (*Crabb Robinson: Blake, Coleridge, Wordsworth, Lamb, etc.*, ed. Morley, 1922, p. 5.)

Swinburne ranks *The Marriage of Heaven and Hell** as not only the greatest of Blake's books, but as 'about the greatest produced by the Eighteenth Century in the line of high poetry and spiritual speculation.'[33] It is Blake's Gospel of Revolution. All his heresies may be traced to old sources, but they are presented in an original and provocative form. The Just Man can no longer tread meekly in the Way of Holiness: Heaven has been usurped by the Angels, the hypocrites who passively obey the laws of reason. Energy the Eternal Delight, imagination, inspiration, impulse, is their Evil, and is punished with eternal torment by their God. They believe in the separate reality of the body and the soul, and that evil proceeds from the one, and good from the other. But the Just Man, become an outcast in his wrath, the Devil, the Genius, the Man in whom God Himself acts and is, knows that the body is only a portion of the soul discerned by the senses, and that if these, the doors of perception, are cleansed, everything will appear infinite as it is, and as the Eagle, the Genius, perceives it to be. No reconciliation is possible between the Angels and the Devils, between those who are in the bonds of reason, and those freed by imagination, the Poetic Genius. The Angels must be converted by Love and understanding of Christ, who was himself no mild slave of the decalogue. 'Jesus was all virtue, and acted from impulse, not from Rules.'[34] *The Marriage of Heaven and Hell* is fragmentary in form, but the Infernal Wisdom of the 'Proverbs of Hell', the dinner party (a satire on Swedenborg's visions) at which Isaiah and Ezekiel uphold the righteousness of honest indignation and the force of an imaginative faith, the excursions with the angel whose dogmatic beliefs and metaphysical arguments reveal nothing but the rottenness of education, religion, and social life among those who can only perceive and inhabit the material world of space and time, all attack conventional religion and ethics.

---

* *The Marriage of Heaven and Hell* is not dated, and it is usually assigned to 1790, as Blake speaks at the beginning of thirty-three years having passed since the coming of Swedenborg's New Age. It is probable that some of the *Songs of Experience* were written after he had at any rate begun it, but I have dealt with it after them because the mood is that which synthesizes the Contrary States and is therefore psychologically later.

In the tractate *All Religions are One*, Blake had stated that all men participate in the Poetic Genius, but now he emphasizes the division between sheep and goats, and proclaims the War of the Devils upon the Angels: 'One Law for the Lion & Ox is Oppression.'[35]

All the known copies of *The Marriage of Heaven and Hell* include 'A Song of Liberty.' It has been suggested that this 'Song' is wrongly regarded as a separate poem, and is really the last section of *The Marriage of Heaven and Hell*. This theory is based on the continuous pagination, the similarity of lettering, the balance which the 'Song' at the end would give to the 'argument' at the beginning, and the fact that the title does not differ materially in appearance from those of other sections of *The Marriage*.

Blake's reputation as a poet rests on a selection from the *Poetical Sketches*, *Songs of Innocence and of Experience*, and on some of the lyrics in the Notebook and the Pickering MS. Even *The Marriage of Heaven and Hell* finds comparatively few readers. Still fewer have attempted the symbolic books and most of these have rejected them as incomprehensible if not the works of a madman. How explain the fact that the greater number of Blake's readers— genuine admirers of his genius though they be—do not even know the titles of many of his writings? Does the fault lie with them or with Blake? Is the gulf between the lyrics and the symbolic books impassable save by a few adventurers, and what rare flowers do they pluck from those terrific crags?*

Had Blake been only a metaphysical poet he might have been content with the synthesis of the *contrary states* which he celebrated in *The Marriage of Heaven and Hell*, embodying his discovery in a series of lyrics such as the later 'Everlasting Gospel'. The mind of the metaphysician at rest, he might even have returned to perfect one or other of the experiments of the *Poetical Sketches*, forestalling the classicism of Landor, or setting free the romantic spirit imprisoned in the verse of Collins. The mysticism of the *Songs of*

---

* These questions were fully justified at the time when the author was writing; she would not have asked them at the present day. [Ed.]

Innocence and of Experience as apprehended by most of Blake's readers without the light reflected from his later writings, might have been merely a passing phase, a picturesque mode of poetical expression. But Blake's mysticism was an overwhelming personal experience, giving rise to an intense spiritual desire to which everything else must be sacrificed. The symbolic books are the wings with which he clove through his own darkness. In them he aimed at transcending the limits of the world of space and time by means of conceptions which should convey eternal truths. As an artist, despite his all-pervading mysticism, he received enthusiastic recognition from his contemporaries—Romney and Lawrence, Fuseli and Flaxman—and from the group of younger artists headed by John Linnell. As a lyrical poet he was acclaimed by Lamb and Landor, by Wordsworth and Coleridge and Southey. But the writer of the symbolic books was alone from first to last. The tares of obscurity flourish in intellectual solitude.

Apart from the blind instinct compelling him to seek salvation at any cost, what is Blake's own account of his intentions? While writing the earlier symbolic books, he did not, it would seem, despair of contemporary sympathy, but later he was avowedly addressing the *Young Men of the New Age*. To them he appeals to 'Go, put off Holiness And put on Intellect,'[36] for them he writes 'Allegory address'd to the Intellectual powers, while it is altogether hidden from the Corporeal Understanding.'[37] He did not believe that God revealed himself to saintly fools, nor that He could be approached through reasoned argument by means of philosophical propositions. Eternal truths could be comprehended only by 'Imagination heightened to vision.' Born himself in the first year of the New Age, he hoped to found a school of mystics to whom his conceptions should be intelligible. But the young men were as apathetic as their predecessors.

Blake's failure may be explained in the terms of a conversation between Wordsworth and Crabb Robinson.* Wordsworth

---

* For this conversation see *Crabb Robinson*, ed. Morley, pp. 49–50. A history of the word 'genius' and 'talent' will be found in Logan Pearsall Smith's *Words and Idioms* (1925), ch. iii.

expressed the opinion that Coleridge's talents were even greater than his genius, and that his excellence lay in the union of so much talent with so much genius. If Crabb Robinson's distinction be accepted, and it was doubtless derived from the most authentic German sources, that 'genius is properly creation and production from within and talent is the faculty of appropriation from without and assimilation,' it may be said that Blake, though supreme in genius, is deficient in talent. Without the mediation of talent which facilitates contact with the minds of others, genius stands aloof, difficult of approach. Talent tides over the inevitable shallows where inspiration has failed, and Blake's deficiency is accountable for the marked unevenness of his work both as poet and artist. Genius, self-absorbed, lacks the power of detached criticism supplied by talent; thus Blake is often strangely blind to the actual results achieved both by himself and others, because he creates mentally what he or they intended. His declaration 'I must Create a System or be enslav'd by another Man's. I will not Reason & Compare: my business is to Create'[38] is indicative of this weakness, but it is also true that he was impelled to make his own myths by lack of suitable material in which to embody his ideas. Greek thought as he knew it, mainly, it may be assumed, through the writings of the Platonists, Henry More and Thomas Taylor, satisfied neither the rebel nor the artist. More, like Blake, was 'Incola Coeli in Terrâ, an Inhabitant of Paradise and Heaven upon Earth—I sport with the Beasts of the Earth; the Lion licks my Hand like a Spaniel; and the Serpent sleeps upon my Lap, and stings me not, I play with the Fowls of Heaven; and the Birds of the Air sit singing on my Fist.' But he distrusted enthusiasm and 'Phansy' became 'Presentifical', he was satisfied with the God of the Timaeus, now the Father of Christ.* Blake, whose irritability over what he failed to assimilate again marks his lack of talent,

---

* These passages are quoted from Richard Ward's *Life of Dr. Henry More* (edition of 1911, pp. 86, 87, 91). More's condemnation would probably have covered Blake's visions. Foster Damon in his commentaries (1924) suggests resemblances to both More and Thomas Vaughan, and emphasizes Blake's knowledge of the *Timaeus*, which he could have read in Thomas Taylor's translation (*The Cratylus, Phaedo, Parmenides and Timaeus of Plato*, 1793).

rejects the Greeks as exalting reason and belittling inspiration: 'The Greek Muses are daughters of Mnemosyne, or Memory, and not of Inspiration or Imagination.'[39] 'The Gods of Greece & Egypt were Mathematical Diagrams—See Plato's Works.'[40]

Rome & Greece swept Art into their maw & destroy'd it; a Warlike State can never produce Art. It will Rob & Plunder & accumulate into one place, & Translate & Copy & Buy & Sell & Criticise, but not Make. Grecian is Mathematic Form: Gothic is Living Form, Mathematic Form is Eternal in the Reasoning Memory: Living Form is Eternal Existence.[41]

A constant student of the Bible and, like his masters, Swedenborg and Boehme, a firm believer in the symbolism of the Old Testament, Blake—unless indeed his *Designs for the Book of Job* be counted among the symbolic books—failed to find material in them adapted to the expression of his spiritual experiences and revolutionary ideas. The general notion of his mythical cosmogony is, on the other hand, plainly influenced by, although not directly derived from, *Paradise Lost*.

Although Blake created his own myths and added symbols to those common to other mystics, he did not apart from these attempt to create or even select any special phraseology for the expression of his mystical ideas. A bitter opponent of conventional Christianity he yet often adopts the religious language of Bunyan and of the followers of Wesley and Whitefield both in his letters and in his symbolic books. The explanation of this is undoubtedly that they stood for faith as opposed to rationalistic questionings. Faith for Blake implied in itself some measure of insight, and therefore the language of evangelical fervour spelt symbolic truth.

The form of the symbolic books is another stumbling block. The poet who had been so bold and felicitous in his prosodic innovations never entirely lost his lyrical gift, but for the earlier symbolic books he adopted the septenary, already used with an iambic basis in *Thel* and *Tiriel*, and with an anapaestic basis in *The French Revolution*. As the modulation of the septenary had been more lyrical in the *Book of Thel*, so it changes with the subject matter of the earlier symbolic books, becoming, for instance, more rich and varied in the *Visions of the Daughters of Albion.*

In the other Lambeth books, *Urizen, Los, Ahania,* and part of *The Song of Los,* Blake substituted for the septenary a new triple-beat measure,* but his treatment of it is even freer than his treatment of the longer metre, and it is only by taking the obstacles—long vowels and massed consonants—at a gallop that the reader can keep the rhythm clear.

In the more poetic passages of *Milton,* where he returns to the septenary, some of which will be quoted in a later chapter, the tendency is still to maintain metrical regularity, but for the rest the process described in the preface to *Jerusalem* has already begun.

When this Verse [i.e., the septenary] was first dictated to me I consider'd a Monotonous Cadence, like that used by Milton & Shakespeare & all writers of English Blank Verse, derived from the modern bondage of Rhyming, to be a necessary and indispensible part of Verse. But I soon found that in the mouth of a true Orator such monotony was not only awkward, but as much a bondage as rhyme itself. I therefore have produced a variety in every line, both of cadences & number of syllables. Every word and every letter is studied and put into its fit place; the terrific numbers are reserved for the terrific parts, the mild & gentle for the mild & gentle parts, and the prosaic for inferior parts; all are necessary to each other. Poetry Fetter'd Fetters the Human Race. Nations are Destroy'd or Flourish in proportion as Their Poetry, Painting and Music are Destroy'd or Flourish! The Primeval State of Man was Wisdom, Art and Science.[42]

In *Jerusalem,* accordingly, all metrical basis disappears save in the occasional lyrics and on plate 77, where he breaks into blank verse, again showing a lack of facility in handling it. It must be left to those who claim Blake as the first *vers-librist* to save the poet as they may: others can still admire the fire and eloquence of the orator, as he now describes himself.

Obscure mythology and inharmonious prosody bar the access

---

* There is possibly some mystical reference in the 7 and 3, and it is curious that the triple-beat measure approximated to the metre of much Hebrew verse as determined by modern scholars. See, for example, the rhythmical translation of Isaiah 10. 1–4, in *Early Religious Poetry of the Hebrews,* by E. G. King, D.D., pp. 106, 107.

to the symbolic books. At a first reading they will appear to most people—and many would never approach them but for their illuminated printing—a smouldering rubbish heap dimly lit by flickering flames of sense and beauty, but the heap will seem so large and the little flames so rare that most of them will pass it by. The few who read and re-read gradually acquire the conviction that there is no nonsense here, that Blake never wrote a word without a meaning perfectly definite to himself. This conviction may be strong enough to dispel the mist by which he had been surrounded, but the mist only drifts over from him to enwreathe his readers; and many obscurities still remain. The step which should have been the first has only just been taken. Ninety-eight years after Blake's death Geoffrey Keynes has edited the first complete and reliable text of Blake's writings.* At least we now know what Blake himself wrote, freed from the tinkerings of subsequent poets and admirers.

Another source of obscurity is that the symbolic books are largely spiritual autobiography demanding as gloss a detailed knowledge of Blake's life. The reliable data are unfortunately rather meagre: the letters and prose writings, invaluable though they be, are unevenly distributed, and for several important years any such record is almost lacking. If, for instance, we knew only of Blake's gratitude to Flaxman for his introduction to Hayley and nothing of the consequent friction between Blake and Hayley, a part of *Milton* would be incomprehensible, or an interpretation would have to be constructed without the essential facts and would certainly be false. Fresh knowledge about Blake's life might therefore throw light on obscure passages in his writings, or even alter well established interpretations. The symbolism personal to himself, such as his use of places, cannot, without a knowledge of Blake's particular associations, be the subject of more than plausible guesswork. Take, for example, the lines:

'The Corner of Broad Street weeps; Poland Street languishes;
To Great Queen Street & Lincoln's Inn all is distress & woe.'[43]

* *The Writings of William Blake*, edited in three volumes by Geoffrey Keynes (Nonesuch Press, 1925).

The more general symbolism presents another difficulty: it is so fluid that any dictionary of Blake's symbols must be used judiciously. Hence, although the best qualified critics may agree as to his main metaphysical doctrines there will remain large loopholes for difference of interpretation and difference of emphasis. Blake can be understood only in so far as his spirit enters into the reader, and every one will tend to believe in the efficacy of his own particular communion.

Blake's use of sex symbolism, in particular, will be stressed in its more literal sense or given a deeper meaning, ignored it cannot be, in accordance with the reader's habit of mind. Blake may be readily pinned through the wings as a choice specimen in the Freudian museum; the adventures of the children in the *Songs of Innocence and of Experience* can be given endless pathological significance, and the Oedipus complex, far from needing patient unravelling, positively prances through his pages. The paucity of information about his relations to his father and mother is also an asset to readers of this school. But even those who are more interested in understanding the books than in attributing complexes to the writer will differ widely in their interpretation of particular passages: some will give a symbolic sexual significance to words or phrases which seems gratuitous to others, or will insist on an application to the problems of sex where other readers will perceive only a meaning on the level where, for Blake, sex does not exist.

Blake accepted Boehme's doctrine that the Eternal Man is androgynous, and believed that sex belongs only to the divided world of time and space.

> Eternity shudder'd when they saw
> Man begetting his likeness
> On his own divided image.[44]

> Humanity knows not of Sex.[45]

> The Sexual is Threefold: the Human is Fourfold.[46]

'Humanity is far above
Sexual organization & the Visions of the Night of Beulah*
Where Sexes wander in dreams of bliss among the Emanations,
Where the Masculine & Feminine are nurs'd into Youth &
Maiden
By the tears & smiles of Beulah's Daughters till the time of Sleep
is past.'[47]

In the etching, which has been replaced in all but two copies
of the *Songs of Innocence and of Experience* by the poem 'To Tirzah',
Blake represents the regenerated, spiritual body as an androgynous
figure borne upwards by cherubs.†

'Sexual' is sometimes equivalent to emotional, and corresponds
to the special attribute of Blake's 'threefold vision.'

> Now I a fourfold vision see,
> And a fourfold vision is given to me;
> 'Tis fourfold in my supreme delight
> And threefold in soft Beulah's night
> And twofold Always. May God us keep
> From Single vision & Newton's sleep![48]

Single vision is purely material perception: in twofold vision
an intellectual value is added, in threefold an emotional, and in
fourfold a spiritual. But the earthly man can know eternity only
through, *through*, be it noted, not *with*, the senses, and the fifth
sense, touch, is identified by Blake with sex. The fairy hidden in
the tulip of Rasselas whose streaks Johnson had declined to count‡

---

* 'Beulah' is the Hebrew word for married, and the Muses are 'Beulah's
Daughters'. See Damon, *Blake*, p. 365. Cf. Isaiah 62. 4 and 5. Blake may also
have had in mind Bunyan's Beulah.

† Reproduced, Nonesuch *Writings*, i, facing p. 292. Russell (*The Engravings
of William Blake*, 1912, p. 71) described the plate as 'Subject Resembling the
Ecstasy of St. Mary Magdalene,' to which Keynes objected that the figure is
that of a man. (*Bibliography*, p. 115, note.) The interpretation given in the text
reconciles these contrary opinions.

‡ The reference is to Dr. Johnson's *The Prince of Abyssinia*, ch. x: 'The
business of a poet, said Imlac, is to examine, not the individual, but the
species, to remark general properties and large appearances: he does not
number the streaks of the tulip, or describe the different shades in the verdure
of the forest.' In the succeeding lines of the Preface to *Europe* 'the cavern'd
man' recalls that Johnson's Rasselas was a prince confined to a Happy Valley

and Reynolds had generalized away, the fairy who will only sing
when a poet makes him tipsy with 'a cup of sparkling poetic
fancies', sang this to Blake:

'Five windows light the cavern'd Man: thro' one he breathes the
    air;*
Thro' one hears music of the spheres; thro' one the eternal vine
Flourishes, that he may recieve the grapes; thro' one can look
And see small portions of the eternal world that ever groweth;
Thro' one himself pass out what time he please; but he will not,
For stolen joys are sweet & bread eaten in secret pleasant.'

So sang a Fairy, mocking, as he sat on a streak'd Tulip,
Thinking none saw him: when he ceas'd I started from the trees
And caught him in my hat, as boys knock down a butterfly.
'How know you this,' said I, 'small Sir? where did you learn this
    song?'
Seeing himself in my possession, thus he answer'd me:
'My master, I am yours! command me, for I must obey.'

'Then tell me, what is the material world, and is it dead?'
He, laughing, answer'd: 'I will write a book on leaves of flowers,
If you will feed me on love-thoughts & give me now and then
A cup of sparkling poetic fancies; so, when I am tipsie,
I'll sing to you to this soft lute, and shew you all alive
The world, when every particle of dust breathes forth its joy.'

I took him home in my warm bosom: as we went along
Wild flowers I gather'd, & he shew'd me each eternal flower:
He laugh'd aloud to see them whimper because they were pluck'd.
They hover'd round me like a cloud of incense: when I came
Into my parlour and sat down and took my pen to write,
My Fairy sat upon the table and dictated EUROPE.[49]

---

surrounded by mountains and to be entered only through 'a cavern that
passed under a rock'. [Ed.]

    * These introductory lines are found only in two of the later copies of
Europe (*Complete Writings*, pp. 237–8). Another reference to Rasselas may be
detected in the amusing visionary head of 'The Man who Built the Pyramids',
obviously not a victim to 'that hunger of imagination which preys incessantly
upon life'. [See a speech by Imlac in *The Prince of Abyssinia*, ch. xxxvii: 'But
for the pyramids no reason has ever been given adequate to the cost and
labour of the work. . . . It seems to have been erected only in compliance
with that hunger of imagination which preys incessantly upon life, and must
be always appeased by some employment.' Ed.]

The Fairy remembers how Raphael,* an Angel, speaking to Adam 'with contracted brow', warned him against the fifth sense. But the Fairy knows better than the Angel: the fifth sense, if its pleasures be not the stolen and secret joys of lust, may, should man so will it, be the great portal of imagination, and while still a dweller in this world of division he may become most nearly the Eternal Man.

'The Imagination is not a State: it is the Human Existence itself. Affection or Love becomes a State when divided from Imagination'.[50]

A perfect marriage had opened the window into the eternal world for Blake and he passed through.† 'And the strong pinion'd Eagle bore the fire of heaven in the night season.' In *Milton* there is an etching of a man and a woman lying on a shelf of rock secure above the sea of space and time; above them hovers the eagle of inspiration, on whom the man's eyes are fixed. This etching and the fairy's words give Blake's account of the matter: his biographers complete the story. Tatham tells how 'he was very much accustomed to get out of his bed in the night to write for hours, & return to bed for the rest of the night, after having committed

---

* *Paradise Lost*, Book VIII, l. 579, etc. Crabb Robinson reports in his Diary that Blake said on one occasion:

'I saw Milton in Imagination And he told me to beware of being misled by his Paradise Lost. In particular he wished me to show the falsehood of his doctrine that the pleasure of *sex* arose from the fall. The fall could not produce any pleasure. I answered the fall produced a state of *evil* in which there was a mixture of good or pleasure. And in that sense the fall may be said to produce the pleasure. But he replied that the fall produced only generation and death. And then he went off upon a rambling state [-ment?] of Union of sexes in Man as in God, an Androgynous state in which I could not follow him—' (Morley, p. 9).

That inestimable reporting angel has unfortunately repeated this conversation in his later 'Reminiscences', changing 'pleasures of sex' into 'sexual intercourse', and hence Blake has been accused of misunderstanding *Paradise Lost*. The reference is, of course, to the Ninth Book, and marks his objection to the inference that the 'pleasures of sex' are enhanced by lust.

† This account of Blake's sex mysticism is based on Foster Damon's 'The Fifth Window' (Damon, *Blake*, ch. xv).

to paper pages & pages of his mysterious Phantasies.'[51] Gilchrist quotes a testimony to his need for his wife's presence:

'She would get up in the night, when he was under his very fierce inspirations, which were as if they would tear him asunder, while he was yielding himself to the Muse, or whatever else it could be called, sketching and writing. And so terrible a task did this seem to be, that she had to sit motionless and silent; only to stay him mentally, without moving hand or foot; this for hours, and night after night.'[52]

Another visionary has said that 'Desire is hidden identity.'* Blake's desire is a reaching out towards spiritual unity. 'The voice of the Devil' had announced that:

Energy is the only life, and is from the Body; and Reason is the bound or outward circumference of Energy. . . .
Those who restrain desire, do so because theirs is weak enough to be restrained; and the restrainer or reason usurps its place & governs the unwilling.
And being restrain'd, it by degrees becomes passive, till it is only the shadow of desire.[53]

Hence Blake's hatred of repression which frustrates the 'hidden identity'. In *A Vision of the Last Judgment* he has said:

Men are admitted into Heaven not because they have curbed & govern'd their Passions or have No Passions, but because they have Cultivated their Understandings. The Treasures of Heaven are not Negations of Passion, but Realities of Intellect, from which all the Passions Emanate Uncurbed in their Eternal Glory. The Fool shall not enter into Heaven let him be ever so Holy. Holiness is not The Price of Enterance into Heaven. Those who are cast out are All Those who, having no Passions of their own because No Intellect, Have spent their lives in Curbing & Governing other People's by the Various arts of Poverty & Cruelty of all kinds.[54]

Blake believed that it was possible to maintain a life of the spirit illuminated by these eternal truths, which appear distorted in the divided world of space and time. 'What are called the vices in the natural world are the highest sublimities in the spiritual world.'[55] But he recognized the limitations of that other earthly life which men must also lead while in the body:

* Cf. A.E., *The Candle of Vision* (1918), p. 2.

Many Persons, such as Paine & Voltaire, with some of the Ancient Greeks, say: 'we will not converse concerning Good & Evil; we will live in Paradise & Liberty.' You may do so in Spirit, but not in the Mortal Body as you pretend, till after the Last Judgment; for in Paradise they have no Corporeal & Mortal Body—that originated with the Fall & was call'd Death & cannot be removed but by a Last Judgment; while we are in the world of Mortality we Must Suffer. The Whole Creation Groans to be deliver'd; there will be as many Hypocrites born as Honest Men, & they will always have superior Power in Mortal Things. You cannot have Liberty in this World without what you call Moral Virtue, & you cannot have Moral Virtue without the Slavery of that half of the Human Race who hate what you call Moral Virtue.[56]

By temperament and conviction alike Blake was the enemy of asceticism; he wrote to George Cumberland:

Now you will, I hope, shew all the family of Antique Borers that Peace & Plenty & Domestic Happiness is the Source of Sublime Art, & prove to the Abstract Philosophers* that Enjoyment & not Abstinence is the food of Intellect.[57]

And again, in *Jerusalem*:

And many of the Eternal Ones laughed after their manner:

'Have you known the Judgment that is arisen among the
Zoas of Albion, where a Man dare hardly to embrace
His own Wife for the terrors of Chastity that they call
By the name of Morality?'[58]

* A letter from Thomas Taylor, the Platonist, to George Cumberland, dated 16 October 1798, quoted by A. Symons, *Saturday Review*, 25 August 1906, suggests that Taylor was one of the 'Abstract Philosophers' referred to. 'With respect to your novel, since you desire me to give you my opinion freely of its merit, I must own that I think it more entertaining than instructive, more ingenious than moral. I will not, indeed I cannot suppose that you would undertake to defend lasciviousness publickly; and yet to me it is as much patronized by the conduct of your Sophisms as by the works of Mrs. Wollstonecraft. You will doubtless excuse the freedom of this Opinion, when you consider that as I am a professed Platonist, love with me is *true* only in proportion as it is pure; or, in other words, in proportion as it rises above the gratification of our brutal part.'

His own lack of austerity is shown amusingly by his pleasure in Mrs. Blake's luck when, seeking her fortune in Bysshe's *Art of Poetry*, she happened on an exuberant description of lovers' joys by Aphra Behn.[59] In spite of his audacious speeches and writings the only breath of scandal touching his life comes from a story, based, perhaps, on some wild saying of his own or reference to Mary Wollstonecraft's passion for Fuseli, that he proposed to add a concubine to his household. If it be true its ending is significant: Mrs. Blake cried and he gave up the idea. Blake's remark that spectators of his 'Last Judgment' will not believe that it was 'Painted by a Madman or by one in a State of Outrageous manners'[60] suggests that he resented this or some similar charge as much as he did that of madness. Mr. Crabb Robinson indeed confides to his diary, and he protects the innocence of his housemaid by confiding it in German, that on the occasion when Blake asserted that he had committed many murders he also advocated community of women.[61] It will be remembered that Dr. Johnson *often* thought how he would clothe a seraglio.[62] Blake's day-dream was bolder and less personal. He dreamt, it would seem, of a time when the return of the Golden Age was very near, when human nature had so changed that selfhood, jealousy, and lust were banished from the earth. Meanwhile he fiercely condemned the repression of natural instincts and desires because he believed in their purity, and because 'Thought is Act,' whereas repression leads to hypocrisy. False love that 'drinks another as a sponge drinks water' depends for its gratification upon the mechanical rules of religion and morality, asking with Bromion:

'And is there not one law for both the lion and the ox?
And is there not eternal fire and eternal chains
To bind the phantoms of existence from eternal life?'[63]

But the only restraint on freedom must come from love itself, love inspired by imagination, and therefore pitiful and forgiving.

I thought Love liv'd in the hot sun shine,
But O, he lives in the Moony light!
I thought to find Love in the heat of day,
But sweet Love is the Comforter of Night.

Seek Love in the Pity of others' Woe,
In the gentle relief of another's care,
In the darkness of night & the winter's snow,
In the naked & outcast, Seek Love there![64]

Blake's accounts of his visions have led some critics to suppose that he suffered from hallucinations or even that he was a medium subject to supermundane control. He himself constantly explained that he saw 'in imagination' or 'here', tapping his forehead, and that he only possessed a power common to others if they chose to exercise it. Linnell comments that Varley, for whom Blake drew the famous visionary heads, believed in the actual presence of the 'sitters' in a sense which was not shared by Blake himself. Blake says in *A Descriptive Catalogue*:

The connoisseurs and artists who have made objections to Mr. B's mode of representing spirits with real bodies, would do well to consider that the Venus, the Minerva, the Jupiter, the Apollo, which they admire in Greek statues are all of them representations of spiritual existences, of Gods immortal, to the mortal perishing organ of sight; and yet they are embodied and organized in solid marble. Mr. B. requires the same latitude, and all is well. The Prophets describe what they saw in Vision as real and existing men, whom they saw with their imaginative and immortal organs; the Apostles the same; the clearer the organ the more distinct the object. A Spirit and a Vision are not, as the modern philosophy supposes, a cloudy vapour, or a nothing: they are organized and minutely articulated beyond all that the mortal and perishing nature can produce. He who does not imagine in stronger and better lineaments, and in stronger and better light than his perishing, mortal eye can see, does not imagine at all. The painter of this work asserts that all his imaginations appear to him infinitely more perfect and more minutely organized than anything seen by his mortal eye. Spirits are organized men.[65]

There is only one instance recorded in which a vision assumed an outward form uncontrolled by imagination. Gilchrist states that, 'When talking on the subject of ghosts, he was wont to say they did not appear much to imaginative men, but only to common minds, who did not see the finer spirits. A ghost was a thing seen by the gross bodily eye, a vision, by the mental. "Did you ever see a ghost?" asked a friend. "Never but once," was the reply. And it befell thus. Standing one evening at his garden-door in Lambeth, and chancing to look up, he saw a horrible grim figure, "scaly, speckled, very awful," stalking downstairs towards him. More frightened than ever before or after, he took to his heels, and ran out of the house.'[66]

Does Blake's own explanation meet the case, and did he merely cultivate or possess ordinary powers to an extraordinary degree? In the first place he clearly had, like all artists, the power of visualizing what he had actually seen and of giving visual form to his ideas.* Most people possess this power to some extent, the complete absence of it would be abnormal, and many can call up at will or on occasion a clear presentment of their friends and enemies, living or dead. This power is apt to be increased by any special emotion and even to escape the control of the imagination, so that they believe the person of whom they are thinking to be present in bodily form. Again, though this is less common, the imagination may be so stimulated by something actually seen that the percipient temporarily loses the power of discriminating between what he sees and what he imagines. The tree and lawn of a town garden are for him a wood and meadows until he returns to dispel the illusion. Blake, it would seem, except in that one instance, never confused spiritual vision with that of the 'gross bodily eye'.

---

* Symons (*William Blake*, 1907, p. 217) records a remark of Rodin's on Blake's drawings:

'I was once showing Rodin some facsimiles of Blake's drawings, and telling him about Blake, I said: "He used to literally see these figures; they are not mere inventions"; "Yes," said Rodin, "he saw them once; he should have seen them three or four times." '

It is probable that Blake's weaker inventions are hasty records of something seen in imagination and not fully and repeatedly visualized, but J. T. Smith records that he often saw a vision of the figure in 'The Ancient of Days' (*Blake Records*, p. 470), and Wicksteed, *The Quest*, vol. iii, nos. 1 and 3, gives instances of the adaptation and improvement of earlier designs. Cf. Galton's account of 'Mental Imagery' in *Inquiries into Human Faculty*.

At one of Mrs. Aders's evening parties he described how 'the other evening, taking a walk, I came to a meadow, and at the further corner of it I saw a fold of lambs. Coming nearer, the ground blushed with flowers; and the wattled cote and its woolly tenants were of an exquisite pastoral beauty. But I looked again, and it proved to be no living flock, but beautiful sculpture.'[67] Artists will not need his explanation to the inquiring lady that he had seen the sculpture *here*, touching his forehead; and many other people must have hung in the galleries of the mind pictures which are not mere direct visual memories, but works of art, of things seen in a moment of imagination, perhaps after the eye and brain have been stimulated by some picture or poem. Everyone must have shared the Blakes' experience of seeing figures in the fire, and understand Blake's saying to Richmond: 'I can look at a knot in a piece of wood till I am frightened at it.'[68] Further it should be noted that Blake's visionary heads were drawn in the late evening, and that he often made visionary sketches at night.[69] This suggests another perfectly normal experience—that of hypnagogic images, things seen on the verge of sleep. Some people may not see these images at all, or only when ill or tired: others welcome their coming as the customary herald of sleep. For some the darkness fashions itself into heads or forms of no special significance, like those seen on a discoloured wall: for others they seem to convey a message from the unconscious mind —a scene, perhaps, which may even have a word, or part of a word, written across the sky. Others—and their experience more closely resembles Blake's—are suddenly shown, as it were, pictures from a magic lantern, representing nothing they have actually seen—some exciting incident, figures as restless as Blake's sitters, unknown peoples, Greeks, Romans, and others, going about their occupations, and beautiful strange flowers. Most people are apt to ignore or minimize all such occurrences, either from the fear of being thought abnormal, or because they do not regard them as of any practical importance. Yet carefully considered these normal experiences go far to support Blake's contention that there was nothing unusual in the nature of his powers.* But he exercised them in such a way as to become a freeman of both worlds without confusing his spiritual and earthly dwelling-places. Analogous experiences are described in *The Candle of Vision*, and the author also keeps his footing firmly in both worlds.† A.E. is a believer in the 'world memory', and those who see hypnagogic images of the magic-lantern variety will be tempted to entertain this hypothesis. The following passage from *A Descriptive Catalogue* implies that Blake believed himself to possess this power:

The two pictures of Nelson and Pitt are compositions of a mythological cast, similar to those Apotheoses of Persian, Hindoo, and Egyptian Antiquity, which are still preserved on rude monuments, being copies from some stupendous originals now lost or perhaps buried till some happier age. The Artist having been taken in vision into the ancient republics, monarchies, and patriarchates of Asia, has seen those wonderful originals called in the Sacred Scriptures the Cherubim, which were sculptured and painted on walls of Temples, Towers, Cities, Palaces, and erected in the highly cultivated states of Egypt, Moab, Edom, Aram, among the Rivers of Paradise, being originals from which the Greeks and Hetrurians copied Hercules Farnese, Venus of Medicis, Apollo Belvidere, and all the grand works of ancient art. They were executed in a very superior style to those justly admired copies, being with their accompaniments terrific and grand in the highest degree. The Artist has endeavoured to emulate the grandeur of those seen in his vision, and to apply it to modern Heroes, on a smaller scale. . . .

Those wonderful originals seen in my visions, were some of them one hundred feet in height; some were painted as pictures,

* In Galton's account of 'Visionaries' in *Inquiries into Human Faculty*, he says: '. . . the familiar hallucinations of the insane are to be met with far more frequently than is commonly supposed, among people moving in society and in good working health.' Herschell describes hypnagogic images of various types in his lecture 'On Sensorial Vision' (*Familiar Lectures on Scientific Subjects*, Lecture IX). Since writing this account I have come across 'An Introductory Study of Hypnagogic Phenomena,' by F. E. Leaning (*Proceedings of the Society for Psychical Research*, May 1925), in which the whole question is fully discussed. Cf. Keats to Reynolds, 25 March 1818.

† This account of the experiences of another visionary will be helpful to those who wish to understand Blake.

and some carved as basso relievos, and some as groupes of statues, all containing mythological and recondite meaning, where more is meant than meets the eye.[70]

Blake's frequent references to his visions in company not capable of understanding him or them, naturally led to the state of affairs thus described by Gilchrist: 'In society, people would disbelieve and exasperate him, would set upon the gentle yet fiery-hearted mystic, and stir him up into being extravagant, out of a mere spirit of opposition. Then he would say things on purpose to startle and make people stare. In the excitement of conversation he would exaggerate his peculiarities of opinion and doctrine, would express a floating notion or fancy in an extreme way, without the explanation or qualification he was, in reality, well aware it needed; taking a secret pleasure in the surprise and opposition such views aroused.'[71]

It may be surmised that earnest persons like Crabb Robinson also had a provocative effect. Moreover, it is possible that Blake retained some of the characteristics of the fantasy life of a child who is easily stimulated to embroider his story by further imaginings. He says that he has seen a fairy. Ask if she was wearing a scarlet cap. 'Of course,' he will reply, 'and a green cloak with a big gold button.'

Blake seems also to have had some power of imaginative hearing. As a boy he heard the chant of a phantom procession in Westminster Abbey: as a man he speaks of 'the sound of harps which I hear before the Sun's rising.'[72] It may well be that he heard Homer and Moses, Dante and Milton, Jesus and Socrates talk with him in as true a sense as he saw their visionary forms. This, again, only implies the possession in a greater degree of a normal power. Some hear music when they read a score, others hear an absent voice reply to an unspoken question. It is interesting to note that Southey, a thoughtful though unsympathetic observer, arrived at this explanation after a long visit to Blake: 'Whoever has had what is sometimes called the vapours, and seen faces and figures pass before his closed eyes when he is lying sleepless in bed, can very well understand how Blake saw what he painted. I am sure I can, from this experience; and from like experience can tell how sounds are heard which have had no existence but in the brain that produced them.'[73]

The notion that, so far as the symbolic books are concerned, Blake was an automatic writer, arose from ignorance of his manuscripts (now dispelled by Geoffrey Keynes's edition of the *Writings*), from lack of perception that the lyrics were also the work of a mystic, and from his own phraseology.

'I write', Blake informed Crabb Robinson, with whom his relations are fully discussed in a later chapter, 'when commanded by the spirits and the moment I have written I see the words fly abt the room in all directions. It is then published & the Spirits can read.'[74] Again he told Butts that he had written 'from immediate Dictation, twelve or sometimes twenty or thirty lines at a time, without Premeditation & even against my Will; the Time it has taken in writing was thus render'd Non Existent, & an immense Poem Exists which seems to be the Labour of a long Life, all produc'd without Labour or Study.'[75]

The hypothesis of automatic script is not only superfluous but is clearly disproved by correction during first drafts, as well as by later revision. Had Blake literally believed that he wrote every word by the command of the spirits, correction would have been obviously a profanity. The preface to *Jerusalem* already quoted is a flat contradiction of the theory; so is his address in the First Book of *Milton* to the Daughters of Beulah, who dwell on the third plane, commanding emotional as well as intellectual and direct vision:

Daughters of Beulah! Muses who inspire the Poet's Song,

    .   .   .   .   .

                          Come into my hand,
By your mild power descending down the Nerves of my right
    arm
From out the Portals of my brain, where by your ministry
The Eternal Great Humanity Divine planted his Paradise,
And in it caus'd the Spectres of the Dead to take sweet forms
In likeness of himself.[76]

The spirits were only an emphatic variation on the popular invocation to the Muse marking the particularity and force of the inspiration. Unlike his modest contemporary who wrote 'Permit the muse to dictate; she means well'* Blake makes no apology, and his comment on the following passage in Reynolds's seventh *Discourse* shows clearly what he meant by dictation. Reynolds wrote: 'To understand literally these metaphors or ideas expressed in poetical language seems to be equally absurd as to conclude, that because painters sometimes represent poets writing from the dictates of a little winged boy or genius, that this same genius did really inform him in a whisper what he was to write; and that he is himself but a mere machine, unconscious of the operations of his own mind.' Blake annotates this with 'How very Anxious Reynolds is to Disprove & Contemn Spiritual Perception!'[77]

The charge of madness has been brought against Blake both during his lifetime and since his death. He has himself said all that it is necessary to say in the first 'Memorable Fancy', where he describes his collection of the 'Proverbs of Hell', 'As I was walking among the fires of hell, delighted with the enjoyments of Genius, which to Angels look like torment and insanity.'[78] None of his intimate friends thought him mad. Neither will any 'devil' who has studied his works. A sympathetic reader of the letters must hear the very voice of the man and feel his essential sanity in spite of eccentricities and whimsicalities. In a letter to Hayley he used the word madness of himself. 'Dear Sir, excuse my enthusiasm or rather madness, for I am really drunk with intellectual vision whenever I take a pencil or graver into my hand, even as I used to be in my youth. . . .'[79] Only in this sense is the word 'mad' permissible, but mystics and other strongly imaginative people may be justly described as unstable because they slip without warning from the world of time and space into the eternal world. And it would be well for those who are so eager to charge genius

---

* David Lloyd, quoted by R. D. Havens in *The Influence of Milton on English Poetry* (1922), p. 398.

with madness to remember that they lay themselves open to the
suspicion of being mentally defective.

> 'Madman' I have been call'd: 'Fool' they call thee.
> I wonder which they Envy, Thee or Me?[80]

IV
LAMBETH

'I must Create a System or be enslav'd by another Man's.
I will not Reason & Compare: my business is to Create.'[1]

There is no record of Blake's relations with his mother after childhood. She died in 1792 at the family home, 28 Broad Street, where she had been living with James, her eldest son. William had left this neighbourhood in the autumn of 1790 and settled at 13 Hercules Buildings,* Lambeth, described by Tatham as 'a pretty, clean house of eight or ten rooms'. In the strip of garden grew a vine with luxuriant leaves and tiny fruit. This vine, Blake's favourite symbol, was never pruned. Is this fact in itself another symbol? Did he feel that his critics set too high a value on a little dish of ripe grapes? The vine veiled an arbour, the scene of an incident related by Gilchrist on the authority of Blake's new friend and patron, Thomas Butts.

'Mr. Butts calling one day found Mr. and Mrs. Blake sitting in this summer-house, freed from "those troublesome disguises" which have prevailed since the Fall. *"Come in!"* cried Blake; *"it's only Adam and Eve, you know!"* Husband and wife had been reciting passages from *Paradise Lost*, in character, and the garden of Hercules Buildings had to represent the Garden of Eden.'†

This story, although in itself of little or no importance, has been the subject of impassioned controversy. Swinburne blew a furious blast on the trumpet of Victorian propriety:

* The row of terrace houses called Hercules Buildings, now destroyed, was on the east side of the street, not, as stated by Gilchrist, on the west. The house is shown by a drawing reproduced in *Blake Records*, pl. lvi. [Ed.]

† (Gilchrist, i, p. 112.) The story has been modified in the second edition quoted above: the first edition has the additional phrase, 'a little to the scandal of wondering neighbours on more than one occasion. However they knew sufficient of the single-minded artist not wholly to misconstrue such phenomena.'

Mr. Linnell, the truest friend of Blake's age and genius, has assured me—and has expressed a wish that I should make public his assurance—that the legend of Blake and his wife, sitting as Adam and Eve in their garden, is simply a legend—to those who knew them, repulsive and absurd; based probably, if on any foundation at all, on some rough and rapid expression of Blake's in the heat and flush of friendly talk, to the effect (it may be) that such a thing, if one chose to do it, would be in itself innocent and righteous—wrong or strange only in the eyes of a world whose views and whose deeds were strange and wrong. So far Blake would probably have gone; and so far his commentators need not fear to go. But one thing does certainly seem to me loathsome and condemnable; the imputation of such a charge as has been brought against Blake on this matter, without ground and without excuse. The oral flux of fools, being as it is a tertian or quotidian malady or ague of the tongue among their kind, may deserve pity or may not, but does assuredly demand rigid medical treatment. The word or thoughts of a fine thinker and a free speaker, falling rather upon than into the ear of a servile and supine fool, will probably in all times bring forth such fruit as this. By way of solace a compensation for the folly which he half perceives and half admits, the fool must be allowed his little jest and his little lie. Only when it passes into tradition and threatens to endure, is it worth while to set foot on it.[2]

E. J. Ellis portentously queries the details as though the precarious life of his 'Real Blake' hung upon the answers.

He [Gilchrist] hints much and tells little. He suggests that Blake and his wife were stark naked in public, and would even invite a friend to see them so together. But there are several things that he does not tell us.

The first is whether he received this story *as he gives it* from Mr. Butts, or from people who 'retailed it about town.'

The second is that he does not say whether Butts walked up to the entrance of the summer-house uninvited and saw Mr. and Mrs. Blake *before* Blake spoke to him, though, from the usual nature of summer-houses, we are able to conjecture this, while Blake's speech seems not to have been an invitation but merely made to cover the embarrassment shown by his indiscreet and intrusive friend.

The third that we are not told is whether Blake and his wife had

gone naked all down to that summer-house from their own door—
it was at the end of the garden—or had disrobed *there*, a thing
which it is clear that they had a perfect right to do.

The fourth is that we are not told whether the couple were
naked at all, a question which the title of this picture,* *Unto Adam
and his Wife did the Lord make coats of skin*, leaves at least open.

The fifth is that, though this story was extensively retailed for
years before Linnell knew Blake, and though when Linnell did
know him he disbelieved it, we are not told whether Linnell's
disbelief was due to the very natural cause that he had asked
Blake whether it was true, and that Blake had said, 'Of course
not.'[3]

This last query has been disposed of by Linnell's own note
showing that he thought Blake must have mentioned such an
incident to him had it occurred. Samuel Palmer also dismissed
it as apocryphal on the ground that it was unlike Blake, whom,
be it noted, he did not meet till 1824.

Were the story true, says Ellis, the indiscretion of Butts is its
worst feature. 'He remains the only person really disgraced by it.
Gilchrist is but lightly smirched in comparison. After all, Blake
and his wife *were married*. And there is still the question of the
"coats of skin made by the Lord".' He is, however, inclined to
reject it on the ground that Mrs. Blake's polite messages to Butts
in Blake's letters to him do not show 'the smallest trace of such
familiarity as must necessarily have sprung from that scene in
the summer-house at Hercules Buildings if there had been anything in it, such as Gilchrist implies, of the nature of a *spicy
secret*.'

Nakedness will always seem an obvious and easy escape from
convention, and *Rousseau-manie* had given it a certain vogue. Dr.
Franklin, a votary of the cult, startled a servant bringing a letter
by coming naked to meet her in the garden. Shelley's friend,
Mrs. Newton, allowed her children to run about the house without
clothes, although she confined her personal observance of the rites
to her own room. Thomas Holcroft believed that he could prolong

---

* The picture, formerly in the Graham Robertson collection, is now in the
Fitzwilliam Museum, Cambridge. [Ed.]

his life by standing naked for an hour or so night and morning.[4] Although the story is reported on the authority of Thomas Butts,* Captain Butts declared that his grandfather emphatically denied it, and an unpublished letter of Samuel Palmer's† suggests that it may well have been a fabrication of Blake's pupil, the recalcitrant Master Tommy. And even if it were true it would tell us nothing significant about William or Catherine Blake.

The Lambeth period was that of Blake's greatest worldly prosperity. Mrs. Blake even tried the experiment of keeping a servant, but afterwards preferred to do the housework herself in addition to helping her husband print his books; sometimes she also helped to colour them. To these years belongs the story of a burglary when sixty pounds' worth of plate and forty pounds' worth of clothes were stolen.[5] Charity was possible on no mean scale. The Blakes noticed that a young man of delicate appearance passed their house daily carrying a portfolio. They made his acquaintance, and during the long illness which preceded his death visited him daily, supplying money, wine, and other necessaries. The gift to a free-thinker already noticed belongs to this period.

It is said that Blake had at this time pupils of high rank who found their master so delightful that, the lesson ended, they often persuaded him to spend the rest of the day in their company, but that after the misguided endeavour of friends to secure for him the post of drawing-master to the royal family he gave up teaching

---

* This information was given by Mrs. Colville-Hyde, widow of Captain Butts. Some account of Captain Butts's hereditary interest in Blake will be found in the fragment of autobiography by his daughter Mary Butts, *The Crystal Cabinet* (1937).

† George C. Smith, Jr., of New York, allowed the author to quote the following passage from a letter of Samuel Palmer to Anne Gilchrist of 22 December 1863, which was then in his possession:

I have one and only one suggestion to make, or rather one protest to lodge against what I believe to be a misconception of Mr. Butts, Junr. concerning the Lambeth garden scene—I most certainly do not believe it as he seems to have related it. Many years ago I remember a wandering rumour of something distantly like it—probably the very thing which, told him by his father, grew unconsciously in his memory. Precisely as he tells it, I disbelieve it, because *it is so very unlike Blake.*

as incompatible with his other work.* The story of George III's
only criticism when some of Blake's drawings were shown to him,
'Take them away! take them away!' bears no date.

In 1793 Blake issued a *Prospectus, To the Public,*† dated 10
October. It opens with the statement that 'The Labours of the
Artist, the Poet, the Musician, have been proverbially attended
by poverty and obscurity; this was never the fault of the Public,
but was owing to a neglect of means to propagate such works as
wholly absorbed the Man of Genius. Even Milton and Shakespeare
could not publish their own works.' Blake goes on to explain with
a cheerful truculence that he has invented a process by which these
difficulties are obviated, and that he has been able to 'bring before
the Public works (he is not afraid to say) of equal magnitude and
consequence with the productions of any age or country.' Then
follows a list containing eight illuminated books and two historical engravings, 'Job'‡ and 'Edward & Elenor'.§ The *Prospectus*
ends with the following intimation: 'No Subscriptions for the
numerous great works now in hand are asked, for none are
wanted; but the Author will produce his works, and offer them
to sale at a fair price.'‖ The prices of the books vary from 10*s.* 6*d.*
to 3*s.* The most expensive item is the engraving of Job—'What
is Man that thou should try him every Moment' (Job 7. 17 and 18),
priced at 12*s.* It is of special interest as the first presentation of a
story which was to be the subject of Blake's greatest series of
engravings. The most beautiful figure is that of Job's wife, whose

---

* Symons (*Blake*, p. 72) says, though giving no authority, that Blake gave
up other pupils from courtesy because he had refused the royal offer, but it is
not clear that the post was actually offered to him.

† No copy of Blake's *Prospectus* is known to have survived. It was seen
by Gilchrist, who is the only authority for the contents. (*Life*, ii, pp. 285–6.)
[Ed.]

‡ The large engraving of 'Job' exists in two states, the later one dated
18 August 1793. For the evolution of this design see Keynes, *The Separate
Plates*, pp. 10–12. The companion plate, 'Ezekiel', is dated 27 October 1794
(ib., pp. 23–4). [Ed.]

§ The large print of 'Edward & Elenor' is known in only one perfect
example, now in the British Museum, Department of Prints and Drawings.
For a description see Keynes, *The Separate Plates*, pp. 17–18. [Ed.]

face and attitude are expressive of deep emotion. The companion print, 'Ezekiel', 'I take away from thee the desire of thine eyes' (Ezekiel 24. 16), which was published in the next year, is as a whole even more impressive. The engraving of 'The Accusers of Theft, Adultery, Murder' had been published in 1793, but does not appear in the list. One state of this print* is inscribed with a quotation from the 'Prologue intended for a Dramatic Piece of King Edward the Fourth' in Blake's *Poetical Sketches*:

> When the senses
> Are shaken, and the soul is driven to madness.[7]

Congenial work was obtainable with less difficulty than during his latter years. In 1794 his old friend, Flaxman, came back to London after seven years in Italy. Gilchrist states that Blake engraved the plates for Flaxman's *Odyssey* (1793) as the original plates by Piroli had been lost, though his name remains on the title-page, but there appears to be no evidence for this assertion. Blake designed, but did not himself engrave, a frontispiece and two vignettes for a translation of Bürger's *Leonora*, published in 1796.

In 1794 Blake printed a *Small Book of Designs* consisting of twenty-three relief etchings from his Illuminated Books, coloured with opaque pigment. About the same time he also issued a *Large Book of Designs*, among which are coloured prints of his early 'Joseph of Arimathea preaching to the inhabitants of Britain'† and of 'Glad Day.' The only complete copies of these books known to exist are in the Print Room at the British Museum, but in each case plates apparently belonging to a second copy have survived. Both books were probably printed in the first instance for Blake's friend and admirer Ozias Humphry, the well-known miniature painter. If this be so, Blake refers to them in his letter to Dawson Turner of 9 June 1818 as 'a selection from the different Books of such as could be Printed without the Writing, tho' to the Loss of

---

* For the three states see Keynes, *The Separate Plates*, pp. 19–22. The two first states are dated 5 June 1793. [Ed.]

† Not to be confused with Blake's print of 'Joseph of Arimathea', engraved when he was an apprentice at James Basire's. [Ed.]

some of the best things. For they when Printed perfect accompany Poetical Personifications & Acts, without which Poems they never could have been Executed.'[8]

Blake's colour-printed drawings rank among his finest and most characteristic work, exhibiting an energy of inspiration akin to that of *The Marriage of Heaven and Hell*. Most of them were produced at Lambeth, many of them during the year 1795. The method is described by A. G. B. Russell in his account of the Graham Robertson Collection*: 'The method was to make the design roughly and swiftly on mill-board in distemper (not oil-colours) and while it was wet take an impression from it on paper. The blotted ground-work of this impression was coloured up by hand. The design could be revived on the mill-board when another impression was wanted.'

This magnificent series included 'Satan exulting over Eve', 'God judging Adam', 'Newton', 'Nebuchadnezzar', 'The House of Death' (the 'Lazar-House' of Milton), 'Hecate', 'Pity' from *Macbeth*, and 'The Elohim Creating Adam'.

His work had now become a subject of interest and controversy among his fellow artists. Farington notes on 19 February 1796 that 'West, Cosway,† and Humphry spoke warmly of the designs

* In the *London Mercury*, July, 1920. Graham Robertson's own account of the process is quoted by Todd in his edition of Gilchrist (1945), p. 397. Robertson's experiments in reconstructing the process were so successful that his copy of one of the colour prints in his collection appeared at a well-known auctioneer's as an original Blake and was only withdrawn when identified by himself.

† Cosway, the miniaturist, was a follower of Swedenborg: he asserted that he could raise the dead, and that the Virgin had sat to him, and God and Christ had conversed with him. (Redgrave, *A Century of English Painters*, i, p. 424.) Cf. Epigram 40, *Complete Writings*, p. 545. Russell, *Letters*, p. 55, quotes from a letter of Richard Cosway's to George Cumberland in which, after praising the outline of a picture by Leonardo which Cumberland had left with Mrs. Cosway, he says:

I hope it will not be long before I shall be able to request a sight of the picture. Why do you not get Blake to make an engraving of it? I should think he would be delighted to undertake such a work, and it would certainly *pay him very well* for whatever time and pains he may bestow upon such a plate, as we have *so very few* of Leonardo's works well engraved, and the composition of this picture is so very graceful and pleasing, I am convinced

of [William] Blake the Engraver, as works of extraordinary genius and imagination. Smirke differed in opinion, from what he had seen, so do I.'

From Farington we hear of Blake's engagement as illustrator of Young's *Night Thoughts*:

June 24th [1796]. Fuseli called on me last night & sat till 12 oClock. He mentioned [William] Blake, the Engraver, whose genius & invention have been much spoken of. Fuseli had known him several years and thinks he has a great deal of invention, but that 'fancy is the end, and not a means in his designs'. He does not employ it to give novelty and decoration to regular conceptions; but the whole of his aim is to produce singular shapes & odd combinations. . . .

Blake has undertaken to make designs to encircle the letter press of each page of 'Youngs night thoughts.' Edwards the Bookseller, of Bond S^{tr} employs him, and has had the letter press of each page laid down on a large half sheet of paper. There are ab^t 900 pages. Blake asked 100 guineas for the whole. Edwards said He could not afford to give more than 20 guineas for which Blake agreed.—Fuseli understands that Edwards proposes to select ab^t 200 from the whole and to have that number engraved as decorations for a new edition.

Farington's entry on 12 January 1797* must also refer to the *Night Thoughts*:

Blakes eccentric designs were mentioned. Stothard supported his claims to Genius, but allowed He had been misled to extravagance in his art, & He knew by whom.†—Hoppner ridiculed the absurdity of his designs, and said nothing could be more easy than

---

he might put almost any price on the print and assure himself of a very extensive sale.

This is probably the cartoon of the Virgin and St. Anne now in the Diploma Gallery. The Secretary informs me that it is referred to in the Council Minutes in 1791 as having been for some time in the possession of the Royal Academy. There is no trace of an engraving by Blake of this or of any other work by Leonardo.

* The two passages from Farington's diary are quoted in *Blake Records*, pp. 51–2, 57–8. [Ed.]

† The reference is probably to Fuseli, who is believed to have written the 'Explanation of the Engravings'.

to produce such.—They were like the conceits of a drunken fellow or a madman. 'Represent a man sitting on the moon, and pissing the Sun out—that would be a whim of as much merit.'—Stothard was angry mistaking the laughter caused by Hoppners description.

The introductory note to these illustrations was probably written by Edwards. The first part only of the edition was published, appearing in the autumn of 1797. It contained plates engraved by Blake from 43 out of his 537 designs. The copy, which belonged to Thomas Butts, was richly coloured by Blake himself.* The muse who dictated the *Night Thoughts* was a daughter of the eighteenth century, but Dr. Edward Young, at the age of seventy-six, caught strange premonitory glimpses of the Daughters of Inspiration, recorded in his *Conjectures on Original Composition*, 1759. If, as is likely enough, Blake read this little treatise, his heart must have warmed towards the author while at work on his illustrations.

The first record of Blake's acquaintance with George Cumberland, a cousin of the dramatist, is a letter of 6 December 1795, but they had probably met some years previously. The friendship lasted till the end of Blake's life; one of his last letters, written in 1827, is to Cumberland, whose home was at Bristol, and Cumberland's little message card or bookplate was his last engraving. Blake gave him some instruction in engraving and assistance in his *Thoughts on Outline*, published in 1796.† This

---

* The water-colour designs are now in the British Museum, Department of Prints and Drawings. For an account of their history see Keynes, *Blake Studies*, pp. 50–8. Nineteen coloured copies are known, the majority done from Blake's key copy by another professional colourist. There is no reason for supposing, as had been suggested, that any were done by Mrs. Blake. [Ed.]

† Cumberland says in an appendix to his *Outlines from the Antients* (1824) in which four of Blake's plates were reprinted (pp. 47–8):

... but one thing may be asserted of this work, which can be said of few others that have passed the hands of an engraver, which is, that *Mr. Blake* has condescended to take upon him the laborious office of making them, I may say, facsimiles of my originals; a compliment, from a man of his extraordinary genius and abilities, the highest, I believe, I shall ever receive:—and I am indebted to his generous partiality for the instruction which encouraged

work exalts 'the inestimable value of chaste outline' and explains
its importance in ancient art: of the 24 designs of classical subjects
drawn by Cumberland 8 were engraved by Blake. He acknowledged Cumberland's gift of the book with the exhortation:

> Go on, Go on. Such works as yours Nature & Providence, the
> Eternal Parents, demand from their children: how few produce
> them in such perfection: how Nature smiles on them: how Provi-
> dence rewards them. How all your Brethren say, 'The sound of his
> harp & his flute heard from his secret forest chears us to the
> labours of life, & we plow & reap forgetting our labour.'[9]

Cumberland was concerned in the movement for founding the
National Gallery, and Blake, who had not yet suffered his reaction
against Greek art, partly from his rejection of Greek philosophy
and partly on account of its supposed subservience to mechanical
canons, was enthusiastic about the project:*

---

me to execute a great part of the plates myself; enabling me thereby to reduce
considerably the price of the book.

He also mentions Blake's engraving in a letter to his son of 17 June 1824
as a model for C. Stothard, who was then doing some work for him:

And as to the possibility of its being done I need only refer to all those
engraved by Blake from my drawings, particularly plates 14 and 19, of which
I sent up the plates to be carefully, I hope, repaired by Blake if they are worn
by printing. He understands me, and how to keep a free and equal outline,
which is always best. I send you, with this, one from Blake's etching with my
own design. . . . I don't want the outlines mended, I don't expect that, except
from such a man as Blake; they may be, and certainly are, defective even as
contours, but if they are copied with feeling they will do very well to explain
my ideas of the system of composition, and we must be content to get them
done as well as we can in this age of very bad engravers. . . .

(B.M. MSS., Cumberland Correspondence, quoted from Keynes, *Bibliography*,
pp. 257-8.)

* Blake in his boyhood had read Fuseli's translation of Winckelmann's
Reflections on the Painting and Sculpture of the Greeks (1765), but in this passage
he was probably thinking of the successive appearance of Stuart and
Revett's *Antiquities of Athens* (first volume 1790), and Chandler and Pars's
Antiquities of Ionia (second volume 1797). He may also have heard of the
arrival in Athens in May 1800 of the staff engaged by Lord Elgin to make
drawings and casts of the Parthenon sculptures. He had himself executed
some engravings after Pars for the third volume of the *Antiquities of Athens*,
published in 1794. Cf. letter to Willey Reveley, October 1791 (*Complete
Writings*, p. 790).

I have to congratulate you on your plan for a National Gallery being put into Execution. All your wishes shall in due time be fulfilled; the immense flood of Grecian light & glory which is coming on Europe will more than realize our warmest wishes. Your honours will be unbounded when your plan shall be carried into Execution as it must be if England continues a Nation. I hear that it is now in the hands of Ministers, That the King shews it great Countenance & Encouragement, that it will soon be before Parliament, & that it *must* be extended & enlarged to take in Originals both of Painting & Sculpture by considering every valuable original that is brought into England or can be purchased Abroad as its objects of Acquisition. Such is the Plan as I am told & such must be the plan if England wishes to continue at all worth notice; as you have yourself observ'd only now, we must possess Originals as well as France or be Nothing.[10]

After the completion of the designs for Young's *Night Thoughts* Cumberland introduced Blake as a possible illustrator to the Revd. John Trusler, author of *Hogarth Moralized* and *The Way to be Rich and Respectable* and many other works,* but, as these titles suggest, the association was not a fruitful one.

I find more & more [writes Blake] that my Style of Designing is a Species by itself, & in this which I send you have been compell'd by my Genius or Angel to follow where he led; if I were to act otherwise it would not fulfil the purpose for which alone I live, which is, in conjunction with such men as my friend Cumberland, to renew the lost art of the Greeks.

I attempted every morning for a fortnight together to follow your Dictate, but when I found my attempts were in vain, resolv'd to shew an independence which I know will please an Author better than slavishly following the track of another, however admirable that track may be. At any rate, my Excuse must be: I could not do otherwise; it was out of my power!

I know I begged of you to give me your Ideas, & promised to build on them; here I counted without my host. I now find my mistake! ... But I hope that none of my Designs will be destitute

---

* Dr. Garnett gives some account of Trusler and his varied activities in 'Letters of William Blake to George Cumberland,' *The Hampstead Annual*, 1903. Blake's 'Malevolence', drawn for him, is reproduced in *Letters*, ed. Keynes, pl. ii.

of Infinite Particulars which will present themselves to the Contemplator. And tho' I call them Mine, I know that they are not Mine, being of the same opinion with Milton when he says That the Muse visits his Slumbers & awakes & governs his Song when Morn purples the East, & being also in the predicament of that prophet who says: I cannot go beyond the command of the Lord, to speak good or bad.[11]

But Dr. Trusler was not pleased: he wanted straightforward illustrations which should be immediately intelligible to himself and his readers. Blake replied to his objections:

I really am sorry that you are fall'n out with the Spiritual World, Especially if I should have to answer for it. I feel very sorry that your Ideas & Mine on Moral Painting differ so much as to have made you angry with my method of Study. If I am wrong, I am wrong in good company. I had hoped your plan comprehended All Species of this Art, & Expecially that you would not regret that Species which gives Existence to Every other, namely, Visions of Eternity. You say that I want somebody to Elucidate my Ideas. But you ought to know that What is Grand is necessarily obscure to Weak men. That which can be made Explicit to the Idiot is not worth my care. The wisest of the Ancients consider'd what is not too Explicit as the fittest for Instruction, because it rouzes the faculties to act. I name Moses, Solomon, Esop, Homer, Plato.

But as you have favor'd me with your remarks on my Design, permit me in return to defend it against a mistaken one, which is, That I have supposed Malevolence without a Cause. Is not Merit in one a Cause of Envy in another, & Serenity & Happiness & Beauty a Cause of Malevolence? But Want of Money & the Distress of a Thief can never be alledged as the Cause of his Thieving, for many honest people endure greater hardships with Fortitude. We must therefore seek the Cause elsewhere than in want of Money, for that is the Miser's passion, not the Thief's.

I have therefore proved your Reasoning Ill proportion'd, which you can never prove my figures to be; they are those of Michael Angelo, Rafael & the Antique, & of the best living Models. I percieve that your Eye is perverted by Caricature Prints, which ought not to abound so much as they do. Fun I love, but too much Fun is of all things the most loathsom. Mirth is better than Fun, & Happiness is better than Mirth. I feel that a Man may be happy in This World. And I know that This World is a World of imagination & Vision. I see Every thing I paint In This World, but Every body does not see alike. To the Eyes of a Miser a Guinea is far more beautiful than the Sun, & a bag worn with the use of Money has more beautiful proportions than a Vine filled with Grapes. The tree which moves some to tears of joy is in the Eyes of others only a Green thing which stands in the way. Some See Nature all Ridicule & Deformity, & by these I shall not regulate my proportions; & Some Scarce see Nature at all. But to the Eyes of the Man of Imagination, Nature is Imagination itself. As a man is, So he Secs. As the Eye is formed, such are its Powers. You certainly Mistake, when you say that the Visions of Fancy are not to be found in This World. To Me This World is all One continued Vision of Fancy or Imagination, & I feel Flatter'd when I am told so. What is it sets Homer, Virgil & Milton in so high a rank of Art? Why is the Bible more Entertaining & Instructive than any other book? Is it not because they are addressed to the Imagination, which is Spiritual Sensation, & but mediately to the Understanding or Reason? Such is True Painting, and such was alone valued by the Greeks & the best modern Artists. Consider what Lord Bacon says: 'Sense sends over to Imagination before Reason have judged, & Reason sends over to Imagination before the Decree can be acted.' See Advancem^t of Learning, Part 2, P. 47 of first Edition.

But I am happy to find a Great Majority of Fellow Mortals who can Elucidate My Visions, & Particularly they have been Elucidated by Children, who have taken a greater delight in contemplating my Pictures than I even hoped. Neither Youth nor Childhood is Folly or Incapacity. Some Children are Fools & so are some Old Men. But There is a vast Majority on the side of Imagination or Spiritual Sensation.[12]

The letter* from which this quotation is taken, an illuminating document to students of Blake, was no less perplexing to the worthy doctor than the design referred to.

Blake's comments in thanking Cumberland for the recommendation to Trusler, despite its failure, close the incident.

* The letter is now among the Cumberland Correspondence in the British Museum, Department of Manuscripts. It is endorsed: 'Blake, dim'd with Superstition', and this has often been attributed to Trusler; it is, however, in Cumberland's hand. [Ed.]

I have made him a Drawing in my best manner; he has sent it back with a Letter full of Criticisms, in which he says It accords not with his Intentions, which are to Reject all Fancy from his Work. How far he Expects to please, I cannot tell. But as I cannot paint Dirty rags & old shoes when I ought to place Naked Beauty or simple ornament, I despair of Ever pleasing one Class of Men. Unfortunately our authors of books are among this Class; how soon we shall have a change for the better I cannot Prophecy. Dr. Trusler says: '*Your Fancy*, from what I have seen of it, & I have seen variety at Mr Cumberland's, seems to be in the other world, or the World of Spirits, which accords not with my Intentions, which, whilst living in This World, Wish to follow *the Nature of it.*' I could not help Smiling at the difference between the doctrines of Dr Trusler & those of Christ. But, however, for his own sake I am sorry that a Man should be so enamour'd of Rowlandson's caricatures as to call them copies from life & manners, or fit Things for a Clergyman to write upon.[13]

The cold reception of the *Night Thoughts* served as a check on Blake's employment as illustrator and engraver, but he fortunately became acquainted with an enthusiastic and self-effacing patron who allowed him to follow his own bent. In the letter to Cumberland about the Trusler affair Blake continues:

As to Myself, about whom you are so kindly Interested, I live by Miracle. I am Painting small Pictures from the Bible. For as to Engraving, in which art I cannot reproach myself with any neglect, yet I am laid by in a corner as if I did not Exist, & Since my Young's Night Thoughts have been publish'd, Even Johnson & Fuseli have discarded my Graver. But as I know that He who Works & has his health cannot starve, I laugh at Fortune & Go on & on. I think I foresee better Things than I have ever seen. My Work pleases my employer, and I have an order for Fifty small Pictures at One Guinea each, which is Something better than mere copying after another artist. But above all, I feel myself happy & contented let what will come; having passed now near twenty years in ups & downs, I am used to them, & perhaps a little practise in them may turn out to benefit. It is now Exactly Twenty years since I was upon the ocean of business, &, Tho' I laugh at Fortune, I am perswaded that She Alone is the Governor of Worldly Riches, & when it is Fit She will call on me; till then I wait with Patience, in hopes that She is busied among my Friends.[14]

The 'employer' referred to was Thomas Butts, 'Muster Master General,'* who filled his house in Fitzroy Square with Blake's work: for many years he was a constant purchaser, sometimes taking a drawing a week. In posterity's debt to him must be reckoned not only the large number of Blake's paintings and drawings which might not have existed without his discerning encouragement, but letters from Blake to him, invaluable as autobiography. A letter of his, quoted in a later chapter, shows the kindly, jovial nature of the man. He came of a distinguished family, one of his ancestors being Sir William Butts, physician to Henry VIII and a patron of Holbein. Blake was engaged at a salary of twenty-six pounds per annum to teach drawing to Thomas Butts, junior, but there is a family tradition that the father profited more than the son from these lessons.† Some relics of them still survive, a copper plate‡ with a classical figure playing a harp, the fragment of another plate, and two sheets of drawings copied by Tommy from Blake's originals. In the centre of one of these is a grasshopper, probably the same which later captivated the children of John Linnell (see p. 340). A charming needlework picture of two rabbits by Mrs. Butts suggests that she too may have benefited by Blake's designs. § There was a close friendship between the two families, and frequent visits were exchanged. The youthful Tommy records, in a pocket diary of 13 May 1800, that 'Mr. and Mrs. Blake and Mr. T. Jones drank tea with mama.'[15] And again on 13 September 'Mr. Blake breakfasted with Mama.' On 14 August

* The title of 'Muster Master General' was given him by his family. In fact he was working as a clerk in this department of the War Office. [Ed.]

† This account of Butts was based on information given to the author by Mrs. Colville-Hyde.

‡ The engraving cabinet from the Butts collection (now in the Rosenwald Collection, Library of Congress, Washington, D.C.) contains the only fragment of Blake's copperplate of the symbolic works known to have survived, a part of one of the cancelled plates for *America*. The large engraving of 'Christ trampling on Satan', was probably the joint work of Blake and the younger Butts. (See Keynes, *The Separate Plates*, pp. 34–5.)

§ The great skill shown in this needlework done in silk and wool has been much admired by experts in this craft. The design and colouring are so entirely Blake-like and so different from other conventional panels by Mrs. Butts that the attribution can scarcely be in doubt. [Ed.]

1809 he writes to his mother: 'This morning I breakfasted with
George before I went to South Molton Street; you wished me to
do so while you and my Father are out of Town. Mr. and Mrs.
Blake are very well, they say I am browner and taller;—they
intend shortly to pay the promised visit at Epsom.'*

Blake's friendship with the elder Butts lasted till the end of his
life: he mentions a call from Butts in 1827.† Thomas Butts,
junior, does not appear to have appreciated either Blake or his
works: he parted with a large number of these after his father's
death, including the original 'Inventions to the Book of Job',
leaving the remainder to his son, Captain Butts, and his daughter,
Mrs. Graham Foster Piggott. Mrs. Piggott stored her share in a
loft, where it is supposed that they were devoured by rats. Captain
Butts, on the other hand, appreciated Blake's work as his grandfather had done: he only sold two or three examples during his
lifetime, but his widow was obliged to part with the collection in
1903.

About 1797 Blake made a series of illustrations for Gray's *Poems,*
these having been commissioned by Flaxman for presentation to
his wife. Blake wrote a dedicatory verse perhaps implying his
gratitude for Flaxman's kind offices with Hayley which resulted in
the move to Felpham. He had shown himself a reader of Gray as
early as 1785, when he exhibited at the Royal Academy 'The Bard,
from Gray', of which he wrote later in the *Descriptive Catalogue.*
And his 'Fly', in the *Songs of Experience*, is reminiscent of Gray's
'Poor Moralist! and what art thou? A solitary fly.' These drawings
show that Blake was attracted by Gray's imagery and humour.‡
Many of them are roughly executed and seem grotesque accom-

* Butts had a cottage at Epsom and another at Hadley. It is believed that
the Blakes stayed with them at both places.

† Gilchrist, i, p. 327, appears to have assumed a coolness between Blake
and Butts for which no evidence exists: his statement that Butts was a
merchant is also erroneous.

‡ The drawings, numbering 116, are now in the Paul Mellon Collection in
the United States. A reproduction, with a few in colour and an introduction
by Sir Herbert Grierson, was published in 1922. Another in full colour is
now (1970) in course of production by the Trianon Press, Paris, for The
Blake Trust. [Ed.]

paniments to the polished verse. Those illustrating 'A Long Story' and the 'Ode on the Death of a Favourite Cat' are, as a whole, the most successful, and are more humorous than any of Blake's other work: the alternations of his sympathy between the cat and the fish, or their 'spiritual forms', are entertaining and characteristic. Such were the occupations of the artist during the Lambeth years, years which were fruitful also for the poet and the mystic.

Visions of the Daughters of Albion, 1793, is the second of the minor symbolic books, usually described as the Lambeth Books.

Thel had personified the human soul gazing fearfully through the door of imagination upon the World of Generation, the *Visions* are concerned with her struggles when she has entered that world. Oothoon, instinct in its natural purity, is torn between Bromion, conventional religion, and morality, and Theotormon, desire restrained by reason and clouded by jealousy. Oothoon, although she has been prostituted by Bromion, implores Theotormon to believe that she is still innocent and pure.

'Silent I hover all the night, and all day could be silent
If Theotormon once would turn his loved eyes upon me.
How can I be defil'd when I reflect thy image pure?
Sweetest the fruit that the worm feeds on, & the soul prey'd on by woe,
The new wash'd lamb ting'd with the village smoke, & the bright swan
By the red earth of our immortal river. I bathe my wings,
And I am white and pure to hover round Theotormon's breast.'

Then Theotormon broke his silence, and he answer'd:—

'Tell me what is the night or day to one o'erflowed with woe?
Tell me what is a thought, & of what substance is it made?
Tell me what is a joy, & in what gardens do joys grow?
And in what rivers swim the sorrows? and upon what mountains
Wave shadows of discontent? and in what houses dwell the wretched,
Drunken with woe forgotten, and shut up from cold despair?

'Tell me where dwell the thoughts forgotten till thou call them
    forth?
Tell me where dwell the joys of old? & where the ancient loves,
And when will they renew again, & the night of oblivion past,
That I might traverse times & spaces far remote, and bring
Comforts into a present sorrow and a night of pain?
Where goest thou, O thought? to what remote land is thy flight?
If thou returnest to the present moment of affliction
Wilt thou bring comforts on thy wings, and dews and honey and
    balm,
Or poison from the desart wilds, from the eyes of the envier?'[16]

    She perceives that Urizen, the restrainer, Blake's God of reason,
who appears for the first time in this poem, is the author of
Bromion's 'one law for both the lion and the ox.'

'O Urizen! Creator of men! mistaken Demon of heaven!
Thy joys are tears, thy labour vain to form men to thine image.
How can one joy absorb another? are not different joys
Holy, eternal, infinite? and each joy is a Love.
            .   .   .   .
'Father of Jealousy, be thou accursed from the earth!
Why hast thou taught my Theotormon this accursed thing?
Till beauty fades from off my shoulders, darken'd and cast out,
A solitary shadow wailing on the margin of non-entity.

'I cry: Love! Love! Love! happy happy Love! free as the moun-
    tain wind!
Can that be Love that drinks another as a sponge drinks water,
That clouds with jealousy his nights, with weepings all the day,
To spin a web of age around him, grey and hoary, dark,
Till his eyes sicken at the fruit that hangs before his sight?
Such is self-love that envies all, a creeping skeleton
With lamplike eyes watching around the frozen marriage bed.
            .   .   .   .
'Does the sun walk in glorious raiment on the secret floor
Where the cold miser spreads his gold; or does the bright cloud
    drop
On his stone threshold? does his eye behold the beam that brings
Expansion to the eye of pity? or will he bind himself
Beside the ox to thy hard furrow? does not that mild beam blot
The bat, the owl, the glowing tyger, and the king of night?
The sea fowl takes the wintry blast for a cov'ring to her limbs,

And the wild snake the pestilence to adorn him with gems & gold;
And trees & birds & beasts & men behold their eternal joy.
Arise, you little glancing wings, and sing your infant joy!
Arise, and drink your bliss, for every thing that lives is holy!'

Thus every morning wails Oothoon; but Theotormon sits
Upon the margin'd ocean conversing with shadows dire.[17]

Blake's belief in the innocence of instinct and his passionate denunciation of the evils of repression in this poem have scandalized the 'angels'. As in some of his drawings for *Vala* he has used sex symbolism in such a way that they were partly obliterated while in Linnell's possession,* so here his words are audaciously innocent. The poem presents a twofold drama, that of the human soul in the world of experience and that of the mythological personages who exhibit her adventures. Critics vary in their emphasis on one or the other element. It must rest with the taste and judgement, and with the sense of humour of the reader to determine whether the 'girls of mild silver, or of furious gold,' whom Oothoon proposes to catch and trap, symbolize joys and instincts which should not be mutually exclusive, or whether Blake is advocating that a woman should generously supply her lover with a blonde and a brunette, and recline cheerfully on a bank watching the results. Yet Blake unmistakably refers to the social problem for which Mary Wollstonecraft was seeking a solution both personally and in her courageous book, when he writes of the tragedy of enforced chastity, and the misery of loveless marriage:

'...Till she who burns with youth, and knows no fixed lot, is bound
In spells of law to one she loathes? and must she drag the chain
Of life in weary lust? must chilling, murderous thoughts obscure
The clear heaven of her eternal spring; to bear the wintry rage
Of a harsh terror, driv'n to madness, bound to hold a rod
Over her shrinking shoulders all the day, & all the night
To turn the wheel of false desire. . . .'[18]

* Max Plowman (*Times Literary Supplement*, 1 April 1926) thinks it probable that Linnell himself was not responsible for the disfigurement of the drawings, but that they fell into the hands of some young or uneducated person, as the pencil markings are unskilled.

This poem, as a whole, is the most powerful and moving of the symbolic books, and it is not obscure if the main symbolism be once grasped. Oothoon exhibits the twofold tragedy of the spiritual conflict of the soul, and of the woman—or of the man—who comes in conflict with the social laws which do not recognize that 'One Law for the Lion & Ox is Oppression.' The answer to her questionings and lamentations is to be found in the words from the *Vision of the Last Judgment* already quoted: in this world only spiritual freedom is possible. The individual, Milton or 'William Bond', for whom some may read William Blake, must work out his own problems with the aid of love inspired by imagination.

Unorganiz'd Innocence: An Impossibility.
Innocence dwells with Wisdom, but never with Ignorance.[19]

America, 1793, the first book with 'Lambeth' on the title-page, is in subject the third of the series in which Los, who is both Time and the Poetic Spirit, plays upon his four harps, the four continents. The Preludium tells in allegory how the spirit of Man must be freed by revolt. Orc,* the terrible adolescent, breaks his chains and embraces nature, the Virgin, the Shadowy Daughter of Urthona, dumb and unfruitful till dominated by him. Then:

... she put aside her clouds & smil'd her first-born smile,
As when a black cloud shews its lightnings to the silent deep.

And spoke:

'I know thee, I have found thee, & I will not let thee go:
Thou art the image of God who dwells in darkness of Africa,
And thou art fall'n to give me life in regions of dark death.

.   .   .   .

'O what limb rending pains I feel! thy fire & my frost
Mingle in howling pains, in furrows by thy lightnings rent.
This is eternal death, and this the torment long foretold.'[20]

Then follows 'a Prophecy', or symbolic poem, describing the American Revolution. Washington, supported by Franklin, Paine, and the others, protests against the tyranny of England; the spirit of Revolt is born:

* Orc is probably an anagram of cor, heart.

And in the red clouds rose a Wonder o'er the Atlantic sea,
Intense! naked! a Human fire, fierce glowing, as the wedge
Of iron heated in the furnace: his terrible limbs were fire
With myriads of cloudy terrors, banners dark & towers
Surrounded: heat but not light went thro' the murky atmosphere.[21]

Orc proclaims the resurrection of Man's saviour, liberty:

'The morning comes, the night decays, the watchmen leave their
    stations;
The grave is burst, the spices shed, the linen wrapped up;
The bones of death, the cov'ring clay, the sinews shrunk & dry'd
Reviving shake, inspiring move, breathing, awakening,
Spring like redeemed captives when their bonds & bars are burst.
Let the slave grinding at the mill run out into the field,
Let him look up into the heavens & laugh in the bright air;
Let the inchained soul, shut up in darkness and in sighing,
Whose face has never seen a smile in thirty weary years,
Rise and look out; his chains are loose, his dungeon doors are
    open;
And let his wife and children return from the oppressor's scourge.

'They look behind at every step & believe it is a dream,
Singing: "The Sun has left his blackness & has found a fresher
    morning,
And the fair Moon rejoices in the clear & cloudless night;*
For Empire is no more, and now the Lion & Wolf shall cease." '[22]

The Angel of Albion challenges him thus:

'Blasphemous Demon, Antichrist, hater of Dignities,
Lover of wild rebellion, and transgressor of God's Law,
Why dost thou come to Angel's eyes in this terrific form?'
The Terror answer'd: 'I am Orc, wreath'd round the accursed tree:
The times are ended; shadows pass, the morning 'gins to break;
The fiery joy, that Urizen perverted to ten commands,
What night he led the starry hosts thro' the wide wilderness,
That stony law I stamp to dust; and scatter religion abroad
To the four winds as a torn book, & none shall gather the leaves;
But they shall rot on desart sands, & consume in bottomless deeps,
To make the desarts blossom, & the deeps shrink to their fountains,
And to renew the fiery joy, and burst the stony roof;
That pale religious lechery, seeking Virginity,

* The sun symbolizes intellect, and the moon the emotions.

May find it in a harlot, and in coarse-clad honesty
The undefil'd, tho' ravish'd in her cradle night and morn;
For every thing that lives is holy, life delights in life;
Because the soul of sweet delight can never be defil'd.
Fires inwrap the earthly globe, yet man is not consum'd;
Amidst the lustful fires he walks; his feet become like brass,
His knees and thighs like silver, & his breast and head like gold.'[23]

England threatens war, the representatives of the States consult together, and Boston's Angel speaks out:

He cried: 'Why trembles honesty, and like a murderer
Why seeks he refuge from the frowns of his immortal station?
Must the generous tremble & leave his joy to the idle, to the
    pestilence,
That mock him? who commanded this? what God? what Angel?
To keep the gen'rous from experience till the ungenerous
Are unrestrain'd performers of the energies of nature;
Till pity is become a trade, and generosity a science
That men get rich by; & the sandy desart is giv'n to the strong?
What God is he writes laws of peace & clothes him in a tempest?
What pitying Angel lusts for tears and fans himself with sighs?
What crawling villain preaches abstinence & wraps himself
In fat of lambs? no more I follow, no more obedience pay!'[24]

England tries to crush the spirit of liberty, but finds in dismay that it is awakening even on her own shores. Urizen, the Restrainer, is alarmed and prevents the 'Demon's Light' from reaching Europe in its full intensity for twelve years, the period between the American and French Revolutions, but:

Stiff shudderings shook the heav'nly thrones! France, Spain, &
    Italy
In terror view'd the bands of Albion, and the ancient Guardians,
Fainting upon the elements, smitten with their own plagues.
They slow advance to shut the five gates of their law-built heaven,
Filled with blasting fancies and with mildews of despair,
With fierce disease and lust, unable to stem the fires of Orc.
But the five gates were consum'd, & their bolts and hinges melted;
And the fierce flames burnt round the heavens, & round the
    abodes of men.[25]

The spirit of man has conquered.

Europe, 1794, is introduced in two copies only by the Fairy's Song, which has been already quoted. The Preludium continues the Preludium of *America*. Nature is worn out with travail, and fears what she may bring forth. But with her 'shady woe' is mingled 'visionary joy'.

'And who shall bind the infinite with an eternal band?
To compass it with swaddling bands? and who shall cherish it
With milk and honey?
I see it smile, & I roll inward, & my voice is past.'

> She ceast, & roll'd her shady clouds
> Into the secret place.[26]

Then follows another 'Prophecy', or symbolic poem. The first verse is in imitation of Milton's 'Hymn to the Nativity':

> The deep of winter came,
> What time the secret child
Descended thro' the orient gates of the eternal day:
War ceas'd, & all the troops like shadows fled to their abodes.[27]

Los, the Spirit of Poetry, rejoices, and tries to conquer by his songs Urizen, Reason, who is usurping the North, the region of the spirit, instead of being content to rule the South, his own domain of intellect. But Los is not at one with his wife Enitharmon, Inspiration and Spiritual Beauty.* She, in her division from Los, sets up false ideals from which repression and hypocrisy result. She sends forth her sons, Rintrah, Wrath, and Palamabron, Pity, saying:

'Go! tell the Human race that Woman's love is Sin;
That an Eternal life awaits the worms of sixty winters
In an allegorical abode where existence hath never come.
Forbid all Joy, & from her childhood shall the little female
Spread nets in every secret path.'[28]

Enitharmon thus renders impossible the spiritual freedom which should have followed from the birth of Christ, and then she, Inspiration, slumbers for 1,800 years.

---

* Enitharmon also symbolizes space.

Meanwhile Urizen, who had already set up the false religion of the Druids—

> Then was the serpent temple form'd, image of infinite
> Shut up in finite revolutions, and man became an Angel,
> Heaven a mighty circle turning, God a tyrant crown'd.[29]

—is lord of man's spirit. The Stone of Night, the Decalogue, is surrounded by trees of blackest leaf, superstition, and overhung by poisonous deadly nightshade, and Urizen unclasps '. . . his brazen Book That Kings & Priests had copied on Earth,' the book of charity uninformed by imagination, sympathy, and forgiveness. England is already threatened by Revolution: justice has become timid and hypocritical: Palamabron and Rintrah, Pity and Wrath, are under the sway of Enitharmon, instead of being as they should on the side of liberty. Then:

> Enitharmon laugh'd in her sleep to see (O woman's triumph!)
> Every house a den, every man bound: the shadows are fill'd
> With spectres, and the windows wove over with curses of iron:
> Over the doors 'Thou shalt not,' & over the chimneys 'Fear' is
>   written:
> With bands of iron round their necks fasten'd into the walls
> The citizens, in leaden gyves the inhabitants of suburbs
> Walk heavy; soft and bent are the bones of villagers.

The angel of Albion, surrounded by the clouds of Urizen and the flames of Orc, is powerless, and 'A mighty Spirit leap'd from the land of Albion, Nam'd Newton,' the spirit of materialism.* His coming rouses Inspiration:

> Then Enitharmon woke, nor knew that she had slept;
> And eighteen hundred years were fled
> As if they had not been.[30]

* At the time of the Newton tercentenary Dr. Charles Singer pointed out in *The Nation* that Blake had been the first to recognize that Newton inaugurated a new phase in the ascendancy of science. It should also be noticed that in Blake's colour print Newton, like the great figure in the frontispiece of *Europe*, holds a pair of compasses. Since it has been generally recognized that the doctrine of materialism no longer affords an adequate basis for the concepts of science, Blake's
> May God us keep
> From Single vision & Newton's sleep!
has acquired new meaning. (Cf. p. 321.)

But she persists in her false ideals 'Till morning oped the eastern gate'; with the light comes the Spirit of Revolution:

But terrible Orc, when he beheld the morning in the east,
Shot from the heights of Enitharmon,
And in the vineyards of red France appear'd the light of his fury.

The sun glow'd fiery red!
The furious terrors flew around
On golden chariots raging with red wheels dropping with blood!
The Lions lash their wrathful tails!
The Tigers couch upon the prey & suck the ruddy tide,
And Enitharmon groans & cries in anguish and dismay.

Then Los arose: his head he rear'd in snaky thunders clad;
And with a cry that shook all nature to the utmost pole,
Call'd all his sons to the strife of blood.[31]

The frontispiece of *Europe* showing Urizen as the Creator is one of Blake's most magnificent designs. The first sketch appears in the Notebook, page 96, with the legend: 'Who shall bind the Infinite?' and on his death-bed he laid aside the print of 'The Ancient of Days Striking the First Circle of the Earth',* which he had coloured for Tatham, with the words: 'There, I have done all I can! It is the best I have ever finished. I hope Mr. Tatham will like it.' The subject of the design is taken from Proverbs 7. 27, 'when he set a compass upon the face of the depth': and from the *Book of Urizen*, vii, 7, 8:

> He form'd a line & a plummet
> To divide the Abyss beneath;
> He form'd a dividing rule;
> He formed scales to weigh,
> He formed massy weights;
> He formed a brazen quadrant;
> He formed golden compasses,
> And began to explore the Abyss.[32]

J. T. Smith tells how 'He was inspired with the splendid grandeur of this figure, by the vision which he declared hovered over his head at the top of his staircase; and he has been frequently heard

* Now in the Whitworth Art Gallery, Manchester.

to say, that it made a more powerful impression upon his mind than all he had ever been visited by. This subject was such a favourite with him, that he always bestowed more time and enjoyed greater pleasure when colouring the print, than any thing he ever produced.'[33]

In the Palgrave copy of *Europe* in the British Museum poetical quotations are written under some of the illustrations. They are not in Blake's handwriting, and may have been inserted by the first owner of the book on his own initiative, but it is possible that they were suggested to him by Blake as explaining the pictures.* The majority of the quotations are from Bysshe's *Art of Poetry*, which Blake possessed.

The First Book of Urizen, 1794, develops one of Blake's most important metaphysical doctrines. Tom Paine had said that the Bible described a devil under the name of God. Blake was equally heretical: 'Thinking as I do that the Creator of this World is a very Cruel Being, & being a Worshipper of Christ, I cannot help saying: "the Son, O how unlike the Father!" First God Almighty comes with a Thump on the Head. Then Jesus Christ comes with a balm to heal it.'[34]

Urizen† is Blake's version of the Jehovah of the Bible. The rational principle usurps the power which should belong to the spiritual, and creates the world by division and constraint. The tyranny of reason leaves no room for freedom which is of the spirit.

The description of the creation and passages in *A Vision of the Last Judgment* suggest that Blake was acquainted with the doctrine of the *Timaeus*, at any rate as expounded by Thomas Taylor. But whereas Plato's God is represented as justified in making the most satisfactory copy of himself possible in time as the proper outlet for his energy, Urizen, the usurper, makes a

---

*This copy of *Europe* had belonged to George Cumberland and the quotations are in his hand, so that it may well be that Blake had a part in choosing them. [Ed.] *Paradise Lost*, VII, lines 225–31, are written under the frontispiece.

† Urizen may be a play on 'You reason' or 'your reason', but the i scans short.

false start, and, unlike the God of the *Timaeus* or of the Bible, he is displeased with the results. His creations are not good in his eyes, because his power over them is limited. Los, Poetry, Imagination, has entered the world of generation with him, and therefore this world has still a passage to eternity:

> Vision or Imagination is a Representation of what Eternally Exists, Really & Unchangeably. . . . This World of Imagination is the world of Eternity; it is the divine bosom into which we shall all go after the death of the Vegetated body. This World of Imagination is Infinite & Eternal, whereas the world of Generation, or Vegetation, is Finite & Temporal. There Exist in that Eternal World the Permanent Realities of Every Thing which we see reflected in this Vegetable Glass of Nature. . . .[35]

> Many suppose that before the Creation All was Solitude & Chaos. This is the most pernicious Idea that can enter the Mind, as it takes away all sublimity from the Bible & Limits All Existence to Creation & to Chaos, To the Time & Space fixed by the Corporeal Vegetative Eye, & leaves the Man who entertains such an Idea the habitation of Unbelieving demons. Eternity Exists, and All things in Eternity, Independent of Creation which was an act of Mercy.[36]

Los, by his struggle with Urizen, made the creation an act of mercy. Imagination defines error in order that it can be cast out: then and only then is spiritual freedom possible.

The Preludium announces the power of the 'primeval Priest', Urizen, over the north, spirit, and so explains the first verse of the poem.

> Lo, a shadow of horror is risen
> In Eternity! Unknown, unprolific,
> Self-clos'd, all repelling: what Demon
> Hath form'd this abominable void,
> This soul-shudd'ring vacuum? Some said
> 'It is Urizen.' But unknown, abstracted,
> Brooding, secret, the dark power hid.[37]

Urizen,

> An activity unknown and horrible,
> A self-contemplating shadow,[38]

proceeds by division and measurement. Separating himself from the Eternals he tries to make everything conform to his own notions:

> 'I have sought for a joy without pain,
> For a solid without fluctuation.'

and imposes his own wisdom:

> 'Here alone I, in books form'd of metals,
> Have written the secrets of wisdom,
> The secrets of dark contemplation,
> By fightings and conflicts dire
> With terrible monsters Sin-bred
> Which the bosoms of all inhabit,
> Seven deadly Sins of the soul.

> 'Lo! I unfold my darkness, and on
> This rock place with strong hand the Book
> Of eternal brass, written in my solitude:

> 'Laws of peace, of love, of unity,
> Of pity, compassion, forgiveness;
> Let each chuse one habitation,
> His ancient infinite mansion,
> One command, one joy, one desire,
> One curse, one weight, one measure,
> One King, one God, one Law.'[39]

Urizen and the world of his creation are cut off:

> And Los, round the dark globe of Urizen,
> Kept watch for Eternals to confine
> The obscure separation alone;
> For Eternity stood wide apart,
> As the stars are apart from the earth.[40]

Urizen has become a 'formless, unmeasurable death', convulsed by awful changes in a dreamless night. But Los gave form to the changes of Urizen, so that he, who had been one of the Eternals, became Man, and God of this world.

> All the myriads of Eternity,
> All the wisdom & joy of life
> Roll like a sea around him,
> Except what his little orbs
> Of sight by degrees unfold.

> And now his eternal life
> Like a dream was obliterated.[41]

Then Los himself, imprisoned with Urizen in the created world,
'suffer'd his fires to decay.' In his anguish he is divided from
Enitharmon, Inspiration, who, in her separation from him, becomes Pity, 'the first female', the 'divided image' of Man. The
separation of the sexes, though, as Blake's fairy knew, it opens a
door into eternity, seems to remove the world of generation still
further:

> 'Spread a Tent with strong curtains around them.
> Let cords & stakes bind in the Void,
> That Eternals may no more behold them.'[42]

Los pursues Enitharmon and begets a child Orc, the spirit of
Revolt and Freedom. But with the division of sex, jealousy has
come into being, and Orc is chained to the Rock, the Decalogue,
'beneath Urizen's deathful shadow.' But, though bound, his very
existence is a sign of hope:

> The dead heard the voice of the child
> And began to awake from sleep;
> All things heard the voice of the child
> And began to awake to life.

> And Urizen, craving with hunger,
> Stung with the odours of Nature,
> Explor'd his dens around.[43]

Then follow the lines already quoted, which are illustrated by
the frontispiece of *Europe*. Los prevents Enitharmon, Pity, from
seeing Urizen and Orc. So Urizen continues his work alone and
creates the four elements, but the world he had made is hateful
to him.

> He in darkness clos'd view'd all his race,
> And his soul sicken'd! he curs'd
> Both sons & daughters; for he saw
> That no flesh nor spirit could keep
> His iron laws one moment.

> For he saw that life liv'd upon death:
> The Ox in the slaughter house moans;

The Dog at the wintry door;
And he wept & he called it Pity,
And his tears flowed down on the winds.

Cold he wander'd on high, over their cities
In weeping & pain & woe;
And where ever he wander'd, in sorrows
Upon the aged heavens,
A cold shadow follow'd behind him
Like a spider's web, moist, cold & dim,
Drawing out from his sorrowing soul,
The dungeon-like heaven dividing,
Where ever the footsteps of Urizen
Walked over the cities in sorrow;

Till a Web, dark & cold, throughout all
The tormented element stretch'd
From the sorrows of Urizen's soul.
And the Web is a Female in embrio.
None could break the Web, no wings of fire,

So twisted the cords, & so knotted
The meshes, twisted like to the human brain.

And all call'd it The Net of Religion.[44]

Restrained by the Net of Urizen the senses are weakened and driven inward, and the giant forms of Urizen's children contract into mortal men.

Six days they shrunk up from existence,
And on the seventh day they rested,
And they bless'd the seventh day, in sick hope,
And forgot their eternal life.

.   .   .   .

No more could they rise at will
In the infinite void, but bound down
To earth by their narrowing perceptions
They lived a period of years;
Then left a noisom body
To the jaws of devouring darkness.

And their children wept, & built
Tombs in the desolate places,
And form'd laws of prudence, and call'd them
The eternal laws of God.[45]

So civilization began with Materialism, the thirty cities of
Egypt, 'Whose Gods are the Powers Of this World, Goddess
Nature, Who first spoil & then destroy Imaginative Art; For their
Glory is War and Dominion.'[46] Those sons of Urizen who had
refused to be restrained by the Net tried to deliver their shrunken
brethren, but, finding persuasion vain, they quitted the 'pendulous
earth', now englobed by the ocean of space and time.

A lyric from the Notebook, written about this time, suggests
that escape from the 'Net' is still possible for man.

> O Lapwing, thou fliest around the heath,
> Nor seest the net that is spread beneath.
> Why dost thou not fly among the corn fields?
> They cannot spread nets where a harvest yields.[47]

The Book of Los, 1795, retells the story from the standpoint
of Los.* The first five stanzas take the place of the Preludium of
the earlier books. Eno, the Earth Mother, laments eternity where
spiritual excess was unrestrained, whereas now the shrunken
sublimities appear as vices in the created world:

> 'O Times remote!
> When Love & Joy were adoration,
> And none impure were deem'd:
> Not Eyeless Covet,
> Nor Thin-lip'd Envy,
> Nor Bristled Wrath,
> Nor Curled Wantonness;

> 'But Covet was poured full,
> Envy fed with fat of lambs,
> Wrath with lion's gore,
> Wantonness lull'd to sleep
> With the virgin's lute
> Or sated with her love;

> 'Till Covet broke his locks & bars
> And slept with open doors;
> Envy sung at the rich man's feast;

---

* Los is presumably the anagram of sol. Blake has used the ordinary
process of etching for *The Book of Los* and *The Book of Ahania*.

> Wrath was follow'd up and down
> By a little ewe lamb;
> And Wantonness on his own true love
> Begot a giant race.'[48]

The story begins in the sixth stanza: Los finds himself cut off from eternity,

> bound in a chain,
> Compell'd to watch Urizen's shadow,[49]

amid the black darkness of the material world. He breaks loose from restraint, but, having as yet no means of combating the new and terrible conditions, he only falls into error:

> Falling, falling, Los fell & fell,
> Sunk precipitant, heavy, down, down,
> Times on times, night on night, day on day—
> Truth has bounds, Error none—falling, falling,
> Years on years, and ages on ages
> Still he fell thro' the void, still a void
> Found for falling, day & night without end;

But gradually thought succeeds the first impotent wrath as of a new-born babe.

> Then aloft his head rear'd in the Abyss
> And his downward-borne fall chang'd oblique
>
> .   .   .   .
>
> Incessant the falling Mind labour'd,
> Organizing itself, till the Vacuum
> Became element, pliant to rise
> Or to fall or to swim or to fly,
> With ease searching the dire vacuity.[50]

Los gives himself form and struggles to separate the 'thin' from the 'heavy', the spiritual from the material. 'Then Light first began,' and he sees the 'Back bone of Urizen.' Imagination is now a power in the Material World: Los can bind Urizen and forge the sun of poetry. He tries to chain Urizen to this sun, but it is only temporal, the poetry of this world, a 'glowing illusion', whose light Urizen quenches. Yet even so his contact with imagination gives him form and life, till he becomes the earthly man:

till a Form
Was completed, a Human Illusion
In darkness and deep clouds involv'd.[51]

Such is Blake's version of the creation of Adam. God has become Man, and so the poem ends without word of the birth of Orc, the spirit of freedom, by whom man shall be saved.

The *Book of Urizen* was entitled by Blake *The First Book of Urizen*, and he must have originally intended that *The Book of Ahania*, 1795,* which continues the story, should be the second book. Fuzon, Passion, one of the sons of Urizen who had refused to be restrained by the net of religion, revolts against his father:

> 'Shall we worship this Demon of smoke,'
> Said Fuzon, 'this abstract non-entity,
> This cloudy God seated on waters,
> Now seen, now obscur'd, King of sorrow?'[52]

He hurls a beam of flame against Urizen, who is protected only by a shield forged in the mills of logic. The beam penetrates the shield, 'the cold loins of Urizen dividing.' Reason, who, unable to synthesize the contraries, had desired 'joy without pain', wounded by passion, casts out his 'parted soul', Ahania, Pleasure.

> He groan'd anguish'd, & called her Sin,
> Kissing her and weeping over her;
> Then hid her in darkness, in silence,
> Jealous, tho' she was invisible.
>
> She fell down a faint shadow wand'ring
> In chaos and circling dark Urizen,
> As the moon anguish'd circles the earth,
> Hopeless! abhorr'd! a death-shadow,
> Unseen, unbodied, unknown,
> The mother of Pestilence.[53]

Pleasure, repressed and separated from reason, is 'Mother of Pestilence' because, as is written in the 'Proverbs of Hell': 'He who desires but acts not, breeds pestilence.'[54] Fuzon's beam is

---

* The unique copy of *Ahania* is now in the Rosenwald Collection in the Library of Congress, except for the original frontispiece, which is in the collection of Sir Geoffrey Keynes.

identified by Blake with the pillar of fire which led the Israelites out of bondage, and, after it had been seized by Los, the Spirit of Time and Poetry, with Christ, the Deliverer. Fuzon, not realizing that Urizen, one of the immortals, cannot die, thinks that he has killed his father, and has become God in his stead. But Urizen slays the serpent of lust, who attacked him when he repressed Pleasure as Sin, and forming a bow of the serpent's ribs, shoots the poisoned Rock of the Decalogue at Fuzon. The body of Fuzon, still alive though he seems to be dead, is crucified by Urizen on the Tree of Mystery, Religion. The 'pale living Corse' of Fuzon is assailed by the arrows of Pestilence, and shapes, the spectres of repressed desires, flutter round the Tree of Mystery. In the *Book of Urizen* civilization began with Africa, Materialized Reason: now Asia rises, Materialized Passion. The lament of Ahania, Pleasure cast out by Reason, with which the poem closes, is one of the most beautiful passages in the Lambeth Books.

The Song of Los, 1795,* which comprises 'Africa' and 'Asia', precedes *America* and *Europe* in subject, although written later. In 'Africa' Adam, the natural man, and Noah, the man of imagination, are described as watching Urizen setting up his different forms of religion. They are diversely affected: 'Adam shudder'd! Noah faded!'[55] These religions are 'Abstract' because the process takes place which had been described in *The Marriage of Heaven and Hell*:

The ancient Poets animated all sensible objects with Gods or Geniuses, calling them by the names and adorning them with the properties of woods, rivers, mountains, lakes, cities, nations, and whatever their enlarged & numerous senses could percieve.

And particularly they studied the genius of each city & country, placing it under its mental deity;

Till a system was formed, which some took advantage of, & enslav'd the vulgar by attempting to realize or abstract the mental deities from their objects: thus began Priesthood;

Choosing forms of worship from poetic tales.

* Five copies of *The Song of Los* are known, all heavily coloured with opaque pigment in a manner unlike that used for any of the other illuminated books, and impossible to reproduce in true facsimile. [Ed.]

And at length they pronounc'd that the Gods had order'd such
things.
Thus men forgot that All deities reside in the human breast.[56]

The symbol shrinks to dogma and so becomes the Philosophy
of Brahma, the Religion of the Jews, and the Aestheticism of the
Greeks. Orc, the spirit of freedom, is in chains, but Oothoon
(Instinct as in the *Visions of the Daughters of Albion*) can still speak:

> And Jesus heard her voice (a man of sorrows) he reciev'd
> A Gospel from wretched Theotormon.[57]

This Gospel withered into monkish Christianity, and Moham-
medanism and the 'Code of War' of Northern Mythology signal-
ized the reaction against asceticism.

Har and Heva, Poetry and Painting, who should have announced
the Gospel of Imagination, shrunk

> Into two narrow doleful forms
> Creeping in reptile flesh upon
> The bosom of the ground;
> And all the vast of Nature shrunk
> Before their shrunken eyes.[58]

So the sons of Har, men, who are all possessors of the Poetic
Genius in varying degrees, were, by their laws and religions,
bound more and more closely to earth:

> Till a Philosophy of Five Senses was complete.
> Urizen wept & gave it into the hands of Newton & Locke.[59]

The Kings of Asia, startled in their religious darkness by the
approach of revolution in Europe, call for still more restraint.
The appeal of these orthodox believers to the God of reason is
Blake's ironical exposition of the social aims and conditions of
his day:

> 'Shall not the King call for Famine from the heath,
> Nor the Priest for Pestilence from the fen,
> To restrain, to dismay, to thin
> The inhabitants of mountain and plain,
> In the day of full-feeding prosperity
> And the night of delicious songs?

'Shall not the Councellor throw his curb
Of Poverty on the laborious,
To fix the price of labour,*
To invent allegoric riches?

'And the privy admonishers of men
Call for fires in the City,
For heaps of smoking ruins
In the night of prosperity & wantonness?

'To turn man from his path,
To restrain the child from the womb,
To cut off the bread from the city,
That the remnant may learn to obey,

'That the pride of the heart may fail,
That the lust of the eyes may be quench'd,
That the delicate ear in its infancy
May be dull'd, and the nostrils clos'd up,
To teach mortal worms the path
That leads from the gates of the Grave?'[60]

But Urizen's books of brass, iron, and gold (charity, war, and economics) are melted by the fires of Orc. Revolution breaks forth that by the trial of a 'Last Judgment' error may be cast out.

The last three of the minor symbolic books known as the Lambeth Books were engraved in 1795, and probably about that time Blake began to write a long mystical poem, with the title of:

VALA
or
The Death and Judgement
of the Ancient Man
A Dream of Nine Nights.

which he afterwards altered to:

---

* Blake's allusion to fixing the price of labour obviously refers to the Spitalfields weavers, whose wages were fixed by the magistrates at this time. Their wages became allegoric because, as a result, the trade tended to leave Spitalfields.

THE FOUR ZOAS
The torments of Love & Jealousy in
The Death and Judgement
of Albion the Ancient Man.

A third title on the back of a drawing may also have been intended
for it: 'The Bible of Hell, in Nocturnal Visions collected. Vol. I.
Lambeth.'[61] This appears likely, as *The Four Zoas* is divided into
Nine Nights, a form which may have been suggested by Young's
Night Thoughts, illustrated by Blake at that time. If this be so,
Vala or *The Four Zoas* is the poem promised in *The Marriage of
Heaven and Hell*. 'I have also The Bible of Hell, which the world
shall have whether they will or no.'[62] But Blake never gave *Vala*
to the world; it remained in manuscript with alternative drafts,
repetitions, and additions, and was not finally revised. John
Linnell received it as a gift from Blake; it is now in the Department of Manuscripts at the British Museum, and the first approximately accurate text was printed by Geoffrey Keynes in the 1925
Nonesuch edition of Blake's *Writings*.* Blake obviously intended
to systematize in this poem the metaphysic which he had been
evolving as he wrote the Lambeth Books. Some of the myths
reappear, and passages are adopted from these books either ver-
batim or with slight alterations. The manuscript was extensively
revised from 1800 to 1803, while Blake was living at Felpham,
and possibly some alterations were made at a still later date. It was

---

* The MS. has presented great difficulties to all editors owing to Blake's
successive changes in his plan without ever arriving at a final form. H. M.
Margoliouth printed what he claimed to be Blake's first version, disentangled
from his later changes (*Blake's Vala*, 1956). He edited this text with great
learning and insight, though making the wise observation that Blake can be
over-interpreted. The whole work has been edited by G. E. Bentley, Jr. with
full-size reproductions of every page of the MS. (1963). There are pencil
drawings on almost every page, some with slight colour-washes added; the
meaning of these presents great difficulty and has given rise to disagreements.
Reference has already been made to erasures of some of the drawings.
Margoliouth thought that these had probably been done by Blake himself
with a view to making them publishable. [Ed.]

apparently abandoned when he decided to complete and engrave *Milton* and *Jerusalem*, as the former contains repetitions and adaptations from it and the latter lengthy excerpts.

The Four Zoas, who give to the poem the title which seems to have been Blake's final choice, are Urizen, Reason; Urthona, Spirit; Luvah, Passion; and Tharmas, the Body. They are associated by Blake with the Four Living Creatures of the Book of Revelation, to which there are frequent allusions. The poem describes the fall, the creation of the world in space and time, the Crucifixion and Resurrection, and consequent redemption and regeneration.* The fall is due to the twofold error of the Zoas, who set themselves up as gods instead of realizing that they are but the servants of the Eternal Man, and also usurp each other's regions, with the result that they fail in the fulfilment of their own functions. Urizen, for example, who in Eternity is faith and certainty, is changed to doubt, and Urthona, spirit, suffers a threefold division into Los, Poetry ineffectual and uninspired, Enitharmon, Inspiration, Spiritual beauty, who is feeble and easily led astray in her isolated state, and the spectre of Urthona, a mere shadow of the Eternal Spiritual Wisdom, which includes all knowledge and all art.

Blake had now begun to use the symbolism which pervades his later work, representing reason or logic by the Spectre, and emotion or inspiration by the Emanation. The simplest expression of his doctrine that before harmony can be attained this fatal division must be transcended is the lyric 'Spectre and Emanation' which he wrote at Felpham.

As in the earlier books there is a twofold drama because the history of the macrocosm is also that of the microcosm, the history of the universe writ small is that of the individual. Those for whom this situation is not already sufficiently complicated may amuse themselves by naming Los William, and Enitharmon Catherine, in order to extract autobiographical significance, deducing that Catherine was anxious that William should play a part

* Saurat, *Blake and Milton* (1920), pp. 13-21, traces a parallel between the plot of *Vala* and that of *Paradise Lost*.

in politics and leave her free for self-realization, and that William
paid her a pretty compliment in referring to the way in which she
coloured his illuminated books.* But as the story of Los and
Enitharmon is largely concerned with the birth of their son Orc
and Los's jealousy of the adolescent, this procedure is necessarily
perfunctory, if not wholly superfluous.

Above the title is written in Greek, the fruit of Felpham
scholarship, Ephesians 6. 12: 'For we wrestle not against flesh
and blood, but against principalities, against powers, against the
rulers of the darkness of this world, against spiritual wickedness
in high places.'

Night the First describes the beginning of the fall. The second
stanza, with a marginal reference to 'John xvii c., 21, 22, 23 v.'
and 'John i c., 14 v.', explains the Four Zoas:

> Four Mighty Ones are in every Man; a Perfect Unity
> Cannot Exist but from the Universal Brotherhood of Eden,
> The Universal Man, to Whom be Glory Evermore. Amen.[63]

Blake had laid down as principles in *All Religions are One* 'That
the Poetic Genius is the true Man,' and that 'As all men are alike
in outward form, So (and with the same infinite variety) all are
alike in the Poetic Genius.' In *Vala* Los, the Poetic Genius, whose
name in Eternity is Urthona, Spirit, is supposed originally to have
dwelt in Man whole and undivided. Blake invokes his Muse to
describe the Fall.

> Daughter of Beulah, Sing
> His fall into Division & his Resurrection to Unity:
> His fall into the Generation of decay & death, & his
> Regeneration by the Resurrection from the dead.[64]

The first to feel the fall into division is Tharmas, the Body, who
is no longer at one with Enion, the Earth Mother and generative
instinct. He has lost his 'emanation', his power of intuition, and
he has become furtive and a prey to self-analysis. He infects
Enion with his dread.

* Cf. Damon, *Blake*, p. 367, commentary on *The Four Zoas*.

Enion said: 'Thy fear has made me tremble, thy terrors have
   surrounded me.
All Love is lost: Terror succeeds, & Hatred instead of Love,
And stern demands of Right & Duty instead of Liberty.
Once thou wast to Me the loveliest son of heaven—But now
Why art thou Terrible? and yet I love thee in thy terror till
I am almost Extinct & soon shall be a shadow in Oblivion,
Unless some way can be found that I may look upon thee & live.
Hide me some shadowy semblance, secret whisp'ring in my Ear,
In secret of soft wings, in mazes of delusive beauty.
I have look'd into the secret soul of him I lov'd,
And in the Dark recesses found Sin & cannot return.'

Trembling & pale sat Tharmas, weeping in his clouds.

'Why wilt thou Examine every little fibre of my soul,
Spreading them out before the sun like stalks of flax to dry?
The infant joy is beautiful, but its anatomy
Horrible, Ghast & Deadly; nought shalt thou find in it
But Death, Despair & Everlasting brooding Melancholy.
Thou wilt go mad with horror if thou dost Examine thus
Every moment of my secret hours. Yea, I know
That I have sinn'd, & that my Emanations are become harlots.
I am already distracted at their deeds, & if I look
Upon them more, Despair will bring self-murder on my soul.
O Enion, thou art thyself a root growing in hell,
Tho' thus heavenly beautiful to draw me to destruction.
Sometimes I think thou art a flower expanding,
Sometimes I think thou art fruit, breaking from its bud
In dreadful dolor & pain; & I am like an atom,
A Nothing, left in darkness; yet I am an identity:
I wish & feel & weep & groan. Ah, terrible! terrible!'[65]

Enion hides from him, but the separation only hastens his fall
into the sea of time and space. There Enion follows the spectre
of Tharmas, who in his division reproaches her with sin, and of
their union, now neither happy nor innocent, are born Los and
Enitharmon. This birth results from the division of Urthona,
Spirit, with whom in eternity they are one. Los and Enitharmon
in their separate entities cannot maintain a state of love and unity
but lapse into shame and jealousy and quarrels. Enitharmon
appeals to Urizen, who takes advantage of their dissension to

proclaim himself God, and claims obedience from Los, who still retains remembrance of the Divine Image.*

'Obey my voice, young Demon; I am God from Eternity to
  Eternity.
Art thou a visionary of Jesus, the soft delusion of Eternity?
Lo I am God, the terrible destroyer, & not the Saviour.
Why should the Divine Vision compell the sons of Eden
To forego each his own delight, to war against his spectre?
The Spectre is the Man. The rest is only delusion & fancy.'
Thus Urizen spoke, collected in himself in awful pride.
Ten thousand thousand were his hosts of spirits on the wind,
Ten thousand thousand glittering Chariots shining in the sky.
They pour upon the golden shore beside the silent ocean,
Rejoicing in the Victory, & the heavens were fill'd with blood.[66]

Los becomes reconciled to Enitharmon, but they forsake Luvah and Vala (passion and nature), and their nuptial song is chanted by the hosts of Urizen, who foretell the destruction of the Eternal Man, call on the spider to spread the Net of Religion, and announce the birth of Orc, revolution: Enion, the Earth Mother, stands aloof in lamentation. The fall of the Eternal Man has now begun, and he can no longer abide in Beulah, the place of repose midway between eternity and the world of space and time, described earlier in the poem.

There is from Great Eternity a mild & pleasant rest
Nam'd Beulah, a soft Moony Universe, feminine, lovely,
Pure, mild & Gentle, given in Mercy to those who sleep,
Eternally created by the Lamb of God around,
On all sides, within & without the Universal Man.
The daughters of Beulah follow sleepers in all their Dreams,
Creating spaces, lest they fall into Eternal Death.†

* As Blake was working on *Vala* at Felpham, it is tempting to ascribe autobiographical significance to this passage, and say that like the 'Bard's Song' in *Milton* it refers to the friction between Hayley and Blake and Mrs. Blake's attempts to reconcile them. Although it is not suggested in *Milton*, which would be the later account, that Blake resented his wife's efforts as mediator, a later letter to Hayley speaks of past division and unhappiness (see p. 211). It is, however, quite possible that this first draft was written before he went to Felpham.

† Here, as elsewhere, Blake regards the creation of the world of space and time as setting a limit to error.

> The Circle of Destiny complete, they gave to it a space,
> And nam'd the space Ulro, & brooded over it in care & love.[67]

He must sink into the death-like sleep of the material world where martyrdom and error await him.

> Now Man was come to the Palm tree & to the Oak of Weeping
> Which stand upon the edge of Beulah, & he sunk down
> From the supporting arms of the Eternal Saviour who dispos'd
> The pale limbs of his Eternal Individuality
> Upon The Rock of Ages, Watching over him with Love & Care.[68]

The first draft of Night the First ends here, and the second draft was not incorporated by Blake with the necessary readjustments, as it would doubtless have been in a final revision. In the second draft the fall is explained to the Council of God in Great Eternity by Messengers from Beulah, who bewail the plight of Albion, the Eternal Man, because Urizen, Reason, having failed to subject Los entirely to his will has proposed to Luvah, Passion, that he himself should usurp the North, the Region of Spirit, and rule Jerusalem, the emanation of Albion, who symbolizes Spiritual Freedom, abandoning his own region, the South, to Passion. Luvah will not agree and Urizen threatens him with death. Urthona, Spirit, has been riven by their strife, the result of his division having been the birth of Los and Enitharmon: Jerusalem, Spiritual Freedom, is in ruins. The outcome of this embassy from Beulah is that Seven Guardians, the Seven Eyes of God, are appointed to watch over the Eternal Man:

> . . . the Seventh is named Jesus,
> The Lamb of God, blessed for ever, & he follow'd the Man
> Who wander'd in mount Ephraim* seeking a Sepulcher,
> His inward eyes closing from the Divine vision, & all
> His children wandering outside, from his bosom fleeing away.[69]

Blake has deleted 'Second' in the title 'Vala, Night the Second', but, in the absence of further alteration or addition, it must be

---

* Damon, *Blake*, p. 368, points out that Mount Ephraim is used by Swedenborg (*Arcana*, 5354) to symbolize the intellectual principle of the Church as opposed to the spiritual and celestial.

treated as the second book of the poem. The Eternal Man, wearied on his Couch of Death, abdicates and gives his sceptre to Urizen, who creates the Mundane Shell, the universe, as a protection against non-existence, the boundlessness of error. The world of matter, Ulro, comes into existence: 'What is within now seen without.'[70] Vala, under the influence of Urizen, turns against Luvah, and Reason seems to have destroyed Passion and even Nature herself. The Material World is ordered by the Sons of Urizen with compasses and scales, but the Eagles of Genius bear their share in the work, though some of them are snared in the net of religion or entrapped by false art.

While far into the vast unknown the strong wing'd Eagles bend
Their venturous flight in Human forms distinct; thro' darkness
    deep
They bear the woven draperies; on golden hooks they hang abroad
The universal curtains & spread out from Sun to Sun
The vehicles of light; they separate the furious particles
Into mild currents as the water mingles with the wine.

While thus the Spirits of strongest wing enlighten the dark deep,
The threads are spun & the cords twisted & drawn out; then the
    weak
Begin their work, & many a net is netted, many a net
Spread, & many a Spirit caught: innumerable the nets,
Innumerable the gins & traps, & many a soothing flute
Is form'd, & many a corded lyre outspread over the immense.
In cruel delight they trap the listeners, & in cruel delight
Bind them, condensing the strong energies into little compass.[71]

Reason raises his Golden Hall, but though he does not exclude from it his emanation, Ahania, the emotion of pleasure, they are no longer one: 'Two wills they had, two intellects, & not as in times of old.'[72] But the Eternal Man in the death of this life is under the guardianship of Jesus: as in *The Song of Los* Jesus receives the Gospel from wretched Theotormon, so here the Incarnation is necessary for the deliverance of man because Passion has been curbed by Reason.

For the Divine Lamb, Even Jesus who is the Divine Vision,
Permitted all, lest Man should fall into Eternal Death;

For when Luvah sunk down, himself put on the robes of blood
Lest the state call'd Luvah should cease; & the Divine Vision
Walked in robes of blood till he who slept should awake.[73]

Meanwhile Los and Enitharmon are represented as still for a
time happy and innocent—a further proof that the poem lacks
final revision as the Nuptial Song for the First Night had shown
another state of things.

For Los & Enitharmon walk'd forth on the dewy Earth
Contracting or expanding their all flexible senses
At will to murmur in the flowers small as the honey bee,
At will to stretch across the heavens & step from star to star,
Or standing on the Earth erect, or on the stormy waves
Driving the storms before them, or delighting in sunny beams,
While round their heads the Elemental Gods kept harmony.[74]

But there is no true union between them: they are soon beset by
jealousy and, though Enitharmon still is able to revive Los from
seeming death, she exults unduly in her power:

'The joy of woman is the death of her most best beloved
Who dies for Love of her
In torments of fierce jealousy & pangs of adoration.'[75]

Los, pursuing Inspiration, delusive in her division from him,
drives away Enion, the generative instinct, who breaks out in
lamentation:

'I am made to sow the thistle for wheat, the nettle for a nourishing
    dainty.
I have planted a false oath in the earth; it has brought forth a
    poison tree.
I have chosen the serpent for a councellor, & the dog
For a schoolmaster to my children.
I have blotted out from light & living the dove & nightingale,
And I have caused the earth worm to beg from door to door.

'I have taught the thief a secret path into the house of the just.
I have taught pale artifice to spread his nets upon the morning.
My heavens are brass, my earth is iron, my moon a clod of clay,
My sun a pestilence burning at noon & a vapour of death in night.

'What is the price of Experience? do men buy it for a song?
Or wisdom for a dance in the street? No, it is bought with the
   price
Of all that a man hath, his house, his wife, his children.
Wisdom is sold in the desolate market where none come to buy,
And in the wither'd field where the farmer plows for bread in vain.

'It is an easy thing to triumph in the summer's sun
And in the vintage & to sing on the waggon loaded with corn.
It is an easy thing to talk of patience to the afflicted,
To speak the laws of prudence to the houseless wanderer,
To listen to the hungry raven's cry in wintry season
When the red blood is fill'd with wine & with the marrow of
   lambs.

'It is an easy thing to laugh at wrathful elements,
To hear the dog howl at the wintry door, the ox in the slaughter
   house moan;
To see a god on every wind & a blessing on every blast;
To hear sounds of love in the thunder storm that destroys our
   enemies' house;
To rejoice in the blight that covers his field, & the sickness that
   cuts off his children,
While our olive & vine sing & laugh round our door, & our
   children bring fruits & flowers.

'Then the groan & the dolor are quite forgotten, & the slave
   grinding at the mill,
And the captive in chains, & the poor in the prison, & the soldier
   in the field
When the shatter'd bone hath laid him groaning among the
   happier dead.

'It is an easy thing to rejoice in the tents of prosperity:
Thus could I sing & thus rejoice: but it is not so with me.'[76]

   Ahania, pleasure, hears the lament of Enion, and, as Los had
hoped, her peace is also destroyed.

   Night the Third opens with Ahania's attempt to relieve her
perplexities by strengthening Urizen's sense of power:

'Why sighs my Lord? are not the morning stars thy obedient Sons?
Do they not bow their bright heads at thy voice? at thy command
Do they not fly into their stations & return their light to thee?

The immortal Atmospheres are thine; there thou art seen in glory
Surrounded by the ever changing Daughters of the Light.
Why wilt thou look upon futurity, dark'ning present joy?'[77]

But Urizen knows that Orc, the Spirit of Revolt, is born and must
in his maturity rule over reason. He sees Vala, Nature, as the
daughter of Enitharmon, Space, and Luvah, Passion, as the son
of Time. Ahania reproaches him with his initial error in letting
Luvah, Passion, drive 'the immortal steeds of light', the horses
of instruction. She tells him of a vision in which she had seen the
Dark'ning Man, as in the death-like sleep of this life he wandered
farther and farther from the light of eternity, and heard his voice
worshipping his own shadow, his desires externalized and become
heaven to him.

'Then Man ascended mourning into the splendors of his palace,
Above him rose a Shadow from his wearied intellect
Of living gold, pure, perfect, holy; in white linen pure he hover'd,
A sweet entrancing self delusion, a wat'ry vision of Man
Soft exulting in existence, all the Man absorbing.

'Man fell upon his face prostrate before the wat'ry shadow,
Saying "O Lord, whence is this change? thou knowest I am
    nothing."
        .   .   .   .

' "O I am nothing when I enter into judgment with thee.
If thou withdraw thy breath I die & vanish into Hades;
If thou dost lay thine hand upon me, behold I am silent;
If thou withhold thine hand I perish like a fallen leaf,
O I am nothing, & to nothing must return again.
If thou withdraw thy breath, behold I am oblivion." '[78]

But Luvah, Passion, revealed himself in the shadow, and strove
for dominion over the Man, prostrating him and covering him
with boils.* Then the Fallen Man drove away Luvah and Vala,
who went forth into the world leaving jealousy and rage in the
Human Heart where Paradise and its joys had abounded. Urizen,
in his anger at Ahania's vision which confirms his own fears,

* A symbol of misery consequent on the misuse of the fifth sense.

casts her out, and she falls into Non-Entity. In the terror and confusion caused by her fall Tharmas, the Body, is materialized. He repudiates Enion, the Generative instinct. She becomes 'only a voice eternal wailing in the Elements'; and then Tharmas knows that ' "Love and Hope are ended".'

Night the Fourth opens with the lament of Tharmas for the loss of Enion. He denounces Reason and Passion—'The all powerful curse of an honest man be upon Urizen & Luvah.'[79]

He calls on Los to rebuild the universe as he directs, but Los refuses, saying that Urizen is God, and since he is now fallen into the Deep, he himself is God. Los boasts that he is all powerful, and Urthona, Spirit, but his shadow. Tharmas carries off Enitharmon, Inspiration, and without his emanation Los is reduced to the Spectre of Urthona: the Poetic Genius has lost his intuition and retains only his logical faculty. The Spectre appeals to Tharmas, who restores Enitharmon, and he becomes Los once more. Then Tharmas sees himself as God, but he would rather be a Man, and he again desires Los to do his work for him. Los, as in *The Book of Urizen*, binds and limits reason.

Meanwhile the Council of God is watching over the Body of the Eternal Man, and the daughters of Beulah are comforted by the Divine Vision.

'Lord Saviour, if thou hadst been here our brother had not died,
And now we know that whatsoever thou wilt ask of God
He will give it thee; for we are weak women & dare not lift
Our eyes to the Divine pavilions; therefore in mercy thou
Appearest cloth'd in Luvah's garments that we may behold thee
And live. Behold Eternal Death is in Beulah. Behold
We perish & shall not be found unless thou grant a place
In which we may be hidden under the shadow of wings.
For if we, who are but for a time & who pass away in winter,
Behold these wonders of Eternity, we shall consume.'

.   .   .   .

The Saviour mild & gentle bent over the corse of Death,
Saying, 'If ye will Believe, your Brother shall rise again.'
And first he found the Limit of Opacity, & nam'd it Satan,
In Albion's bosom, for in every human bosom these limits stand.

And next he found the Limit of Contraction, & nam'd it Adam,
While yet those beings were not born nor knew of good or Evil.

And
                                                    Limit
Was put to Eternal Death.[80]

Satan, Error, must be limited that he may be cast out: error is
opaque because impenetrable by the light of truth: contraction
must also be limited that return from the finite to the infinite
and eternal may not be impossible. But Los himself was changed
by his labours:

               he became what he beheld:
He became what he was doing: he was himself transform'd.[81]

   Night the Fifth shows the changed Los dancing in mad triumph
on the mountains until he and Enitharmon shrink and wither on
the Rocky Cliff of the material world. They are no longer re-
sponsive to beauty as in their age of innocence, but 'Their senses
unexpansive in one stedfast bulk remain.'[82] Then, as Urizen had
foretold, Orc, the Spirit of Revolt, is born, and is acclaimed as a
lower form of Luvah, Passion. 'Luvah, King of Love, thou art the
King of rage & death.' Luvah himself does not recognize his
incarnation, and assails him with the weapons of reason. Los is
aghast, but Enitharmon nourishes her child. When Orc reaches
the age of adolescence Los becomes jealous of his love for his
mother and binds him with a chain. But his vitality is unquench-
able: fettered though he be his very existence transforms the world.

His limbs bound down mock at his chains, for over them a flame
Of circling fire unceasing plays; to feed them with life & bring
The virtues of the Eternal worlds, ten thousand thousand spirits
Of life lament around the Demon, going forth & returning.
At his enormous call they flee into the heavens of heavens
And back return with wine & food, or dive into the deeps
To bring the thrilling joys of sense to quell his ceaseless rage.
His eyes, the lights of his large soul, contract or else expand:
Contracted they behold the secrets of the infinite mountains,
The veins of gold & silver & the hidden things of Vala,
Whatever grows from its pure bud or breathes a fragrant soul:

Expanded they behold the terrors of the Sun & Moon,
The Elemental Planets & the orbs of eccentric fire.
His nostrils breathe a fiery flame, his locks are like the forests
Of wild beasts; there the lion glares, the tyger & wolf howl there,
And there the Eagle hides her young in cliffs & precipices.
His bosom is like starry heaven expanded; all the stars
Sing round; there waves the harvest & the vintage rejoices; the
  springs
Flow into rivers of delight; there the spontaneous flowers
Drink, laugh & sing, the grasshopper, the Emmet & the Fly;
The golden Moth builds there a house & spreads her silken bed.
His loins inwove with silken fires are like a furnace fierce:
As the strong Bull in summer time when bees sing round the heath
Where the herds low after the shadow & after the water spring,
The num'rous flocks cover the mountain & shine along the valley.
His knees are rocks of adamant & rubie & emerald:
Spirits of strength in Palaces rejoice in golden armour
Armed with spear & shield they drink & rejoice over the slain.
Such is the Demon, such his terror in the nether deep.[83]

Los and Enitharmon repent, but fail to undo their work and set
Orc free, because the chain of jealousy is now so deeply rooted in
the foundations of the world that it cannot be torn up. This
Night ends with the recantation of Urizen, who realizes, though
only for the moment, that his degradation is the result of his own
pride and misuse of his powers. He had refused the services which
were asked of him for the guidance of the Eternal Man: the power
of Spirit was weakened, and Passion and Nature had withered up
under his rule.

'I well remember, for I heard the mild & holy voice
Saying, "O light, spring up & shine," & I sprang up from the
  deep.
He gave to me a silver scepter, & crown'd me with a golden
  crown,
& said, "Go forth & guide my Son who wanders on the ocean."

'I went not forth: I hid myself in black clouds of my wrath;
I call'd the stars around my feet in the night of councils dark;
The stars threw down their spears & fled naked away.
We fell. I siez'd thee, dark Urthona. In my left hand falling

'I siez'd thee, beauteous Luvah; thou art faded like a flower
And like a lilly is thy wife Vala wither'd by winds.'[84]

But Urizen's repentance brings him hope:

'. . . perhaps this is the night
Of Prophecy, & Luvah hath burst his way from Enitharmon.
When Thought is clos'd in Caves Then love shall shew its root in
deepest Hell.'[85]

In Night the Sixth Urizen sets forth on his travels through the
material world, and meets his three daughters, who symbolize the
loins, heart, and head. They shrink and hide in material forms
when they recognize their father, and he curses them because
Tharmas, the body, is their God. Tharmas attempts to confront
Urizen, but flies from him in terror, praying for death because he
can create only monstrous forms. Urizen pursues his way to his
own region, the South, aghast at the horror and misery and degradation he beholds on all sides:

He knew they were his Children ruin'd in his ruin'd world.

.   .   .   .

He saw them curs'd beyond his Curse: his soul melted with fear.
He could not take their fetters off, for they grew from the soul,
Nor could he quench the fires, for they flam'd out from the heart,
Nor could he calm the Elements, because himself was subject;
So he threw his flight in terror & pain, & in repentant tears.[86]

Then he visits the East, vacant because Luvah no longer rules
there, and falls into the void. But 'The ever pitying one who
seeth all things' allows his life to be renewed, and bearing his
books of brass and iron and gold he goes on his way and tries to
reorganize the world that it may obey his will, dragging the net of
religion behind him. Next he falls into the West, the region of
Tharmas, who fled in pursuit of Enion and from terror of Urizen.
Urthona alone of the four Zoas remains in his own region, the
North, but only in his divided, spectral form. Urizen attempts to
invade the North, but he is repelled by the Spectre of Urthona,
aided by Tharmas, and four Sons of Urizen, the four elements.
Defeated by Spirit, Reason withdraws into the net of religion.

There are two versions of Night the Seventh of which that
marked (a) is probably the later.* As Reason could not prevail
over Spirit, even in its darkened form, so Spirit in its division
cannot wholly conquer Reason. Urizen, no longer pursued by the
Spectre of Urthona, goes to the South, his own region, where
Orc, Revolt, lies bound. Orc, despite his fetters, is vital and inspired, and both Urizen and Los are filled with envy. While Reason
sits brooding coldly over Revolt, the root of Mystery sends up
branches into the heaven of Los, the Poet, and Urizen himself
escapes with difficulty and pain, leaving his iron book of war for
safety in its shade. He offers Orc his pity and advice, but Orc, who
is both genius and revolutionist, replies by jeers—'my fierce fires
are better than thy snows.'[87] Urizen commands his daughters to
knead the bread of sorrow, materialism, for Orc, and reads from
the book of brass his Gospel of charity:

'Listen, O Daughters, to my voice. Listen to the Words of Wisdom,
So shall [you] govern over all; let Moral Duty tune your tongue.
But be your hearts harder than the nether millstone.
To bring the Shadow of Enitharmon beneath our wondrous tree,
That Los may Evaporate like smoke & be no more,
Draw down Enitharmon to the Spectre of Urthona,
And let him have dominion over Los, the terrible Shade.
Compell the poor to live upon a Crust of bread, by soft mild arts.
Smile when they frown, frown when they smile; & when a man
    looks pale
With labour & abstinence, say he looks healthy & happy;
And when his children sicken, let them die; there are enough
Born, even too many, & our Earth will be overrun†
Without these arts. If you would make the poor live with temper
    [ance],
With pomp give every crust of bread you give; with gracious
    cunning
Magnify small gifts; reduce the man to want a gift, & then give
    with pomp.
Say he smiles if you hear him sigh. If pale, say he is ruddy.
Preach temperance: say he is overgorg'd & drowns his wit

* The ordering in the Complete Writings does not agree with this opinion.
[Ed.]
    † Probably an allusion to the doctrines of Malthus.

In strong drink, tho' you know that bread & water are all
He can afford. Flatter his wife, pity his children, till we can
Reduce all to our will, as spaniels are taught with art.'[88]

Orc curses the hypocrisy of Urizen who at last recognizes Luvah,
Passion, in him, but Orc himself now finds his escape in hypocrisy
and becomes the serpent. Next follows a difficult and subtle
passage in which the divided spirit communes with itself, the
psychological states changing as they speak—these are Los and
Enitharmon, Poetry and Inspiration, their shadows, the logical
form of poetry devoid of intuition and suppressed inspiration,
and the Spectre of Urthona, Spirit, in its logical form. Enitharmon,
Spiritual Beauty, brings forth Vala, the Shadowy Female, Material
Beauty, thus giving complete fulfilment to the prophecy of Urizen.
Spirit in division enacts the drama of the fall in its Biblical version
with Orc, the serpent, in the part of tempter. Los would have
united with Enitharmon and the spectre of Urthona, but inspiration flies for refuge to the tree of Mystery, the tree of the knowledge
of Good and Evil. She has already eaten of the fruit:

'It was by that I knew that I had Sinn'd, & then I knew
That without a ransom I could not be sav'd* from Eternal
    death:'[89]

and persuades Los to eat also. The knowledge of Good and Evil
fills the poet with despair, but spiritual logic comforts him with the
hope of the eventual reunion of Spirit, and he has a vision of the
Lamb of God, the Redeemer. But Enitharmon, convinced of sin,
can only behold the Lamb as Avenger, 'nor will the Son of God
redeem us, but destroy.'[90] Los, who better understood the meaning
of the Vision and knew that redemption would come through
sacrifice of self, persuades Enitharmon to help him in building
Golgonooza,† the City of Art, which he had already begun under
the inspiration of the Divine Mercy:

* Enitharmon is deceived by the false doctrine of vicarious atonement, and
has not apprehended the true gospel of the forgiveness of sins. Cf. *Jerusalem*,
61 (*Complete Writings*, p. 694).

† Golgonooza may be a corruption of Golgotha because art involves
self-sacrifice.

                                    'Stern desire
I feel to fabricate embodied semblances in which the dead
May live before us in our palaces & in our gardens of labour,
Which now, open'd within the Center, we behold spread abroad
To form a world of sacrifice of brothers & sons & daughters,
To comfort Orc in his dire sufferings; look, my fires enlume
    afresh
Before my face ascending with delight as in ancient times!'[91]

Art brought comfort to the Spirit of Revolt and reconciled Poetry
with his enemy, Reason.

    The alternative version also continues the story from the Sixth
Night, but in so different a form that Blake can scarcely have
intended to combine them. The details are less finished, and it does
not therefore fall into place so readily as version (a), though it
contains passages of great force and beauty. Urizen returns to his
own region and determines that as God he will shape the world to
his own ends.

First Trades & Commerce, ships & armed vessels he builded
    laborious
To swim the deep; & on the land, children are sold to trades
Of dire necessity, still labouring day & night till all
Their life extinct they took the spectre form in dark despair;
And slaves in myriads, in ship loads, burden the hoarse sounding
    deep,
Rattling with clanking chains; the Universal Empire groans.[92]

    He institutes the worship of Chastity, and since chastity is sex
repressed, sex itself is worshipped disguised or in secret.*

And Urizen laid the first Stone, & all his myriads
Builded a temple in the image of the human heart.
And in the inner part of the Temple, wondrous workmanship,
They form'd the Secret place, reversing all the order of delight,
That whatsoever enter'd into the temple might not behold
The hidden wonders, allegoric of the Generations
Of secret lust, when hid in chambers dark the nightly harlot

---

* Blake believed that the division of sex was temporal only: therefore sex,
and still less the repression of sex, was no fit object of worship. The illustration shows figures bowing before the phallus.

Plays in Disguise in whisper'd hymn & mumbling prayer. The
    priests
He ordain'd & Priestesses, cloth'd in disguises beastial,
Inspiring secrecy; & lamps they bore: intoxicating fumes
Roll round the Temple; & they took the Sun that glow'd o'er
    Los*
And, with immense machines down rolling, the terrific orb
Compell'd. The Sun, redd'ning like a fierce lion in his chains,
Descended to the sound of instruments that drown'd the noise
Of the hoarse wheels & the terrific howlings of wild beasts
That drag'd the wheels of the Sun's chariot; & they put the Sun
Into the temple of Urizen to give light to the Abyss,
To light the War by day, to hide his secret beams by night,
For he divided day & night in different order'd portions,
The day for war, the night for secret religion in his temple.[93]

Strife and Religious Hypocrisy are rampant. Revolt, loving
nature and jealous of her subjection, breaks loose from his fetters
but in the violence of his triumph he misdirects the force of Spirit,
already darkened, and defeats himself:

They sound the clarions strong, they chain the howling captives,
They give the Oath of blood, they cast the lots into the helmet,
They vote the death of Luvah & they nail'd him to the tree,
They pierc'd him with a spear & laid him in a sepulcher
To die a death of Six thousand years, bound round with desolation.

The sun was black & the moon roll'd, a useless globe, thro'
    heaven.[94]

After this Urizen rules unmolested, hence the increasing conflict
and complexity of life which culminates in the industrial revolution, the mockery of nature.

Then left the sons of Urizen the plow & harrow, the loom,
The hammer & the chisel & the rule & compasses.
They forg'd the sword, the chariot of war, the battle ax,
The trumpet fitted to the battle & the flute of summer,
And all the arts of life they chang'd into the arts of death.
The hour glass contemn'd because its simple workmanship
Was as the workmanship of the plowman, & the water wheel
That raises water into Cisterns, broken & burn'd in fire

---

* The sun is symbolic of spirit and of poetry.

Because its workmanship was like the workmanship of the
   shepherd,
And in their stead intricate wheels invented, Wheel without
   wheel,
To perplex youth in their outgoings & to bind to labours
Of day & night the myriads of Eternity, that they might file
And polish brass & iron hour after hour, laborious workmanship,
Kept ignorant of the use that they might spend the days of wisdom
In sorrowful drudgery to obtain a scanty pittance of bread,
In ignorance to view a small portion & think that All,
And call it demonstration, blind to all the simple rules of life. [95]

Nature herself, perverted, revels in the conflict, and: 'No more
remain'd of Orc but the Serpent round the tree of Mystery.' [96]

But Tharmas, the body, retains his innocence in the midst of
despair:

            'O Vala, once I liv'd in a garden of delight;
I waken'd Enion in the morning, & she turned away
Among the apple trees; & all the gardens of delight
Swam like a dream before my eyes. I went to seek the steps
Of Enion in the gardens, & the shadows compass'd me
And clos'd me in a wat'ry world of woe where Enion stood
Trembling before me like a shadow, like a mist, like air.
And she is gone, & here alone I war with darkness & death.
I hear thy voice, but not thy form see; thou & all delight
And life appear & vanish, mocking me with shadows of false hope.
Hast thou forgot that the air listens thro' all its districts,* telling
The subtlest thoughts shut up from light in chambers of the
   Moon?' [97]

Nature, repentant, laments that passion is hidden from her in
'that Outrageous form of Orc'.

The body blames nature, but she, Material Beauty, though her
face is shadowy, is the true daughter of Spiritual Beauty, and her
forms have life which opens within to eternity.

And she went forth & saw the forms of life & of delight
Walking on Mountains or flying in the open expanse of heaven.
She heard sweet voices in the winds & in the voices of birds

  * Allusion to the World Memory, cf. p. 76 and Damon, *Blake*, Commentary
on *The Four Zoas*, p. 383.

That rose from waters; for the waters were as the voice of Luvah,
Not seen to her like waters or like this dark world of death,
Tho' all those fair perfections, which men know only by name,
In beautiful substantial forms appear'd & Served her
As food or drink or ornament, or in delightful works
To build her bowers; for the Elements brought forth abundantly
The living soul in glorious forms, & every one came forth
Walking before her Shadowy face & bowing at her feet.
But in vain delights were poured forth on the howling melancholy.
For her delight the horse his proud neck bow'd & his white mane,
And the strong Lion deign'd in his mouth to wear the golden bit,
While the far beaming Peacock waited on the fragrant wind
To bring her fruits of sweet delight from trees of richest wonders,
And the strong pinion'd Eagle bore the fire of heaven in the night
    season.[98]

Nature's range is as wide as that of reason: moreover there is no
gulf fixed between her and the land of Beulah, which lies midway
between the material world and eternity.

The daughters of Beulah, 'Waiting with patience for the fulfil-
ment of the Promise Divine,' see undoubting the errors of the
World, which must be seen to be cast out. 'These they nam'd
Satans, & in the Aggregate they nam'd them Satan.'[99]

Night the Eighth again proves the lack of revision by the repetition of some incidents which have been already described. The
Council of God, in their unity as Jesus, meets over the Fallen Man,
who is guarded by Beulah as two angels, one at his head and one
at his feet. He begins to awake, and the Divine Vision is beheld
again by Los and Enitharmon. They help to waken the Man by
clothing with form 'the poor wondering spectres' who have been
tempted to leave Beulah and enter the material world:

Astonish'd, comforted, Delighted, in notes of Rapturous Extacy
All Beulah stood astonish'd, looking down to Eternal Death.
They saw the Saviour beyond the Pit of death & destruction;
For whether they look'd upward they saw the Divine Vision,
Or whether they look'd downward still they saw the Divine
    Vision
Surrounding them on all sides beyond sin & death & hell.[100]

Urizen is perplexed and terrified because he sees that the

Saviour is an incarnation of Luvah, and yet Luvah is also present in his own world in the degraded form of Orc, the serpent, still feeding on the bread of materialism. He declares war on Los and Enitharmon, but, although he did not intend it, Doubt arises, 'a Shadowy hermaphrodite, black & opake.' Reason becomes 'Himself tangled in his own net, in sorrow, lust, repentance.'* Meanwhile Enitharmon gives universal form to the emanation which has been lacking to the spectres, Jerusalem, Spiritual Freedom, who conceives the Lamb of God.

Then sang the sons of Eden round the Lamb of God, & said,
'Glory, Glory, Glory to the holy Lamb of God
Who now beginneth to put off the dark Satanic body.
Now we behold redemption. Now we know that life Eternal
Depends alone upon the Universal hand, & not in us
Is aught but death In individual weakness, sorrow & pain.'[101]

'We now behold the Ends of Beulah, & we now behold
Where death Eternal is put off Eternally.
Assume the dark Satanic body in the Virgin's womb,
O Lamb Divine! it cannot thee annoy. O pitying one,
Thy pity is from the foundation of the World, & thy Redemption
Begun Already in Eternity. Come then, O Lamb of God,
Come, Lord Jesus, come quickly.'[102]

The Lamb of God is brought to trial by Reason.

As it is written, he was number'd among the transgressors.

Thus was the Lamb of God condemn'd to Death.
They nail'd him upon the tree of Mystery, weeping over him
And then mocking & then worshipping, calling him Lord & King.[103]

Los takes the Body from the Cross and buries it in a sepulchre which he had hewn for his own burial from the rock of Eternity, Jerusalem weeping the while. But the death of the Lamb has

* Reason gives rise to contradictions which cannot be solved, symbolized by the separate existence of both sexes in the hermaphrodite, whereas contraries are capable of synthesis as sexes disappear by the union in the Eternal Man.

revealed the falsity of the religion of Mystery, which condemns individuals instead of the one thing beyond redemption, error, the 'State nam'd Satan'. Passion passing through revolt, which had not been capable of self-sacrifice, had sunk into this state as the serpent of hypocrisy, but now error is defined by the death of Jesus, who had sacrificed himself. Reason has lost his power, and has become half repentant, half stupefied. Body and Spirit, weakened and depressed by the shadow of materialism, give allegiance to Poetry and Inspiration, though these are suffering from the general stupor.

> Thus in a living death the nameless shadow all things bound:
> All mortal things made permanent that they may be put off
> Time after time by the Divine Lamb who died for all,
> And all in him died, & he put off all mortality.[104]

The Night ends with the lamentation of Ahania, Pleasure, who had not yet beheld the Divine Vision, and the reply of Enion, who foresees the time when she herself, as the Generative Instinct, shall be 'as a thing Forgotten' when the mortal passes into immortality. She tells of what has happened in the World of Generation.

> '"Listen. I will tell thee what is done in the caverns of the grave.
> The Lamb of God has rent the Veil of Mystery, soon to return
> In Clouds & Fires around the rock & the Mysterious tree.
> As the seed waits Eagerly watching for its flower & fruit,
> Anxious its little soul looks out into the clear expanse
> To see if hungry winds are abroad with their invisible army,
> So Man looks out in tree & herb & fish & bird & beast
> Collecting up the scatter'd portions of his immortal body
> Into the Elemental forms of every thing that grows.
> He tries the sullen north wind, riding on its angry furrows,
> The sultry south when the sun rises, & the angry east
> When the sun sets; when the clods harden & the cattle stand
> Drooping & the birds hide in their silent nests, he stores his
>   thoughts
> As in a store house in his memory; he regulates the forms
> Of all beneath & all above, & in the gentle West
> Reposes where the Sun's heat dwells; he rises to the Sun
> And to the Planets of the Night, & to the stars that gild

The Zodiac, & the stars that sullen stand to north & south,
He touches the remotest pole, & in the center weeps
That Man should Labour & sorrow, & learn & forget, & return
To the dark valley whence he came, to begin his labours anew.
In pain he sighs, in pain he labours in his universe,
Screaming in birds over the deep, & howling in the wolf
Over the slain, & moaning in the cattle, & in the winds,
And weeping over Orc & Urizen in clouds & flaming fires,
And in the cries of birth & in the groans of death his voice
Is heard throughout the Universe: wherever a grass grows
Or a leaf buds, The Eternal Man is seen, is heard, is felt,
And all his sorrows, till he reassumes his ancient bliss." '105

But 'Jerusalem wept over the Sepulcher two thousand years.'*
The religion of Mystery continues to prevail till 'Satan divided
against Satan'; error is not cast out but a new error replaces the
old.

The Ashes of Mystery began to animate; they call'd it Deism
And Natural Religion; as of old, so now anew began
Babylon again in Infancy, call'd Natural Religion.106

In 'Night the Ninth Being The Last Judgment' error is realized
and cast out. Los and Enitharmon build up Jerusalem, Spiritual
Freedom, but, not knowing that Jesus has risen from the dead and
is with them in spirit, they still weep over the sepulchre and over
the crucified body. In his agony of grief Los destroys the material
world, and then:

The heavens are shaken & the Earth removed from its place,
The foundations of the Eternal hills discover'd:
The thrones of Kings are shaken, they have lost their robes &
    crowns,
The poor smite their oppressors, they awake up to the harvest,
The naked warriors rush together down to the sea shore
Trembling before the multitude of slaves now set at liberty:
They are become like wintry flocks, like forests strip'd of leaves:
The oppressed pursue like the wind; there is no room for escape.107

The summons has sounded for the Last Judgment. The universe is consumed in the purifying 'flames of mental fire', and the

* Roughly the period between the Crucifixion and Blake's own time.

Man, now awakened from the sleep that is life in the world of space and time, remembers his happiness in Eternity, contrasting it with the present misery.

'O weakness & O weariness! O war within my members!
My sons, exiled from my breast, pass to & fro before me.
My birds are silent on my hills, flocks die beneath my branches.
My tents are fallen, my trumpets & the sweet sound of my harp
Is silent on my clouded hills that belch forth storms & fire.
My milk of cows & honey of bees & fruit of golden harvest
Are gather'd in the scorching heat & in the driving rain.
My robe is turned to confusion, & my bright gold to stone.
Where once I sat, I weary walk in misery & pain,
For from within my wither'd breast grown narrow with my woes
The Corn is turned to thistles & the apples into poison,
The birds of song to murderous crows, My joys to bitter groans,
The voices of children in my tents to cries of helpless infants,
And all exiled from the face of light & shine of morning
In this dark world, a narrow house, I wander up & down.
I hear Mystery howling in these flames of Consummation.
When shall the Man of future times become as in days of old?
O weary life! why sit I here & give up all my powers
To indolence, to the night of death, when indolence & mourning
Sit hovering over my dark threshold? tho' I arise, look out
And scorn the war within my members, yet my heart is weak
And my head faint. Yet will I look again unto the morning.
Whence is this sound of rage of Men drinking each other's blood,
Drunk with the smoking gore, & red, but not with nourishing
    wine?'

The Eternal Man sat on the Rocks & cried with awful voice:
'O Prince of Light, where art thou? I behold thee not as once
In those Eternal fields, in clouds of morning stepping forth
With harps & songs where bright Ahania sang before thy face
And all thy sons & daughters gather'd round my ample table.
See you not all this wracking furious confusion?
Come forth from slumbers of thy cold abstraction! Come forth,
Arise to Eternal births! Shake off thy cold repose,
Schoolmaster of souls, great opposer of change, arise!
That the Eternal worlds may see thy face in peace & joy,
That thou, dread form of Certainty, maist sit in town & village
While little children play around thy feet in gentle awe,
Fearing thy frown, loving thy smile, O Urizen, Prince of Light.'[108]

But Reason does not answer, and the Man, who knows that the Zoas must be his servants, threatens that he shall be cast out from Eternity unless he repents, because the error of reason is more insidious and deadly than that of passion.

'My anger against thee is greater than against this Luvah,
For war is energy Enslav'd, but thy religion,
The first author of this war & the distracting of honest minds
Into confused perturbation & strife & honour & Pride,
Is a deciet so detestable that I will cast thee out
If thou repentest not, & leave thee as a rotten branch to be burn'd
With Mystery the Harlot & with Satan for Ever & Ever.
Error can never be redeemed in all Eternity,
But Sin, Even Rahab, is redeem'd in blood & fury & jealousy—
That line of blood that stretch'd across the windows of the
    morning—
Redeem'd from Error's power. Wake, thou dragon of the
    deeps!'[109]

Then Urizen repents and renounces his mistaken rule over the other Zoas. Immediately his youth is renewed, and Ahania, his Emanation, joins him, but she dies from excess of joy: the time for Pleasure is not yet. After Urizen has confessed his error the universe is convulsed in the pangs of new birth. The Zoas, now acknowledging themselves the servants of Man, take on again their eternal forms and carry on joyfully the work of regeneration, symbolized as sowing, reaping, threshing, and grinding corn for the Bread, and treading the grapes for the Wine. They know that 'the Eternal Man is Risen,' though the Human harvest cannot share their joy until the Last Judgment is over, until there is neither chaff in the bread of knowledge, nor lees in the wine of ecstasy.

                                         Nature in darkness groans
And Men are bound to sullen contemplation in the night:
Restless they turn on beds of sorrow; in their inmost brain
Feeling the crushing Wheels, they rise, they write the bitter words
Of Stern Philosophy & knead the bread of knowledge with tears
    & groans.

But at last the night of Time is past:

The Sun has left his blackness & has found a fresher morning,
And the mild moon rejoices in the clear & cloudless night,
And Man walks forth from the midst of the fires: the evil is all
    consum'd.
His eyes behold the Angelic spheres arising night & day;
The stars consum'd like a lamp blown out, & in their stead, behold
The Expanding Eyes of Man behold the depths of wondrous
    worlds!
One Earth, one sea beneath; nor Erring Globes wander, but Stars
Of fire rise up nightly from the Ocean; & one Sun
Each morning, like a New born Man, issues with songs & joy
Calling the Plowman to his labour & the Shepherd to his rest.
He walks upon the Eternal Mountains, raising his heavenly voice,
Conversing with the Animal forms of wisdom night & day,
That, risen from the Sea of fire, renew'd walk o'er the Earth;
For Tharmas brought his flocks upon the hills, & in the Vales
Around the Eternal Man's bright tent, the little Children play
Among the wooly flocks. The hammer of Urthona sounds
In the deep caves beneath; his limbs renew'd, his Lions roar
Around the Furnaces & in Evening sport upon the plains.
They raise their faces from the Earth, conversing with the Man:

'How is it we have walk'd thro' fires & yet are not consum'd?
How is it that all things are chang'd, even as in ancient times?'

The Sun arises from his dewy bed, & the fresh airs
Play in his smiling beams giving the seeds of life to grow,
And the fresh Earth beams forth ten thousand thousand springs
    of life.
Urthona is arisen in his strength, no longer now
Divided from Enitharmon, no longer the Spectre Los.
Where is the Spectre of Prophecy? where the delusive Phantom?
Departed: & Urthona rises from the ruinous Walls
In all his ancient strength to form the golden armour of science
For intellectual War. The war of swords departed now,
The dark Religions are departed & sweet Science reigns.[110]

The myth is intricate, the symbolism remote, the allusions to
and reminiscences of the Bible, Plato, Milton, as obscure as they
are abundant. Obscurer still and often unfathomable are Blake's
own associations with places and people whom he introduces. A
summary can be but a handful of gleanings nor can the gleaner
pretend to have chosen these impersonally and with a perfect

discretion. *Vala* will only yield its harvest to the reader who is diligent as well as receptive. Some critics appear to have expected the crisp drama of a morality play, and have in their disappointment transferred their own confusion of mind to Blake. It is essential to realize that Blake is making an attempt, impossible or absurd though it may be deemed, to describe experience, universal and individual, in its process and particularity, its psychological advances and retrogressions, without what he held to be the delusive and meretricious aid of logical dialectic, categories, and formulae. The student will often doubt his own intelligence, but his faith in Blake's will increase.

The manuscript of *Vala* was given to Linnell by Blake toward the close of his life: it contains some of his most beautiful drawings.

It will have been seen that Blake's tale of work during the Lambeth period is almost incredible. During these seven years he had been employed by the booksellers, though to a less extent after the commercial failure of the *Night Thoughts*; he had issued independently the series of printed drawings, and had produced the Lambeth Books with their numerous designs and ornaments. Moreover, he had created in them and in *Vala* a new and complex mythology, the product not only of intellectual effort, but of intense personal experience and emotional conflict. The self-assertion of the *Prospectus* and other of his references to his own work masks the essential fear and trembling of which he spoke to the young Palmer, and is of the nature of a reaction and a reassurance. A sentence in the Notebook suggests that moments of superhuman energy were followed by desperate physical exhaustion. 'I say I shan't live five years, And if I live one it will be a Wonder. June 1793.'[111]

He allowed himself no relaxation and yet he loved laughter: laughter is perhaps what his life most lacked, and more sympathy and a little ease: he did not need to ride in the coach with pictured panels:* but above all more laughter. His letter to Cumberland of 2 July 1800 shows signs of mental fatigue, and also a dread of isolating himself in his absorption: 'I begin to Emerge from a

* The precursor of the Rolls Royce, affected by Sir Joshua.

Deep pit of Melancholy, Melancholy without any real reason for it, a Disease which God keep you from & all good men. . . . I have been too little among friends which I fear they will not Excuse & I know not how to apologize for.'

And again: 'I feel very strongly that I neglect my Duty to my Friends, but It is not want of Gratitude or Friendship but perhaps an Excess of both.'[112]

Blake the man might well need change of scene, human sympathy, and relief from anxiety about the means of existence, and a *deus ex machina* was even then descending, beneficent in intention, if somewhat obsolete in pattern. But the marriage bells of Heaven and Hell, announcing revolution to the sound of laughter, had now ceased to ring. Blake's *particular friend*, the Angel so easily converted into a Devil, and the light-hearted Fairy of the Introduction to *Europe*, had failed him. Their places had been taken by those vehement and unhuman abstractions Urizen, Los, and the rest; even Orc, the Secret Child, was not yet identified with that other child whose birth was the symbol of regeneration and of peace. Blake the mystic had passed into the Dark Night of the Soul which, illumined now and then by dreams of dawn, would still last for some years.

V

FELPHAM

And all this Vegetable World appear'd on my left Foot
As a bright sandal form'd immortal of precious stones &
    gold:
I stooped down & bound it on to walk forward thro'
    eternity.[1]

Hayley is indeed a true poet; he has the fire and the invention of
Dryden, without any of his absurdity; and he has the wit and ease
of Prior. If his versification is a degree less polished than Pope's,
it is more various. We find the numbers sweet and flowing, and I
think sufficiently abundant in the graces of harmony.[2]

So spake the Swan of Lichfield of the Bard of Sussex, Anna
Seward of William Hayley, who was to be Blake's employer and
constant companion for three years. Lest the curiosity of a too
hopeful reader be aroused by Miss Seward's praise it must be
added that Hayley's laurels are withered irrevocably: no critic will
ever freshen them up and make them sappy with his praise: the
last word is with Lord Byron, 'For ever feeble and for ever tame.'
But Hayley took his vocation seriously enough: in the monumental memoirs of himself and his son, for which he received a
substantial annuity during the last twelve years of his life on condition that they were to be left ready for publication at his death,
he is always the Poet, the Bard, the Hermit. He vented all his
feeble thoughts and facile emotions in verse, priding himself on
ease and rapidity of composition. His opinions on History,
Painting, Sculpture, Music, and Epic Poetry were expressed in
Poetic Epistles; his sepulchral tribute to the dead was paid in a
hundred or more epitaphs; he was accustomed to compose on his
pillow brief nocturnal poems, and was even known to emit before
breakfast four devotional stanzas. His most popular poem, *The
Triumphs of Temper*, was undertaken because 'his observation of
the various effects of spleen on the female character induced him

to believe that he might render an important service to social life, if his poetry could induce his young and fair readers to cultivate the gentle qualities of the heart and maintain a constant flow of humour.'3 The persuasive influence of his 'soft Serena' upon the peevish fair rewarded the poet's labours, but her power has passed away.

Hayley was not only a professional poet, he was also an amateur in art. During his Cambridge days he had taken lessons in water-colour and miniature painting with results very pleasing to himself and his friends. A letter to Cowper's cousin, the Revd. John Johnson, shows his taste in matters artistic:

What negligent idle rogues are you, and your painter: . . . Cannot your artist devise any neat and graceful mode of uniting the portraits of Milton and Cowper in one plate? Surely it may be done, either as busts, or as medallions. In the latter case, he might sketch an eagle, holding in his beak a ribband, or ring, from which may descend a medallion of Milton, and a dove, as its companion, with a similar image of Cowper. Or, if you prefer their busts, they may be placed on terms, or pilasters, forming the entrance to a bower, in which, at a distance, you should discover the Muse Urania in a pensive attitude, with her harp, and a Bible: the figure of the Muse much smaller than the features of the busts.

If your artist has any dexterity of hand, and exercise of fancy, he may make something expressive and pleasing from these simple ideas, or he may draw two neat altars, inscribed *to Piety*, in the shady recess of a garden, placing the bust of Milton on one, and that of Cowper on the other; the first, near a *Cedar* or a *Palm*; the second, near a *Cypress*.4

Hayley numbered Gibbon, Romney, Flaxman, and Cowper among his friends, and to his creditable exertions Cowper owed his pension of £300. Flaxman had sent the Bard a copy of his young friend Blake's *Poetical Sketches*, remarking in the spirit of the Mathew preface: 'his education will plead sufficient excuse to your Liberal mind for the defects of his work & there are few so able to distinguish & set a right value on the beauties as yourself.'5

Hayley's verdict on the poems is not recorded, but some fifteen years later, thanks again to Flaxman, he employed Blake to execute three engravings for his *Essay on Sculpture*, one from a bust of

Pericles, one after a drawing by his illegitimate son of 'The Death of Demosthenes', and the third after a medallion by Flaxman of this Thomas Alphonso, the 'dear diminutive Phidias', who had been a pupil of Flaxman's. Flaxman writes to Hayley, 29 January 1800, 'I have delivered the Drawing of Demosthenes to Mr Blake with the right orthography of the Dedication to Neptune';[6] and again, 26 March 1800;

It is equally Surprizing & unaccountable that you have had no farther news of the Engravings, for Mr Howard finished a beautiful drawing from the Medallion of my Friend Thomas I think four weeks ago, since which time it has been in the hands of Mr Blake & the copper plate from it is most likely done by this time, as well as that of the head of Pericles; but perhaps You are not acquainted with Mr Blake's direction? it is No 13 Hercules Buildings near the Asylum, Surry Side of Westminster Bridge.[7]

On the 1st April Blake despatched his engraving of the medallion of Tom, who was then mortally ill.

                                    Hercules Buildings, Lambeth
                                              1 April 1800
Dear Sir,
    With all possible Expedition I send you a proof of my attempt to Express your & our Much Beloved's Countenance. Mr. Flaxman has seen it & approved of my now sending it to you for your remarks. Your Sorrows and your dear son's May Jesus and his Angels assuage & if it is consistent with his divine providence restore him to us & to his labours of Art & Science in this world. So prays a fellow sufferer & Your humble Servant,
                                              Willm Blake

But Hayley was dissatisfied with the result: in a letter about his son's illness to Samuel Rose, written the 2nd April, he says:

Here is the long-expected medallion arrived today from the Engraver Blake—& I must endeavour to be a Hero in another way & bear a most mortifying disappointment with serenity, for mortifying you will allow it to be when I tell you the portrait instead of representing the dear juvenile pleasant Face of yr Friend exhibits a heavy sullen sulky Head which I can never present to the public Eye as the Image of a Being so tenderly &

so justly beloved. I believe I must have a fresh outline & a mere outline instead of it—but I shall consult the dear artist himself on his own Head to-morrow—.[9]

The engraving was sent back to Blake, who writes again, 6 May, after the boy's death:

I am very sorry for your immense loss, which is a repetition of what all feel in this valley of misery & happiness mixed. I send the Shadow of the departed Angel; hope the likeness is improved. The lips I have again lessened as you advised & done a good many other softenings to the whole. I know that our deceased friends are more really with us than when they were apparent to our mortal part. Thirteen years ago I lost a brother & with his spirit I converse daily & hourly in the Spirit & See him in my remembrance in the regions of my Imagination. I hear his advice & even now write from his Dictate. Forgive me for Expressing to you my Enthusiasm which I wish all to partake of Since it is to me a Source of Immortal Joy: even in this world by it I am the companion of Angels. May you continue to be so more & more & to be more & more perswaded that every Mortal loss is an Immortal Gain. The Ruins of Time builds Mansions in Eternity.[10]

Hayley acknowledged his sympathy by the gift of Alphonso's copy of *The Triumphs of Temper* with this characteristic inscription:

> Accept, my gentle visionary, Blake,
>   Sublimely fanciful & kindly mild;
> Accept, and fondly keep for Friendship's sake,
>   This favoured vision, my poetic Child!
>
> Rich in more grace than Fancy ever won,
>   To thy most tender mind this Book will be,
> For it belong'd to my departed son;
>   So from an Angel it descends to Thee.
>
>   W. H. July, 1800[11]

But he was not yet content with the portrait of Tom, and Blake paid a visit to Felpham in order to make a further attempt under his supervision. On 16 July he writes to Flaxman:

as I find our good enthusiastic Friend Blake will (in his Zeal to render the Portraits of our beloved scholar more worthy of Him)

extend the time of his Residence in the south* a little longer than
we at first proposed, I shall not wait to transmit my Thanks to you
for a Letter of infinite Kindness by the worthy Engraver on his
Return.[12]

After a reference to his plans for the mother of the lamented
Thomas Alphonso, 'I hope she will pass a respected & tranquill
evening of mortal existence in a neat and comfortable little man-
sion near the Grave of that justly idolized youth...'[13] he continues:
'The good Blake is taking great pains to render all the Justice in
his Power to Romneys exquisite Portrait of Him, & I hope the
two next prints will atone for all the defects of the engraved
Medallion.'[14] The end of the letter is torn, but is to the effect that
'the good Blake' will give Flaxman a history of what he has 'done
in the South on his Return,' and Hayley sends Nancy Flaxman a
book which 'shall travel to Her by the Favor of Blake.'

Cowper had died a week earlier than Tom, and the afflicted
Hayley determined to devote himself to immortalizing the memories of his friend and his son. He invited Blake to engrave the
plates for his *Life of Cowper*, suggesting that he should live for a
time at Felpham while employed on this and other work: this
proposal no doubt originated during Blake's visit. Hayley himself
had just moved from the family property at Eartham to a 'Marine
Villa' at Felpham in order to retrench his expenses. Blake, as we
have seen, was in the mood to welcome such a change. In August
he went again to Felpham, and rented a cottage from the landlord
of the Fox Inn for £20 a year.† His gratitude to Flaxman for the
introduction to Hayley which led to this arrangement was boundless; one of its expressions is to be found in the lines beginning
'I bless thee, O Father of Heaven & Earth, that ever I saw Flaxman's face,'[15] a hymn of thanksgiving for his friends, earthly and
heavenly, in which Hayley, the last recruit, joins Ezra and Isaiah,

* This visit of Blake's to Hayley appears to have escaped the attention of
biographers hitherto. [The letter is among the voluminous Hayley correspondence now in the Fitzwilliam Museum, Cambridge. Extracts relating to
Blake are printed in *Blake Records*. Ed.]

† This rent—equivalent to about £80 at the present (1927) value of money
—seems surprisingly high.

Shakespeare and Milton, Boehme and Paracelsus, Flaxman and Fuseli. It is well that Blake did not read Flaxman's letter of 19 August to Hayley about the migration to Felpham or he would have accounted this corporeal friend a spiritual enemy.

You may naturally suppose that I am highly pleased with the exertion of Your usual Benevolence in favour of my friend Blake & as such an occasion offers you will perhaps be more satisfied in having the portraits engraved under your own eye, than at a distance, indeed I hope that Blake's residence at Felpham will be a Mutual Comfort to you & him, & I see no reason why he should not make as good a livelihood there as in London, if he engraves & teaches drawing, by which he may gain considerably as also by making neat drawings of different kinds but if he places any dependence on painting large pictures, for which he is not qualified, either by habit or study, he will be miserably decieved.[16]

Mrs. Blake also wrote to Mrs. Flaxman of their plans for a summer visit from the Flaxmans: '... & we not only talk, but behold! the Angels of our journey have inspired a song to you'; then follow Blake's verses 'To My Dear Friend, Mrs Anna Flaxman':

This Song to the flower of Flaxman's joy,
To the blossom of hope, for a sweet decoy:
Do all that you can or all that you may,
To entice him to Felpham & far away.

Away to Sweet Felpham, for Heaven is there;
The Ladder of Angels descends thro' the air;
On the Turret its spiral does softly descend,
Thro' the village then winds, at My Cot it does end.

You stand in the village & look up to heaven;
The precious stones glitter on flights seventy seven;
And My Brother is there, & My Friend & Thine,
Descend & Ascend with the Bread & the Wine.

The Bread of sweet Thought & the Wine of Delight
Feeds the Village of Felpham by day & by night;
And at his own door the bless'd Hermit* does stand,
Dispensing Unceasing to all the whole Land.

* The turret is that of Hayley's house, and the Hermit Hayley himself.
With 'the Ladder of Angels' may be associated Blake's drawing, 'Jacob's Ladder'.

Mrs. Blake was worn out by pleasurable excitement and domestic cares. Blake tells Hayley on 16 September that 'My Dear & too careful & over joyous Woman has Exhausted her strength. . . .'[18] None the less, two days later they set out for Felpham between 6 and 7 a.m., accompanied by Miss Blake. The journey lasted till 11.30 p.m., involving six changes of chaise and driver for themselves and their sixteen heavy boxes and portfolios, yet 'All was Chearfulness & Good Humour on the Road.'[19] The cottage, which is still standing, a six-roomed thatched cottage facing south with a verandah running the length of the house, smiled false promises in the summer weather.

We are safe arrived at our Cottage, which is more beautiful than I thought it, & more convenient. It is a perfect Model for Cottages &, I think, for Palaces of Magnificence, only Enlarging, not altering its proportions, & adding ornaments & not principals. Nothing can be more Grand than its Simplicity & Usefulness. Simple without Intricacy, it seems to be the Spontaneous Effusion of Humanity, congenial to the wants of Man. No other formed House can ever please me so well; nor shall I ever be perswaded, I believe, that it can be improved either in Beauty or Use.[20]

The village seemed a haven of peace and inspiration to the travellers.

Felpham is a sweet place for Study, because it is more Spiritual than London. Heaven opens here on all sides her Golden Gates; her windows are not obstructed by vapours; voices of Celestial inhabitants are more distinctly heard, & their forms more distinctly seen, & my Cottage is also a Shadow of their houses.[21]

The omens were propitious; the implements of labour and the very words of the labourers were symbols of promise.

Work will go on here with God speed.—A roller & two harrows lie before my window. I met a plow on my first going out at my gate the first morning after my arrival, & the Plowboy said to the Plowman, 'Father, The Gate is Open.'[22]

Heaven was scarcely veiled; surely here invention would be inspired, and Execution, 'the Chariot of Genius', would move with speed and ease.

And Now Begins a New life, because another covering of Earth is shaken off. I am more famed in Heaven for my works than I could well concieve. In my Brain are studies & Chambers fill'd with books & pictures of old, which I wrote & painted in ages of Eternity before my mortal life; & those works are the delight & Study of Archangels. Why, then, should I be anxious about the riches or fame of mortality. The Lord our father will do for us & with us according to his Divine will for our Good.[23]

Mr. Butts, whom Blake had addressed as 'Dear Friend of My Angels,' is delighted with his luck. His letter shows the easy relations between the two households, and also his concern about Blake's heterodox opinions.*

September 1800, Marlborough Street

Dear Sir,
    I cannot immediately determine whether or no I am dignified by the Title you have graciously conferred on me.—You cannot but recollect the difficulties that have unceasingly arisen to prevent my discerning clearly whether your Angels are black, white, or grey, and that of the three on the whole I have rather inclined to the former opinion and considered you more immediately under the protection of the black-guard; however, at any rate I should thank you for an introduction to his Highness's Court, that, when refused admittance into other Mansions, I may not be received as a Stranger in this.
    I am well pleased with your pleasures, feeling no small interest in Your Happiness, and it cannot fail to be highly gratifying to me and my affectionate Partner, to know that a Corner of your Mansion of Peace is asylumed to Her, & when invalided & rendered unfit for service who shall say she may not be quarter'd on your Cot—but for the present she is for active Duty and satisfied with requesting that if there is a Snug Berth unoccupied in any Chamber of your warm Heart, that her Portrait may be suspended there, at the same time well aware that you, like me, prefer the Original to the Copy.
    Your good Wife will permit, & I hope may benefit from, the Embraces of Neptune, but she will presently distinguish betwixt

---

* Butts's letter is printed from a draft which he kept among the letters he had received from Blake. The whole collection, formerly owned by W. Graham Robertson, is now in the Kerrison Preston Blake Library in the Westminster Public Library. [Ed.]

the warmth of his Embraces & yours, & court the former with
caution. I suppose you do not admit of a third in that concern,
or I would offer her mine even at this distance. Allow me before I
draw a Veil over this interesting Subject to lament the frailty of
the fairest Sex for who alas! of us, my good Friend, could have
thought that so good a Woman would ever have exchanged
Hercules Buildings for Neptune's Bed,—

So Virtuous a Woman would ever have fled
from Hercules Buildings to Neptune's Bed?

Whether you will be a better Painter or a better Poet from your
change of ways & means I know not, but this I predict, that you
will be a better Man—excuse me, as you have been accustomed
from friendship to do, but certain opinions imbibed from reading,
nourish'd by indulgence, and rivetted by a confined Conversation,
and which have been equally prejudicial to your Interest & Happiness, will now, I trust, disperse as a Day-break Vapour, and you
will henceforth become a Member of that Community of which
you are at present, in the opinion of the Archbishop of Canterbury,
but a Sign to mark the residence of dim incredulity, haggard
suspicion, & bloated philosophy—whatever can be effected by
sterling sense, by opinions which harmonize society and beautify
creation, will in future be exemplified in you, & the time I trust
is not distant, and that because I truly regard you, when you will
be a more valorous Champion of Revelation & Humiliation than
any of those who now wield the Sword of the Spirit; with your
natural & acquired Powers nothing is wanting but a proper direction of them, & altho' the way is both straight & narrow I know
you too well to fear your want of resolution to persevere & to
pursue it—you have the Plough & the Harrow in full view & the
Gate you have been prophetically told is Open; can you then
hesitate joyfully to enter into it?

I have much to congratulate you on. Meat cheap, Music for
nothing, a command of the Sea, and brotherly affection fluttering
around ye—The Arts have promised to be propitious and the
Graces will courtesy to your wishes—

Happy, happy, happy Pair,
On Earth, in Sea, or eke in Air,
In morn, at noon, & thro' the Night
From Visions fair receiving light,

> Long may ye live, your Guardians' Care,
> And when ye die may not a Hair
> Fall to the lot of Demons black,
> Be singed by Fire, or heard to crack,
> But may your faithful Spirit upward bear
> Your gentle Souls to Him whose care
> Is ever sure and ever nigh
> Those who on Providence rely,
> And in his Paradise above
> Where all is Beauty, Truth & Love,
> O May ye be allowed to chuse
> For your firm Friend a Heaven-born Muse,
> From purest Fountains sip delight,
> Be cloathed in Glory burning bright,
> For ever blest, for ever free,
> The loveliest Blossoms on Life's Tree.

I have no more Nonsense for you just now, but must assure you that I shall always sincerely devote myself to your service when my humble endeavours may be useful.

Mrs. Butts greets your Wife & charming Sister with a holy Kiss and I, with old Neptune, bestow my Embraces there also—for yourself I commend you to the protection of your Guard & am,

Dear Sir,

Yours most cordially

& faithfully[24]

Blake exchanges for 'your very beautiful & encouraging Verses' 'a return of verses, such as Felpham produces by me, tho' not such as she produces by her Eldest Son.' No, indeed, poor Hayley! They are the lines beginning:

> To my Friend Butts I write
> My first Vision of Light,
> On the yellow sands sitting.[25]

But Blake was too happy for irony. Hayley was still a poet and a brother.*

---

* Gilchrist, *Life*, i, p. 356, gives an instance of Blake's courtesy to an inferior painter. He was showing one of his pictures to a visitor and said: 'Mr. Blake once paid me a high compliment on that picture. It was on the

One of Blake's first tasks was to decorate Hayley's new library at Felpham with eighteen heads nearly life size,* among them Shakespeare, Homer, Camoens, Sir Philip Sidney, Cowper with his favourite dog, Thomas Alphonso Hayley encircled by doves, Ercilla, Ariosto, and Spenser. These paintings are now in the possession of the Manchester Corporation Art Gallery. He also illustrated, and printed with Mrs. Blake's help, Hayley's ballad, *Little Tom the Sailor*,† which was sold for the benefit of a Folkestone widow whose husband had been drowned. For a time things went gaily enough. Blake was even a little suspicious of his unwonted high spirits.

Time flies very fast and very merrily. I sometimes try to be miserable that I may do more work, but find it is a foolish experiment. Happinesses have wings and wheels; miseries are leaden legged, and their whole employment is to clip the wings and to take off the wheels of our chariots. We determine, therefore, to be happy and do all that we can, tho' not all that we would.[26]

He became Hayley's pupil in miniature painting, and sent Mrs. Butts a portrait of her husband,‡ but was dissatisfied with the memory picture—'for I have now discovered that without Nature before the painter's Eye, he can never produce any thing in the walks of Natural Painting.' For a time at least miniature painting

---

last occasion when the old gentleman visited me, and his words were, "Ah! that is what I have been trying to do all my life—to paint *round* and never could." '

* Reproduced by the Blake Society, 1925. K. Povey (*Notes and Queries*, 24 July 1926) discusses these heads, suggesting that several are now wrongly named. There may have been two more, now lost. The full list of subjects of the heads is as follows: Camoens, Geoffrey Chaucer, Cicero, William Cowper, Dante Alighieri, Demosthenes, John Dryden, Ercilla, Thomas Hayley, Homer, Friedrich Klopstock, John Milton, Thomas Otway, Alexander Pope, William Shakespeare, Edmund Spenser, Torquato Tasso, and Voltaire.

† Produced by the method which Blake called 'wood cutting on pewter.' Cf. Memoranda from the Notebook (*Complete Writings*, p. 440).

‡ Blake painted miniatures of Thomas and Mrs. Butts with one of their son Tom; there are also two of Cowper and one of his cousin, John Johnson (see Keynes, *Blake Studies*, pp. 111–12). There must have been others of Hayley's friends at present unidentified. [Ed.]

was a pleasant change from engraving, and he had numerous sitters from the neighbourhood, but as Hayley made progress with his *Life of Cowper* Blake's time was mainly occupied in engraving the illustrations,* printing them in his own excellent press, which had cost £40. He was delighted with Cowper's letters, 'Perhaps, or rather Certainly, the very best letters that were ever published.'[27] Did not the delightful letter recording a dream, in which Milton appeared 'very gravely, but very neatly attired in the fashion of his day' and they talked about *Paradise Lost*, bring the first suggestion of Blake's symbolic book of *Milton*? It is not recorded whether he shared that enthusiasm for the 'Yardley Oak' which moved Hayley to send for 'a large lump' of the roots to be made into 'nice little boxes, for the toilette of the fair.'

His sympathy with Cowper is shown by a later note.

Cowper came to me and said: 'O that I were insane always. I will never rest. Can you not make me truly insane? I will never rest till I am so. O that in the bosom of God I was hid. You retain health and yet are as mad as any of us all—over us all—mad as a refuge from unbelief—from Bacon, Newton and Locke.'†

Cowper's cousin, the Revd. John Johnson, who had been with him during his last illness, paid a visit to Felpham that he might give Hayley some help with the *Life of Cowper*. Blake describes him as 'a happy Abstract, known by all his Friends as the most innocent forgetter of his own Interests.'[28] He painted a miniature of Johnson,‡ and panels for his chimney- piece at Yaxham Rectory of 'Winter', 'Evening', and 'Olney Bridge'. §

* The illustrations in the three volumes (1803–4) include portraits of Cowper after Romney and Lawrence, of Cowper's mother after Heins, and two of Cowper's monument in East Dereham church. Only one is from a design by Blake himself—the 'Weather House' with Cowper's tame hares. [Ed.]

† Notes on Spurzheim's *Observations on the Deranged Manifestations of the Mind, or Insanity* (*Complete Writings*, p. 772). The lines to 'William Cowper, Esqre,' p. 551, are obviously a gibe at the tardiness of the assistance given to Cowper by the pension which Hayley was instrumental in securing.

‡ Johnson (*Memoirs of William Hayley*, 1823, ii, p. 32) dates his visit January 1802, but Blake's reference is from a letter to Butts of 11 September 1801. (*Complete Writings*, p. 808.)

§ The splendid panels of 'Winter' and 'Evening' painted with a tempera medium in pale colours are still in the keeping of a descendant of Johnson.

Blake rejoiced in the negotiations which led to the Peace of
Amiens, and had dreams of a visit to Paris, a project which was
never carried out. In a letter to Flaxman of 19 October 1801 he
says:

The Reign of Literature & the Arts Commences. Blessed are
those who are found studious of Literature & Humane & polite
accomplishments. Such have their lamps burning & such shall
shine as the stars. . . .
Now I hope to see the Great Works of Art, as they are so near to
Felpham, Paris being scarce further off than London. But I hope
that France & England will henceforth be as One Country and
their Arts One, & that you will Ere long be erecting Monuments
In Paris—Emblems of Peace.[29]

In the same letter he speaks of sending Flaxman his designs for
Comus* when finished. Hayley had written to Flaxman the day
before: 'it is with great delight I assure you, that our good Blake
grows more & more attach'd to this pleasant marine village, &
seems to gain in it a perpetual Increase of improving Talents, &
settled Comfort.'[30]

But the first hint of trouble had already appeared in a letter to
Butts of 11 September. The fussy, possessive Hayley has begun to
constitute himself Blake's mentor. We can hear the echo of his
voice in Blake's playful self-depreciation:

Time flies faster (as seems to me) here than in London. I labour
incessantly & accomplish not one half of what I intend, because
my Abstract folly hurries me often away while I am at work,
carrying me over Mountains & Valleys, which are not Real, in a
Land of Abstraction where Spectres of the Dead wander. This I
endeavour to prevent & with my whole might chain my feet to the

---

The painting of 'Olney Bridge' has been destroyed. [Ed.] The two former
illustrate the lines from *The Task*, iv:

> O Winter, ruler of the inverted year,
> Thy scattered air with sleet-like ashes filled.

and

> Come Ev'ning once again season of Peace
> Return sweet Ev'ning and continue long.

* Blake painted two series for *Comus*, each in eight water colours; both are
now in the United States.

world of Duty & Reality; but in vain! the faster I bind, the better is the Ballast, for I, so far from being bound down, take the world with me in my flights, & often it seems lighter than a ball of wool rolled by the wind. Bacon & Newton would prescribe ways of making the world heavier to me, & Pitt would prescribe distress for a medicinal potion; but as none on Earth can give me Mental Distress, & I know that all Distress inflicted by Heaven is a Mercy, a Fig for all Corporeal! Such Distress is My mock & scorn. Alas! wretched, happy, ineffectual labourer of time's moments that I am! who shall deliver me from this Spirit of Abstraction & Improvidence? Such, my Dear Sir, Is the truth of my state, & I tell it you in palliation of my seeming neglect of your most pleasant orders.[31]

Meanwhile Hayley, self-satisfied, sentimental, and insensitive, was indulging his old-lady-like propensities—

> Of H's birth this was the happy lot
> His Mother on his Father him begot—[32]

by treating his long-suffering protégé as little better than a hired companion. His presence was indispensable while Hayley was composing.

I say *we*, for the warm-hearted indefatigable Blake works daily at my side, on the intended decorations of our biography. Engraving, of all human works, appears to require the largest portion of patience, and he happily possesses more of that inestimable virtue, than I ever saw united before to an imagination so lively and so prolific.[33]

Blake's patience was also required to carry out bright little ideas of Hayley's own. For instance, Hayley was not pleased with Flaxman's sketches for Cowper's tomb,

and presumptuously have tried myself to out-design my dear Flaxman* himself on this most animating occasion. I form'd there-

---

* On 18 January Hayley had added at the end of a letter to Flaxman about the Cowper monument that Blake 'allows me to inclose one of his *unfinish'd* Engravings, that we think you may wish to see for the purpose of forming a medallion—Be kind enough to keep it in *friendly privacy* & tell us your *frank opinion* of it, in its *present unfinish'd state*: we shall *both* thank you heartily for *any suggestions that may improve it*.' (*Blake Records*, p. 88.)

fore a Device of *the Bible upright* supporting '*The Task*' with a Laurel Wreath & *Palms*, such as I send you neatly copied by our Kind Blake. . . . If her Ladyship [Lady Hesketh] & Flaxman are as much pleasd with my Idea, as the good Blake & Pauline of Lavant *are*, all our difficulties on this *grand monumental Contention* will *end most happily*.[34]

Sometimes he even acted as amanuensis to Hayley, whose eyes were weak, but not too weak to inflict his favourite Klopstock on his companion. Blake, it would appear, had already recorded his opinion of Klopstock, usually printed in these polite days in an expurgated form, and must have exercised some control in not pouring out the full torrent of the original on Hayley's head. The MS. 'Genesis The Seven Days of the Created World', about two hundred lines of blank verse, obviously not by Blake himself, is probably a translation of Klopstock by Hayley, transcribed by Blake.* Hayley's own opera, nocturnal and diurnal, also formed part of his patient companion's pabulum, 'the Verses that Hayley sung When my heart knock'd against the root of my tongue.'[35] The Greek lessons based on Cowper's translation of the *Iliad* must have been some alleviation, and perhaps also the morning ride, Hayley, with his umbrella, leading, no doubt, on a charger, and Blake paying sufficient attention to the physical world to follow him in safety on Bruno, the pony lent to him by Miss Harriet Poole of Lavant,† with whom Hayley was in the habit of breakfasting twice a week.[36] Together they visited neighbours such as Miss Poole and were present at the death-bed of Hayley's old servant, William. Hayley's friends were as blind as himself in their patronage. Lady Bathurst, to whose children Blake had given some drawing lessons, proposed to engage him as salaried painter in ordinary to the family, and the only order he ever refused, a set of handscreens, is supposed to have been hers.[37]

* Kenneth Povey proved in 1952 (*Times Literary Supplement*, 3 October) that this MS. is a translation, probably by Hayley, of Tasso's *Le Sette Giornale del Mondo Creato*, Blake acting as amanuensis. [Ed.]

† Miss Poole is referred to as 'the Lady of Lavant' and as 'Paulina', possibly a variant of 'Poolina'. Henrietta (Harriet) Poole was the daughter of William Poole, Receiver-General of the Stamp Office. For further information about her see Morchard Bishop's *Blake's Hayley* (1951), pp. 187–8, etc.

Enough has been said to show that the atmosphere of Felpham would have been sufficiently trying to any person of aesthetic and ecstatic tendencies, intolerable to the poet and artist, and still more intolerable to the mystic whose absorbing spiritual conflicts must of themselves precipitate him suddenly from high heavenly places into caverns of seemingly endless gloom. 'The Visions were angry with me at Felpham,'[38] Blake used to say in after years. In Lambeth it had at least been possible to secure solitude, but at Felpham Hayley was all-pervasive. Well might the spiritual form of his umbrella frighten visions away.

It is to Blake's credit that the storm was so slow in bursting. In his letter to Butts of 10 January 1802 there is an ominous rumble. He begins by saying that he has been ill, and Mrs. Blake, who had been constantly plagued by ague and rheumatism, very ill. Then he confides to Butts that:

When I came down here, I was more sanguine than I am at present; but it was because I was ignorant of many things which have since occurred, & chiefly the unhealthiness of the place. Yet I do not repent of coming on a thousand accounts; & Mr H., I doubt not, will do ultimately all that both he & I wish—that is, to lift me out of difficulty; but this is no easy matter to a man who, having Spiritual Enemies of such formidable magnitude, cannot expect to want natural hidden ones.

Then follows a refusal of pecuniary help from Butts: 'our expenses are small, & our income, from our incessant labour, fully adequate to them at present.'

Later in the same letter he recurs to his confidences and enlarges on the situation:

But you have so generously & openly desired that I will divide my griefs with you, that I cannot hide what it has now become my duty to explain.—My unhappiness has arisen from a source which, if explor'd too narrowly, might hurt my pecuniary circumstances, As my dependence is on Engraving at present, & particularly on the Engravings I have in hand for Mr H.: & I find on all hands great objections to my doing any thing but the meer drudgery of business, & intimations that if I do not confine myself to this, I shall not live; this has always pursu'd me

You will understand by this the source of all my uneasiness. This from Johnson & Fuseli brought me down here, & this from Mr H. will bring me back again; for that I cannot live without doing my duty to lay up treasures in heaven is Certain & Determined, & to this I have long made up my mind, & why this should be made an objection to Me, while Drunkenness, Lewdness, Gluttony & even Idleness itself, does not hurt other men, let Satan himself Explain. The Thing I have most at Heart—more than life, or all that seems to make life comfortable without— Is the Interest of True Religion & Science, & whenever any thing appears to affect that Interest (Especcially if I myself omit any duty to my Station as a Soldier of Christ), It gives me the greatest of torments. I am not ashamed, afraid, or averse to tell you what Ought to be Told: That I am under the direction of Messengers from Heaven, Daily & Nightly; but the nature of such things is not, as some suppose, without trouble or care. Temptations are on the right hand & left; behind, the sea of time & space roars & follows swiftly; he who keeps not right onward is lost, & if our footsteps slide in clay, how can we do otherwise than fear & tremble? but I should not have troubled You with this account of my spiritual state, unless it had been necessary in explaining the actual cause of my uneasiness, into which you are so kind as to Enquire; for I never obtrude such things on others unless question'd, & then I never disguise the truth.—But if we fear to do the dictates of our Angels, & tremble at the Tasks set before us; If we refuse to do Spiritual Acts because of Natural Fears or Natural Desires! Who can describe the dismal torments of such a state!—I too well remember the Threats I heard!—If you, who are organised by Divine Providence for Spiritual communion, Refuse, & bury your Talent in the Earth, even tho' you should want Natural Bread, Sorrow & Desperation pursues you thro' life, & after death shame & confusion of face to eternity. Every one in Eternity will leave you, aghast at the Man who was crown'd with glory & honour by his brethren, & betray'd their cause to their enemies. You will be call'd the base Judas who betray'd his Friend!—Such words would make any stout man tremble, & how then could I be at ease? But I am no longer in That State, & now go on again with my Task, Fearless, and tho' my path is difficult, I have no fear of stumbling while I keep it.

My wife desires her kindest Love to Mrs Butts, & I have permitted her to send it to you also; we often wish that we could unite again in Society, & hope that the time is not distant when we shall do so, being determin'd not to remain another winter here, but to return to London.

> I hear a voice you cannot hear, that says I must not stay,
> I see a hand you cannot see, that beckons me away.*

Naked we came here, naked of Natural things, & naked we shall return; but while cloth'd with the Divine Mercy, we are richly cloth'd in Spiritual & suffer all the rest gladly. . . .[39]

Blake's miniatures help us to picture Mr. and Mrs. Butts receiving this letter; she, perhaps, thought it a trifle fantastic, and he, though his eyes twinkled a little, damned Hayley for a fool: there was no taint of 'holiness' or 'officious brotherhood' in Mr. Butts, despite his respect for the Archbishop of Canterbury. Blake's two letters to him of 22 November 1802 were written in the lull before the storm:

> And now let me finish with assuring you that, Tho' I have been very unhappy, I am so no longer. I am again Emerged into the light of day; I still & shall to Eternity Embrace Christianity and Adore him who is the Express image of God; but I have travel'd thro' Perils & Darkness not unlike a Champion. I have Conquer'd, and shall still Go on Conquering. Nothing can withstand the fury of my Course among the Stars of God & in the Abysses of the Accuser. My Enthusiasm is still what it was, only Enlarged and confirm'd.[40]

The second letter encloses some verses written a year before 'which My Wife desires me to Copy out & send you with her kind love & Respect', the lines beginning 'With happiness stretch'd across the hills', the history of an hour in the three years' struggle amid the incompatibilities of Felpham,

> With Angels planted in Hawthorn bowers
> And God himself in the passing hours,[41]

and Hayley reading his own verses aloud. The poem ends with one of those triumphs of the spirit which prolonged the struggle:

---

* The couplet (really four lines) is from 'Lucy and Colin,' by Thomas Tickell, included in Percy's *Reliques* (1765), iii, p. 308.

Now I a fourfold vision see,
And a fourfold vision is given to me;
'Tis fourfold in my supreme delight
And threefold in soft Beulah's night
And twofold Always. May God us keep
From Single vision & Newton's sleep![42]

Blake's confidences to Butts must be supplemented by his
account of the quarrel in the symbolic book of *Milton*, partly
written at Felpham. The story can be deciphered from the Bard's
Song in the earlier pages of the First Book, where certain states
or aspects of the persons concerned are personified. Hayley, in
the aspect inimical to Blake's spiritual welfare and poetic and
artistic inspiration, figures as Satan; Blake forbearing and pitiful
as Palamabron, indignant with Hayley and fighting for his spiritual
interests symbolized by Michael, as Rintrah; Mrs. Blake, the
peacemaker, as Enitharmon; Hayley's feeble muse as Leutha;
and Blake's poetic inspiration as Elynittria. For the division into
Angels and Devils of *The Marriage of Heaven and Hell* is substituted
a fourfold classification, the Elect, the conventionally moral and
religious, the Reprobate or Transgressors, 'who never cease to
Believe,' corresponding to the Devils of the *Marriage of Heaven
and Hell*, and an intermediate class of the Redeemed 'Who live in
doubts & fears perpetually tormented by the Elect,'[43] 'They are
the Two Contraries & the Reasoning Negative.'[44] But the Eternal
Man is none of these:

Here the Three Classes of Men take their Sexual texture, Woven;
The Sexual is Threefold: the Human is Fourfold.[45]

Hayley, of course, belonged to the Elect, Blake as Palamabron
to the Redeemed, but as Rintrah to the Reprobate. Hayley's
interference is described as:

'. . . Satan's mildness and his self-imposition,
Seeming a brother, being a tyrant, even thinking himself a brother
While he is murdering the just:'[46]

Blake is in a dilemma; if he shows anger Hayley will accuse him
of ingratitude, but he has not forgotten the truth of his Song of
Experience, 'A Poison Tree,' and reflects that:

'If you account it Wisdom when you are angry to be silent and
Not to shew it, I do not account that Wisdom, but Folly.
Every Man's Wisdom is peculiar to his own Individuality.'[47]

He attempts a persuasive explanation. Hayley, annoyed but tear-
fully sentimental, asserts that the fault is on Blake's side, and
denies that he has exercised any restraint. They come to an understanding that Blake shall not curb himself 'in pity false' or Hayley
be active 'in officious brotherhood'. But Blake cannot keep his
originality out of his work for Hayley and Hayley, incapable of
giving him a free hand, is dissatisfied with the results. Blake is
angry and there is a crisis—'this mournful day Must be a blank in
Nature'; no work is done, but the Blakes and Hayley fruitlessly
discuss the situation. Hot words on both sides might have led to
a genuine reconciliation, but Blake, now 'reprobate', is indignant
at Hayley's soft dissimulation of friendship. Exhausted by spiritual
conflict Blake prays in despair.

'O God, protect me from my friends, that they have not power
    over me.
Thou hast giv'n me power to protect myself from my bitterest
    enemies.'[48]

Hayley, 'not having the Science of Wrath, but only of Pity'
(which may be translated as sentimentality where Blake uses the
word in a bad sense), finally lost his temper, and, as Blake had
feared, accused him of ingratitude and malice. Mrs. Blake, who
apparently had some sympathy to spare for Hayley, as Enitharmon
is described as having 'kissed Satan', tries in vain to make peace.
Then Blake comes to the conclusion which is voiced by Hayley's
muse, Leutha, that Hayley's 'admiration join'd with envy' of
Blake had caused the trouble; hence the provoking attempts to
tyrannize over Blake which had caused Hayley:

'To do unkind things in kindness, with power arm'd to say
The most irritating things in the midst of tears and love:'[49]

Finally the quarrel ended with a friendly agreement that the
Blakes should return to London, as Blake tells Butts in his letter
of 25 April 1803:

And now, My Dear Sir, Congratulate me on my return to London, with the full approbation of Mr Hayley & with Promise —But, Alas!

Now I may say to you, what perhaps I should not dare to say to any one else: That I can alone carry on my visionary studies in London unannoy'd, & that I may converse with my friends in Eternity, See Visions, Dream Dreams & prophecy & speak Parables unobserv'd & at liberty from the Doubts of other Mortals; perhaps Doubts proceeding from Kindness, but Doubts are always pernicious, Especially when we Doubt our Friends. Christ is very decided on this Point: 'He who is Not With Me is Against Me.' There is no Medium or Middle state; & if a Man is the Enemy of my Spiritual Life while he pretends to be the Friend of my Corporeal, he is a Real Enemy—but the Man may be the friend of my Spiritual Life while he seems the Enemy of my Corporeal, but Not Vice Versa.[50]

In a further letter to Butts of 6 July 1803 Blake returns to the subject:

As to Mr H., I feel myself at liberty to say as follows upon this ticklish subject: I regard Fashion in Poetry as little as I do in Painting; so, if both Poets & Painters should alternately dislike (but I know the majority of them will not), I am not to regard it at all, but Mr H. approves of My Designs as little as he does of my Poems, and I have been forced to insist on his leaving me in both to my own Self Will; for I am determin'd to be no longer Pester'd with his Genteel Ignorance & Polite Disapprobation. I know myself both Poet & Painter, & it is not his affected Contempt that can move me to any thing but a more assiduous pursuit of both Arts. Indeed, by my late Firmness I have brought down his affected Loftiness, & he begins to think I have some Genius: as if Genius & Assurance were the same thing! but his imbecile attempts to depress Me only deserve laughter. I say thus much to you, knowing that you will not make a bad use of it. But it is a Fact too true That, if I had only depended on Mortal Things, both myself & my Wife must have been Lost. I shall leave every one in This Country astonish'd at my Patience & Forbearance of Injuries upon Injuries; & I do assure you that, if I could have return'd to London a Month after my arrival here, I should have done so, but I was commanded by my Spiritual friends to bear all, to be silent, & to go thro' all without murmuring, &, in fine, hope, till my three years should be almost accomplish'd; at which time I was set at liberty to remonstrate against former conduct & to demand Justice & Truth; which I have done in so effectual a manner that my antagonist is silenc'd completely, & I have compell'd what should have been of free-dom—My Just Right as an Artist & as a Man; & if any attempt should be made to refuse me this, I am inflexible & will relin-quish any engagement of Designing at all, unless altogether left to my own Judgment, As you, My dear Friend, have always left me, for which I shall never cease to honour & respect you.

When we meet, I will perfectly describe to you my Conduct & the Conduct of others toward me, & you will see that I have labour'd hard indeed, & have been borne on angel's wings.[51]

In the interval before these last two letters to Butts Blake had written a long letter to his brother James. It is the only letter extant to a member of his own family. Two projects are men-tioned which came to nothing, another country home and lucra-tive publication on a large scale. Blake had been much impressed by Hayley's business capacity, though the master stroke by which he secured a handsome annuity from his publisher was yet to come.

Felpham,
Janʸ, 30, 1803

Dear Brother,

Your Letter mentioning Mʳ Butts' account of my Ague sur-prized me because I have no Ague, but have had a Cold this Winter. You know that it is my way to make the best of every thing. I never make myself nor my friends uneasy if I can help it. My Wife has had Agues & Rheumatisms almost ever since she has been here, but our time is almost out that we took the Cottage for. I did not mention our Sickness to you & should not to Mʳ Butts but for a determination which we have lately made, namely To leave This Place, because I am now certain of what I have long doubted, Viz that H. is jealous as Stothard was & will be no further My friend than he is compell'd by circumstances. The truth is, As a Poet he is frighten'd at me & as a Painter his views & mine are opposite; he thinks to turn me into a Portrait Painter as he did Poor Romney, but this he nor all the devils in hell will never do. I must own that seeing H. like S., Envious (& that he is I am now certain) made me very uneasy, but it is over & I now defy the worst & fear not while I am true to myself which I will be. This is the uneasiness I spoke of to Mr Butts, but I did not tell him so plain & wish you to keep it a secret & to burn this letter because it speaks so plain. I told Mr Butts that I did not wish to Explore too much the cause of our determination to leave Felpham because of pecuniary connexions between H. & me—Be not then uneasy on any account & tell my Sister not to be uneasy, for I am fully Employ'd & Well Paid. I have made it so much H's interest to employ me that he can no longer treat me with indifference & now it is in my power to stay or return or remove to any other place that I choose, because I am getting before hand in money matters. The Profits arising from Publications are immense, & I now have it in my power to commence publication with many very formidable works, which I have finish'd & ready. A Book price half a guinea may be got out at the Expense of Ten pounds & its almost certain profits are 500 G. I am only sorry that I did not know the methods of publishing years ago, & this is one of the numerous benefits I have obtain'd by coming here, for I should never have known the nature of Publication unless I had known H. & his connexions & his method of managing. It now would be folly not to venture publishing. I am now Engraving Six little plates for a little work of M^r H's,* for which I am to have 10 Guineas each, & the certain profits of that work are a fortune such as would make me independent, supposing that I could substantiate such a one of my own & I mean to try many. But I again say as I said before, We are very Happy sitting at tea by a wood fire in our Cottage, the wind singing above our roof & the sea roaring at a distance, but if sickness comes all is unpleasant.

But my letter to Mr Butts appears to me not to be so explicit

---

* 'Mr. H's little Work' is *The Triumphs of Temper* (1803), for which Blake engraved six plates after designs by Maria Flaxman, sister of the sculptor. It would appear that at this time Hayley proposed to print all Cowper's MS. relating to Milton, but later only his translations of Milton's Latin and Italian poems with the fragmentary dissertation on *Paradise Lost*. Cf. *Life of Cowper*, iv, pp. 439–42. In 1790 Johnson had intended to publish Cowper's edition of Milton with engravings after Fuseli's Milton gallery, and it was proposed that Blake should engrave 'Adam and Eve observed by Satan', but the scheme fell through owing to Cowper's illness (Knowles, *Life and Writings of Henry Fuseli*, 1831, i, p. 172). Hayley writes to Johnson, 6 August 1801, that Blake 'has a great wish that you should prevail on Cowper's dear Rose [Mrs. Anne Bodham] to send her portrait of the beloved bard, by Abbot, to Felpham, that Blake may engrave it for the Milton we meditate. . . .' (*Memoirs of Hayley*, ii, p. 124.)

as that to you, for I told you that I should come to London in
the Spring to commence Publisher & he has offer'd me every
assistance in his power without knowing my intention. But since
I wrote yours we had made the resolution of which we inform'd
him, viz to leave Felpham entirely. I also told you what I was
about & that I was not ignorant of what was doing in London in
works of art. But I did not mention Illness because I hoped to
get better (for I was really very ill when I wrote to him the last
time) & was not then perswaded as I am now that the air tho'
warm is unhealthy.

However, this I know will set you at ease. I am now so full
of work that I have had no time to go on with the Ballads, & my
prospects of more & more work continually are certain. My
Heads of Cowper for M^r H's life of Cowper have pleas'd his
Relations exceedingly & in Particular Lady Hesketh & Lord
Cowper—to please Lady H. was a doubtful chance who almost
ador'd her Cousin the poet & thought him all perfection, & she
writes that she is quite satisfied with the portraits & charm'd
by the great Head in particular, tho' she never could bear the
original Picture.

But I ought to mention to you that our present idea is: To
take a house in some village further from the Sea, Perhaps Lavant,
& in or near the road to London for the sake of convenience.
I also ought to inform you that I read your letter to Mr H. & that
he is very afraid of losing me & also very afraid that my Friends
in London should have a bad opinion of the reception he has
given to me. But My Wife has undertaken to Print the whole
number of the Plates for Cowper's work, which She does to
admiration, & being under my own eye the prints are as fine as
the French prints & please every one: in short I have Got every
thing so under my thumb that it is more profitable that things
should be as they are than any other way, tho' not so agreeable,
because we wish naturally for friendship in preference to interest.
—The Publishers are already indebted to My Wife Twenty
Guineas for work deliver'd; this is a small specimen of how we
go on: then fear nothing & let my Sister fear nothing because it
appears to me that I am now too old & have had too much experience to be any longer imposed upon, only illness makes all
uncomfortable & this we must prevent by every means in our
power.

I send with this 5 Copies of N 4 of the Ballads for Mrs Flaxman
& Five more, two of which you will be so good as to give to

Mr^s Chetwynd if she should call or send for them. These Ballads
are likely to be Profitable, for we have Sold all that we have had
time to print. Evans the Bookseller in Pallmall says they go off
very well, & why should we repent of having done them? it is
doing Nothing that is to be repented of & not doing such things
as these.

Pray remember us both to Mr Hall when you see him.

I write in great haste & with a head full of botheration about
various projected works & particularly a work now Proposed to
the Public at the End of Cowper's Life, which will very likely
be of great consequence; it is Cowper's Milton, the same that
Fuseli's Milton Gallery was painted for, & if we succeed in our
intentions the prints to this work will be very profitable to me &
not only profitable, but honourable at any rate. The Project
pleases Lord Cowper's family, & I am now labouring in my
thoughts Designs for this & other works equally creditable. These
are works to be boasted of, & therefore I cannot feel depress'd,
tho' I know that as far as Designing & Poetry are concern'd I am
Envied in many Quarters, but I will cram the dogs, for I know that
the Public are my friends & love my works & will embrace them
whenever they see them. My only Difficulty is to produce fast
enough.

I go on Merrily with my Greek & Latin; am very sorry that I
did not begin to learn languages early in life as I find it very Easy;
am now learning my Hebrew אבג. I read Greek as fluently as an
Oxford scholar & the Testament is my chief master: astonishing
indeed is the English Translation, it is almost word for word, &
if the Hebrew Bible is as well translated, which I do not doubt it
is, we need not doubt of its having been translated as well as
written by the Holy Ghost:

my wife joins me in Love to you both.

I am, Sincerely yours,
W. Blake⁵²

The Ballads founded on Anecdotes Relating to Animals, which
are referred to in this letter, were written by Hayley and illustrated
by Blake. The intention was to publish them in half-crown parts,
each containing one ballad and three engravings, but the enterprise was a failure and only four parts were issued. The Preface
by Hayley explains that Blake had come from London in order to
engrave the plates for his *Life of Cowper*, and that 'there is hardly

any kind of ingenious employment in which the mind requires more to be cleared and diverted, than the slow, and sometimes very irksome, progress of engraving; Especially, when that art is exercised by a person of varied talents and of a creative imagination.' He had therefore written these ballads 'to Amuse the Artist in his patient labour,' and wished that he should profit by the illustrations he had made for them. In 1805 another edition was published by Phillips, containing five plates of reduced size but more finished execution, two of which had not appeared before. Hayley had suggested that Blake should write an advertisement for this issue, and in a letter of 25 April 1805 Blake says:

Simplicity, as you desired has been my first object. I send it for your Correction or Condemnation, begging you to supply its deficiency or to New Create it according to your wish.

——————

The public ought to be inform'd that These Ballads were the Effusions of Friendship to Countenance what their Author is kindly pleased to call Talents for Designing and to relieve my more laborious engagement of Engraving those Portraits which accompany The Life of Cowper. Out of a number of Designs I have selected Five [and] hope that the Public will approve of my rather giving few highly labour'd Plates than have a greater number & less finish'd. If I have succeeded in these more may be added at Pleasure.[53]

But Philips would have none of it: 'Mr. Phillips objects altogether to the insertion of my Advertisement, calling it an appeal to charity, and says it will hurt the sale of the work. . . .'[54]

This edition was also a failure. Southey ridiculed the Ballads in a notice in the *Annual Review* for 1805, adding:

The Poet has had the singular good fortune to meet with a painter capable of doing full justice to his conceptions; and, in fact, when we look at the delectable frontispiece to this volume which represents Edward starting back, fido *volant*, and the crocadile *rampant*, with a mouth open like a boot-jack to receive him, we know not whether most to admire the genius of Mr. William Blake or of Mr. William Hayley.[55]

Half a century later a better judge paid an amusing tribute to the illustrations. D. G. Rossetti, writing to thank Allingham for a copy of the Ballads, says:

Old Blake is quite as lovable by his oddities as by his genius, and the drawings to the ballads abound with both. The two nearly faultless are the 'Eagle' and the 'Hermit's Dog.' Ruskin's favourite (who has been looking at it) is the 'Horse'; but I can't quite myself get over the intensity of comic decorum in the brute's face. He seems absolutely snuffing with propriety. The lion seems singing a comic song with a pen behind his ear, but the glimpse of distant landscape below is lovely. The only drawing where the comic element riots almost unrebuked is the one of the dog jumping down the crocodile.[56]

A ridiculous but in those days alarming incident, graphically described in a letter to Butts of 16 August 1803, made the parting with Hayley more friendly than it might otherwise have been.

I am at Present in a Bustle to defend myself against a very unwarrantable warrant from a Justice of Peace in Chichester, which was taken out against me by a Private* in Captn Leathes's troop of 1st or Royal Dragoons, for an assault & Seditious words. The wretched Man has terribly Perjur'd himself, as has his Comrade†; for, as to Sedition, not one Word relating to the King or Government was spoken by either him or me. His Enmity arises from my having turned him out of my Garden, into which he was invited as an assistant by a Gardener at work therein, without my knowledge that he was so invited. I desired him, as politely as was possible, to go out of the Garden; he made me an impertinent answer. I insisted on his leaving the Garden; he refused. I still persisted in desiring his departure; he then threaten'd to knock out my Eyes, with many abominable imprecations & with some contempt for my Person; it affronted my foolish Pride. I therefore took him by the Elbows & pushed him before me till I had got him out; there I intended to have left him, but he, turning about, put himself into a Posture of Defiance, threatening & swearing at me. I, perhaps foolishly & perhaps not, stepped out at the Gate, &, putting aside his blows, took him again by the Elbows, &, keeping his back to me, pushed him forwards down the road about fifty yards—he all the while endeavouring to turn round & strike me, & raging & cursing, which drew out several neighbours; at length, when I had got him to where he was Quarter'd, which was very quickly done, we were met at the Gate by the

* John Scolfield, or Schofield.   † John Cock.

Master of the house, The Fox Inn (who is the proprietor of my Cottage), & his wife & Daughter & the Man's Comrade & several other people. My Landlord compell'd the Soldiers to go in doors, after many abusive threats against me & my wife from the two Soldiers; but not one word of threat on account of Sedition was utter'd at that time. This method of Revenge was Plann'd between them after they had got together into the Stable. This is the whole outline. I have for witnesses: The Gardener, who is Hostler at the Fox & who Evidences that, to his knowledge, no word of the remotest tendency to Government or Sedition was utter'd: Our next door Neighbour, a Miller's wife, who saw me turn him before me down the road, & saw & heard all that happen'd at the Gate of the Inn, who Evidences that no Expression of threatening on account of Sedition was utter'd in the heat of their fury by either of the Dragoons; this was the woman's own remark, & does high honour to her good sense, as she observes that, whenever a quarrel happens, the offence is always repeated. The Landlord of the Inn & His Wife & daughter will Evidence the same, & will evidently prove the Comrade perjur'd, who swore that he heard me, while at the Gate, utter Seditious words & D—— the K——, without which perjury I could not have been committed; & I had no witness with me before the Justices who could combat his assertion, as the Gardener remain'd in my Garden all the while, & he was the only person I thought necessary to take with me. I have been before a Bench of Justices at Chichester this morning; but they, as the Lawyer who wrote down the Accusation told me in private, are compell'd by the Military to suffer a prosecution to be enter'd into: altho' they must know, & it is manifest, that the whole is a Fabricated Perjury. I have been forced to find Bail. Mr Hayley was kind enough to come forwards, and Mr Seagrave, Printer at Chichester; Mr H. in 100£, & Mr S. in 50£; & myself am bound in 100£ for my appearance at the Quarter Sessions, which is after Michaelmass. So I shall have the satisfaction to see my friends in Town before this Contemptible business comes on. I say Contemptible, for it must be manifest to every one that the whole accusation is a wilful Perjury. Thus, you see, my dear Friend, that I cannot leave this place without some adventure; it has struck a consternation thro' all the Villages round. Every Man is now afraid of speaking to, or looking at, a Soldier; for the peaceable Villagers have always been forward in expressing their kindness for us, & they express their sorrow at our departure as soon as they hear of it. Every one here is my Evidence for Peace & Good Neighbourhood; & yet, such is the present state of things, this foolish accusation must be tried in Public. Well, I am content, I murmur not & doubt not that I shall recieve Justice, & am only sorry for the trouble & expense. I have heard that my Accuser is a disgraced Sergeant; his name is John Scholfield; perhaps it will be in your power to learn somewhat about the Man.* I am very ignorant of what I am requesting of you; I only suggest what I know you will be kind enough to Excuse if you can learn nothing about him, & what, I as well know, if it is possible, you will be kind enough to do in this matter.[57]

Impressed by Hayley's genuine kindness Blake feels that his own personality has been largely responsible for the friction with him, so continues:

Dear Sir, This perhaps was suffer'd to Clear up some doubts, & to give opportunity to those whom I doubted to clear themselves of all imputation. If a Man offends me ignorantly & not designedly, surely I ought to consider him with favour and affection. Perhaps the simplicity of myself is the origin of all offences committed against me. If I have found this, I shall have learned a most valuable thing, well worth three years' perseverance. I have found it. It is certain that a too passive manner, inconsistent with my active physiognomy, had done me much mischief. I must now express to you my conviction that all is come from the spiritual World for Good, & not for Evil.

Give me your advice in my perilous adventure; burn what I have peevishly written about any friend. I have been very much degraded & injuriously treated; but if it all arise from my own fault, I ought to blame myself.

O why was I born with a different face?
Why was I not born like the rest of my race?
When I look, each one starts! when I speak, I offend;
Then I'm silent & passive & lose every Friend.

Then my verse I dishonour, My pictures despise,
My person degrade & my temper chastise;
And the pen is my terror, the pencil my shame;
All my Talents I bury, and dead is my Fame.

* That is, as an official in the office of the Muster-Master General, or Commissary General of the Musters, and so concerned with registration of troops. Butts did not help Blake in his trouble as far as is known. [Ed.]

I am either too low or too highly priz'd;
When Elate I am Envy'd, When Meek I'm despis'd.

This is but too just a Picture of my Present state. I pray God to keep you & all men from it, & to deliver me in his own good time.[58]

Shortly before the trial Hayley, the chief witness as to Blake's character and peaceful habits, had been pitched on his head, having perhaps frightened his horse by unfurling the inevitable umbrella, but had maintained that 'living or dying' he would be present. This noble behaviour called forth expressions of anxiety and gratitude from his 'devoted rebel':

I write immediately on my arrival. Not merely to inform you that I am safe arriv'd, but also to inform you that in a conversation with an old Soldier who came in the Coach with me I learned: that no one: not even the most expert horseman: ought ever to mount a Trooper's Horse;* they are taught so many tricks such as stopping short, falling down on their knees, running sideways, & in various & innumerable ways endeavouring to throw the rider, that it is a miracle if a stranger escapes with Life, —All this I learn'd with some alarm & heard also what the soldier said confirm'd by another person in the coach. I therefore as it is my duty beg & intreat you never to mount that wicked horse again, nor again trust to one who has been so Educated. God our Saviour watch over you & preserve you. . . . Pray my dear Sir favour me with a line concerning your health & how you have escaped the double blow both from the wicked horse & from your innocent humble servant, whose heart & soul are more & more drawn out towards you & Felpham & its kind inhabitants. I feel anxious, & therefore pray to my God & father for the health of Miss Poole: & hope that the pang of affection & gratitude is the Gift of God for good. I am thankful that I feel it; it draws the soul towards Eternal life & conjunction with Spirits of just men made perfect by love & gratitude—the two angels who stand at heaven's gate ever open, ever inviting guests to the marriage. O foolish Philosophy! Gratitude is Heaven itself;

* On 27 April 1804, Blake writes: 'We feel much easier to hear that you have parted with your horse,' but it does not appear whether this is the same tricky charger or another dangerous mount of Hayley's. (*Complete Writings*, p. 843.)

there could be no heaven without Gratitude.* I feel it & I know it. I thank God & Man for it & above all You, My dear friend & benefactor in the Lord.[59]

Blake had awaited his trial with considerable anxiety. In a letter to Hayley of 13 December 1803 he says: 'Business comes in & I shall be at ease if this infernal business of the soldier can be got over.' Flaxman, who doubtless felt some responsibility for the difficulties in which Hayley had been involved by his introduction to Blake, makes some pious comments on the situation in a letter to Hayley of 2 January 1804.

I sincerely wish with You that the Tryal was over, that our poor friend's peace of mind might be restored, altho' I have no doubt from what I have heard of the Soldier's character and the merits of the case that the bill will at least be thrown out by the Court as groundless & vexatious—Blake's irritability as well as the Association & arrangement of his ideas do not seem likely to be Soothed or more advantageously disposed by any power inferior to That by which man is originally endowed with his faculties.[60]

After the trial Blake wrote that Flaxman had 'welcom'd Me with kind affection & generous exultation in my escape from the arrows of darkness.'[61]

The information laid by Schofield was as follows:

The Information and Complaint of John Schofield, a Private Soldier in His Majesty's First Regiment of Dragoons, taken upon his Oath, this 15th Day of August, 1803, before me, One of His Majesty's Justices of the Peace, in and for the County aforesaid.

Who saith, that on the twelfth Day of this Instant August, at the Parish of Felpham, in the County aforesaid, one—Blake, a Miniature Painter, and now residing in the said Parish of Felpham, did utter the following seditious expressions, viz., that we (meaning the People of England) were like a Parcel of Children, that they would play with themselves till they got scalded and burnt, that the French Knew our Strength very well, and if Bonaparte should come he would be Master of Europe in an Hour's Time, that England might depend upon it, that when he set his Foot

* The remarks about gratitude are probably an allusion to Godwin's rejection of gratitude as a virtue.

on English Ground that every Englishman would have his choice whether to have his Throat cut, or to join the French, and that he was a strong Man, and would certainly begin to cut Throats, and the strongest Man must conquer—that he damned the King of England—his country, and his subjects, that his Soldiers were all bound for Slaves, and all the Poor People in general—that his Wife then came up, and said to him, this is nothing to you at present, but that the King of England would run himself so far into the Fire, that he might get himself out again, and altho' she was but a Woman, she would fight as long as she had a drop of blood in her—to which the said—Blake said, My Dear, you would not fight against France—she replyed no, I would for Bonaparte as long as I am able—that the said—Blake, then addressing himself to this Informant, said, tho' you are one of the King's Subjects, I have told what I have said before greater People than you, and that this Informant was sent by his Captain to Esquire Hayley to hear what he had to say, and to go and tell them—that his Wife then told her said Husband to turn this Informant out of the garden—that this Informant thereupon turned round to go peaceably out, when the said—Blake pushed this Deponent out of the Garden into the Road down which he followed this Informant, and twice took this Informant by the Collar, without this Informant's making any Resistance and at the same Time the said Blake damned the King, and said the Soldiers were all Slaves.

John Schofield[62]

Blake was not legally represented at the hearing by the magistrates,* but afterwards refuted the charge himself in a businesslike memorandum. He indicates the weak points in Schofield's statement and the nature of the evidence which he will be able to bring forward on his own behalf, ending with the protest:

If such a Perjury as this can take effect, any Villain in future may come and drag me and my Wife out of our House, and beat us in the Garden or use us as he please or is able, and afterwards go and swear our Lives away.

Is it not in the Power of any Thief who enters a Man's Dwelling

---

* An application on 25 December 1803, by Richard Dally, a Chichester solicitor, for a copy of the indictment against Blake shows that he was not legally represented at the hearing before the Chichester bench. (*Blake Records*, pp. 136–7.)

and robs him, or misuses his Wife or Children, to go and swear
as this Man has sworn?[63]

Blake, who had left Felpham before 19 September 1803, went
back to stand his trial for high treason at the Chichester Quarter
Sessions on 11 January 1804. Hayley had engaged Cowper's friend,
Samuel Rose, as counsel. His speech, as it survives from a shorthand report, is clear and effective, but contains no addition to the
facts contained in Blake's memorandum except the discrepancy
between the evidence of Schofield and his comrade, Cock, the
latter swearing that the seditious words had been uttered outside
the Fox Inn, instead of in the garden, as alleged by Schofield.

The *Sussex Weekly Advertiser* of 16 January records that:

Charles [*sic*] Blake, an engraver, at Felpham, was tried on a
charge exhibited against him by two soldiers, for having uttered
seditious and treasonable expressions, such as 'D--n the King,
d—n all his subjects, d—n his soldiery, they are all slaves; when
Bonaparte comes, it will be cut throat for cut throat, and the
weakest must go to the wall; I will help him, &c.'[64]

Blake, his eyes flashing, shouted 'False' at the more pre-
posterous accusations, and, after a lengthy hearing, was finally
acquitted amid uproarious applause. Hayley carried off 'the delivered artist' to a late supper with Miss Poole. Gilchrist,[65] without naming his authority, states that Blake afterwards believed
that Schofield had been employed to entrap him by the Government or someone in high place who knew of his former connection with Paine and the radical set, but it is unlikely that Blake
seriously entertained this improbable theory.*

Nearly a year after the trial Blake lamented the death of his able
counsel, who had suffered from prolonged ill-health. Writing to
Hayley, he says:

---

* J. Bronowski, *William Blake: A Man without a Mask* (1944), p. 74, has
an interesting discussion of the trial and some information about the Chair-
man of the Quarter Sessions, the Duke of Richmond. The book itself deals
with the social and political background of Blake's lifetime, as does also
Mark Schorer's *William Blake* (1946), and David Erdman's *Blake: Prophet
against Empire*.

The Death of so Excellent a Man as my Generous Advocater is a Public Loss, which those who knew him can best Estimate, & to those who have an affection for him like Yours, is a Loss that only can be repair'd in Eternity, where it will indeed with such abundant felicity, in the meeting Him a Glorified Saint who was a Suffering Mortal, that our Sorrow is swallow'd up in Hope. Such Consolations are alone to be found in Religion, the Sun & the Moon of our Journey; & such sweet Verses as yours in your last beautiful Poem must now afford you their full reward.*

Farewell, Sweet Rose! thou has got before me into the Celestial City. I also have but a few more Mountains to pass; for I hear the bells ring & the trumpets sound to welcome thy arrival among Cowper's Glorified Band of Spirits of Just Men made Perfect.[66]

Thus was Hayley, by the warmth of his absence, restored, at least for the moment, to the lost position of poet and brother.

Mrs. Blake must have been thankful to leave Felpham. She had suffered from constant ill-health. Miss Blake's visits were probably a further trial as the tradition that they did not get on well together is supported by Blake's lines, composed on his way to meet Miss Blake:

> 'Must my Wife live in my Sister's bane,'
> 'Or my Sister survive on my Love's pain?'[67]

Blake himself had required his wife's sympathy in his difficulties with Hayley, and also her assistance in his labour in 'Felpham's Old Mill'. She must have been exhausted by her efforts at peace-making, and was, as a climax, 'much-terrified' by the Schofield incident.

For Blake himself the 'three years' Slumber on the banks of the Ocean' were fruitful despite the tame Hayley, the damp cottage, and work unworthy of his genius. His knowledge of the country hitherto had been confined to long walks and occasional short expeditions from London. The water-colour drawing, 'The Spirit of God moved upon the Face of the Waters', must have

---

* Hayley's verses are presumably his epitaph on Rose.

been inspired by this his first sight of the open sea.* Not only
are his Felpham letters full of references to his enjoyment of his
surroundings, but *Milton* shows an intimate observation of nature
which is not present in his earlier books.

Thou seest the Constellations in the deep & wondrous Night:
They rise in order and continue their immortal courses
Upon the mountain & in vales with harp & heavenly song,
With flute & clarion, with cups & measures fill'd with foaming
    wine.
Glitt'ring the streams reflect the Vision of beatitude,
And the calm Ocean joys beneath & smooths his awful waves:[68]

These are the Sons of Los, & these the Labourers of the Vintage.
Thou seest the gorgeous clothed Flies that dance & sport in
    summer
Upon the sunny brooks & meadows: every one the dance
Knows in its intricate mazes of delight artful to weave:
Each one to sound his instruments of music in the dance,
To touch each other & recede, to cross & change & return:
These are the Children of Los; thou seest the Trees on mountains,
The wind blows heavy, loud they thunder thro' the darksom sky,
Uttering prophecies & speaking instructive words to the sons
Of men: These are the Sons of Los: These the Visions of Eternity,
But we see only as it were the hem of their garments
When with our vegetable eyes we view these wondrous Visions.[69]

Thou hearest the Nightingale begin the Song of Spring.
The Lark sitting upon his earthy bed, just as the morn
Appears, listens silent; then springing from the waving Cornfield,
    loud
He leads the Choir of Day: trill, trill, trill, trill,
Mounting upon the wings of light into the Great Expanse,
Reechoing against the lovely blue & shining heavenly Shell.
His little throat labours with inspiration; every feather
On throat & breast & wings vibrates with the effluence Divine.
All Nature listens silent to him, & the awful Sun
Stands still upon the Mountain looking on this little Bird
With eyes of soft humility & wonder, love & awe.

* This small drawing in Indian ink is otherwise known as "The waters
prevailed upon the earth' (Genesis 7. 19). It was reproduced in the Nonesuch
edition of this *Life* and remains in private possession in this country. On the
verso is a drawing of a human-limbed elephant, believed to be a caricature
of Blake's later friend, John Varley. [Ed.]

Then loud from their green covert all the Birds begin their Song:
The Thrush, the Linnet & the Goldfinch, Robin & the Wren
Awake the Sun from his sweet reverie upon the Mountain.
The Nightingale again assays his song, & thro' the day
And thro' the night warbles luxuriant, every Bird of Song
Attending his loud harmony with admiration & love.
This is a Vision of the lamentation of Beulah over Ololon.

Thou percievest the Flowers put forth their precious Odours,
And none can tell how from so small a center comes such sweets,
Forgetting that within that Center Eternity expands
Its ever during doors that Og & Anak fiercely guard.
First, e'er the morning breaks, joy opens in the flowery bosoms,
Joy even to tears, which the Sun rising dries; first the Wild
    Thyme
And Meadow-sweet, downy & soft waving among the reeds,
Light springing on the air, lead the sweet Dance: they wake
The Honeysuckle sleeping on the Oak; the flaunting beauty
Revels along upon the wind; the White-thorn, lovely May,
Opens her many lovely eyes listening; the Rose still sleeps,
None dare to wake her; soon she bursts her crimson curtain'd bed
And comes forth in the majesty of beauty; every Flower,
The Pink, the Jessamine, the Wall-flower, the Carnation,
The Jonquil, the mild Lilly, opes her heavens; every Tree
And Flower & Herb soon fill the air with an innumerable Dance,
Yet all in order sweet & lovely. Men are sick with Love.
Such is a Vision of the lamentation of Beulah over Ololon.[70]

He knows the host of insects whom his contemporary, John
Clare, also loved:

Timbrels & violins sport round the Wine-presses; the little Seed,
The sportive Root, the Earth-worm, the gold Beetle, the wise
    Emmet
Dance round the Wine-presses of Luvah: the Centipede is there,
The ground Spider with many eyes, the Mole clothed in velvet,
The ambitious Spider in his sullen web, the lucky golden Spinner,
The Earwig arm'd, the tender Maggot, emblem of immortality,
The Flea, Louse, Bug, the Tape-Worm, all the Armies of Disease,
Visible or invisible to the slothful vegetating Man.
The slow Slug, the Grasshopper that sings & laughs & drinks:
Winter comes, he folds his slender bones without a murmur.
The cruel Scorpion is there, the Gnat, Wasp, Hornet & the
    Honey Bee,

The Toad & venomous Newt, the Serpent cloth'd in gems & gold.
They throw off their gorgeous raiment: they rejoice with loud
     jubilee
Around the Wine-presses of Luvah, naked & drunk with wine.[71]

A deleted passage in *Vala*, too, particularizing Imlac's 'verdure
of the forest', may date from Felpham.

The barked Oak, the long limb'd Beech, the Chestnut tree, the
     Pine,
The Pear tree mild, the frowning Walnut, the sharp Crab, &
     Apple sweet,
The rough bark opens; twittering peep forth little beaks & wings,
The Nightingale, the Goldfinch, Robin, Lark, Linnet & Thrush.[72]

Though his visionary life was interrupted by the conditions of
his companionship to Hayley, yet as he wandered by the sea he
communed with the great poets of the past, beholding them as
'majestic shadows, gray but luminous, and superior to the common
height of men.'[73] The overwhelming vision recorded in *Milton*
appeared to him and it was at Felpham that he saw a fairy's
funeral.

'Did you ever see a fairy's funeral, madam?' he once said to a
lady, who happened to sit by him in company. 'Never, sir!' was
the answer. 'I have,' said Blake, 'but not before last night. I was
walking alone in my garden, there was great stillness among the
branches and flowers and more than common sweetness in the
air; I heard a low and pleasant sound, and I knew not whence it
came. At last I saw the broad leaf of a flower move, and underneath I saw a procession of creatures of the size and colour of
green and gray grasshoppers, bearing a body laid out on a rose
leaf, which they buried with songs, and then disappeared. It was a
fairy funeral.'[74]

His unfettered works for Mr. Butts, although it had often to
give way to the exigencies of the 'Mills', was a relief and pleasure
to Blake. 'Your approbation of my pictures is a Multitude to Me.'[75]
He appears to have sent Butts several drawings toward the end
of 1801, eight others in the summer of 1803, and to have brought
back from Felpham ten in a more or less finished state.*

* Most of these were formerly in the Graham Robertson collection, but
have now been dispersed to a variety of galleries. [Ed.]

In his letter to Dr. Trusler of 16 August 1799 he had spoken of himself as 'a Scholar of Rembrandt & Teniers, whom I have Studied no less than Rafael & Michael angelo.'[76] But at Felpham he freed himself from both Dutch and Venetian influences, and returned to his youthful ideal, uniformity of colour and long continuation of lines. He tells Butts on 10 January 1802:

One thing of real consequence I have accomplish'd by coming into the country, which is to me consolation enough: namely, I have recollected all my scatter'd thoughts on Art & resumed my primitive & original ways of Execution in both painting & engraving, which in the confusion of London I had very much lost & obliterated from my mind.[77]

On 22 November he elaborates this theme:

I have now given two years to the intense study of those parts of the art which relate to light & shade & colour, & am Convinc'd that either my understanding is incapable of comprehending the beauties of Colouring, or the Pictures which I painted for you Are Equal in Every part of the Art, & Superior in One, to any thing that has been done since the age of Rafael.—All Sʳ J. Reynolds's discourses to the Royal Academy will shew that the Venetian finesse in Art can never be united with the Majesty of Colouring necessary to Historical beauty.[78]

Blake then quotes with approval Sir Joshua's letter to William Gilpin, printed in the latter's *Three Essays on Picturesque Beauty* (1792), and goes on to say that:

. . . I have now proved that the parts of the art which I neglected to display in those little pictures & drawings which I had the pleasure & profit to do for you, are incompatible with the designs. . . . I would not send you a Drawing or a Picture till I had again reconsider'd my notions of Art, & had put myself back as if I was a learner. I have proved that I am Right, & shall now Go on with the Vigor I was in my Childhood famous for. . . . You will be tempted to think that, as I improve, The Pictures, &ᶜ, that I did for you are not what I would now wish them to be. On this I beg to say That they are what I intended them, & that I know I never shall do better; for, if I was to do them over again, they would lose as much as they gain'd, because they were done in the heat of My Spirits.[79]

Nor was the poet idle. The references in his letters to a poem of
great length composed at Felpham have been variously applied to
Vala, to *Milton*, and to his later epic, *Jerusalem*. Internal evidence
suggests that *Milton* was partly written at Felpham, but it is
unlikely that *Jerusalem* took shape before his return to London,
as it represents a later stage in the development of his ideas, and
is metrically more irregular. Blake says in a letter to Butts of
25 April 1803:

But none can know the Spiritual Acts of my three years' Slumber on the banks of the Ocean, unless he has seen them in the
Spirit, or unless he should read My long Poem descriptive of those
Acts; for I have in these three years composed an immense
number of verses on One Grand Theme, Similar to Homer's Iliad
or Milton's Paradise Lost, the Persons & Machinery intirely new
to the Inhabitants of Earth (some of the Persons Excepted). I have
written this Poem from immediate Dictation, twelve or sometimes twenty or thirty lines at a time, without Premeditation &
even against my Will; the Time it has taken in writing was thus
render'd Non Existent, & an immense Poem Exists which seems
to be the Labour of a long Life, all produc'd without Labour or
Study. I mention this to shew you what I think the Grand Reason
of my being brought down here.[80]

And again in a later letter of 6 July 1803:

Thus I hope that all our three years' trouble Ends in Good Luck
at last & shall be forgot by my affections & only remember'd by
my Understanding; to be a Memento in time to come, & to speak
to future generations by a Sublime Allegory, which is now
perfectly completed into a Grand Poem. I may praise it, since I
dare not pretend to be any other than the Secretary; the Authors
are in Eternity. I consider it as the Grandest Poem that this World
Contains. Allegory address'd to the Intellectual powers, while it is
altogether hidden from the Corporeal Understanding, is My
Definition of the Most Sublime Poetry; it is also somewhat in
the same manner defin'd by Plato. This Poem shall, by Divine
Assistance, be progressively Printed & Ornamented with Prints
& given to the Public. But of this work I take care to say little to
Mr H., since he is as much averse to my poetry as he is to a
Chapter in the Bible. He knows that I have writ it, for I have
shewn it to him, & he has read Part by his own desire & has looked

with sufficient contempt to inhance my opinion of it. But I do not wish to irritate by seeming too obstinate in Poetic pursuits. But if all the World should set their faces against This, I have Orders to set my face like a flint (Ezekiel iiiC, 9v) against their faces, & my forehead against their foreheads.[81]

The poem shown to Hayley was probably *Vala*,* which answers best to the above description, but even had it been the first book of *Milton*, containing the account of their quarrel, as supposed by some critics, the assumption that Blake thought the subject matter so concealed that Hayley could not recognize it is unnecessary. In *Milton* these earthly happenings are treated *sub specie æternitatis*, not as they appeared to the writer in a passing mood. The Bard's Song is a work of art, detached, impartial. It would not have occurred to Blake that Hayley, if he perceived its drift, would think it unkind and personal. Moreover, Blake never blames individuals; where he appears to do so he is using them, as for example he uses Sir Joshua and Newton, to represent some doctrine which he considers pernicious. The personages of *Milton* are not individuals disguised under false names, but embodied 'states'. The epigrams on Hayley belong to a different category. They are ebullitions by which Blake relieved his irritability in a private notebook, intended neither for the eye of the victim nor for publication. Blake would have said of them as of a letter to Butts—'burn what I have peevishly written about any friend.'[82] One of these epigrams has been variously interpreted:

> When H—y finds out what you cannot do,
> That is the very thing he'll set you to.
> If you break not your Neck, 'tis not his fault,
> But pecks of poison are not pecks of salt.
> And when he could not act upon my wife
> Hired a Villain to bereave my Life.[83]

The fifth line no doubt refers to some attempt of Hayley's to

---

* Max Plowman, in a letter to the *Times Literary Supplement* of 30 April 1925, points out that *Milton* is mainly concerned with the 'spiritual acts' of Milton, not of Blake, and that *Vala* is a much longer poem, dealing with one grand theme, the redemption of man.

secure Mrs. Blake's support in his efforts to confine her husband
to the Mill; the sixth suggests that, having failed, he instigated
some one else to deprive Blake of spiritual life by urging his
worldly interest. There is no clue to the identity of this tool, but
Hayley's immediate kindness and Blake's gratitude rule out the
matter-of-fact interpretation that Blake suspected Hayley of con-
triving the Schofield incident in order that he might be hanged for
high treason.

Some of the most interesting and beautiful of Blake's later lyrics
were written at Felpham. Besides those in his letters already
mentioned, several pages of the Notebook are ascribed to the
years 1800–3, and the *Pickering MS.* to 1803.

'My Spectre around me night & day,'[84] in the Notebook, expresses in lyrical form the division and discord between spectre
and emanation, reason and imagination, logic and intuition, the
conscious and the unconscious mind, which is elaborated in *Vala*
and in *Milton*.

Nine of the stanzas of 'I saw a Monk of Charlemaine' reappear
in the *Pickering MS.* as 'The Grey Monk,'[85] and seven in 'To the
Deists' of *Jerusalem*. All three have that famous and exquisite
verse:

> 'For a Tear is an Intellectual Thing,
> And a Sigh is the Sword of an Angel King,
> And the bitter groan of the Martyr's woe
> Is an Arrow from the Almightie's Bow.'[86]

'Beneath the white thorn, lovely May' is the earlier version of
'The Golden Net'[87] of the *Pickering MS.*: the net, like the net of
religion, is from the factory of Urizen, and symbolizes the repression of desire by the moral law.

The *Pickering MS.* consists of eleven leaves, and contains fair
copies of ten poems. The MS. seems to have been kept by Blake
and after his death it came into the possession of Frederick
Tatham. He sold it to a bookseller, Francis Harvey, who offered
it to various customers for 25 guineas, but failed to find a buyer.*
It was lent to Gilchrist for Rossetti's use about 1863, and in 1866

* For further details see Keynes, *Blake Studies*, pp. 155–7. [Ed.]

it was purchased by Basil Montagu Pickering, son of William Pickering, who had published an edition of the *Songs of Innocence and of Experience* in 1839. B. M. Pickering reissued the *Songs* in 1866, adding the poems from his MS. in a more accurate text than that printed by Rossetti in the second volume of Gilchrist's *Life*. Dr. Sampson, who printed the first authoritative text of all the poems in his edition of 1905, assigns them to the Felpham period on the ground that earlier versions of two poems are among the lyrics in the Notebook written at that time, some lines from 'Mary' were quoted in Blake's letter to Butts of 16 August 1803, and various phrases are repeated in *Milton* and *Jerusalem*. All the poems have Blake's own titles, whereas in the Notebook titles are frequently lacking.

'The Mental Traveller' presents a fascinating problem, of which no satisfactory solution has yet been offered. Damon[88] identifies the mental traveller with the mystic and endeavours to trace the five stages of the mystic way, but, even if this part of his argument carries conviction, the one thing clear about the poem is that it is dealing with a cycle. The mystic way is not a cycle: it is a figure for progress towards a definite goal through five states or regions traversed by every mystic. W. M. Rossetti's ingenious interpretation seems to come nearer to the mark:

The 'Mental Traveller' indicates an Explorer of mental phaenomena. The mental phaenomenon here symbolized seems to be the career of any great Idea or intellectual movement—as, for instance, Christianity, chivalry, art, etc.—represented as going through the stages of—1, birth, 2, adversity and persecution, 3, triumph and maturity, 4, decadence through over-ripeness, 5, gradual transformation, under new conditions, into another renovated Idea, which again has to pass through all the same stages. In other words, the poem represents the action and re-action of ideas upon society, and society upon Ideas.

Argument of the stanzas: 2, The idea, conceived with pain, is born amid enthusiasm. 3, If of masculine, enduring nature, it falls under the control and ban of the already existing state of society (the woman old). 5, As the Idea develops, the old society becomes moulded into a new society (the old woman grows young). 6, The Idea, now free and dominant, is united to Society, as it were in wedlock. 8, It gradually grows old and effete, living now only upon the spiritual treasures laid up in the days of its early energy. 10, These still subserve many purposes of practical good, and outwardly the Idea is in its most flourishing estate, even when sapped at its roots. 11, The halo of authority and tradition, or prestige, gathering round the Idea, is symbolized in the resplendent babe born on his hearth. 13, The prestige deserts the Idea itself, and attaches to some individual, who usurps the honour due only to the Idea (as we may see in the case of papacy, royalty, etc.); and the Idea is eclipsed by its own very prestige, and assumed living representative. 14, The Idea wanders homeless till it can find a new community to mould ('until he can a maiden win'). 15 to 17, Finding whom, the Idea finds itself also living under strangely different conditions. 18, The Idea is now 'beguiled to infancy'—becomes a *new* Idea, in working upon a fresh community, and under altered conditions. 20, Nor are they yet thoroughly at one; she flees away while he pursues. 22, Here we return to the first state of the case. The Idea starts upon a new course— is a babe; the society it works upon has become an old society— no longer a fair virgin, but an aged woman. 24, The Idea seems so new and unwonted that, the nearer it is seen, the more consternation it excites. 26, None can deal with the Idea so as to develop it to the full, except the old society with which it comes into contact; and this can deal with it only by misusing it at first, whereby (as in the previous stage, at the opening of the poem) it is to be again disciplined into ultimate triumph.[89]

Another explanation may be tentatively suggested.* The dichotomy of male and female throughout the poem is analogous to that of spectre and emanation. The old woman ill-treats the frowning babe who, as youth, 'binds her down for his delight.' The female babe is pursued by her lover. There is a continuing cycle with no true and harmonious union. The frowning babe suggests Orc, the spirit of Revolt, and the 'little female babe', too precious to be touched, moral and religious ideals. Does Blake who, whatever may have been the illusions of the 'Liberty Boy',

* This difficult poem has had many other interpreters. One of the most recent, Miss Kathleen Raine, offers an interesting variation in her book, *Blake and Tradition* (1968), i, pp. 306–21. She regards the theme as being the cyclic nature of history, relating it to the mythology of Dionysus, derived probably from Thomas Taylor's translation of Plato's *Politicus*, published in 1804. [Ed.]

now only believed in spiritual freedom through the imagination, here deny the possibility of progress in the world of space and time, since it seems to him to consist only in the vain and fruitless alternation of revolutionary and of moral and religious ideals, which in their turn beguile mankind with false hopes?

The possible reference of 'Mary' to Mary Wollstonecraft has already been mentioned, and the verses in the poem also applied by Blake to his own case have been quoted. 'The Crystal Cabinet' symbolizes the threefold state of love, bodily, intellectual, and emotional, but lacking the spiritual which is needed to strengthen and perfect the sexual.*

The 'Auguries of Innocence' opens with the lovely quatrain:

> To see a World in a Grain of Sand
> And a Heaven in a Wild Flower,
> Hold Infinity in the palm of your hand
> And Eternity in an hour.[91]

It is followed by couplets treating of various subjects, possibly jottings for different uncompleted poems, which are not consecutively arranged. Whatever may have been Blake's intention, Dr. Sampson's rearrangement enables the poem to be read as a whole.†

* Cf.
> Altho' our Human Power can sustain the severe contentions
> Of Friendship, our Sexual cannot . . .
> > *Milton*, pl. 41, ll. 32–3.[90]

† The couplet:
> He who the ox to wrath has mov'd
> Shall never be by Woman lov'd

is one of the many instances in which a saying of Blake's has been dismissed as nonsense by ignorant or careless critics. It was a common custom in the East End of London, on which evidence was given before a Parliamentary Committee in 1828, to turn an ox loose in the street, bait it to madness, and hunt it to death. Coleridge has also uttered his protest in the 'Sibylline Leaves':

> The frightened beast ran through the town;
> All follow'd, boy and dad,
> Bull-dog, parson, shopman, clown:
> The publicans rush'd from the Crown,
> 'Halloo! hamstring him! cut him down!'
> They drove the poor Ox mad.

(Cf. Spencer Walpole, *History of England*, chapter xii.) Wicksteed, *The Quest*,

The *Pickering MS.* ends with two ballads. The first, 'Long John Brown & Little Mary Bell,'[92] is the only writing of Blake's which leaves a bad taste in the mouth: it has a brutality quite absent from the coarseness of *An Island in the Moon*. 'William Bond'[93] has often been given an autobiographical significance by critics from D. G. Rossetti onwards: Ellis,[94] surpassing himself in irresponsible ingenuity, finds in it the cause of Catherine Blake's childlessness. Whether the story recalls any experience in the lives of William and Catherine Blake no one can say, but the meaning of the poem is clear. William Bond is restrained by a sense of duty (the angels of Providence) from being unfaithful to his sweetheart, Mary Green, but this mechanical observance of a moral law does not bring peace in the renewal of his love for her. She, on the other hand, is ready to sacrifice herself when she knows that he loves another woman, and by her unselfishness and her piteous grief she regains his love.*

There is no indication whether Blake intended to engrave the poems in the *Pickering MS.* He meant, it may be, to add others to their number, for instance, a final version of 'Spectre and Emanation'. With the addition of this and other poems from the Notebook, the *Pickering MS.* carries on the tradition of the *Songs of Innocence and of Experience* and of *The Marriage of Heaven and Hell*, a tradition which should have been perfected by *The Everlasting Gospel*, had not that great poem been unfortunately left in a fragmentary form. These lyrics are more obscure and more obviously mystical than Blake's earlier work, but the poet has successfully subdued his stubborn material; in phrasing and in metre they are the lineal successors of the *Songs* and of the earlier lyrics in the Notebook, showing no trace of the idiosyncrasy of word and thought which marks the symbolic books. They need no defence as poetry since they are difficult only where the ideas expressed are difficult of apprehension. They are not scarred by

---

iii, no. 1 (October 1911), p. 88, interprets Blake's lines as meaning that the action of men in irritating an animal deprived by them of virility, argues a lack of chivalry for which they should forfeit woman's love.

* The last two verses have been already quoted, p. 72.

the mystic's strife on his way towards the unitive life, which prevents the symbolic books from achieving the detachment essential to great art. These books are an integral part of the life of the man, William Blake: the lyrics and *The Marriage of Heaven and Hell* are the work of a poet, mystic though he be, who needs no name, whose personality calls for no explanation.

The greater part of the symbolic book *Milton* was also probably drafted at Felpham, although additions were made after Blake's return to London in 1803, and no copy was issued till after August 1808. Blake presumably began to engrave it in 1804, the date on the title-page. Two books only of *Milton* are extant, although in one copy it is clearly entitled *Milton, a Poem in 12 Books*. It is improbable that others were ever written.* The motto below the title, 'To justify the Ways of God to Men,' is taken from *Paradise Lost*.

In the Preface occur the beautiful quatrains beginning:

> And did those feet in ancient time
> Walk upon England's mountains green?[95]

erroneously known to the public as *Jerusalem*. These verses have been set to music,† and are sung at religious and social assemblies, when the 'dark Satanic Mills' doubtless suggest to the audience not Hayley's quiet library at Felpham or Urizen's logic, but factory labour with its attendant evils. Blake appeals in this Preface to the young men of the New Age to restore the Muses to their rank as Daughters of Inspiration from that of Daughters of Memory to which they had been degraded by the Greeks and

---

* Binyon (*The Engraved Designs*, p. 121) points out that, although in the New York copy (C) the figure 1 might be part of the decoration, it is clear in the Windus copy (D) and has been painted out in the Print Room copy (A). It is, however, difficult to believe that Blake intended to write ten more books, as the poem appears to reach its culmination at the end of the second book.

† By Sir Hubert Parry. For musical settings of other of Blake's lyrics see Keynes, *Bibliography*, pp. 290–2. Blake appears to have adopted the idea common among the Celtic revivalists of his day that England was the birthplace of the 'patriarchal religion' from which all later forms of religion were derived. See note on pp. 296–7.

Romans, an error into which Milton himself had fallen. Many years later Blake spoke to Crabb Robinson of Milton 'as being at one time a sort of classical Atheist,' and in *The Marriage of Heaven and Hell* he had written:

Those who restrain desire, do so because theirs is weak enough to be restrained; and the restrainer or reason usurps its place & governs the unwilling.

And being restrain'd, it by degrees becomes passive, till it is only the shadow of desire.

The history of this is written in Paradise Lost, & the Governor or Reason is call'd Messiah.

And the original Archangel, or possessor of the command of the heavenly host, is call'd the Devil or Satan, and his children are call'd Sin & Death. . . .

But in Milton, the Father is Destiny, the Son a Ratio of the five senses, & the Holy-ghost Vacuum![96]

Yet Blake's fundamental sympathy with Milton is characteristically expressed in the note to this section:

The reason Milton wrote in fetters when he wrote of Angels & God, and at liberty when of Devils & Hell, is because he was a true Poet and of the Devil's party without knowing it.[97]

The theme of the poem is a particular instance of a Last Judgment, the recognition of error, and consequent redemption. The hero is Milton, whom Blake had always admired beyond all other poets.* 'Milton lov'd me in childhood & show'd his face.'[98] Milton is 'unhappy tho' in heav'n' because he remembers his errors while on earth. He recognizes that he had been divided against himself, allowing himself to be dominated by his spectre, reason, and that one of the results had been his unsatisfactory emotional relations with his wives and daughters, his 'sixfold emanation'. Moved by the story of the quarrel between Blake and Hayley and its causes, he determines to return in spirit to earth.

---

* For a detailed examination of the influence of Milton on Blake see Denis Saurat, *Blake and Milton*, and R. D. Havens, *The Influence of Milton on English Poetry*, pp. 217–28. (Saurat's *Blake and Modern Thought* appeared too late for the author to profit from it. This applies also to Milton O. Percival's interpretation of Blake's system, *William Blake's Circle of Destiny*.)

And Milton said: 'I go to Eternal Death! The Nations still
Follow after the detestable Gods of Priam, in pomp
Of warlike selfhood contradicting and blaspheming.
When will the Resurrection come to deliver the sleeping body
From corruptibility? O when, Lord Jesus, wilt thou come?
Tarry no longer, for my soul lies at the gates of death.
I will arise and look forth for the morning of the grave:
I will go down to the sepulcher to see if morning breaks:
I will go down to self annihilation and eternal death,
Lest the Last Judgment come & find me unannihilate
And I be siez'd & giv'n into the hands of my own Selfhood.

> .   .   .   .

'What do I here before the Judgment? without my Emanation?
With the daughters of memory & not with the daughters of
     inspiration?
I in my Selfhood am that Satan: I am that Evil One!
He is my Spectre! in my obedience to loose him from my Hells,
To claim the Hells, my Furnaces, I go to Eternal Death.'[99]

Passing through Beulah he enters into his own shadow, leaving
'His real and immortal Self, . . . as One sleeping on a couch Of
gold,' and he sees the eternal man in the death of the life to which
he is himself returning.

First Milton saw Albion upon the Rock of Ages,
Deadly pale outstretch'd and snowy cold, storm cover'd,
A Giant form of perfect beauty outstretch'd on the rock
In solemn death: the Sea of Time & Space thunder'd aloud
Against the rock, which was inwrapped with the weeds of death.[100]

His spirit enters into Blake, who is enabled by his sympathetic
communion to follow the experience of Milton on his return to
earth. Milton, who in Eternity had known the fourfold vision,
the Human, now realizes that though as a poet in his former
existence he had possessed the threefold vision of Beulah, he had
failed to annihilate his selfhood, and hence the errors in his
relations to his wives and daughters. The Zoas, who, as in *Vala*,
have been striving and intriguing among themselves for dominion, instead of fulfilling their own functions, are disturbed by the
return of the 'immortal Man', and 'the Shadowy Female', who
may here be best interpreted as the spirit of the age, distracted
by the terrors of revolution, expresses her alarm:

'I will lament over Milton in the lamentations of the afflicted:
My Garments shall be woven of sighs & heart broken lamentations:
The misery of unhappy Families shall be drawn out into its border,
Wrought with the needle with dire sufferings, poverty, pain & woe
Along the rocky Island & thence throughout the whole Earth;
There shall be the sick Father & his starving Family, there
The Prisoner in the Stone Dungeon & the Slave at the Mill.
I will have writings written all over it in Human Words
That every Infant that is born upon the Earth shall read
And get by rote as a hard task of a life of sixty years.
I will have Kings inwoven upon it & Councellors & Mighty Men:
The Famine shall clasp it together with buckles & Clasps,
And the Pestilence shall be its fringe & the War its girdle.
To divide into Rahab & Tirzah that Milton may come to our tents.*
For I will put on the Human Form & take the Image of God,
Even Pity & Humanity, but my Clothing shall be Cruelty:
And I will put on Holiness as a breastplate & as a helmet,
And all my ornaments shall be of the gold of broken hearts,
And the precious stones of anxiety & care & desperation & death
And repentance for sin & sorrow & punishment & fear,
To defend me from thy terrors, O Orc, my only beloved!'[101]

Milton's spirit goes toward the 'Universe of Los and Enitharmon', poetry and inspiration, but he is obstructed by Urizen. His 'Redeemed portion', 'the Reasoning Negative', tries to form a philosophy, while still

within that portion
His real Human walk'd above in power and majesty,
Tho' darken'd, and the Seven Angels of the Presence attended him.[102]

He resists the temptation to return to the world of generation and division to which he is enticed by promises of intellectual kingship. But since Milton's spectre is not yet united to his Emanation, he is absorbed by abstract reasoning and seeks God 'beyond the

* Rahab symbolizes sexual licence and Tirzah sexual repression.

skies', instead of seeing through 'fourfold vision' that everything is holy.

Seest thou the little winged fly, smaller than a grain of sand?
It has a heart like thee, a brain open to heaven & hell,
Withinside wondrous & expansive: its gates are not clos'd:
I hope thine are not: hence it clothes itself in rich array:
Hence thou art cloth'd with human beauty, O thou mortal man.
Seek not thy heavenly father then before the skies,
There Chaos dwells & ancient Night & Og & Anak old.
For every human heart has gates of brass & bars of adamant
Which few dare unbar, because dread Og & Anak guard the gates
Terrific: and each mortal brain is wall'd and moated round
Within, and Og & Anak watch here: here is the Seat
Of Satan in its Webs: for in brain and heart and loins
Gates open behind Satan's Seat to the City of Golgonooza,
Which is the spiritual fourfold London in the loins of Albion.[103]

The Eternals are wroth at Milton's spiritual error and force the Seven Eyes of God and the 'Shadowy Eighth', Milton's own essential individuality, who are guarding the Golden Couch in Beulah, to follow him into space and time. The Spirit of Milton enables Blake to see anew the beauty of the material world. The spirit shown in the illustration as a star, enters Blake's left foot because he is in the material world, left and right being accredited symbols of the material and the spiritual. Another illustration represents the star entering the right foot of Blake's beloved brother Robert: there is no reference to this in the text, but by it Blake implies that Robert's spirit is giving him aid and sympathy. The inspiration of Milton so invigorates Blake that he becomes one with the Poetic Genius.

And I became One Man with him arising in my strength.
'Twas too late now to recede. Los had enter'd into my soul:
His terrors now posses'd me whole! I arose in fury & strength.[104]

Los takes Blake to his City of Art, Golgonooza, but they are met at the Gate by two sons of Los, Rintrah, Wrath, and Palamabron, Pity, who resent the entry of Blake both as revolutionist, and as influenced by Milton, whose religion, Puritanism, they regard as the origin of present errors. But Los tries to reassure them:

> 'O noble Sons, be patient yet a little!
> I have embrac'd the falling Death, he is become One with me:*
> O Sons, we live not by wrath, by mercy alone we live!
> I recollect an old Prophecy in Eden recorded in gold and oft
> Sung to the harp, That Milton of the land of Albion
> Should up ascend forward from Felpham's Vale & break the Chain
> Of Jealousy from all its roots; be patient therefore, O my Sons!
>
> .   .   .   .
>
> O when shall we tread our Wine-presses in heaven and Reap
> Our wheat with shoutings of joy, and leave the Earth in peace?
> Remember how Calvin and Luther in fury premature
> Sow'd War and stern division between Papists & Protestants.
> Let it not be so now! O go not forth in Martyrdoms & Wars!
> We were plac'd here by the Universal Brotherhood & Mercy
> With powers fitted to circumscribe this dark Satanic death,
> And that the Seven Eyes of God may have space for Redemption.
> But how this is as yet we know not, and we cannot know
> Till Albion is arisen; then patient wait a little while.
> Six Thousand years are pass'd away, the end approaches fast:
> This mighty one is come from Eden, he is of the Elect
> Who died from Earth & he is return'd before the Judgment. This thing
> Was never known, that one of the holy dead should willing return.
> Then patient wait a little while till the Last Vintage is over.'[105]

Under the guidance of Los, Blake sees the descent of Souls to the material world, and their generation in the region of Bowlahoola and Allamanda, the digestive, assimilative, and the nervous, perceptive systems, and the treading of the 'Human Grapes' in the wine-press of war. Yet all the while, as Blake never wearies of saying, whatever the misery of the world of generation

> . . . the poor indigent is like the diamond which, tho' cloth'd
> In rugged covering in the mine, is open all within
> And in his hallow'd center holds the heavens of bright eternity.[106]

---

* Milton, whose spirit has entered into Blake.

And in the City of Golgonooza

. . . Enitharmon and her Daughters take the pleasant charge
To give them to their lovely heavens till the Great Judgment
    Day.[107]

The first book of *Milton* contains Blake's most precise description of Los in his twofold symbolism as Time and the Poetic Genius.

Los is by mortals nam'd Time, Enitharmon is nam'd Space:
But they depict him bald & aged who is in eternal youth
All powerful and his locks flourish like the brows of morning:
He is the Spirit of Prophecy, the ever apparent Elias.
Time is the mercy of Eternity; without Time's swiftness,
Which is the swiftest of all things, all were eternal torment.
All the Gods of the Kingdoms of Earth labour in Los's Halls:
Every one is a fallen Son of the Spirit of Prophecy.
He is the Fourth Zoa that stood around the Throne Divine.[108]

This is further defined by Los's account of himself as the Guardian of the World Memory:

'I am that Shadowy Prophet who Six Thousand Years ago
Fell from my station in the Eternal bosom. Six Thousand Years
Are finish'd. I return! both Time & Space obey my will.
I in Six Thousand Years walk up and down; for not one Moment
Of Time is lost, nor one Event of Space unpermanent,
But all remain: every fabric of Six Thousand Years
Remains permanent, tho' on the Earth where Satan
Fell and was cut off, all things vanish & are seen no more,
They vanish not from me & mine, we guard them first & last.
The generations of men run on in the tide of Time,
But leave their destin'd lineaments permanent for ever & ever.'[109]

And by the beautiful description of Time, every moment of which is of equal value with the whole period since the creation of the world:

But others of the Sons of Los build Moments & Minutes &
    Hours
And Days & Months & Years & Ages & Periods, wondrous
    buildings;

And every Moment has a Couch of Gold for soft repose,
(A Moment equals a pulsation of the artery),
And between every two Moments stands a Daughter of Beulah
To feed the Sleepers on their Couches with maternal care.
And every Minute has an azure Tent with silken Veils:
And every Hour has a bright golden Gate carved with skill:
And every Day & Night has Walls of brass & Gates of adamant,
Shining like precious Stones & ornamented with appropriate
    signs:
And every Month a silver paved Terrace builded high:
And every Year invulnerable Barriers with high Towers:
And every Age is Moated deep with Bridges of silver & gold:
And every Seven Ages is Incircled with a Flaming Fire.
Now Seven Ages is amounting to Two Hundred Years.
Each has its Guard, each Moment, Minute, Hour, Day, Month &
    Year.
All are the work of Fairy hands of the Four Elements:
The Guard are Angels of Providence on duty evermore.
Every Time less than a pulsation of the artery
Is equal in its period & value to Six Thousand Years,
For in this Period the Poet's Work is Done: & all the Great
Events of Time start forth & are conciev'd in such a Period,
Within a Moment, a Pulsation of the Artery.[110]

The second book opens with a description of Beulah, 'a place
where Contrarieties are equally True' and where 'no dispute can
come.' It was created that the emanations might have repose
while their spectres are in the World of Generation. In their
divided state they are too feeble to face the mental war and 'Fury
of Poetic Inspiration' in Eternity itself:

              the life of Man was too exceeding unbounded.
His joy became terrible to them; they trembled & wept,
Crying with one voice: 'Give us a habitation & a place
In which we may be hidden under the shadow of wings:
For if we, who are but for a time & who pass away in winter,
Behold these wonders of Eternity we shall consume:
But you, O our Fathers & Brothers, remain in Eternity.
But grant us a Temporal Habitation, do you speak
To us; we will obey your words as you obey Jesus
The Eternal who is blessed for ever & ever. Amen.'

So spake the lovely Emanations, & there appear'd a pleasant
Mild Shadow above, beneath, & on all sides round.
Into this pleasant Shadow all the weak & weary
Like Women & Children were taken away as on wings
Of dovelike softness, & shadowy habitations prepared for them.
But every Man return'd & went still going forward thro'
The Bosom of the Father in Eternity on Eternity,
Neither did any lack or fall into Error without
A Shadow to repose in all the Days of happy Eternity.[111]

Ololon, Milton's Emanation, whom he sought, at first described as 'a sweet River of Milk & liquid pearl,' but later a
'a Virgin of twelve years', had already bewailed Milton's return
to earth and had been moved to follow him.

She now descends, and a part of the lovely lamentation of
Beulah has been already quoted:

There is a Moment in each Day that Satan cannot find,
Nor can his Watch Fiends find it; but the Industrious find
This Moment & it multiply, & when it once is found
It renovates every Moment of the Day if rightly placed.
In this Moment Ololon descended to Los & Enitharmon
Unseen beyond the Mundane Shell, Southward in Milton's track.[112]

Meanwhile the sleeping Milton, 'His real and immortal Self',
converses in dream and vision with his Guardians, the Seven
Angels of the Presence, and in this dialogue Blake explains the
distinction between states and the individuals who pass through
them, between the Identity, the Poetic Genius, the Imagination,
which is Eternal, and the Selfhood which has been created and
must be annihilated.

'I have turned my back upon these Heavens builded on cruelty;
My Spectre still wandering thro' them follows my Emanation,
He hunts her footsteps thro' the snow & the wintry hail & rain.
The idiot Reasoner laughs at the Man of Imagination,
And from laughter proceeds to murder by undervaluing calumny.'

Then Hillel,* who is Lucifer, replied over the Couch of Death,
And thus the Seven Angels instructed him, & thus they converse:

* The Jewish scholar, called by Blake Lucifer, the morning star, because
he was a forerunner of Jesus, the Sun.

'We are not Individuals but States, Combinations of Individuals.
We were Angels of the Divine Presence, & were Druids in
  Annandale,
Compell'd to combine into Form by Satan, the Spectre of Albion,
Who made himself a God & destroyed the Human Form Divine.
But the Divine Humanity & Mercy gave us a Human Form
Because we were combin'd in Freedom & holy Brotherhood,
While those combin'd by Satan's Tyranny, first in the blood of
  War
And Sacrifice & next in Chains of imprisonment, are Shapeless
  Rocks
Retaining only Satan's Mathematic Holiness, Length, Bredth &
  Highth,
Calling the Human Imagination, which is the Divine Vision &
  Fruition
In which Man liveth eternally, madness & blasphemy against
Its own Qualities, which are Servants of Humanity, not Gods or
  Lords.
Distinguish therefore States from Individuals in those States.
States Change, but Individual Identities never change nor
  cease.
You cannot go to Eternal Death in that which can never
  Die.
Satan & Adam are States Created into Twenty-seven Churches,
And thou, O Milton, art a State about to be Created,
Called Eternal Annihilation, that none but the Living shall
Dare to enter, & they shall enter triumphant over Death
And Hell & the Grave: States that are not, but ah! Seem to
  be.

'Judge then of thy Own Self: thy Eternal Lineaments explore,
What is Eternal & what Changeable, & what Annihilable.
The Imagination is not a State: it is the Human Existence itself.
Affection or Love becomes a State when divided from Imagina-
  tion.
The Memory is a State always, & the Reason is a State
Created to be Annihilated & a new Ratio Created.
Whatever can be Created can be Annihilated: Forms cannot:
The Oak is cut down by the Ax, the Lamb falls by the Knife,
But their Forms Eternal Exist For-ever. Amen. Hallelujah!'[113]

One of the illustrations shows Blake's cottage at Felpham and
the descent of Ololon.

Walking in my Cottage Garden, sudden I beheld
The Virgin Ololon & address'd her as a Daughter of Beulah:

'Virgin of Providence, fear not to enter into my Cottage.
What is thy message to thy friend? What am I now to do?
Is it again to plunge into deeper affliction? behold me
Ready to obey, but pity thou my Shadow of Delight:*
Enter my Cottage, comfort her, for she is sick with fatigue.'

The Virgin answer'd: 'Knowest thou of Milton who descended
Driven from Eternity? him I seek, terrified at my Act
In Great Eternity which thou knowest: I come him to seek.'[114]

Immediately Milton's shadow appears, 'clothed in black, severe &
silent he descended.' Blake, inspired by Ololon, now recognizes
fully the errors of Milton's religious thought, and its connections
with other false religions and morality, which are all a Tabernacle
for Satan and a covering for him to do his Will.

Milton himself, although he has not yet perceived the presence
of his Emanation, frees himself from the domination of his
Spectre, declaring that he will:

'. . . put off
In Self annihilation all that is not of God alone. . . .'[115]

Satan, Reason as Error, makes another attempt to conquer his
soul,

Saying: 'I am God the judge of all, the living & the dead.
Fall therefore down & worship me, submit thy supreme
Dictate to my eternal Will, & to my dictate bow.
I hold the Balances of Right & Just & mine the Sword.
Seven Angels bear my Name & in those Seven I appear,
But I alone am God & I alone in Heav'n & Earth
Of all that live dare utter this, others tremble & bow,
Till All Things become One Great Satan, in Holiness
Oppos'd to Mercy, and the Divine Delusion, Jesus, be no more.'[116]

Then the Starry Seven, whose name Satan has taken in vain,
appear in a column of fire, and call on the Eternal Man to waken.

* His wife.

'Awake, Albion* awake! reclaim thy Reasoning Spectre. Subdue
Him to the Divine Mercy. Cast him down into the Lake
Of Los that ever burneth with fire ever & ever, Amen!
Let the Four Zoas awake from Slumbers of Six Thousand Years.'[117]

Milton can now perceive Ololon, who questions him, fearing that
the error he has cast out may but give rise to new errors, and he
replies:

'Obey thou the Words of the Inspired Man.
All that can be annihilated must be annihilated
That the Children of Jerusalem may be saved from slavery.
There is a Negation, & there is a Contrary:
The Negation must be destroy'd to redeem the Contraries.
The Negation is the Spectre, the Reasoning Power in Man:
This is a false Body, an Incrustation over my Immortal
Spirit, a Selfhood which must be put off & annihilated alway.
To cleanse the Face of my Spirit by Self-examination,
To bathe in the Waters of Life, to wash off the Not Human,
I come in Self-annihilation & the grandeur of Inspiration,
To cast off Rational Demonstration by Faith in the Saviour,
To cast off the rotten rags of Memory by Inspiration,
To cast off Bacon, Locke & Newton from Albion's covering,
To take off his filthy garments & clothe him with Imagination,
To cast aside from Poetry all that is not Inspiration,
That it no longer shall dare to mock with the aspersion of
    Madness
Cast on the Inspired by the tame high finisher of paltry Blots
Indefinite, or paltry Rhymes, or paltry Harmonies,
Who creeps into State Government like a catterpiller to destroy;
To cast off the idiot Questioner who is always questioning
But never capable of answering, who sits with a sly grin
Silent plotting when to question, like a thief in a cave,
Who publishes doubt & calls it knowledge, whose Science is
    Despair,
Whose pretence to knowledge is Envy, whose whole Science is
To destroy the wisdom of ages to gratify ravenous Envy
That rages round him like a Wolf day & night without rest:
He smiles with condescension, he talks of Benevolence & Virtue,
And those who act with Benevolence & Virtue they murder time
    on time.

* Albion symbolizes the Eternal Man, Fourfold Humanity, and England.
The Mental fire of Imagination and Inspiration consuming error.

These are the destroyers of Jerusalem, these are the murderers
Of Jesus, who deny the Faith & mock at Eternal Life,
Who pretend to Poetry that they may destroy Imagination
By imitation of Nature's Images drawn from Remembrance.
These are the Sexual Garments, the Abomination of Desolation
Hiding the Human Lineaments as with an Ark & Curtains
Which Jesus rent & now shall wholly purge away with Fire
Till Generation is swallow'd up in Regeneration.'[118]

Then Ololon recognizes that:

'Altho' our Human Power can sustain the severe contentions
Of Friendship, our Sexual cannot,'[119]

and sacrificing her selfhood she is united with Milton's shadow.
Their union is followed by that of the Starry Eight as 'One Man,
Jesus the Saviour': Milton, 'the Shadowy Eighth', is now united
with Jesus who is God.

But the Last Judgment and redemption of Milton are only a
prelude of what is to come.

Jesus wept & walked forth
From Felpham's Vale clothed in Clouds of blood, to enter into
Albion's Bosom, the bosom of death, & the Four* surrounded
him
In the Column of Fire in Felpham's Vale; then to their mouths the
Four
Applied their Four Trumpets & them sounded to the Four
winds.

Terror struck in the Vale I stood at that immortal sound.
My bones trembled, I fell outstretch'd upon the path
A moment, & my Soul return'd into its mortal state
To Resurrection & Judgment in the Vegetable Body,
And my sweet Shadow of Delight stood trembling by my side.

Immediately the Lark mounted with a loud trill from Felpham's
Vale,†
And the Wild Thyme from Wimbleton's green & impurpled
Hills. . . .[120]

* The Four Zoas.
† Cf. the lovely illustration of 'L'Allegro', 'Night Startled by the Lark',
Milton's Poems in English (Nonesuch Press, 1926), ii, facing p. 28.

The revelation through Blake of Milton's error, which has been the error of the Created World, has prepared the way for 'the Great Harvest & Vintage of the Nations.'

Milton is the most personal of the symbolic books, and contains some of the finest of Blake's later poetry, splendid rhetoric, and unforgettable phrases. The vitality of the text is equalled by that of the illustrations.

VI
FAILURE

The spirit said to him, 'Blake be an artist and nothing
else. In this there is Felicity.'

But Los hid Enitharmon from the sight of all these things
Upon the Thames whose lulling harmony repos'd her soul.[1]

In other words the Blakes came back to London and lodged at
17 South Molton Street, where Mrs. Blake gradually recovered
health. On 26 October 1803 Blake writes to Hayley: 'My wife
continues poorly, but fancies she is better in health here than by
the seaside.'[2] The agony of apprehension which she suffered
during Blake's absence for his trial at Chichester in the following
January brought her very low. 'My poor wife has been near the
Gate of Death as was supposed by our kind & attentive fellow
inhabitant, the young & very amiable Mrs Enoch, who gave my
wife all the attention that a daughter could pay to a mother, but
my arrival has dispell'd the formidable malady & my dear & good
woman again begins to resume her health & strength.'[3]

She was treated by a surgeon, John Birch, who was also a
friend of Mr. Butts, and is mentioned in Blake's letters to him of
11 September 1801 and 25 April 1803, and on 23 October 1804
Blake says: 'She is surprisingly recovered. Electricity is the
wonderful cause; the swelling of her legs and knees is entirely
reduced. She is very near as free from rheumatism as she was five
years ago, and we have the greatest confidence in her perfect
recovery.'[4] This hope seems to have been realized, as he wrote
again on 18 December: 'My wife continues well, thanks to Mr
Birch's Electrical Magic, which she has discontinued these three
months.'[5]

The only description of the Blakes' home in South Molton
Street known to me is given in a note by Martin Cregan, afterwards President of the Royal Hibernian Academy, who visited
them in 1809: 'I had the felicity of seeing this happy pair in their

one apartment in South Molton Street. The Bed on one side and picture of Aldred and the Danes on the wall.'*

Blake was exhilarated by his return to London, as he had at first been by the change of surroundings at Felpham.

The shops in London improve; everything is elegant, clean, and neat; the streets are widened where they were narrow; even Snow Hill is become almost level, and is a very handsome street, and the narrow part of the Strand near St. Clement's is widened and become very elegant.[6]

In a letter to Hayley of 7 October 1803 he writes:†

. . . some say that Happiness is not Good for Mortals, & they ought to be answer'd that Sorrow is not fit for Immortals & is utterly useless to any one; a blight never does good to a tree, & if a blight kill not a tree but it still bear fruit, let none say that the fruit was in consequence of the blight. When this Soldier-like danger is over I will do double the work I do now, for it will hang heavy on my Devil who terribly resents it; but I soothe him to peace, & indeed he is a good natur'd Devil after all & certainly does not lead me into scrapes—he is not in the least to be blamed for the present scrape, as he was out of the way all the time on other employment seeking amusement in making Verses, to which he constantly leads me very much to my hurt & sometimes to the annoyance of my friends.[7]

Hayley was certainly one species of blight; did Blake account for the survival of friendly feeling towards him by the presence of a 'good natur'd Devil' in himself? After his return from the trial he wrote: 'Hope earnestly that you have entirely escaped the brush of my Evil Star, which I believe is now for ever fallen into the Abyss.'[8] His belief in Hayley's power of understanding the spiritual conflicts he had endured would be amazing, were it not

* The author found this note in the London Library copy of Redgrave's *A Century of Painters*, which contained other notes by Cregan (1788–1870), who went to London in 1808. Mr Dermod O'Brien, then President of the Royal Hibernian Academy, tried to obtain further information about this visit from a descendant of Cregan's, but the note quoted above appeared to be the only record. [The picture mentioned is not now known. Ed.]

† When the author was writing, this letter was known only in a fragment quoted in a sale catalogue. Since then it has been found and printed in full. [Ed.]

more probable that the need for self-expression—with perhaps a little help from the good-natured Devil—had blurred the image of his correspondent. His letter of 23 October 1804 celebrates his deliverance.

For now! O Glory! and O Delight! I have entirely reduced that spectrous Fiend to his station, whose annoyance has been the ruin of my labours for the last passed twenty years of my life. He is the enemy of conjugal love and is the Jupiter of the Greeks, an iron-hearted tyrant, the ruiner of ancient Greece. I speak with perfect confidence and certainty of the fact which has passed upon me. Nebuchadnezzar* had seven times passed over him; I have had twenty; thank God I was not altogether a beast as he was; but I was a slave bound in a mill among beasts and devils; these beasts and these devils are now, together with myself, become children of light and liberty, and my feet and my wife's feet are free from fetters. O lovely Felpham, parent of Immortal Friendship, to thee I am eternally indebted for my three years' rest from perturbation and the strength I now enjoy. Suddenly, on the day after visiting the Truchsessian Gallery† of pictures, I was again enlightened with the light I enjoyed in my youth, and which has for exactly twenty years been closed from me as by a door and by window-shutters. Consequently I can, with confidence, promise you ocular demonstration of my altered state on the plates I am now engraving after Romney, whose spiritual aid has not a little conduced to my restoration to the light of Art. O the distress I have undergone, and my poor wife with me; incessantly labouring and incessantly spoiling what I had done well. Every one of my friends was astonished at my faults, and could not assign a reason; they knew my industry and abstinence from every pleasure for the sake of study, and yet—and yet—and yet there wanted the proofs of industry in my works. I thank God with entire confidence that it shall be so no longer—he is become my servant who domineered over me, he is even as a brother who was my enemy. Dear Sir, excuse my enthusiasm or rather madness, for I am really drunk with intellectual vision whenever I take a pencil or graver into my hand, even as I used

* Nebuchadnezzar's madness symbolizes the dominion of the 'vegetable world', the materialism of the rationalists.

† This collection of pictures was brought to England by Joseph, Count Truchsess, and exhibited in London in August 1803. See below, p. 208. [Ed.]

to be in my youth, and as I have not been for twenty dark, but very profitable years. I thank God that I courageously pursued my course through darkness. In a short time I shall make my assertion good that I am become suddenly as I was at first, by producing the Head of Romney and the Shipwreck* quite another thing from what you or I ever expected them to be. In short, I am now satisfied and proud of my work, which I have not been for the above long period.[9]

And again, a few weeks later:

I have indeed fought thro' a Hell of terrors & horrors (which none could know but myself) in a Divided Existence; now no longer Divided nor at war with myself I shall travel on in the strength of the Lord God as Poor Pilgrim says.[10]

Blake had traversed the fourth stage of the Way, the most terrible to him as to all mystics, and had entered on the last, the Unitive Life. Poverty and neglect he had still to face, but it would seem that in spite of such crises as that recorded in the Notebook: 'Tuesday, Jan^ry. 20, 1807, between Two & Seven in the Evening —Despair,'[11] what had been doubt had become faith and certainty, and henceforth the Divine Vision was not long absent from him. In writing of the redemption of man in *Vala* he had redeemed himself, and won spiritual freedom for his divided soul; the devils, the Four Zoas, had become the Children of Light and the servants of Man. Los, the Poetic Genius, tortured by doubts and failures, knew again that his name in Eternity was Urthona, Spirit, and that on Earth he had power to build the Palace of Art. Blake was beginning to engrave *Milton* (probably finished in 1808), telling his own story of the struggle to free his genius from those who were corporeal friends but spiritual enemies, and the story of Milton's conquest of spiritual unity which was also his own story of an inspired visionary knowledge of the Unitive Life. Moreover, the conception of his last symbolic

* Blake engraved one of Romney's drawings ('The Shipwreck') for Hayley's *Life of Romney*, 1809. His head of Romney was not used and may never have been completed. [Ed.]

book, *Jerusalem*, the epic of spiritual freedom, was already taking shape in his mind.

The conflict between reason and imagination which had beset the mystic was reflected in the divided inspiration of the artist. Of this he had already spoken to Butts in a letter from Felpham: but the flame of his early inspiration suddenly burnt clear after this visit to the Truchsessian Gallery. These pictures were the property of a Count Truchsess, who purported to have lost a large fortune in the French Revolution, and wished to found a company for the purchase of his pictures as the nucleus of a permanent gallery. Farington writes in his Diary, 21 August 1803:

> Lawrence has been this morning to see the exhibition of Count Truchesis pictures near the New Road, Marybone. He gave a most unfavourable account of them,—saying there was scarcely an original picture of a *Great Master* among them. . . . There are 1,000 pictures & Lawrence does not think the whole are worth £2,000. The Count values them at £60,000.

The judgement of so famous a collector as Lawrence must be accepted. Blake, who had been recovering his youthful inspiration at Felpham, went to the Gallery with creative eyes: young genius, and Blake's genius never aged, is often stimulated by something of little worth: how many of those prints after old masters by which his imagination had been fired would have been thought worthy by Sir Thomas of a place in his portfolios? Blake speaks of twenty years of darkness which, if taken literally, would carry him back to 1784, but he was apt to deal in round numbers, and doubtless means that the happiness and certainty which produced the *Songs of Innocence* and the engraving of 'Glad Day' had returned to him. Since then he had lived through the contrary state of experience and the dark tumult of Lambeth and Felpham, only broken by the laughter of *The Marriage of Heaven and Hell*. Mr. Foster Damon, however, does not allow even this approximate accuracy to Blake's 'exactly twenty years', reducing the time to less than half by dating it from the completion of *Ahania*— 'Judging by Blake's own works, the terrible period of sterility had lasted only nine years.'[12] But Blake is not speaking of a period of sterility, if indeed the years during which he wrote *Vala*, and at least conceived the idea of *Milton*, can fairly be called sterile; on the contrary he calls those years 'very profitable' though darkened by conflict and division. He respected the process of his own development, however painful that process might have been, and he knew what he had gained by it even though he was returning to his old ideas: his movement was synthetic, though he was furiously casting out what seemed to him error because it was foreign to his own genius. He had cautioned Butts against thinking that the pictures he had painted for him were not what he now wished them to be: moreover, he did not destroy his 'experiment pictures' but exhibited them in 1809 with the comment:

These Pictures, among numerous others painted for experiment, were the result of temptations and perturbations, labouring to destroy Imaginative power, by means of that infernal machine called Chiaro Oscuro, in the hands of Venetian and Flemish Demons, whose enmity to the Painter himself, and to all Artists who study in the Florentine and Roman Schools, may be removed by an exhibition and exposure of their vile tricks. They cause that every thing in art shall become a Machine. They cause that the execution shall be all blocked up with brown shadows. They put the original Artist in fear and doubt of his own original conception. The spirit of Titian was particularly active in raising doubts concerning the possibility of executing without a model, and when once he had raised the doubt, it became easy for him to snatch away the vision time after time, for, when the Artist took his pencil to execute his ideas, his power of imagination weakened so much and darkened, that memory of nature, and of Pictures of the various schools possessed his mind, instead of appropriate execution resulting from the inventions; like walking in another man's style, or speaking, or looking, in another man's style and manner, unappropriate and repugnant to your own individual character; tormenting the true Artist, till he leaves the Florentine, and adopts the Venetian practice, or does as Mr. B. has done, has the courage to suffer poverty and disgrace, till he ultimately conquers.[13]

Many of the pictures which belonged to Mr. Butts are now in

the Graham Robertson collection.* 'The River of Life,' with its clear, radiant colour, is supposed to have been painted after Blake's visit to the Truchsessian Gallery, and 'The Four and Twenty Elders casting down their crowns before the Divine Throne,' which specially impressed Rodin, was executed in 1805. On the other hand some of those pre-eminently remarkable for invention, such as 'The Soldiers Casting Lots for Christ's Garments', or for colour, as 'The Death of the Virgin Mary' and its companion picture 'The Death of St. Joseph', belong to the earlier group. Blake, as A. G. B. Russell pointed out, stands almost alone as a great imaginative painter of figures in water colour.[14] He has, in fact, accomplished a more difficult and a far rarer feat than that of the early imaginative landscape painters in water colour. The originality of his inventions, as, for instance, that of the angels flying downwards on each side of the figure of Christ in 'The Ascension', is usually singled out as the main characteristic of his genius. The brilliance and subtlety, the opalescence, the iridescence of his colouring at its best are inevitably lost in reproductions. Another quality which is at least easier to detect in the originals because it is induced by such slight variations in tone, is the sculpturesque, a legacy from those years spent in Westminster Abbey: often a group of two or three figures becomes in memory, like Blake's fold of lambs, beautiful sculpture. Some of the pictures painted for Mr. Butts are far less successful than others. All Blake's work except, perhaps, the series of colour-printed drawings, is uneven, but it is impossible to divide it into two groups, pre- and post-Truchsessian, as this enthusiastic pronouncement suggests.

In his letter Blake speaks, too, of that 'spectrous Fiend' as the 'enemy of conjugal love', and says that his wife's feet also are now free from fetters. This implies that Mrs. Blake's doubts had been added to his own, and even, perhaps, that her sympathy

* The Graham Robertson collection, derived largely from that of Thomas Butts, was sold at auction by Christie's 22 July 1949 and dispersed. A catalogue of the collection, with Graham Robertson's descriptions, was compiled by Kerrison Preston and published for the William Blake Trust in 1949. [Ed.]

with Hayley may have gone a little further than Blake could have wished. The obvious interpretation—and doubtless Hayley's reading—of his apostrophe to Felpham as 'parent of Immortal Friendship' is that the good-natured Devil had urged him to an exaggerated expression of his feeling for Hayley, but the allusions to his wife suggest a subtler meaning. Blake sometimes uses friendship as the name for love in eternity, and in *A Vision of The Last Judgment* there is a sentence which recalls what those who knew her toward the end of her life say of Catherine Blake—'Also On the right hand of Noah A Female descends to meet her Lover or Husband, representative of that Love, call'd Friendship, which Looks for no other heaven than their Beloved & in him sees all reflected as in a Glass of Eternal Diamond.'[15] Blake may then be referring to a more perfect relationship with his wife as one outcome of his spiritual victory. But on the other hand gratitude and the relief from Hayley's presence may have temporarily induced a belief in their immortal friendship, witness the characteristic scrap from a sale catalogue: 'Reading in the Bible of the Eyes of the Almighty, I could not help putting up a petition for yours.'*

The rest from perturbation means, of course, the freedom from financial anxiety of Felpham of which he had assured Butts. The peacefulness of Felpham had now become a refreshing memory:

Remembering our happy Christmas at lovely Felpham, our spirits seem still to hover round our sweet cottage and round the beautiful Turret. I have said *seem*, but am persuaded that distance is nothing but a phantasy. We are often sitting by our cottage fire, and often we think we hear your voice calling at the gate. Surely these things are real and eternal in our eternal mind and can never pass away.[16]

Blake's letters are full of references to the *Life of Romney* as he was assisting Hayley by collecting material and interviewing various persons concerned. This brought him into renewed relations with Flaxman, who was one of the principal persons to be

* From a letter to Hayley dated 17 May 1805 (*Complete Writings*, p. 860), the original of which has not yet been found. [Ed.]

consulted on Hayley's behalf, and he writes: 'My admiration of Flaxman's genius is more and more—his industry is equal to his other great powers.'[17] And again, after the death of Banks, the sculptor, in 1805, 'Now I concieve Flaxman stands without a competitor in Sculpture.'[18] In a letter dated 4 December Blake wrote:

I have mention'd your Proposal to our Noble Flaxman whose high & generous Spirit relinquishing the whole to me was in some measure to be Expected, but that he has reasons for not being able to furnish any designs You will readily believe; he says his Engagements are so multiform that he should not be able to do them Justice, but that he will overlook & advise.[19]

One of the owners of Romney's pictures upon whom Blake called was Adam Walker, author and inventor, who showed him some family portraits:

But above all, a picture of Lear and Cordelia, when he awakes and knows her,—an incomparable production, which Mr. W. bought for five shillings at a broker's shop; it is about five feet by four, and exquisite for expression; indeed, it is most pathetic; the heads of Lear and Cordelia can never be surpassed, and Kent and the other attendant are admirable; the picture is very highly finished.[20]

Another, Daniel Braithwaite,* thought Blake's own engraving of Romney 'a very great likeness'. This portrait, which Blake mentions several times as acceptable to those who had known Romney, was intended for Hayley's Life, but was not used. His only contribution was 'The Shipwreck', after a sketch by Romney, for which he took Fittler's illustrations of Falconer's poem, The Shipwreck, as a model.† On 4 May 1804 he had written to Hayley:

I thank you sincerely for Falconer, an admirable poet, and the admirable prints to it by Fittler. Whether you intended it or not,

* Daniel Braithwaite, controller of the Foreign Department of the Post Office, was Romney's earliest patron in 1762. Hayley's Life of Romney was dedicated to him.

† A. G. B. Russell, The Engravings, p. 179, considers that 'The Shipwreck' is an uncharacteristic and laborious piece of work, as the result of Blake's attempt to imitate Fittler's methods.

they have given me some excellent hints in engraving; his manner of working is what I shall endeavour to adopt in many points.[21]

Blake's old partner, James Parker, was among those whom he consulted about engraving plates for the Romney *Life*. Parker was now apparently very prosperous: Blake quotes him as saying: 'I have to-day turned away a Plate of 400 Guineas because I am too full of work to undertake it, & I know that all the Good Engravers are so Engaged that they will be hardly prevail'd upon to undertake more than One of the Plates on so short a notice.'[22] It may be that Blake is comparing his own lot with Parker's in a sentence in a sale catalogue* which follows another concerning the Romney *Life*—'Money flies from me. Profit never ventures upon my Threshold, tho' every other man's doorstone is worn down into the very Earth by the footsteps of the fiends of commerce.'[23]

Blake was also finishing the plates for the Cowper *Life* and writes on 23 February 1804:

The plates of Cowper's Monument are both in great forwardness, & you shall have Proofs in another week. I assure you that I will not spare pains, & am myself very much satisfied that I shall do my duty & produce two Elegant plates; there is, however, a great deal of work in them that must & will have time.[24]

And again three weeks later:

Engraving is Eternal work; the two plates are almost finish'd. You will recieve proofs of them for Lady Hesketh, whose copy of Cowper's letters ought to be printed in letters of Gold & ornamented with Jewels of Heaven, Havilah, Eden & all the countries where Jewels abound. I curse & bless Engraving alternately, because it takes so much time & is so untractable, tho' capable of such beauty & perfection.[25]

Hayley is fussing over the non-arrival of the plates and on 31 March Blake says:

I hope you will believe me when I say that my solicitude to

* From a letter to Hayley of 7 August 1804. The original has not been recovered. [Ed.]

bring them to perfection has caused this delay, as also not being quite sure that you had Copies ready for them. I could not think of delivering the 12 Copies without giving the last touches, which are always the best. . . . I remain In Engraver's hurry, which is the worst & most unprofitable of hurries,

Your Sincere & Affectionate,

Will Blake[26]

When he first went back to London Blake expected to procure work as an engraver without difficulty. On 26 October 1803 he wrote to Hayley: 'I have got to work after Fuseli for a little Shakespeare. Mr. Johnson, the bookseller, tells me that there is no want of work. So far you will be rejoiced with me, and your words *"Do not fear you can want employment!"* were verified the morning after I received your kind letter. . . .'[27] The reference is to Alexander Chalmers' edition of *Shakespeare's Works*, 1805, for which Blake engraved two plates after Fuseli, 'Queen Catherine's Dream'* and 'Romeo and the Apothecary', receiving £25 for each plate. And early in the New Year he says:

My Dear Sir, I write now to satisfy you that all is in a good train. I am going on briskly with the Plates, find every thing promising. Work in Abundance; &, if God blesses me with health doubt not yet to make a Figure in the Great dance of Life that shall amuse the Spectators in the Sky.[28]

He engraved plates for two books by Prince Hoare, painter and dramatist, whose acquaintance he made at this time. Hoare had studied in Rome under Mengs with Fuseli in 1776, and became Foreign Secretary of the Royal Academy in 1799. Blake writes to Hayley on the 23 February 1804:

I inclose likewise the Academical Correspondence of Mr Hoare the Painter, whose note to me I also inclose, for I did but express to him my desire of sending you a Copy of his work, & the day after I reciev'd it with the note Expressing his pleasure in your

---

* The pencil drawing made by Blake for this engraving is now in the Rosenwald Collection, National Gallery, Washington, D.C. In 1807 Blake himself painted a water-colour design of the same subject, now in the Fitzwilliam Museum, Cambridge, and made three others soon afterwards. [Ed.]

wish to see it. You would be much delighted with the Man, as I assure myself you will be with his work.[29]

The frontispiece of the *Correspondence* is 'Two Views of a Statue of Ceres' engraved by Blake after Flaxman. Blake also engraved the frontispiece for Hoare's *An Inquiry into the Requisite Cultivation and Present State of the Arts of Design in England*, published in 1806. The subject of this is the 'Graphic Muse' sketched from the picture by Sir Joshua Reynolds on the ceiling of the library of the Royal Academy, which has now been transferred to the Council Chamber of Burlington House. This is Blake's only known work after Reynolds, and his opinion of his task is not recorded.

He exhibits great interest in a scheme for which it is difficult to understand his enthusiasm, except that he doubtless thought it would give Hayley pleasure. Richard Phillips, bookseller and editor of the *Monthly Magazine*, had proposed that Hayley should be responsible for the conduct of a literary enterprise, and Blake was commissioned by Prince Hoare to act as intermediary. He endorses a note of Phillips's terms, saying:

Knowing your aversion to Reviews & Reviewing, I consider the Present Proposal as peculiarly adapted to your Ideas; it may be call'd a Defence of Literature against those pests of the Press & a bulwark for Genius, which shall with your good assistance disperse those Rebellious Spirits of Envy & Malignity. In short: If you see it as I see it, you will embrace this Proposal on the Score of Parental Duty. Literature is your Child. She calls for your assistance! You: who never refuse to assist any, how remote soever, will certainly hear her voice.[30]

Either because Hayley wished to delegate some of his duties or for another cause the scheme fell through.

Blake's courteous and easy references to money matters mark his friendly relations with Hayley:

Now, My Dear Sir, I will thank you for the transmission of ten Pounds to the Dreamer over his own Fortunes: for I certainly am that Dreamer; but tho' I dream over my own Fortunes, I ought not to Dream over those of other Men, & accordingly have given a look over my account Book, in which I have regularly written down Every Sum I have reciev'd from you; & tho' I never can balance the account of obligations with you, I ought to do my best at all times & in all circumstances. I find that you was right in supposing that I had been paid for all I have done; but when I wrote last requesting ten pounds, I thought it was Due on the Shipwreck (which it was), but I did not advert to the Twelve Guineas which you Lent Me when I made up 30 Pounds to pay our Worthy Seagrave in part of his Account. I am therefore that 12 Guineas in your Debt: Which If I had consider'd, I should have used more consideration, & more ceremony also, in so serious an affair as the calling on you for more Money; but, however, your kind answer to my Request makes me Doubly Thank you.[31]

And, again, when the arrangements with Phillips for the ill-fated second edition of the *Ballads* were under discussion:

I consider myself as only put in trust with this work, and that the copyright is for ever yours. I therefore beg that you will not suffer it to be injured by my ignorance, or that it should in any way be separated from the grand bulk of your literary property. Truly proud I am to be in possession of this beautiful little estate; for that it will be highly productive I have no doubt, in the way now proposed; and I shall consider myself a robber to retain any more than you at any time please to grant. In short, I am tenant at will, and may write over my door, as the poor barber did, Money for live here.[32]

Towards the end of the year he refers again to the *Ballads*:

I cannot give you any Account of our Ballads, for I have heard nothing of Phillips this Age. I hear them approved by the best, that is, the most serious people, & if any others are displeas'd it is also an argument of their being Successful as well as Right, of which I have no Doubt; for what is Good must Succeed first or last, but what is bad owes success to something beside or without itself, if it has any.[33]

Before Blake had been back in London for a year he found that, however much the appearance of the town had improved, human nature was the same, and he exposes to Hayley the attempts of Johnson and Phillips to decry the work of the Chichester printer, Seagrave, whom Hayley had employed, in their own interests, adding:

I could not avoid saying thus much in justice to our good Seagrave, whose replies to Mr. Johnson's aggravating letters have been represented to Mr. Rose in an unfair light, as I have no doubt; because Mr. Johnson has, at times, written such letters to me as would have called for the sceptre of Agamemnon rather than the tongue of Ulysses, and I will venture to give it as my settled opinion that if you suffer yourself to be persuaded to print in London you will be cheated every way; but, however, as some little excuse, I must say that in London every calumny and false-hood utter'd against another of the same trade is thought fair play. Engravers, Painters, Statuaries, Printers, Poets, we are not in a field of battle, but in a City of Assassinations. This makes your lot truly enviable, and the country is not only more beautiful on account of its expanded meadows, but also on account of its benevolent minds.[34]

Hayley, it would seem, quoted these remarks to Flaxman with a little embroidery, as the latter comments on them in a letter of 2 August 1804:

. . . with respect to Blake's remark upon 'Assassinations' I suppose he may have been acquainted with wretches capable of such practices, but I desire it may be understood that I am not one of them, & 'tho I do not deal in 'barbarous Stilettos' myself I am willing to acknowledge the benevolence & soundness of Blake's general observation as well as the point & keenness with which it was applied; but this was only a poetic jeu d'esprit which neither did nor intended harm.[35]

The fashionable enthusiasm of the moment appealed to him as little as the self-interested commercialism of Johnson, Phillips & Co.

Few memoirs or essays of this time can be without their references, favourable or adverse, to that well-advertised phenomenon, the actor Betty, who did not fulfil his boyhood's promise. Here is Blake's comment:

The Town is Mad: Young Roscius like all Prodigies is the talk of Every Body. I have not seen him & perhaps never may. I have no curiosity to see him, as I well know what is within compass of a boy of 14, & as to Real Acting it is Like Historical Painting, No Boy's Work.[36]

Towards another infant prodigy he shows more sympathy. In
1806 Dr. Benjamin Heath Malkin, head master of Bury Grammar
School, and author of *Scenery, Antiquities, and Biography of South
Wales* and other works, published an account of the precocious
little Thomas Malkin, who died in 1802, in his seventh year.
Reference has already been made to Dr. Malkin's account of
Blake in the dedicatory epistle to Johnes of Hafod, translator of
Froissart, which serves as introduction to *A Father's Memoirs of
his Child*. Dr. Malkin supports his own view of the originality
of his little boy's drawings by adding Blake's testimony. Blake
praises the 'firm, determinate outline', and concludes: 'All his
efforts prove this little boy to have had that greatest of all blessings,
a strong imagination, a clear idea, and a determinate vision of
things in his own mind.'[37]

One of Thomas's productions was a Map of Allestone, an
imaginary country, with places named Bubblebob, Punchpeach,
Le Grassebank, and so forth, of which he also wrote the history.
Blake may have known little Thomas before he went to Felpham
in 1800, and encouraged him in the creation of a mythical region,
but it is more likely that Cromek introduced him to Dr. Malkin
in 1805. The frontispiece of the memoir has a portrait of the child
after a miniature by Paye, surrounded by a design after Blake which
represents an angel conducting the child heavenward; he takes
leave of his mother, who is kneeling on the edge of a cliff. The
objects lying beside her may have been suggested to Blake by a
passage in one of the child's own letters. 'Also, I think my Pocket-
Book, is a very nice thing, especially; for in it, there is a tweasers,
bodkin, scissors, and a knife to cut with, pencil to write memoran-
dums with upon the asses skin, and there is a clasp to it on the
outside to open and shut the pocket-book with.'[38] Gilchrist states
that the design was originally engraved by Blake himself, but was
re-engraved by Cromek. The reviewers were not attracted by the
specimens of Blake's poetry quoted by Dr. Malkin: in the *Monthly
Review* for October 1806 he is described as 'certainly very inferior
to Dr. Watts,' while the writer in the *Monthly Magazine* of January
1807 considers that 'the poetry of Mr. Blake, inserted in the

dedication, does not rise above mediocrity; as an artist he appears to more advantage.' The variant of the last line of the third verse of 'The Tyger': 'What dread hand forged thy dread feet?' for 'What dread hand? & what dread feet?'[39] is interesting because Malkin had derived his information direct from Blake.

The only letters of Blake's which have been preserved from the time of his return to London till the end of 1805 are addressed to Hayley, and are chiefly concerned with Hayley's work and his own. They contain a few allusions to books; a letter of 16 July 1804 has:

I omitted to get Richardson till last Friday having call'd thrice unsuccessfully & before publication, have only had time to skim it but cannot restrain myself from speaking of Mrs Klopstock's letters Vol. 3,* which to my feelings are the purest image of Conjugal affection honesty & Innocence I ever saw on paper. Richardson has won my heart. I will again read Clarissa &c., they must be admirable.[40]

His reference to a *Life of Washington* (4 December 1804) which he is sending on to Hayley suggests that his enthusiasm for the American Revolution is on the wane. Did he see Urizen's Prohibition, one law for the lion and the ass, approaching to condemn his shadowy pint of porter?

I suppose an American would tell me that Washington did all that was done before he was born, as the French now adore Buonaparte and the English our poor George; so the Americans will consider Washington as their god. This is only Grecian, or rather Trojan, worship, and perhaps will be revised [?] in an age or two. In the meantime I have the happiness of seeing the Divine countenance in such men as Cowper and Milton more distinctly than in any prince or hero.[41]

Blake's last two letters to Hayley are reserved for later quotation, as they introduce Hayley's successor, an employer who better deserved the name of Satan than the well-intentioned Bard.

* *The Correspondence of Samuel Richardson*, selected by Anne Laetitia Barbauld, 6 vols. (1804). See vol. iii, pp. 139–58 for the letters to and from Mrs. Klopstock. [Ed.]

Although no further letters have come to light Blake's lines 'On H—the Pick thank'

> I write the Rascal Thanks till he & I
> With Thanks & Compliments are quite drawn dry[42]

show that the correspondence continued for some years, since this and his other epigrams on Hayley are in the section of the Notebook ascribed to *circa* 1808–11. Some critics have spoken of these epigrams as though Blake, after signing one of his affectionate letters of 1803–5, had opened his MS. book and then and there scribbled lines of a grossly opposite character. This is inaccurate and misleading. The breach with Hayley gradually widened until all and more than all the Felpham bitterness revived and overflowed in lines which, be it remembered, were never intended for publication. It is clear from Blake's letters that he was expecting a considerable share in engraving the plates for the Romney *Life*; his position as Hayley's agent in collecting material for illustrations also gives colour to such an expectation: and yet he is only represented by one plate, that of 'The Shipwreck.'* The portrait to which reference has been made was discarded, and none of the other illustrations was allotted to him. In a letter of 27 April 1804 he says: 'Engraving is of so slow process, I must beg of you to give me the earliest possible notice of what engraving is to be done for the *Life of Romney*.'[43] On 4 May of the same year he writes: 'Mr. Flaxman agrees with me that somewhat more than outline is necessary to the execution of Romney's designs, because his merit is eminent in the art of massing his lights and shades. I should propose to etch them in a rapid but firm manner, somewhat, perhaps, as I did the Head of Euler†...'[44]

He discusses the same subject in the letter of 22 June, supporting

---

* Blake's sepia drawing made for his engraving after the picture by Romney is now in the British Museum, Department of Prints and Drawings. The drawing for the portrait of Romney was sold at Sotheby's in 1862, but its present whereabouts is not known. (A. G. B. Russell, *The Engravings*, p. 175.)

† Engraved as frontispiece to Euler's *Elements of Algebra*, published by Joseph Johnson, 1797.

his own opinion by that of Parker and Flaxman, though it would appear that, at any rate by that date, Blake did not look forward to undertaking all the work for the *Life* himself. He says:

. . . it is certain that the Pictures deserve to be Engraved by the hands of Angels, & must not by any means be done in a careless or too hasty manner. The Price Mr Parker has affix'd to each is Exactly what I myself had before concluded upon. Judging as he did that if the Fuseli Shakespeare is worth 25 Guineas, these will be at least worth 30, & that the inferior ones cannot be done at any rate under 15.

Mr Flaxman advises that the best Engravers should be engaged in the work, as its magnitude demands all the Talents that can be procured.[45]

He then gives a list of eight subjects chosen by Flaxman, and adds: 'I hope . . . you will soon recieve such documents as will enable you to decide on what is to be done in our desirable & arduous task of doing Justice to our admired Sublime Romney.'[46]

The proposals referred to in Blake's letter of December 1804 may be assumed to refer to the *Life of Romney*, and it was probably suggested that he should engrave a certain number of plates, possibly those afterwards allotted to Caroline Watson, under Flaxman's supervision. They cannot refer to a book which was later under consideration for the benefit of Samuel Rose's widow, as Blake's letter about his death is dated 20 December of this year. A letter of Flaxman's of 12 August 1805 relates to this suggestion, which apparently came to nothing, at any rate so far as Blake was concerned. He offers to give five drawings of his own, adding:

. . . concerning the Edward the first, I have seen two or three noble Sketches by Blake which might be drawn in outline by him in a manner highly creditable to your book & I would overlook them so far as to see that they should be Suitable to the other designs.

Later in the same letter he says:

. . . the day after I recieved your last letter, Blake brought a present of two Copies of the Songs,* it is a beautiful work, Nancy and I are

* The 'Songs' are no doubt the *Ballads*, 1805 edition.

equally thankful for this present and equally delighted with your bounty to the Poet-Artist. . . .[47]

This letter shows that while Flaxman was a genuine admirer of Blake's powers he considered that his engraving was too individual in character to combine easily with work by other hands; but it was not his doing that Hayley employed Caroline Watson instead of Blake as he had expressed a poor opinion of her work as far back as 18 June 1804.* In the same letter he recommended Cromek as an alternative, mentioning 'The Shipwreck' as a specially suitable subject for him, but it is fair to assume that he did

---

* Flaxman writes:

Notwithstanding your apparent determination and reasons given, for having the drawing engraved by the Lady you have mentioned I cannot communicate that commission untill I have given my reasons for delay, I like You, delight in paying a large portion of respect and preference to Female Talent but if I am to execute a commission for a Friend it ought to be done faithfully with a view to his satisfaction and advantage, at least not to his hurt, and really I have seen two children's heads with the abovementioned lady's name lately copied from pictures by Sr. Wm. Beechy, but so miserably executed that similar engraving instead of being a decoration, would be a blemish in your Book I am very sure the fault could not be in the pictures, for the Painter is a man of great merit if after this information you still continue in the same resolution as at first I will deliver your commission but there my interference must cease and all further communication must be between the engraver and yourself, because I foresee that the conclusion of such an engagement must be unsatisfactory to all parties concerned;

The Engraver mentioned in my last as having been casually consulted is Mr. Cromak with whom I believe you have no acquaintance, he has engraved several pictures and drawings of Stothards which in beauty, far exceed any other prints from that Artist's works, and I am very sure that he would engrave in strokes the man on horseback saving the people in the ship-wreck or any other *colored picture* of Romney's for your book in very great perfection. . . .

Hayley was apparently annoyed by Flaxman's strictures on Caroline Watson, as Flaxman writes again on 2 August 1804:

. . . concerning Caroline Watson's engraving, I should have acted more judiciously if I had desired you to see her last works for the regulation of your own judgment rather than to have sent any opinion of my own, I confess my own want of taste in Richardson's portrait for tho it is delicately engraven, it dont come up to my Idea of Highmore's portraits, notwithstanding if you are inclined to have a plate engraved by this artist, the only sentiment I can feel on the occasion will be satisfaction at seeing an ingenious Lady engaged in a respectable employment this is the only kind of 'atonement' which seems requisite for an opinion delivered upon works publicly exhibited. . . . (Fairfax Murray Collection, Fitzwilliam Museum.)

not at that time know that Blake was engraving 'The Shipwreck', and on the 18th December Blake reports to Hayley that Flaxman approves much of his plate. Hayley's first transference of work from Blake to Caroline Watson was the substitution in the octavo edition of 1805 of the *Life of Cowper* of her engraving after Romney's drawing of Cowper for Blake's, which had appeared in the first edition. Blake, it would seem, did not know of her engraving till April 1805, and it is not clear that he was then informed that it was to be used in the new edition. His courteous comment is: 'The Idea of Seeing an Engraving of Cowper by the hand of Caroline Watson is, I assure you, a pleasing one to me; it will be highly gratifying to see another Copy by another hand & not only gratifying, but Improving, which is better.'[40]

The *Life of Romney* was published in 1809. Most of the plates were executed by Caroline Watson, who assumed the role of engraver-in-chief originally intended for and expected by Blake. There is, however, no evidence of an actual breach of agreement, nor can it be determined at what point Blake realized that he had been finally ousted. It is possible that the fresh venture on which he was embarking was considered by Hayley and his adviser, Flaxman, as a sufficient excuse for ignoring the indefinite arrangement with him.

There are no private letters for 1806 to 1807, but in June of the former year a letter to Richard Phillips, as Editor, appeared in the *Monthly Magazine* protesting against a criticism in *Bell's Weekly Messenger* of Fuseli's 'Count Ugolino', exhibited at the Royal Academy, in which the treatment of the subject and also the colouring had been censured. After a vigorous defence of both Blake concluded:

A gentleman who visited me the other day, said, 'I am very much surprised at the dislike that some connoisseurs shew on viewing the pictures of Mr. Fuseli; but the truth is, he is a hundred years beyond the present generation.' Though I am startled at such an assertion, I hope the contemporary taste will shorten the hundred years into as many hours; for I am sure that any person consulting his own eyes must prefer what is so super-eminent; and I am as sure that any person consulting his own reputation, or the reputation of his country, will refrain from disgracing either by such ill-judged criticisms in future.[49]

On 14 October 1807 Blake addressed another letter to Phillips, both as Editor and as Sheriff, demanding an enquiry into the alleged imprisonment of an astrologer. 'We are all subject to Error': writes Blake. 'Who shall say, Except the Natural Religionists, that we are not all subject to Crime?'[50] This letter was not published.

Flaxman first informed Hayley of Blake's new prospects in a letter of 18 October 1805:

. . . Mr. Cromak has employed Blake to make a set of 40 drawings from Blair's poem of the Grave,* 20 of which he proposes [to] have engraved by the Designer and to publish them with the hope of rendering Service to the Artist, several members of the Royal Academy have been highly pleased with the specimens and mean to encourage the work, I have seen several compositions, the most Striking are, The Gambols of Ghosts according with their affections previous to the final Judgment—A widow embracing the turf which covers her husband's grave— Wicked Strong man dying—the good old man's Soul recieved by Angels.[51]

In a later letter he added the acrimonious comment:

. . . you will be glad to hear that Blake has his hands full of work for a considerable time to come and if he will only condescend to give that attention to his worldly concerns which every one does that prefers living to Starving, he is now in a way to do well. . . .[52]

Cromek† is the engraver already mentioned whom Flaxman had recommended to Hayley in connection with the Romney Life. He was a pupil of Bartolozzi's, and had engraved many book illustrations after Stothard, but was now trying—partly, it would

---

* More than forty drawings and water-colours related to these designs are known, but have been widely distributed. [Ed.]

† Gilchrist, Life, i, pp. 283–90, gives some account of Cromek's career including his supposed theft from Sir Walter Scott of an autograph letter from Ben Jonson to Drummond of Hawthornden.

appear, on account of indifferent health—to set up for himself as a publisher of engravings and illustrated books. He must be credited with a certain measure of artistic discernment as well as with commercial acumen of a less creditable kind.

Blake himself announces his undertaking in a letter to Hayley dated 27 November 1805:

> Mr Cromek the Engraver came to me desiring to have some of my Designs; he nam'd his Price & wish'd me to Produce him Illustrations of The Grave, A Poem by Robert Blair; in consequence of this I produced about twenty Designs which pleas'd so well that he, with the same liberality with which he set me about the Drawings, has now set me to Engrave them. He means to Publish them by Subscription with the Poem as you will see in the Prospectus which he sends you in the same Pacquet with the Letter. You will, I know, feel as you always do on such occasions, not only warm wishes to promote the Spirited Exertions of my Friend Cromek. You will be pleased to see that the Royal Academy have Sanctioned the Style of work. I now have reason more than ever to lament your Distance from London, as that alone has prevented our Consulting you in our Progress, which is but of about two Months Date.[53]

Blake's reply to Hayley's congratulations, which closes the surviving correspondence between them, shows that he expected to be delivered from pecuniary anxiety by the arrangement with Cromek, and also believed that his opportunity had at last come for obtaining wider recognition as a 'Prophet of True Art'.

> I cannot omit to Return you my sincere & Grateful Acknowledgments for the kind Reception you have given my New Projected Work. It bids fair to set me above the difficulties I have hitherto encounter'd. But my Fate has been so uncommon that I expect Nothing. I was alive & in health & with the same Talents I now have all the time of Boydell's, Macklin's, Bowyer's, & other Great Works. I was known by them & was look'd upon by them as Incapable of Employment in those Works; it may turn out so again, notwithstanding appearances. I am prepared for it, but at the same time sincerely Grateful to Those whose Kindness & Good opinion has supported me thro' all hitherto. You, Dear Sir, are one who has my Particular Gratitude, having conducted me

thro' Three that would have been the Darkest Years that ever Mortal Suffer'd, which were render'd thro' your means a Mild & Pleasant Slumber. I speak of Spiritual Things, Not of Natural; Of Things known only to Myself & to Spirits Good & Evil, but Not known to Men on Earth. It is the passage thro' these Three Years that has brought me into My Present State, & *I know* that if I had not been with You I must have Perish'd. Those Dangers are now Passed & I can see them beneath my feet. It will not be long before I shall be able to present the full history* of my Spiritual Sufferings to the Dwellers upon Earth & of the Spiritual Victories obtain'd for me by my Friends. Excuse this Effusion of the Spirit from One who cares little for this World, which passes away, whose Happiness is Secure in Jesus our Lord, & who looks for Suffering till the time of complete deliverance. In the mean While I am kept Happy, as I used to be, because I throw Myself & all that I have on our Saviour's Divine Providence. O What Wonders are the Children of Men! Would to God that they would consider it,That they would consider their Spiritual Life, Regardless of that faint Shadow call'd Natural Life, & that they would Promote Each other's Spiritual Labours, Each according to its Rank, & that they would know that Recieving a Prophet As a Prophet is a Duty which If omitted is more Severely Avenged than Every Sin & Wickedness beside. It is the Greatest of Crimes to Depress True Art & Science. I know that those who are dead from the Earth, & who mock'd and Despised the Meekness of True Art (and such, I find, have been the situations of our Beautiful Affectionate Ballads), I know that such Mockers are Most Severely Punished in Eternity. I know it, for I see it & dare not help. The Mocker of Art is the Mocker of Jesus. Let us go on, Dear Sir, following his Cross: let us take it up daily, Persisting in Spiritual Labours & the Use of that Talent which it is Death to Bury, & of that Spirit to which we are called.[54]

It appears from the first of these letters, as also from Flaxman's account, that Cromek had definitely commissioned Blake to make designs from Blair's *Grave*. Gilchrist's statement, supported by J. T. Smith, that he had already made some drawings, intending to engrave and publish them himself, may therefore be erroneous. The letter of 27 November, and this is a more im-

* This probably refers to his poem, *Milton*, completed about three years later. [Ed.]

portant point, confirms J. T. Smith's statement that the drawings
were sold to Cromek on the express understanding that Blake was
to engrave them himself, though Cromek's prospectus, to which
Gilchrist refers, announcing that the engravings were to be from
Blake's own hand, has disappeared. Cromek purchased twelve
instead of twenty of Blake's designs for the sum of twenty guineas,
and breaking his contract with Blake, handed them over to
Schiavonetti, a second-rate engraver, who had been a fellow-pupil
of his under Bartolozzi. Blake, according to Gilchrist, had actually
engraved one or two plates,* and he obviously expected to derive
his profit mainly from engraving, as the price of a single plate
would have exceeded that of the whole set of drawings. After his
designs had been transferred to Schiavonetti he offered Cromek an
exquisite drawing intended to accompany the lines in which he
had dedicated his illustrations to the Queen,† at £4 4s., a price
higher than he had charged for the others on the understanding
that he should be their engraver. Cromek's reception of this
moderate proposal is both mean and insolent:

64, Newman Street. May 1807‡

Mr. Blake—Sir, I received not without great surprise, your letter

* Samuel Palmer says in a letter to William Abercrombie of 5 February
1881, which was sold in the Shaw collection at Sotheby's 29 July 1925:

To render the list of type-printed designs complete, you can, if you please,
insert the mention of a very fine version of age entering the tomb, & the
spiritual body sitting above; the same invention which appears in the Blair's
Grave—it is not coloured.
My Son has an impression which, so far as we know, is unique.
[This print was exhibited by A. H. Palmer at the Victoria and Albert
Museum in 1926, was sold at Christie's 2 February 1928, and is now in a
private collection in the United States. See Keynes, *The Separate Plates*, where
it is also reproduced. The plate is executed in a rugged style which would
have been unlikely to catch the public fancy in 1808. Cromek was no doubt
right in judging that Schiavonetti's smoother style would prove more
popular. Ed.]
† The lines are those beginning 'The Door of Death is made of Gold'
(*Complete Writings*, p. 442), and the drawing is now in the Print Room of the
British Museum.
‡ Published in the *Gentleman's Magazine*, February 1852, pp. 149–50.
Symons printed in the *Saturday Review* of 25 August 1906 a later letter

demanding four guineas for the *sketched* vignette dedicated to the Queen. I have returned the drawing with this note, and I will briefly state my reasons for so doing. In the first place I do not think it merits the price you affix to it *under any circumstances*. In the next place I never had the remotest suspicions that you would for a moment entertain the idea of writing *me* to supply money to create an honour in which I cannot possibly participate. The Queen allowed *you*, not *me*, to dedicate the work to *her*! The honour would have been yours exclusively; but that you might not be deprived of any advantage likely to contribute to your reputation, I was willing to pay Mr. Schiavonetti *ten* guineas for etching a plate from the drawing in question.

Another reason for returning the sketch is that I *can do without it*, having already engaged to give a greater number of etchings than the price of the book will warrant; and I neither have nor ever had any encouragement from *you* to place you before the public in a more favourable point of view than that which I have already chosen. You charge me with *imposing upon you*. Upon my honour I have no recollection of anything of the kind. If the world and I were to settle accounts to-morrow, I do assure you the balance would be considerably in my favour. In this respect I am more sinned against than sinning, but, if I cannot recollect any instances wherein I have imposed upon *you*, several present themselves in which I have imposed upon *myself*. Take two or three that press upon me.

When I first called on you, I found you without reputation; I *imposed* on myself the labour, and a herculean one it has been, to create and establish a reputation for you. I say the labour was herculean, because I had not only to contend with, but I had to battle with a man who had predetermined not to be served. What

---

of Cromek's to Cumberland, showing him still impudent and impenitent.

14th August, 1808.

. . . Through the d——d carelessness of my Printer your Name is omitted in the list, a misfortune that I deplored, & almost raved about for three Days and three Nights.

You are the only person in Bristol who thoroughly understands the Inventions of Blake. Your Name has also some influence, & consequently the affair is to the last degree unlucky. However, it is past. I need not ask you to speak of the Book as you may think it ought to be spoken of. . . .

Your Packet went to Blake. I sent him 2 Copies, but he has not had the common politeness to thank me for them.

public reputation you have, the reputation of eccentricity excepted, I have acquired for you, and I can honestly and conscientiously assert that if you had laboured thro' life for yourself as zealously and as earnestly as I have done for you your reputation as an artist would not only have been enviable but it would have put it out of the power of an individual as obscure as myself, either to add to or to take from it. *I also imposed on myself* when I believed what you have so often told me, that your works were equal, nay superior, to a Raphael or to a Michael Angelo! Unfortunately for me as a publisher the public awoke me from this state of stupor, this mental delusion. That public is willing to give you credit for what real talent is to be found in your productions, *and for no more.*

I have imposed on myself yet more grossly in believing you to be one altogether abstracted from this world, holding converse with the world of spirits!—simple, unoffending, a combination of the *serpent* and the *dove.* I really blush when I reflect how I have been cheated in this respect. The most effectual way of benefiting a designer whose aim is general patronage, is to bring his designs before the public, through the medium of engraving. Your drawings have had the *good fortune* to be engraved by one of the first artists in Europe, and the specimens already shown have already produced you orders that I verily believe you otherwise would not have received. Herein I have been gratified, for I was determined to bring you food as well as reputation, tho' from your late conduct I have some reason to embrace your wild opinion, that to manage genius, and to cause it to produce good things, it is absolutely necessary to starve it; indeed, this opinion is considerably heightened by the recollection that your best work, the illustration of *The Grave,* was produced when you and Mrs. Blake were reduced so low as to be obliged to live on half-a-guinea a week.

Before I conclude this letter, it will be necessary to remark, when I gave you the order for the drawings from the poem of *The Grave,* I paid you for them more than I could then afford; more in proportion than you were in the habit of receiving, and what you were perfectly satisfied with, though, I must do you the justice to confess much less than I think is their real value. Perhaps you have friends and admirers who can appreciate their merit and worth as much as I do. I am decidedly of opinion that the twelve for *The Grave* should sell at the least for sixty guineas. If you can meet with any gentleman who will give you this sum for them, I will deliver them into his hands on the publication of the poem. I will deduct the twenty guineas I have paid you from that sum, and the remainder forty ditto shall be at your disposal.[55]

The book was published in 1808, and was issued to 589 subscribers at 2½ guineas, some proof copies being priced at 4 guineas.* Cromek announces in his Advertisement that he had submitted the drawings before they were engraved to eleven members of the Royal Academy, including West, the President, Flaxman, and Lawrence. The dull little introduction is by Fuseli, and the descriptions of the plates probably by Cromek himself. The frontispiece is an engraving of Blake by Schiavonetti after the portrait by T. Phillips, R.A., now in the National Portrait Gallery. A comparison between this painting and the life mask in the same gallery suggests that Phillips has softened, weakened, and conventionalized Blake's head as much as Schiavonetti has softened, weakened, and conventionalized his designs. Allan Cunningham, in *The Cabinet Gallery of Pictures*, tells an anecdote about this picture, which, like others in Cunningham's version of the Blake legend, suggests embellishment:

Blake, who always saw in fancy every form he drew, believed that angels descended to painters of old, and sat for their portraits. When he himself sat to Phillips for that fine portrait so beautifully engraved by Schiavonetti, the painter, in order to obtain the most unaffected attitude, and the most poetic expression, engaged his sitter in a conversation concerning the sublime in art. 'We hear much,' said Phillips, 'of the grandeur of Michael Angelo; from the engravings, I should say he has been over-rated; he could not paint an angel so well as Raphael.' 'He has not been over-rated, Sir,' said Blake, 'and he could paint an angel better than Raphael.' 'Well, but' said the other, 'you never saw any of the paintings of Michael Angelo; and perhaps speak from the opinions of others; your friends may have deceived you.' 'I never saw any of the paintings of Michael Angelo,' replied Blake, 'but I speak from the opinion of a friend who could not be mistaken.' 'A valuable friend

* The remainder and copyright were sold in 1812 by Cromek's widow for £120 to R. Ackermann, who re-issued it in 1813. The plates were also used by him in 1826 to illustrate a Spanish poem by José Joaquin, and (according to Gilchrist, *Life*, i, p. 271) were afterwards used again for the American edition of Mark Tupper's *Proverbial Philosophy*. (Keynes, *Bibliography*, p. 221.)

truly,' said Phillips, 'and who may he be I pray?' 'The arch-angel Gabriel, Sir,' answered Blake. 'A good authority surely, but you know evil spirits love to assume the looks of good ones; and this may have been done to mislead you.' 'Well now, Sir,' said Blake, 'this is really singular; such were my own suspicions; but they were soon removed—I will tell you how. I was one day reading Young's Night Thoughts, and when I came to that passage which asks "who can paint an angel," I closed the book and cried, "Aye! who can paint an angel?" A voice in the room answered, "Michael Angelo could." "And how do *you* know," I said, looking round me, but I saw nothing save a greater light than usual. "I *know*," said the voice, "for I sat to him: I am the arch-angel Gabriel." "Oho!" I answered, "you are, are you; I must have better assurance than that of a wandering voice; you may be an evil spirit—there are such in the land." "You shall have good assurance," said the voice, "can an evil spirit do this?" I looked whence the voice came, and was then aware of a shining shape, with bright wings, who diffused much light. As I looked, the shape dilated more and more: he waved his hands; the roof of my study opened; he ascended into heaven; he stood in the sun, and beckoning to me, moved the universe. An angel of evil could not have *done that*—it was the arch-angel Gabriel.' The painter marvelled much at this wild story; but he caught from Blake's looks, as he related it, that rapt poetic expression which has rendered his portrait one of the finest of the English school.[56]

Fate, it would seem, took a malignant revenge on Blake for his disbelief in the reality of time; she never secured him ease or even a modest measure of prosperity: she made him wait for his due share of fame. And now when, through the publication of his series of designs for Blair's *The Grave*, he made his first and only appeal to a contemporary public wider than the little group of his fellow-artists and admirers, his work was dishonoured, his true art depressed, by inadequate interpretation. Possibly Cromek was wise in his generation and a larger public was then only able to assimilate Blake diluted by Schiavonetti, but he is none the less guilty not only of cheating Blake but of defrauding the world of the setting which befitted his jewel.

Although the Blair designs were Blake's only work with any

pretensions to popularity in his own day, they were too imaginative to be wholly acceptable. Cunningham, who himself awards them tepid praise, says that 'The frontispiece—a naked Angel descending headlong and rousing the Dead with the Sound of the last Trumpet—alarmed the devout people of the north, and made maids and matrons retire behind their fans.'[57] Crabb Robinson was disturbed because Blake's 'greatest enjoyment consists in giving bodily form to spiritual beings.' He mentions the engravings which represent the soul as hovering over the body or uniting with it as 'about the most offensive of his inventions.'

Robert Hunt, in the *Examiner*, agrees with Crabb Robinson in admiring the 'Death of the Wicked Man', but considers that 'nearly all the allegory is not only far fetched but absurd, inasmuch as a human body can never be mistaken in a picture for its soul.' Two of the designs are, however, worse than silly—'The Day of Judgment' and 'The Meeting of a Family in Heaven'— as 'here an appearance of libidinousness intrudes itself upon the holiness of our thoughts, and counteracts their impression. . . . At the awful day of Judgment, before the throne of God himself, a male and female figure are described in most indecent attitudes. It is the same with the salutation of a man and his wife meeting in the pure mansions of Heaven.'[58] It is, perhaps, of the supersensuality of this reviewer that Blake was thinking when he wrote that a man could no longer embrace his own wife without being condemned as unchaste.[59] James Montgomery* was also scandalized by some of the plates: he sold his copy at the subscription price as unfit to lie on the parlour table, but regretted his haste when the work became rarer and more valuable.[60]

Not content with this, Cromek undoubtedly made Blake the victim of a second piece of trickery, though it is impossible to determine the truth of certain details from the various accounts given of the incident. Gilchrist† says that Cromek, some time in

---

* See p. 336 for further reference to James Montgomery. William Paulet Carey has an enthusiastic appreciation of the designs for *The Grave* in his *Critical Description*, etc.; see p. 234, and Keynes, *Bibliography*, pp. 467–8.

† *Life*, i, p. 250.

1806, saw in Blake's work-room 'a pencil drawing from a hitherto virgin subject—the *Procession* of Chaucer's *Canterbury Pilgrims*; Chaucer being a poet read by fewer then than now. Cromek "appeared highly delighted" with Blake's sketch, says Smith, as being an original treatment of an original subject. In point of fact, he wanted to secure a finished drawing from it, for the purpose of having it engraved, and *without* employing Blake, just as he had served him over the designs of *The Grave*; as I learn from other sources, on sifting the matter. However, Blake was not to be taken in a second time. Negotiations on that basis failed; but, as Blake understood the matter, he received a commission, tacit or express, from Cromek to execute the design.' Smith mentions that Blake showed Cromek 'the designs sketched out for a fresco picture'[61] of the Canterbury Pilgrims, but does not say if Cromek made an offer for it, or gave a commission for the engraving, or even that Blake had expressed an intention of engraving it himself. Allan Cunningham states that 'Blake declared that Cromek had actually commissioned him to paint the Pilgrimage before Stothard thought of his; to which Cromek replied, that the order had been given in a vision, for he never gave it.'[62]

Gilchrist unfortunately gives no authority for his additions to Smith's story. It is, at least, clear that Cromek had seen the drawing in 1806, and knew of Blake's intention to carry it further. Cromek thereupon—and here there is no question about the facts—suggested the subject to Stothard and ordered an oil picture from him for the sum of sixty, afterwards increased to a hundred, guineas, with the intention of having it engraved by Bromley, for whom Schiavonetti was substituted later.* A certain general resemblance between the composition of the two paintings may be due, as Gilchrist suggests, to Cromek's hints to Stothard based on his examination of Blake's drawing. Blake, not suspecting Cromek's treachery, saw and politely praised Stothard's unfinished picture, and Stothard talked of introducing his portrait. By May 1807 Stothard's 'Cabinet Picture' was exhibited, and at the end of

---

* Schiavonetti died before the plate was finished and it was completed by other hands.

the month Hoppner* wrote an appreciation of it in a letter to Cumberland which was printed in Prince Hoare's paper, *The Artist*, and quoted by Cromek in his prospectus of the engraving. A proposal for publishing an engraving of the picture by subscription was inserted at the end of Blair's *Grave*, and a *Critical Description* of Stothard's picture was published by William Paulet Carey, an engraver, art critic, and dealer, who was apparently ignorant of Blake's grievance, as he refers incidentally to his designs for Blair's *Grave* with enthusiasm.† Blake was furious when he realized that Stothard's painting was undertaken at Cromek's suggestion, naturally regarding it as a rival enterprise which had been pushed on to thwart his own intention. His anger is explicable whether negotiations with Cromek had taken place or not. There is, as we have seen, no direct evidence of an agreement with Cromek, but Gilchrist and Cunningham both indicate that Blake rightly or wrongly believed that there was one. He no doubt assumed too hastily that Stothard was a fellow conspirator of Cromek's and had known of his drawing from the beginning. It must also be remembered in explanation, if not in palliation, of Blake's rancour that Stothard had undoubtedly been considerably influenced by him—in short, like Fuseli, he had found Blake 'damned good to steal from'—and his easily acquired popularity had probably been a source of some irritation before this incident.

It appears from Gilchrist's account that Blake had not begun to paint his fresco until after the exhibition of Stothard's picture. Gilchrist adds, without giving his authority, that Blake, finding his drawing, which had been hanging above a door, a good deal effaced, attributed this to some malignant spell of Stothard's

---

* Hoppner, in a letter to Prince Hoare, which appears to have been written about this time, says: 'Respecting Blake's Poems, will you believe me? The merit was all vanished, in my mind at least, on reading them next morning. I therefore took no copy—but if you wish for them Cromek can now refuse you nothing—so I hope you will be modest in your demands of favours of him.' There is nothing to show to which poems Hoppner refers. (*Times Literary Supplement*, 7 October 1926.)

† Blake's description of his own 'Canterbury Pilgrims' in the *Descriptive Catalogue* may have been a counterblast to this pamphlet.

until Flaxman pointed out that it was the usual fate of pencil drawings exposed to air and dust. If Blake ever made such a remark it would assuredly have been in jest, but Flaxman's matter of fact reply is quite in character. Be this as it may Blake finished his fresco* in time for his Exhibition in May 1809; the account of it in *A Descriptive Catalogue* closes with a denunciation of Stothard, alike for his misconception of Chaucer's characters and for a false style of execution, and it must be admitted that Blake has expressed himself offensively. He retained the characteristics of a child in his anger as in his lovelier moods. His own drawing of Los with his hammer would have been a fitting tail-piece. Later in the *Catalogue*, commenting on his picture of 'The Bard', he describes more temperately the difference between Stothard's treatment of the subject and his own intentions.

Weaving the winding sheet of Edward's race by means of sounds of spiritual music and its accompanying expressions of articulate speech, is a bold, and daring, and most masterly conception, that the public have embraced and approved with avidity. Poetry consists in these conceptions; and shall Painting be confined to the sordid drudgery of fac-simile representations of merely mortal and perishing substances, and not be as poetry and music are, elevated into its own proper sphere of invention and visionary conception? No, it shall not be so! Painting, as well as poetry and music, exists and exults in immortal thoughts. If Mr. B's Canterbury Pilgrims had been done by any other power than that of the poetic visionary, it would have been as dull as his adversary's.[63]

A Prospectus of the Engraving of Chaucer's Canterbury Pilgrims was also issued in May 1809, announcing that:

The Designer proposes to Engrave, in a correct and finished Line manner of Engraving, similar to those original Copper

---

* The 'fresco', or tempera painting, was bought by Butts. When it was sold by his son in 1853, it was acquired by Sir William Stirling-Maxwell for his collection at Pollak House, Glasgow, where it is now on permanent exhibition. Butts also bought about 1809 the water-colour of 'The Whore of Babylon', now in the British Museum, Department of Prints and Drawings. [Ed.]

Plates of Albert Durer, Lucas, Hisben, Aldegrave and the old original Engravers, who were great Masters in Painting and Designing, whose method, alone, can delineate Character as it is in this Picture, where all the Lineaments are distinct.

The Blair's *Grave* controversy is referred to in the words:

It is hoped that the Painter will be allowed by the Public (notwithstanding artfully disemminated insinuations to the contrary) to be better able than any other to keep his own Characters and Expressions. . . .[64]

The draft for a further Prospectus is bound in with the Notebook. The Prospectus, printed about 1810, is a revision of this draft, with the omission of the first paragraph. The description of the engraving in both repeats with slight variations the opening of Number III in *A Descriptive Catalogue*, but the revised prospectus contains two additional paragraphs referring to the continued existence of the Tabarde Inn under the name of the Talbot, and to St. Thomas's Hospital.[65]

Blake, according to Gilchrist, began the engraving in September or October 1809, and the plate was issued on the 8th October 1810. It was re-worked by Blake, with the result that the later impressions are rather black and heavy: he also tinted a few copies in water colour.*

Early in 1812 a further attempt was made to advertise the engravings by the publication of a pamphlet containing Chaucer's

---

*The first state, lighter in effect, is very rarely found. Two copies, very beautifully painted with water colours, are now in private collections; the colouring follows very closely that of the original painting. One of these was exhibited with the tempera at the National Library of Scotland in August 1969. The second, darkened, state would not have been suitable for colouring. The final state was modified by Blake to resemble the first state, but is not known to have been coloured. See Keynes, *The Separate Plates*, pp. 45–9, where three states are reproduced, so that they may be distinguished. Blake's copper-plate was acquired by Colnaghi about 1880 and reprinted as required. It is now in the United States. [Ed.]

The engraving of Stothard's version was delayed by the death of Schiavonetti and of Cromek himself, and did not appear until two years later, when it became exceedingly popular. (Gilchrist, *Life*, i, pp. 288–90.)

Introduction to the Canterbury Tales in the original and also in a modernized version from Ogle's edition of 1741, illustrated by a portion of the engraving, with slight variation of detail, and a vignette, also by Blake and probably representing Canterbury Cathedral.[66] The Preface, which Gilchrist suggests may have been written by Dr. Malkin, contains an appreciation of the larger engraving, and explains that a part of Chaucer's poem is given 'that the heads as represented by Mr. Blake may be compared with the lineaments drawn by Chaucer, and I think the merit of the artist will be acknowledged.'

The section of the Notebook written about 1810 contains a note that 'This day is Publish'd Advertizements to Blake's Canterbury Pilgrims from Chaucer, Containing Anecdotes of Artists. Price 6ᵈ'[67] but this pamphlet was probably neither issued nor completed. The raw material for it exists in the so-called *Public Address* of the Notebook. In this disjointed set of notes Blake sets forth that good draughtsmanship is the essential foundation of both engraving and painting.

Painting is drawing on Canvas, & Engraving is drawing on Copper, & Nothing Else; & he who pretends to be either Painter or Engraver without being a Master of drawing is an Imposter.[68]

Blake complains that Heath and Stothard, Flaxman and even Romney held that drawing

. . . spoils an Engraver; for Each of these Men have repeatedly asserted this Absurdity to me in Condemnation of my Work & approbation of Heath's lame imitation, Stothard being such a fool as to suppose that his blundering blurs can be made out & delineated by any Engraver who knows how to cut dots & lozenges equally well with those little prints which I engraved after him five & twenty years ago & by which he got his reputation as a draughtsman.[69]

As always he contends that great art must be imaginative.

Men think they can Copy Nature as Correctly as I copy Imagination; this they will find Impossible, & all the Copiers or Pretended Copiers of Nature, from Rembrandt to Reynolds, Prove that Nature becomes to its Victim nothing but Blots & Blurs. Why are Copiers of Nature Incorrect, while Copiers of Imagination are Correct? this is manifest to all. . . . While the Works of Pope & Dryden are look'd upon as the same Art with those of Milton & Shakespeare, while the Works of Strange & Woollett are look'd upon as the same Art with those of Rafael & Albert Durer, there can be no Art in a Nation but such as is Subservient to the interest of the Monopolizing Trader. . . .

Nor can an Original Invention Exist with Execution, Organized & minutely delineated & Articulated, Either by God or Man. I do not mean smooth'd up & Niggled & Poco-Pen'd, and all the beauties pick'd out & blurr'd & blotted, but Drawn with a firm & decided hand at once, like Fuseli & Michael Angelo, Shakespeare & Milton.[70]

Blake hopes that this engraving will remove the misconception which has existed as to his own lack of execution:

the Lavish praise I have recieved from all Quarters for Invention & drawing has Generally been accompanied by this: 'he can concieve but he cannot Execute'; this Absurd assertion has done me, & may still do me, the greatest mischief. I call for Public protection against these Villains. I am, like others, Just Equal in Invention & in Execution as my works shew.[71]

The best comment on these notes is his own: 'Resentment for Personal Injuries has had some share in this Public Address, But Love to My Art & Zeal for my Country a much Greater.'[72]

The history of Blake's efforts to gain public acceptance for his 'Canterbury Pilgrims' has been set out at some length because it occupied much of his thoughts and energies. The most unfortunate result of the controversy was his breach with Stothard, and for a time with Flaxman, which rendered his isolation during the ensuing years greater, and also materially affected his chance of getting work as an engraver. Flaxman, who took Stothard's part, exonerating him from complicity with Cromek,* writes to Hayley

* Professor E. J. Morley informed the author in her selections from Crabb Robinson's *Reminiscences*, p. 20, that the passage concerning Flaxman should read, 'wh. Flaxman considered to have been *not* the wilful act of Stoddart'. She had accidentally omitted the negative.

on 4 May 1808—'. . . at present I have no intercourse with Mr. Blake.'* According to J. T. Smith Stothard was unaware of Blake's treatment of the subject until he knew of his engraving in 1810. This is difficult to credit as Blake's own fresco was exhibited in 1809 and his *Descriptive Catalogue* contains allusions to the work of his rival,† which were likely to have been brought to Stothard's notice. Moreover, the end of Cromek's letter, the earlier part of which has been already quoted, shows that Blake had expressed his indignation in 1807:

I will not detain you more than one minute. Why should you so *furiously rage* at the success of the little picture of 'The Pilgrimage'? Three thousand people have now *seen it and have approved of it.* Believe me, yours is *'the voice of one crying in the wilderness!'*

You say the subject is *low* and *contemptibly treated.* For his excellent mode of treating the subject the poet has been admired for the last 400 years! The poor painter has not yet the advantage of antiquity on his side, therefore, with some people, an apology may be necessary for him. The conclusion of one of Squire Simkin's letters to his mother in the *Bath Guide* will afford one. He speaks greatly to the purpose:

'I very well know
Both my subject and verse is exceedingly low;
But if any *great critic* finds fault with my letter,
He has *nothing to do but to send you a better.'*

With much respect for your talents, I remain, Sir, your real friend and well-wisher.

R. H. Cromek[73]

It seems probable from what is known of Stothard's character that he was not a party to Cromek's trickery, but that he was

* Flaxman wrote about the engravings for Cowper's translation of Milton's Italian Poems '. . . concerning the engravings Mr Raimbach thought very modestly that Mr Blake would execute the *outlines* better than himself but it was not possible to take the commission from the person that brought it to town, besides at present I have no intercourse with Mr Blake'. (*Blake Records*, pp. 189–90.)

† Gilchrist, *Life*, i, p. 250, expresses the view that Stothard did not know of Cromek's previous overtures to Blake, 'nor of the fact that a subscription paper for an engraving of the *Canterbury Pilgrims* had been circulated by Blake's friends.' He implies that this was circulated as early as 1806, but gives no further details. Blake's own *Prospectus* was not printed till May 1809.

induced to believe that Cromek had neither seen a drawing of the
Pilgrims by Blake nor given him an order for an engraving, and
that Blake, after admiring his own picture, had stolen the idea and
invented the rest of the story. To take Cromek's word as against
Blake's was, to say the least of it, a serious error of judgement in
one who had known Blake for years, and the tenacity with which
he clung to his opinion and nursed his wrath suggests that he was
unable to forgive Blake's strictures on his pictures in the *Descriptive Catalogue*. Gilchrist states on the authority of Linnell, an eye-
witness, that Blake some years later offered to shake hands
with Stothard at a gathering of artists, but was repulsed, and
again that Blake called on him when he was ill, but was refused
admittance. Gilchrist's statement was, however, controverted by
Stothard's son, who wrote to *The Athenaeum* in 1863:

I cannot admit Mr. Gilchrist's assertion that there was any
apparent ill-will between my father and Blake; for on one occasion
I was sent to Blake with a message from my father, when I found
him living in a court off the Strand, and met him on the stairs,
saying to me 'he had a battle with the devil below to obtain the
coals' which seemed to me to indicate madness.*

* 'Stothard and Blake,' by Robert T. Stothard, *The Athenaeum*, December
1863. R. T. Stothard also defends Cromek in a fashion which gives rise to
the suspicion that his facts may be as loose as his grammar:

Cromek was at that time very frequently at my father's, either for the
purpose of getting him to touch a proof for him, or on other matters of which
I then knew not the exact nature. I have heard it stated by my father that
Cromek got Blake to make for him a series of drawings from Blair's 'Grave';
Cromek found and explained to my father, that he had etched one of the
subjects but so indifferently and so carelessly [see Cumberland's 'Thoughts
on Outline' as an instance in that particular branch of his (Blake's) carelessness as an engraver] that he employed Schrovenitti [*sic*] to engrave them.
Cromek's success by their sale induced him to speculate farther, and he
employed my father (who had no time for going about and seeing what other
artists were employed upon or engaged in, and therefore his seeing Blake's
design of the 'Pilgrimage to Canterbury' is doubtful) to paint that picture for
him soon after he had completed the Burleigh staircase commission for the
Marquis of Exeter. Whether Cromek had seen it or not dates will prove; this
of which I am speaking was in 1804-5. Cromek was daily with my father,
living then as he was opposite nearly, at 64, and my father at 28 Newman
Street.
What I think proper to state, and as it may not be uninteresting to those
who are lovers of Art (for I was commissioned to write my father's life) I
shall begin, as will be seen in it, by stating that Cromek agreed to give my

Epigrams in the Notebook show Blake's exasperation with his old companions. Some of these have been already quoted. They have little or no merit apart from their value as autobiography: one of the happier efforts is the parallel suggested between Hayley's belief that Pope's translation is finer than Homer's original and the persuasion of Flaxman and Stothard that Blake's designs are improved by the interpretation of Schiavonetti:

Thus Hayley on his Toilette seeing the sope
Says, 'Homer is very much improv'd by Pope.'
Flaxman & Stothard, smelling a sweet savour,
Cry, 'Blakified drawing spoils painter & Engraver.'
While I looking up to my Umbrella,
Resolv'd to be a very Contrary Fellow,
Cry, looking up from Skumference to Center,
'No one can finish so high as the original inventor.' . . .
Thus Poor Schiavonetti died of the Cromek
A thing that's tied about the Examiner's neck.[74]

Blake's friendship with Fuseli was happily unaffected by Cromek's knavery, as the epigram in the Notebook shows. It is likely enough that Fuseli had openly supported Blake: he can scarcely have avoided expressing an opinion, at least in the matter of the Blair illustrations, for which he had written an introduction. It has been suggested that the writer of the attack on Fuseli in the *Weekly Messenger* was Robert Hunt,* brother of Leigh Hunt, and that he avenged himself for Blake's protest by the spiteful personalities of his articles in the *Examiner*. This hypothesis is strengthened by the epigram 'To H.'

You think Fuseli is not a Great Painter. I'm glad:
This is one of the best compliments he ever had.[75]

---

father for a painting from Chaucer 100 L. or 100 guineas, as that Author was a favourite with him, so much so that he could often relate stories from him. They determined on the 'Pilgrimage to Canterbury,' for there had been a little vignette of the same subject engraved for him, I think, before. In 1805 or 1806 the painting was shown to the public at Cromek's house. . . .

* Symons shows in *The Athenaeum* of 16 November 1907, by quoting a letter from John Hunt to Haydon (*Correspondence and Table-Talk*, vol. i, p. 358), that art criticisms in the *Examiner*, signed R. H., were by Robert Hunt.

Blake himself did not exhibit again in the Academy till 1808, after an interval of nine years, and for the last time. His two water-colours, 'Christ in the Sepulchre guarded by Angels' and 'Jacob's Dream', were hung in the Drawing and Miniature Room. Some of the pictures shown in his Exhibition of 1809 were painted in the years immediately preceding it, and his only known litho-graph, 'Enoch'*, belongs to 1806. Three water-colour drawings of the Ghost from *Hamlet*, Caesar's Ghost, and Jacques and the wounded Stag, were executed in 1806. These are bound up in a second folio Shakespeare, which was interleaved and illustrated by various artists while in the possession of the Revd. Joseph Thomas.† The volume contains three other drawings by Blake: Richard III and the Ghosts who appeared to him, a stiff and sym-metrical version of the 'Dream of Queen Catherine', dated 1809, and a symbolical design of a woman reclining on a cloud and reading a book, with a flying figure of a man below her, and in the bottom right-hand corner a horse on its hind legs on the edge of a cliff. This last drawing is also dated 1809, and appears to be

* This lithograph was contributed to Sennefelder's 'Specimens of Polyautography', which was published by G. J. Vollweiler in 1806. The print was formerly known as 'Job in Prosperity', the design being related to an earlier water-colour on this subject, but it was pointed out by J. H. Wicksteed that the Hebrew inscriptions proved it to represent Enoch, whose descendant Noah, with his sons Shem and Japheth, were identified by Blake with Poetry, Painting, and Music. See Keynes, *The Separate Plates*, pp. 43–4, with a reproduction of the lithograph. [Ed.]

† This Shakespeare folio was seen by the author when it was in the possession of George Macmillan. It is now in the British Museum, Depart-ment of Prints and Drawings, and the designs by Blake have been taken out so that they can be exhibited. [Ed.]

The author found that the volume contained illustrations said to be by Hamilton, Ker Porter, Harlow, Thurston, and Mulready, but they were not all signed. Blake's are signed with his name or initials. Gilchrist reproduces the Ghost from *Hamlet*, *Life*, vol. i, facing p. 272, but his reference on that page is inaccurate, since he says that the illustrations were executed for the Revd. Ker Porter. Robert Ker Porter, artist and traveller, was one of those who contributed to the volume. In an album in the British Museum Print Room, are drawings—'Had he not resembled my Father, I had done it'—with another study of Lady Macbeth's figure at the back, and 'Hamlet ad-ministering the Oath to his Friends', which Blake may have also intended for this book.

the same subject as that of Number VI in *A Descriptive Catalogue*—
'A Spirit vaulting from a cloud to turn and wind a fiery Pegasus.—
Shakspeare. The Horse of Intellect is leaping from the cliffs of
Memory and Reasoning; it is a barren Rock: it is also called the
Barren Waste of Locke and Newton.'

Blake's first set of illustrations for *Paradise Lost*, sometimes
known as the Liverpool set, belong to 1807, and in the following
year he designed another series of nine drawings which were
bought by Thomas Butts.*

During 1807 he had also painted a small tempera of 'The Last
Judgment' for the Countess of Egremont, a more elaborate version than that of the same subject in Blair's *Grave*.† This is described in a letter of 18 January 1808, to Ozias Humphry,[76]
through whom he had obtained the commission, although it
would appear that he had known Lord Egremont during his
Felpham days. The verses in the Notebook beginning 'The
Caverns of the Grave I've seen,'[77] refer to this painting, but it is
not known whether Lady Egremont received a dedicatory copy
of them.

Ozias Humphry was another friend with whom Blake's relations
remained undisturbed. Humphry was a well-known miniature
painter who spent some years in India: towards the end of his life
his sight began to fail and he took to crayon portraits, being
appointed in 1792 Painter in Crayons to His Majesty. He had himself secured in 1805 (four years and a half before his death) an
annuity of £100 from Lord Egremont as a compromise on his
proposed charge of six hundred guineas for the copy of a portrait
which he made while in Italy. He had been intimate with Romney,
and the oil painting sold in 1912 as 'Mrs. Siddons and Miss
Kemble', by Romney, was decided in the ensuing lawsuit to be
the work of Humphry and to represent the Ladies Waldegrave.

Another friend still faithful to Blake was George Cumberland,

---

* The Liverpool set is now in the H. E. Huntington Library, the Butts set
in the Boston Museum of Fine Arts.

† The painting is still at Petworth House in the keeping of the Earl of
Egremont.

and this in spite of the fact that his son was actually boarding for a time with Cromek.* On 18 December 1808 he wrote to ask Blake whether he could obtain for a gentleman, whose name he does not mention, a complete set of the illuminated books. He refers to some sketches from Raphael which he had sent to Blake through his son, and regrets that young George had seized the opportunity of asking for a drawing. 'The Holy family is like all your designs full of Genius and originality—I shall give it a handsome frame and shew it to all who come to my house.'† There follow some sentences referring to a plan of Blake's, which apparently came to nothing. 'When you answer this pray tell me if you have been able to do any thing with the Bookseller— something of that kind would be no bad thing, and might turn out a great one if a competition could be raised by this means among the genuine qymeliars‡ of talents of every sort.' He adds:

You talked also of publishing your new method of engraving— send it to me and I will do my best to prepare it for the Press.— perhaps when done you might with a few specimens of Plates make a little work for subscribers of it—as Du Crow did of his Aqua tinta,—selling about 6 Pages for a guinea to non Subbscriers —but if you do not chuse this method, we might insert it in Nicholsons Journal or the Monthly Magazine,—with reference to you for explanations.[78]

* Young George Cumberland testifies against the Cromeks. He wrote to his father on 20 December 1808: '. . . . it is very unpleasant at Mrs Cromek's. if you are coming to town after Christmas let me know or otherwise your advice they take great liberty's with me, my home & abroad amusements & Study's are frustrated by their selfish dispositions, *true Yorkshire.*' ('Letters of William Blake to George Cumberland, edited by Richard Garnett,' *The Hampstead Annual,* 1903, and *Blake Records,* p. 209 n.)

† Symons printed in the *Saturday Review* of 25 August 1906 some correspondence between Cumberland and his son, from which it appears that the sketches referred to were 'a few old Tracings from Raphael's Pictures in Fresco.' Young George says: 'I thought it a good opportunity to ask him for the Holy Family, which he gave very readily,' to which the elder Cumberland replies: 'I hope you did not ask Blake for the Picture very *importunately.*' (*Blake Records,* p. 210.)

‡ This word may be intended for 'cymeliarchs' from the Greek for 'treasurer' or 'storekeeper'. See *Letters,* ed. Keynes, p. 134 n. (*Blake Records,* p. 211, prints it 'appre[cia]tors'.) [Ed.]

Blake replies promptly:

I am very much obliged by your kind ardour in my cause, & should immediately Engage in reviving my former pursuits of printing if I had not now so long been turned out of the old channel into a new one, that it is impossible for me to return to it without destroying my present course. New Vanities, or rather new pleasures, occupy my thoughts. New profits seem to arise before me so tempting that I have already involved myself in engagements that preclude all possibility of promising anything. I have, however, the satisfaction to inform you that I have Myself begun to print an account of my various Inventions in Art, for which I have procured a Publisher, & am determined to pursue the plan of publishing what I may get printed without dis-arranging my time, which in future must alone be devoted to Designing & Painting. . . .[79]

This letter, with the exception of that to Humphry wholly con-cerned with a description of his painting of the Last Judgment, is the first private letter of Blake's extant since those to Hayley of 1805, and is therefore of special interest. It shows him in a posi-tion to decline a fairly lucrative commission, but there is no other information throwing light on his 'engagements', by which he may only mean preparations for his exhibition of 1809, and orders for paintings from Mr. Butts and others. The six water-colour drawings for the 'Hymn on the Nativity', now in the Whitworth Institute Gallery, Manchester, were executed in 1809, and a second series, now in the H. E. Huntington Library, probably about the same time. Nothing is known of the projected account of his Inventions in Art, either published or unpublished. He cannot refer to the *Descriptive Catalogue* of his Exhibition, as he speaks in the Advertisement of 'a Work on Art, now in the Press'.*

Blake's annotations to Reynolds's *Discourses* were also written

* It appears from passages in the Cumberland papers in the British Museum that Blake had indeed requested Cumberland to see through the press a work he had prepared on his 'Inventions in Art'; he afterwards decided to do this himself, though in the end the project was abandoned. See Geoffrey Keynes, 'George Cumberland', in *The Book Collector*, March 1970. [Ed.]

about 1808.* They give expression to his rebellion against the established convention, and were doubtless affected by his own recent experiences. 'This Man was Hired to Depress Art,' he says of Reynolds, who had died in 1792 but was still in Blake's eyes responsible for the prevalence of false ideals.

Having spent the Vigour of my Youth & Genius under the Opression of Sʳ Joshua & his Gang of Cunning Hired Knaves Without Employment & as much as could possibly be Without Bread, The Reader must Expect to Read in all my Remarks on these Books Nothing but Indignation & Resentment. While Sʳ Joshua was rolling in Riches, Barry was Poor & Unemploy'd except by his own Energy; Mortimer was call'd a Madman, & only Portrait Painting applauded & rewarded by the Rich & Great. Reynolds & Gainsborough Blotted & Blurred one against the other & Divided all the English World between them. Fuseli, Indignant, almost hid himself. I am hid.[80]

After such an opening the reader will not expect a judicial attitude, but Blake's notes bring out the main points at issue between the orthodox and the ecstatic, namely, the emphasis laid by the former on generalization, and their tendency to set industry above inspiration, a tendency probably stressed by Reynolds as salutary for the students of the Royal Academy to whom his *Discourses* were addressed. Reynolds, for example, says that 'there is a rule, obtained out of general nature, to contradict which is to fall into deformity.' Blake annotates this: 'What is General Nature? is there Such a Thing? what is General Knowledge? is there such a Thing? Strictly Speaking All Knowledge is Particular.'[81]

For Blake the Particular is the expression of individuality and accordingly Reynolds's dictum: 'If you mean to preserve the most perfect beauty in its most perfect state, you cannot express the passions . . .' calls for violent dissent.

What Nonsense!
Passion & Expression is Beauty Itself. The Face that is Incapable of Passion & Expression is deformity Itself. Let it be

* Blake's copy of the second edition of the *Discourses* is now in the Reading Room of the British Museum. The first volume only contains the marginalia, the other notes being in the Notebook.

Painted & Patch'd & Praised & Advertised for Ever, it will only
be admired by Fools.[82]

In the margin of the fifth page of the first *Discourse* Blake has
written:

Reynolds's Opinion was that Genius May be Taught & that all
Pretence to Inspiration is a Lie & a Deceit, to say the least of it.
For if it is a Deceit, the whole Bible is Madness. This Opinion
originates in the Greeks' calling the Muses Daughters of
Memory.[83]

And when Reynolds writes 'My notion of nature comprehends
not only the forms which nature produces, but also the nature and
internal fabrick and organization . . . of the human mind and
imagination,' Blake annotates 'Here is a Plain Confession that he
Thinks Mind & Imagination not to be above the Mortal &
Perishing Nature. Such is the End of Epicurean or Newtonian
Philosophy; it is Atheism.'[84]

Reynolds, who knows nothing of the Golden Age, ruined by
Satanic reason, which Art and Poetry, inspired by Imagination,
can alone restore, holds that 'The regular progress of cultivated
life is from necessaries to accommodations, from accommodations
to ornaments.' Blake dissents:

The Bible says That Cultivated Life Existed First. Uncultivated
Life comes afterwards from Satan's Hirelings. Necessaries, Accomodations & Ornaments are the whole of Life. Satan took away
Ornament First. Next he took away Accomodations, & Then he
became Lord & Master of Necessaries.[85]

Yet Blake is sometimes in agreement, but when this is the case
he usually points out that Reynolds has been inconsistent with
his own doctrines. For instance, on 'A firm and determined outline is one of the characteristics of the great style in painting;
and let me add, that he who possesses the knowledge of the
exact form which every part of nature ought to have, will be
fond of expressing that knowledge with correctness and precision

in all his works,' Blake notes: 'A Noble Sentence! Here is a
Sentence, Which overthrows all his Book.'[86]

Mention of the Venetian, Dutch, and Flemish schools provokes,
of course, much railing, but Reynolds and his annotator are united
in their admiration of Poussin. Several of the Epigrams in the
Notebook question the genuineness of Reynolds's admiration for
Michelangelo, and it is interesting to note that Farington represents Northcote, his biographer, as entertaining a similar suspicion:

Oct. 18, 1803
Northcote doubted his having any real feeling for the excel-
lencies of Michael Angelo, & thought his praise was in compliance
with established opinion.

One perceives in these annotations to Reynolds's *Discourses* a
jarring note of resentment for personal injuries which is frankly
admitted in Blake's *Public Address*. The same feeling was to
prompt him to his one great effort to secure public recognition for
himself as the representative of imaginative art, his Exhibition
of 1809. His lyric ecstasy had fallen years ago on deaf ears, the
last words of his mystic gospel were not yet written. With poets
and mystics he was not in daily rivalry, but the art of painting,
as he conceived it, had been mocked in his own person, the true
prophet had been feebly interpreted and forestalled by the false:
it was as a painter, therefore, that he struggled for the suffrage of
his contemporaries. He stood like a child with his back to the wall
waving his little flag in a corner and shouting with pathetic
truculence. But the child's voice has been heard at last, what
matter if his words are petulant and a little absurd? He was in
truth the genius above the age, his flag the banner of imaginative
art. Whatever the changes of fashion, however his faults and
failures may be exaggerated or minimized from time to time,
his claim is never likely to be seriously gainsaid by those qualified
to judge. Imperfect though his vessel may be, in it he indeed
bore the divine fire.

The Exhibition was held at James Blake's house in Broad
Street, Golden Square, and was open from May till September.

The motto of the Advertisement, 'Fit audience find tho' few,' disclaims competition with the curious crowd who, as Cromek boasted, had been to see Stothard's Canterbury Pilgrims. Besides naming the chief pictures the Advertisement explains the advantages of a 'Portable Fresco' for the decoration of buildings, and promises an account of Blake's recovery of the lost art of fresco painting. As this account has disappeared or was never written, J. T. Smith's description may be quoted:

Blake's modes of preparing his ground, and laying them over his panels for painting, mixing his colours, and manner of working, were those which he considered to have been practised by the earliest fresco-painters, whose productions still remain, in numerous instances, vivid and permanently fresh. His ground was a mixture of whiting and carpenter's glue,* which he passed over several times in thin coatings: his colours he ground himself, and also united them with the same sort of glue, but in a much weaker state. He would, in the course of painting a picture, pass a very thin transparent wash of glue-water over the whole of the parts he had worked upon, and then proceed with his finishing.

This process I have tried, and find, by using my mixtures warm, that I can produce the same texture as possessed in Blake's pictures of the Last Judgment, and others of his productions, particularly in Varley's curious picture of the personified Flea. Blake preferred mixing his colours with carpenter's glue, to gum, on account of the latter cracking in the sun, and becoming humid in moist weather.[87]

Gilchrist gives Linnell's explanation, which supplements Smith's in some respects:

He evidently founded his claim to the name *fresco* on the material he used, which was water-colour on a plaster ground (literally glue and whiting); but he always called it either fresco, gesso, or plaster. And he certainly laid this ground on too much like plaster on a wall. When so laid on to canvas or linen, it was sure to crack, and, in some cases, for want of care and protection from damp, would go to ruin. Some of his pictures in this material on board

---

* A. H. Palmer speaks of ' "Blake's white," a pigment for making which Blake gave my father the recipe.' (*Life and Letters of Samuel Palmer*, 1892, p. 51.)

have been preserved in good condition, and so have a few even on cloth. They come nearer to *tempera* in process than to anything else, inasmuch as white was laid on and mixed with the colours which were tempered with common carpenter's glue.[88]

Linnell also said that he had lent Blake a copy of Cennino Cennini's Treatise,* and Blake had told him that his materials and methods were the same as those described by Cennini. Blake complains in his Advertisement that his pictures had been regularly refused at the Royal Academy. He may refer only to the exclusion of his frescoes from the main rooms where the oil paintings were hung, as he had exhibited five times in the drawing and miniature room. On the other hand his last exhibits were two water-colour drawings, and it is possible that his frescoes had been actually refused during the nine years in which he was not represented. He alludes to a description of his work as 'but an unscientific and irregular Eccentricity, a Madman's Scrawls'[89]: this may refer to some Press criticism which has not yet been traced, as it is inapplicable to the first attack in the *Examiner*, and the Exhibition itself was the excuse for the second. The last sentence sounds his challenge:

If Italy is enriched and made great by RAPHAEL, if MICHAEL ANGELO is its supreme glory, if Art is the glory of a Nation, if Genius and Inspiration are the great Origin and Bond of Society, the distinction my Works have obtained from those who best understand such things, calls for my Exhibition as the greatest of Duties to my Country.[90]

The *Descriptive Catalogue*, included in the 2s. 6d. charge for admission to the Exhibition, is a duodecimo volume of thirty-eight leaves in a grey paper wrapper: only eighteen copies of it have been recorded.† Nine frescoes, including some of the 'experiment pictures' to which reference has already been made, and seven water-colour drawings were shown, including the 'Penance

* For a note written in Cennini's *Trattato della Pittura* see *Complete Writings*, p. 779.
† The Stirling-Maxwell copy of the *Descriptive Catalogue* at Pollak House, Glasgow, has bound up with it an Advertisement of the *Catalogue* itself. See *Complete Writings*, p. 562.

of Jane Shore', painted about 1779. Four of the frescoes and one of the drawings have disappeared: the remainder are reproduced in the third volume of the Nonesuch Edition, 1925.

The Catalogue is not merely a commentary on the sixteen exhibits, it is a manifesto eulogizing Raphael and Michelangelo at the expense of Titian and Correggio, Rubens and Rembrandt. In reading Blake's fierce and foolish denunciations of Rubens as 'a most outrageous demon', and Correggio as 'a soft and effeminate, and consequently a most cruel demon, whose whole delight is to cause endless labour to whoever suffers him to enter his mind,' two facts must be borne in mind. Blake had seen very few original paintings by old masters: his opinions were based mainly on bad copies, or on prints, not always of the best. He was, therefore, really attacking the supposed influence of those masters, whom he ignorantly condemned, on the moderns whose style he disliked. Moreover, as already hinted, he had little talent for discriminating assimilation, and the failure of any such effort was regarded by him, not as the result of his own limitations, but as manful resistance to temptation by 'blotting and blurring demons' and insidious attacks by the spirits of Titian and Correggio. In his furious casting-out of error he did not distinguish between bad art and art foreign to his own genius. Blake has double dotted the 'i' in this mistake, but he is by no means the only artist who has made it. He states his case in the Preface:

The quarrel of the Florentine with the Venetian is not because he does not understand Drawing, but because he does not understand Colouring. How should he? he who does not know how to draw a hand or a foot, know how to colour it?

Colouring does not depend on where the Colours are put, but on where the lights and darks are put, and all depends on Form or Outline, on where that is put; where that is wrong, the Colouring never can be right; and it is always wrong in Titian and Correggio, Rubens and Rembrandt. Till we get rid of Titian and Correggio, Rubens and Rembrandt, We never shall equal Rafael and Albert Durer, Michael Angelo, and Julio Romano.[91]

His exposition is continued in the course of comments on his various pictures.

The Venetian and Flemish practice is broken lines, broken masses, and broken colours. Mr. B's practice is unbroken lines, unbroken masses, and unbroken colours. Their art is to lose form; his art is to find form, and to keep it. His arts are opposite to theirs in all things.[92]

And again:

If losing and obliterating the outline constitutes a Picture, Mr. B. will never be so foolish as to do one. Such art of losing the outlines is the art of Venice and Flanders; it loses all character, and leaves what some people call expression; but this is a false notion of expression; expression cannot exist without character as its stamina; and neither character nor expression can exist without firm and determinate outline.[93]

In his campaign against 'generalization' he raises the importance of outline to a mystic truth:

The great and golden rule of art, as well as of life, is this: That the more distinct, sharp, and wirey the bounding line, the more perfect the work of art; and the less keen and sharp, the greater is the evidence of weak imitation, plagiarism, and bungling. Great inventors, in all ages, knew this; Protogenes and Apelles knew each other by this line. Rafael and Michael Angelo and Albert Dürer are known by this and this alone. The want of this determinate and bounding form evidences the want of idea in the artist's mind, and the pretence of the plagiary in all its branches. How do we distinguish the oak from the beech, the horse from the ox, but by the bounding outline? How do we distinguish one face or countenance from another, but by the bounding line and its infinite inflexions and movements? What is it that builds a house and plants a garden, but the definite and determinate? What is it that distinguishes honesty from knavery, but the hard and wirey line of rectitude and certainty in the actions and intentions? Leave out this line, and you leave out life itself; all is chaos again, and the line of the almighty must be drawn out upon it before man or beast can exist.[94]

The Catalogue closes quietly with a dignified expression of self-confidence:

If a man is master of his profession, he cannot be ignorant that he is so; and if he is not employed by those who pretend to encourage art, he will employ himself, and laugh in secret at the pretences of the ignorant, while he has every night dropped into his shoe, as soon as he puts it off, and puts out the candle, and gets into bed, a reward for the labours of the day, such as the world cannot give, and patience and time await to give him all that the world can give. [95]

It may be left to professional critics to discuss how far Blake's own achievements justify his pretensions. His absorption in great imaginative conceptions sometimes made him blind to actual results: his reckless statement to Crabb Robinson that the diagrams in Law's translation of Boehme could not have been bettered by Michelangelo illustrated this confusion. But if his frequent boasts of his equality with Michelangelo and Raphael excite a smile it must be remembered that he never had the chance for which he longed of executing great decorative frescoes, and it may be that had he been enabled to work on a large scale he would himself have recognized and amended some of his weaknesses and defects. And—fruitless wish—could John Hawkins but have sent Blake not to Rome, but to Borgo San Sepolcro and Arezzo! Was not Piero della Francesca the master from whom he would have learnt the most? He writes of four of the drawings, 'The Body of Abel found by Adam and Eve', 'The Soldiers casting lots for Christ's Garments', 'Jacob's Ladder', and 'Ruth':

The above four drawings the Artist wishes were in Fresco on an enlarged scale to ornament the altars of churches, and to make England, like Italy, respected by respectable men of other countries on account of Art. It is not the want of Genius that can hereafter be laid to our charge; the Artist who has done these Pictures and Drawings will take care of that; let those who govern the Nation take care of the other. The times require that every one should speak out boldly: England expects that every man should do his duty, in Arts, as well as in Arms, or in the Senate. [96]

There is no indication whether the Exhibition was a success in point of either quality or quantity of visitors. Blake sent Ozias Humphry a ticket of admission and also a copy of the *Catalogue*, with a note saying that it explained the difference between their theories of art. [97] Humphry had, perhaps, deprecated the lack of colour in the 'Last Judgment', which Blake had painted for Lady Egremont.* Cumberland, hearing of the exhibition from his son, wrote at once for two copies of the *Catalogue*, but there is no record of a visit. Southey quotes the greater part of Blake's commentary on 'The Ancient Britons' in *The Doctor*, and he refers to it as 'one of his worst pictures.'⁹⁸ In 1830 he wrote of the Exhibition: 'The colouring of all was as if it had consisted merely of black and red ink in all intermixture. Some of the designs were hideous, especially those which he considered as most supernatural in their conception and likenesses. In others you perceived that nothing but madness had prevented him from being the sublimest painter of this or any other country.'⁹⁹ Crabb Robinson, who had as yet no personal acquaintance with Blake, had undertaken to write a paper on his work for a German magazine, the *Vaterländisches Museum*, and therefore went to 28 Broad Street in search of copy. He wrote in his Reminiscences of Blake, dated the 19th February 1852, and based on an account written in 1825:

> These paintings filled several rooms of an ordinary dwelling-house, and for the sight a half-crown was demanded of the visitor, for which he had a catalogue. This catalogue I possess, and it is a very curious exposure of the state of the artist's mind. I wished to send it to Germany and to give a copy to Lamb and others, so I took four, and giving 10*s*. bargained that I should be at liberty to go again. 'Free! as long as you live,' said the brother, astonished at such liberality, which he had never experienced before, nor I dare say did afterwards.†

His description of the pictures themselves, as might be expected after his comments on the Blair illustrations, is unsympathetic and inaccurate:

---

* It would appear from the index to the Royal Academy Catalogue that Blake also exhibited in 1800 'The Last Judgment' and 'The Loaves and Fishes'.

† Symons, *Blake*, p. 283, states that 'like' is first written, and replaced by 'live'. In the earlier reminiscences of the year 1810, ibid., p. 279, is a short reference to the Exhibition: in this Robinson gives a less dramatic and probably more accurate account of his conversation with James Blake. 'I took 4—telling the brother I hoped he would let me come in again. He said, "Oh! as often as you please." '

There were about thirty oil-paintings, the colouring excessively dark and high, the veins black, and the colour of the primitive men like that of the Red Indians. In his estimation they would probably be the primitive men. Many of his designs were unconscious imitations. This appears also in his published works, the designs of *Blair's Grave*, which Fuseli and Schiavonetti highly extolled—and in his designs to illustrate Job, published after his death for the benefit of his widow.

It will be observed that Robinson gets the number of pictures and the medium wrong, and his general allegation of unconscious imitation means no more than that he had seen other pictures of similar subjects of which he was reminded. His remark about Red Indians probably applies chiefly to the fresco of 'The Ancient Britons', as he says in his article that in this picture the 'naked forms are almost crimson,' at the same time describing it as Blake's 'greatest and most perfect work.' Of the 'Canterbury Pilgrims' he says that 'Lamb preferred it greatly to Stodart's, and declared that Blake's description was the finest criticism he had ever read of Chaucer's poem.'

Charles Lamb himself, induced no doubt to visit the Exhibition by the gift of the Catalogue, is more enthusiastic than Crabb Robinson about Blake's work. On 15 May 1824 he wrote to Bernard Barton:

Blake is a real name, I assure you, and a most extraordinary man, if he be still living. He is the Robert Blake, whose wild designs accompany a splendid folio edition of the Night Thoughts, which you may have seen, in one of which he pictures the parting of soul & body by a solid mass of human form floating off God knows how from a lumpish mass (fac simile to itself) left behind on the dying bed. He paints in water colours, marvellous strange pictures, visions of his brain which he asserts that he has seen. They have great merit. He has *seen* the old welch bards on Snowdon —he has seen the Beautifullest, the Strongest, & the Ugliest Man, left alone from the Massacre of the Britons by the Romans, & has painted them from memory (I have seen his paintings) and asserts them to be as good as the figures of Raphael & Angelo, but not better, as they had precisely the same retrovisions & prophetic visions with himself. The painters in Oil (which he will have it that neither of them practised) he affirms to have been the ruin of art, and affirms that all the while he was engaged in his water-paintings, Titian was disturbing him, Titian the Ill Genius of oil Painting. His Pictures, one in particular the Canterbury Pilgrims (far above Stothard's) have great merit, but hard, dry, yet with grace. He has written a Catalogue of them, with a most spirited criticism on Chaucer, but mystical and full of Vision.[100]

Lamb kept his copy of the *Catalogue*, binding it in one cover with Elia's *Confessions of a Drunkard*, Southey's *Wat Tyler*, and the *Poems* of Rochester and Lady Winchelsea.[101] He also possessed an engraving of the Pilgrims, one of the two copies which Crabb Robinson bought from Mrs. Blake after her husband's death. The last paragraphs of Blake's description of his fresco of the 'Canterbury Pilgrims' (concerning which Cromek's parlour boarder wrote gleefully to his father, 'He has given Stothard a compleet set down') have already been referred to, but it is in the earlier part that Blake's enjoyment and understanding of Chaucer, so sympathetic to Lamb, appears unalloyed by controversial matter. W. P. Ker has suggested that 'Milton's Samson may help to explain what Blake meant when he insisted that great ideal figures are not abstract.' So Blake's own comments on the 'Canterbury Pilgrims' help to explain why he attaches so much importance to 'minute particulars', and the distinction between 'minute particulars' and irrelevant details. He writes:

The characters of Chaucer's Pilgrims are the characters which compose all ages and nations: as one age falls, another rises, different to mortal sight, but to immortals only the same; for we see the same characters repeated again and again, in animals, vegetables, minerals, and in men; nothing new occurs in identical existence; Accident ever varies, Substance can never suffer change nor decay.

Of Chaucer's characters, as described in his Canterbury Tales, some of the names or titles are altered by time, but the characters themselves for ever remain unaltered, and consequently they are the physiognomies or lineaments of universal human life, beyond which Nature never steps. Names alter, things never alter. I have known multitudes of those who would have been monks in the age of monkery, who in this deistical age are deists. As Newton

numbered the stars, and as Linneus numbered the plants, so
Chaucer numbered classes of men. . . . Thus the reader will observe, that Chaucer makes every one of his characters perfect in
his kind; every one is an Antique Statue; the image of a class,
and not of an imperfect individual.[102]

It is tempting to linger over Blake's delightful descriptions of
Chaucer's different personages, but the whole should be read and
compared with the engraving. One sample must serve here:

The principal figure in the next groupe is the Good Parson; an
Apostle, a real Messenger of Heaven, sent in every age for its light
and its warmth. This man is beloved and venerated by all, and
neglected by all: He serves all, and is served by none; he is,
according to Christ's definition, the greatest of his age. Yet he is a
Poor Parson of a town. Read Chaucer's description of the Good
Parson, and bow the head and the knee to him, who, in every age,
sends us such a burning and a shining light. Search, O ye rich and
powerful, for these men and obey their counsel, then shall the
golden age return: But alas! you will not easily distinguish him
from the Friar or the Pardoner; they, also, are 'full solemn men,'
and their counsel you will continue to follow.[103]

The most striking picture in the exhibition, now unfortunately
lost, was apparently 'The Ancient Britons', representing the only
three who escaped from the battle of Camlan, the Strongest Man,
the Beautifullest Man, and the Ugliest Man. In his own description of this fresco Blake says:

The Strong Man represents the human sublime. The Beautiful
Man represents the human pathetic, which was in the wars of
Eden divided into male and female. The Ugly Man represents the
human reason. They were originally one man, who was fourfold;
he was self-divided, and his real humanity slain on the stems of
generation, and the form of the fourth* was like the Son of
God.[104]

* It will be noted that this explanation introduces Blake's customary fourfold division, the fourth factor being the eternal, which has the power of
uniting and transfiguring the whole. Maung Ba-Han (*William Blake, His
Mysticism*, pp. 77–80) traces a correspondence with the Four Zoas. Crabb
Robinson, in describing the painting, refers to 'Owen's Triads', and
Mr. J. E. Lloyd, Hon. Librarian of the University of North Wales, Bangor,
sent the author a translation of this triad which is no. 85, first series, in the

Blake goes on to say that the Beautiful Man represents his own idea of intellectual Beauty, and 'acts from duty and anxious solicitude for the fates of those for whom he combats.' The Strong Man is 'a receptacle of Wisdom, a sublime energizer,' and 'acts from conscious superiority, and marches on in fearless dependance on the divine decrees, raging with the inspirations of a prophetic mind.' The Ugly Man, on whose villainous aspect Blake dwells with gusto, 'acts from love of carnage, and delight in the savage barbarities of war, rushing with sportive precipitation into the very teeth of the affrighted enemy.' The battlefield is strewn with dead and dying, armed Roman and naked Britons, and the blood-red sun sets behind mountains, among which rise Druid temples.

Fortunately a young art student, whose memories of Blake are reserved for a later chapter, has left some account of this painting, although he does not mention a visit to the exhibition. Seymour Kirkup says in a letter to Lord Houghton of 25 March 1870:

I thought it his best work—a battle from the Welsh Triads. The three last men who remained of Arthur's army, and who defeated the enemy—the strongest man, the handsomest man, and the ugliest man. As he was an enemy to oil painting, which he said was the ruin of painting, he invented a method of applying fresco to canvas, and this life-size picture was the result. It made so great an impression on me that I made a drawing of it fifty years afterwards, which I gave to Swinburne. You can see it. It (the picture) must have been about 14 feet by 10. In texture it was rather mealy, as we call it, and was too red; the sun seemed setting in blood. It was not Greek in character. Though the figures reminded one of Hercules, Apollo, and Pan, they were naked Britons. If you should ever hear of it, it is worth seeking. There is more power and drawing in it than in any of his works that I have known, even in Blair's grave, respecting which he was enraged against Schiavonetti for correcting some defects.[105]

Myvyrian Archaeology, ii, issued by William Owen, Owen Jones, and Edward Williams in 1801: 'Three men escaped from Camlan, Morfran son of Tegid, Sanddef Angel-face, and Glewlwyd of the Mighty Grasp: Morfran, by reason of his ugliness—all thought he was a devil and avoided him: Sanddef was so fair and beautiful that none lifted a hand against him, deeming him an angel; Glewlwyd was so huge and powerful that all fled before him.' See p. 269

The drawing to which Kirkup refers has unluckily not been discovered among Swinburne's papers. His testimony is the more interesting as he was not an admirer of Blake's work. He describes himself as belonging to 'the opposite party of colourists', and says that his *beau ideal* was the union of Phidias and Titian.' 'Blake', he writes to W. M. Rossetti, 'had but little effect in the works that I remember. I should have liked the heads more British and less Grecian.'[106]

It would seem from these references that 'The Ancient Britons' and the 'Pilgrims' made most impression on the minds of Blake's contemporaries: Crabb Robinson observed, but dares not describe in his article, 'The Spiritual Form of Pitt guiding Behemoth and The Spiritual Form of Nelson guiding Leviathan':* the water-colour drawings—lovely as we know some of them to be—attract no special attention. A second article in the *Examiner*, far more intemperate than the first, was probably also written by Robert Hunt. A few extracts will account for Blake's bitter indignation.

If beside the stupid and mad-brained political project of their rulers, the sane part of the people of England required fresh proof of the alarming increase of the effects of insanity, they will be too well convinced from its having lately spread into the hitherto sober region of Art. I say hitherto, because I cannot think with many, that the vigorous genius of the present worthy Keeper of the Royal Academy is touched, though no one can deny that his Muse has been on the verge of insanity, since it has brought forth, with more legitimate offspring, the furious and disturbed beings of extravagant imagination. But, when the ebullitions of a distempered brain are mistaken for the sallies of genius by those whose works have exhibited the soundest thinking in art, the malady has indeed attained a pernicious height, and it becomes a duty to endeavour to arrest its progress. Such is the case with the productions and admirers of William Blake, an unfortunate lunatic, whose personal inoffensiveness secures him from confinement, and, consequently, of whom no public notice would have

* Both are now in the Tate Gallery. The former was exhibited several years later at the Royal Academy absurdly entitled 'The Right Hon. William Pitt.' Cf. *Life of Samuel Palmer*, p. 347.

been taken, if he was not forced on the notice and animadversion of the *Examiner*, in having been held up to public admiration by many esteemed amateurs and professors as a genius in some respect original and legitimate. The praises which these gentlemen bestowed last year on this unfortunate man's illustrations of *Blair's Grave*, have, in feeding his vanity, stimulated him to publish his madness more largely, and thus again exposed him, if not to the derision, at least to the pity of the public. . . . Thus encouraged, the poor man fancies himself a great master, and has painted a few wretched pictures, some of which are unintelligible allegory, others an attempt at sober character by caricature representation, and the whole 'blotted and blurred,' and very badly drawn. These he calls an Exhibition, of which he has published a Catalogue, or rather a farrago of nonsense, unintelligibleness, and egregious vanity, the wild effusions of a distempered brain. . . . That insanity should elevate itself to this fancied importance, is the usual effect of the unfortunate malady; but that men of taste, in their sober senses, should mistake its unmeaning and distorted conceptions for the flashes of genius, is indeed a phenomenon.[107]

Blake's comment on this outrageous attack is to be found in the *Public Address* of the Notebook:

The manner in which my Character has been blasted these thirty years, both as an artist & a Man, may be seen particularly in a Sunday Paper cal'd the Examiner, Publish'd in Beaufort Buildings (We all know that Editors of Newspapers trouble their heads very little about art & science, & that they are always paid for what they put in upon these ungracious Subjects), & the manner in which I have routed out the nest of villains will be seen in a Poem concerning my Three years' Herculean Labours at Felpham, which I will soon Publish. Secret Calumny & open Professions of Friendship are common enough all the world over, but have never been so good an occasion of Poetic Imagery. When a Base Man means to be your Enemy he always begins with being your Friend. Flaxman cannot deny that one of the very first Monuments he did, I gratuitously designed for him; at the same time he was blasting my character as an Artist to Macklin, my Employer, as Macklin told me at the time; how much of his Homer & Dante he will allow to be mine I do not know, as he went far enough off to Publish them, even to Italy, but the Public will know & Posterity will know.

Many People are so foolish [as] to think that they can wound Mr Fuseli over my Shoulder; they will find themselves mistaken; they could not wound even Mr Barry so.[108]

Blake here suggests that the *Examiner* is the paid agent of those who have injured his reputation, of 'that nest of villains' with whom he has already dealt in a poem concerning his labours at Felpham. This may refer to some poem now lost, but it is possible that Blake is alluding to those pages of *Milton* in which he describes the struggle to free himself from the interference of 'spiritual enemies', and that in the phrase 'Herculean Labours' he refers to the 'fight thro' a Hell of terrors and horrors . . .' in a divided existence which was rewarded by the visionary knowledge of spiritual unity symbolized by the end of the poem. It was one of the unfortunate results of the Cromek controversy that he had revived old grudges against Flaxman and now regarded him as having always been a false friend. Three of the four known copies of *Milton* had probably been printed by 1808, but there is no evidence that any of them had been 'published', that is, issued by Blake, before the *Public Address* was written. In the *Public Address* Blake expresses respect for Hogarth as an original painter whose execution can be neither copied nor improved. He had engraved 'When my Hero in Court Appears' (from the *Beggar's Opera*) after Hogarth in 1790 for Boydell,* and his water-colour drawing of 'Satan, Sin and Death at Hell's Gate' follows closely Hogarth's treatment of the same subject.†

It would seem that neither criticism nor any disillusion as to the fitness of his audience prevented Blake from entertaining the idea of another exhibition. The notes in the Notebook known as *A Vision of the Last Judgment*, written about 1810, have as subtitle: 'For the year 1810. Additions to Blake's Catalogue of Pictures &c'[109] and are chiefly concerned with a fresco of the Last Judgment, a different rendering of the subject from that painted

---

* See Keynes, *The Separate Plates*, pp. 73–4.

† This large water-colour drawing, properly entitled 'Satan comes to the Gates of Hell', is now in the H. E. Huntington Library and Art Gallery. Two versions in pencil are also known. [Ed.]

for the Countess of Egremont and described in the letter to Ozias
Humphry.

W. M. Rossetti states that this fresco measured seven feet by
five and was estimated to contain 1000 figures. J. T. Smith is
enthusiastic about it.

Had he fortunately lived till the next year's exhibition at
Somerset-house, the public would then have been astonished at
his exquisite finishing of a Fresco picture of the Last Judgment,
containing upwards of one thousand figures, many of them wonder-
fully conceived and grandly drawn. The lights of this extraordinary performance have the appearance of silver and gold;
but upon Mrs. Blake's assuring me that there was no silver used, I
found, upon a closer examination, that a blue wash had been
passed over those parts of the gilding which receded, and the
lights of the forward objects, which were also of gold, were
heightened with a warm colour, to give the appearance of the
two metals.[110]

From his allusion to Mrs. Blake as his informant it would
appear that Smith saw the fresco after her husband's death; much
importance need not therefore be attached to a story told by
Gilchrist. 'Blake, on looking up one day at this *fresco*, which
hung in his front room, candidly exclaimed, as one who was
present tells me, "I spoiled that—made it darker; it was much
finer, but a Frenchwoman here [a fellow-lodger] didn't like it." '
Gilchrist also says that the painting was a favourite of Blake's
and that he lavished finishing touches on it during his last years.
The fresco has now unfortunately disappeared, but sketches
probably used for it are still in existence.*

The conception of a Last Judgment made a special appeal to
Blake, both as artist and as mystic, because he believed that error
must take definite shape before it could be cast out: however bad

---

* George Cumberland junior with his brother called on Blake at 17 South
Molton Street on 30 January 1815 and reported to his father about this
picture: 'he received us well & shewed his large drawing in Water colors of
the last Judgement; he has been labouring at it till it is nearly as black as
your Hat—the only lights are those of a *Hellish Purple*'. (*Blake Records*,
p. 235.) [Ed.]

things might be there was the consoling thought that an essential development was taking place. In these notes he explains that:

The Last Judgment [will be] when all those are Cast away who trouble Religion with Questions concerning Good & Evil or Eating of the Tree of those Knowledges or Reasonings which hinder the Vision of God, turning all into a Consuming Fire. When Imagination, Art & Science & all Intellectual Gifts, all the Gifts of the Holy Ghost, are look'd upon as of no use & only Contention remains to Man, then the Last Judgment begins, & its Vision is seen by the [Imaginative Eye] of Every one according to the situation he holds. . . . The Last Judgment is one of these Stupendous Visions. I have represented it as I saw it; to different People it appears differently as everything else does; for tho' on Earth things seem Permanent, they are less permanent than a Shadow, as we all know too well.[111]

The Last Judgment is an Overwhelming of Bad Art & Science' Mental Things are alone Real; what is call'd Corporeal, Nobody Knows of its Dwelling Place: it is in Fallacy, & its Existence an Imposture. Where is the Existence Out of Mind or Thought? Where is it but in the Mind of a Fool? Some People flatter themselves that there will be No Last Judgment & that Bad Art will be adopted & mixed with Good Art, That Error or Experiment will make a Part of Truth, & they Boast that it is its Foundation; these People flatter themselves: I will not Flatter them. Error is Created. Truth is Eternal. Error, or Creation, will be Burned up, & then, & not till Then, Truth or Eternity will appear. It is Burnt up the Moment Men cease to behold it. I assert for My Self that I do not behold the outward Creation & that to me it is hindrance & not Action; it is as the Dirt upon my feet, No part of Me. 'What,' it will be Question'd, 'When the Sun rises, do you not see a round disk of fire somewhat like a Guinea?' O no, no, I see an Innumerable company of the Heavenly host crying 'Holy, Holy, Holy is the Lord God Almighty.' I question not my Corporeal or Vegetative Eye any more than I would Question a Window concerning a Sight. I look thro' it & not with it.[112]

Blake explains in the course of these notes that all the personages depicted symbolize not individuals but states through which man passes like a traveller.

It ought to be understood that the Persons, Moses & Abraham, are not here meant, but the States Signified by those Names, the Individuals being representatives or Visions of those States as they were reveal'd to Mortal Man in the Series of Divine Revelations as they are written in the Bible; these various States I have seen in my Imagination; when distant they appear as One Man, but as you approach they appear Multitudes of Nations.[113]

Some of the figures are purely symbolical.

Sin is also represented as a female bound in one of the Serpent's folds, surrounded by her fiends. Death is Chain'd to the Cross, & Time falls together with death, dragged down by a demon crown'd with Laurel. . . .[114]

His interpretation is not without humour:

The Ladies will be pleas'd to see that I have represented the Furies by Three Men & not by three Women. . . . The Spectator may suppose them Clergymen in the Pulpit, scourging Sin instead of Forgiving it.[115]

These notes abound in passages which throw light on Blake's metaphysics: several have already been quoted. Another extract, pathetically autobiographical, may be given here:

Some People & not a few Artists have asserted that the Painter of this Picture would not have done so well if he had been properly Encourag'd. Let those who think so, reflect on the State of Nations under Poverty & their incapability of Art; tho' Art is Above Either, the Argument is better for Affluence than Poverty; & tho' he would not have been a greater Artist, yet he would have produc'd Greater works of Art in proportion to his means.[116]

Blake hated money, but money is as obtrusive by its absence as by its excess, and it is one of the tragic elements in his life that his old age was even less free from pecuniary care than his youth had been. It is probably true enough that he would have done greater work had he but met with a few more patrons as generous and as self-effacing as Thomas Butts. To imagine him peacefully engaged on public work for State or Church is more difficult. Is there even yet a committee or dean and chapter who could be relied on not to obstruct the path of genius?

VII
YEARS OF NEGLECT

I rose up at the dawn of day—
Get thee away! get thee away!
Pray'st thou for Riches? away! away!
This is the Throne of Mammon grey.

Said I, 'this sure is very odd.
I took it to be the Throne of God.
For every Thing besides I have:
It is only for Riches that I can crave.

I have Mental Joy & Mental Health
And Mental Friends & Mental wealth;
I've a Wife I love & that loves me;
I've all But Riches Bodily.

I am in God's presence night & day,
And he never turns his face away.
The accuser of sins by my side does stand
And he holds my money bag in his hand.

For my worldly things God makes him pay,
And he'd pay for more if to him I would pray;
And so you may do the worst you can do;
Be assur'd Mr devil I won't pray to you.

Then If for Riches I must not Pray,
God knows I little of Prayers need say.
So as a Church is known by its Steeple,
If I pray it must be for other People.

He says, if I do not worship him for a God,
I shall eat coarser food & go worse shod;
So as I don't value such things as these,
You must do, Mr devil, just as God please.'[1]

Thus wrote Blake after his failure to secure public recognition as a prophet of imaginative art, and it was decreed that neither riches nor fame should be his lot.

Only one letter has been preserved for the years 1810–17, but this is not remarkable as he had few regular correspondents who kept any of his letters. Communication with Hayley had probably ceased before 1811. Flaxman and Thomas Butts were both at hand: Ozias Humphry had died in 1810. There remains George Cumberland, whose son was now a convenient messenger, and Cumberland does not appear to have hoarded all Blake's letters: only six are extant, five written before 1809, and the last in 1827. A few references by his contemporaries and the drawings and engravings which can be dated are, therefore, the chief sources of information about Blake's life between 1810 and 1818.*

Seymour Kirkup, whose description of the large fresco, 'The Ancient Britons', has been quoted, left an interesting account of his acquaintance with Blake in letters to Lord Houghton, Swinburne, and W. M. Rossetti.† Kirkup, a friend of Landor, Trelawny, and the Brownings, settled in Florence about 1817. He discovered the lost portrait of Dante by Giotto, and was dignified in consequence by the title of Barone. Like Elizabeth Barrett Browning and that indefatigable writer, old Mrs. Trollope, he fell a victim to 'Sludge the Medium', Daniel Home, and it may be inferred that his spiritualistic experiences gave him retrospectively some sympathy with Blake, which he had lacked as a boy. Swinburne visited him in Florence in 1864 in order to glean memories of Blake for his *Critical Essay*. Kirkup had been a student in the Antique School at the Royal Academy from 1810–16. He was an old school fellow of the younger Butts, and told Lord Houghton that during these

---

* Todd, Gilchrist, p. 388, quotes a notice of and references to Blake as 'an eccentric but very ingenious artist' from *A Biographical Dictionary of the Living Authors of Great Britain and Ireland,* published by Henry Colburn in 1816. John Gibson, R.A., visited Blake in 1817. See Lady Eastlake's *Life of John Gibson, R.A. Sculptor* (1870), p.42, and *Times Literary Supplement*, 3 April 1937. See also *Blake Records,* p. 245 n.2.

† In a letter to Swinburne, 30 November 1865, Kirkup says: ' . . . as I always treated him with respect, and did not presume to contradict him, he was very kind and communicative to me, and so I believe he was to everybody except Schiavonetti.' The account of Kirkup's relations with Blake is taken from a letter of 25 March 1870, printed in *The Life of Richard Monckton Milnes, 1st Lord Houghton,* by T. Wemyss Reid; a letter to W. M. Rossetti of 27 February 1866, in *Rossetti Papers;* and from 'Swinburne and Kirkup,' by Edmund Gosse, C.B., *London Mercury,* iii, no. 14 (December 1920).

years he was much with Blake, regretting that he did not sufficiently prize his qualities, or learn as much from him as he might
have done.

. . . Besides, I thought him mad. I do not think so now. I never
suspected him of imposture. His manner was too honest for that.
He was very kind to me, though very positive in his opinion,
with which I never agreed. His excellent old wife was a sincere
believer in all his visions. She told me seriously one day, 'I have
very little of Mr. Blake's company; he is always in Paradise.' She
prepared his colours, and was as good as a servant. He had no
other.[2]

It has been suggested that Kirkup was actually a pupil of
Blake's, but this seems improbable as he laments in a letter to
W. M. Rossetti that he 'neglected sadly the opportunities the
Buttses threw in my way. I only heard of him as engraving-master
to my old schoolfellow Tommy.' Kirkup thought that the Butts
family did not value Blake as they should have done, but this
impression may have been derived chiefly from the irreverent
Tommy.

Another remark of Kirkup shows that in spite of his epigrams
Blake still spoke generously of Flaxman's work. 'I used to wonder
[at] his praise of Fuseli and Flaxman,* my two first masters, for
their tastes were so different to his, w^h Fuseli especially disliked &
he was a magnanimous fellow though a sharp critic.'[3] Fuseli must
have made some adverse comment on a particular design or
characteristic of Blake's in Kirkup's hearing, as there is ample
evidence that he was in general an enthusiastic admirer.

Though in boyhood Kirkup thought Blake mad, as the young
Stothard had done, and perhaps on equally trivial grounds, there
was apparently nothing in his description to Swinburne which
supported this impression:

Mr. Kirkup also speaks of the courtesy with which, on occasion,
Blake would waive the question of his spiritual life, if the subject
seemed at all incomprehensible or offensive to the friend with him:
he would no more obtrude than suppress his faith, and would

* See p. 355.

practically accept and act upon the dissent or distaste of his companions without visible vexation or the rudeness of a thwarted fanatic.[4]

It may have been from Kirkup that Swinburne heard a story of Blake as Don Quixote which only appears in the *Critical Essay*:

Seeing once, somewhere about St. Giles, a wife knocked about by some husband or other violent person, in the open street, a bystander saw this also—that a small swift figure coming up in full swing of passion fell with such counter violence of reckless and raging rebuke upon the poor ruffian, that he recoiled and collapsed, with ineffectual cudgel; persuaded, as the bystander was told on calling afterwards, that the very devil himself had flown upon him in defence of the woman; such Tartarean overflow of execration and objurgation had issued from the mouth of her champion. It was the fluent tongue of Blake which had proved too strong for this fellow's arm: the artist, doubtless, not caring to remember the consequences, proverbial even before Molière's time, of such interference with conjugal casualties.[5]

Southey, who had been interested in Blake's Exhibition, called on him in South Molton Street in the summer of 1811. Crabb Robinson records in his Diary for 24 July:

Late to C. Lamb's. Found a very large party there. Southey had been with Blake & admired both his designs & his poetic talents at the same time that he held him for a decided madman. Blake, he says, spoke of his visions with the diffidence that is usual with such people & did not seem to expect that he shd. be believed. He showed S[outhey] a perfectly mad poem called *Jerusalem*. Oxford Street is in Jerusalem.

No more severe intelligence test could be devised than the casual introduction of *Jerusalem* at afternoon tea, and some such topographical detail is as much as the startled guest would be likely to carry away.

Nearly twenty years later Southey described this visit to Caroline Bowles, who had been interested by Cunningham's *Life* of Blake.

I have nothing of Blake's but his designs for Blair's *Grave*, which were published with the poem. His still stranger designs for his own compositions in verse were not ready for sale when I saw him, nor did I ever hear that they were so. Much as he is to be admired, he was at that time so evidently insane, that the predominant feeling in conversing with him, or even looking at him, could only be sorrow and compassion. His wife partook of his insanity in the same way (but more happily) as Taylor the pagan's wife caught her husband's paganism. And there are always crazy people enough in the world to feed and foster such craziness as his. My old acquaintance William Owen, now Owen Pugh, who, for love of his native tongue, composed a most laborious Welsh Dictionary, without the slightest remuneration for his labour, when he was in straitened circumstances, and has, since he became rich, translated *Paradise Lost* into Welsh verse, found our Blake after the death of Joanna Southcote, one of whose four-and-twenty elders he was. Poor Owen found everything which he wished to find in the Bardic system, and there he found Blake's notions, and thus Blake and his wife were persuaded that his dreams were old patriarchal truths, long forgotten, and now re-revealed. They told me this, and I, who well knew the muddy nature of Owen's head, knew what his opinion upon such a subject was worth. I came away from the visit with so sad a feeling that I never repeated it. . . .

. . . You could not have delighted in him—his madness was too evident, too fearful. It gave his eyes an expression such as you would expect to see in one who was possessed.[6]

The last dated entry in the Notebook was written a few days later than Crabb Robinson's account of Southey's visit to Blake. It is an extract from *Bell's Weekly Messenger* of 4 August 1811 referring to Peter le Cave, an artist then in Wilton Gaol who declared that Morland had sold many of his paintings as his own. Blake's comment on the paragraph is: 'It confirms the Suspition I entertain'd concerning those two I Engraved From for J. R. Smith—That Morland could not have Painted them, as they were the works of a Correct Mind & no Blurrer.' Blake's reference is probably to the 'Industrious Cottager' and 'The Idle Laundress', engraved by him in 1788.

In 1812 Blake exhibited at the fifth and last Exhibition of the 'Associated Artists in Water Colour' his 'Pitt', 'Nelson', and 'Canterbury Pilgrims'.

Another glimpse of him, as seen through Flaxman's eyes, is given in Crabb Robinson's Diary for 30 January 1815:

Flaxman was very chatty and pleasant. He related some curious anecdotes of Sharp the engraver, who seems the ready dupe of any and every religious fanatic & imposter who offers himself. . . . Sharp, tho' deceived by Brothers, became a warm partisan of Joanna Southcott. He endeavoured to make a convert of Blake the engraver, but as Fl. judiciously observed, such men as B[lake] are not fond of playing the 2nd. fiddle. Hence B[lake] himself a seer of visions & a dreamer of dreams would not do homage to a rival claimant of the privilege of prophecy.* B[lake] told F[laxman] that he had had a violent dispute with the Angels on some subjects and had driven them away . . . excessive pride equally denoted Blake and Barry [another seer of visions].

About 1815 Blake gave William Ensom, the engraver, some sittings, as that year Ensom was awarded the silver medal of the Royal Society of Arts for a pen-and-ink portrait of him. This drawing cannot be traced. Tatham told Gilchrist that Blake came to the Antique School at the Royal Academy in 1815 to copy the cast of the Laocoön,† and was greeted by Fuseli, then Keeper, with the words: 'What! You here, *Meesther Blake*? We ought to come and learn of you, not you of us!' Gilchrist adds: 'Blake took his place with the students, and exulted over his work, says Mr. Tatham, like a young disciple; meeting his old friend Fuseli's congratulations and kind remarks with cheerful, simple joy.'9

About 1816 we catch sight of him again calling on Isaac D'Israeli's friend, the Revd. Thomas Dibdin, who gives an account of the visit in his *Reminiscences of a Literary Life*.

. . . pupil of no Master, but a most extraordinary artist in his own particular element: although I believe he professed to have been

---

* Cf. Blake's epigram 'On the Virginity of The Virgin Mary & Johanna Southcott,' written at Felpham:

Whate'er is done to her she cannot know,
And if you ask her she will swear it so.
Whether 'tis good or evil none's to blame:
No one can take the pride, no one the shame.

† Blake had made this drawing in order to include an engraving of it on a plate for Rees's *Cyclopaedia* mentioned on p. 274. [Ed.]

a pupil of Flaxman and Fuseli—artists, as opposite in all respects as a chaste severity differs from wild exuberance of style. . . . I soon found the amiable but illusory Blake far beyond my ken or sight. In an instant he was in his 'third heaven'—flapped by the wings of seraphs, such as his own genius only could shape, and his own pencil embody. The immediate subject of our discussion—and for which indeed he professed to have in some measure visited me—was 'the minor poems of Milton.' Never were such 'dreamings' poured forth as were poured forth by my original visitor:—his stature mean, his head big and round, his forehead broad and high, his eyes blue, large, and lambent—such as my friend Mr. Phillips has represented him upon his imperishable canvas. 'What think you, Mr. Blake, of Fuseli's Lycidas—asleep, beneath the opening eyelids of the morn?' 'I don't remember it.' 'Pray see it, and examine it carefully. It seems to me to be the pencil of poetry employed to give intelligence and expression to the pen of the poet'—or words to this effect were, I think, pronounced. I learnt afterwards that my Visitor had seen it—but thought it 'too tame'—tameness from Fuseli! I told Mr. Blake that our common friend, Mr. Masquerier, had induced me to purchase his '*Songs of Innocence*,' and that I had no disposition to 'repent my bargain.' This extraordinary man sometimes—but in good sooth very rarely—reached the sublime; but the sublime and the grotesque seemed, somehow or the other, to be for ever amalgamated in his imagination; and the choice or result was necessarily doubtful. . . .[10]

Dibdin had originally intended to give a much longer account of Blake's work, and asked Isaac D'Israeli to lend him the designs in his possession. D'Israeli refused on the ground that he had too many to send, a hundred and sixty, and that in any case Blake's drawings baffled description. Some critics have supposed that D'Israeli's reply indicated a large and valuable collection, still unknown, but it seems clear that he was only referring to the copies of the symbolic books in his possession.[11]

Meagre as these references are they suggest that Blake had entered on the period of tranquil acceptance of his fate, which, from all accounts, distinguished his latter years. He was living in obscurity, and even in old age he was never patent to the public eye, like Lawrence, Fuseli, or Flaxman. William Paulet Carey, writing in 1817 of his designs for the *Grave*, says:

I never had the good fortune to see him; and so entire is the uncertainty, in which he is involved, that after many inquiries, I meet with some in doubt whether he is still in existence. But I have accidentally learned from a Lady, since I commenced these remarks, that he is, certainly, now a resident in London. I have, however, heard enough to warrant my belief that his professional encouragement has been very limited, compared with his powers.[12]

The records of Blake's work during these years are an additional warrant to this belief, and it is difficult to see how he managed to support himself and his wife. It is possible that other drawings or notes of commissions may be found which will make his position more explicable. So far as present information goes it seems clear that he was sometimes in actual want. The account with Butts* shows a total of £339 5s. 6d. for 1805–10, the average for 1807–10 being higher than for the two previous years. No receipts have been preserved later than 1810, but as none exists before 1805, although Blake had then been working for Butts for some years, it is probable that a further account was opened. Kirkup's letters suggest that Tommy Butts continued to be Blake's pupil. Captain Butts believed his grandfather to have been a steady purchaser of Blake's work for thirty years, and Mr. Butts certainly gave further commissions as the designs for 'L'Allegro' and 'Il Penseroso', executed about 1816, were his property. Samuel Palmer's eulogy of Butts in the letter to William Abercrombie, part of which has been already quoted,† confirms this view. Palmer writes:

Were I illustrating the book, my great object would be some likeness of Mr. Butts—through his son Captain Butts, if he could

* Two records of Blake's dealings with Mr. Butts were preserved among the letters to Butts and are now with these in the Westminster Public Library. The first is a Debtor and Credit account showing the prints and drawings which Blake did for Butts in 1805. It is interesting since it enables certain drawings to be accurately dated, and also gives their prices. The second is a collection of receipts for the period from January 1805 till December 1810, signed by Blake, with the exception of No. X, which bears Mrs. Blake's signature. [All the existing accounts between Blake and Butts are printed in *Blake Records*, pp. 570–8. Ed.]

† See p. 227 n.

be found; ... because the father for years stood between the greatest designer in England & the workhouse, that designer being, of all men whom I ever knew, the most practically sane, steady, frugal and industrious.

For the rest the unpublished engraving of Earl Spencer after the portrait by Phillips may have been executed in 1811, as a proof in the Print Room is water-marked with that year.* The smaller engraving of the Canterbury Pilgrims was published in 1812. A relief-etching, similar in subject to that of the third plate of *America*, is dated 1812.† Copies of several of the Illuminated Books were issued about 1813–15. In 1814 he began to engrave plates for Flaxman's *Hesiod*, which was published in 1817.‡ Gilchrist says that Blake did not take Flaxman's recommendation of him to Longmans, publishers of the book, quite in good part as he would have preferred to be recommended as a designer, but he gives no authority for this statement. Flaxman, who had designed some crockery for Josiah Wedgwood, also secured for Blake, about 1815, the task of engraving it for a catalogue, § work still less worthy of his powers than the *Hesiod*, or even than the hand-screens he had refused to paint at Felpham.¶ Some of the plates

* There is evidence found in the Cumberland papers that this plate was executed in 1813. (*Blake Records*, p. 232.) [Ed.]

† A pencil drawing of this subject in the British Museum is inscribed by Blake, 'Chaining of Orc'. The print is very rare. See Keynes, *The Separate Plates*, pp. 50–2. [Ed.]

‡ Professor G. E. Bentley Jr. found among records kept by Longmans, the publishers, that the contract for engraving the *Hesiod* plates was signed on 24 February 1816. Blake received between September 1814 and February 1817 a total of £224. 17. 6 for the 37 plates, which were therefore an important source of income in those years. See *Blake Records*, pp. 578–80. [Ed.]

§ For a full account of this episode see Keynes, *Blake Studies*, pp. 61–5. These drawings, now in the Pierpont Morgan Library, were first reproduced in the Nonesuch edition of *Milton's Poems*, 1926. [Ed.]

¶ Another effort of Flaxman's to provide Blake with work had been unsuccessful. K. Povey (*Notes and Queries*, 20 November 1921) draws attention to a letter of Flaxman's to John Bischoff of Leeds, dated 19 August 1814, printed in *Memoranda of Art and Artists* by Joseph Sandell. Flaxman offers to give Dr. Whitaker for his *History of Leeds* an outline drawing of the monument to Captains Walker and Beckett, continuing: 'The engraving, including the copper-plate, will cost six guineas if done by Mr. Blake, the best engraver of outlines.'

for Rees's *Cyclopaedia* were engraved and others both drawn and engraved in 1815 and 1816. A water-colour drawing, 'The Judgment of Paris', is dated 1817. The series of twelve designs for 'L'Allegro' and 'Il Penseroso' are on paper watermarked with the date 1816, and his visit to Dibdin no doubt related to these. His description of his illustrations would therefore have been written in that year. The twelve designs for *Paradise Regained* were probably executed about the same time.

An explanation of the scanty information about Blake's life during these years furnished by an article in the *Revue Britannique* for 1833 seems even less plausible than when attention was first drawn to it in 1912,* as some of the facts recorded above had been unknown before the publication of the Keynes *Bibliography*. The article is headed '*Hôpital des Fous à Londres*', and purports to describe a visit, the date of which is not mentioned, to Bethlem Hospital, and an interview there with Blake 'surnommé le Voyant'. Blake, who was under five foot six inches in height, is described as a big pale man who was engaged in drawing the ghost of a flea when the visitor entered, in itself a suspicious circumstance. There are other references to the visionary heads which Blake actually drew for Varley, and to conversations with Moses and Michelangelo, and an appropriate allusion to '*ce pauvre Job*'. The writer mentions as another interesting inmate Jonathan Martin, brother of John Martin the artist, who set fire to York Minster as a warning to the card-playing and theatre-going clergy of England; but Martin was tried for arson and committed to Bedlam on 13 March 1829, nearly two years after Blake's death.[13] The whole interview reads like a fabrication, perhaps concocted from the *Life* by Cunningham, which appeared in 1830, with the addition of a little current gossip. There is no mention of a Blake in the asylum records 1815–35, and no corroboration of the story elsewhere. Blake, in 1818, was still living in South Molton Street, where he had settled after his return from Felpham.

* Keynes, *Bibliography*, p. 375. The extract is reprinted in Appendix III. Cf. 'Was Blake ever in Bedlam? A Strange Discovery', by William T. Horton, *Occult Review*, November 1912.

During these years Blake was writing the last of his symbolic books, *Jerusalem, The Emanation of the Giant Albion*. It is probable that this poem was begun in 1804, as the title-page bears that date, but that the greater part of it was written after the completion of *Milton* in 1808. Southey saw something of it in 1811, but none of the known copies is printed on paper watermarked earlier than 1818. Five copies are recorded printed in black and uncoloured, and one in orange very beautifully painted with water colours and gold.* This is probably the copy to which Blake refers in his letter to George Cumberland of 12 April 1827: 'The Last Work I produced is a Poem Entitled Jerusalem the Emanation of the Giant Albion, but find that to Print it will Cost my Time the amount of Twenty Guineas. One I have Finish'd. It contains 100 Plates but it is not likely I shall get a Customer for it.'[14]

Blake was right, and this copy passed into the hands of Frederick Tatham after Mrs. Blake's death. Two posthumous copies were printed, probably by Tatham. Another coloured copy is said to have been sold to Ruskin, and some fragments at one time in the British Museum Print Room may have been part of it as Ruskin had a curious craze for cutting up illuminated MSS.†

Jerusalem is dedicated 'SHEEP To the Public GOATS', Blake maintaining the distinction he had drawn years before in *The Marriage of Heaven and Hell*:

Thus one portion of being is the Prolific, the other the Devouring: to the Devourer it seems as if the producer was in his chains; but it is not so, he only takes portions of existence and fancies that the whole. . . . Note: Jesus Christ did not wish to unite, but to seperate them, as in the Parable of sheep and goats! & he says: 'I came not to send Peace, but a Sword.'[15]

* This book, formerly in the possession of General Archibald Stirling of Keir, is now in the Paul Mellon collection. It was reproduced in facsimile for the Blake Trust in 1949. [Ed.]

Allan Cunningham says that Blake 'wrought incessantly upon what he counted his masterpiece, the Jerusalem, tinting and adorning it, with the hope that his favourite would find a purchaser. No one, however, was found ready to lay out twenty-five guineas on a work which no one could have any hope of comprehending, and this disappointment sank to the old man's heart.' (Symons, *Blake*, p. 428.)

† See Keynes, *Blake Studies*, p. 118. [Ed.]

The reference to Felpham in the first sentence, 'After my three years slumber on the banks of the Ocean, I again display my Giant forms to the Public,' is additional evidence that Blake began to write *Jerusalem* after his return to London. Aggressive in his claim as an artist, he does not pose as a slighted poet, though his paintings had clearly excited far more attention than his lyrics or symbolic books.

My former Giants & Fairies having reciev'd the highest reward possible, the love and friendship of those with whom to be connected is to be blessed, I cannot doubt that this more consolidated & extended Work will be as kindly recieved.[16]

It would seem that the fitness of the audience had made up for their being but very few, and these few can then have numbered two or three at most beyond the little circle of his personal friends.

Jerusalem, the longest of the symbolic books, is indeed a Giant form, ungainly, amorphous. Who can listen to his terrific voice without confusion and alarm? Who will not regret the sweet and ordered accents of the lyric Fairies? Had Blake left us more of these perhaps they would have said for him all that he needed to say, and the Giants might have been reserved for the eye curious in technique and psychology as colossal rough drafts which could convey their full meaning only to the writer. But, fairies failing, those who would understand Blake's mystic gospel must listen also to this giant.

The inscription at the head of Chapter I, Μονος ὁ Ιεσους [*sic*], is anticipated by the statement in the dedication that Jesus is 'the God of Fire and Lord of Love' . . . 'The Spirit of Jesus is continual forgiveness of Sin: he who waits to be righteous before he enters into the Saviour's kingdom, the Divine Body, will never enter there.'[17] A fairy's voice is heard for a moment telling of Jesus as the God of Fire.

Again he speaks in thunder and in fire!
Thunder of Thought, & flames of fierce desire:
Even from the depths of Hell his voice I hear
Within the unfathom'd caverns of my Ear.[18]

The dedication ends with the note already quoted, on the measure in which the poem is written.

As *Milton* records Blake's rebellion against the conditions of his life at Felpham, so the substance of *Jerusalem* is affected by the agony of mind he had suffered in awaiting his trial for high treason. This experience had impressed on him the cruelty of men to men, their readiness to accuse and judge; he saw more clearly than before that freedom is only attainable through imaginative understanding and mutual forgiveness. The theme of *Jerusalem* is stated in the first lines:

> Of the Sleep of Ulro!* and of the passage through
> Eternal Death! and of the awaking to Eternal Life.[19]

Jesus through the words of Blake appeals to Albion, the Eternal Man, to awaken from his deathful sleep, and hide no longer his emanation, Jerusalem, spiritual freedom, which is the outcome of imagination.

> 'I am not a God afar off, I am a brother and friend;
> Within your bosoms I reside, and you reside in me:
> Lo! we are One, forgiving all Evil, Not seeking recompense.'[20]

But the Man denies spiritual freedom, and puts reason and moral law in her place.

> 'Jerusalem is not! her daughters are indefinite:
> By demonstration man alone can live, and not by faith.
> .   .   .   .
>   . . . here will I build my Laws of Moral Virtue.
> Humanity shall be no more, but war & princedom & victory!'[21]

Blake, seeing that without spiritual freedom and imagination learning has become abstract and religion narrow, asks for divine inspiration that he may describe the building of Golgonooza, the City of Art, and also the present state of misery brought about by the Man's inhumanity.

> Trembling I sit day and night, my friends are astonish'd at me,
> Yet they forgive my wanderings. I rest not from my great task!

* Ulro symbolizes the material world.

To open the Eternal Worlds, to open the immortal Eyes
Of Man inwards into the Worlds of Thought, into Eternity
Ever expanding in the Bosom of God, the Human Imagination.
O Saviour pour upon me thy Spirit of meekness & love!
Annihilate the Selfhood in me: be thou all my life![22]

Jerusalem in her misery becomes the companion of Vala,
Nature, and Los, the Poet, embodied by Blake himself, hears her
lamentations. Los, whose name in Eternity is Urthona, Spirit, is
divided from his Spectre, Reason, who is described later in the
poem:

The Spectre is the Reasoning Power in Man, & when separated
From Imagination and closing itself as in steel in a Ratio
Of the Things of Memory, It thence frames Laws & Moralities
To destroy Imagination, the Divine Body, by Martyrdoms & Wars.

Reason tries to destroy the Poet, and then to terrify him by his
pessimism and his gibes, but Los refuses to be alarmed.

'Comfort thyself in my strength; the time will arrive
When all Albion's injuries shall cease, and when we shall
Embrace him, tenfold bright, rising from his tomb in immortality.
They have divided themselves by Wrath, they must be united by
Pity; let us therefore take example & warning, O my Spectre.
O that I could abstain from wrath! O that the Lamb
Of God would look upon me and pity me in my fury,
In anguish of regeneration, in terrors of self annihilation!'[24]

The last words sound a personal note in reply to the Spectre's
taunt which, it would seem, refers to the neglect of Blake as an
artist and to the Cromek and Stothard controversies.

Los recognizes the Spectre as his own 'Pride & Self-righteous-
ness'; he will labour in hope, exposing error:

'That he who will not defend Truth may be compell'd to defend
A Lie: that he may be snared and caught and snared and taken:
That Enthusiasm and Life may not cease; arise Spectre, arise!'[25]

The prevailing error is plain enough:

They take the Two Contraries which are call'd Qualities, with
    which
Every Substance is clothed: they name them Good & Evil;

From them they make an Abstract, which is a Negation
Not only of the Substance from which it is derived,
A murderer of its own Body, but also a murderer
Of every Divine Member: it is the Reasoning Power,
An Abstract objecting power that Negatives every thing.
This is the Spectre of Man, the Holy Reasoning Power,
And in its Holiness is closed the Abomination of Desolation.[26]

Los, therefore, compels the unwilling Spectre to labour with him:

'I must Create a System or be enslav'd by another Man's.
I will not Reason & Compare: my business is to Create.'[27]

Then follows a description of how Los, 'Striving with Systems to deliver Individuals from those Systems,' builds the Eternal City of Art, Golgonooza, which has four gates, and in which all things are fourfold. Outside Golgonooza lies the world of materialistic science, with its symbols, the Cave, the Rock, the Tree, and so forth.

And all that has existed in the space of six thousand years,
Permanent & not lost, not lost nor vanish'd, & every little act,
Word, work & wish that has existed, all remaining still
    .   .   .   .
For every thing exists & not one sigh nor smile nor tear,
One hair nor particle of dust, not one can pass away.[28]

Blake, appalled by the condition of the material world, makes another appeal for inspiration.

I see the Four-fold Man, The Humanity in deadly sleep
And its fallen Emanation, The Spectre & its cruel Shadow.
I see the Past, Present & Future existing all at once
Before me. O Divine Spirit, sustain me on thy wings,
That I may awake Albion from his long & cold repose;
For Bacon & Newton, sheath'd in dismal steel, their terrors hang
Like iron scourges over Albion: Reasonings like vast Serpents
Infold around my limbs, bruising my minute articulations.[29]

I turn my eyes to the Schools & Universities of Europe
And there behold the Loom of Locke, whose Woof rages dire,
Wash'd by the Water-wheels of Newton: black the cloth
In heavy wreathes folds over every Nation: cruel Works

Of many Wheels I view, wheel without wheel, with cogs tyrannic
Moving by compulsion each other, not as those in Eden, which,
Wheel within Wheel, in freedom revolve in harmony & peace.[30]

After contemplating the existing misery Blake recalls that Los is
not only the builder of the City of Art, but also the Guardian of the
World Memory.

All things acted on Earth are seen in the bright Sculptures of
Los's Halls, & every Age renews its powers from these Works
With every pathetic story possible to happen from Hate or
Wayward Love; & every sorrow & distress is carved here,
Every Affinity of Parents, Marriages & Friendships are here
In all their various combinations wrought with wondrous Art,
All that can happen to Man in his pilgrimage of seventy years.
Such is the Divine Written Law of Horeb & Sinai,
And such the Holy Gospel of Mount Olivet & Calvary.[31]

The poet dominates his reason lest he should destroy Enitharmon, Inspiration, but at the same time makes use of reason to
withstand the seductions of the Daughters of Albion, unimagina-
tive and therefore false conceptions of beauty. Hand and Hyle,
Sons of Albion, the rationalist and the bad artist,* deny the
spiritual freedom of imagination:

'Cast, Cast ye Jerusalem forth! The Shadow of delusions!
The Harlot daughter! Mother of pity and dishonourable
    forgiveness!
Our Father Albion's sin and shame!'[32]

They proclaim Vala, Nature, their Mother. The first chapter ends
with the mutual reproaches of Jerusalem and Vala, who now see
that they are incompatible with one another, and Albion blames
them both for his fall from eternity. He seeks salvation in
hypocrisy: 'All is Eternal Death unless you can weave a chaste
Body over an unchaste Mind!'

* Hand is believed to be a name covering the brothers, Robert and Leigh
Hunt, who had attacked Blake in their newspaper, *The Examiner*. David
Erdman has pointed out that Leigh Hunt used a 'printer's fist', or pointing
hand, as his editorial signature. (*Blake: Prophet against Empire*, p. 459.) Hyle
is probably Hayley, who had attempted to divert Blake from his true mission
as an artist. [Ed.]

He rejects Jerusalem as sin, and seizes Vala's Veil, Matter, that the souls of men may be ensared. He only knows God 'wide separated from the Human Soul,' the god of vengeance and moral law. Then, suddenly, he realizes that he has fallen from Eternity because he has forsaken freedom:

'O Human Imagination, O Divine Body I have Crucified,
I have turned my back upon thee into the Wastes of Moral Law.'[33]

He dies into the World of Generation asking for forgiveness, and the daughters of Beulah, the region below eternity where Albion had been sleeping, the first stage in his fall, utter their lamentation:

'Why did you take Vengeance, O ye Sons of the mighty Albion,
Planting these Oaken Groves, Erecting these Dragon Temples?
Injury the Lord heals, but Vengeance cannot be healed.
As the Sons of Albion have done to Luvah, so they have in him
Done to the Divine Lord & Saviour, who suffers with those that suffer;
For not one sparrow can suffer & the whole Universe not suffer also
In all its Regions, & its Father & Saviour not pity and weep.
But Vengeance is the destroyer of Grace & Repentance in the bosom
Of the Injurer, in which the Divine Lamb is cruelly slain.
Descend, O Lamb of God, & take away the imputation of Sin
By the Creation of States & the deliverance of Individuals Evermore.
Amen.'[34]

The preface to Chapter II is dedicated 'To the Jews'. The first paragraph is elucidated by the description of an aged patriarch in *A Vision of the Last Judgment*. 'He is Albion, our Ancestor, patriarch of the Atlantic Continent, whose History preceded that of the Hebrews & in whose Sleep, or Chaos, Creation began.'[35] After the fall of Albion the false religion of sacrifice, which Blake always calls 'Druid', was common to the whole earth, but these Druids had none the less handed down the tradition 'that Man anciently contain'd in his mighty limbs all things* in Heaven & Earth.'[36]

* Damon, *Blake*, pp. 446, 447, discusses Blake's familiarity, direct or indirect, with the doctrines of the Kabala, and points out that Albion is identical with Adam Kadmon, whose limbs had once contained all things.

The first six verses of the lyric describe the golden age of innocence, when Jerusalem, Freedom, was familiar to all.

> She walks upon our meadows green,
> The Lamb of God walks by her side,
> And every English Child is seen
> Children of Jesus & his Bride.[37]

Then comes the age of experience when Satan, Error, rules for a time though he cannot gain a final victory.

> He wither'd up the Human Form
> By laws of sacrifice for sin,
> Till it became a Mortal Worm,
> But O! translucent all within.

> The Divine Vision still was seen,
> Still was the Human Form Divine,
> Weeping in weak & mortal clay,
> O Jesus, still the Form was thine.

> And thine the Human Face, & thine
> The Human Hands & Feet & Breath,
> Entering thro' the Gates of Birth
> And passing thro' the Gates of Death.

> And O thou Lamb of God, whom I
> Slew in my dark self-righteous pride,
> Art thou return'd to Albion's Land?
> And is Jerusalem thy Bride?

> Come to my arms & never more
> Depart, but dwell for ever here:
> Create my Spirit to thy Love:
> Subdue my Spectre to thy Fear.

> Spectre of Albion! warlike Fiend!
> In clouds of blood & ruin roll'd,
> I here reclaim thee as my own,
> My Self-hood! Satan! arm'd in gold.

> Is this thy soft Family-Love,
> Thy cruel Patriarchal pride,
> Planting thy Family alone,
> Destroying all the World beside?

A man's worst enemies are those
Of his own house & family;
And he who makes his law a curse,
By his own law shall surely die.

In my Exchanges every Land
Shall walk, & mine in every Land,
Mutual shall build Jerusalem,
Both heart in heart & hand in hand.[38]

In the last verses Blake shows that he regarded exclusive family love and patriotism as a form of selfhood. The last verse but one refers back to the lines in Albion's lament of the previous chapter:

'O my Children,
I have educated you in the crucifying cruelties of Demonstration
Till you have assum'd the Providence of God & slain your Father.'[39]

Chapter II opens with Albion's conviction of sin, which he hardens into a doctrine dividing men against each other. The Divine Vision appears and announces that Albion's sleep of death must last until the hidden Satan, the Secret Error, is exposed. Then 'two Immortal forms' leave Albion, the spectre and emanation of Los. As they escape they give with slight alterations the same account of Albion as Ahania had given in *Vala* of her vision of the 'Dark'ning Man.' Since they have fled from Error they are now reunited with Los, the Poet, who tries to comprehend the degradation of Albion, but error is still hidden from him, although he sees that:

Every Universal Form was become barren mountains of Moral
Virtue, and every Minute Particular harden'd into grains of sand,
And all the tendernesses of the soul cast forth as filth & mire: . . .[40]

Now that Albion has fallen into the World of Generation, his Spectre, Chaos, Satan, who, as Error, is 'the Great Self-hood' and represents memory as opposed to imagination, addresses him in the language of materialism.

'I am your Rational Power, O Albion, & that Human Form
You call Divine is but a Worm seventy inches long
That creeps forth in a night & is dried in the morning sun,

In fortuitous concourse of memorys accumulated & lost.
It plows the Earth in its own conceit, it overwhelms the Hills
Beneath its winding labyrinths, till a stone of the brook
Stops it in midst of its pride among its hills & rivers.'[41]

Vala, Nature, appears from Chaos; now that Albion is in the
material world she, and not Jerusalem, is his emanation. She
obscures the Divine Vision for Albion, claiming that she alone
is Beauty, and that the Eternal, the Imaginative Human form is her
own creation. Los is appalled at the domination of Nature over
Man.

'There is a Throne in every Man, it is the Throne of God;
This, Woman has claim'd as her own, & Man is no more!
Albion is the Tabernacle of Vala & her Temple,
And not the Tabernacle & Temple of the Most High.'[42]

As in *Vala* the Divine hand sets two limits of opacity and
contraction for created man in the world of generation, but in
Jerusalem the Divine voice also announces the creation of States,
through which the individual passes leaving error behind him.

'Albion goes to Eternal Death. In Me all Eternity
Must pass thro' condemnation and awake beyond the Grave.
No individual can keep these Laws, for they are death
To every energy of man and forbid the springs of life.
Albion hath enter'd the State Satan! Be permanent, O State!
And be thou for ever accursed! that Albion may arise again.
And be thou created into a State! I go forth to Create
States, to deliver Individuals evermore! Amen.'[43]

Meanwhile the world of generation becomes more and more
divided, and illusion is all powerful until the Divine Body,
Imagination, shall redeem man.

    . . . 'What seems to Be, Is, To those to whom
It seems to Be, & is productive of the most dreadful
Consequences to those to whom it seems to Be, even of
Torments, Despair, Eternal Death; but the Divine Mercy
Steps beyond and Redeems Man in the Body of Jesus. Amen.
And Length, Bredth, Highth again Obey the Divine Vision.
        Hallelujah.'[44]

The fallen Albion, though he has steeled his heart against 'Universal Love', is not cut off from eternity, for the Saviour follows him, as in *Vala*:

Displaying the Eternal Vision, the Divine Similitude,
In loves and tears of brothers, sisters, sons, fathers and friends,
Which if Man ceases to behold, he ceases to exist,

Saying, 'Albion! Our wars are wars of life, & wounds of love
With intellectual spears, & long winged arrows of thought.
Mutual in one another's love and wrath all renewing
We live as One Man; for contracting our infinite senses
We behold multitude, or expanding, we behold as one,
As One Man all the Universal Family, and that One Man
We call Jesus the Christ; and he in us, and we in him
Live in perfect harmony in Eden, the land of life,
Giving, recieving, and forgiving each other's trespasses.
He is the Good shepherd, he is the Lord and master,
He is the Shepherd of Albion, he is all in all,
In Eden, in the garden of God, and in heavenly Jerusalem.
If we have offended, forgive us; take no vengeance against us.'45

But Albion fled from the Divine Vision, seeking a refuge in the doctrine of Atonement instead of in forgiveness of sins.* The poet is still his friend:

Los said to Albion: 'Whither fleest thou?' Albion reply'd:

'I die! I go to Eternal Death! the shades of death
Hover within me & beneath, and spreading themselves outside
Like rocky clouds, build me a gloomy monument of woe.
Will none accompany me in my death, or be a Ransom for me
In that dark Valley? I have girded round my cloke, and on my feet
Bound these black shoes of death, & on my hands, death's iron
    gloves.
God hath forsaken me & my friends are become a burden,
A weariness to me, & the human footstep is a terror to me.'

Los answered troubled, and his soul was rent in twain:
'Must the Wise die for an Atonement? does Mercy endure
    Atonement?
No! It is Moral Severity & destroys Mercy in its Victim.'46

---

* Cf. Morley, *Crabb Robinson*, p. 26. 'Speaking of the Atonement in the ordinary Calvinist sense, he said "It is a horrible doctrine; if another pay your debt, I do not forgive it." '

But Blake recalls for his own comfort that even in the world of generation there is a window opening on Eternity of which the Fairy had told him.

There is a Grain of Sand in Lambeth* that Satan cannot find,
Nor can his Watch Fiends find it; 'tis translucent & has many
   Angles,
But he who finds it will find Oothoon's palace; for within
Opening into Beulah, every angle is a lovely heaven.
But should the Watch Fiends find it, they would call it Sin
And lay its Heavens & their inhabitants in blood of punishment.[47]

Los continues to remonstrate vainly with Albion, and then, despite his own doubt and despair, implores the other Zoas, 'Urizen cold & scientific, Luvah pitying & weeping, Tharmas indolent & sullen,'[48] to help him in the eternal Man, describing in a long and vehement speech the evil and degradation and cruelty and error which have resulted from his fall. They respond to the appeal of Los and together they try to bear Albion back to eternity, but they cannot succeed against his will: they are winged with vision and imagination, but the 'Starry Wheels' of Albion, reason and logic, roll him back into the material world in spite of their efforts to raise him.

Albion again abandons hope, and Jerusalem, his emanation, like Ololon in *Milton*, descends to earth in order to save him, while the Daughters of Beulah implore the Lamb of God to come and take away the remembrance of sin.

The third chapter is dedicated 'To the Deists', self-righteous believers in natural virtue, who accuse religious men like Whitefield of hypocrisy because they confess their sins, promoters of warfare, who will not understand that 'The Glory of Christianity is To Conquer by Forgiveness.'[49] The dedication ends with the second half of the 'Monk of Charlemaine' from the MS. Book. The monk is the 'image of his Lord', who is slain by those who have forcibly divided the moral law from the gospel of forgiveness.

* Lambeth, here the place of Blake's inspiration, where several of the earlier symbolic books had been written, changes its connotation where the allusion is to Bedlam or to the Archbishop's Palace.

Early in Chapter III Blake defines Jerusalem in her universal relation to men.

In Great Eternity every particular Form gives forth or Emanates
Its own peculiar Light, & the Form is the Divine Vision
And the Light is his Garment. This is Jerusalem in every Man,
A Tent & Tabernacle of Mutual Forgiveness, . . .[50]

But men are still the victims of passion: unreleased by imagination, which ensures mutual forgiveness, they are bound by the iron chains of Sexual Love, and the 'cold constrictive Spectre' of Reason imposes doubt instead of faith.* As in *Vala* and *Milton* the Seven Eyes of God are appointed to watch, the first six representing the states through which man must pass before he is prepared for the seventh, Jesus, the recognition of truth. The eighth, the 'Shadowy Eighth' of *Milton*, the eternal individuality of Man, is lost in the forest of error and does not answer to the call. The Living Creatures, the Four Zoas, wage war against the indefinite, the abstract:

'He who would do good to another must do it in Minute Particulars:
General Good is the plea of the scoundrel, hypocrite & flatterer,
For Art & Science cannot exist but in minutely organized Particulars
And not in generalizing Demonstrations of the Rational Power.
The Infinite alone resides in Definite & Determinate Identity;
Establishment of Truth depends on destruction of Falsehood
    continually,
On Circumcision, not on Virginity, O Reasoners of Albion!'[51]

Circumcision, Blake's symbol for sacrifice of the selfhood, must take the place of Virginity, abstinence and unnatural repression. Los, the Poet, takes comfort in the thought that man is cast in the image of the divine Infant:

'He who is an Infant and whose Cradle is a Manger
Knoweth the Infant sorrow, whence it came and where it goeth
And who weave it a Cradle of the grass that withereth away.
This World is all a Cradle for the erred wandering Phantom,
Rock'd by Year, Month, Day & Hour; and every two Moments
Between dwells a Daughter of Beulah to feed the Human
    Vegetable.[52]

* Cf. Damon, *Blake*, pp. 388–9.

Los here and elsewhere deplores the dominance of the Female Will, the Moral Law, which, like freedom and inspiration on the higher plane and nature on the lower, is represented as feminine. Jerusalem, a captive in the Mills of reason, is mad with despair, and Vala, Nature and materialistic religion, triumphs over her rival. Nevertheless Jerusalem often beheld the Divine Vision and said:

'O Lord & Saviour, have the Gods of the Heathen pierced thee,
Or hast thou been pierced in the House of thy Friends?
Art thou alive, & livest thou for evermore? or art thou
Nought but a delusive shadow, a thought that liveth not?
Babel mocks, saying there is no God nor Son of God,
That thou, O Human Imagination, O Divine Body, art all
A delusion; but I know thee, O Lord, where thou arisest upon
My weary eyes, even in this dungeon & this iron mill.
The Stars of Albion cruel rise; thou bindest to sweet influences,
For thou also sufferest with me, altho' I behold thee not;
And altho' I sin & blaspheme thy holy name, thou pitiest me
Because thou knowest I am deluded by the turning mills
And by these visions of pity & love because of Albion's death.'[53]

But she is comforted by a visionary knowledge that the birth of the Divine Child was itself an occasion for forgiveness. She hears Mary appeal to Joseph in her own name, as a sign that she also will be forgiven and reinstated, fallen though she be:

... 'Art thou more pure
Than thy Maker who forgiveth Sins & Calls again Her that is
Lost?'[54]

Blake, in *A Vision of the Last Judgment*, had included the Virgin Mary among the 'innocently gay & thoughtless,* not being among the condemn'd because ignorant of crime in the midst of a corrupted Age.'[55] He believed that Jesus was conceived by the Holy Ghost, not in a miraculous sense but because Mary, like Oothoon in *Visions of the Daughters of Albion*, had yielded to an instinct pure in itself.

Jerusalem receives the Divine Child from Mary at his birth, but again despairs at the Crucifixion:

* Cf. Blake's remark to Crabb Robinson that 'careless gay people are better than those who think'. (Morley, *Crabb Robinson*, p. 13.)

'Shall Albion arise? I know he shall arise at the Last Day!
I know that in my flesh I shall see God; but Emanations
Are weak, they know not whence they are nor whither tend.'

Jesus replied, 'I am the Resurrection & the Life.
I Die & pass the limits of possibility as it appears
To individual perception. . . .
Come now with me into the villages, walk thro' all the cities;
Tho' thou art taken to prison & judgment, starved in the streets,
I will command the cloud to give thee food & the hard rock
To flow with milk & wine; tho' thou seest me not a season,
Even a long season, & a hard journey & a howling wilderness,
Tho' Vala's cloud hide thee & Luvah's fires follow thee,
Only believe & trust in me. Lo, I am always with thee!'[56]

But in the meantime the world is ruled by Vala, Nature, and
the Spectre, Reason, in the false union which does not synthesize
the contraries and is always called by Blake hermaphroditic as
opposed to androgynous.

The description of the industrial revolution is repeated from
Vala. The Eternal Man will not hear the voice of the poet, but
Los continues his work, creating the prophets to defeat the kings
of the material world, and he is aided by 'all the gentle Souls Who
guide the great Wine-press of Love', among them Fénelon, Mme
Guyon, Saint Teresa, Whitefield, and Hervey.* The chapter ends
with another cry from Blake for inspiration, while he ponders over
all that has happened in the world of time and space.

The fourth chapter is dedicated 'To the Christians.' Blake con-
trasts the doctrines of the Evangelicals with his own religion of
art in forcible prose. This passage must be quoted in full, and
needs no comment.

Devils are	I give you the end of a golden string,
False Religions.	Only wind it into a ball,
'Saul, Saul,	It will lead you in at Heaven's gate
Why persecutes	Built in Jerusalem's wall.
thou me?'	

We are told to abstain from fleshly desires that we may lose no

* Hervey was the author of *Meditations among the Tombs*, the subject of an
elaborate painting by Blake now in the Tate Gallery.

time from the Work of the Lord: Every moment lost is a moment
that cannot be redeemed; every pleasure that intermingles with
the duty of our station is a folly unredeemable, & is planted like
the seed of a wild flower among our wheat: All the tortures of
repentance are tortures of self-reproach on account of our leaving
the Divine Harvest to the Enemy, the struggles of intanglement
with incoherent roots. I know of no other Christianity and of no
other Gospel than the liberty both of body & mind to exercise the
Divine Arts of Imagination, Imagination, the real & eternal World
of which this Vegetable Universe is but a faint shadow, & in
which we shall live in our Eternal or Imaginative Bodies when
these Vegetable Mortal Bodies are no more. The Apostles knew
of no other Gospel. What were all their spiritual gifts? What is the
Divine Spirit? is the Holy Ghost any other than an Intellectual
Fountain? What is the Harvest of the Gospel & its Labours?
What is that Talent which it is a curse to hide? What are the
Treasures of Heaven which we are to lay up for ourselves, are they
any other than Mental Studies & Performances? What are all the
Gifts of the Gospel, are they not all Mental Gifts? Is God a Spirit
who must be worshipped in Spirit & in Truth, and are not the
Gifts of the Spirit Every-thing to Man? O ye Religious, dis-
countenance every one among you who shall pretend to despise
Art & Science! I call upon you in the Name of Jesus! What is the
life of Man but Art & Science? is it Meat & Drink? is not the
Body more than Raiment? What is Mortality but the things relating to the Body which Dies? What is Immortality but the things
relating to the Spirit which Lives Eternally? What is the Joy of
Heaven but Improvement in the things of the Spirit? What are the
Pains of Hell but Ignorance, Bodily Lust, Idleness & devastation
of the things of the Spirit? Answer this to yourselves, & expel
from among you those who pretend to despise the labours of Art
& Science, which alone are the labours of the Gospel. Is not this
plain & manifest to the thought? Can you think at all & not
pronounce heartily That to Labour in Knowledge is to Build up
Jerusalem, and to Despise Knowledge is to Despise Jerusalem &
her Builders. And remember: He who despises & mocks a Mental
Gift in another, calling it pride & selfishness & sin, mocks Jesus
the giver of every Mental Gift, which always appear to the
ignorance-loving Hypocrite as Sins; but that which is a Sin in the
sight of cruel Man is not so in the sight of our kind God. Let every
Christian, as much as in him lies, engage himself openly &
publicly before all the World in some Mental pursuit for the
Building up of Jerusalem.[57]

Some of the sentences surrounding the Laocoön carry further the idea that the pursuit of art leads to freedom of spirit and imagination.

A Poet, a Painter, a Musician, an Architect: the Man Or Woman* who is not one of these is not a Christian.
You must leave Fathers & Mothers & Houses & Lands if they stand in the way of Art.
>Prayer is the Study of Art.
>Praise is the Practise of Art.
>Fasting &c., all relate to Art.
>The outward Ceremony is Antichrist.

Jesus & his Apostles & Disciples were all Artists. Their Works were destroy'd by the Seven Angels of the Seven Churches in Asia, Antichrist Science.[58]

Then Blake tells how he beheld a vision of the fiery wheel of religion, and was told that 'Jesus died because he strove Against the current of this Wheel.' He was himself bidden to follow the example of Christ, the Man of Imagination, and not that of the Pharisees, who were led astray by the self-righteous spectre of reason.

>'Go therefore, cast out devils in Christ's name,
>Heal thou the sick of spiritual disease,
>Pity the evil, for thou art not sent
>To smite with terror & with punishments
>Those that are sick, like to the Pharisees
>Crucifying & encompassing sea & land
>For proselytes to tyranny & wrath;
>But to the Publicans & Harlots go,
>Teach them True Happiness, but let no curse
>Go forth out of thy mouth to blight their peace;
>For Hell is open'd to Heaven: thine eyes beheld
>The dungeons burst & the Prisoners set free.'[59]

Then follows an appeal to England to waken at the call of spiritual freedom.

With the beginning of the fourth chapter things are at their worst. The 'Sleeping Humanity' of Albion, the shadowy eighth,

* 'Or' is a good instance of Blake's use of a capital letter for emphasis.

who cannot awaken till the seventh state, the recognition of truth, has been passed through, is attacked, but Los protects the eternal individuality of Man. Jerusalem is in utter despair.

'Encompass'd by the frozen Net and by the rooted Tree
I walk weeping in pangs of a Mother's torment for her Children.
I walk in affliction. I am a worm and no living soul!
A worm going to eternal torment, rais'd up in a night
To an eternal night of pain, lost! lost! lost! for ever!'[60]

Vala, Nature, also laments because she wrongly believes that the awakening of the Man will mean the death of Luvah, Passion, whose emanation she is: she does not understand that then the Zoas will live as the servants of man, and strife between him and them will cease. False ideals hold in subjection the reasoner and the artist, threatening freedom and preventing the recognition of truth. On plate 81 these false ideals are represented by a group of female figures; one of them points to lines written in reversed writing:

In Heaven the only Art of Living
Is Forgetting & Forgiving
Especially to the Female.

But if you on Earth Forgive
You shall not find where to Live.[61]

Enitharmon, Inspiration, is again separated from Los, the Poet, and his efforts are, therefore, wasted. The Spectre, Reason, rejoices at the division, but his triumph is short-lived, for now the Antichrist appears; the covering cherub, who had once guarded the truth but had been mistaken for it, is known as false doctrine. Error is revealed, and can, therefore, be destroyed. The poet, though still toiling in darkness, begins to perceive and proclaim the truth.

'It is easier to forgive an Enemy than to forgive a Friend.
The man who permits you to injure him deserves your vengeance:
He also will recieve it; go Spectre! obey my most secret desire
Which thou knowest without my speaking. Go to these Fiends of
    Righteousness,
Tell them to obey their Humanities & not pretend Holiness

When they are murderers: as far as my Hammer & Anvil permit.
Go, tell them that the Worship of God is honouring his gifts
In other men: & loving the greatest men best, each according
To his Genius: which is the Holy Ghost in Man; there is no other
God than that God who is the intellectual fountain of Humanity.
He who envies or calumniates, which is murder & cruelty,
Murders the Holy-one. Go, tell them this, & overthrow their cup,
Their bread, their altar-table, their incense & their oath,
Their marriage & their baptism, their burial & consecration.
I have tried to make friends by corporeal gifts but have only
Made enemies. I never made friends but by spiritual gifts,
By severe contentions of friendship & the burning fire of thought.
He who would see the Divinity must see him in his Children,
One first, in friendship & love, then a Divine Family, & in the
    midst
Jesus will appear; so he who wishes to see a Vision, a perfect
    Whole,
Must see it in its Minute Particulars, Organized, & not as thou,
O Fiend of Righteousness, pretendest; thine is a Disorganized
And snowy cloud, brooder of tempests & destructive War.
You smile with pomp & rigor, you talk of benevolence & virtue;
I act with benevolence & Virtue & get murder'd time after time.
You accumulate Particulars & murder by analyzing, that you
May take the aggregate, & you call the aggregate Moral Law,
And you call that swell'd & bloated Form a Minute Particular;
But General Forms have their vitality in Particulars, & every
Particular is a Man, a Divine Member of the Divine Jesus.'[62]

Los dominates the Spectre, and confines reason to his proper
functions, declaring:

'I care not whether a Man is Good or Evil; all that I care
Is whether he is a Wise Man or a Fool. Go, put off Holiness
And put on Intellect, or my thund'rous Hammer shall drive thee
To wrath which thou condemnest, till thou obey my voice.'[63]

Enitharmon, Inspiration, fears that when the Man is no longer
asleep in the world of generation her task will be over, but Los
reassures her; their division will be at an end but she will not
perish. The awakening of Albion is not a cause of terror.

'Fear not, my Sons, this Waking Death; he is become One with me.
Behold him here! We shall not Die! we shall be united in Jesus.

Will you suffer this Satan, this Body of Doubt that Seems but Is
    Not,
To occupy the very threshold of Eternal Life? if Bacon, Newton,
    Locke
Deny a Conscience in Man & the Communion of Saints & Angels,
Contemning the Divine Vision & Fruition, Worshiping the Deus
Of the Heathen, The God of This World, & the Goddess Nature,
Mystery, Babylon the Great, The Druid Dragon & hidden Harlot,
Is it not that Signal of the Morning which was told us in the
    Beginning?'[64]

Britannia, the emotional emanation of Albion, is the first to
awake: her lament for her errors rouses him, and in anger he
compels the three Zoas, Luvah, Urizen, and Tharmas, the
Emotions, the Reason, and the Senses, to serve him and fulfil
their true functions. But the fourth Zoa, Los, the Poet, is honoured
above the rest.

Urthona he beheld, mighty labouring at
His Anvil, in the Great Spectre Los unwearied labouring &
    weeping:
Therefore the Sons of Eden praise Urthona's Spectre in songs,
Because he kept the Divine Vision in time of trouble.[65]

Then Jesus himself appears to Albion in the similitude of Los,
and tells him that his own death is necessary if the eternal man is
to live. Albion is perplexed—'Cannot Man exist without Mysterious Offering of Self for Another? is this Friendship &
Brotherhood?'

Jesus said: 'Wouldest thou love one who never died
For thee, or ever die for one who had not died for thee?
And if God dieth not for Man & giveth not himself
Eternally for Man, Man could not exist; for Man is Love
As God is Love; every kindness to another is a little Death
In the Divine Image, nor can Man exist but by Brotherhood.'[66]

The covering cherub,* the cloud of error, divides them. Albion
forgets himself in terror at the danger for his Friend, throwing
himself into the Furnaces of affliction, and immediately:

All was a Vision, all a Dream: the Furnaces became
Fountains of Living Waters flowing from the Humanity Divine.

* Cf. Damon, *Blake*, pp. 408-9.

And all the Cities of Albion rose from their Slumbers, and All
The Sons & Daughters of Albion on soft clouds, waking from
  Sleep.
Soon all around remote the Heavens burnt with flaming fires,
And Urizen & Luvah & Tharmas & Urthona arose into
Albion's Bosom. Then Albion stood before Jesus in the Clouds
Of Heaven, Fourfold among the Visions of God in Eternity.[67]

Then the eternal man wakens Spiritual Freedom:

'Awake, Awake, Jerusalem! O lovely Emanation of Albion,
Awake and overspread all Nations as in Ancient Time;
For lo! the Night of Death is past and the Eternal Day
Appears upon our Hills. Awake, Jerusalem, and come away!'[68]

He takes his bow, which appears as fourfold, a bow in the hands
of each of the four Zoas, and Error is annihilated. Then the truth
of both science and art is revealed. Bacon, Newton, and Locke are
the companions in eternity of Milton, Shakespeare, and Chaucer.

The end of *Jerusalem* is obscure. Though the old earth has
passed away, the new heaven has its complement in a new earth.
Blake, it would seem, conceives a golden age of regeneration, an
imaginative creation which involves no Fall. The Four Living
Creatures are described as 'going forward, forward irresistible
from Eternity to Eternity.'

And they conversed together in Visionary forms dramatic
  which bright
Redounded from their Tongues in thunderous majesty, in Visions
In new Expanses, creating exemplars of Memory and of Intellect,
Creating Space, Creating Time, according to the wonders Divine
Of Human Imagination throughout all the Three Regions
  immense
Of Childhood, Manhood & Old Age; & the all tremendous
  unfathomable Non Ens
Of Death was seen in regenerations terrific or complacent, varying
According to the subject of discourse; & every Word & every
  Character
Was Human according to the Expansion or Contraction, the
  Translucence or
Opakeness of Nervous fibres: such was the variation of Time &
  Space
Which vary according as the Organs of Perception vary . . .[69]

Every man has become Fourfold, Human: even Nature herself, 'the Wondrous Serpent', is 'Humanized'. Nothing save error is destroyed, as Blake had declared earlier in the poem. 'Every thing has as much right to Eternal Life as God, who is the Servant of Man.'[70]

The new order is hailed by a great cry from all the earth, from the men of all nations, and from those who had laboured to build the city of art in the shadowy world of generation: all things, united by the bond of spiritual freedom, enjoy their own individualities without let or restraint.

All Human Forms identified, even Tree, Metal, Earth & Stone: all
Human Forms identified, living, going forth & returning wearied
Into the Planetary lives of Years, Months, Days & Hours; reposing,
And then Awaking into his Bosom in the Life of Immortality.

And I heard the Name of their Emanations: they are named
   Jerusalem.[71]

This imperfect account only aims at giving the gist of *Jerusalem*. To summarize the poem adequately within reasonable limits is impossible as the 'minute particulars' require, though they frequently resist, a detailed interpretation. The number of proper names, both of places and of persons, scriptural, mythological, and modern, used as symbols, causes much confusion. Instead of contenting himself with a few striking allusions and personifications Blake's study of Biblical prophecy has resulted in an ugly and hybrid shorthand. For instance, the haunting effects of his trial are shown by the frequent references to Schofield and his comrade, and to the magistrates concerned, as typifying the accuser and the judge of sin. Any attempt to deal with this symbolism in a few lines would leave the reader in the same condition of mind as poor Southey. Those who attack the poem itself will be well advised to consult Mr. Foster Damon's synopsis,* and his

* Damon, *Blake*, pp. 183–95 and 433–75. Denis Saurat in an interesting article ('Blake et Les Celtomanes', *Modern Philology*, xxiii, November 1925) has explained many obscure passages both in *Jerusalem* and in *A Descriptive Catalogue* by connecting them with theories prevalent among contemporary

commentary with its table of correspondences, but no one should venture on *Jerusalem* who is not familiar with the other symbolic books. The outline of the poem is indeterminate: there are fewer fine passages of verse than in *Vala* or *Milton*, and of these some of the best have been transferred from the former book. These defects may be partly due to age, but it is also probable that Blake's small audience had been interested in the form of the illuminated books rather than their purport, and he had, therefore, failed to receive intelligent criticism and fruitful questioning which would have revealed to himself the depths of his own obscurity, and made it worth while to strive for a clearer expression of his ideas. He admitted in a conversation with Crabb Robinson on 18 February 1826 that during those last years, when he was producing some of his best and most famous work as engraver and draughtsman, he was writing only for his own spiritual relief and no longer even desired readers.

He will not print any more. 'I write,' he says, 'when commanded by the spirits and the moment I have written I see the words fly abt the room in all directions. It is then published & the Spirits can read. My M.S.S. [are] of no further use. I have been tempted to burn my M.S.S. but my wife won't let me.' 'She is right,' said I. 'You have written these, not from yourself but by a higher order. The M.S.S. are theirs, not your property. You cannot tell what purpose they may answer unforeseen to you.' He liked this & said he wd not destroy them.*

But *Jerusalem* shows no abatement of energy or enthusiasm.

Celtic antiquaries, with whom Blake may have come in contact early in life through Basire's connection with them. It was a current belief among them that Britain was the birthplace of the human race and of the patriarchal religion, the Druids being the originators of derivative religions and civilizations throughout the world.

Maung Ba-Han deals at length with the later symbolic books in *William Blake, His Mysticism.*

* Morley, *Crabb Robinson*, pp. 12, 13. Perhaps Blake's praise of Fouqué's *Sintram*—'This is better than my things'—may be taken also as an admission of his failure to reach the public through his symbolic books. (Symons, *Blake*, p. 271.)

Blake is still as fearless and uncompromising in his refusal to
accept conventional standards and ideals as when he wrote *The
Marriage of Heaven and Hell*. No longer the politician of *The French
Revolution* and *America*, he is still the unflinching champion of
freedom, of spiritual freedom which involves a more complete
change of things as they are, or even as most reformers wish them
to be, than any political programme. It is noteworthy that Blake
criticized Christ's political activities in conversation with Crabb
Robinson. 'He was wrong in suffering himself to be crucified. He
should not have attacked the Govt. He had no business with such
matters.'[72] And again, ' "Christ," said he, "took much after his
mother [the law], and in that respect was one of the worst of men."
On my requiring an explanation he said, "There was his turning
the money-changers out of the Temple. He had no right to do
that." Blake then declared against those who sat in judgment on
others.'[73]

Some of the finest designs in Blake's illuminated books are to
be found in *Jerusalem*, notably 'Christ Crucified Adored by
Albion,'[74] which ranks among the most impressive and moving
representations of the Crucifixion. The dead Christ is nailed to the
Tree of Good and Evil, and below stands the solitary figure of
Man, himself adopting the cruciform attitude which symbolizes
the sacrifice of the selfhood. Among the most striking of the
smaller designs are the serpent chariot drawn by the human-
headed bulls, the swan woman, and the figure of Beulah en-
throned on the sunflower of desire, which suggests Blake's
transcription of the Buddha seated on the lotus flower.

Jerusalem is mentioned with inappropriate flippancy in the
London Magazine for September 1820 under the heading of 'Mr.
Janus Weathercock's Private Correspondence.'

Talking of articles, my learned friend Dr. Tobias Ruddicombe,
M.D. is, at my earnest entreaty, casting a tremendous piece of
ordnance,—*an eighty-eight pounder!* which he proposeth to fire off in
your next. It is an account of an ancient, newly discovered illuminated manuscript, which has to name 'Jerusalem the Emanation
of the Giant Albion!!!' It contains a good deal anent one *'Los,'*

who, it appears, is now, and hath been from the creation, the *sole* and fourfold dominator of the celebrated city of *Golgonooza*! The doctor assures me that the redemption of mankind hangs on the universal diffusion of the doctrines broached in this M.S.—But, however, that is'nt the subject of this *scrinium*, scroll, or scrawl, or whatever you may call it.[75]

The proposed exposition of *Jerusalem* was probably unacceptable to John Scott, then editor of the *London*, as no such article appeared. This is to be regretted since Blake's own voice might have been audible through the 'tricked and tinselled style' of the interpreter, as Lamb's 'light-hearted Janus', Thomas Griffiths Wainewright, journalist, painter, and murderer, was a friend and admirer of Blake's. He had purchased one of the most beautiful copies of the *Songs of Innocence and of Experience*, and although no other reference of his to Blake's work has been found, he was a supporter of imaginative art after his fashion.

'We are now in the great room, reader,' he writes of the Royal Academy Exhibition of 1821, 'where, if you have no objection, we will sit down behind this gay party, who seems to be dealing about their remarks as freely as you and I do. "Whose is that?" "Fuseli's."—"La! What a frightful thing! I hate his fancies of fairies and spirits and nonsense. One can't understand them." (Speak for yourself, miss!) "It's foolish to paint things which nobody ever saw, for how is one to know whether they're right? Isn't it, Mr. D——?" "Ha, Ha! very good indeed—'pon my life, you're very severe." '[76]

Samuel Palmer gives a little picture of Blake at the Academy pointing out a painting of Wainewright's illustrating Walton's *Angler* as 'very fine'. 'While so many moments better worthy to remain are fled, the caprice of memory presents me with the image of Blake looking up at Wainewright's picture; Blake in his plain black suit and *rather* broad-brimmed, but not quakerish hat, standing so quietly among all the dressed-up, rustling, swelling people, and myself thinking "How little you know *who* is among you!" '[77]

It was not till three years after Blake's death that Wainewright

took the first step in the criminal career which led to his transportation to Australia, by insuring his sister-in-law's life and
poisoning her with strychnine after securing a will in his own
favour.

While Blake was engraving *Jerusalem* he was writing in the
manuscript book notes for a poem which, if finished and revised,
would have been as forcible an expression of his later doctrine as
the *Marriage of Heaven and Hell* was of the earlier. *The Everlasting
Gospel* is neither Giant nor Fairy: it embodies the mature wisdom
of that converted angel who as devil became Blake's particular
friend. Unfortunately it exists only in overlapping fragments.[78]
Two additional passages with a prose preface were first printed in
1925.* This valuable addition, which has all the appearance of an
exordium, makes it easier to conceive what the finished poem
would have been. But the order in which the various fragments
were to have been placed cannot be recovered. The metre is the
octosyllable of 'L'Allegro', but handled with the freedom which
Blake had practised from his earliest youth. The effect is therefore
very like that of *Christabel*, Blake's lines being somewhat more
regular but considerably rougher in texture.

In the introduction, which is as lucid as *Jerusalem* is obscure,
Blake states his thesis: the moral virtues were an old story; Jesus
came to announce one Gospel only, forgiveness of sins, thus
bringing to light Life and Immortality, because only through
forgiveness can man realize his eternal nature; vengeance is the
betrayal of this nature, the 'Murder of the Divine Image.'

> The Accuser, Holy God of All
> This Pharisaic Worldly Ball,[79]

identified with Lucifer, demands the Crucifixion of Jesus because
forgiveness of sins is destructive of his daughters, the moral
virtues, who owe their birth to accusations of sin. Blake is ob-

---

* The manuscript had been known to Swinburne, who summarized its
contents in his *William Blake: A Critical Essay* (1868), pp. 175–6. It was then
lost to sight until it was sold with the E. J. Shaw collection at Sotheby's in
1925. It is now in the Rosenbach Foundation in Philadelphia. [Ed.]

viously trying to express himself in simple and popular language. For instance, he has deleted

> 'Jerusalem' he said to me

and has substituted

> It was when Jesus said to Me,
> 'Thy Sins are all forgiven thee.'[80]

and the 'Mysterious Tree' is clearly defined as that 'Of Good & Evil & Misery And Death & Hell. . . .' The fragment lettered *a* is the original opening of the poem as it stands in the Notebook. It has been suggested on the strength of the 'great hook nose' that Stothard is the person addressed, but it is more probable that Blake simply chose a type unlike himself to represent those whose interpretation of the Bible differs widely from his own. A note in the MS. book gives comic expression to his habit of regarding Christ as an ideal self. 'I always thought that Jesus Christ was a Snubby or I should not have worship'd him, if I had thought he had been one of those long spindle nosed rascals.'[81] The rest of the fragments elaborate the reply of the Devil in the last 'Memorable Fancy' to the Angel who asked whether Christ had not approved the decalogue:

. . . 'now hear how he has given his sanction to the law of ten commandments: did he not mock at the sabbath, and so mock the sabbath's God? murder those who were murder'd because of him? turn away the law from the woman taken in adultery? steal the labor of others to support him? bear false witness when he omitted making a defence before Pilate? covet when he pray'd for his disciples, and when he bid them shake off the dust of their feet against such as refused to lodge them? I tell you, no virtue can exist without breaking these ten commandments. Jesus was all virtue, and acted from impulse, not from rules.'[82]

The fragments *b*, *c*, and *d* are different treatments of the same theme, Jesus' lack of gentleness or humility as shown by the events of his life; *d*, the latest version, is the longest and fullest. Above it is written the title, *The Everlasting Gospel*. The lines

> 'Thou art a Man, God is no more,
> Thy own humanity learn to adore,
> For that is my Spirit of Life.'[83]

may be compared with Blake's reply when Crabb Robinson asked his view concerning the divinity of Jesus. 'He said—*He is the only God*—But then he added—"And so am I & so are you." '84

Fragment *e* describes the episode of the woman taken in adultery, who is identified with Mary Magdalene. Here Blake, through the mouth of Christ, makes his fiercest attack on the God of the Old Testament.

> 'Thou art Good, & thou Alone;
> Nor may the sinner cast one stone.
> To be Good only, is to be
> A God or else a Pharisee.'85

But the day of God, the Creator and lawgiver, is over.

> 'Tho' thou wast so pure & bright
> That Heaven was Impure in thy Sight,
> Tho' thy Oath turn'd Heaven Pale,
> Tho' thy Covenant built Hell's Jail,*
> Tho' thou didst all to Chaos roll
> With the Serpent for its soul,
> Still the breath Divine does move
> And the breath Divine is Love.'86

The dialogue between Jesus and Mary which follows is the finest passage in the poem.

> 'Mary, Fear Not! Let me see
> The Seven Devils that torment thee:
> Hide not from my Sight thy Sin,
> That forgiveness thou maist win.
> Has no Man Condemned thee?'
> 'No Man, Lord:' 'then what is he
> Who shall Accuse thee? Come Ye forth,
> Fallen fiends of Heav'nly birth
> That have forgot your Ancient love
> And driven away my trembling Dove.
> You shall bow before her feet;
> You shall lick the dust for Meat;
> And tho' you cannot Love, but Hate,
> Shall be beggars at Love's Gate.

---

* Cf. 'Prisons are built with stones of Law, Brothels with bricks of Religion.' (*The Marriage of Heaven and Hell*, 'Proverbs of Hell'.)

What was thy love? Let me see it;
Was it love or Dark Deceit?'
'Love too long from Me has fled;
'Twas dark deceit, to Earn my bread;
'Twas Covet, or 'twas Custom, or
Some trifle not worth caring for;
That they may call a shame & Sin
Love's temple that God dwelleth in,
And hide in secret hidden Shrine
The Naked Human form divine,
And render that a Lawless thing
On which the Soul Expands its wing.
But this, O Lord, this was my Sin
When first I let these Devils in
In dark pretence to Chastity:
Blaspheming Love, blaspheming thee.
Then Rose Secret Adulteries,
And thence did Covet also rise.
My sin thou hast forgiven me,
Canst thou forgive my Blasphemy?
Canst thou return to this dark Hell,
And in my burning bosom dwell?
And canst thou die that I may live?
And canst thou Pity & forgive?'[87]

In the fragment lettered *i* Blake questions the doctrine of the Virgin birth,* but his treatment of the subject is less sympathetic and original than in *Jerusalem*, and he does not here associate the birth of Jesus with forgiveness of sin. But as he implies that the birth of Jesus was not miraculous, so, too, he denies that Jesus shared the cold inhuman purity of God, the Creator.

Or what was it which he took on
That he might bring Salvation?
A Body subject to be Tempted,
From neither pain nor grief Exempted?
Or such a body as might not feel
The passions that with Sinners deal?
Yes, but they say he never fell.
Ask Caiaphas; for he can tell.[88]

* Cf. 'On the Virginity of the Virgin Mary and Johanna Southcott', Notebook, p. 6 (*Complete Writings*, p. 418).

Then follows a summary of Christ's offences against the decalogue and social conventions. This is the last fragment and it is vain to conjecture how Blake would have ended the poem.

He turned, it would seem, from the unfinished *Everlasting Gospel* to his old picture book, *For Children: The Gates of Paradise*. But his concern is now no longer with the innocent, the instinctively pure; and accordingly he engraved another title-page, *For the Sexes: The Gates of Paradise*. He also wrote a Prologue, verses explaining the emblems, which he called 'The Keys of the Gates', and an Epilogue, and made some additions to the legends below the emblems.

The first lines of the Prologue:

> Mutual Forgiveness of each Vice,
> Such are the Gates of Paradise.[89]

are an echo of lines in the second set of supplementary verses to *The Everlasting Gospel*:

> The Christian trumpets loud proclaim
> Thro' all the World in Jesus' name
> Mutual forgiveness of each Vice,
> And oped the Gates of Paradise.[90]

Why, Blake asks, when Jehovah himself repented writing the decalogue and hid it beneath his Mercy Seat, have Christians exalted it? Then follow the sixteen emblems. The couplet engraved between 'The Keys' and 'Of the Gates' refers to the frontispiece and is a slightly different version of two lines in the 'Auguries of Innocence.' The rest of these verses explain the emblems in turn, the number in the margin showing to which the lines refer. The symbolism will be clear to readers of the preceding pages on *Jerusalem* and *The Everlasting Gospel*.

The Epilogue is addressed to 'The Accuser', who does not distinguish the individual from the state, the Antichrist and God of this World.

> The Son of Morn in weary Night's decline,
> The Lost Traveller's Dream under the Hill.[91]

VIII
FRIENDS AND OBSERVERS

The Man who never in his Mind & Thoughts travel'd to
Heaven Is No Artist.[1]

In 1818 Blake formed the first of those friendships with men
much younger than himself who were to gather round him during
the last years of his life. John Linnell describes their meeting in
his autobiographical notes.

At Rathbone Place, 1818* . . . here I first became acquainted
with William Blake, to whom I paid a visit in company with the
younger Mr. Cumberland. Blake lived then in South Molton
Street, Oxford Street, second floor. We soon became intimate, and
I employed him to help me with an engraving of my portrait of
Mr. Upton, a Baptist preacher,† which he was glad to do, having
scarcely enough employment to live by at the prices he could
obtain; everything in Art was at a low ebb then.

John Linnell, then aged twenty-six and already a successful
artist, was friend rather than disciple, as his work shows no direct
traces of Blake's influence. He is now best known as a landscape
painter, but in early manhood he supported his family mainly by
painting portraits. During Blake's lifetime Linnell was a member
of the Baptist community; later he contemplated for a time becoming a member of the Society of Friends, and was a Plymouth
Brother for a few years, but finally he severed his connection with
all religious bodies, though he maintained to the last his own
evangelical fervour. A precocious boy, he had been a pupil of
John Varley's when he was twelve years old, and it was probably
early in 1819 that he introduced Blake to his former master.

Varley, Blake's junior by twenty years, was a well-known

* Gilchrist, Life, i, p. 293, erroneously dates this meeting as about 1813,
and confuses the elder George Cumberland with his son.

† Blake received 15 guineas out of the 50 guineas paid to Linnell. (Story,
The Life of John Linnell, 1892, i, p. 159, and Blake Records, p. 607.)

teacher: he was one of the founders of the Society of Painters in Water Colours, and his best work ranks high among the water-colour landscapes of the period. He was a big, unwieldy man, fond of boxing, like his brother-in-law Mulready, so extravagant and happy-go-lucky that though he made a large income he was constantly in money difficulties and died in poverty. His spirits were irrepressible, he was three times burnt out of house and home; he had also a fatal attraction for furious bulls, and his son was mentally defective, but each of these troubles in turn seemed to him a crowning mercy. 'All these troubles are necessary to me. If it were not for my troubles I should burst with joy!' Varley had a passion for the dubious sciences. He was a palmist and an astrologer, and had the remarkable luck of predicting truly his own misfortunes and those of his friends. He arrived at his results by means of mathematical calculations; Blake's attraction for him was the possession of the visionary faculty which he himself lacked. Blake had tried to protest publicly against the ill-treatment of an astrologer; he would doubtless have done the same for the most rationalistic disciple of Newton and Locke, but he seems to have had little respect for astrology with its values of worldly weal. 'Your fortunate nativity', he would say, 'I count the worst. You reckon to be born in August, and have the notice and patronage of Kings to be the best of all; whereas, the lives of the Apostles and martyrs, of whom it is said the world was not worthy, would be counted by you as the worst, and their nativities those of men born to be hanged.'

Most of Blake's famous visionary heads were drawn at night in the company of Varley and Linnell. Cunningham's account may be quoted as the first and freshest, with the warning that though he applied to Linnell for assistance in his memoir,* he appears to

---

* See Story's *Life of Linnell*, p. 246, for a letter in which Cunningham, after saying that he has received 'much valuable information' from Varley, asks for Linnell's help, adding 'I know Blake's character, for I know the man. I shall make a *judicious* use of my materials, and be merciful where sympathy is needed.' Linnell complains to Bernard Barton in a letter of 3 April 1830: '. . . I am sorry Mr Cunningham did not avail himself of the information I offered him as he might have made his very interesting memoirs the more

have relied more on Varley's information, and that probably lost nothing in the telling.

To describe the conversations which Blake held in prose with demons and in verse with angels, would fill volumes, and an ordinary gallery could not contain all the heads which he drew of his visionary visitants. That all this was real, he himself most sincerely believed; nay, so infectious was his enthusiasm, that some acute and sensible persons who heard him expatiate, shook their heads, and hinted that he was an extraordinary man, and that there might be something in the matter. One of his brethren, an artist of some note, employed him frequently in drawing the portraits of those who appeared to him in visions. The most propitious time for those 'angel-visits' was from nine at night till five in the morning; and so docile were his spiritual sitters, that they appeared at the wish of his friends. Sometimes, however, the shape which he desired to draw was long in appearing, and he sat with his pencil and paper ready and his eyes idly roaming in vacancy; all at once the vision came upon him, and he began to work like one possest.

He was requested to draw the likeness of Sir William Wallace— the eye of Blake sparkled, for he admired heroes. 'William Wallace!' he exclaimed, 'I see him now—there, there, how noble he looks—reach me my things!' Having drawn for some time, with the same care of hand and steadiness of eye, as if a living sitter had been before him, Blake stopt suddenly and said, 'I cannot finish him—Edward the First has stept in between him and me.' 'That's lucky,' said his friend, 'for I want the portrait of Edward too.' Blake took another sheet of paper, and sketched the features of Plantagenet; upon which his majesty politely vanished, and the artist finished the head of Wallace. 'And pray, Sir,' said a gentleman, who heard Blake's friend tell his story—'was Sir William Wallace an heroic-looking man? And what sort of personage was Edward?' The answer was, 'there they are, Sir, both framed and hanging on the wall behind you, judge for yourself.' 'I looked (says my informant) and saw two warlike heads of the size of common life. That of Wallace was noble and heroic, that of Edward stern and bloody. The first had the front of a god, the latter the aspect of a demon.'

---

instructive & far more creditable to Mr Blake by the alteration of some things & the addition of others with which I c^d have furnished him'. (*Blake Records*, p. 395.)

The friend who obliged me with these anecdotes on observing the interest which I took in the subject, said, 'I know much about Blake—I was his companion for nine years. I have sat beside him from ten at night till three in the morning, sometimes slumbering and sometimes waking, but Blake never slept; he sat with a pencil and paper drawing portraits of those whom I most desired to see. I will show you, Sir, some of these works.' He took out a large book filled with drawings, opened it, and continued, 'Observe the poetic fervour of that face—it is Pindar as he stood a conqueror in the Olympic games. And this lovely creature is Corinna, who conquered in poetry in the same place. That lady is Lais, the courtesan—with the impudence which is part of her profession, she stept in between Blake and Corinna, and he was obliged to paint her to get her away. There! that is a face of a different stamp—can you conjecture who he is?' 'Some scoundrel, I should think, Sir.' 'There now—that is a strong proof of the accuracy of Blake—he is a scoundrel indeed! The very individual task-master whom Moses slew in Egypt. And who is this now—only imagine who this is?' 'Other than a good one, I doubt, Sir.' 'You are right, it is a fiend—he resembles, and this is remarkable, two men who shall be nameless; one is a great lawyer, and the other—I wish I durst name him—is a suborner of false witnesses. This other head now?—this speaks for itself—it is the head of Herod; how like an eminent officer in the army!'

He closed the book, and taking out a small panel from a private drawer, said, 'this is the last which I shall show you; but it is the greatest curiosity of all. Only look at the splendour of the colouring and the original character of the thing!' 'I see,' said I, 'a naked figure with a strong body and a short neck—with burning eyes which long for moisture, and a face worthy of a murderer, holding a bloody cup in his clawed hands, out of which it seems eager to drink. I never saw any shape so strange, nor did I ever see any colouring so curiously splendid—a kind of glistening green and dusky gold, beautifully varnished. But what in the world is it?' 'It is a ghost, Sir—the ghost of a flea—a spiritualization of the thing!' 'He saw this in a vision then,' I said. 'I'll tell you all about it, Sir. I called on him one evening, and found Blake more than usually excited. He told me he had seen a wonderful thing—the ghost of a flea! And did you make a drawing of him? I inquired. No, indeed, said he, I wish I had, but I shall, if he appears again! He looked earnestly into a corner of the room, and then said, here he is—reach me my things—I shall keep my eye on him. There he comes! his eager tongue whisking out of his mouth, a cup in his hand to hold blood, and covered with a scaly skin of gold and green;—as he described him so he drew him.'*

These stories are scarcely credible, yet there can be no doubt of their accuracy. Another friend, on whose veracity I have the fullest dependence, called one evening on Blake, and found him sitting with a pencil and a panel, drawing a portrait with all the seeming anxiety of a man who is conscious that he has got a fastidious sitter; he looked and drew, and drew and looked, yet no living soul was visible. 'Disturb me not,' said he, in a whisper, 'I have one sitting to me.' 'Sitting to you!' exclaimed his astonished visitor, 'where is he, and what is he?—I see no one.' 'But I see him, Sir,' answered Blake haughtily, 'there he is, his name is Lot— you may read of him in the Scripture. *He* is sitting for his portrait.'[2]

Varley's own description of the ghost of a flea from his *Zodiacal Physiognomy* is given in Appendix I, together with Blake's Horoscope and Nativity. Gilchrist's account is more temperate, and he refers to various visionary heads not mentioned by Cunningham. A head of Solomon is particularly striking: it is as direct and definite in psychological conception as the portrait of a living sitter.

A note in one edition of *The Scottish Chiefs*, by Jane Porter, herself a lioness and swift in the pursuit of lions, affords a curious proof of the obscurity in which Blake lived. Her brother, Robert Ker Porter, was a member of the 'Brothers', a society of young painters founded by Francia and Girtin; she herself was often present at their meetings, and among her intimate friends was Sir Benjamin West.†

The preceding note having been appended to the first edition of this work, at the same time of its answering date; an extraordinary circumstance which occurred a few years afterwards, regarding certain portraitures of Sir William Wallace and Robert Bruce, the author of these pages is tempted to repeat now, as

* For a full account of Varley and the Ghost of a Flea see Keynes, *Blake Studies*, pp. 130-5.

† See p. 242 n. For an account of Jane Porter and her novels see *These were Muses*, by Mona Wilson (1924), pp. 119-42.

being a something strange and romantic story. The original relater of it was Mr. Blake, a young painter of remarkable talents; but which were at times, carried away into wild fancies; a mirage of waking dreams, which he gravely asserted, on describing them, were real visions from the departed world. Soon after the publication of the 'Scottish Chiefs,' his ardent nature had deeply interested him in their fate; but most particularly in that of Wallace; of whose unjust doom he was often in the habit of speaking to a friend of the author of the book, and with a force of language, and indignation at the fact, as if the noble victim's death had been only an event of yesterday.

In one of my friend's calls on the young painter, he found him in an almost breathless ecstasy, which he explained to him, by telling him that he had just achieved two sketches—one of Sir William Wallace, the other of his enemy, Edward the First! Both chiefs have actually appeared to him successively and had successively stood, at his earnest request, to allow him to make a hasty sketch of their forms.

While he related this, he placed a small canvas, of the common portrait size, on his easel, before my friend; on which was drawn, in a bold and admirable manner, the head of a young warrior in the prime of his days: as Wallace is described to have been, even at the time in which he was cut off. . . . [Here follows a long description of the portrait.]

While my friend was contemplating this extraordinary portrait, its enraptured artist had described its origin, in this wise:—'He was sitting, meditating, as he had often done, on the heroic actions and hard fate of the Scottish hero, when, like a flash of lightning, a noble form stood before him; which he instantly knew, by a something within himself, to be Sir William Wallace. He felt it was a spiritual appearance; which might vanish away as instantly as it came; and, transported at the sight, he besought the hero to remain a few moments till he might sketch him. The warrior Scot, in this vision, seemed as true to his historical mental picture, as his noble shade was to the manly bearing of his recorded person; for, with his accustomed courtesy, he smiled on the young painter; and the sketch was outlined, with a tint or two besides. But, while eagerly proceeding, the artist bent his head once too often, to replenish his pencil, and turning again to pursue the noble contour, the spirit of the "stalworth knight" had withdrawn from mortal ken. But (Blake proceeded to say), it had not left a vacancy! Edward the First stood in its place; armed from head to foot, in a close and superb suit of mail; but with the visor of his helmet open!'

The artist, it appears, had as little difficulty in recognizing the royal hero as when, his heart, as well as his eyes bowing before the august figure just departed, told him it was the Caledonian patriot he beheld. His English loyalty, however, made him rise before the royal apparition. Nevertheless, he saluted the monarch with the same earnest privilege of enthusiastic genius which had dictated his request to the Scottish chief; and he asked the stern-looking, but majestic warrior-king of England, to allow him to make a corresponding sketch. This too, was accorded. And he had arrived at about the same point, as in the former portrait, when the British hero also disappeared;—and Blake was left—not so disappointed at not having accomplished all he wished, as enraptured at having been permitted to behold two such extraordinary characters; and to have thus far, identified their personal presence to himself; and to the world, to all posterity! For such was his own conviction. The vast expanse of life's energies, wrought in this young man by the over-active exercise of his talents and the burning enthusiasm, which almost ever over-stimulated their action, swiftly consumed his constitution and not very long after the painting of these two visionary portraits, he died of a rapid decline—my friend purchased them both; and subsequently showed them to me, recounting the little history, I have just repeated.*

It will be observed that Miss Porter's account and Cunningham's differ in various particulars: the one is exploiting Varley for journalistic purposes, the other instinctively enhances the romance of the situation. But the most striking feature of Miss Porter's note is her description of Blake's early death; this is obviously her own characteristic contribution, but it proves that Blake's name and reputation were entirely unknown to her, although she was familiar with a number of artists.

In Linnell's amusing sketch of Blake and Varley arguing† Blake seems almost a votary of Urizen beside the eager, credulous

* Postscript to Appendix of *The Scottish Chiefs*, May 1841, quoted from Keynes, *Bibliography*, pp. 173–5, where the note is printed in full. Linnell possessed these two visionary heads, but he copied them in oil for Varley who may therefore have been Jane Porter's informant. (Story, *Linnell*, i, p. 168.)

† Now with other drawings of Blake by Linnell in the Fitzwilliam Museum. [Ed.]

Varley, and Linnell himself remarks that 'Varley believed in the reality of Blake's visions more than even Blake himself.' Varley, it would seem, believed that Blake actually summoned the spirits of the dead to sit for their portraits in a bodily form invisible to others, and this in spite of Blake's own explanations. Linnell says:

Even to John Varley, to whom I had introduced Blake, and who readily devoured all the marvellous in Blake's most extravagant utterances—even to Varley Blake would occasionally explain, unasked, how he believed that both Varley and I could see the same visions as he saw—making it evident to me that Blake claimed the possession of some powers, only in a greater degree than all men possessed, and which they undervalued in themselves, and lost through love of sordid pursuits, pride, vanity, and the unrighteous Mammon.[3]

Blake, it may be inferred, did not, like Varley, regard himself as a spiritualistic medium in the ordinary sense. He believed that he, and others who chose to cultivate the power, could have visionary intercourse with the spirits of the dead, because he believed in the timeless union of all things in the Divine Mind, and hence that the living could command the world memory to a greater or less extent. He visualized and drew these heads just as many people can visualize and draw a well-known face or landscape. It has already been suggested that this power, which was most active at night, was connected with the ordinary phenomenon of hypnagogic images which are very rarely under the voluntary control of the subject.

Linnell does not record his own opinion of the visionary heads: it is possible that he was more interested in Blake's power of visualizing his conceptions for practical purposes than in the likeness of the portraits to their originals. Be this as it may, he evidently thought the drawings executed under these conditions of considerable interest, as he bought those of the flea and thirty-six others from Blake, and also painted some of them in oil for Varley from Blake's drawings.*

* For further accounts of Blake's 'visionary heads' see Keynes, *Blake Studies*, pp. 130–1, and *The Blake-Varley Sketchbook of 1819*, ed. Martin Butlin (1969), where part of the book is reproduced in facsimile. Several of the

He was so strongly attracted to Blake that, although in later years disposed to accentuate his heterodoxy, he made a genuine effort to fathom his darkest sayings:

I soon encountered Blake's peculiarities, and was sometimes taken aback by the boldness of some of his assertions. I never saw anything the least like madness. I never opposed him spitefully, as many did. But being really anxious to fathom, if possible, the amount of truth that there might be in his most startling assertions, I generally met with a sufficiently rational explanation in the most really friendly and conciliatory tone.[4]

Linnell's attitude towards Blake was from first to last that of a sensible and affectionate son. They were good companions, and enjoyed going together to theatres and to see paintings and prints. Linnell introduced Blake to his friends, and put him in the way of obtaining work, although it was not till later that he realized how poor Blake was. The illuminated books were still a source of income, and Blake's wider acquaintance probably made it possible to dispose of a few more of these, but the expense of materials prevented his keeping a store of them in hand for casual disposal. A letter of June 1818 to Dawson Turner of Great Yarmouth, botanist, antiquary, and patron of art, shows that he considered them 'unprofitable enough to me, tho' Expensive to the Buyer.' After giving a list of books and prints he says:

The few I have Printed & Sold are sufficient to have gained me great reputation as an Artist, which was the chief thing Intended. But I have never been able to produce a Sufficient number for a general Sale by means of a regular Publisher. It is therefore necessary to me that any Person wishing to have any or all of them should send me their Order to Print them on the above terms, & I will take care that they shall be done at least as well as any I have yet Produced.[5]

A comparison of this list with that of Blake's Prospectus of 1793 shows a considerable rise in the prices: that of *America* has increased from 10*s.* 6*d.* to 5 guineas, *The Book of Thel* from 3*s.* to

---

drawings in Linnell's collection had been removed from this book as well as others now dispersed. [Ed.]

2 guineas, both the *Songs of Innocence* and the *Songs of Experience* from 5*s.* to 3 guineas. The list in a letter to George Cumberland nine years later shows a further increase of a guinea or two guineas in most cases.

In 1820 Blake engraved a portrait of Mrs. Quentin, one of the Regent's mistresses, after Huet Villiers.[6] About the same time he executed a series of twenty-one water-colour drawings illustrating the Book of Job for his old patron, Thomas Butts.* These were afterwards engraved at Linnell's instance. The print of the Laocoön surrounded by mystical sentences was engraved about 1820.† Only two copies of this are known, and it can scarcely have been a remunerative publication.[7]

The annotations to Berkeley's *Siris*‡ and the one-page leaflet *On Homer's Poetry* and *On Virgil* were written about the same time.[8] Only six copies of the latter are known. They are printed in black and uncoloured: to the left of the second heading is a small drawing of Homer playing a harp, while a group of four figures listens. The substance of all these utterances is the same and may be summed up in the last notes on the *Siris*. 'Man is All Imagination. God is Man & exists in us & we in him.' 'What Jesus came to Remove was the Heathen or Platonic Philosophy, which blinds the Eye of Imagination, The Real Man.'[9]

Through Linnell or otherwise Blake had become acquainted with Lady Caroline Lamb, and there is a glimpse of him at one of her parties in Lady Charlotte Bury's diary for 20 January 1820:

I dined at Lady C. L—'s. She had collected a strange party of artists and literati, and one or two fine folks, who were very ill assorted with the rest of the company, and appeared neither to give nor receive pleasure from the society among whom they mingled. Sir T. Lawrence, next whom I sat at dinner, is as courtly

* These drawings were later in the collection of Lord Houghton and of his son, the Marquis of Crewe. They are now in the Pierpont Morgan Library, New York. A replica set was made for John Linnell in 1821. [Ed.]

† This was probably engraved from the drawing made for Rees's *Cyclopaedia*, 1820, already mentioned (p. 270). See Keynes, *The Separate Plates*, pp. 56–7, with full-size reproduction. [Ed.]

‡ This copy of *Siris*, 1744, is now in the Rothschild Library, Trinity College, Cambridge. [Ed.]

as ever. His conversation is agreeable, but I never feel as if he was saying what he really thought. . . .

Besides Sir T., there was also present of this profession Miss M[ee], the miniature painter, a modest, pleasing person; like the pictures she executes, soft and sweet. Then there was another eccentric little artist, by name Blake; not a regular professional painter, but one of those persons who follow the art for its own sweet sake, and derive their happiness from its pursuit. He appeared to me to be full of beautiful imaginations and genius; but how far the execution of his designs is equal to the conceptions of his mental vision, I know not, never having seen them. *Main-d'œuvre* is frequently wanting where the mind is most powerful. Mr. Blake appears unlearned in all that concerns this world, and from what he said, I should fear he was one of those whose feelings are far superior to his situation in life. He looks care-worn and subdued; but his countenance radiated as he spoke of his favourite pursuit, and he appeared gratified by talking to a person who comprehended his feelings. I can easily imagine that he seldom meets with any who enters into his views; for they are peculiar, and exalted above the common level of received opinions. I could not help contrasting this humble artist with the great and powerful Sir Thomas Lawrence, and thinking that the one was fully if not more worthy of the distinction and fame to which the other has attained, but from which *he* is far removed. Mr. Blake, however, though he may have as much right, from talent and merit, to the advantages of which Sir Thomas is possessed, evidently lacks that worldly wisdom and that grace of manner which make a man gain an eminence in his profession, and succeed in every society. Every word he uttered spoke the perfect simplicity of his mind, and his total ignorance of all worldly matters. He told me that Lady C— L— had been very kind to him. 'Ah!' said he, 'there is a deal of kindness in that lady.' I agreed with him, and though it was impossible not to laugh at the strange manner in which she had arranged this party, I could not help admiring the goodness of heart and discrimination of talent which had made her patronise this unknown artist. Sir T. Lawrence looked at me several times whilst I was talking with Mr. B., and I saw his lips curl with a sneer, as if he despised me for conversing with so insignificant a person. It was very evident that Sir Thomas did not like the company he found himself in, though he was too well-bred and too prudent to hazard a remark upon the subject.[10]

Sir Thomas, after his dinner-table courtesies, may have resented

Lady Charlotte's obvious preference for the society of a shabby old man whom he probably did not know by sight, but when introduced to Blake about two years later by Linnell he proved his admiration by buying a copy of the *Songs of Innocence and of Experience* and two drawings, 'Queen Catherine's Dream'* and 'The Wise and Foolish Virgins', at fifteen guineas apiece. Gilchrist's irresponsible saying that Lawrence considered it 'almost giving the money' is falsified by a note in a friend's diary to the effect that the latter 'was Sir Thomas' favourite drawing,' and that 'he commonly kept it on his table in his studio, as a study.' This was a genuine tribute from the possessor of a famous collection of drawings by old masters.

In 1820 Blake began his illustrations for Dr. Thornton's edition of Virgil's Pastorals, adapted for use in schools. Thornton was a well-known physician and botanist. Linnell probably suggested the commission as Thornton was his family doctor. The edition has 230 illustrations from various hands. Blake's contributions are six engravings from his own drawings of the busts of Theocritus, Virgil, Augustus, Agrippa, Julius Caesar, and Epicurus, a woodcut of a drawing after Poussin, and twenty woodcuts from his own designs, only seventeen of which were executed by himself.† The latter, the only woodcuts he is known to have attempted, narrowly escaped the fate of his designs for Blair's *Grave*. The publishers, according to Gilchrist, were for rejecting the seventeen, and having them re-cut by another hand.‡ Dr. Thornton was luckily

---

* This drawing is now in the Lessing Rosenwald Collection, National Gallery, Washington, D.C. W. M. Rossetti (Gilchrist, ii, p. 223) says that Lawrence also possessed the water-colour, 'The Rich Man in Purgatory', or 'Dives in Hell', but the present location of this is not known.

† Reproduced in *The Illustrations of William Blake for Thornton's Virgil*, with Introduction by Geoffrey Keynes (1937).

‡ The three plates which were executed by a professional woodcutter have become smooth and characterless in the process. One of the designs cut by Blake was also cut by a professional, and impressions from the two blocks were printed to illustrate an article in *The Athenaeum* for 21 January 1843, a date at which Blake was in general little appreciated, in order to point the moral that the artist himself can alone give full expression to his own genius. See Keynes, *Blake Studies*, p. 139, with reproductions.

reassured as to their merit by a party of artists, among whom were Lawrence, James Ward, and Linnell, but thought it necessary to add a propitiatory note which recalls Blake's first introduction to the public by the Revd. A. S. Mathew.

The illustrations of this English Pastoral are by the famous *Blake*, the illustrator of Young's *Night Thoughts*, and Blair's *Grave*; who designed and engraved them himself. This is mentioned as they display less of art than of genius, and are much admired by some eminent painters.

The twarted publishers avenged themselves by allowing some of the blocks to be worked over, and also by cutting down sixteen of Blake's seventeen blocks in order to fit their pages. Much of the beauty and spaciousness of the original designs, of which proofs remain in eight instances, is lost in the mutilated prints. So carefully had Blake planned his designs for the effect he wished to produce that his original drawings* are considered by some critics inferior to the woodcuts, whatever these may lack in technical efficiency. (The influence of these woodcuts on the group of young painters who nicknamed themselves the 'Ancients' is discussed in a later chapter.)

In 1821 Blake's landlord in South Molton Street retired, and the Blakes removed to 3 Fountain Court, Strand,† where they rented the first floor of a house occupied by Mr. Baines, Mrs. Blake's brother-in-law. During the first months in his new home Blake seems to have had serious financial difficulties, as he sold his entire collection of prints to Messrs. Colnaghi. Linnell, on realizing his position, made representations to Lawrence, Collins, and some other Royal Academicians, who induced the Council to vote in

---

* The volume of original sepia drawings was sold with the Linnell collection in 1918; it was then taken to the United States, where the leaves were separated and dispersed. The frontispiece was lacking, but there was one extra drawing which was not engraved. The majority were reproduced in the volume edited by Keynes for the Nonesuch Press, 1937. [Ed.]

† The house is described by Symons (*Blake*, p. 227) as being in a narrow slit between the Strand and the Thames. The name was changed to Southampton Buildings in 1883, and the houses were pulled down in 1902. [Ed.]

1822 a donation of £25, which was transmitted to Blake by Linnell. *

Blake issued, in 1822, a dramatic poem,

THE GHOST of ABEL

A Revelation In the Visions of Jehovah Seen by William Blake

This was the last time he made use of his invention of relief-etching, and after the date in the colophon are the words 'Blake's Original Stereotype was 1788.'† Four copies only are known, printed in black and uncoloured. The dedication offers his solution of the *Mystery* to the author of *Cain*, still wandering in the wilderness of error.‡ Adam refuses to hear the voice of Jehovah, and immediately the Ghost of Abel, like those in *Vala* who were murdered before the Last Judgment has been passed and error cast out, calls for vengeance, but Eve knows intuitively that it is not the real Abel. For Adam:

It is all a Vain delusion of the all creative Imagination.
Eve, come away, & let us not believe these vain delusions.
Abel is dead, & Cain slew him. We shall also Die a Death,
And then, what then? be, as poor Abel, a Thought, or as
This! O, what shall I call thee, Form Divine, Father of Mercies,
That appearest to my Spiritual Vision? Eve, seest thou also?

Eve's reply is Blake's own: it is also a clear explanation of the nature of his visions, and of his faith in them as the highest expression of his spiritual imagination.

I see him plainly with my Mind's Eye. I see also Abel living,
Tho' terribly afflicted, as We also are, yet Jehovah sees him
Alive & not Dead; were it not better to believe Vision
With all our might & strength, tho' we are fallen & lost?[11]

* Collins and Abraham Cooper recommended him for the grant; the mover and seconder of the resolution were Baily and R. Bone. (Gilchrist, *Life*, i, p. 328.)

† This has been supposed to indicate an earlier issue of 'The Ghost of Abel'. Sampson (*The Poetical Works of William Blake*, 1905, p. xvii) pointed out that it refers to Blake's first use of the process.

‡ Cf. Damon, *Blake*, chapter xxxi. Blake's Exhibition had included 'The Body of Abel, found by Adam and Eve. Cain fleeing away'.

When the Ghost of Abel defies God and sinks into the grave still demanding blood for blood, Satan, the Accuser, is revealed, and claims the great vengeance, the sacrifice of God on Calvary. But Jehovah condemns him to 'Eternal Death In Self Annihilation, even till Satan, Self-subdu'd, Put off Satan. . . .'[12] Satan, it should be noted, is not here conceived as error only, but as the Accuser who can be redeemed when he will listen to the Everlasting Gospel, and cast out his error. The chorus of Angels hails the acceptance by the Heathen Gods, the Avengers, of Jehovah's Covenant of the Forgiveness of Sins. God is named Jehovah in this poem because he is not yet known in time as Jesus.

A commission from Linnell in 1821 led to Blake's greatest achievement as an engraver and his most likely known work as an artist. He had borrowed from Mr. Butts the series of water-colour drawings illustrating the Book of Job, hoping to obtain orders for replicas. Linnell alone responded, and in September himself traced the outlines from Butts's drawings, which Blake completed with some variations from the originals. As no further orders were forthcoming Linnell suggested that Blake should produce a book of engravings from these designs as a more saleable alternative, and offered to bear the risk of the undertaking.* Blake therefore made a set of reduced pencil sketches, and began to engrave the plates in 1823. The terms of the agreement between himself and Linnell were as follows:

* Full information about the Job designs will be found in *Illustrations of the Book of Job by Blake*, reproduced in facsimile with Introduction by Laurence Binyon and Geoffrey Keynes (New York, The Pierpont Morgan Library, 1935). See also Keynes, *Blake Studies*, and *Blake Records*. The additional plate is the title-page. Seventeen of the water-colour drawings commissioned by Linnell are now in the Boston Museum of Fine Arts; the pencil drawings are in the Fitzwilliam Museum. Sets of the prints in original boards are usually marked: 'Prints £3. 3s. Proofs £5. 5s.' Linnell mentioned the transaction in a letter to Bernard Barton of 3 April 1830 (*Blake Records*, p. 395), discounting his own generosity on the ground that he had expected, and still hoped for, profit. This hope was fully realized in 1918 when his Blake collection was sold at auction for over £22,000.

Memorandum of Agreement between William Blake and John Linnell.
March 25th 1823—
W. Blake agrees to Engrave the Set of Plates from his own Designs of Job's Captivity in number twenty, for John Linnell— and John Linnell agrees to pay William Blake five Pounds p^r Plate or one hundred Pounds for the set part before and the remainder when the Plates are finished, as Mr Blake may require it, besides which J. Linnell agrees to give W. Blake one hundred pounds more out of the Profits of the work as the receipts will admit of it.

Signed J. Linnell   Willm Blake

N.B. J. L. to find Copper Plates.*

The book was published in March 1826, and although no profits resulted, Linnell paid Blake an additional sum of £50 by instalments between March 1823 and October 1825. A receipt for the total of £150, dated 14 July 1826, sets forth that this sum was paid 'for the copyright and plates [22 in number] of the "Job," published March 1825, by William Blake, author.'

Cumberland had made a special study of Bonasone, and Linnell possessed his large print of Michelangelo's 'Last Judgment', and probably a selection of Marcantonio's work. Blake's growing familiarity with the style of these engravers had enabled him to rid himself of the heavy mechanical manner derived from Basire, his imagination had long been possessed by the Book of Job, as his earlier drawing, engraving, and lithograph testify, and more-over he was free in this venture from commercial interference. The omens, for once, were wholly favourable.

These illustrations have been so frequently reproduced that any description would be unnecessary had not a modern critic shown that the designs are not mere straightforward comments on the Bible story, but the vehicle for Blake's own gospel. These Inventions are, as Mr. Joseph Wicksteed has shown, the greatest of the symbolic books, the only one of the Giants who has attained form and proportion. Blake himself gives a hint of his intention

* The MS. of this document, printed here as it is given in *Blake Records*, p. 277, is in the Yale University Library, New Haven, Conn [Ed.].

to George Cumberland, who had been vainly trying to dispose of a copy to the Bristol booksellers:

> I thank you for the Pains you have taken with Poor Job. I know too well that a great majority of Englishmen are fond of The Indefinite, which they Measure by Newton's Doctrine of the Fluxions of an Atom, A Thing that does not Exist. These are Politicians & think that Republican Art is Inimical to their Atom. For a Line or Lineament is not formed by Chance. A Line is a Line in its Minutest Subdivisions: Straight or Crooked It is Itself, & Not Intermeasurable with or by any Thing Else. Such is Job, but since the French Revolution Englishmen are all Intermeasurable One by Another. Certainly a happy state of Agreement to which I for One do not Agree. God keep me from the Divinity of Yes & No too, The Yea Nay Creeping Jesus, from supposing Up & Down to be the same Thing as all Experimentalists must suppose.[13]

This passage alone would suggest that Blake's preoccupation with the contrast between the eternal, the spiritual, and the material, the illusory, finds expression in the Inventions. But there are also frequent indications both in his verse and drawings that if up and down must not be confused neither must right and left: the right had been customarily esteemed the propitious direction and the honourable position, and Blake followed other mystics in extending the meaning of right and left to spiritual and material.* The use of this symbolism is probably more deliberate and consistent in the Job than elsewhere, but it must not be forgotten that in *A Vision of the Last Judgment* Blake had entreated the Spectator

---

* This clue has been both suggested and followed up by Joseph Wicksteed in *Blake's Vision of the Book of Job* (1910). Few readers of his elaborate argument will doubt Blake's symbolic use of right and left, although they may feel that Wicksteed's explanation is unconvincing in a few instances. Wicksteed also shows that God all through the book, except where he is the image of Eliphaz, is the reflection of Job's own spiritual state, and he relates the texts and symbols in the margins with the central designs. His valuable book, of which free use has been made in the account of *Job* given here, should be read by all students of Blake (2nd ed., 1925). Damon, *Blake*, chapter xxx, writing after the publication of the first edition of Wicksteed's book, has added several contributions to the symbolic interpretation of the illustrations, notably the suggestion, borne out by the title-page, that Blake again makes use of the Seven States, the Seven Eyes of God, and by his comparison with the Tarot Cards.

to attend to the hands and feet. Some of the variations on the water-colour drawings tend to increase the symbolic significance of the engravings, but the main proof that their meaning does not lie on the surface is to be found in the texts and designs in the borders, which always throw light on the central design. Moreover, readers of *Jerusalem* and Blake's other writings of the same period will recognize the pictorial expression of symbols with which they are already familiar.

Job in the Bible is the just man who eschews evil and observes the ceremonies of religion, tested and humiliated that God may convince Satan of Job's allegiance to himself. Job is rewarded for his constancy and his unnecessary suffering by a renewal of God's favour and the restoration and increase of his worldly prosperity: his only spiritual satisfaction besides a confirmation of his belief in God's power is the conviction of his own inability to understand the ways of the Almighty.

Blake's Job, on the other hand, passes from the state of innocence because he cultivates a rigid and repressive holiness and fails to offer the only sacrifice which avails anything, that of the selfhood. His sufferings in the contrary state of experience are at once the result of his own error and the means through which he attains full spiritual stature. In the first illustration the sun is setting behind the 'living form' of a Gothic cathedral: Job, with his wife and children, surrounded by the flocks which mark his material prosperity, is shown in the solemn exercise of family prayers: the letter which killeth is symbolized by the heavy books open on the parents' knees, and the spirit which giveth life by the joyful instruments of music, discarded and hung up on the tree behind them. This is followed by a revelation of Job's spiritual condition. Above the family group a smug God in Job's own image sits in his heaven with a book of the precepts which Job obeys open on his knees; the records of Job's good deeds are being handed about from earth to heaven in order to justify him against Satan, the Accuser of Sin, while on the other side of Satan the self-satisfied faces of Job and his wife bear witness to his spiritual error. Job next sends the winged accuser of his own thought against his sons, who are the victims of the excesses which he has made attractive to them by restraint and repression. Then come two messengers, left foot foremost, announcing the destruction of his property, while the figure of a third in the far distance with the right foot in advance, shows that material disaster will be followed by spiritual.

In the fifth design the 'living form' of the cathedral is replaced by a Druid altar. God is seated less firmly in his heaven, while Satan, the spiritual error in Job's own mind, is beginning his attack on Job himself. Below, Job, with a sanctimonious expression, retains the loaf in his right hand, while he gives that in his left to a beggar. On either side hover two angels of holiness betraying his self-approving thoughts. Then Satan descends on him in full fury. The four arrows show that he has killed four of the senses, and he is smiting the fifth, touch and sex. He is standing on Job's right leg to signify that the disease is spiritual. Job ignores his wife, who has hitherto been completely united with him, and she is weeping at his feet. The design is similar to the painting in the Tate Gallery, but a great thunder-cloud takes the place of Satan's wings, showing that the Accuser has not been sent forth by Job against others as in the third illustration, but is besetting Job himself.

Next comes the arrival of the three corporeal friends who are spiritual enemies. After that Job, in the absence of all spiritual consolation, curses the day when he was born. Then Eliphaz concentrates the argument of the three friends by narrating his vision of the God of Justice. God is here in the image of Eliphaz and his arms are bound by his own law. Next, the Accuser, whom Job had sent against his sons, comes upon him from the outside, personified by the three friends. His wife crouches by his side and touches him with her right hand in token of sympathy, but he takes no notice of her.* In the eleventh design God, revealing

* It is difficult to forgive Wicksteed's treatment of Job's wife in his commentary on this design. Although he has pointed out that she has been one with her husband, never counselling him to 'curse God, and die,' as in the Bible story, he here fancies her as strengthening the friends' case against Job.

himself as Satan by his cloven hoof, but still in Job's image, swoops down upon him in the coils of the serpent of materialism, and points to the stone tables of the law in his heaven. Next comes Elihu, who brings instead of false sympathy that opposition which is true friendship. He is indignant because Job does not submit himself to the decrees of his God, Urizen, the 'starry king'. Job, strengthened in spirit, can now pass into the last state of the Seven Eyes of God, Jesus. God, typifying this state, descends from heaven in a whirlwind to answer Job's appeal. The friends abase themselves in terror, but Job and his wife can behold his face. The other six Eyes of God are depicted in the margin, and one of them stretches out his hand towards another figure which is just rising: this is the 'shadowy eighth',* Job's eternal individuality, now ready to join the rest.

The fourteenth design, which belongs also to the seventh state, Jesus, 'When the morning Stars sang together, and all the Sons of God shouted for joy,'† is Blake's best-known work. God, the poetic genius, is in the centre, and under his immediate control Apollo drives the horses of Intellect, and Diana guides the dragons of Desire. The other Zoas, spirit and body, are symbolized by the line of angels above, endless, thanks to Blake's afterthought in adding the arms of others to right and left which appear in the engraving only, and the group on earth.‡ In the next invention

---

Had the engraving belonged to the Felpham days Blake might have been so tempted, but such a suggestion is now a treachery to Catherine Blake.

(Mr. Wicksteed resented this note, and the author afterwards agreed that her sympathy with Job's wife, whose spiritual sufferings must have been even greater than Job's, had betrayed her into undue vehemence.)

* The beginning of this figure is discernible in the left-hand margin.

† Sir C. Holmes has reproduced this design in his volume on the *Italian School* in the National Gallery, on the same page as Botticelli's Nativity. Blake is the only modern artist thus associated with the old masters, and it may be hoped that this honour has been duly published in heaven. Samuel Palmer writes: 'I asked him how he would like to paint on glass, for the great West window (i.e., of Westminster Abbey), his *Sons of God Shouting for Joy*, from his designs in the Job. He said, after a pause, "I could do it!" kindling at the thought'. (Gilchrist, *Life*, i, p. 56.)

‡ The addition of the arms of other angels to right and left is a recurrence

God is explaining the world of nature, in which Pitt's Behemoth and Nelson's Leviathan reappear. Then Job's Error is cast out at a Last Judgment. As Blake had said some years before, 'Whenever any Individual Rejects Error & Embraces Truth, a Last Judgment passes upon that Individual.'[14] Satan, Error, is cast out, and with him the embodied errors of Job and his wife fall into the pit of annihilation. They look on in calm thankfulness, while their friends on the other side are terrified. In the design which follows Job and his wife are with God above the cloud and he is blessing them. The friends, still in the material world, have turned their backs, unable to bear the light. The contrast recalls the lines in the 'Auguries of Innocence':

> God Appears & God is Light
> To those poor Souls who dwell in Night,
> But does a Human Form Display
> To those who Dwell in Realms of day.[15]

Blake had told Crabb Robinson that Jesus is the only God, 'And so am I and so are you'; and the texts below are evidently intended to identify God with Jesus and with Job, who has now cast out spiritual error.

Then Job, in the cruciform attitude of self-sacrifice, prays for the friends whom he has forgiven. The cubical altar and pyramidal flame probably symbolize body and soul, a refinement on the water colour in which the irregular flame is cut off by the top of the drawing. The palette, brushes, and scrolls in the margin recall the sentence on the Laocoön print: 'Prayer is the Study of Art'; perhaps also Blake intended to show that he had himself forgiven those who had slighted him as an artist. The next design shows Job and his wife receiving their neighbours, who are loaded with offerings, signifying that Job has now learnt to accept as well as to give. In that which follows, Job is telling his daughters of the State of Experience, pointing to panels on the wall which illustrate

---

to one of Blake's designs for the *Night Thoughts*. In 1818 Blake engraved 'The Child of Nature' and 'The Child of Art' after Charles Burckhart: details in Keynes's *Separate Plates*.

it. The tessellated floor, with intersecting circles bounded by one great circle, doubtless symbolizes the perfect spiritual relation of men to one another and to God.

It has been suggested that Job's daughters, who were not involved in the disaster of their brothers, since the number of the women in the third illustration shows them to be intended for wives or concubines and not the three sisters, may symbolize the three modes of art, but there is no definite indication of this either here or in the next design. The last invention is in marked contrast to the first. The sun rises and the family are joyfully making music: two of the daughters are singing from scrolls, light in the hand, but the heavy books of holiness which define and restrain have disappeared.

Among the new friends whom Blake owed to Linnell were Mr. and Mrs. Aders of Euston Square. Mrs. Aders, a beautiful and gifted woman, was a daughter of Raphael Smith, the mezzotint engraver. She married a wealthy merchant of German extraction, who had acquired a remarkable collection of early Italian, Flemish, and German paintings, which he was obliged to part with later as the result of business reverses. The Aderses were hospitable, delighting in the society of artists and literary men, and Mrs. Aders, who lived till old age, always retained an affectionate memory of Blake. At their house in 1825 he met Crabb Robinson, journalist and barrister-at-law, and, like his hosts, a friend of Wordsworth, Coleridge,* and Lamb. Although not personally acquainted with him hitherto, Robinson had been interested in Blake since the appearance of Dr. Malkin's book, and in the spring of 1810 he chose Blake as the subject for an article in the *Vaterländisches Museum*. It was translated by Dr. Julius, who was particularly successful in his rendering of 'The Tyger.'† The

* Coleridge's poem, 'The Two Founts', was addressed to Mrs. Aders. Lamb wrote some verses 'To C. Aders, Esq., On his Collection of Paintings by the old German Masters' (Charles and Mary Lamb, *Poems and Plays*, edited by E. V. Lucas, p. 85).

† See Sampson, *Poetical Works* (1905), p. 115, for the German version.

original has not been found among the Crabb Robinson papers, but the article has been retranslated from the German.* The first paragraph shows the spirit in which Robinson approached his task, and was later to approach Blake himself.

Of all the conditions which arouse the interest of the psychologist, none assuredly is more attractive than the union of genius and madness in single remarkable minds, which, while on the one hand they compel our admiration by their great mental powers, yet on the other move our pity by their claims to supernatural gifts. Of such is the whole race of ecstatics, mystics, seers of visions and dreamers of dreams, and to their list we have now to add another name, that of William Blake.

In his *Reminiscences* he is more explicit, as he speaks of 'writing an account of the insane poet & painter engraver, *Blake*.'[16] After some reference to Blake's early life, for which Malkin was no doubt his authority, Robinson discusses his paintings and engravings, quoting excerpts from the *Descriptive Catalogue*, which he regards as 'a very curious exposure of the state of the artist's mind.' He has one anecdote of Blake which does not appear elsewhere:

He told a friend, from whose mouth we have the story, that once when he was carrying home a picture which he had done for a lady of rank, and was wanting to rest in an inn, the angel Gabriel touched him on the shoulder and said, 'Blake, wherefore art thou here? Go to, thou shouldst not be tired.' He arose and went on unwearied.

The greater part of the *Poetical Sketches* are dismissed as 'singularly rough and unattractive', but 'there is a wildness and loftiness of imagination in certain dramatic fragments which

* By K. M. Esdaile, in *The Library*, vol. v, 1 July 1914, pp. 229–56. Her translation is quoted here. Mrs. Esdaile found some notes which Robinson had used in compiling his article; among others, quotations from the *Advertisement (Complete Writings*, pp. 560–1), which was not reprinted till 1921 (Keynes, *Bibliography*, facing pp. 84, 85). She points out that Blake's early reputation in Germany was due to Crabb Robinson's article. The greater part of Cunningham's *Life* was translated in the *Zeitgenossen* in 1830, and considerable space was devoted to Blake in Nagler's *Kunstler-Lexicon*, 1835. Mrs. Esdaile's article is entitled 'An Early Appreciation of William Blake.'

testifies to genuine poetical feeling.' 'To the Muses' is quoted with the ambiguous comment that it 'may serve as a measure of the inspiration of the poet at this period.' *The Songs of Innocence and of Experience* he considers 'a still more remarkable little book.'

These miniature pictures are of the most vivid colours, and often grotesque, so that the book presents a most singular appearance. It is not easy to form a comprehensive opinion of the text, since the poems deserve the highest praise and the gravest censure.

Though he regards some of the *Songs of Innocence* as 'excessively childish' and the *Songs of Experience* as metaphysical riddles, he accords more praise than censure, and his interpretation of 'The Garden of Love' shows insight and sympathy:

The following Song of Experience probably represents man after the loss of his innocence, as, found by the commandment and the priests its servants, he looks back longing to his earlier state, where before was no commandment, no duty, and nought save love and voluntary sacrifice.

Europe and *America*, the only two of the symbolic books which he had come across, are frankly too much for him; he is doubtful whether they are intended for prose or verse. He concludes that in Blake:

all the elements of greatness are unquestionably to be found, even though those elements are disproportionately mingled. . . . We will only recall the phrase of a thoughtful writer, that those faces are the most attractive in which nature has set something of greatness which she had yet left unfinished; the same may hold good of the soul.

The article is the most appreciative and careful estimate of Blake as poet and painter which appeared during his lifetime.

In the interval between writing of Blake and meeting him at the Aderses', Crabb Robinson had heard Southey and Flaxman talk about him, and had read some of his poems to Wordsworth, who 'was pleased with some of them and considered [Blake] as having the elements of poetry a thousand times more than either Byron or Scott. . . .' In 1825 he added that Wordsworth* had said after reading a number of the *Songs of Innocence and of Experience*: 'There is no doubt this poor man was mad, but there is something in the madness of this man which interests me more than the sanity of Lord Byron and Walter Scott!'[18]

It is clear, therefore, that Crabb Robinson had made up his mind before seeing Blake that he was mad: when they met on the 10th December 1825 he seems surprised that his mental condition was not more obvious. In his Diary he asks 'Shall I call him Artist or Genius—or Mystic or Madman? Probably he is all,' and he adds in the *Reminiscences*:

He had a broad, pale face, a large full eye with a benignant expression;† at the same time a look of languor except when excited, & then he had an air of inspiration, but not such as without a previous acquaintance with him, or attending to *what* he said, would suggest the notion that he was insane. There was nothing *wild* about his look and though very ready to be drawn out to the assertion of his favourite ideas, yet with no warmth as if he wanted to make proselytes. Indeed one of the peculiar features of his scheme as far as it was consistent was indifference and a very extraordinary degree of tolerance & satisfaction with what had taken place, a sort of pious & humble optimism, not the scornful optimism of *Candide*.[19]

Robinson himself was puzzled by his own interest in mystics. 'It is strange,' he says in his Diary, 'that I, who have no imagination, nor any power beyond that of a logical understanding, should yet have great respect for the mystics.' Unfortunately he

---

* Cf. letter of Samuel Palmer to Mrs. Gilchrist (*Life of Samuel Palmer*, p. 248): 'Wordsworth said to a friend, "I called the other day while you were out, and stole a book out of your library—*Blake's Songs of Innocence*." He read, and read, and took it home to read, and read again.' In a letter to Dorothy Wordsworth of February 1826 Crabb Robinson wrote: 'I gave your brother some poems in MS & they interested him—as well they might, for there is an affinity between the regulated imagination of a wise poet & the incoherent dreams of a poet.' It has been suggested (Keynes, *Bibliography*, p. 46) that the 'poems in MS' may have been the *Pickering MS*.

† Cunningham (Symons, *Blake*, p. 429) describes him as 'of low stature and slender make, with a high pallid forehead, and eyes large, dark, and expressive'.

exercised his logical understanding in trying to isolate Blake's metaphysical doctrines from what he regarded as the insane expression of them, in order that he might classify them, and he finds it 'hard to fix Blake's station between Christianity, Platonism and Spinozism.' There were, sometimes, congenial moments as when, for example, Robinson expressed the view that an immortal being could not be created. 'His eye brightened on my saying this. And he eagerly concurred. "To be sure it is impossible. We are all coexistent with God, Members of the Divine body. We are all partakers of the divine nature." ' Robinson could deal comfortably with this since Blake had but 'adopted an ancient Greek idea Qy. of Plato.'

But Blake's talk of visions and voices, and 'the same half crazy crochets about the two worlds' made him feel that 'there being really no system or connection in his mind, all his future conversation will be but varieties of wildness and incongruity.'[21] For this reason he tantalizes us by imperfect accounts of his later interviews. He pleased Blake by seeming to assent to his statement that all men possess in some degree the faculty of vision; had he not presupposed insanity he might have genuinely accepted this view, contenting himself with a psychological analysis of Blake's visionary experiences which would have led him, like Linnell, to a less extreme conclusion. As it is he defends himself for thinking it worth while to record Blake's sayings on the ground that he was not a mere madman, but a monomaniac. Robinson's interlocutions were evidently conducted in a kindly and conciliatory spirit; he never tried to provoke Blake, and he never obtruded his own opinions, but he sometimes notes that Blake had made no reply to his observations. He remarks with disapproval that Masquerier,* an acquaintance of longer standing than himself, commented on Blake's opinions 'as if they were those of a man of ordinary notions,' and doubts 'whether Flaxman sufficiently tolerates Blake.'[22] His own policy was to humour the mental case, and this was doubtless obvious enough to the patient, who demanded opposition from his friends. What did Blake think of

* John James Masquerier (1778–1855), portrait painter.

Robinson? Did he confide to Mrs Blake that the visitor was a good creature but something of a bore?

Yet in spite of this mutual want of sympathy Crabb Robinson has given by far the most detailed and convincing report of Blake's conversations. His account has been already quoted as explaining passages in the poems, but Blake's talk with Voltaire and his refusal to be floored by the astute barrister are too characteristic to omit:

'. . . he understands by the Bible the spiritual sense. For as to the natural sense, that Voltaire was commissioned by God to expose. I have had much intercourse with Voltaire and he said to me I blasphemed the Son of Man it shall be forgiven me. But *they* (the enemies of V[oltaire]) blasphemed the Holy Ghost in me And it shall not be forgiven them.' I asked in what language Voltaire spoke. He gave an ingenious answer. 'To my sensations it was English. It was like the touch of a musical key. He touched it probably French, but to my ear it became English!'[23]

Crabb Robinson's description of the Blakes' home in Fountain Court must be discounted; he and his friends were all in comparatively easy circumstances and he doubtless failed to perceive the gulf set between simplicity and squalor.*

He was at work engraving in a small bedroom, light & looking out on a mean yard—everythg. in the room squalid, & indicating poverty except himself. And there was a natural gentility about, & an insensibility to the seeming poverty which quite removed the impression. Besides, his linen was clean, his hands white & his air

---

* The shorter and earlier account in the Diary, p. 8, is more emphatic; Crabb Robinson even speaks of 'filth'. It appears from a passage on page 25 of *The Richmond Papers*, edited by A. M. W. Stirling (1926), as though George Richmond was in agreement with Crabb Robinson rather than Palmer, but the opinion given is based on second-hand information, and Mrs. Stirling kindly informs me that the story about Mrs. Blake was told to her by Mrs. Arthur Severn's niece. [This story at second-hand is as follows: 'George Richmond once told Mr Severn—'never have I known an artist so spiritual, so devoted, so single-minded or so full of vivid imagination as he. Before Blake began a picture he used to fall on his knees and pray that his work might be successful. The room was squalid and untidy. And once Mrs Blake, in excuse for the general lack of soap and water, remarked to me "You see, Mr Blake's skin don't dirt".' Ed.]

quite unembarrassed when he begged me to sit down, as if he were in a palace. There was but one chair in the room besides that on wh. he sat. On my putting my hand to it, I found that it would have fallen to pieces if I had lifted it. So, as if I had been a Sybarite, I said with a smile, 'Will you let me indulge myself?' And I sat on the bed and near him. And during my short stay there was nothing in him that betrayed that he was aware of what to other persons might have been even offensive, not in his person, but in all about him.

His wife I saw at this time, & she seemed to be the very woman to make him happy. She had been formed by him. Indeed otherwise she cd. not have lived with him. Notwithstanding her dress, wh. was poor & dirty, she had a good expression in her countenance—& with a dark eye, had remains of beauty in her youth.[24]

Gilchrist read this passage from the *Reminiscences*, which Robinson had lent him, to Samuel Palmer, who wrote on 3 May 1860:

Late as we parted last night, I awaked at dawn with the question in my ear, Squalor?—squalor? Crush it; it is a roc's egg to your fabric. It gives a notion altogether false of the man, his house, and his habits.

No, certainly;—whatever was in Blake's house, there was no squalor. Himself, his wife, and his rooms, were clean and orderly; everything in its place. His delightful working corner had its implements ready—tempting to the hand. The millionaire's upholsterer can furnish no enrichments like those of Blake's enchanted rooms.*

George Richmond, more than fifty years after Blake's death, thus described the arrangement of the room which had impressed Crabb Robinson so unfavourably:

The fire-place was in the far right-hand corner opposite the window; their bed in the left hand, facing the river; a long engraver's table stood under the window (where I watched Blake engrave the *Book of Job*. He worked facing the light), a pile of portfolios and drawings on Blake's right near the only cupboard;

* From *Anne Gilchrist: Her Life and Writings*, ed. H. H. Gilchrist (1887). Palmer wrote to Gilchrist in 1855 that he remembered a finished picture after Giulio Romano from Ovid's *Metamorphoses* hanging in Blake's room, 'and, close by his engraving table, Albert Dürer's *Melancholy the Mother of Invention*.' (Gilchrist, i, pp. 346–7.)

and on the poet-artist's left—a pile of books placed flatly one on another; no bookcase.[25]

In reply to the question whether there were many pictures on the walls Richmond answered, 'No, not many in the work-room but a good number in his show-room, which was rather dark.'

On the other hand Crabb Robinson's description of Blake's amiability and charm of manner confirms all that his younger friends say of him. He was anxious to bring Blake and Wordsworth together, but there is no evidence that they ever met. Blake annotated some of the poems lent him by Crabb Robinson, and also gave him some notes on *The Excursion*. These must be read with Crabb Robinson's Diary and *Reminiscences* and his letter to Dorothy Wordsworth, as, taken by themselves, they scarcely do justice to Blake's profound admiration for Wordsworth, whom he held to be 'the greatest poet of the age.' He was overwhelmed by the 'Ode on the Intimations of Immortality', which Robinson read aloud to him:

I had been in the habit when reading this marvellous Ode to friends, to omit one or two passages, especially that beginning

> But there's a tree, of many one

lest I shd. be rendered ridiculous, being unable to explain precisely *what* I admired—not that I acknowledged this to be a fair test. But with Blake I cd. fear nothing of the kind, & it was this very Stanza wh. threw him almost into a hysterical rapture. His delight in W's poetry was intense. Nor did it seem less notwithstanding by the reproaches he continually cast on W. for his imputed worship of nature, wh. in the mind of Blake constituted Atheism.[26]

The first passage which Blake has noted in the *Excursion* brought on an attack of illness because he gained from it the impression that the '*only poet* of the age' felt himself superior to God, and was therefore no Christian in Blake's sense.* In the annotations to the

* Crabb Robinson notes, 19 December 1814, that Flaxman had also objected to Wordsworth's phrase, 'seeing Jehovah unalarmed.' 'If my brother had written that,' said Flaxman, 'I should say, "Burn it." ' But he admitted that Wordsworth could not mean anything impious in it. (*Crabb Robinson: Diary, Remininiscences and Correspondence*, ed. Sadler, 1869.)

poems he quotes Wordsworth's own rendering of Michelangelo's sonnet, a part of which he inscribed about the same time in William Upcott's autograph album,* to prove that 'W. must know that what he writes valuable is not to be found in Nature.' He condemns the Prefaces, excepting the close of the supplementary Preface, as the opinions of a 'landscape painter'. 'Imagination is the divine vision not of the World, or of Man, nor from Man as he is a natural man, but only as he is a spiritual Man. Imagination has nothing to do with memory.'

The main cause of offence is doubtless Wordsworth's use of the word 'imagination' as signifying merely the creative faculty; for Blake imagination was the corner-stone of his religion, the Divine Body, the Mystic Word which alone had power to dispel error and reveal eternal truth. Coleridge and he would have agreed, perhaps did agree, that Wordsworth was no true mystic.†

... I will not conceal from *you* [writes Coleridge] that this inferred dependency of the human soul on accidents of birth-place and abode, together with the vague, misty, rather than mystic, confusion of God with the world, and the accompanying nature-worship, of which the asserted dependence forms a part, is the trait in Wordsworth's poetic works that I most dislike as unhealthful, and denounce as contagious; while the odd introduction of the popular, almost the vulgar, religion in his later publications (the popping in, as Hartley says, of the old man with a beard), suggests the painful suspicion of worldly prudence—at best a justification of masking truth (which, in fact, is a falsehood substituted for a truth withheld) on the plea of expediency—carried into religion. At least it conjures up to my fancy a sort of Janus head of Spinosa & Dr. Watts, or 'I and my brother the dean.'27

Coleridge had read the *Songs of Innocence and of Experience* in 1818 when Charles Augustus Tulk, a well-known Swedenborgian, lent him the copy he had bought from Blake. He returns 'Blake's poesies metrical and graphic' with some severe strictures on the drawings and a list of the poems elaborately marked in order of

---

* Upcott was an illegitimate son of Ozias Humphry.
† Cf. *Mysticism*, by Evelyn Underhill (1912), p. 286.

merit. 'The Little Black Boy' gets top marks, and several are highly commended. Much as he admires 'Infant Joy' he wishes to amend the last lines. 'For a babe two days old does not, cannot smile, & innocence and the very truth of Nature must go together. Infancy is too holy a thing to be ornamented.' 'A Little Girl Lost' he would have omitted, 'not for the want of innocence in the poem, but from the too probable want of it in many readers.' He is perplexed by 'The Little Vagabond':

. . . yet still I disapprove the mood of mind in this wild poem so much less than I do the servile, blind-worm, wrap-rascal, scurf-coat of *fear* of the *Modern* Saint (whose whole being is a lie to themselves as well as to their brethren), that I should laugh with good conscience in watching a Saint of the new stamp, one of the first stars of our Eleemosynary advertisements, groaning in the windpipe! and with the whites of his eyes upraised at the *audacity* of this poem![28]

In 1826 Crabb Robinson tells Dorothy Wordsworth that Coleridge has visited Blake '& I am told talks finely about him,' but we catch no echo of this talk. The only account of their meeting is in a critical review of Cunningham's *Life of Blake* by an anonymous writer in the *London University Magazine* for 1830,*

* Vol. ii, p. 323. Keynes, *Bibliography*, p. 375, suggests that the article may have been written by Palmer, Richmond, or Calvert. The writer complains 'first of the insertion of stories which are falsely coloured; then of the stealing, borrowing, or copying a considerable portion of the life from Nolleken's Own Times; and, last of all, of a smile of contempt when speaking of Blake's private sentiments and feelings, which certainly is not becoming or respectful in a fellow artist.' He remarks that had Blake lived in Germany he would have had 'commentators of the highest order upon every one of his effusions. . . .'
Commenting on *Jerusalem*, 'We are perfectly aware of the present state of public opinion on this kind of men, but we know at the same time, that every genius has a certain end to perform, and always runs before his contemporaries, and for that reason is not generally understood.' The article contains comments on several of the poems, including the following reference to *Jerusalem*:

For instance, Albion, with which the World is very little acquainted, seems the embodying of Blake's ideas on the present state of England; he viewed it, not with the eyes of ordinary men, but contemplated it rather as a promise of one grand man, in which diseases and crimes are continually engendered, and on this account he poured forth his poetical effusions somewhat in the style of Novalis, mourning over the crimes and errors of his dear country:

who adds in a footnote: 'Blake and Coleridge, when in company, seemed like congenial beings of another sphere, breathing for a while on our earth; which may easily be perceived from the similarity of thought pervading their works.'

The writer does not attempt to report the dialogue, or was it rather the two monologues?

No meeting between Lamb and Blake is recorded, but Lamb also knew some of the *Songs*. He had heard 'The Tyger' recited and speaks of it to Bernard Barton as 'glorious', adding that 'the man is flown, whither I know not—to Hades or a Mad House. But I must look on him as one of the most extraordinary persons of the age.'[29] Lamb, it must be remembered, was present when Southey described Blake as the mad author of a mad poem. The reciter of 'The Tyger' was probably Crabb Robinson, whose performance at the Aderses' so much impressed Linnell that he used to imitate it.

The 'Chimney Sweeper' Lamb sent to James Montgomery for insertion in *The Chimney Sweeper's Friend, and Climbing Boy's Album*, altering 'Tom Dacre' in the fifth line to 'Tom Toddy'. He considers Blake's 'the Flower of the set,' but deprecates Montgomery's awkward paraphrase of the 'Dream'.

Bernard Barton, the Quaker poet, to whom Lamb's letter about Blake is addressed, was another admirer to whom Blake was unknown personally. After Blake's death Barton wrote a sonnet* prefaced by Cunningham's exaggerated reference to 'a miserable garret and a crust of bread', and dedicated it to Linnell. This elicited the interesting letter already quoted in which Linnell describes Blake's circumstances and his own relations to him.

Another friend of Lamb and Crabb Robinson, Edward Fitzgerald, may have heard of Blake in his school days at Bury St. Edmunds under Dr. Malkin. He bought a copy of the *Songs*

---

and it is more extraordinary still that, like Novalis, he contemplated the natural world as the mere outbirth of the thought, and lived and existed in that world for which we are created.

* The sonnet is printed by Story, *Linnell*, i, p. 194. Story also prints a letter from Barton acknowledging a copy of Blake's *Job*, and regretting that he cannot afford to buy one of the visionary heads (i, p. 192).

of Innocence in 1833, and his comments show that he had heard of the visionary heads and accepted the view of Blake's mental condition current in his own set.[30] Walter Savage Landor did not apparently know the poems till later. His biographer says that in 1836 he picked up some volumes in Bristol by which he was 'strangely fascinated' and proposed to make a collection of Blake's work, a project which came to nothing.*

'He protested that Blake has been Wordsworth's prototype, and wishes they could have divided his madness between them; for that some accession of it in the one case, and something of a diminution of it in the other would very greatly have improved both.'

Crabb Robinson had read some of the *Songs of Innocence and of Experience* to Hazlitt in 1811, who thought them 'beautiful, & only too deep for the vulgar', but added: 'He is ruined by vain struggles to get rid of what presses on his brain—he attempts impossibles.'[31]

Hazlitt, after speaking of Flaxman as a 'profound mystic', adds:

This last is a character common to many other artists in our days—Loutherbourg, Cosway, Blake, Sharp, Varley, &c.—who seem to relieve the literalness of their professional studies by voluntary excursions into the regions of the preternatural, pass their time between sleeping and waking, and whose ideas are like a stormy night, with the clouds driven rapidly across, and the blue sky and stars gleaming between![32]

Bulwer Lytton wrote in 1835 with admiration for Blake's verse and engravings, speaking of his 'delightful vein of madness.'†

It would seem then that Blake's literary contemporaries found his poems strange, disturbing, beautiful, and the readiest solution

---

* John Forster, *Walter Savage Landor*, ii, pp. 322–3. Crabb Robinson records, 20 May 1838, that Blake had furnished the chief matter for talk at a breakfast party when Landor, Milnes, and Talfourd were present, and that Landor had maintained him to be the greatest of poets. (Sadler, *Crabb Robinson*.)

† *The Student*, ii, pp. 152–3. The heroine of Bulwer Lytton's *A Strange Story*, who is for a time insane, occupies herself with 'strange and fantastic drawings resembling Blake's illustrations of the *Night Thoughts* and the *Grave*' (chapter lxiv).

of their own perplexity was to call him a genius, but insane. To-day, when everyone is familiar with Blake's *Songs* in anthologies or in selections from his own verse, the timid and ambiguous acceptance of them by his distinguished contemporaries comes as a surprise, but Wordsworth and Coleridge, Keats and Shelley have been, in truth, precursors of Blake's influence and fame. Educated by them, readers are prepared to perceive at once the beauty of his *Songs*, even when his mystic doctrine escapes them.

Artists were more ready to accord unqualified recognition during Blake's lifetime, and this not only because his paintings and engravings were more accessible than his poems. Those who, in the course of their own professional work, were accustomed to visualize their memories and their conceptions, were less likely to be disturbed by Blake's assertion of his visionary powers. More-over, a number of them knew the man familiarly in casual daily intercourse. Their opinions are, therefore, more responsible. Flaxman found him provokingly neglectful of his worldly interests and difficult to help, but the intolerance, of which Crabb Robinson complains, is in itself a proof that he did not imagine himself to be dealing with a madman. J. T. Smith begins his *Biographical Sketch* by indignantly dismissing the suggestion, while Cunningham, though he makes the most of Blake's eccentricities and deplores his excess of imagination, does not hint at insanity. Linnell found him able and willing to give a reasonable explanation of his paradoxes and experiences. James Ward and Cornelius Varley emphatically denied that he was mad. The boy artists for whom the two rooms in Fountain Court became the 'House of the Inter-preter' are equally explicit: their testimony will be given later.

IX
OLD AGE

But when once I did descry
The Immortal Man that cannot Die,
Thro' evening shades I haste away
To close the Labours of my Day.[1]

Blake's letters to Linnell from 1824 onwards contain many references to his failing health. He suffered from periodical rigors, which he describes as 'shivering fits' and 'this abominable ague or whatever it is,' and later from jaundice, both symptoms of gall-stones, the disease which caused his death. Linnell had taken lodgings at North End, Hampstead, for his wife and children in 1822 and again the following year. In 1824 he rented permanently one end of the Home Farm on the Wylde's Estate,* the property of Eton College, living there himself but retaining the old home in Cirencester Place as a studio.

Blake's intercourse with him was not interrupted by the move to Collins' Farm, so called after the dairyman tenant. Linnell was sometimes entertained in Fountain Court before a journey to the provinces, and Blake would see him off. He gives an amusing description of one such occasion when, absorbed in conversation with Linnell and another passenger, he started involuntarily for Gloucester.[2] Sunday expeditions to North End took the place of the long walks south of the Thames which had been his delight in his younger days, and this in spite of his firm persuasion that Hampstead was inimical to his health. He writes to Linnell on the 1 February 1826 that he is unable to visit them:

For I am again laid up by a cold in my stomach; the Hampstead Air, as it always did, so I fear it always will do this, Except it be the Morning air; & That, in my Cousin's time,† I found I could

* See an article by Mrs. Arthur Wilson, 'Wyldes and its Story', in *The Hampstead Annual*, 1903.

† This cousin and the aunt buried in Bunhill Fields (Gilchrist, *Life*, i, p. 405) are the only relatives apart from Blake's immediate family to whom reference is made.

bear with safety & perhaps benefit. I believe my Constitution to be a good one, but it has many peculiarities that no one but myself can know. When I was young, Hampstead, Highgate, Hornsea, Muswell Hill, & even Islington & all places North of London, always laid me up the day after, & sometimes two or three days, with precisely the same Complaint & the same torment of the Stomach, Easily removed, but excruciating while it lasts & enfeebling for some time after. Sr Francis Bacon would say, it is want of discipline in Mountainous Places. Sr Francis Bacon is a Liar. No discipline will turn one Man into another, even in the least particle, & such discipline I call Presumption & Folly. I have tried it too much not to know this, & am very sorry for all such who may be led to such ostentatious Exertion against their Eternal Existence itself, because it is Mental Rebellion against the Holy Spirit, & fit only for a Soldier of Satan to perform.[3]

But foolish as Sir Francis Bacon's repressive arguments might be, the attractions of North End prevailed. Years before he had marked Lavater's aphorism, 'Keep him at least three paces distant who hates bread, music, and the laugh of a child,' 'The best in the book!' And now there were children at Collins' Farm watching for his signal. He was interested in their childish drawings, and once showed them an old sketch-book of his own containing a lifelike grasshopper. He used to tell them stories, sterling stuff if we may judge by a surviving nursery rhyme:*

> The sow came in with the saddle,
> The little pig rocked the cradle,
> The dish jumped o' top of the table
> To see the brass pot swallow the ladle.
> The old pot behind the door
> Called the kettle a blackamoor.
> 'Odd bobbs,' said the Gridiron, 'Can't you agree?
> I'm the head constable, bring them to me.'[4]

---

* An early MS. of this rhyme, on a loose sheet, was in the copy of the *Songs of Innocence and of Experience* which belonged to Dr. Jebb, Bishop of Limerick, and was later in the possession of E. M. Forster. It is copied on paper bought at Reigate, which suggests that it may have come from the Linnells, who lived at Redhill. [This copy of the *Songs* is now in the library of King's College, Cambridge, but the MS. of the rhyme has disappeared. Ed.]

And the music was there too. Mrs. Linnell moved him by her
rendering of Scottish melodies, and, in return, he still, as long ago
in Mrs. Mathew's drawing-room, would chant his songs to tunes
of his own making. With the same filial kindness which marked
her husband's relation to Blake Mrs. Linnell used to wrap him in
a shawl on cold evenings and send the servant with a lantern to
light him across the heath. During the summer of 1826 the Blakes
spent some days at Hope Cottage, North End, a former lodging
of the Linnells. They drove up luxuriously in a cabriolet as Blake
had been suffering from piles, and compared himself in one letter
to 'a young Lark without feathers,' saying in the next that he is
'only bones & sinews, All strings & bobbins like a Weaver's
Loom.'⁵

Among Linnell's artist friends, besides John Varley, his brother
Cornelius, and brother-in-law Mulready, were Holmes, Byron's
pet portrait-painter, Richter,* an ardent student of Kant, and the
correct Collins, who cut Blake carrying his pint of porter in the
Strand. Constable may have been also an occasional visitor, as
there is a tradition that Blake, seeing a drawing of fir trees on
Hampstead Heath in one of Constable's sketch-books, exclaimed,
'Why, this is not drawing, but inspiration': to which Constable
characteristically replied, 'I meant it for drawing.'† But it was the
younger generation who lightened the burden of his years by
welcoming him as one of themselves. Both in their corporate form
as the 'Ancients', a group of artists who met monthly for discussion in town and painted in company at Shoreham, and
individually, these boys, Palmer and Calvert, Richmond and
Finch,‡ Walter and Tatham, took possession of Fountain Court,

---

* There seems to be no foundation for Gilchrist's statement, *Life*, i, p. 296,
that Holmes and Richter influenced Blake's colouring.

† Constable was 'much concerned' at Blake's death, as he wrote to Linnell
on 14 August 1827. He suggested that the charitable funds of the Royal
Academy should be used to give help to Mrs. Blake. (*Blake Records*, p. 343.)
[Ed.]

‡ Cf. *The Followers of William Blake*, by Laurence Binyon (1925); *Life of
Samuel Palmer; A Memoir of Edward Calvert; Memorials of F. O. Finch*. George
Richmond said that the Ancients always kissed the bell-handle before entering
Blake's house. (*The Richmond Papers*, ed. Stirling, p. 25.)

sought help and advice, and sometimes induced Blake to return their visits.

Several accounts have been given of the 'Ancients', the 'Extollagers' as the Shoreham villagers called them, coining a word as expressive in its way as the 'Academinions' of Linnell's landlady. Armed with that new implement the camp-stool, they roamed about the country by night as well as by day, wore strange garments, and recited poetry. Samuel Palmer's father gave up his book-shop and retired to the 'Water-house', and on one occasion at least Blake spent a night or two in the village. He joined Palmer and Calvert in a nocturnal expedition to the haunted castle, where the ghost revealed itself as a large snail crawling up a mullion and tapping on the window-pane. Calvert gives an instance of Blake's telepathic power, more striking than his warning to Paine, a divination requiring little more than common sense. While they were at Shoreham young Palmer left them to go up to London. An hour after he had started Blake put his hand to his forehead and said, 'Palmer is coming; he is walking up the road.' The others protested, but after a while Blake said again, 'He is coming through the wicket—there!' and in another minute Palmer, whose journey had been frustrated by a breakdown of the coach, walked in.

All these young men professed a lifelong devotion to Blake's memory. They were stimulated both by his personality and by his imaginative art, but they were in no sense imitators: none of their drawings has passed as his like those of his earlier friends, Flaxman and Fuseli, Romney and Stothard.* To Samuel Palmer, Blake's Virgil woodcuts were a revelation: their influence upon his early work is obvious, and after a middle period of more conventional painting, his later drawings and etchings, more particularly his own designs for Virgil, show an emotional quality again reminiscent of Blake. When only fourteen, five years before he met Blake, he had exhibited paintings at the British Gallery and at the

---

* Binyon (*The Followers of William Blake*, pp. 1–2) says that drawings by William Young Ottley have probably also been attributed to Blake, and that Tom Hood was influenced by him.

Royal Academy. He describes as his first interview a call with Linnell on the 9th October 1824:*

> We found him lame in bed, of a scalded foot (or leg). There, not inactive, though sixty-seven years old, but hard-working on a bed covered with books sat he up like one of the Antique patriarchs, or a dying Michael Angelo. Thus and there was he making in the leaves of a great book (folio) the sublimest designs from his (not superior) Dante. He said he began them with fear and trembling. I said, 'O! I have enough of fear and trembling.' 'Then,' said he, 'you'll do.'[6]

Palmer had been brought up as a Baptist, though he afterwards became a member of the Church of England. His memoranda after meeting Blake, are a curious mixture of orthodox evangelical language with phrases and sentences of no doubtful origin, such as, for instance:

> We must not begin with medium, but think always on excess, and only use medium to make excess more abundantly excessive.
> Genius is the unreserved devotion of the whole soul to the divine, poetic arts, and through them to God; deeming all else, even to our daily bread, only valuable as it helps us to unveil the heavenly face of Beauty. . . .
> Nature is not at all the standard of art, but art is the standard of nature. The visions of the soul, being perfect, are the only true standard by which nature must be tried. The corporeal executive is no good thing to the painter, but a bane.[7]

Palmer seems to have treated Blake's visionary experiences lightly. In a letter published by Gilchrist he writes: '. . . materialism was his abhorrence: and if some unhappy man called in question the world of spirits, he would answer him "according to his folly," by putting forth his own views in their most extravagant and startling aspect. This might amuse those who were in the secret, but it left his opponent angry and bewildered.'[8]

He also instances Blake's exclamation when irritated by some scientific talk about the vastness of space. 'It is false, I walked the

* This date is wrong, if, as seems probable, Blake did not begin the Dante designs till October 1825. See *Blake Records*, p. 291.

other evening to the end of the earth, and touched the sky with my fingers.' He found Blake's talk far from monotonous, and the languid manner was apparently reserved for Crabb Robinson. In the letter to Gilchrist he says:

His knowledge was various and extensive, and his conversation so nervous and brilliant, that, if recorded at the time, it would now have thrown much light upon his character, and in no way lessened him in the estimation of those who know him only by his works. . . . He was energy itself, and shed around him a kindling influence; an atmosphere of life, full of the ideal.

. . . in conversation he was anything but sectarian or exclusive, finding sources of delight throughout the whole range of art; while as a critic, he was judicious and discriminating.

In 1875 Palmer wrote a vigorous defence of Blake's sanity.*

* *Athenaeum*, 11 September 1875. The allusion is to an essay by Dr. Richardson quoted in *The Cornhill Magazine*, August 1875.

Dr. Richardson, in an interesting essay on hallucinations, mentions a singular illustration of this faculty in the case of Wm. Blake. This artist once 'produced three hundred portraits from his own hand in one year.' When asked on what this peculiar power of rapid work depended, he answered 'that when a sitter came to him, he looked at him attentively for half-an-hour, sketching from time to time on the canvas; then he put away the canvas and took another sitter. When he wished to resume the first portrait, he said, I took the man, and put him in the chair where I saw him as distinctly as if he had been before me in his own proper person. When I looked at the chair, I saw the man.' It may be well to mention that the exercise of this faculty is fraught with danger in some cases. Blake, after a while, began to lose the power of distinguishing 'between the real and imaginary sitters, so that [the *sequitur* is not quite manifest, however] he became actually insane, and remained in an asylum for thirty years. Then his mind was restored to him and he resumed the use of the pencil; but the old evil threatened to return, and he once more forsook his art, soon afterwards to die.' ('On Some Strange Mental Feats,' *Cornhill Magazine*, vol. xxii, pp. 157–68.)

Dr. Richardson may have based his assertion on the article in the *Revue Britannique* (see Appendix III), or have derived it from some common source. The above statement that Blake produced three hundred portraits in a year may have inspired the perpetrator of the portraits of Shelley and others described in 'An Unknown Collection of Portraits by William Blake; the Genius of the Pre-Raphaelite Movement,' by J. E. Robinson, *Arts and Decorations*, January 1918, pp. 100–5, 130. The twelve reproductions in the article show that the portraits are not Blake's work. A modern alienist has treated Blake as a typical case of manic-depressive insanity ('William Blake,' by Herbert J. Norman, *Journal of Mental Science*, April 1915). Dr. Norman

Without alluding to his writings, which are here not in question, I remember William Blake, in the quiet consistency of his daily life, as one of the sanest, if not the most thoroughly sane man I have ever known. The flights of his genius were scarcely more marvellous than the ceaseless industry and skilful management of affairs, which enabled him on a very small income to find time for very great works. And of this man the public are informed that he passed thirty years in a mad-house!

The opening phrase is significant. Blake had taken the excitable boy by storm. His religious phraseology had for the time being masked his heresies, and had but heightened the pious ardour which was Palmer's natural attitude toward his art. But later on Palmer was disturbed by Blake's writings. He advises a friend to read Gilchrist's *Life*, but disavows 'all adherence to some of the doctrines put forth in the poems, which seem to me to savour of Manicheism'; he expresses the belief that Blake had been 'misled by erroneous spirits', and regrets that 'he should sometimes have suffered fancy to trespass within sacred precincts.' Yet while advising Mrs. Gilchrist to omit parts of *The Marriage of Heaven and Hell* as likely to scare reviewers and exclude the book from every drawing-room table in England, he makes a pathetic, muddle-minded attempt to explain that not only is it not nearly as bad as it seems, but Blake's real views, though equally outrageous, were completely opposed to those expressed in it.

Blake has said the same kind of thing to me; in fact almost everything contained in the book; and *I* can understand it in

---

appears to accept Ellis's *Real Blake* as a historic account of the man, and he ignores some of the opinions expressed by Blake's contemporaries. Although his knowledge of mental pathology is presumably profound, Dr. Norman permits alarmingly little licence to the normal man. His imaginative experiences are rigidly circumscribed, nor must he, apparently, remain celibate since Blake's lack of nephews and nieces is taken to indicate the tendency to sterility of a degenerating family. Dr. Norman cites some of Blake's writing as obviously the work of a madman, but his acquaintance with the symbolic works would not appear to be exhaustive, as he alludes to the child-bearing Enitharmon as male. It is unnecessary to examine the article in detail because readers of this book, who wish to refer to it, will be able to determine for themselves whether Dr. Norman's treatment of the subject is adequate.

relation to my memory of the whole man, in a way quite different to that roaring lion the 'press', or that led lion the British Public.

Blake wrote often in anger and rhetorically; just as we might speak if some *pretender* to Christianity whom we knew to be hypocritical, were *canting* to us in a pharisaical way. We might say, 'If this is your Heaven, give me Hell.' We might say this in temper, but without in the least meaning that that was our deliberate preference.

.   .   .   .

His real views would now be considered extravagant on the opposite side to that apparently taken in the *Marriage*, for he quite held forth one day to me, on the Roman Catholic Church being the only one which taught the forgiveness of sins; and he repeatedly expressed his belief that there was more *civil* liberty under the Papal Government, than any other Sovereignty; nor did I ever hear him express any admiration for the American republic.[9]

He adds in the same letter:

If madness and absurdity be synonyms, which they are not, then Blake would be as 'mad as a March hare,' his love for art was so great that he would see nothing *but art* in anything he loved; and so, as he loved the Apostles and their divine Head (for so I believe he did), he must needs say that they were all artists.

Edward Calvert was a few years older than Palmer, and had been in the navy before making art his profession. His stockbroker was Palmer's cousin, John Giles, whose enthusiasm for everything ancient gave the brotherhood its name. He denounced modern pictures as too finished: 'no room to get a thought in edgewise. Wretched work, Sir!' and told Calvert of the 'divine Blake' who 'had seen God, sir, and had talked with angels.' Through Giles, Calvert came to know both 'The Ancients' and Blake himself. His work was already imaginative in character, but he was for a time directly influenced by Blake. Some of his woodcuts are surrounded by mystic sentences which reveal their source as clearly as Palmer's notes. Miss Linnell used to relate how Calvert showed her one of his drawings, saying solemnly, 'These are God's fields, this is God's brook, and these are God's sheep and lambs.' 'Then why don't you mark them with a big G?' asked Linnell, who, never himself an 'Ancient', was sometimes exas-

perated by the 'real Greeks from Hackney and Lisson Grove.'
Calvert, like Palmer, went through a conventional period; later he
became a romantic Parnassian, painting golden-toned sketches of
Greek subjects, idyllic and mythological, which might bear for
their legend:

> We lack not songs, nor instruments of joy,
> Nor echoes sweet, nor waters clear as heaven,
> Nor laurel wreaths against the sultry heat.[10]

Calvert went to Fountain Court, and Blake sometimes visited
him and his wife at Brixton. His memoir contains reminiscences,
of Blake's courtesy and consideration for the feelings of others,
and he recalled how Blake, when he felt his energies diverted from
his work, would say that 'he was being devoured by jackals and
hyenas.' Calvert retained a most affectionate memory of Blake. In
his later years he painted a study from one of the Virgil woodcuts,* and said, when nearly eighty: 'I want to take a little
pilgrimage to Fountain Court, that I may once more gaze upon
that divine window where the blessed man did his work.'
Although a religious man he was not a sectarian, and does not
show the same tendency as Palmer to criticize and condemn what
he did not understand. His son says that 'he made the most tender
allusion to the visions and visitations, the ecstasies and wild
indignations that made up the Visionary's life. . . . There was no
assumption of occult mystery about Blake. All was a serious
reality, yet abnormal and strange to others.'[11] Questioned by
Gilchrist about Blake's supposed madness he replied: 'I saw
nothing but sanity, saw nothing mad in his conduct, actions or
character.'

George Richmond, a boy of sixteen when he first met Blake at
the Tathams, went back with him to Fountain Court, feeling 'as
if he were walking with the prophet Isaiah.'[12] Like Palmer he
enjoyed Blake's conversation, and he found it possible to argue

* 'Pilgrim and Milestone', now in the British Museum, Department of
Prints and Drawings.

and disagree as though with a youth of his own age. Once, distressed by a temporary failure in his power of invention, he asked Blake's advice. Blake turned to his wife and said: 'It is just so with us, is it not, for weeks together, when the visions forsake us? What do we do then, Kate?' 'We kneel down and pray, Mr. Blake.' Richmond was at the time more strongly influenced by Blake than any of the others.* His early paintings, notably 'The Creation of Light', resemble Blake's both in spirit and in technique, but the imaginative phase of his work was short-lived, and he became exclusively a painter of portraits. Richmond, then the only survivor of the 'Ancients', showed H. H. Gilchrist a replica of Deville's life mask of Blake, taken because the phrenologist considered the imaginative faculty specially prominent. Richmond's remarks about the mask are interesting:

That is not like dear Blake's mouth, such a look of severity was foreign to him—an expression of sweetness and sensibility being habitual: but Blake experienced a good deal of pain when the cast was taken, as the plaster pulled out a quantity of his hair. Mrs. Blake did not like the mask, perhaps the reason being that she was familiar with varying expressions of her husband's fine face, from daily observation: indeed it was difficult to please her with any portrait—she never liked Phillips's portrait; but Blake's friends liked the mask.†

* Binyon, *The Followers of William Blake*. H. H. Gilchrist, in his *Memoir of Anne Gilchrist*, p. 261, says that Richmond showed him his first picture, 'The Shepherd Abel', and told him how Blake had made a drawing for him in correction of the shepherd's arm. [This drawing by Blake, made on a leaf of a sketch-book of Palmer's, is now in my collection. It is accompanied by Richmond's posthumous drawing of Blake. Ed.]

† *Anne Gilchrist*, pp. 258–62. Richmond does not really account for the mouth being unlike as the pain would have been a later occurrence. H. H. Gilchrist also says: 'Mr. Richmond drew our attention to the position of Blake's ear, which is low down, away from the face near the back of the neck, showing an immense height of head above: . . .' He prints a letter from Samuel Palmer, p. 58, saying, 'I forgot I think to mention that in the late Sir R. Peel's copy of the "Europe and America" there is a pencil drawing by Mr. Richmond (a disciple of Blake's), done soon after Blake's decease, while the memory was fresh, and assisted by the cast of which I spoke; most probably this is the closest likeness existing.' Mr. Sydney Morse has a drawing acquired from the Richmond family, which is said to be a mask of Blake.

Richmond confirms the report of Blake's outrageous sayings to 'those who did not and never would understand either him or his works.'[13] He remarked of the article which drew Palmer's defence: 'What a strange assertion! I must say, I think Dr. Richardson is more deluded about Blake than dear old Blake ever was about anything himself.' 'Never,' he told Gilchrist, 'have I known an artist so spiritual, so devoted, so single-minded, or cherishing imagination as he did.'[14]

Francis Oliver Finch had been a pupil of John Varley. His landscapes, though of an imaginative character, are not obviously affected by his admiration of Blake. A Swedenborgian, he was, in Palmer's view, more inclined than the others to believe in Blake's spiritual intercourse. He told Gilchrist that Blake 'struck him as *a new kind of man*, wholly original and in all things. Whereas most men are at the pains of softening down their extreme opinions, not to shock those of others, it was the contrary with him.'[15] Blake's name is not mentioned in *Memorials of F. O. Finch* by his wife, although the book contains an account of the 'Ancients'. A possible explanation of this curious omission is that Mrs. Finch regarded Blake as a renegade Swedenborgian.

No special record seems to have been preserved of Henry Walter's friendship with Blake, and again, his work bears no mark of Blake's direct influence.

Frederick Tatham was the son of C. H. Tatham, an architect. Blake had some previous acquaintance with the father as a copy of *America* is inscribed 'From the author to C. H. Tatham, Oct. 7, 1799.' The younger Tatham, a sculptor and miniature painter, does not appear to have known Blake till he was about twenty. He wrote a *Life of William Blake* which is bound up with

---

The mouth is sensitive and full, but the nose is a third as long as Blake's nose in the life mask. It is therefore doubtful whether it is the drawing of Blake to which Palmer refers. Peel's copies of *Europe* and *America* have not been identified. [The original cast of Blake's head, formerly in the possession of the Richmond family, is now in the Fitzwilliam Museum, Cambridge. A replica is in the National Portrait Gallery and a few casts of this have been made in bronze. Ed.]

the only complete coloured copy of *Jerusalem*,* and was published by A. G. B. Russell in 1906 with Blake's letters. It is one of the most important contemporary records of Blake, and reference has already been made to it. His account of Blake's personality is in accord with those of the other 'Ancients.'

His disposition was cheerful & lively, & was never depressed by any cares, but those springing out of his Art. . . . He was every thing but subtle, the serpent had no share in his nature. Secresy was unknown to him. He would relate those things of himself that others make it their utmost endeavour to conceal.[16]

And, like the rest, he thinks that many of the reports of Blake's eccentricity arose from his enigmatic replies to idle questions. Tatham's genuine respect and affection for Blake are perceptible through his ridiculous verbiage, yet he lies under the suspicion of having wrongfully appropriated and afterwards destroyed some of Blake's manuscripts and drawings. Gilchrist says that Mrs. Blake bequeathed the remaining stock of her husband's works to Tatham.† Linnell wrote an emphatic contradiction of this in his copy of the *Life*. In his *Life of Blake*, which bears no date but was probably written some years later, though he doubtless made notes for it during the lifetime both of Blake and his wife, Tatham

---

* Now in the Paul Mellon Collection. Reproduced in facsimile by the William Blake Trust in 1949. [Ed.]

† The following note by Joseph Hogarth was discovered by Mr. Wilfrid Partington in his copy of *Nollekens and His Times* (*Times Literary Supplement*, 28 January 1939):

Fred Tatham was Blake's executor and possessed several of his drawings, many of which I purchased from him (these were sold at Southgate and Barrett's, 7th June 1854). Mrs. Blake was hardly the passive creature here described—at all events Tatham did not find her so for she was opposed to everything he did for her benefit and when she submitted to his views it was always with the words 'she had no help for it'—that at last Tatham, tired with her opposition, threw the Will behind the fire and burnt it saying, 'There now you can do as you like for the Will no longer exists,' and left her. Early the following morning she called upon him saying William had been with her all night and required her to come to him and renew the Will which was done and never after did she offer any opposition to Tatham's proceedings.

[For an account of Tatham's relations with John Linnell and Mrs. Blake after Blake's death see Keynes, *Blake Studies*, pp. 224–8. Ed.]

takes up the position that Blake not only mentioned him on his deathbed to Mrs. Blake 'as a likely person to become the manager of her affairs,' but that she actually bequeathed to him both manuscripts and pictures. He refers to a copy of the *Songs* 'which work the Author of this is now in possession of by the kindness of Mrs Blake who bequeathed them to him as well as all of his Works that remained unsold at his [i.e. her] Death being writings, paintings, & a very great number of Copperplates, of whom Impressions may be obtained.[17] He also alludes to a bequest from Mrs. Blake of Blake's library, and again of all she possessed.

Be this as it may, Tatham obtained possession of Blake's effects legally or illegally. It is probable that he destroyed some of the manuscripts, but here again the facts are obscure. Samuel Calvert says that his father, hearing of Tatham's intention, remonstrated, but thinks that in spite of this intervention Tatham had destroyed 'blocks, plates, drawings, and MSS.' This appears to have been also Linnell's impression. The allegations made by the Gilchrists are rather less serious. Gilchrist states that some of the remaining stock of Blake's works were destroyed after Mrs. Blake's death, and Anne Gilchrist, in a letter to William Rossetti, speaks of 'the actual Tatham who knew Blake and enacted the holocaust of Blake's manuscripts—not designs, I think, as I have heard from his own lips.'* Dr. Garnett had an interview about 1860 with Tatham, who told him that he had some of Blake's manuscripts which he was selling from time to time, and Mr. Symons says that Dr. Garnett spoke to him of an admission from Tatham that he had destroyed some MSS.[18] There seems little doubt, therefore, that Tatham was responsible for the destruction of some of Blake's papers, but its extent has probably been exaggerated, and it is even possible that some of the lost manuscripts may still be discovered. Tatham became a follower of Edward Irving, that Irving of whom Blake himself has said all that needs saying: 'He is a highly gifted man. He is a sent man, but they who are sent

---

* *Anne Gilchrist*, p. 129. She also said that Tatham admitted selling the works for thirty years at good prices. Tatham wrote to W. M. Rossetti: '. . . I have sold Mr. Blake's Works for thirty years'. (*Rossetti Papers*, p. 16.)

sometimes go further than they ought.'[19] It is supposed that some of his fellow members of the Catholic Apostolic Church induced him to burn manuscripts containing what they considered dangerous doctrines, but Carlyle was sure that Irving himself was not responsible. Tatham's own remarks on Blake's writings suggest that he had succeeded in persuading himself that Blake was an orthodox believer, betrayed into doubt only by his controversial pen:

He wrote much upon controversial subjects, & like all controversies these writings are inspired by doubt & made up of vain conceits & whimsical Extravagancies. A bad cause requires a long Book. Generally advocating one in which there is a flaw, the greatest controversialists are the greatest doubters. They are trembling needles between extreme points.—Irritated by hypocrisy & the unequivocal yielding of weak & interested men, he said & wrote unwarrantable arguments, but unalloyed & unencumbered by opposition, he was in all essential points orthodox in his belief, but he put forth ramifications of doubt, that by his vigorous & creative mind, were watered into the empty enormities of Extravagant & rebellious thoughts.[20]

It may be assumed, then, that Tatham persuaded himself that he was only burning the doubts and riddles and perversities into which Blake was provoked by idle opponents, and which Blake, the true believer, would have disclaimed in his calmer moments. There could be no betrayal of the master by one who had never been a disciple.*

The contents of Tatham's holocaust can be only a matter for conjecture. A book named *Outhoun* was offered for sale by Mrs. Blake, after her husband's death, to Mr. Ferguson, a Tynemouth artist.[21] No copy of this work was known either to Gilchrist or Linnell. This is likely to have been one of the works Tatham either sold or destroyed. The reference in the Notebook to the *Book of Moonlight* suggests that a work of that name actually

---

* Tatham furnished Gilchrist (*Life*, i, p. 421) with an account of the process by which Blake executed his printed drawings. Its accuracy was disputed by Linnell but has been confirmed by Graham Robertson's experiments. Tatham also corresponded on the subject with W. M. Rossetti. (*Rossetti Papers*, Letter No. 15.)

existed, but no trace of it has been found. Another book which has disappeared is mentioned by Crabb Robinson:

He showed me his Version (for so it may be called) of Genesis, 'As understood by a Christian Visionary,' in which in a style resembling the Bible, The spirit is given. He read a passage at random. It was striking.*

On this occasion he told Robinson that he had written '6 or 7 Epic poems as long as Homer, & 20 Tragedies as long as Macbeth.' Whether these were invented to amaze the questioner, or existed but as conceptions in Blake's mind, or were sold or destroyed by Tatham, will probably never be known. It should, however, be noted that among Cunningham's additions to his *Life* in the second edition† is the statement that Blake 'has left volumes, amounting it is said to nearly a hundred, prepared for the press.'
Tatham says of Blake that:

His mental acquirements were incredible, he had read almost every thing in whatsoever language, which language he always taught himself. . . . It is a remarkable fact that among the Volumes bequeathed by Mrs Blake to the Author of this Sketch, the most thumbed from use are his Bible & those books in other languages.[22]

Tatham's statement must, of course, be discounted, but Blake had some knowledge of French, Latin, Italian, Greek, and Hebrew. Samuel Palmer writes to Anne Gilchrist that he can give her no help with Blake's French—'W. B. *was* mad about languages.'[23] Some of Blake's French is obviously dog French, used as a joke. Hebrew he quotes fairly often and with unimpeachable accuracy. The researches of students of the symbolic books shows that many of his ideas were derived from Oriental, Greek, mediaeval,

---

* Morley, *Crabb Robinson*, p. 12. An album in the British Museum Print Room contains a design for a title-page inscribed in elaborate lettering 'Visions of Eternity.' It may possibly have been intended for this book, but is as likely to have been a title-page for *Vala*.

† These additions were noticed for the first time by Keynes, *Bibliography*, p. 320. Cunningham has quoted Lamb's letter to Barton of 15 May 1824, and has given a more detailed criticism of Blake's poetry.

and Celtic sources, but there is little indication as to what he actually read, and it is, therefore, impossible to draw the line between the results of study and coincidence of mystic ideas. Books annotated by him have been dealt with in chronological order, as also those to which he alludes in letters or notes, and it may be assumed that he read all the books illustrated by himself. In addition to these the following are known to have been in his possession: Potter's translation of Aeschylus, Chapman's Homer, Walpole's *Catalogue of the Royal and Noble Authors of England,* Bowles's *Sonnets and Other Poems, Tragedies* by William Sotheby; a copy of the *Works of Peter Pindar* is also said to bear his autograph. Tatham says that he 'was very fond of Ovid, especially the *Fasti,*' and Samuel Palmer that he often quoted the works of St. Teresa,* and other writers on the interior life; among the latter were probably Fénelon and Mme Guyon. He doubtless read Law's own works as well as his translation of Boehme, and was familiar with Bunyan.† His name is among the subscribers to the posthumous edition of *Poems* by the Revd. James Hurdis, D.D., Professor of Poetry at Oxford and friend of Cowper and Hayley.‡

Blake, it is clear, delighted in the company of the 'Ancients'. He had the gift of being happy and of being himself in any society not openly hostile or provocative: these boys gave him love and

---

* Abraham Woodhead's life of St. Teresa (1671) was available at the time; cf. *Jerusalem (Complete Writings,* p. 712):

> . . . . . the Four-fold Gate
> Towards Beulah is to the South. Fenelon, Guion, Teresa,
> Whitefield & Hervey guard that Gate. . . .

It is possible that St. Teresa's writings were the origin of Blake's fantasies about the help given him by the saints.

† Cf. *A Vision of the Last Judgment (Complete Writings,* p. 604): 'Note here that Fable or Allegory is seldom without some Vision. Pilgrim's Progress is full of it'. Twenty-eight designs for *The Pilgrim's Progress* on paper dated 1824 in the possession of Lord Crewe, but never exhibited, were reproduced in an edition of *The Pilgrim's Progress* edited by Geoffrey Keynes for the Limited Editions Club, New York, 1941. They are now in the Frick Gallery, New York. For a description see Keynes, *Blake Studies,* pp. 165–75.

‡ For an account of books owned by Blake see Keynes, *Blake Studies,* and G. E. Bentley, Jr., 'Additions to Blake's Library', *Bulletin of the New York Public Library,* lxiv (1960), 595–605.

admiration: perfect intellectual sympathy he must long have ceased to expect. It would be unjust to accuse them of unfaithfulness to his memory. They had admired the artist, and wellnigh worshipped the man, but they were not the young men of the New Age to whom he had appealed some twenty years before. The seals of his mystic books had never been broken by them, and it is very sure that Blake himself knew this.

Blake would have been lonely indeed without Linnell and the 'Ancients'. Fuseli had died in 1825 and Flaxman followed next year. No letters to Fuseli have been preserved and none to Flaxman after the Felpham days, but it would appear from the references to them by Tatham and Palmer that Blake had continued to see something of his old friends. Though Fuseli and Flaxman, especially the latter, had found Blake exasperating at times, they were enthusiastic admirers of his art. J. T. Smith says in his *Biographical Sketch* of Blake that they both predicted 'That a time will come when Blake's finest works will be as much sought after and treasured up in the portfolios of men of mind, as those of Michel Angelo are at present.'[24]

Farington and Sir Thomas Lawrence had solemnly agreed that Fuseli was an impossible person who could not be safely introduced to their friends, especially the ladies.[25] Flaxman had complained of Fuseli's foul language and asked what Blake did when Fuseli swore. 'What do I do?' asked Blake. 'Why I swear again! and he says, astonished, "Vy, Blake, you are svaring!" but he leaves off himself!'[26] Whether Fuseli rushed into a corner if someone came in whom he disliked, stopped the coach when a proud parent boasted of his daughter's painting on velvet,[27] or wept in the presence of Sir Thomas Lawrence over the beauty of the Farnese Hercules,[28] Blake's serenity was not likely to be disturbed. An anecdote told by Cunningham suggests not only that Blake did not mind if Fuseli were 'artificially very ill natured,'[29] but also that stories of this type about his visions may have been originally similar pleasantries. Fuseli remarked of one of his productions 'now some one has told you this is very fine.' 'Yes,' said Blake, 'the Virgin Mary appeared to me and told me it was very fine:

what can you say to that?' 'Say?' exclaimed Fuseli, 'why nothing, only her ladyship has not an immaculate taste.'*

Whatever the value of Fuseli's achievements, and he himself regretted that he could not 'paint up to what he *saw*', he, like Blake, had given his life to the cause of imaginative art; his Milton Gallery had been a failure and his pictures did not sell. None the less he declared himself to have been a happy man because he had always been well and had always been employed in doing what he liked.

Flaxman thought Blake's poems as great as his paintings, but it is not clear how far this judgement comprehended the symbolic books. Would not the Revd. John Flaxman, as Fuseli dubbed him, have found *The Marriage of Heaven and Hell* distinctly blasphemous? Yet it is likely enough that Flaxman, himself a Swedenborgian, was in closer sympathy with Blake's writings than any of his other friends.† *The Knight of the Blazing Cross*,‡ which he wrote and illustrated for his wife, shows his own mystical leanings, as well as Blake's influence in the drawings. Moreover, Blake's verses in a letter dated 12 September 1800 suggest that Flaxman had known and understood his spiritual experiences while he was writing the prophetic books.

The American War began. All its dark horrors passed before my
    face
Across the Atlantic to France. Then the French Revolution
    commenc'd in thick clouds,
And My Angels have told me that seeing such visions I could not
    subsist on the Earth,
But by my conjunction with Flaxman, who knows to forgive
    Nervous Fear.[30]

* Cunningham, *Lives*, ii, p. 309. Some of these stories were doubtless fabrications. Gilchrist, *Life*, i, pp. 364–5, instances one said to have been told by Leigh Hunt, of Blake taking off his hat and bowing low in Cheapside, explaining that he had seen St. Paul.

† Crabb Robinson, speaking of 1810, when he was writing his article on Blake, says: 'I knew that Flaxman thought highly of him, and though he did not venture to extol him as a genuine Seer, yet he did not join in the ordinary derision of him as a madman'. (Morley, *Crabb Robinson*, p. 19.)

‡ Now in the Fitzwilliam Museum, Cambridge.

When Flaxman died in 1826 Crabb Robinson, always curious to observe Blake's reactions, tried the experiment of bringing the news himself: the result confirmed his view that little was to be gained by frequent intercourse between them. 'It was as I expected. He had been ill during the summer, & he said with a smile, "I thought I shd. have gone first." He then said, "I cannot think of death as more than the going out of one room into another." And Flaxman was no longer thought of. He relapsed into his ordinary train of thinking.'[31] But Blake's memory was not failing as Robinson supposed; four months later he speaks to his old friend, Cumberland, of Flaxman's death, though perhaps these words also would have seemed casual, callous, or insane to Robinson:

Flaxman is Gone, & we must All soon follow, every one to his Own Eternal House, Leaving the Delusive Goddess Nature & her Laws to get into Freedom from all Law of the Members into The Mind, in which every one is King & Priest in his own House. God send it so on Earth as it is in Heaven.[32]

To Linnell he might write: 'I go on without daring to count on Futurity, which I cannot do without doubt & Fear that ruins Activity, & are the greatest hurt to an Artist such as I am.'[33] But Linnell had not known, like Fuseli and Flaxman, the hopes and fears, the doubts and disappointments of Blake's youth and prime. He was patient and kind, kind in 'minute particulars', but he was no mystic, and as years went by he seems to have become more isolated in his angular evangelicism, and the gulf between his views and Blake's widened in his memory. In 1830 he had written to Bernard Barton:

There is one thing I must mention: I never in all my conversations with him could for a moment feel there was the least justice in calling him insane; he could always explain his paradoxes satisfactorily when he pleased, but to many he spoke so that 'hearing they might *not* hear.' He was more like the ancient patterns of virtue than I ever expected to see in this world; he feared nothing so much as being rich, lest he should lose his spiritual riches. He was at the same time the most sublime in his expressions, with the simplicity of a child, though never wanting in energy when called for.[34]

Linnell never altered his mind about Blake's sanity, and was as indignant with Dr. Richardson's article[35] as Palmer and Richmond, but the statement dated 1855 found among his papers suggests that Blake's heterodoxy seemed more shocking when seen down the vista of years than in the days of their constant companionship:

A saint amongst the infidels, and a heretic with the orthodox. With all the admiration [possible] for Blake, it must be confessed that he said many things tending to the corruption of Christian morals, even when unprovoked by controversy, and when opposed by the superstitious, the crafty, or the proud, he outraged all common-sense and rationality by the opinions he advanced, occasionally even indulging in the support of the most lax interpretations of the precepts of the Scriptures.[36]

In October 1825 Linnell gave Blake a folio of fine Dutch paper and commissioned him to make designs from Dante and also to engrave them. The arrangement was that he should take his own time over them and be paid by instalments;* some of these are

* After Blake's death Mrs. Blake, according to Linnell's biographer, sent the book of Dante designs to Linnell with a note saying that they were his as he had already paid for them, but Tatham demanded that they should be returned to him (ibid., p. 241). Anne Gilchrist says that Linnell fetched them away, but that Mrs. Blake asserted that a considerable sum was still due which Tatham claimed first on her behalf and afterwards on his own (*Anne Gilchrist*, p. 130). Mr. John Linnell, the painter's son, told Mr. Ellis that his father had paid Blake a total of £103 5s. 6d., and had made a subsequent payment of about £26 to Mrs. Blake in respect of the Dante designs (*The Real Blake*, p. 410). Crabb Robinson (Morley, *Crabb Robinson*, pp. 2, 22, 217) hints that Linnell was retaining the designs in order to make a profit on them when Blake became famous, but Linnell is cleared from this imputation by a letter to Lord Egremont in which he offers to sell him the designs, engaging to hand over to Mrs. Blake the difference between their price and the sum he had paid for them. The designs were dispersed at the Linnell sale and most of them were distributed among public galleries. The copper-plates of the seven engravings were sold without the knowledge of the trustees and are now in the Rosenwald Collection, National Gallery, Washington, D.C. A limited number of sets of prints from these had been issued while they were in possession of the Linnell family. [For details of the above see Keynes, *Blake Studies*, pp. 228–9. Ed.]

acknowledged in his letters to Linnell. The subject of the fifteenth plate of the *Gates of Paradise*, Ugolino in the Tower of Famine, had been taken from Dante, and it is probable that the head devouring a human figure, which appears several times in the Notebook, represents Lucifer with Judas, but Blake had not hitherto read Dante in the original. With the help of his small Latin he is said to have learnt enough Italian for his purpose in a few weeks. There are several references in his letters to his progress and to the pleasure he took in his work. His invention showed no signs of flagging, and, had he lived, the Dante illustrations might have been the crowning work of his life, an achievement comparable with the Job. The water-colour drawings, many of which were made while he was obliged to stay in bed, number 102, and are often unfinished, some of them mere sketches. Blake had only engraved seven plates, and some of these were not finished. They were issued at two guineas, and Blake notes in a letter to Linnell that Mr. Butts, who had been calling on him, had ordered a proof copy for three guineas; 'this is his own decision, quite in Character.' One set is painted in water colour, possibly by Mrs. Blake after her husband's death, but more probably by Birkett Foster, in whose possession it had been.*

Götzenberger, the German artist, who said, on returning to his own country, that he had seen many men of talent in England, 'but only 3 men of Genius, Coleridge, Flaxman and Blake, and of these Blake was the greatest,' was enthusiastic about the designs, but Crabb Robinson, who introduced him to Blake, modestly remarks: 'They were too much above me.' He was not, however,

---

* Facsimile reproductions of the Dante designs were published by the National Art Collections Fund in 1922. They were also reproduced in Albert S. Roe's volume, *Blake's Illustrations to the Divine Comedy* (1953). The originals were sold at auction with the Linnell collection in 1918 and were distributed among seven galleries, the largest number going to the National Gallery of Victoria, Melbourne. The design of 'Ugolino in Prison', mentioned above, is represented in the series only by a rough pencil sketch, but Blake painted it in tempera on a panel (now in my collection), referring to it in his letter to Linnell of 25 April 1827: 'As to Ugolino, &c, I never supposed that I should sell them; my Wife alone is answerable for their having Existed in any finished state' (*Complete Writings*, p. 79). [Ed.]

afraid to ask whether Blake considered Dante's moral character pure.* '*Pure*,' said Blake, 'do you think there is any purity in God's eyes. The angels in heaven are no more so than we.' Blake's opinion of Dante can be gathered from his conversation with Crabb Robinson and from the sentences written on some of the designs. He thought that Dante had made the same mistake as Swedenborg in believing that 'in this World is the Ultimate of Heaven. This is the most damnable Falsehood of Satan & his Antichrist.' Dante was, therefore, like Wordsworth, an atheist in Blake's sense. 'Dante saw Devils where I see none. I see only Good.' 'He was the slave of the world & time. But Dante & Wordsw. in spight of their Atheism were inspired by the Holy Ghost. . . .' Blake made use of Cary's translation of Dante, and had some acquaintance with Cary,[37] to whom he was probably introduced by Wainewright. Cary told Gilchrist that he gave up his preconceived theory of Blake's madness after he came to know him personally, regarding him only as an enthusiast.

Blake was also illustrating Genesis for Linnell. He had transcribed the text up to the end of the fifteenth verse of the fourth chapter. The manuscript consists of two designs for title-pages and eleven pages of text with illustrations. The title-pages and some of the leaves are coloured, the text of the latter being illuminated in green.† W. M. Rossetti describes six of the designs as follows: '1. A Title-page, with God the Father and Son, the four living creatures used as the Evangelical Symbols, and Adam; 2. Similar subject; 3. The Creator; 4. The Trinity creating Adam; 5. The Creation of Eve; 6. God setting the mark upon Cain.' Blake interprets the Elohim of Genesis as the Trinity, and the brand of Cain as the kiss of forgiveness. The chapter headings also show that his interpretation of Genesis would have been as original and as mystical as his interpretation of Job.

---

* But in his Diary he remarks: 'He showed me his designs, of which I have nothing to say but that they evince a power of grouping & of throwing grace & interest over conceptions most monstrous and disgusting, which I shd. not have anticipated.'

† The illuminated MS. was sold with the Linnell collection in 1918 and is now in the H. E. Huntington Library and Art Gallery.

Chap. I. The Creation of the Natural Man.

Chap. II. The Natural Man divided into Male & Female, & of the Tree of Life, & of the tree of Good and Evil.

Chap. III. Of Sexual Nature, & its Fall into Generation and Death.

Chap. IV. How Generation and Death took Possession of the Natural Man & Of the Forgiveness of Sins written on the Murderer's Forehead.

It was probably about this time that Blake began a series of illustrations for the apocalyptic Book of Enoch, of which the first English translation appears in 1821. Five pencil drawings on folio sheets are extant:* these inventions, like those for the Book of Job, not only illustrate the text, but are a vehicle for Blake's symbolism.

The only book annotated by Blake during the last year of his life, which has been discovered so far, is the *New Translation of the Lord's Prayer*† published in 1827 by the versatile Dr. Thornton. His rendering, intended to check the mechanical repetition of the prayer, is treated by Blake as 'a Most Malignant & Artful attack upon the Kingdom of Jesus By the Classical Learned, thro' the Instrumentality of Dr Thornton.'[38]

The excerpts printed by Geoffrey Keynes with Blake's annotations do not give the cumulative effect of the worthy doctor's pedantry, or do justice to his notion of God, the Creator, who, 'by the mere act of volition, produces substances the *most solid*,' and will only be fully appreciated with the aid of more powerful telescopes.

Exasperated by Thornton's endorsement of Dr. Johnson's view that the Bible is unintelligible to the ignorant, and of Byron's comparison of Christ with Socrates as a great ethical teacher, as also by his own description of God as 'uncontrollably powerful',

* The drawings were sold with the Linnell collection in 1918 and are now in a private collection in the United States.

† The book has the same history as the Genesis MS. The annotations were first printed in full in the Nonesuch edition, 1925.

Blake reads into the translation all the worst errors of the materialist followers of Urizen, and brings them out into the open in his parody: 'Our Father Augustus Caesar, who art in these thy Substantial Astronomical Telescopic Heavens, Holiness to thy Name or Title, & reverence to thy Shadow'[39]—and so forth. Blake's own version of the Lord's Prayer is addressed to Jesus as also the Father and the Holy Ghost, asking that the reign of the God of this World, the Accuser, shall be ended by the forgiveness of sins. The next sentence, which is unfortunately only partly legible, appears to be a prayer for our 'Money bought Bread' and for all things in common without money or tax or value or price, and must be interpreted by the suggestion in Thornton's retranslation of the prayer that he is only occupied with material good, which can be bought, and priced and valued and taxed, and not with spiritual good. Since 'Everything has as much right to Eternal Life as God, who is the Servant of Man,' God, the tyrant, must also be consumed by forgiveness. This is followed by a prayer for deliverance from Parsimony and from the Natural Man.

If Blake and the worthy doctor, who had indeed raised the devil by saying the Lord's Prayer backwards, gave their accustomed signals some Sunday morning to the watching children from Collins' Farm, the meeting may well have been the occasion for some of Blake's most mystifying utterances, likely to be remembered by Linnell and Palmer in after years as outrageous and blasphemous.

Early in 1827 Linnell, seeing how feeble Blake had become, suggested that the Blakes should look after his house, 6 Cirencester Place, at the upper end of Tichfield Street, where he himself spent the day in his studio, and lived there rent free. The neighbourhood would, he thought, be healthier than the low-lying Fountain Court. But Blake could not face the sacrifice of solitude and independence. Perhaps, too, he remembered that he would no longer be able to look up from his work-table and see the Thames through his window 'like a bar of gold'.

In February he wrote to Linnell declining his offer:

I have thought & thought of the Removal & cannot get my Mind out of a state of terrible fear at such a step; the more I think, the more I feel terror at what I wish'd at first & thought it a thing of benefit & Good hope; You will attribute it to its right Cause—Intellectual Peculiarity, that must be Myself alone shut up in Myself, or Reduced to Nothing. I could tell you of Visions & dreams upon the Subject. I have asked & intreated Divine help, but fear continues upon me, & I must relinquish the step that I had wish'd to take, & still wish, but in vain.[40]

He had a severe attack of illness during the spring as he says to Cumberland in a letter of the 12th April:

I have been very near the Gates of Death & have returned very weak & an Old Man, feeble & tottering, but not in Spirit & Life, not in The Real Man The Imagination which Liveth for Ever. In that I am stronger & stronger as this Foolish Body decays.[41]

In the same letter he refers to the card or bookplate which Cumberland had commissioned him to engrave. This has the name, 'Mr. Cumberland', in the centre, surrounded by an allegorical design; on the left an angel with a sickle is swooping down on two boys, one with a snare, and the other flying two birds tied to strings: on the right a figure with a distaff is soaring towards three angels and a child bowling a hoop through the sky. Cumberland did not receive the plate till after Blake's death. He sent his son to call on Mrs. Blake, and wrote to him later:*

I suppose by her charging three guineas he had made a new plate instead of the old one, which I sent to be ornamented in the margin; ... I long much to see what he has done, but if it is ever so trifling take it at her price, as it is the last I shall have on that feeling which I am often forced to restrain.

Young Cumberland answers that Mrs. Blake had told him that the plate would have been more finished had her husband lived, and that it was the last engraving he attempted. Cumberland

* For a full account of Blake's relations with Cumberland and his sons see Geoffrey Keynes, 'George Cumberland', *in Blake Studies,* pp. 230–52. Cumberland had become rather impecunious at the time of Blake's death and this tended to affect his relations with Mrs. Blake. [Ed.]

replies that he shall use proofs from the plate 'to spread my old friend's fame and promote his wife's interest by making him thus the subject of conversation; and his works.'

Blake's last letter to Linnell is dated 3 July: in it he speaks of a relapse caused by a visit to Collins' Farm the previous Sunday. 'I find I am not so well as I thought. I must not go on in a youthful Style. . . .' But, as he had told Cumberland, 'The Real Man The Imagination' was still strong, and he was able to sit up in bed and work on at the Dante designs in the folio book. A few days before his death he finished colouring a relief etching of the 'Ancient of Days' for Tatham. Then, turning to his wife he said: 'Stay! keep as you are! *you* have ever been an *angel* to me, I will draw you.'* A few days later, 12 August, he died at six o'clock in the afternoon. The dying Boehme had asked his son to open the door as he heard strains of distant music: William Blake welcomed death with joyful songs, saying to his wife: 'My beloved, they are not mine—no—they are not mine.'

George Richmond wrote to Samuel Palmer a few days later:†

* This account has been taken from Smith's *Biographical Sketch* (*Blake Records*, pp. 455–76) who, according to Gilchrist, had it from Mrs. Blake. Tatham (Russell, *Letters*, pp. 34, 35) writes as though the etching had been coloured and the portrait drawn on the day of his death. Tatham described the drawing to Gilchrist (*Life*, i, p. 404) as a 'phrenzied sketch of some power, highly interesting but not like.' It was at one time in his possession, but has not been traced. Smith, who probably saw it also, speaks of it as 'a most spirited likeness of her.'

Cunningham calls it 'a fine likeness'. He gives two additional speeches of the dying Blake to his wife which sound like his own embellishments.

'I glory,' he said, 'in dying, and have no grief but in leaving you, Katherine; we have lived happy, and we have lived long; we have been ever together, but we shall be divided soon. Why should I fear death? Nor do I fear it. I have endeavoured to live as Christ commands, and have sought to worship God truly—in my own house, when I was not seen of men.' [And] 'Kate,' he said, 'I am a changing man—I always rose and wrote down my thoughts, whether it rained, snowed, or shone, and you arose too and sat beside me— this can be no longer.' (*Blake Records*, 501–2.)

† The original of this letter was in the possession of A. H. Palmer, and was exhibited at the Victoria and Albert Museum in 1926. Richmond seems to have been present at Blake's death, as H. H. Gilchrist speaks of him as the man who 'when a student, closed the poet's eyes and kissed William Blake

15 August 1827
My Dear Friend, Wednesday Even^g

Lest you should not have heard of the Death of Mr. Blake I have Written this to inform you—He died on Sunday Night at 6 O'clock in a most glorious manner. He said He was going to that Country he had all His life wished to see & expressed Himself Happy hoping for Salvation through Jesus Christ—Just before he died His countenance became fair—His eyes Brighten'd and He burst out in Singing of the things he saw in Heaven. In truth He Died like a Saint as a person who was standing by Him Observed—He is to be Buryed on Fridayay [*sic*] at 12 in morn^g—Should you like to go to the Funeral—If you should there there [*sic*] will be Room in the Coach.

Yrs. affection^y.
G. Richmond[42]

Catherine Blake did the last offices for her husband and made the necessary arrangements courageously and even with a smile. He had told her that it was no real parting, and he should always be there to take care of her.

Blake was buried in Bunhill Fields on 17 August.* In answer to his wife's questions he had replied that he did not himself mind where he lay, but it might as well be where others of his family had been buried, and that he would wish the service to be that of the Church of England. Calvert, Richmond, Tatham, and a clergyman brother of his were present at the funeral.† The grave was not marked by a stone, but the site has been identified.‡

Obituary notices appeared in the *Literary Gazette*, the *Gentleman's Magazine*, and the *Annual Register*. The first assumes that readers will know the illustrations of Blair's *Grave* and quotes a part of Fuseli's preface. Flaxman and Lawrence are also cited as

in death' (*Anne Gilchrist*, pp. 258–9). The other person present was a neighbour helping Mrs. Blake, referred to by Gilchrist, *Life*, i, p. 405, as saying afterwards, 'I have been at the death, not of a man, but of a blessed angel.'

* For details of the funeral expenses see *Blake Records*, pp. 342–3. [Ed.]

† Linnell's presence is not mentioned, but his son told Ellis that the additional £26 paid to Mrs. Blake for the Dante drawings included £10 18s. which he had advanced for the funeral. See Keynes, *Blake Studies*, pp. 221–2.

‡ The late Herbert Jenkins described his investigations in *William Blake, Studies of His Life and Personality*, chapter ix.

admirers of Blake's work. After a melodramatic description of his poverty and physical condition the notice goes on:

... even yet was his eye undimmed, the fire of his imagination unquenched, and the preternatural, never-resting activity of his mind unflagging. He had not merely a calmly resigned, but a cheerful and mirthful countenance; in short, he was a living commentary on Jeremy Taylor's beautiful chapter on Contentedness. He took no thought for his life, what he should eat, or what he should drink; nor yet for his body, what he should put on; but had a fearless confidence in that Providence which had given him the vast range of the world for his recreation and delight.[43]

The article ends by drawing attention to the destitute state of the widow and suggesting assistance for her.

The notice in the *Gentleman's Magazine* contains a fuller account of Blake's work, including the earlier illuminated books, but otherwise is condensed like that in the *Annual Register*, from the *Literary Gazette*.

Blake left no debts and no effects except the stock of copperplates, illuminated books, pictures, and manuscripts. About a month after his death Mrs. Blake went to look after Linnell's house in Cirencester Place, until he moved in the following April to 26 Porchester Terrace. After that she lived for a time with Frederick Tatham, taking charge of his domestic arrangements, and then moved into lodgings at No. 17 Upper Charlotte Street, Fitzroy Square.* Princess Sophia sent her a gift of £100 which she returned, saying that there were others who needed it more.† She supplied her wants by disposing of her husband's work, avoiding, as a good saleswoman should, the display of too large a choice to her customers. She also coloured some of the engraved books with Tatham's help, and, to Linnell's distress, finished some of Blake's drawings. Linnell, Richmond, J. T. Smith, and others helped her by sending purchasers. Lord Egremont paid eighty

---

* Tatham says that she went back to her former lodgings which Ellis (*The Real Blake*, p. 438) takes to mean Fountain Court. She may therefore have lived for a few weeks in Upper Charlotte Street before or after being at Cirencester Place.

† Swinburne (*A Critical Essay*, p. 89) heard this from Seymour Kirkup.

guineas for a water-colour drawing of 'The Characters of Spenser's *Faerie Queen*',* a companion picture to the 'Canterbury Pilgrims', but did not accept Linnell's offer of the Dante drawings. Haviland Burke bought several works himself, and also selected a copy of the *Songs of Innocence and of Experience* and two prints of Job and Ezekiel for Dr. Jebb, Bishop of Limerick, who paid her £20 for them. Cary purchased a drawing of 'Oberon and Titania',† and James Ferguson, to whom she offered the lost *Outhoun*, three or four of the illuminated books. Crabb Robinson went to see her at Linnell's house, and bought two prints of the 'Canterbury Pilgrims' and asked her to look out some engravings for him. Barron Field, who was with him, took a proof of the Pilgrims.‡

In October 1831 mortification set in as a consequence of a neglected attack of inflammation of the bowels. She sent for Mr. and Mrs. Tatham and gave instructions that she should be buried in Bunhill Fields, and that the arrangements should be like those for her husband's funeral: she also asked that no one but themselves should see her after death, and that a bushel of slaked lime should be put in the coffin. After bidding good-bye to Miss Blake, she spent the few hours that remained happy and tranquil, 'repeating texts of Scripture, and calling continually to her William, as if he were only in the next room, to say that she was coming to him, and would not be long now.' She died in Mrs Tatham's arms on the morning of the 18th October. The Tathams, the Richmonds, Denham, a sculptor, and Bird, an artist, attended her funeral. §

* The picture is still at Petworth House, Sussex.

† This water colour is now in the Tate Gallery.

‡ The Diary account (Symons, *Blake*, p. 272) is here used as it is not clear from that in the *Reminiscences* (Morley, *Crabb Robinson*, p. 26) that she was then living at Cirencester Place. The other facts are taken from Gilchrist, *Life*, i, pp. 409–11; Story, *Linnell*, i, pp. 242–5; and Russell, *Letters*, p. 48.

§ These facts are taken from Gilchrist, *Life*, i, p. 411 and Russell, *Letters*, p. 49. A copy of *For the Sexes: The Gates of Paradise*, now in the H. E. Huntington Library, bears the inscription, 'Frederick Tatham to Mr. Bird on his attendance at the Funeral, Oct. 23rd, 1831, being the day on which the widow of the author was Buried in Bunhill Fields church yard' (Keynes, *Bibliography*, p. 177). *Anne Gilchrist* (pp. 129–30) repeats some gossip to W. M. Rossetti to the effect that Mrs. and Miss Blake did not get on well and latterly never met at all. The last part of the statement is contradicted by the

There is little independent record of Catherine Blake, nor is it needed. No one can understand Blake's life without being aware of the significance of her helpful and faithful figure, nor is it possible to think of him with a different type of wife without loss, even without the utter destruction of the fabric of his life. And what other test is there of a perfect marriage? If the gossip about early dissensions, for which there is but a slender basis, be accepted, it only shows the greater victory for love and imagination.* Blake's own words but prove that the doubts and mental distress, which had for a time clouded his life, had cast a shadow over hers also, and that they were both the freer and the happier for his renewed confidence in himself. His love for her was no selfish dependence, the love 'that drinks another as a sponge drinks water,' but that friendship of which he speaks so often as outlasting sexual love. The woman who had signed her name with a cross in the marriage register at Battersea Church had learnt from him, aided by her own love and belief in him, to share his work† and to be his constant stay in spiritual as well as in material things. Even when he was away from her in a visionary Paradise, her bodily presence was necessary to him. Her life was one with his.

---

account of Mrs. Blake's death in Gilchrist's *Life*, to which reference has been made. She says that Miss Blake died in penury and that there was even a rumour that she committed suicide, and blames Tatham for leaving her in want, even if his inheritance of the Blake effects were legally sound.

* See p. 72. Gilchrist, *Life*, i, p. 359, says: 'There *had* been stormy times in years long past, when both were young; discord by no means trifling while it lasted. But with the cause (jealousy on her side, not wholly unprovoked), the strife had ceased also.' J. T. Smith, on the other hand, writes: 'Blake and his wife were known to have lived so happily together, that they might unquestionably have been registered at Dunmow' (*Blake Records*, p. 474).

† Gilchrist, *Life*, i, p. 359, says that Mrs. Blake also had visions: she saw 'processions of figures wending along the river, in broad daylight; and would give a start when they disappeared in the water.' Two paintings by her were formerly in the Graham Robertson collection: 'A Face in the Fire,' watercolour, inscribed 'A drawing made by Mrs. Blake, taken from something she saw by the fire during her residence with me. Curious as by her. Frederick Tatham'; and a tempera on canvas, inscribed by Blake 'Agnes. From the novel of *The Monk*. Designed and painted by Catherine Blake, and presented by her in Gratitude and Friendship to Mrs. Butts.' [Both paintings are now in my collection. Ed.]

X
THE TIDE RETREATS

Hear the voice of the Bard!
Who Present, Past, & Future, sees;
Whose ears have heard
The Holy Word
That walk'd among the ancient trees,

Calling the lapsed Soul,
And weeping in the evening dew;
That might controll
The starry pole,
And fallen, fallen light renew![1]

From the lyrics of his boyhood till those last triumphant songs rang through the little room where he lay dying, from the radiant dawn of 'Glad Day' till the evening shades fell and the folio book was closed, from the time when the youth flaunted the red cap of revolution till the seer wrote his epic on the eternal liberty of the spirit, Blake had kept the Divine Vision. Fate has decreed that lyric poets die young, but if, passing over as we must the unfulfilled promise of *The Everlasting Gospel* and those last unwritten songs, Blake's span of lyric life be taken as ending about the time of his return from Felpham, it was not shorter than that of most of his fellows. Some critics will have it that the mystic slowly stifled the poet, but did he not rather guard the sacred fire, when youth had fled and it was burning low, to create in another medium the poem of the inventions to the Book of Job?

Other men, born later than he, had also toiled in building anew the City of Art, some using marble richly veined and handling it with a cunning greater than his. But he had outlasted them all. He was a poet twenty years before Wordsworth had met Coleridge. When he died the inspiration of Wordsworth and Coleridge was wellnigh spent: Keats and Shelley were dead; Byron had left the wilderness in which he wandered to give his life for the only

liberty he knew.* None of these, his fellow labourers, influenced
Blake. There is, indeed, no evidence that he knew the work of
Coleridge, Shelley, or Keats.† Neither did he affect them: so far as
we know only Wordsworth and Coleridge read any of his poems.
Wordsworth he never met, and he probably had but two or three
talks with Coleridge. In this there is little to regret. Shelley was
the man with whom communion would have been possible and
fraught with mutual good. The sympathy of thought between
Blake and Shelley has been often remarked. Shelley, as he freed
himself from the fetters of Godwin, who was in truth for him
Urizen personified, was gradually developing a philosophy akin
to Blake's. 'Imagination is as the immortal God which should
assume flesh for the redemption of mortal passion.' This sentence
comes not from *A Vision of the Last Judgment*, but from the
Preface to *The Cenci*. And Shelley defends poetry in words which
might be Blake's. 'It is as it were the interpenetration of a diviner
nature through our own . . . it strips the veil of familiarity from
the world, and lays bare the naked and sleeping beauty which is
the spirit of its forms.'² Prometheus bears his sufferings in the
spirit of *The Everlasting Gospel*, and Jupiter cries:

> Oh,
> That thou wouldst make mine enemy my judge,
> Even where he hangs sear'd by my long revenge,
> On Caucasus! he would not doom me thus.
> Gentle, and just, and dreadless is he not
> The monarch of the world?

We may imagine Shelley stretched at Blake's feet listening to a
discourse, well seasoned with Proverbs of Hell, on the Fourfold
Vision, those Last Judgments when the individual casts out error
which he would recognize so readily, the dangers of repressed
desire, and the Human Friendship which transcends sexual love.

* T. Sturge Moore, *Art and Life*, p. 209, detects an improvement of style
in *The Ghost of Abel*, which he thinks may have been due to the influence of
Byron.

† Amy Lowell (*John Keats*, i, pp. 405, 561, 583-5) tries to trace the
influence of Blake on Keats. C. W. Dilke possessed a copy of the *Songs of
Innocence*, but there is no evidence that he acquired it during Keats's lifetime.

Mary Shelley shivers at the old man's talk while Catherine Blake, in her wisdom, smiles. And Shelley, the lover of Aeschylus and Euripides, the scholar and the Platonist, takes fire at Blake's ignorant abuse of the Greeks. Shelley, truly the young man of the New Age for whom Blake had looked in vain, might have restored the music and sense of proportion which the lonely creator of Giants had lost. The beauty of Shelley, mysterious rather than obscure, makes the wider appeal. But the divine imagination of the two poets is not to be measured by a silver rod or poured out in a golden bowl. Yet this may be said, that for good and for evil Blake's visionary faculty was the stronger. His intimacy with his own mythological creations gives them a substantiality which Shelley's 'figures of indistinct and visionary delineation' lack.* The psychological subtleties of Urizen, a possession to those with patience to discover them, are not attempted by Shelley's Jupiter: Enitharmon is richer in suggestion than the lady of the dissolving arms in *Alastor* or the intellectual beauty of Asia.

But the abnormal strength of this faculty was in itself a hindrance to perfection. It is the pressure of visionary material that deforms and obscures the symbolic books and compelled Blake again and again to throw his work aside unfinished. Yet instinctively he made the wisest use of this power. Had he repressed it the balance of his mind might indeed have been lost: he protected himself against its dangers by accepting and availing himself of all that it brought him. '. . . he sometimes thought that if he wrote less, he must necessarily do more graving & painting & he has debarred himself of his pen for a month or more, but upon comparison has found by no means so much work accomplished & the little that was done by no means so vigorous.'[3] The vine was unpruned, but would it not have bled to death under the knife? When he was painting and designing, the very relief from the drudgery of engraving no doubt increased his mental excitement, and made it harder to submit to the discipline necessary for the

* Preface to *Hellas*. It is interesting to note that Shelley thought of writing a dramatic poem on the Book of Job.

attainment of technical excellence. Yet, although his work as an artist is full of blemishes due, at least in part, to haste and crowded vision, his genius has here been easier of recognition than in his writings. It is the mark of the true mystic that, after his initiation into the mysteries of the unitive life, he is impelled in some way to serve his fellow men. Blake's letters after his return from Felpham, his words to Crabb Robinson, and passages in his prose writings, show that he dedicated himself to the restoration of imaginative art as passionately as Teresa and Catherine of Siena to religious or political reform. Tricked and obstructed he seemed to fail, but the originality of his inventions has impressed his fellow artists of all schools, beginning with some of his most distinguished contemporaries, and has gradually won its way with a wider public. The insistence of certain modern critics that he must be judged as an artist and not as a mystic has only increased his reputation.

Of the mystic it is harder to speak. Blake did not offer a new creed for universal acceptance. He had no illusions about the goats and the fools, and no belief in political panaceas. He only knew of individual regeneration attained through doubts and exaltations and sacrifices of self, and of release from the bonds of the material world by a spiritual struggle which tolerated no compromise.

I shd. be sorry if I had any earthly fame for whatever natural glory a man has is so much detracted from his spiritual glory. I wish to do nothing for profit. I wish to live for art. I want nothing whatever. I am quite happy.[4]

The account which he has given of his mental experiences in the symbolic books can only be understood by those who 'put off Holiness, and put on Intellect,' and are also capable of intimate communion with him; unless spectre and emanation are united in the reader he will reproduce Blake's doctrines in a distorted form. Banish, if you will, the symbolic books from the City of Art, not as mad or meaningless, but to be pondered over in the hermit's cell just outside the city walls. But even so, remember that the man who wrote them had allowed no compromise with the material world to cloud his sight.

'You shall not bring me down to believe such fitting & fitted. I know better & please your Lordship—' he wrote with a youthful vehemence in his annotations to *The Excursion*. 'Does not this Fit, & is it not Fitting most Exquisitely too, but to what?—not to Mind, but to the Vile Body only & to its Laws of Good & Evil & its Enmities against Mind.'[5]

'*C'est une étoile très pure et très lointaine dont les rayons commencent seulement à nous atteindre.*' The poet and the artist may often have failed to embody his thought and inventions in a perfect form, and who shall be sure that he has read the message of the mystic aright? To recognize and assail the evils of repression, of law and morality, to perceive and denounce the errors of rulers, teachers, employers, and philanthropists, needs less insight and less boldness in our day than in his. But all this, he would have said, is nothing without the healing power of constructive imagination: the moral judgement must submit itself to the Fourfold, Human Vision. 'I have never known a very bad man who had not something very good about him.'[6] It was through faith in that Shadowy Eighth, the Eternal Individuality of the wanderer through the states of error, that he came to the Forgiveness of Sins which he had once found so difficult, but which in the end he learnt to be the key of Paradise. So the old man, whose wish for a little child was that God might make this world as beautiful to her as it had been to him, whose eyes, bright with the visions he had seen, another child remembered all her life,* the old man who worked

---

* *Three-score Years and Ten: Reminiscences of the late Sophia Elizabeth De Morgan*, edited by Mary A. De Morgan, pp. 66–8.

When I was about ten years old I was walking with my father in the Strand, when we met a man who had on a brown coat, and whose eyes, I thought, were uncommonly bright. He shook hands with my father, and said:

'Why don't you come and see me? I live down here,' and he raised his hand and pointed to a street which led to the river.

Each said something about visiting the other as they parted. I asked who that gentleman was, and was told:

'He is a strange man; he thinks he sees spirits.'

'Tell me his name,' I said.

'William Blake.'

on till the end and died with the gaiety of a saint, had solved the riddle for himself and found his own happiness. 'If asked,' wrote Samuel Palmer to Gilchrist, 'whether I ever knew, among the intellectual, a happy man, Blake would be the only one who would immediately occur to me.'[7]

When William Blake died the Daughters of Inspiration had again yielded their place to the Daughters of Memory. Once more:

> The languid strings do scarcely move!
> The sound is forc'd, the notes are few![8]

In 1826 a young poet had written:

The disappearance of Shelley from the world, seems, like the tropical setting of that luminary (*aside*, I hate that word) to which his poetical genius can alone be compared with reference to the companions of his day, to have been followed by instant darkness and owl-season; whether the vociferous Darley is to be the comet, or tender full-faced L. E. L. the milk-and-watery moon of our darkness, are questions for the astrologers: if I were the literary weather-guesser for 1825 I would safely prognosticate fog, rain, blight in due succession for its dullard months.*

His prophecy was true of more years than the one. No voice yet proclaimed a new revelation. We might fancy that Los, Time Spirit, and Genius of Poetry, had ordained a solemn pause to honour the death of a beloved son before the current of things resumed its course:

> For the spent hurricane the air provides
> As fierce a successor, the tide retreats
> But to return out of its hiding-place
> In the great deep; all things have second birth:
> The earthquake is not satisfied at once.[9]

But the poets, when they came, were inspired by the later leaders of the first and greater revolutionary movement, Byron and Shelley and Keats. The Pre-Raphaelites indeed hailed the spirit of

---

* Thomas Lovell Beddoes in *Letters*, ed. E. Gosse (1894), pp. 33-4.

Blake, but as a bold breaker of idols rather than a master in the art of poetry; Rossetti's amended texts are in the manner of the Mathew Preface.

A lonely guardian of the Divine Vision while he lived, the young men of the newer ages have left Blake lonely still. His are not the excellences of a schoolmaster; his genius of its very nature stands aloof and solitary.

APPENDICES, REFERENCES, AND INDEX

APPENDIX I

EXTRACTS FROM VARLEY'S
ZODIACAL PHYSIOGNOMY AND *URANIA*

With respect to the vision of the Ghost of the Flea, seen by Blake, it agrees in countenance with one class of people under Gemini, which sign is the significator of the Flea; whose brown colour is appropriate to the colour of the eyes in some full-toned Gemini persons. And the neatness, elasticity, and tenseness of the Flea are significant of the elegant dancing and fencing sign Gemini. This spirit visited his imagination in such a figure as he never anticipated in an insect. As I was anxious to make the most correct investigation in my power, of the truth of these visions, on hearing of this spiritual apparition of a Flea, I asked him if he could draw for me the resemblance of what he saw: he instantly said, 'I see him now before me.' I therefore gave him paper and a pencil, with which he drew the portrait, of which a facsimile is given in this number. I felt convinced by his mode of proceeding that he had a real image before him, for he left off and began on another part of the paper to make a separate drawing of the mouth of the Flea, which the spirit having opened, he was prevented from proceeding with the first sketch, till he had closed it. During the time occupied in completing the drawing, the Flea told him that all fleas were inhabited by the souls of such men as were by nature blood-thirsty to excess, and were therefore providentially confined to the size and form of insects; otherwise, were he himself, for instance, the size of a horse, he would depopulate a great portion of the country. He added, that if in attempting to leap from one island to another, he should fall into the sea, he could swim, and should not be lost. This spirit afterwards appeared to Blake, and afforded him a view of his whole figure; an engraving of which I shall give in this work.

The engraving was not included in the unfinished *Treatise*, but the drawing was found in a sketch-book which had belonged to Varley, and was reproduced in 'A Varley-and-Blake Sketch-Book,' by W. B. Scott (*The Portfolio*, vol. ii, 1871), and in a recent facsimile (see p. 312 n.).

An account of Varley's rare pamphlet will be found in Keynes's *Bibliography*, pp. 315–18 and his *Blake Studies* (1970).

From *Urania or the Astrologer's Chronicle, and Mystical Magazine*
Edited by Merlinus Anglicus, Jun. (London, 1825)

NATIVITY OF MR. BLAKE,

𝕿𝖍𝖊 𝕸𝖞𝖘𝖙𝖎𝖈𝖆𝖑 𝕬𝖗𝖙𝖎𝖘𝖙.

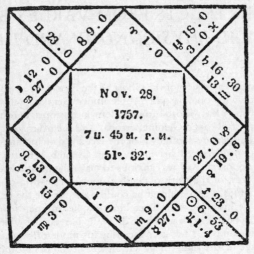

PLANETS LATITUDE

☽ 2.20 S   ♄ 1.14 S   ♃ 0.42 N   ♂ 2.02 N
                  ♀ 2.10 S   ☿ 0.40 N

The above horoscope is calculated for the *estimate* time of birth, and Mr.
Blake, the subject thereof, is well known amongst scientific characters, as
having a most peculiar and extraordinary turn of genius and vivid imagination. His illustrations of the Book of Job have met with much and deserved
praise; indeed, in the line which this artist has adopted, he is perhaps equalled
by none of the present day. Mr. Blake is no less peculiar and *outré* in his ideas,
as he seems to have some curious intercourse with the invisible world; and
according to his own account (in which he is certainly, to all appearances,
perfectly sincere), he is continually surrounded by the spirits of the deceased
of all ages, nations, and countries. He has, as he affirms, held actual conversations with Michael Angelo, Raphael, Milton, Dryden, and the worthies of
antiquity. He has now by him a long poem nearly finished, which he affirms
was recited to him by the spirit of Milton; and the mystical drawings of this
gentleman are no less curious and worthy of notice, by all those whose
minds soar above the cloggings of this terrestrial element, to which we are

most of us too fastly chained to comprehend the nature and operations of the world of spirits.

Mr. Blake's pictures of the last judgment, his profiles of Wallace, Edward the Sixth, Harold, Cleopatra, and numerous others which we have seen, are really wonderful for the spirit in which they are delineated. We have been in company with this gentleman several times, and have frequently been not only delighted with his conversation, but also filled with feelings of wonder at his extraordinary faculties, which, whatever some may say to the contrary, are by no means tinctured with superstition, as he certainly believes what he promulgates. Our limits will not permit us to enlarge upon this geniture, which we merely give as an example worthy to be noticed by the astrological student in his list of remarkable nativities. But it is probable that the extraordinary faculties and eccentricities of idea which this gentleman possesses, are the effects of the Moon in Cancer in the twelfth house (both sign and house being mystical), in trine to Herschell from the mystical sign Pisces, from the house of science, and from the mundane trine to Saturn in the scientific sign Aquarius, which latter planet is in square to Mercury in Scorpio, and in quintile to the Sun and Jupiter, in the mystical sign Sagittarius. The square of Mars and Mercury, from fixed signs, also, has a remarkable tendency to sharpen the intellects, and lay the foundation of extraordinary ideas. There are also many other reasons for the strange peculiarities above noticed, but these the student will no doubt readily discover.

APPENDIX II

BLAKE'S CALLIGRAPHY

Blake's calligraphy does not seem to have received the attention it deserves, and some experts in penmanship have been good enough to give me their opinions.

Professor Selwyn Image writes:

The excellence of his MS. writing has always seemed to me to lie in these two facts. First, it is extremely easy to read—the beauty of its form does not over-assert itself, and, so to say, get in the way between you and the matter of the poem. Secondly—it is essentially a *current* script based on ordinary handwriting—and this, at least to my thinking, is much in its favour for the purpose of illuminated poems as against the more formal MS. type, incomparable as this latter is for inscriptions, addresses, records—and so forth. . . .

Rossetti, if I remember right, was a great admirer of Blake's writing in his illuminated work, and perhaps more or less founded his own on it—as, for example, in his design for his sonnet on The Sonnet, beginning 'A Sonnet is a Moment's Monument.'

Mr. Graily Hewitt, on the other hand, considers Blake's script slovenly and unpleasing:

I imagine he wrote the etched plates in reverse—a thing no pen of a right-handed scribe can do and retain the essential pen character—for all ordinary *pull* strokes have then to become *push* strokes, a fact which essentially alters them. I have at times seen some of the writing on the plates, & marvelled, I fear, more at the labour of the whole process than admired the result. . . . I was in town this last week, and had time (though only an hour) to renew my impression of Blake's etched writing in the British Museum Print Room. I looked at the *Songs of Innocence & Experience*, the *Book of Thel, Europe*, and *America*. My former opinion remains that the writing, though clear and neat, is commonplace and undistinguished; an imitation of printed types, upright and italic; as of one unaware or regardless of the manner of mediaeval manuscripts. Just the efficient work of a competent engraver.

I am no judge of 'design' (and you do not ask me about that), but no scribe is ignorant of that amount of design which concerns the arrangement of matter on a page and the relation of pages to each other. Blake makes his pages with no such reference (it seems to me). They are all like miniature broadsheets, independent. Perhaps the difficulty of printing back to back led to his disregard of a book as a series of diptyches.

His arrangement of matter on the pages is independent of those traditions, which a scholarly scribe may not see ignored without offence. The pleasure of peace too does not seem to have been of value to him in a thing to be read. A love of flickering twigs as in a wind, or flutter of flame, or else a weary drooping of stems or pendulous lines, seems to have suggested to him his accompaniments of writing. Even the writing itself sometimes gives forth little streamers most fidgettingly, from heads and tails. It is best where it is plainest. Even then it can commit the careless errors of the worker-backwards, so that the Y of the title to 'Europe' appears thus. The writing is perfunctory (in as good a sense as that word holds), by which I mean that he seems to have thought little of it as a means to his ends, and to have just planted it on as decently or insignificantly as he could. His unawareness of the Mediaeval works at least saved him from affectations of imitation. And yet—how might he not have applied a serious study of them and the potentialities of fine penmanship! As it is I can't help thinking the foolish tree stems in the page (from *Songs of Innocence*) of that ineffable song of 'The Lamb', so terribly futile as to be sacrilege, or impudently inept. There is a dreadful bushy tree in the background also, cut out by the song itself; and the whole page, to a *book*-lover is defiled by its slip-shod de-composition.

I am sorry to shock you so. But that a man should be able to write as well as this, and then should care so little for the effect of writing and its relation to the page, is one of the things at which one's perceptive patience goes; as it does with artists who paint masterpieces with pigments they have made no enquiry and taken no care about.

Mr. Charles Ricketts allows Blake's writing more merit:

I have ever considered it as of the utmost interest, in its time, and for the singularity of its achievement in the various difficult mediums he employed. His writing is often shapely and vivid but not without flaws in taste: it is often unpleasant when treated fantastically or ornamentally in tiles, etc. I doubt if an exigent standard can be applied to it: it is however very personal and very much alive and both these qualities are of the utmost importance.

The example of Blake's script given below will enable readers to make their own comments on these diverse opinions.

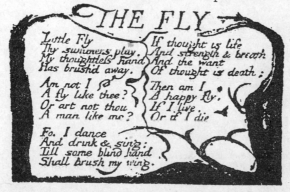

APPENDIX III

EXTRACT FROM
*REVUE BRITANNIQUE**

Les deux plus célèbres habitans de l'hôpital de Bethlem, sont l'incendiare Martin, frère aîné du peintre Martin, et Blake surnommé le Voyant. Lorsque j'eus passé en revue et soumis à mon examen toute cette populace de criminels et d'insensés, je me fis conduire à la cellule de Blake. C'était un homme grand et pâle, parlant bien, vraiment éloquent; dans toutes les annales de la démonologie, rien n'est plus extraordinaire que les visions de Blake.

Il n'était pas victime d'une simple hallucination, il croyait fermement, profondément à la réalité de ses visions; il conversait avec Michel-Ange, il causait avec Moïse, il dînait avec Sémiramis; rien de charlatanique chez lui; il était convaincu. Le passé lui ouvrait ses portes ténébreuses; le monde des ombres accourait chez lui; tout ce qui avait été grand, étonnant, célèbre, venait poser devant Blake.

Cet homme s'était constitué le peintre des Spectres; devant lui, sur sa table, des crayons et des pinceaux se trouvaient toujours placés, et lui servaient à reproduire les physionomies et les attitudes des ses héros qu'il n'évoquait pas, disait-il, mais qui venaient le prier d'eux-mêmes de faire leurs portraits. J'ai compulsé de gros volumes remplis de ces effigies parmi lesquelles j'ai remarqué le portrait du Diable et celui de sa mère. Quand j'entrai dans sa cellule, il dessinait une puce dont le spectre, à ce qu'il prétendait, venait de lui apparaître.

Edouard III était un des habitués les plus assidus; pour reconnaître cette condescendance du monarque, il avait fait à l'huile, son portrait, en trois séances. Je lui adressai des questions qui devaient l'étonner, maix auxquelles il répondit naïvement et sans aucun trouble.

'— Ces messieurs se font-ils annoncer? lui demandai-je. Ont-ils soin de vous envoyer leur carte?

—Non, mais je les reconnais dès qu'ils paraissent. Je ne m'attendais pas à voir Marc-Antoine hier au soir, mais j'ai reconnu le Romain dès qu'il a mis le pied chez moi.

—A quelle heure vos illustres morts vous rendent-ils visite?

—A uneheū quelquefois leur visites sont longues, quelquefois courtes. J'ai vu ce pauvre Job avant-hier; il n'a voulu rester que deux minutesù j'ai à peine eu le temps d'en faire une esquisse que j'ai ensuite copiée à l'eau forte. . . . Mais chut. . . . Voici Richard III.

—Où le voyez-vous?

—En face de vous, de l'autre côté de la table. C'est sa première visite.

* (Paris, 1833) troisième Série, tome IV, pp. 183–6. This article is a translation, but the source of the English original is not given.

—*Comment savez-vous son nom?*

—*Mon esprit le reconnaît, mais je ne sais pas comment.*

—*Quelle est sa physionomie?*

—*Rude, mais belle: je ne vois encore que son profil. Le voici de trois quarts; ah! maintenant il se tourne vers moi; il est terrible à contempler.*

—*Pouvez-vous le questionner?*

—*Assurément, que voulez-vous que je lui demande?*

—*S'il prétend justifier les meutres qu'il a commis pendant sa vie?*

—*Votre demande lui est déjà parvenue, nous conversons d'âme à âme, par intuition et par magnétism. Nous n'avons pas besoin de paroles.*

—*Quelle est la réponse de Sa Majesté?*

—*La voici, un peu plus longue qu'il ne me l'a donnée: vous ne comprendriez pas le langage des esprits. Il vous dit que ce que vous appelez meurtre et carnage n'est rien; qu'en égorgeant quinze ou vingt mille hommes on ne leur fait aucun mal; que la partie mortelle de leur être non seulement se conserve, mais passe dans un meilleur monde, et que l'homme assassiné qui adresserait des reproches à son assassin se rendrait coupable d'ingratitude, puisque ce dernier n'a fait que lui procurer un logement plus commode et une existence plus parfaite. Mais laissez-moi, il pose très bien maintenant, et si vous dites un mot il s'en ira.'*

Je quittai cet homme auquel on n'avait rien à reprocher et qui ne manquait pas de talent comme graveur et comme dessinateur.

The legend of Blake's confinement in Bedlam has its source in this article in the *Revue Britannique*. Dr. Richardson's reckless assertion that Blake had been in an asylum for thirty years (cf. pp. 344-5, 349) was probably also indirectly derived from this article. I have now discovered the origin of the article in a paper in the *Monthly Magazine* for March 1833, entitled 'Bits of Biography: Blake, the Vision Seer, and Martin, the York Minster Incendiary.' The first part is entirely concerned with Blake: the second describes a visit to Bedlam, where Martin was the most famous of the inmates. I will quote the first part in full that readers may have the opportunity of comparing it with the description of the interview with Blake in the French article. It will be observed that all the visionary sitters, except Richard III, introduced in the *Revue Britannique* have been alluded to in the *Monthly Magazine*, and that the conversation with the royal sitter is an almost literal translation, but the French writer has inadvertently substituted the Crookback for the handsome Edward III. He has also drawn on his imagination for the erroneous description of Blake as a tall, pale man, but has ignored the interesting addition to contemporary accounts of Catherine Blake.

Blake was an embodied sublimity. He held converse with Michael Angelo, yea, with Moses; not in dreams, but in the placid still hours of night— alone—awake—with such powers as he possessed in their full vigour. Semiramis was often bodily before him; he chatted with Cleopatra, and the Black Prince sate to him for a portrait. He revelled in the past; the gates of the spiritual world were unbarred at his behest, and the great ones of bygone ages, clothed in the flesh they wore on earth, visited his studio. He painted from spectres. I have seen several of his pictures—of men who died 'many anno-dominis ago,' taken from their ghosts. The shadow of a flea once appeared to him, and he drew it.

His may be deemed the most extraordinary case of spectral illusion that has hitherto occurred. Is it possible that neither Sir Walter Scott, nor Sir David Brewster, the authors of 'Demonology and Witchcraft' and 'Natural Magic,' ever heard of Blake? Allan Cunningham, unless I am grossly mistaken, had, even prior to the appearance of the former work, introduced the Vision-seer to the public—in which of his productions, however, I cannot recollect; so that, being unable to refer to what he has narrated on the subject, I am in danger 'of repeating upon him.' But this shall not daunt me.

Blake was not the victim of a mere optical delusion. He firmly believed in what he seemed to see. He had no doubt but that the spectre of Edward the Third frequently visited him. He painted the Monarch, in oil, at three sittings. Bruce would now and then call to converse with him. He recognized at a glance the ghost of any great personage the moment it appeared. He had no doubt of its identity. His friend Marc Antony had not sent in his card; no one had announced him: yet he knew the Roman, and named him at sight.

About midnight the illustrious dead used to drop in upon him: sometimes their visits were short, but, frequently, as protracted as he could wish. I have been present on these occasions. One night, while we were engaged in criticizing his own extravagant, yet occasionally sublime illustrations of the book of Job, engraved by himself, he suddenly exclaimed, 'Good God! here's Edward the Third.' 'Where?' 'On the other side of the table; *you* can't see him, but I do; it's his first visit.' 'How do you know him?' 'My spirit knows him—how I cannot tell.' 'How does he look?' 'Stern, calm, implacable; yet still happy. I have hitherto seen his profile only, he now turns his pale face toward me. What rude grandeur in those lineaments!' 'Can you ask him a question?' 'Of course I can; we have been talking all this time not with our tongues but with some more subtle, some undefined, some telegraphic organ; we look and we are understood. Language to spirits is useless.' 'Tell him that you should like to know what he thinks of the butcheries of which he was guilty in the flesh.' 'I have while you have been speaking.' 'What says his majesty?' 'Briefly this: that what you and I call *carnage* is a trifle unworthy of notice: that destroying five thousand men is doing them no real injury; that their important part being immortal, it is merely removing them from one state of existence to another; that mortality is a frail tenement, of which the sooner they get quit the better, and that he who helps them out of it is entitled to their gratitude. For, what is being hewn down to the chine to be compared with the felicity of getting released from a dreary and frail frame?' 'His doctrines are detestable and I abhor them.' 'He bends the battlement of his brow upon you; and if you say another word, will vanish. Be quiet, while I take a sketch of him.'

His widow, an estimable woman, saw Blake frequently after his decease: he used to come and sit with her two or three hours every day. These hallowed visitations were her only comforts. He took his chair and talked to her, just as he would have done had he been alive: he advised with her as to the best mode of selling his engravings. She knew that he was in the grave; but she felt satisfied that his spirit visited, condoled, and directed her. When he had been dead a twelvemonth, the devoted and affectionate relict would acquiesce in nothing 'until she had had an opportunity of consulting Mr. Blake.'

The second part also corresponds closely with the account of Bedlam and of Jonathan Martin in the *Revue Britannique*, although the latter has been somewhat curtailed. By unscrupulously stringing together the two bits of biography the French writer has put Blake into Bedlam, and so created a legend which may now be regarded as completely disproved.

The article in the *Monthly Magazine* is unsigned, but a comparison with the extract from *Urania*, quoted in Appendix I, suggests that it may well have been from the same hand. R. C. Smith (Merlinus Anglicus) no doubt owed his introduction to Blake to his fellow astrologer, Varley, and the view taken of Blake's powers by the writer in the *Monthly Magazine* is consonant with Varley's.

REFERENCES

LIST OF ABBREVIATIONS

Anne Gilchrist
Anne Gilchrist, Her Life and Writings, ed. H. H. Gilchrist (London, 1887)

Blake Records
G. E. Bentley, Jr., *Blake Records* (Oxford, 1969)

Damon
S. Foster Damon, *William Blake, His Philosophy and Symbols* (London, 1924)

Ellis
E. J. Ellis, *The Real Blake: A Portrait Biography* (London, 1907)

Ellis and Yeats
The Works of William Blake, ed. with a Memoir by E. J. Ellis and W. B. Yeats, 3 vols. (London, 1893)

Fairfax Murray
Correspondence of William Hayley, Fairfax Murray Collection, Fitzwilliam Museum, Cambridge

Farington Diary
Joseph Farington, R.A., *The Farington Diary*, ed. James Greig, 8 vols. (London, 1922–8)

Gilchrist
Alexander Gilchrist, *The Life of William Blake*, 2nd ed., 2 vols. (London, 1880)

Hayley
Memoirs of the Life and Writings of William Hayley by himself, ed. John Johnson, 2 vols. (London, 1823)

Keynes, *Bibliography*
Geoffrey Keynes, *A Bibliography of William Blake* (New York: The Grolier Club of New York, 1921)

Keynes, *Blake Studies*
Geoffrey Keynes, *Blake Studies*, 2nd ed. revised and enlarged (Oxford, 1971)

Keynes, *Separate Plates*
Engravings by William Blake: The Separate Plates, a Catalogue Raisonnée compiled by Geoffrey Keynes (Dublin, 1956)

Letters
The Letters of William Blake, ed. Geoffrey Keynes, 2nd ed. (London, 1968)

Morley
Crabb Robinson: Blake, Coleridge, Wordsworth, Lamb, etc., Being Selections from the Remains of Henry Crabb Robinson, ed. Edith J. Morley (Manchester, 1922)

OSAB   *Blake: Complete Writings*, with Variant Readings, ed. Geoffrey Keynes, Oxford Standard Authors (London, 1966); new impression with corrections, Oxford Paperbacks, 1971

Palmer   A. H. Palmer, *The Life and Letters of Samuel Palmer* (London, 1892)

Richmond Papers   A. M. W. Stirling, *The Richmond Papers*, from the correspondence and manuscripts of George Richmond, R.A. (London, 1926)

Rossetti Letters   *Letters of Dante Gabriel Rossetti to William Allingham, 1854–1870*, ed. George Birkbeck Hill (London, 1897)

Rossetti Papers   *Rossetti Papers 1862–1870*, a Compilation by William Michael Rossetti (London, 1903)

Russell, *Engravings*   A. G. B. Russell, *The Engravings of William Blake* (London, 1912)

Russell, *Letters*   *The Letters of William Blake, together with a Life by Frederick Tatham*, ed. A. G. B. Russell (London, 1906)

Story, *Blake*   A. T. Story, *William Blake, His Life, Character and Genius* (London, 1893)

Story, *Linnell*   A. T. Story, *The Life of John Linnell*, 2 vols. (London, 1892)

Swinburne   A. C. Swinburne, *William Blake: A Critical Essay*, new ed. (London, 1906)

Symons   Arthur Symons, *William Blake* (London, 1907)

Underhill   Evelyn Underhill, *Mysticism: A Study in the Nature and Development of Man's Spiritual Consciousness*, 2nd ed. (London, 1912)

CHAPTER I

1 OSAB, 10–11
2 Symons, 39
3 Story, *Blake*, preface
4 Ellis and Yeats, i, 3
5 OSAB, 187
6 Symons, 26–8; *Blake Records*, 553–4
7 Gilchrist, i, 5
8 *Anne Gilchrist*, 129
9 Ellis, 105
10 Morley, 22
11 Gilchrist, i, 8
12 Gilchrist, i, 15
13 OSAB, 450
14 OSAB, 591–5r
15 *Blake Records*, 422–3
16 Palmer, 245
17 Gilchrist, i, 18
18 *Blake Records*, 572
19 Symons, 372
20 OSAB, 604
21 OSAB, 798
22 OSAB, 476–7
23 Keynes, *Blake Studies*, 29
24 OSAB, 6
25 OSAB, 151
26 OSAB, 119
27 OSAB, 215
28 OSAB, 212
29 OSAB, 8–9
30 OSAB, 3
31 OSAB, 2
32 *Blake Records*, 432
33 OSAB, 449
34 Gilchrist, i, 314
35 Gilchrist, i, 95
36 OSAB, 207
37 Russell, *Engravings*, 53–4, 68
38 OSAB, 160
39 Keynes, *Bibliography*, 198
40 OSAB, 543–4
41 OSAB, 551
42 OSAB, 446
43 OSAB, 553
44 OSAB, 554
45 *Works of James Barry* (1809), i. 536
46 Gilchrist, i. 54
47 *Blake Records*, 27
48 *Blake Records*, 482
49 OSAB, 801
50 Notebook, 4
51 OSAB, 527
52 Gilchrist, i. 59
53 OSAB, 743
54 Reynolds, *Discourses*, VII, 1798
55 J. T. Smith, *Nollekens and his Times*, ed. Whitten (1920), ii. 351–2
56 J. T. Smith, *A Book for a Rainy Day* (1845), 83
57 Letter to Mrs. Elizabeth Carter, late '70s or early '80s
58 OSAB, 738
59 OSAB, 157
60 *Blake Records*, 456
61 *Blake Records*, 457
62 OSAB, 452–3
63 OSAB, 54
64 OSAB, 44–5
65 OSAB, 49–51
66 OSAB, 48–9
67 Gilchrist, i. 57
68 OSAB, 577
69 OSAB, 797
70 OSAB, 62
71 *Blake Records*, 460, 472–3
72 Keynes, *Bibliography*, 10
73 W. E. A. Axon, 'Thomas Taylor the Platonist', *The Library*, ii (1890), p. 248
74 OSAB, 154

CHAPTER II

1 OSAB, 149
2 OSAB, 111
3 Underhill, 231
4 OSAB, 518
5 Watts, *Horae Lyricae* (1764), 122 ('Grace Shining', iv)
6 OSAB, 431
7 Damon, 268
8 Damon, 40
9 OSAB, 125
10 Damon, 269
11 OSAB, 98
12 Damon, 256
13 OSAB, 804
14 OSAB, 118–19
15 OSAB, 109
16 OSAB, 110
17 OSAB, 130
18 OSAB, 129
19 H. M. Morris, *Flaxman, Blake, and Coleridge* (1915), 89
20 OSAB, 152
21 OSAB, 164
22 *Rossetti Letters*, i. 109–10
23 OSAB, 161
24 OSAB, 168
25 OSAB, 163
26 OSAB, 168
27 OSAB, 171

CHAPTER III

1 OSAB, 149
2 Gilchrist, i. 56, 59
3 Gilchrist, i, 93
4 Gilchrist, i. 358
5 S. T. Coleridge, *Poems*, ed. E. H. Coleridge (1912), 123 n. (In 'Religious Musings', version of 1796)
6 J. Knowles, *Life and Writings of Henry Fuseli* (1831), i. 165–8
7 Damon, 101
8 *Blake Records*, 521
9 OSAB, 383
10 OSAB, 385
11 OSAB, 387
12 OSAB, 390
13 OSAB, 393
14 OSAB, 392
15 OSAB, 391–2
16 OSAB, 396
17 OSAB, 400
18 OSAB, 402
19 OSAB, 456
20 OSAB, 470
21 OSAB, 157
22 Swinburne, 17
23 OSAB, 138
24 OSAB, 65–88
25 OSAB, 88
26 OSAB, 92
27 OSAB, 90
28 Underhill, 120, 121, 142
29 OSAB, 97
30 OSAB, 98
31 OSAB, 133
32 OSAB, 506
33 Swinburne, 227
34 OSAB, 158
35 OSAB, 158
36 OSAB, 739
37 OSAB, 825
38 OSAB, 629
39 OSAB, 565–6
40 OSAB, 776
41 OSAB, 778
42 OSAB, 621
43 OSAB, 729
44 OSAB, 232
45 OSAB, 656
46 OSAB, 483
47 OSAB, 721
48 OSAB, 818

[49] OSAB, 237–8
[50] OSAB, 522
[51] *Blake Records*, 525
[52] Gilchrist, i. 359
[53] OSAB, 149–50
[54] OSAB, 615
[55] Morley, 51
[56] OSAB, 615–16
[57] OSAB, 790
[58] OSAB, 663
[59] OSAB, 440–41
[60] OSAB, 598
[61] Morley, 13
[62] J. Boswell, *Tour to the Hebrides* (1785), 261 (16 Sept. 1746)
[63] OSAB, 192
[64] OSAB, 436
[65] OSAB, 576
[66] Gilchrist, i. 125
[67] Gilchrist, i. 362–3
[68] Palmer, 24
[69] Gilchrist, i. 300
[70] OSAB, 565
[71] Gilchrist, i. 370
[72] OSAB, 835
[73] *Correspondence of Southey with Caroline Bowles*, ed. E. Dowden (1881), 194; *Blake Records*, 399
[74] Morley, 12
[75] OSAB, 823
[76] OSAB, 481
[77] OSAB, 473
[78] OSAB, 150
[79] OSAB, 852
[80] OSAB, 538

CHAPTER IV

[1] OSAB, 629
[2] Swinburne, 333
[3] Ellis, 192–3
[4] Elbridge Colbey, *Life of Holcroft*, (1925), xxxiii
[5] *Blake Records*, 207–8
[7] OSAB, 33
[8] OSAB, 867
[9] OSAB, 791
[10] OSAB, 797–8
[11] OSAB, 791–2
[12] OSAB, 793–4
[13] OSAB, 794–5
[14] OSAB, 795
[15] *Blake Records*, 67
[16] OSAB, 191–2
[17] OSAB, 192–5
[18] OSAB, 193
[19] OSAB, 380
[20] OSAB, 196
[21] OSAB, 197
[22] OSAB, 198
[23] OSAB, 198–9
[24] OSAB, 200
[25] OSAB, 203
[26] OSAB, 239
[27] OSAB, 239
[28] OSAB, 240
[29] OSAB, 241
[30] OSAB, 243
[31] OSAB, 244–5
[32] OSAB, 233–4
[33] *Blake Records*, 470–1 n.
[34] OSAB, 617
[35] OSAB, 604–5
[36] OSAB, 614
[37] OSAB, 222
[38] OSAB, 223
[39] OSAB, 224
[40] OSAB, 226
[41] OSAB, 230
[42] OSAB, 231
[43] OSAB, 233
[44] OSAB, 235
[45] OSAB, 236
[46] OSAB, 777
[47] OSAB, 168
[48] OSAB, 256
[49] OSAB, 256
[50] OSAB, 258
[51] OSAB, 260
[52] OSAB, 249

[53] OSAB, 250
[54] OSAB, 151
[55] OSAB, 245
[56] OSAB, 153
[57] OSAB, 246
[58] OSAB, 246
[59] OSAB, 246
[60] OSAB, 247
[61] OSAB, 897
[62] OSAB, 158
[63] OSAB, 264
[64] OSAB, 264
[65] OSAB, 265
[66] OSAB, 273
[67] OSAB, 266–7
[68] OSAB, 277
[69] OSAB, 279
[70] OSAB, 281
[71] OSAB, 284
[72] OSAB, 285
[73] OSAB, 287
[74] OSAB, 288
[75] OSAB, 289
[76] OSAB, 290–1
[77] OSAB, 291
[78] OSAB, 293
[79] OSAB, 298
[80] OSAB, 304
[81] OSAB, 305
[82] OSAB, 305

[83] OSAB, 308
[84] OSAB, 310–11
[85] OSAB, 311
[86] OSAB, 315
[87] OSAB, 322
[88] OSAB, 323
[89] OSAB, 329
[90] OSAB, 331
[91] OSAB, 331
[92] OSAB, 333
[93] OSAB, 333
[94] OSAB, 337
[95] OSAB, 337
[96] OSAB, 338
[97] OSAB, 339
[98] OSAB, 340
[99] OSAB, 340
[100] OSAB, 342
[101] OSAB, 346
[102] OSAB, 347
[103] OSAB, 348–9
[104] OSAB, 353
[105] OSAB, 355–6
[106] OSAB, 357
[107] OSAB, 357
[108] OSAB, 359–60
[109] OSAB, 361
[110] OSAB, 379
[111] OSAB, 187
[112] OSAB. 798

CHAPTER V

[1] OSAB, 503
[2] E. V. Lucas, *A Swan and her Friends* (1909), 183
[3] Hayley, i. 207–8
[4] Hayley, ii. 165–6
[5] *Blake Records*, 27
[6] *Blake Records*, 63
[7] *Blake Records*, 64
[8] OSAB, 796
[9] *Blake Records*, 64
[10] OSAB, 797
[11] *Letters*, 36
[12] *Blake Records*, 70
[13] Fairfax Murray

[14] *Blake Records*, 70
[15] OSAB, 799
[16] *Blake Records*, 72
[17] OSAB, 800
[18] OSAB, 801
[19] OSAB, 802
[20] OSAB, 801–2
[21] OSAB, 802
[22] OSAB, 803
[23] OSAB, 802
[24] *Letters*, 43–5
[25] OSAB, 804
[26] OSAB, 807
[27] OSAB, 816

[28] OSAB, 809
[29] OSAB, 811
[30] *Blake Records*, 84
[31] OSAB, 809
[32] OSAB, 539
[33] Hayley, ii. 126
[34] *Blake Records*, 90
[35] OSAB, 816–17
[36] Hayley, ii. 133
[37] Gilchrist, i. 162
[38] Gilchrist, i. 184
[39] OSAB, 811–13
[40] OSAB, 815–16
[41] OSAB, 817
[42] OSAB, 818
[43] OSAB, 511
[44] OSAB, 484
[45] OSAB, 483
[46] OSAB, 489
[47] OSAB, 483
[48] OSAB, 489
[49] OSAB, 493
[50] OSAB, 822
[51] OSAB, 825–6
[52] OSAB, 819–22
[53] OSAB, 860
[54] OSAB, 861
[55] *Blake Records*, 177
[56] *Rossetti Letters*, 8 Jan. 1856
[57] OSAB, 826–8
[58] OSAB, 828–9
[59] OSAB, 833–4
[60] *Blake Records*, 138
[61] OSAB, 833
[62] *Letters*, 71–2
[63] *Letters*, 77
[64] *Blake Records*, 146
[65] Gilchrist, i. 195–9
[66] OSAB, 854
[67] OSAB, 818
[68] OSAB, 511
[69] OSAB, 512
[70] OSAB, 520
[71] OSAB, 513
[72] OSAB, 269–70
[73] *Blake Records*, 488
[74] *Blake Records*, 489

[75] OSAB, 811
[76] OSAB, 792
[77] OSAB, 812
[78] OSAB, 814
[79] OSAB, 814
[80] OSAB, 823
[81] OSAB, 824–5
[82] OSAB, 828
[83] OSAB, 544
[84] OSAB, 415
[85] OSAB, 418–20
[86] OSAB, 420, 430
[87] OSAB, 421–2, 424
[88] Damon, 131–2
[89] Gilchrist, ii. 112–13
[90] OASB, 533
[91] OSAB, 431
[92] OSAB, 434
[93] OSAB, 434–6
[94] Ellis, 91
[95] OSAB, 480
[96] OSAB, 149–50
[97] OSAB, 150
[98] OSAB, 799
[99] OSAB, 495
[100] OSAB, 497
[101] OSAB, 499
[102] OSAB, 502
[103] OSAB, 502
[104] OSAB, 505
[105] OSAB, 507
[106] OSAB, 515
[107] OSAB, 517
[108] OSAB, 509–10
[109] OSAB, 505
[110] OSAB, 516
[111] OSAB, 519
[112] OSAB, 526
[113] OSAB, 521
[114] OSAB, 527
[115] OSAB, 530
[116] OSAB, 530
[117] OSAB, 530
[118] OSAB, 532–3
[119] OSAB, 533
[120] OSAB, 534

CHAPTER VI

[1] OSAB, 491
[2] OSAB, 832
[3] OSAB, 833
[4] OSAB, 851
[5] OSAB, 854
[6] OSAB, 831
[7] OSAB, 830
[8] OSAB, 835
[9] OSAB, 851-2
[10] OSAB, 935
[11] OSAB, 440
[12] Damon, 8
[13] OSAB, 582
[14] Russell, *Letters*, xxxvii
[15] OSAB, 610
[16] OSAB, 853-4
[17] OSAB, 829
[18] OSAB, 860
[19] OSAB, 935
[20] OSAB, 843-4
[21] OSAB, 843
[22] OSAB, 848
[23] OSAB, 849
[24] OSAB, 837
[25] OSAB, 837
[26] OSAB, 840
[27] OSAB, 831
[28] OSAB, 835
[29] OSAB, 836
[30] OSAB, 841-2
[31] OSAB, 854
[32] OSAB, 858
[33] OSAB, 862
[34] OSAB, 847
[35] *Blake Records*, 155
[36] OSAB, 859
[37] OSAB, 439
[38] Malkin, *A Father's Memoirs of his Child* (1806), 17-18
[39] Ibid., xxxix
[40] OSAB, 934
[41] OSAB, 845
[42] OSAB, 549
[43] OSAB, 842

[44] OSAB, 844
[45] OSAB, 848
[46] OSAB, 849
[47] *Blake Records*, 165
[48] OSAB, 859
[49] OSAB, 864
[50] OSAB, 865
[51] *Blake Records*, 166
[52] *Blake Records*, 167
[53] OSAB, 861
[54] OSAB, 862-3
[55] *Letters*, 125-7
[56] *Blake Records*, 182-3
[57] *Blake Records*, 491
[58] *Blake Records*, 196-7
[59] OSAB, 663
[60] *Blake Records*, 194
[61] *Blake Records*, 464
[62] *Blake Records*, 491
[63] OSAB, 576
[64] OSAB, 586
[65] OSAB, 590
[66] Keynes, *Bibliography*, 209-11
[67] OSAB, 591
[68] OSAB, 594
[69] OSAB, 592
[70] OSAB, 594-5
[71] OSAB, 601
[72] OSAB, 594
[73] *Letters*, 126-7
[74] OSAB, 555
[75] OSAB, 538
[76] OSAB, 442-4
[77] OSAB, 558
[78] *Letters*, 134; *Blake Records*, 211
[79] OSAB, 865-6
[80] OSAB, 445
[81] OSAB, 459
[82] OSAB, 466
[83] OSAB, 452
[84] OSAB, 475
[85] OSAB, 446
[86] OSAB, 461
[87] *Blake Records*, 472

[88] Gilchrist, i. 413–14
[89] OSAB, 561
[90] OSAB, 561
[91] OSAB, 563
[92] OSAB, 573
[93] OSAB, 585
[94] OSAB, 585
[95] OSAB, 586
[96] OSAB, 584
[97] OSAB, 866
[98] Blake Records, 226
[99] Blake Records, 399
[100] Blake Records, 284–5
[101] Keynes, Blake Studies, 73
[102] OSAB, 567, 570–1

[103] OSAB, 570
[104] OSAB, 578
[105] Blake Records, 222
[106] Rossetti Papers, 178
[107] Blake Records, 215–17
[108] OSAB, 592
[109] OSAB, 604–17
[110] Blake Records, 467–8
[111] OSAB, 604–5
[112] OSAB, 617
[113] OSAB, 607
[114] OSAB, 606
[115] OSAB, 608
[116] OSAB, 612

CHAPTER VII

[1] OSAB, 558–9
[2] Blake Records, 221
[3] Blake Records, 220
[4] Swinburne, 89 n.
[5] Swinburne, 86–7
[6] Correspondence of Southey with Caroline Bowles, 193–4; Blake Records, 398–9
[7] OSAB, 553
[8] J. L. Roget, History of the Old Water Colour Society (1891), i. 27
[9] Gilchrist, i. 297
[10] Dibdin, Reminiscences (1836), 784–9; Blake Records, 242–3
[11] Blake Records, 243–4 n.
[12] W. Paulet Cary, Critical Description of Death on the Pale Horse (1817), 130
[13] Keynes, Bibliography, 375
[14] OSAB, 878
[15] OSAB, 155
[16] OSAB, 620
[17] OSAB, 621
[18] OSAB, 621
[19] OSAB, 622
[20] OSAB, 622
[21] OSAB, 622
[22] OSAB, 623

[23] OSAB, 714
[24] OSAB, 626
[25] OSAB, 628
[26] OSAB, 629
[27] OSAB, 629
[28] OSAB, 634
[29] OSAB, 635
[30] OSAB, 636
[31] OSAB, 638
[32] OSAB, 640
[33] OSAB, 647
[34] OSAB, 648
[35] OSAB, 609
[36] OSAB, 649
[37] OSAB, 650
[38] OSAB, 651
[39] OSAB, 648
[40] OSAB, 657
[41] OSAB, 659
[42] OSAB, 661
[43] OSAB, 662
[44] OSAB, 663
[45] OSAB, 664
[46] OSAB, 666
[47] OSAB, 668
[48] OSAB, 671
[49] OSAB, 683
[50] OSAB, 684

51 OSAB, 687
52 OSAB, 688
53 OSAB, 693
54 OSAB, 694
55 OSAB, 610
56 OSAB, 696
57 OSAB, 716
58 OSAB, 776–7
59 OSAB, 718
60 OSAB, 721
61 OSAB, 724
62 OSAB, 737–8
63 OSAB, 739
64 OSAB, 741
65 OSAB, 742
66 OSAB, 743
67 OSAB, 744
68 OSAB, 744
69 OSAB, 746
70 OSAB, 788
71 OSAB, 747

72 Morley, 3
73 Symons, 271
74 *Jerusalem*, pl. 76
75 *Blake Records*, 265–6
76 *London Magazine*, July 1826
77 Gilchrist, i. 323
78 OSAB, 748–59
79 OSAB, 758
80 OSAB, 758
81 OSAB, 555
82 OSAB, 158
83 OSAB, 752
84 Morley, 3
85 OSAB, 754
86 OSAB, 754
87 OSAB, 754–5
88 OSAB, 756
89 OSAB, 761
90 OSAB, 758
91 OSAB, 771

CHAPTER VIII

1 OSAB, 458
2 *Blake Records*, 496–9
3 Story, *Linnell*, i. 160
4 Story, *Linnell*, i. 159–60
5 OSAB, 867
6 Keynes, *Separate Plates*, 84
7 OSAB, 775–7
8 OSAB, 778
9 OSAB, 775
10 *Blake Records*, 249–50
11 OSAB, 780
12 OSAB, 781
13 OSAB, 878
14 OSAB, 613
15 OSAB, 434
16 Morley, 17
17 Morley, 1
18 Morley, 18
19 Morley, 21
20 Morley, 3

21 Morley, 8
22 Symons, 269
23 Morley, 12
24 Morley, 21–2
25 *Anne Gilchrist*, 262
26 Morley, 23
27 *Letters, Conversations and Recollections of S. T. Coleridge*, ed. T. Allsopp (1864), i. 107
28 *Letters of Coleridge*, ed. E. H. Coleridge (1895), ii. 685–8
29 *Works of Charles and Mary Lamb*, ed. E. V. Lucas (1912), vii. 642–3
30 *Letters of Edward Fitzgerald*, ed. W. A. Wright (1894), i. 25–6
31 *Blake Records*, 229
32 W. Hazlitt, *The Plain Speaker*, ix, 'On the Old Age of Artists' (1826), 223–4

CHAPTER IX

1 OSAB, 771
2 OSAB, 869
3 OSAB, 870–1
4 Keynes, *Bibliography*, 125–6
5 OSAB, 875
6 Palmer, 9–10
7 Palmer, 16–17
8 Gilchrist, i. 344–7
9 Palmer, 244–5
10 OSAB, 2
11 Gilchrist, i. 366
12 Gilchrist, i. 342–3
13 Palmer, 23
14 Gilchrist, i. 343
15 Gilchrist, i. 343
16 *Blake Records*, 529
17 *Blake Records*, 533
18 R. S. Garnett, *Portfolio Monograph on Blake* (1895), 71–2
19 Morley, 6
20 *Blake Records*, 530
21 Keynes, *Bibliography*, 187
22 *Blake Records*, 526
23 Palmer, 248
24 *Blake Records*, 467
25 *Farington Diary*, iv. 57–8 (18 Dec. 1806)
26 *Richmond Papers*, 8
27 Palmer, 383
28 *Farington Diary*, v. 118 (24 Feb. 1809)
29 OSAB, 798
30 OSAB, 799
31 Morley, 25
32 OSAB, 879
33 OSAB, 879
34 Russell, *Letters*, 229
35 *Athenaeum*, 11 Sept. 1875, 'Fictions concerning William Blake'
36 Story, *Linnell*, i. 247
37 R. W. King, *Life of Cary* (1925), 170
38 OSAB, 786
39 OSAB, 788
40 OSAB, 876
41 OSAB, 878
42 *Letters*, 165
43 *Blake Records*, 349

CHAPTER X

1 OSAB, 210
2 Shelley, *A Defence of Poetry*
3 *Blake Records*, 525
4 Morley, 5
5 OSAB, 784
6 Morley, 26
7 Gilchrist, i. 352
8 OSAB, 11
9 Wordsworth, *The Prelude*, Bk x.

INDEX

Bold-face references indicate main entries; Blake is shortened to 'B' throughout.

Southey, Robert, 61, 77-8, 170, 254, 268-9, 275, 296, 328, 336
'Spectre and Emanation', 189
Spencer, Earl, 273
Spenser, Edmund, 8, 155
'Spirit of God moved upon the Face of the Waters, The', 178-9
'Spiritual Form of Pitt guiding Behemoth', 259, 269
'Spiritual Form of Nelson guiding Leviathan', 259, 269
Spitalfields, 116n.
Spurzheim, J. G., *Observations on . . . Insanity*, B's annotations to, 156
Stirling, Gen. Archibald, of Keir, 275n.
Stirling-Maxwell, Sir William, collection of, 235n., 250n.
Stokes, Dr., 23n.
Story, A. T., see Linnell, J., *Life of*
Stothard, C., 90n.
Stothard, R. T., 240-1
Stothard, Thomas, 14, 15, 26, 88-9, 166, 222n., 224, 233-5, 236n., 237, 238-41, 249, 256, 267, 278, 301, 342; *Life of Thomas Stothard* (Mrs. A. E. Bray), 15n.
Strange, R., 4
Sussex Weekly Advertiser, 177
Swedenborg, Emanuel, 2n., 4, 51, 54, 56-8, 59, 63, 122n., 360; followers of, 15, 45n., 87n., 334, 349, 356
— *Wisdom of Angels concerning Divine Love and Divine Wisdom*, B's annotations to, 56
— *Wisdom of Angels concerning Divine Providence*, B's annotations to, 57-8
Swedenborgian Society, Great Eastcheap, 56
Swinburne, Algernon Charles, 41-2, 52, 59, 258-9, 266
— *William Blake: A Critical Essay*, 41, 81-2, 266, 267-8, 300n., 366n.
Symons, Arthur, 2, 71n., 227n., 241n., 244n., 351
— *William Blake*, xi-xii, 74n., 254n., 317n.

Talfourd, Thomas Noon, 337n.
Tasso, Torquato, 155n.; *Le Sette Giornale del Mondo Creato*, 159
Tate Gallery, 259n., 289n., 323, 367
Tatham, C. H., 349

Tatham, Frederick, 19n., 45n., 47n., 105, 185, 270, 275, 341, 347, 349-52, 358n., 364, 365, 366-7, 368n.
— 'Life of William Blake', xii, 2n., 3, 16, 26, 47-8, 54n., 69-70, 81, 349-51, 352, 353, 355, 364n.
Taylor, Thomas, B's landlord, 19n.
Taylor, Thomas, the Platonist, 23, 29, 37, 62, 71n., 106, 187n., 269
Teniers, David, 182
Teresa, St., 289, 354, 372
Thel, Book of, see *Book of Thel, The*
'Then she bore Pale Desire', 7n.
There is No Natural Religion, 29, 33, 57
Thomas, Revd. Joseph, 242
Thomson, James, 8
Thornton, Dr. Robert John, 316-17; see also Virgil, *Pastorals*
— *A New Translation of the Lord's Prayer*, B's annotations to, 361-2
'Thou hast a lap full of seed', 42
Tickell, Thomas, 162n.
Tiriel, 35-7, 38, 63
Titian, 251, 256
'To the Deists', 185, 286
'To the Muses', 10, 328
'To Nobodaddy', 42
'To Tirzah', 3, 40, 67
'To Venetian Artists', 17
Todd, Ruthven, xiii; Everyman edition of Gilchrist, *Life of Blake*, 87, 266n.
treason, B's trial for, 171-8, 276
Trianon Press, Paris, 96n.
Trotter, engraver, 15n.
Truchsess, Joseph, Count, 206n., 208; Truchsessian Gallery, 206, 208-10
Trusler, Revd. John, 91, 92, 93n., 94; B's letters to, 51n., 91-3, 182
Tulk, Charles Augustus, 334-5
Turner, Dawson, B's letter to, 86, 313
'Two Views of a Statue of Ceres', 215
'Tyger, The', 38, 219, 326, 336

'Ugolino in Prison', 359
Underhill, Evelyn, *Mysticism*, 334n.
'Unto Adam and his Wife . . .', 83
Upcott, William, 334
Upton, Revd. James, 305
Urania, 380-1, 387
Urizen, B's god of reason, 42, 52, 98, 102, 103-4, 106-11, 144, 185, 190,

"We are witnessing the climax of America's longest war—the culture war. Born in the nascent years of both Ronald Reagan's presidency and the religious right, Jonathan Wilson-Hartgrove was a trained culture warrior—until he turned coat and ditched the delusion of moral grandeur revealed by mercenary politics. *Revolution of Values* is a gift to every person straining for clarity in the fog of the culture war's climax. Read this book. Share it. Talk about it. Both the witness of the church and the future of our nation depends on our capacity to see through the fog right now."

Lisa Sharon Harper, president of Freedom Road and author of *The Very Good Gospel*

"Not only is Jonathan Wilson-Hartgrove one of my best friends, he is also one of the most dynamic Christian leaders in the United States. Rooted out of his Rutba House community in North Carolina, Jonathan has become one of the most prominent leaders in the moral movement and the Poor People's Campaign with Rev. William Barber—a shining star in the revolution of Jesus around the world. His newest book calls us to join the revolution."

Shane Claiborne, author, activist, cofounder of Red Letter Christians

"Jonathan Wilson-Hartgrove is a prophetic voice for our times. Through a combination of storytelling, biblical reflection, and cultural criticism, *Revolution of Values* sheds light on the human victims of an immoral presidency defined by nativism, racism, militarism, Christian nationalism, and anti-intellectualism. Evangelicals can no longer stand on the sidelines and watch the injustice from afar. It is time to join the revolution."

John Fea, historian and author of *Believe Me: The Evangelical Road to Donald Trump*

"*Revolution of Values* promises to be a conversion experience for Christians seeking to live faithfully in an era in which our faith has been hijacked for partisan gain, obfuscating the teachings at the very heart of the gospel. It's a critical read for those coming out of the wilderness of white Christianity's captivity to political operatives. This is a clarion call for us to return to Jesus' mission bringing good news to the poor and freedom to the oppressed."

Jennifer Butler, CEO, Faith in Public Life

"Are you one of the 81 percent of evangelicals who voted for Donald Trump in 2016, thinking you were making the Christian and biblical choice? Or one of the mainline Protestants or Roman Catholics who joined them? Are you having some second thoughts? Here's the story of a young evangelical who rethought his decision to be a foot soldier in the religious right and is now a leader in a revolution of values that you may want to join too."

Brian D. McLaren, author of *The Great Spiritual Migration*

"*Revolution of Values* is a clarion call for those who believe in the liberation message of Jesus. The book upends the association in the United States of Christianity with the religious right and offers a powerful Christian vision for a more just world. Wilson-Hartgrove takes the battle straight to those who have hijacked the gospel for their own selfish ends. I am fired up after reading it! I suspect you will be too."

Eddie S. Glaude Jr., James S. McDonnell Distinguished University Professor, Princeton University

"At this critical and highly problematic time for both the nation and the church, Wilson-Hartgrove offers a compelling set of stories and analyses to stimulate a fresh Christian imagination for justice and the public square. Woven through it is his personal journey of transformation, as well as inspiring examples of ordinary people who have leaned into the public square with faith, resilience, humility, and courage. This is the *Revolution of Values* he offers: how slaveholder religion can be dismantled and replaced by the vivifying truth and justice of Jesus for all. May we learn and follow."

Mark Labberton, president of Fuller Theological Seminary

"*Revolution of Values* puts words to the inarticulate frustrations, confusion, and righteous anger many have felt in response to the increasingly visible distance between the teachings of Jesus Christ and the actions of his followers. Jonathan Wilson-Hartgrove aims a pointed critique at the way some Christians have weaponized the Bible to promote policies that work against the poor, the immigrant, and people of color. He puts a face to the systemic and institutional abuses that have occurred over the past several decades by sharing the stories of people he personally knows. This book encourages all of us to work for nothing less than a revolution in our morality that will usher in more justice, equity, and love in the twenty-first century."

Jemar Tisby, president of The Witness, author of *The Color of Compromise*

"Jonathan Wilson-Hartgrove's urgent message for the church is both a return to Jesus and a call for the body of Christ to no longer be held captive by the politics of our day. *Revolution of Values* returns to the heart of the Christian message—to follow Jesus, love our neighbor, bless those who persecute us, and pursue justice on behalf of the least of these. *Revolution* is an inspiring and prophetic book at a critical time in our country's history!"

Mae Elise Cannon, executive director of Churches for Middle East Peace, author of *Social Justice Handbook* and *Just Spirituality*

JONATHAN WILSON-HARTGROVE

REVOLUTION OF VALUES

RECLAIMING PUBLIC FAITH
FOR THE COMMON GOOD

An imprint of InterVarsity Press
Downers Grove, Illinois

InterVarsity Press
P.O. Box 1400, Downers Grove, IL 60515-1426
ivpress.com
email@ivpress.com

InterVarsity Press® is the book-publishing division of InterVarsity Christian Fellowship/USA®, a movement of students and faculty active on campus at hundreds of universities, colleges, and schools of nursing in the United States of America, and a member movement of the International Fellowship of Evangelical Students. For information about local and regional activities, visit intervarsity.org.

All Scripture quotations, unless otherwise indicated, are taken from The Holy Bible, New International Version®, NIV®. Copyright © 1973, 1978, 1984, 2011 by Biblica, Inc.™ Used by permission of Zondervan. All rights reserved worldwide. www.zondervan.com. The "NIV" and "New International Version" are trademarks registered in the United States Patent and Trademark Office by Biblica, Inc.™

While any stories in this book are true, some names and identifying information may have been changed to protect the privacy of individuals.

Published in association with the literary agency of Daniel Literary Group, Brentwood, TN.

Cover design and image composite: David Fassett
Interior design: Daniel van Loon

Images: cardboard texture: © Katsumi Murouchi / Moment Collection / Getty Images
yellowed paper: © ke77kz / iStock / Getty Images Plus
colorful oil paint: © photominus / iStock / Getty Images Plus
blue and red abstract: © oxygen / Moment Collection / Getty Images
US flag: © Poligrafistka / Digital Vision Vectors / Getty Images
colorful collage: © CurvaBezier / iStock / Getty Images Plus

ISBN 978-0-8308-4593-4 (print)
ISBN 978-0-8308-3648-2 (digital)

Printed in the United States of America ♾

InterVarsity Press is committed to ecological stewardship and to the conservation of natural resources in all our operations. This book was printed using sustainably sourced paper.

Library of Congress Cataloging-in-Publication Data
Names: Wilson-Hartgrove, Jonathan, 1980- author.
Title: Revolution of values : reclaiming public faith for the common good / Jonathan Wilson-Hartgrove.
Description: Westmont : IVP, an imprint of InterVarsity Press, 2019. | Includes bibliographical references.
Identifiers: LCCN 2019036714 (print) | LCCN 2019036715 (ebook) | ISBN 9780830845934 (print) | ISBN 9780830836482 (digital)
Subjects: LCSH: United States—Church history—20th century. | Christian conservatism—United States. | Christianity and culture—United States. | Church work with the poor--United States. | Church work with people with social disabilities--United States.
Classification: LCC BR526 .W575 2019 (print) | LCC BR526 (ebook) | DDC 261.70973—dc23
LC record available at https://lccn.loc.gov/2019036714
LC ebook record available at https://lccn.loc.gov/2019036715

| P | 20 | 19 | 18 | 17 | 16 | 15 | 14 | 13 | 12 | 11 | 10 | 9 | 8 | 7 | 6 | 5 | 4 | 3 | 2 | 1 |
| Y | 36 | 35 | 34 | 33 | 32 | 31 | 30 | 29 | 28 | 27 | 26 | 25 | 24 | 23 | 22 | 21 | 20 | 19 |

FOR ALL THE SAINTS WHO'VE GONE BEFORE

"There is a river . . ."

CONTENTS

MORAL CLARITY AND THE FOG OF WAR

War is the realm of uncertainty; three quarters of the factors on which action in war is based are wrapped in a fog of greater or lesser uncertainty. A sensitive and discriminating judgment is called for; a skilled intelligence to scent out the truth.

CARL VON CLAUSEWITZ, ON WAR

When the Son of Man comes in his glory, and all the angels with him, he will sit on his glorious throne. All the nations will be gathered before him, and he will separate the people one from another as a shepherd separates the sheep from the goats. . . .

Then the righteous will answer him, "Lord, when did we see you hungry and feed you, or thirsty and give you something to drink? When did we see you a stranger and invite you in, or needing clothes and clothe you? When did we see you sick or in prison and go to visit you?"

The King will reply, "Truly I tell you, whatever you did for one of the least of these brothers and sisters of mine, you did for me."

JESUS, MATTHEW 25:31-32, 37-40

Since the late 1970s in America, political operatives have invested money and energy in framing the cultural concerns of conservative white Christians as *the* moral issues in our public life. This framing was the explicit agenda of many

of the organizations that built the religious right, but it has become commonplace across political and religious divides in America's public square. Whether you agree with them or not, conservative white evangelicals serve as the spokespersons for morality on the evening news.

This was not always the case. Just half a century ago, the most famous religious leader in America was the Reverend Dr. Martin Luther King Jr. In the context of the civil and human rights movements of the 1960s, voting rights, equal protection under the law, economic justice, peace, and the environment were widely recognized as moral issues. Americans from different racial and religious groups certainly did not agree on how to address these issues, but they were consistently addressed as moral issues.

I grew up in the Southern Baptist church in the 1980s and 1990s, during the heyday of the Moral Majority movement and the emergence of the Christian Coalition, both of which mobilized conservative white evangelicals to join the Republican Party and hold onto "traditional values." In that context, I learned to understand myself as a Christian at war with the dominant culture. Anxious that our way of life was passing away as the world around us became more diverse, my white evangelical culture taught me to turn to the Bible for solace and direction. As in any battle, our leaders argued about strategy. Should we seek political power to influence legislation or try to influence popular culture? Should we engage more in public life or retreat to spaces where we could avoid the culture's corrupting influence? Should we attempt to use culture, try to change culture, or build a counterculture?

These questions animated a lively debate within white evangelicalism for decades. But amid the back and forth about strategy and tactics, most people came to agree that Americans were, in fact, at war. James Davison Hunter, a sociologist attuned to the ways elites and institutions were shaping public conversations in the late twentieth century, named the phenomenon in his 1991 book *Culture Wars*: "America is in the midst of a culture war that has had and will continue to have reverberations not only within public life but within the lives of ordinary Americans everywhere."

Describing the institutions that had lined up across from one another in American public life, Hunter noted that historic divisions in the nation had shifted. Religious people no longer divided themselves along the denominational lines that had shaped public engagement for most of American history. Increasingly, Hunter observed, Americans saw themselves on one side or the other of a war between traditional morality and progressive values. This wasn't just about Left versus Right in politics, though the culture wars inevitably shaped where people stood with regard to partisan issues. The divide between orthodoxy and progressivism was more fundamental, Hunter argued. People on each side increasingly understood their way of seeing the world as fundamentally incompatible with their enemies across the battle line.

In the realignment that Hunter described, Americans who look to the Bible for moral authority were asked to line up against progressive values and policy proposals that sought to expand rights and alleviate poverty. In the name of defending traditional morality and a biblical worldview, I was

taught to fight against policy proposals advocated by marginalized and vulnerable sisters and brothers crying out for justice in public life. On the front lines of the culture war, many who had committed to follow Jesus as Lord realized we had been deployed to fight against the people through whom Jesus promised to be present in Matthew 25.

How did white Christian nationalists wrest America's public moral narrative away from the civil rights movement and persuade many people of faith to defend white cultural values in the name of Jesus? This question has haunted me since, as a young man on my way out of the religious right, I met black Christians who taught me another way of following Jesus in public. Twenty years later, after the election of Donald Trump, I wrote *Reconstructing the Gospel: Finding Freedom from Slaveholder Religion* to say what I had learned from the black-led freedom movement about how white identity politics distorted American Christianity's understanding of everything from personal salvation to shared public witness. But as I taught that long history in churches and seminaries across the country, I quickly realized that slaveholder religion's more recent impact on American public life was *the* pressing concern, not only for Christians struggling to understand public witness but also for the wider American public that simply could not comprehend how white Christians who claimed to be concerned about morality could stand by a president who was so obviously and egregiously immoral.

I wrote this book both for those who share my experience in white Christian institutions and for the many who do not

because the false moral narrative of the tradition I was raised in has impacted everyone caught up in the American story. *Revolution of Values* is a search for clarity on behalf of a people who lost our way in the midst of the culture wars. Such confusion is not uncommon in the fog of war, veterans remind us. "A sensitive and discerning judgment is called for," Carl von Clausewitz writes in his famous treatise *On War*, "a skilled intelligence to scent out the truth." My methodology has been to scent out the truth of what happened to faith in public life by examining the political and economic interests that invested in winning the political allegiance of white evangelicals in the late twentieth century. The prophets and apostles who warn us against false teachers in Scripture call for such discernment. But it is not easy to question the authority of teachers who tell you that the fate of your very soul is at stake.

I know this because I was trained as a foot soldier in the culture wars. I was taught to vilify liberals, environmentalists, and civil and women's rights advocates, not as a strategy to gain political power but as a religious duty. The true aim of social justice warriors, I was warned, is a squishy tolerance that, in the end, can stand anything but a true Christian. My memory verses in Sunday school taught me to love my enemies, but the culture war taught me to be on guard. Love someone too much and it might cost you your moral grounding.

I did not defect from the moral crusade I was trained to fight because I lost my faith. I went AWOL when I realized Jesus was present to me in the people I had been taught to

fear. Poor and marginalized people's desire for justice had been written off as "progressive" and "atheistic." But they showed me how to read the Bible as both a vision for God's justice and a story about how justice comes through people who've been rejected.

So this is not only a book about how the religious right taught America to misread the Bible. It's also an introduction to the people who can teach us to hear God's Word anew. Each chapter tells the story of someone who has been directly harmed by the policy agenda of politicians who promised to stand for "biblical" and traditional values. Each, in real and painful ways, is a victim of the culture war. But these individuals are more than that. They have been my teachers, and my account of their stories here is the result of interviews I have conducted with them for this book, conversations we have shared over years, and background research into their context and the broader forces that shape their individual biographies. In the light of God's plan to bring justice and mercy through marginalized people, these women and men are prophets who show us a better way. They are heralds of an America that has never yet been.

And they are not alone. While this book focuses on the revolution of values we need because of the disproportionate influence of white Christian nationalists in American public life, it draws from the wisdom of people both within and outside the Christian tradition. While America's distorted moral narrative has overrepresented white cultural values, wisdom from black, native, Latinx, Asian, and progressive white communities has also shaped traditions of rich moral reflection in

America. Faith in these traditions, combined with the growing subset of unaffiliated Americans who want nothing to do with religion, represents far more people than the roughly 17 percent of Americans who self-identify as evangelical Protestant.

In the fog of war, people often become confused about where battle lines lie and who the real enemy is. Those who've known physical combat are honest about this. Clarity is hard to come by in the heat of battle. But at the Last Judgment, Jesus says, nations will be measured by how we treat the least among us (Matthew 25:31-46). Such an apocalypse isn't meant to inspire fear; rather, it intends to offer clarity about which side to take in confusing times. When we stand with people who are hungry and thirsty, naked and far from home, sick and incarcerated, we stand with Jesus.

The culture warriors who challenged me to practice my faith in public life were not wrong to suggest that the gospel of Jesus is political. Their error was in believing that the enemy of morality was progressive values and not the genocidal white supremacy and patriarchy that have compromised Christian witness throughout US history. This was not an innocent miscalculation. As this book shows, people of considerable means invested an incredible amount of resources in encouraging this particular lie.

No lie can live forever, but this lie has brought us, four centuries after the first enslaved Africans were brought to this land, to a moral crisis unlike anything America has experienced since its families, churches, and government were rent by civil war. Now, as then, it is uncertain whether a democratic political arrangement can endure without addressing the

fundamental division in our common life—not an irreconcilable difference of worldviews but a growing breach between the extremes of inequality. If a multiethnic democracy is possible in twenty-first-century America, it will depend on a moral movement that resists the false gods of Christian nationalism and rediscovers a biblical vision for justice and mercy in our common life.

I am convinced that such a vision for faith in public life has always been present in the American story, however marginalized and overlooked it has been. I have had the opportunity to learn from and with communities that received this vision and passed it on. This book is an invitation to draw deeply from the freedom-movement streams that have nurtured me and to join the present struggle for the heart and soul of our democracy. It is, I pray, an invitation you will accept and share with others. In the fierce urgency of our present moral crisis, the well-being of millions and the viability of our common home are at stake.

WADE IN THE WATER

In the West Texas borderlands of the Rio Grande Valley, El Paso, is one side of a city that straddles two nations, a river running through it. Annexed by the United States as a part of the Republic of Texas in 1845, El Paso was officially separated from Juárez, Mexico, in 1848, though the border remained fluid well into the mid-twentieth century. It is a river after all. During the Kennedy administration, in an effort to establish a dividing line more precise than the water's ebb and flow, the US government constructed large concrete embankments on each side of the Rio Grande between El Paso and Ciudad Juárez, creating a manmade canyon that is spanned by three footbridges that connect the people of El Paso/Juárez to this day.

María lives and works on the El Paso side. A grandmother whose dark black hair is streaked with natural silver highlights, she has spent her adult life watching the distance grow between her and her family in Juárez, across the concrete canyon. Since 2002, she has not been able to visit with her children and grandchildren who live just across the border.

During a regular check-in with US Immigration and Customs Enforcement (ICE) in 2016, María's husband was deported without notice, released on the Juárez side of the now heavily militarized border. Though able to reunite with family he had not seen in years, he is now separated from María. Their family, like the living waters of the Rio Grande, does not fit within the boundaries imposed upon them.

I met María on a Sunday morning in the fall of 2017, when the Border Network for Human Rights (BNHR), an advocacy group organized by dozens of women like María, invited a delegation of preachers to join them for a family reunion they called "Hugs Not Walls." After Donald Trump's 2016 presidential campaign popularized the idea of a wall between the United States and Mexico as a symbol of his proposed America First policy, Pope Francis exhorted the faithful around the world to "build bridges, not walls." But anything as permanent as a bridge would require permits that María and her colleagues with the BNHR cannot get. Still, they are not powerless. Where a bridge is impossible, a hug might still happen.

But hugs cannot happen without the help of Border Patrol. Before we can get to the concrete canyon from the El Paso side of the border, we have to travel through a no-man's land behind chainlink fences, under constant video-camera surveillance. Our escorts on this journey are community relations officers from the US Border Patrol. Some years ago, after the *El Paso Times* published an exposé on illegal home invasions and human rights abuses that had been chronicled by the BNHR, local Border Patrol officials asked BNHR for a meeting. "We learned that we have to turn our needs into

rights," one of María's colleagues told me. By honestly confronting the Border Patrol on its violations of the Fourth
Amendment's prohibition against "illegal searches and sei-
zures," BNHR began a sustained conversation about how
Border Patrol can do its job while also respecting the dignity
of the people they encounter.

Thus, some years later, while living apart from her family
under an administration committed to extreme immigration
enforcement, María is willing to get in a van with Border
Patrol agents and lead our small delegation to the northern
rim of El Paso's concrete canyon. Descending by foot on ramps
built into the cement embankment, we reach the water's edge,
where a makeshift set of iron stairs offers an entry point into
the Rio Grande. Twenty yards across, on the river's Mexican
shore, María can see her husband, two sons, and son-in-law
climbing backwards down another set of stairs. As she waves
to them and smiles, I notice a quiver in her cheek. It is the first
time they've all been this close to one another in sixteen years.

Families that are separated long to be together. The people
of Border Patrol understand this as well as María does. They
insist that their job is only to enforce the law, not to keep
families apart. In the ongoing conversation between Border
Patrol and the BNHR, someone asked an important question:
In all the apparatus that has been built around the river over
the past half a century, where precisely is the border? The official answer: in the middle of the Rio Grande.

Looking out across the river, I notice a small island—
a sandbar, really—halfway between our set of stairs and
the small gathering of people on the other side. This is our

destination—a place in the middle where we can straddle two nations. As we step down into the brown water, we hold hands and join our voices to sing,

Wade in the water,
Wade in the water, children.
Wade in the water,
God's gonna trouble the water.

The river isn't very deep here, but the surface beneath is unpredictable, swallowing our legs in mud as we search for a foothold with each step. With an absence of any clear path forward, we find our way together, pausing for anyone who loses their balance or needs a moment to catch up. By the time we climb onto the sandbar, María's husband is already there to pull her into his arms. As they embrace, their sons quickly form a circle around them. I watch tears stream down their cheeks and fall to the water that swirls around our ankles. They only have five minutes—ten, if we can stretch it—for this family reunion; then we'll each have to return to the side of the river we came from. We haven't built a bridge, just a tenuous way toward this temporary embrace.

"Hugs Not Walls," the BNHR calls it. For me, it is a second baptism.

MORAL CRISIS IN OUR PUBLIC LIFE

Capitalizing on decades of Republican outreach to conservative Christian communities, Donald Trump won an unprecedented majority of white evangelicals' votes in the 2016 presidential election while at the same time alienating the vast majority

of black and brown people—and consistently receiving the disapproval of a majority of Americans. Embracing Steve Bannon, an avowed nationalist, as his chief counselor, President Trump appealed to the fear and anxiety of aggrieved white Americans, promising to "Make America Great Again." When his administration acted in its first year to implement his America First policy by imposing a travel ban on several majority Muslim countries, enacting extreme immigration enforcement, rolling back civil rights protections for the LGBTQ community, publicly attacking NFL players who protested police brutality, and disregarding US allies in foreign affairs, both fans and detractors saw Trump's rejection of norms as confirmation of their views. To crowds who had chanted "build that wall" at campaign rallies, Trump was keeping his promises. To the resistance that emerged in airport terminals and on the streets, Trump's administration was a cruel Frankenstein, called to life by his extreme campaign rhetoric wreaking havoc in public life.

Among many white Christians, I noted a quiet anxiety. All my adult life, I've shared the message of Jesus with one foot in the white evangelical world that raised me and the other in the black Baptist church I now call home. I know the tensions within these different yet often overlapping church cultures. But something was different now. I was straddling a border that had become more rigid, feeling in my gut something of what María must feel, watching her family torn in two by powers beyond her control.

Black sisters and brothers in the church were aghast. How could white people who call themselves Christian endorse

outright bigotry? President Trump defended Nazis after Heather Heyer was run over by a white nationalist in Charlottesville, saying there were "very fine people on both sides." At a rally in Alabama, he called black NFL players who knelt during the national anthem to protest the killing of unarmed black people "sons of bitches."

Many white Christians I talked to cringed. They told me they felt torn and confused. Despite a faithful track record in the United Methodist Church, Hillary Clinton had been consistently demonized by conservative religious media outlets for three decades. Though people who considered "family values" a central issue in public life had been uncomfortable with a thrice-married reality TV star who publicly flaunted his promiscuity, many said they just couldn't have voted for Clinton. In their moral imagination, she symbolized a liberal establishment that could never be trusted. "I had to hold my nose, but I voted for him," one Presbyterian elder told me. "We'll see. Maybe God can do something new through an unconventional president."

However compromised their reasoning, white Christians I talked to were anxious, even cautious. They asked for prayers that America would "make it through this difficult time" and lamented growing partisanship. I spent much of the first year of Trump's presidency both asking white Christians to rethink what they thought they knew, and praying with black folks who had no doubt that God opposed the nonsense we were all watching play out before us. In my preaching and teaching, I asked white Christians to lean into their uncertainties and listen to people whose experiences

taught them to question when, precisely, America had ever been great for them.

Meanwhile, the coalition of religious nationalists who'd rallied to support Trump's campaign offered a contrasting clarity of purpose. "When I think of you, President-elect Trump," the Southern Baptist pastor Robert Jeffress preached on the morning of Trump's inauguration, "I am reminded of another great leader God chose thousands of years ago in Israel." Jeffress recalled how God called Nehemiah to rebuild Jerusalem's broken city walls after the exiles returned from Babylonian captivity, before declaring with triumphal delight: "You see, God is NOT against building walls!"

On the Christian Broadcasting Network (CBN) and Fox News, Jeffress regularly joined Christian media mogul Pat Robertson, Pentecostal prosperity preacher Paula White, Jerry Falwell Jr. of Liberty University, and Franklin Graham, the son of evangelist Billy Graham, to defend Trump against his critics. After leading "nonpartisan" prayer rallies at all fifty state capitols during the 2016 campaign, Graham declared President Trump an answer to prayer and offered general amnesty for any past moral failings, regularly quoting verses on forgiveness. When Falwell invited President Trump to address the graduating class of 2017 at Liberty University, he called Trump evangelicals' "dream president."

Historian John Fea has dubbed this circle of Christian preachers who stood ready to defend Trump against all critics "court evangelicals," evoking the image of a king who ruled absolutely by divine right. At any rate, the loudest Christian voices in American public life were not exhorting the faithful

to dwell on their concerns about this president. They were using the Bible to defend him.

Observing the contrast between the spiritual struggle people were facing in their real lives as they grappled with the rupture of the Trump presidency and the manufactured certainty of these "court evangelicals," I began to ask whether teachers in the church like myself had done enough to equip people for faithful citizenship. "God is not a Republican or a Democrat," I'd often said in pulpits, challenging people to see through the either/or of a partisan imagination to a beloved community where God prepares a table before us, even in the presence of our political enemies. But María knew that political difference wasn't just a difference of opinion. She and her family couldn't sit down and enjoy God's heavenly banquet with enemies who think the same God wants a wall to permanently separate them. To worship God, María had to reject the false teaching of enemies who were using the Bible against her.

I remembered a letter I'd come across while researching slaveholder religion in which the Reverend Robert Dabney, a Presbyterian minister in mid-nineteenth-century Virginia, explained to one of his colleagues why using the Bible to defend slavery was so important. "Here is our policy then: to push the Bible argument continually, drive abolitionism to the wall, and compel it to assume an anti-Christian position. By doing so we compel the whole Christianity of the North to array itself to our side." I realized, whether they know it or not, this is what the court evangelicals are doing. Recognizing the moral force of the resistance to Trump, the court evangelicals were pushing the Bible argument continually. They

knew they would never change the minds of people in the streets who were protesting family separation and the subversion of democratic norms. But if they could frame that resistance as anti-Christian—if they could undermine the moral force of its argument—then they could, at the very least, persuade the hesitant and concerned Christians to stay out of their way. This was not new. It was the pattern of slaveholder religion playing out all over again.

THE DANGER OF FALSE TEACHING

The moral crisis of the Trump administration has revealed the danger of false teachers who misuse the Bible and twist its words to whitewash injustice. Since the mid-2000s, when George W. Bush was reelected by an overwhelming majority of white evangelicals, political strategists like Kevin Phillips have warned of an "American theocracy," and good journalists like Michelle Goldberg, Chris Hedges, and Sarah Posner have chronicled the networks of corporately funded religious right programs and media networks that have used the Bible to simultaneously promote a "Christian worldview" and pro-corporate ideologies. Many have endeavored to expose the false teachers of extremism, but most teachers in the church have ignored them.

At the same time, polling and reporting for at least a decade have suggested that millennial evangelicals reject many of the political assumptions of the religious right. While small government and family values were considered sacred by our parents' generation, many evangelicals under forty have experienced care for creation, justice for the poor, and radical

welcome of marginalized neighbors as central to their experience of Jesus. When I visited the studios of Trinity Broadcasting Network (TBN) outside of Nashville during the Obama years, it felt like a relic from the past. The gold spray paint was chipping off the angelic statues, exposing the cheap concrete underneath. I thought anyone could see that the emperor had no clothes.

But on the set of *The Apprentice*, Donald Trump had learned what the folks at TBN always knew—that people don't believe the emperor's lies because they are convincing or well-framed. We believe them—or go along with them, at least—because no one does what only the child in the fable was able to do: stand in the middle of the street and point out the obvious. Outside the mainstream in most of our faith traditions, religious nationalists seemed like fringe fanatics. To take them on, we reasoned, would only legitimize them. Meanwhile, powerful political and corporate interests were more than happy to take them seriously. They laid the foundation for the resurgence of Christian nationalism we all witnessed in the Trump administration.

For María, the lie of Christian nationalism is obvious. When I took her hand and followed her into the middle of the Rio Grande, I saw how America First and family values cannot coexist. But the experience was more than a political education. It was a challenge to reclaim the Bible from the religious right.

"Before the coming of this faith," Paul says, "we were held in custody under the law, locked up" (Galatians 3:23). That bondage was visceral as I stood in the middle of the river with

a family divided by my nation's laws. My country's broken history and immigration system had separated this family, and Robert Jeffress's claim that God blesses walls was keeping them apart. Yet here was a mother who had learned to put faith into action—to link up with others and build a temporary bridge of bodies, where no permits were available, by turning needs into rights. Here was an embodiment of another way of reading the Bible.

"For all of you who were baptized into Christ have clothed yourselves with Christ," Paul explained to the Galatians in his meditation on baptism, "for you are all one in Christ Jesus" (Galatians 3:27, 28). To go down into the waters with Christ is to die to our old ways of seeing the world. To come out of the waters of baptism is to see the whole world anew. "Therefore, if anyone is in Christ," Paul writes elsewhere, "the new creation has come: The old has gone, the new is here!" (2 Corinthians 5:17).

Paul, the religious terrorist turned apostle for Christ, knew better than most how Scripture can be used to prop up laws that condemn, separate people, and reinforce harmful ways of seeing the world. But after Jesus knocked him off his horse, stood in the middle of the road, and pointed out the obvious—"Why do you persecute me?"—Paul apprenticed himself to Ananias and the apostles and learned to read the Bible anew (Acts 9).

It's not enough to say that the court evangelicals and their religious media apparatus have hijacked the Bible. We must understand how these false teachers twist Scripture, what corporate interests have supported their work, and how

many in American public life have been willing to go along with their demonization of others as long as it didn't impact them. While this critical assessment of false teaching is part of the work a book aims to do, critical work alone is not enough. For anyone who wants to follow the way of Jesus, our essential task is to learn a better way of reading the Bible in public life. We who are uncomfortable with Christian nationalism cannot retreat to a private faith; if policy violence is being implemented in the name of Jesus, we have a particular obligation to show up, resist, and demonstrate a better way.

The good news is that people like María know how to read the Bible as a story of freedom for those who have been oppressed and as a vision for justice in public life. In the story of the God who raised Israel out of Egypt before raising Jesus from the dead, poor and marginalized people in America know the good news that both offers hope to people suffering injustice and equips us to stand up and fight in the power of the Spirit. It's not enough to read the scholars and journalists who can explain how the Bible was taken captive by corporate and political powers. We must also apprentice ourselves to sisters like María in order to learn how the Bible comes to life when we are baptized in the waters of resistance.

After María and I climbed out of the Rio Grande on that Sunday morning in the fall of 2017, I sat down on the concrete embankment, wiped the mud off my legs, and put the shoes back on that I'd removed before going down into the water. Then I climbed the embankment on the El Paso side, thinking about what it meant to carry María's story with me. I looked across the river to the Juárez side. There on the

mountain, in large white stones, someone had written, "La Biblia es la verdad. Léela." (The Bible is the truth. Read it.)

People of faith must take up the Bible and read it again if we are to name the forces that hold its message captive and discover its power to give hope and vision despite that manipulation. Most of Scripture was written by and about imprisoned, exiled, and occupied people who knew their God was powerful, even if evil forces controlled the seats of power. An incredible amount of money has been invested to tame that subversive message. Even still, it speaks to us, offering a way out of no way for those who will receive it.

Half a century ago, the Reverend Dr. Martin Luther King Jr. said we needed a "revolution of values" if we were to become the nation we have never yet been. King was able to name our moral crisis because he had learned the Bible's revolutionary vision of a whole new world among the poor and disposed. If we are willing, we can join him and María and millions with them in the freedom church of the poor. But first we must rediscover the revolutionary movement that has outlasted every worldly regime.

Dr. King believed that a revolution of values would necessarily be led by America's poor, coming together across dividing lines that have been used to pit us against one another. He based this belief on a reading of American history that understood how every stride toward a more perfect union in US history—from abolition to ending child labor to women's suffrage to civil rights—happened because people who were impacted by injustice came together to challenge those in power. But King, the preacher, also based this vision on a

reading of the Bible. "The stone the builders rejected has become the cornerstone" (Psalm 118:22). For anyone ready to hear its good news, King taught the Bible's vision of God working through the poor and rejected to introduce a whole new world. "God chose the lowly things of this world," Paul wrote, "and the despised things—and the things that are not—to nullify the things that are" (1 Corinthians 1:28). Like all the prophets before him, King knew that a Poor People's Campaign must not only tear down but also build up. Deconstruction is prelude to the work of reconstruction.

To mark the fiftieth anniversary of this prophetic vision in American public life, twenty-five thousand people gathered on the National Mall in June of 2018 to recommit themselves to the Poor People's Campaign: A National Call for Moral Revival. My family and I boarded a bus in Durham, North Carolina, at 3:00 a.m. that Saturday and arrived in Washington, DC, as the sun was rising, meeting dozens of other buses at a Metro station where black, white, and brown people were singing freedom songs on the platform, awaiting the next train. As we boarded the train, traveled to the Smithsonian station, and ascended the escalator to the National Mall, we joined a sea of people carrying signs that said, "Everybody Has a Right to Live" and "Healthcare Is a Moral Issue." One after another, women and men like María, who've experienced the violence of immoral policies, testified about why America needs a revolution of values. In response to these cries, the Poor People's Campaign was born again in the summer of 2018.

Co-led by the Reverend Dr. William J. Barber II and the Reverend Dr. Liz Theoharis, this Poor People's Campaign: A

National Call for Moral Revival is a network of state-based coalitions made up of thousands of member organizations, from the Border Network for Human Rights in Texas to labor unions, native tribal councils, environmental activists, civil rights organizations, service workers, healthcare advocates, formerly incarcerated activists, and homeless encampments in forty states. Rooted in local communities, we have pledged to build a movement that stands together for a moral economy in which everyone can thrive and a public life where our deepest moral and constitutional values guide policy decisions.

Standing among those thousands of founders of this new Poor People's Campaign on a hot summer day in DC, I thought about my second baptism in the Rio Grande. I knew there was room in this movement for everyone—even for me. But I also knew I had found my way into this movement for a revolution of values because people like María showed me the way. Whether black, white, or brown; documented or undocumented; Republican, Democrat, or unaffiliated, these too-often-neglected neighbors bear witness to why we need a revolution to save us from Christian nationalism's subversion of democracy. We have not simply failed to hear our neighbors' cry for justice. We have been taught to ignore them as a matter of religious duty.

Rather than argue against systemic justice issues, the religious right has driven the Bible argument continually to insist that the primary "moral" issues in America are abortion, gay marriage, and transgender rights. This is intentional. Just as racial identity was written into law during the birth of the plantation economy in order to prevent poor black and poor

white people from uniting in common cause against elite plantation owners, so also have political operatives used the pro-life/pro-choice debate and the politicization of sexuality to keep Americans from building broad coalitions that can challenge extreme inequality and injustice today. We need a revolution of values that makes clear how equal protection under the law and religious liberty are not incompatible but instead are essential to a shared common life where gay and straight, conservative and liberal neighbors can flourish.

Before we talk about "voting our values," we must let people who've been systemically devalued by faith communities help us read the Bible again. Only then can we understand what the Bible really values. Only then can we reclaim the distorted public moral narrative that has turned faith against itself in American public life.

THE WISDOM OF POOR WOMEN

The 1980s were a difficult time to be poor in America. The decade began with news stories about "the homeless," a rapidly growing class of citizens who were visibly present on America's streets due to a dramatic reduction in affordable housing after most single-room occupancy (SRO) high rises were shuttered in the nation's largest cities. Poor people hadn't been this visible in America's public life since the "hobos" of the Great Depression. But poverty hadn't gone away in the intervening half century.

Dr. Martin Luther King Jr., along with dozens of other poor people's organizations, had sought to unite impoverished people of every race during the late 1960s. The original Poor People's Campaign hoped to dramatize inequality through direct actions that would compel the federal government to address the fact that there were, as the Kerner Commission highlighted at the time, two Americas—one for the white suburban middle-class families people saw on TV sit-coms and another for the masses who did not have access to the basic necessities of life. The original Poor People's

Campaign did not win all of its demands, and King was assassinated in the midst of it. But it had served to increase and expand investment in anti-poverty programs during America's War on Poverty.

Riding a wave of conservative backlash against these programs, Ronald Reagan came to the White House in 1981 advocating trickle-down economics that optimistically promised to lift all boats by helping the richest Americans afford bigger yachts. The rhetoric of Reaganomics was always about prosperity for everyone, but the president blamed "welfare queens" for fleecing everyday Americans through their dependence on anti-poverty programs that had been fought for and won by, well, everyday Americans. Reagan certainly didn't spend much time with the "everyday people" Sly and the Family Stone sang about, but he had played them on the silver screen. A Hollywood actor who knew how to talk like the common man became the mouthpiece for corporate America's crusade against "Big Government."

Poverty is always hard, but it became especially difficult as religious leaders and conservative pundits throughout the 1980s blamed poor people for their poverty, even as the federal government worked to dismantle the programs that had demonstrated real progress toward greater equality over the previous decade. Hand in hand with the Moral Majority, Reagan-era conservatives made being poor a sin from which self-reliant individuals must save themselves. Televangelist Robert Tilton told viewers of his *Success-N-Life* program, which brought in $80 million a year in the early 1990s, that listening to President Reagan talk about prosperity in America had made him

want to be a prosperity preacher. As if it weren't enough that the yuppies ignored poor people on the streets, corporate elites poured money into "Christian ministries" like Tilton's that told Americans it would be ungodly to "enable" the moral failing of homeless neighbors by trying to help them.

Julia Dinsmore spent the 1980s raising kids and trying to hold a community together in the Twin Cities of Minnesota. Born into generational poverty, Dinsmore was never under the illusion that she had chosen the circumstances in which she lived—nor that she could simply choose to leave them. She knew she hadn't decided to be a single mother, but she could also see there weren't enough living-wage jobs for fathers to support a family in her community. Poverty wasn't a bad choice that millions of people made over and over again, Dinsmore observed. It was the cruel necessity of an economic systemic we all participate in.

Rather than accept Reagan's label as a welfare queen, Dinsmore became an organizer. She worked with other single parents in her community to form a Mother's Union and identified a shared priority: affordable housing. Over the course of eighteen months, she and the other mothers built principled partnerships with community institutions and raised $65,000 to start a cooperative housing project that would prioritize their children's need for stable housing. This wasn't charity work for others; it was the common work of poor women who wanted to interrupt the systems that were tearing their families apart.

To begin their building project, the Mother's Union needed a fiscal agent. They weren't asking anyone to bankroll them;

they just needed an organizational home to receive and distribute the funds they had already secured. They reached out to a congregation in town that had a reputation for being socially minded and had offered to help in any way they could. By this time, Reagan had spent eight years cutting anti-poverty programs, and his vice president, George H. W. Bush, was in the White House. Prospects were grim for poor folks, but the Mother's Union still hoped it could launch an affordable-housing project in liberal Minnesota.

Still, Dinsmore and her colleagues had learned the hard way that condescension toward poor people isn't partisan. Though they knew better than anyone what they needed, they also knew a well-to-do white church would want to hear from an expert. So they brought two when they went to meet with the church's finance committee about the fiscal partnership. Their resources were in place. Their plan was clear. Their housing experts were on hand and happy to take questions. But the chair of the committee couldn't imagine where they were coming from. "*Those people* don't need homes," Dinsmore remembers him saying. "We give them turkeys at Christmas and Thanksgiving."

Dinsmore knew she and her children could not live in a turkey. She also knew this church wasn't going to help them.

"Entitlement is a disease," Dinsmore told me twenty-five years later, reflecting on the experience that had revealed to her how captive so many Christians are to the dehumanizing assumptions of our society's broken economic systems. "Privilege has convinced people they already know everything and should therefore be imparting themselves on everyone else."

Dinsmore quoted Rigoberta Menchú, the Nobel Peace Prize laureate from Guatemala: "The world needs to start listening to poor women." Despite the fact that women like Dinsmore often speak out, loud and clear, a false moral narrative in our public life mutes their wisdom and redirects our attention to less challenging voices. To understand why the chair of the finance committee at a liberal church in the early 1990s couldn't even hear Julia, we need to go back fifty years in the story of faith in American public life.

A GOD TO REDEEM CAPITALISM

Just before Christmas, in December of 1940, the National Association of Manufacturers (NAM) held its annual meeting at the Waldorf Astoria Hotel in New York City. As business-men who had navigated America's Great Depression for the past decade, members of the NAM were eager to hear from the titans of industry who saw better days ahead. But each man in that room knew that business faced a public relations crisis in 1940: poor people had seen through the hubris of the Gilded Age. Poor people, and especially poor women, had borne the weight of the stock market's crash, sewing feed sacks into clothing for millions of children while learning to stretch every dollar they and their husbands could earn in an economy where jobs were scarce. Poor and working people did not trust corporations after the Great Depression. They had just rejected the NAM's man, Wendell Willkie, for president in that fall's election, opting instead to give Franklin Delano Roosevelt and his New Deal a third term in the White House.

Though it may be difficult to imagine today, FDR's New Deal, which sought to relieve poverty through government programs, was strongly supported by preachers in the 1930s. While fundamentalists largely stayed away from issues of public concern, many mainstream faith leaders in the 1930s embraced the Social Gospel, which argued that the government has a moral responsibility to pursue justice for the poor. Part of that responsibility, Social Gospel preachers insisted, was checking the inherent greed of those at the top of modern society by making sure corporations paid their fair share. For them, the New Deal was an attempt to put that conviction into practice.

The dilemma the NAM's five thousand members gathered to consider before returning home to celebrate the birth of Jesus was, in a nutshell, that most people in America trusted Social Gospel preachers more than they trusted businessmen. And yet, many of these businessmen remembered the thrill of seemingly limitless profit margins and winters in Saint Augustine, Florida, in the Roaring Twenties. They still believed in the promise of a free market. They just needed to find a way to make America trust the invisible hand of capitalism over the hard-earned wisdom of poor women.

Their answer that December at the Waldorf Astoria was delivered by a preacher, the Reverend Dr. James W. Fifield Jr., who bore some resemblance to the movie stars he pastored in Southern California. Though he was no fundamentalist, Fifield had rejected the Social Gospel to preach a broad-minded, pro-corporate message to his well-heeled congregants at First Congregational Church in Los Angeles. Among his most ardent

supporters was D. W. Griffith, the filmmaker who had turned Southern Baptist preacher Thomas Dixon Jr.'s novel *The Clansman* into *The Birth of a Nation*, a film that romanticized the Ku Klux Klan and became its chief recruiting tool in the Jim Crow era. Just as Griffith had redeemed the Lost Cause on the big screen, Fifield believed clergymen could redeem capitalism in American public life. After he laid out his vision to the NAM, a reporter wrote that the applause was so loud it could be heard across the river in Hoboken, New Jersey.

In his book *One Nation Under God: How Corporate America Invented Christian America*, Princeton University professor Kevin Kruse chronicles how Fifield's speech to the NAM launched a movement that wove Christianity and capitalism together in the public imagination of twentieth-century America. Fifield served as a charismatic leader of this movement, inviting thousands of clergy from every major denomination in America to join him through his organization, Spiritual Mobilization. But he wasn't alone.

Before members of the NAM had even had the chance to cheer Fifield's vision in the banquet hall of the Waldorf Astoria, a Norwegian immigrant named Abraham Vereide had already invited some of them to join his Bible studies for the "up and out," as he called them. Troubled by the disruption of massive labor strikes on the West Coast in 1934, Vereide had reached out to powerful businessmen in Seattle and had begun gathering them to talk about how God had chosen them to restore America to a righteous path. In his book *The Family*, journalist Jeff Sharlet tells the story of the secretive network of elites that grew from Vereide's small Seattle circle

into a worldwide network of faith-based power brokers. "Power," Sharlet says Vereide learned as he became simply "Abram" to wealthy elites, "has nothing to do with forcing the devil behind you or making the company increase your wages. Power lies in things as they are. God had already chosen the powerful, his key men. *There they are*, Jesus whispered in Abram's ear; *go and serve them.*"

Serve them Vereide did, joining forces with Fifield and many others who were happy to take corporate donations to build ministries that told corporate leaders—and anyone else who would listen—how God was at work in the world through them. They wrote Bible studies and devotions, launched think tanks, and established fellowships for young Christians to integrate faith and business. Fifield's Spiritual Mobilization even sponsored national preaching contests, offering a financial prize for the most pro-capitalist sermons. By the 1980s, when Ronald Reagan joined hands with the Moral Majority to lift up America as a "city on a hill," a moral narrative united millions of American Christians around the conviction that God works through the good of capitalism. The idea that God has blessed the rich and will do the same for the poor if and when they take responsibility for themselves didn't fall down from heaven or spring spontaneously into the minds of American Christians. It was the result of a well-funded campaign, which reached from corporate board-rooms to secretive Bible studies in the halls of Congress to the finance committee of a socially active church in Minne-apolis, Minnesota. It was an idea sown in the public imagi-nation over decades, producing a culture in which ignoring

Julia Dinsmore and the Mother's Union was not only possible but expected. The chair of the church finance committee did not think he was falling short of Christ's compassion when he insisted his church had already done enough for "those people." He was, instead, steeped in an imagination that allowed him to think he was affirming Dinsmore's freedom and dignity by refusing to help her.

THE BIBLE IN THE HANDS OF RICH MEN

While Dinsmore and the Mother's Union were struggling to find a fiscal sponsor for their affordable-housing project in liberal Minnesota, wealthy Christian businessmen who felt the Reagan years had not done enough to free Americans from the regulatory state paid a Texan named Marvin Olasky to write a revisionist history of American social policy that he called *The Tragedy of American Compassion.* "Throughout the nineteenth century," Olasky imagined, "the rock on which compassion stood was undergoing erosion." In this narrative of America's moral decline, the benevolence of faith communities that cared for poor people in local communities during the nineteenth century had been supplanted by religious liberalism and political socialism in the twentieth century. Like Fifield and Vereide before him, Olasky despised the New Deal because, as he imagined, it taught people to trust government rather than God. In his mythology, dependence on human systems diminished an individual's freedom, making citizens reliant on a nanny state that could in turn manipulate and control them. The compassionate—in fact, the righteous— thing to do, Olasky insisted, is to hold individuals responsible

for their personal choices in a free market. "An emphasis on
freedom also should include a willingness to step away for a
time and let those who have dug their own hole 'suffer the
consequences of their misconduct,'" Olasky asserted, applying his mythology as a critique of government-run anti-
poverty programs.

Olasky in the early 1990s sounded a lot like Russell
Conwell, the American Baptist Civil War veteran who had
preached the good of capitalism during America's Gilded Age.
"The men who get rich may be the most honest men you find
in the community," Conwell wrote in his famous "Acres of
Diamonds" sermon, which he delivered over six thousand
times on the same Chautauqua circuit that made famous his
fellow preacher, Thomas Dixon, the defender of Lost Cause
religion and white supremacy. Throughout the twentieth
century, Christian businessmen shared printed copies of
Conwell's message with their associates and mentees in
spaces dominated by white men. "Ninety-eight out of one
hundred of the rich men of America are honest. That is why
they are rich. That is why they are trusted with money. That
is why they carry on great enterprises and find plenty of
people to work with them," Conwell explained. "I sympathize
with the poor, but the number of poor who are to be sympa-
thized with is very small." When a retired businessman asked
to have lunch and learn more about my ministry after hearing
a sermon I preached in 2010, he handed me a pocket-sized
edition of *Acres of Diamonds*. Nearly a century after the sermon's publication, this man told me it was the most important book he'd ever read.

If you already know that rich people are godly and poor people are morally suspect, then the Bible's complex collection of multiple genres of literature can be distilled into basic instructions for climbing the ladder of success in a capitalist society—as long as you don't pay too close attention to the details. The Bible's wisdom literature is often the most quotable: "Lazy hands make for poverty, but diligent hands bring wealth," Proverbs 10:4 says. For the businessman who's driven by a desire to create wealth, it can seem as if passages of Scripture are written specifically for him: "Whatever you do, work at it with all your heart, as working for the Lord, not for human masters, since you know that you will receive an inheritance from the Lord as a reward" (Colossians 3:23-24). The psalms also have lines that seem to reflect a simple connection between upright living and material blessings. "I was young and now I am old," Psalm 37:25 says, "yet I have never seen the righteous forsaken or their children begging bread."

Read in context, none of these verses explicitly affirms the rich and powerful of the world. King David, the identified author of Psalm 37, was a poor shepherd and a guerrilla fighter when he was young. Looking back in his elder years, he celebrates the miraculous provision of God's abundance in times of scarcity as a way of encouraging all people to trust God. Paul in Colossians is exhorting service workers to see their despised labor as something more significant—an opportunity to bear witness to the transformative love of Christ. And the Proverbs are folk wisdom to teach children basic lessons for personal growth, not justification for any particular public policy.

None of these passages is an explicit endorsement of the Protestant work ethic because there simply wasn't a Protestant work ethic in the ancient Near East. But the Bible in the hands of rich men became divorced from its social and political context. Key to avoiding its prophetic challenge of economic inequality and the exploitation of poor people in ancient economies was a focus on the Bible's "spiritual" message. On this spiritual reading, all of Hebrew Scripture, with its prophets in long beards and hair shirts confronting greedy kings, becomes little more than a morality play meant to demonstrate each individual's need for redemption from sin. If wealth is the visible sign that you are blessed, then poor people are the spiritually needy. When rich men gather to read a spiritualized Bible, their thoughts turn not to repentance but to charity.

Thus the Bible's concern for justice toward all people and mercy for the poor became a reminder to rich men that it was important to sit on nonprofit and foundation boards. Helping poor souls wasn't only about making sure they had food to eat or a place to sleep; it was ultimately about imparting spiritual blessing on them, holding out the hope that they too might pull themselves up by their bootstraps and be saved. "When you did it to the least of these you did it unto me," wasn't Jesus' summary statement about how the nations of the earth will be judged at the last day (a straightforward reading of what Matthew 25 actually says). It was, instead, a reminder that industrialists must also be philanthropists— great men who prove their spiritual greatness by publicly offering to bestow it on anyone who aspires to be like them.

The Bible in the hands of rich white men became spiritual wrapping paper to make whatever was good for business look like a gift from heaven above. Unfortunately, this is the only Bible many middle-class Christians have heard about for generations in America.

READING AMERICA BIBLICALLY

Meanwhile, poor women have always read the Bible for themselves—or, to be more precise, poor people who heard hope in the story the Bible tells have always read America biblically. "People from generational poverty come from an oral culture," Julia Dinsmore told me. "We gravitate to the Bible's stories and to the people who live them out because that's how we understand the world." It is, in fact, how almost everyone in the Bible understood the world as well. Contemporary biblical scholars tell us that most of the Hebrew Bible wasn't written down until the Babylonian exile, when people who had been ripped from their homeland by an imperial power decided to write down the sacred stories that had been passed down to them in hope that their truth might outlast the present regime.

For poor folks who are used to telling stories and singing songs that question the rich and powerful, there has always been power in the tales of David bringing down Goliath and Israel coming out of Egypt, defeating Pharaoh's army, and bringing down the walls of Jericho without a weapon in their hands. "Didn't my Lord deliver Daniel, then why not every man?" enslaved people sang in brush arbors on the edges of the plantations that built the economic power of America in

the nineteenth century. Long after King Cotton's heyday, those songs were passed down to sharecroppers and mill workers, resonating across racial lines because they echoed biblical stories that rang true. Even when the Social Gospel was squeezed out of America's seminaries and pulpits, it was sung by millions of mothers to their children as they struggled to keep hope alive: "This little light of mine, I'm gonna let it shine."

On any honest reading, the Bible cannot be a straight-forward endorsement of capitalism. Its stories, songs, proverbs, and doctrine were written down and canonized as holy writ centuries before any current economic system or policy proposal had been developed. But from the perspective of poor people who saw themselves in the Bible's stories, Scripture was always a testimony to the otherwise—a bold declaration that the way things are is not the way things have to be and that, in a world scarred by gross inequality, God is decidedly on the side of the poor.

Whatever well-paid ministers and Christian businessmen said about the uprightness of the rich, the prophet Amos still declared,

> You levy a straw tax on the poor
>   and impose a tax on their grain.
> Therefore, though you have built stone mansions,
>   you will not live in them. (Amos 5:11)

Scholars and popular writers did intellectual gymnastics to explain to themselves and their funders why economic in-justice, which was an inevitable feature of ancient economies,

had been addressed by the miracle of capitalism. But their self-congratulatory justifications mattered little to members of Dinsmore's Mother's Union, and millions like them, who knew from experience that capitalism had little good news for them.

Still, the Bible itself warns about religious leaders who use faith to prop up unjust authorities. After comparing the political leadership of his day to "wolves tearing their prey," who "shed blood and kill people to make unjust gain," the prophet Ezekiel points out that false prophets "whitewash these deeds for them by false visions and lying divinations" (Ezekiel 22:27-28). Jesus' harshest words are reserved for religious leaders who used their spiritual authority to cover for political leaders and business elites. "Hypocrites," he calls them—people who wear the mask of religion but underneath are serving their own interests. Jesus' most direct action of disruption was to destroy the booths of moneychangers who exploited poor people at the temple in Jerusalem, where Roman currency wasn't accepted.

While much of the New Testament is in the form of letters written to the early church about religious controversies, it is important to remember that those in the early Christian movement practiced a radical economics that challenged the status quo of their communities. "All the believers were together and had everything in common," the Acts of the Apostles attests. "They sold property and possessions to give to anyone who had need" (Acts 2:44-45).

Writing to a young Christian community at Corinth, the apostle Paul makes this economic practice a matter of

doctrine: "At the present time your plenty will supply what they need, so that in turn their plenty will supply what you need. The goal is equality" (2 Corinthians 8:14). Over the centuries, Christians have worked in different ways, depending upon their social location and role, to achieve this goal of economic equality. But to read America biblically is to know that the extreme inequality of America's economy, where an elite fraction of 1 percent owns half of America's wealth while nearly half of Americans don't earn a living wage, isn't a manifestation of God's will but an affront to the Bible's concern for the poor.

To read America biblically with Julia Dinsmore and the Mother's Union—with poor women, whose wisdom is too often ignored—is to see that Paul's language about salvation and reconciliation in Christ rings hollow if it doesn't hit the ground today in stories like the one we read in Acts 19. When Paul was visiting the early Christian community in Ephesus, Acts 19:23 says that "there arose a great disturbance" when a local business leader named Demetrius rallied a mob to protest Paul's preaching. His concern: "You know, my friends, that we receive a good income from this business," Demetrius declared (Acts 19:25), observing that the Christian movement's faith in a crucified Messiah was cutting into his profit. Christianity, Demetrius could see, was bad for business as usual.

When the Bible's message is preached as the good news to the poor that both Jesus and the prophets proclaimed, it disrupts the unjust economic relationships of our broken world and challenges us to embrace both personal choices and public

policies that pursue the goal of equality. Any effort to domesticate this disruption and make the Scriptures into spiritual wrapping for the status quo is not only an affront to poor people—it's a rejection of the God who has been working through the ages to love us into a community that provides enough for everyone's need. To learn the history of how the Bible has been read in America is to know that each of us must choose which Good Book we're going to trust as we work out our faith in the world today: the rich man's Bible or the wisdom of poor women who call us to read America biblically.

LIVING TOWARD A MORAL ECONOMY

No one would have ever heard the story of Jesus' resurrection were it not for the women who went to his tomb early on Easter morning and carried the good news to all the rest of us. Now, as then, the good news we all need is being carried by women like Dinsmore, who may not be commissioned by a missionary organization but are nevertheless linking up with others to build homes for people experiencing homelessness and coalitions that work together for a society in which everyone is housed. These are the leaders we've been waiting for. Their Mother's Unions and similar self-help collectives offer models for what the church might become as we follow Jesus together toward freedom. When we follow their lead, we have the chance to rediscover the church as a space for moral formation in the world.

When Muslim workers at the Hertz rental car company in SeaTac, Washington, were denied time off to pray, they reached out to the local Service Employees International

Union (SEIU). Rather than simply argue their case as a basic workers' rights issue, organizers from the union reached out to local clergy—both Muslim and Christian—and invited them to stand with the workers in their struggle for religious freedom in the work place. A workers' struggle became a moral movement. And when they were successful in winning break time for prayers, they continued to work together and built a coalition that included both faith communities and service workers to demand a living wage of $15 an hour. The Fight for $15 was born as a national movement for living wages and union representation when this local coalition won a $15 per hour minimum wage at the SeaTac airport in 2013.

In cities across America, Fight for $15 activists have engaged in walk-outs from fast-food restaurants and other service industries, insisting at every action that they "cannot survive on $7.25." Standing alongside workers, faith leaders have borne witness to Scripture's economic vision even as we learn from those most directly impacted how far we are from a moral economy. At 6:00 a.m. rallies in the winter cold, I've run into neighbors I didn't even know had joined the Fight for $15. They have taught me how hard we must fight for a country where everyone has as a right to live.

When the Poor People's Campaign conducted an audit of economic conditions in America in 2018, we learned that there is not a city in the country where someone working full time at minimum wage can afford to rent a two-bedroom apartment. Dinsmore is right: charity in the face of this reality is a slap in the face. People cannot live in a turkey, but we can work together to create options for affordable housing, ensure

a living wage for our neighbors, and support unions that will continue to advocate for the rights of workers in a political system dominated by corporate interests. We can do this by following the leadership of women like Dinsmore in our communities, by supporting local service workers when they strike for a living wage, and by demanding that our political representatives recognize the voices of poor people in our common life. If such work feels disruptive to people of faith, we need only look again to the Bible for guidance. We are the heirs of those who disrupted systems that make people poor to insist that God made enough for all our needs.

GIVE US THE BALLOT

Rosanell Eaton was twenty-one years old in 1942 when she hitched her mule to the family wagon in rural North Carolina and rode to the Franklin County courthouse. All along the two-hour journey, she repeated to herself the Preamble to the United States Constitution—lines she had been memorizing for weeks. A young black woman in the Jim Crow South, Eaton knew the literacy test that three white men would administer to her was designed to prevent her from voting. With only 3 percent of black citizens registered to vote in North Carolina in 1942, she understood that her chances of gaining access to the ballot were slim. But Eaton also knew that the Fifteenth Amendment to the US Constitution guaranteed that she, as a citizen of the United States, could not be denied the right to participate in the democratic process simply because she had been born black. Between the promise of America's Constitution and the reality of its persistent inequality, Eaton's faith gave her courage to stand flat-footed, stare straight ahead, and recite the Preamble's hope that America might become a "more perfect Union," guaranteeing the "Blessings of Liberty" to all.

An embodiment of that hope, Eaton became a registered voter in North Carolina in 1942. She went on to become a voting-rights advocate and community organizer in the unsung generation of Southern black women who built organizations and strategies that made the civil rights movement possible a quarter century later. Working at times with Ella Baker, a fellow eastern North Carolina native who would go on to serve as both the first executive director of Martin Luther King Jr.'s Southern Christian Leadership Conference (SCLC) and a key adviser to the Student Nonviolent Coordinating Committee (SNCC), Eaton personally registered over four thousand people to vote in North Carolina. For her, the Voting Rights Act of 1965, which established federal oversight to guarantee African Americans access to the ballot box, was a vindication of the struggle for which she and so many like her had shed blood, sweat, and tears.

But in the summer of 2013, when Ms. Eaton was ninety-two years old, the Supreme Court ruled in Shelby County v. Holder that the Voting Rights Act's formula for determining which counties need federal supervision was outdated (never mind that the law allowed for any county that could demonstrate a decade without any evidence of voter suppression to be removed from federal oversight). If Congress wanted the Justice Department to continue to review voting rules in counties with a history of discrimination, Chief Justice John Roberts said they would have to pass new legislation to determine which counties require preclearance. In her dissenting opinion, Justice Ruth Bader Ginsberg likened the 5-4 decision to "throwing away your umbrella in a rainstorm because you are not getting wet."

The Republican supermajorities that controlled the legislature in Eaton's home state of North Carolina had followed the Shelby case closely. Before the umbrella of voting-rights protections had made it to the metaphorical landfill of history, they passed a downpour of legislation to wash away every measure that had expanded the electorate in North Carolina over the previous decade. Among the dozens of changes was a harsh voter identification requirement insisting that the name on each voter's registration card precisely match the name on their state-issued ID. Seven decades after she'd defied Jim Crow to become a registered voter, Eaton, who was registered as everyone in Franklin County knew her (Rosanell Eaton), was disenfranchised because her driver's license gave her name as Rosa Johnson Eaton.

When I met Eaton in the spring of 2013, she was indignant about the lack of public attention to a fundamental attack on democracy by people who had sworn to uphold the constitution. "I raised my family and have lived on the same piece of land for the past seventy-two years," Eaton told me. "You know who Dr. King was, don't you? Well, I marched with him. We had to work real hard for integration. But we won back then." She knew she could win again. Together with the North Carolina NAACP, Eaton sued her state's governor after he signed the legislature's omnibus voter-suppression law in 2013, launching a legal battle that would last until the summer of 2017, when the US Supreme Court upheld a lower court's ruling that said lawmakers had targeted African American voters like Eaton with "almost surgical precision."

When I read the news story, I remembered my conversation with Eaton five years earlier. She had been frustrated that she and her daughter were the only people from Franklin County who had driven to Raleigh to protest the legislature's action. I recalled Eaton staring off in the distance with a clenched jaw that day, listening to speakers who tried to raise the alarm about what was really going on with the hastily passed omnibus bill. Her presence bore witness to the gravity of what was happening, outlasting any of the arguments I heard against twenty-first-century forms of voter suppression. One line I underlined in my notebook summed up the wisdom of this nonagenarian black woman who knew what it meant to fight for freedom. Taking it upon herself to make sure I understood the history she had lived, Eaton looked at me and said, "This is my second time around, you know."

THE SECOND CAREER OF JAMES CROW, ESQUIRE

In a 1955 book that Dr. King celebrated as the "historical Bible of the Civil Rights movement," *The Strange Career of Jim Crow* by Dr. C. Vann Woodward chronicled the history of the anti-democratic Southern politics that Rosanell Eaton faced her first time around. Woodward published his history just after the Supreme Court's unanimous opinion in *Brown v. Board of Education of Topeka*, a monumental decision that overturned the court's "separate but equal" doctrine from its 1896 decision in the case of *Plessy v. Ferguson*. As a historian, Woodward knew *Brown* was about much more than the desegregation of public schools in the South. To explain the

significance of the court's ruling for American life, he had to go back to the era of Reconstruction.

Following the end of the Civil War in 1865, a political battle ensued to determine how states that had been divided by the Confederacy might become united once again. This was the first political struggle in US history to seriously include the voices of black people. Many of those voices were black preachers who had become leaders in their communities through the church. In North Carolina, the first public gathering of free black people elected the Reverend J. W. Hood as its president in 1865. In his inaugural address at the "Lincoln Church" in Raleigh, North Carolina, he summed up the political aspirations of those gathered: First and foremost, "Equal Rights under Law." Then, as assurance that equality would be preserved through real political power, Hood insisted that formerly enslaved people be allowed to serve on juries, testify in court, and vote. "These are the rights we will contend for," Hood concluded, "and these rights will we have, God being our helper."

To recall Rev. Hood's demands is to recognize how important the Fifteenth Amendment was to the experiment in democracy that had begun with both an expressed desire for the "Blessings of Liberty" and the assignment of enslaved black people to the status of property. By 1869—just four years after Hood's address to the North Carolina freedmen's gathering—the US Congress had passed the Thirteenth and Fourteenth Amendments, abolishing slavery (except for the incarcerated), granting citizenship to the formerly enslaved, and guaranteeing "equal protection under the law" to all people. But what

would protect these new and fragile promises in the South, where federal troops were still stationed to ensure the promises of Reconstruction?

Nothing was more important than the ballot. Long before the Black Power movement of the late 1960s, black people in the South understood that America could never become a multiethnic democracy without the guarantee of real political power to nonwhite people. Of course, the rich white men who controlled both the plantations of the South and corporations in the North understood this also. A simple guarantee of voting rights for all people wasn't politically achievable in 1870, so the Fifteenth Amendment, which was ratified that year, was a compromise. It ensured that "the right of citizens of the United States to vote shall not be denied or abridged . . . on account of race, color or previous condition of servitude," but left the door open for white men to maintain political control through the continued disenfranchisement of women, the poor, and even the formerly enslaved—so long as access to the ballot box wasn't denied based on race.

Thus began the strange career of Jim Crow, a system of state-based segregation laws and two-tiered public accommodations that allowed white men who had fought as Confederate soldiers to strip the influence of black political power from public life. When necessary, those men used the violence and intimidation of the Ku Klux Klan and other terrorist organizations. But following the Republican Party's compromise with Southern Democrats in 1876, Jim Crow was increasingly able to write white supremacy into election law through an array of poll taxes, literacy tests,

and grandfather clauses, all carefully designed to suppress the votes of African Americans. Jim Crow was genteel, civil, and always careful to say that it had the best interests of its black neighbors in mind. After 1896, *Plessy*'s "separate but equal" provided the legal cover needed for Jim Crow to maintain control of a nation that now counted black people as citizens.

For a black woman like Rosanell Eaton, who had been a voting-rights advocate in the rural South for over a decade when the Supreme Court unanimously rejected the ruse of "separate but equal," the *Brown* decision offered a second chance at Reconstruction. If schools could be desegregated, then it was possible to again imagine an integrated society in which the rights of all citizens would be protected under the law. With a preacher, in the person of Dr. Martin Luther King Jr., again serving as spokesperson, the civil rights movement insisted on the same basic demands Rev. Hood had listed a hundred years before: equal protection under the law and real political power through equal access to the ballot. The Civil Rights Act of 1964 addressed Jim Crow's subversion of the Fifteenth Amendment. For the first time in American history, the Voting Rights Act of 1965 promised federal protection of the franchise for all citizens.

But just as former Confederates had prayed for God to "redeem" them from black political power after the Civil War, white men gathered in board rooms after the *Brown* decision to plot how they might subvert this Second Reconstruction's expansion of democracy. The John Birch Society (JBS), which pitched itself as an anticommunist organization, counted

Fred C. Koch among its founding board members in 1958. A conservative oil man who was enraged by the *Brown* decision, Koch and his colleagues sponsored an essay contest for college students to develop legal arguments for why Chief Justice Earl Warren should be impeached. Though they were out of the mainstream in the 1960s and 1970s, JBS and other organizations like it built a national network of wealthy white men who reimagined the "Blessings of Liberty" not as freedom and justice for all citizens but rather as freedom *from* a federal government that would impose the demands of equality on states and corporations.

In her book *Democracy in Chains*, which was a finalist for the National Book Award in 2017, Nancy MacLean traces today's complex efforts to subvert democracy through voter-suppression bills like the one passed in North Carolina to the network of organizations currently sponsored by Fred Koch's sons, Charles and David Koch. On this, Eaton recognizes the repetition of family names. James Crow, Esq., has extended the family business into the twenty-first century. By manipulating voter data about race and party affiliation, legislators now gerrymander voting districts to choose their voters rather than waiting for the voters to choose them (or not) at the next election. Gerrymandering in Eaton's North Carolina is so extreme that in the 2014 midterms, when just over half of North Carolinians cast ballots for Democrats in Congressional races, ten of thirteen House seats still went to Republicans.

But gerrymandering is only one instrument in the high-tech tool set of James Crow, Esq. In the 2016 election, voter

suppression measures in twenty-three states led to at least 868 fewer polling places in poor and African American communities. Combined with targeted voter-roll purges in key precincts, these tactics have suppressed hundreds of thousands of votes in swing states across the South and Midwest. In the 2016 election, Donald Trump lost the popular vote by nearly three million votes and won the Electoral College by only tens of thousands of votes in Michigan, Wisconsin, and Pennsylvania—all states where James Crow, Esq., had been busily at work.

Though Eaton won her case against North Carolina's voter-suppression law, she died in 2018 knowing that the multiethnic democracy she had spent her life working toward was under assault. Eaton understood from hard-won experience that protecting access to the ballot isn't only a fight for democracy; it's also a struggle for the political power that is necessary to ensure equal treatment for the people she loved. For Eaton, access to the ballot was sacred. It was about faith and family and everything that matters most.

THE WORK OF THE CULTURE WARS

Republican lawmakers who spent five years and millions of tax dollars fighting Eaton in court also talk about faith, family, and moral values. But after a federal court found in *North Carolina NAACP v. McCrory* that the all-white and avowedly Christian leadership of the North Carolina General Assembly had engaged in intentional racism, neither their faith nor their expressed respect for the rule of law compelled lawmakers to repent. During the same 2018 session in which they

mandated that public schools post signs saying "In God We Trust," North Carolina's Republican legislative supermajority overturned the Democratic governor's veto to put a voter-identification requirement on the ballot as a referendum. If Eaton's faith sustained her struggle over seven decades, it's also true that a very different kind of Christian faith fueled the fight against her.

During the early voting period of the 2016 election in North Carolina, I volunteered with the North Carolina NAACP to help inform clergy and faith communities about their rights amid ongoing voter-suppression efforts. Our mission was to make sure people knew how to access the ballot that Ms. Eaton and many others had fought to protect. Four days before the election, CNN invited me to share about our work opposite Alice Stewart, a Christian conservative who had served as deputy secretary of state in Arkansas before working on the Mike Huckabee and Ted Cruz campaigns. Though Stewart was no longer working for Arkansas Secretary of State Mark Martin, his office had defended a voter-ID requirement like the one Eaton and the North Carolina NAACP had challenged. In their case, the attempt to suppress votes by imposing a voter-ID requirement had been found unconstitutional by the Arkansas Supreme Court.

When I explained on-air why I didn't believe it should be a partisan issue to say that voter suppression is wrong, Stewart assured viewers that she cared about "free and fair elections." But she denied that there was anything wrong with voting-law changes that both state and federal courts had ruled against. The important thing, she insisted, was for viewers to

understand that this election was possibly the most conse-
quential of their lifetime.

Her pivot was to the rallying cry of conservative Christian
voices in the 2016 election. Just a few weeks earlier, Michele
Bachmann had given an interview on the Christian Broadcasting Network that offered some transparency about the
urgency that Stewart and many others imagined. "It's a math
problem," Bachmann told CBN's David Brody. "If you look at
the numbers of people who vote and who lives [sic] in the
country and who Barack Obama and Hillary Clinton want to
bring in to the country, this is the last election when we even
have a chance to vote for somebody who will stand up for
godly moral principles." Appealing to the faith of fellow white
conservatives, Bachmann wanted to lift up issues that have
fueled the culture wars since the emergence of a religious right
in the late 1970s. But the math she was talking about was
racial demographics. When more black and brown people have
access to the ballot, then "vote your values" doesn't necessarily keep conservatives in power. Black and brown Christians often have different values when it comes to public policy.

To say that religious values challenge the assumptions of
modern secular society is not necessarily a conservative political position. Yes, the belief that people who make
promises in marriage are not only accountable to their
partners and communities but also to God fosters family
values that resist the market's incessant appeal to sexual
desire and individual gratification. But a conviction that all
people are created in the image of God can also inspire com-
munal values that lead people of faith to challenge systemic

injustice, the disposability of poor people, and any nation's claim on our ultimate allegiance. Religious values aren't only conservative values; they also lead people of faith to liberal and progressive political positions. From abolition to women's suffrage to labor and civil rights, faith has fueled social change in American history just as much as it has backed conservative values.

Why, then, do white conservatives like Bachmann imagine "godly moral principles" under threat in a multiethnic democracy? The short answer is fear. It's no secret that the mass movement Eaton was part of in the 1960s challenged established systems of power in America, just as federally imposed Reconstruction shook the South after the Civil War. To read the history of white Southerners' desire to "redeem" the South and overcome the "immorality" imposed upon them by federal Reconstruction in the 1870s is to watch the prequel to the culture wars that emerged in the 1970s. In both stories, fear of change rooted in nonwhite political power fueled reactionary movements that imagined themselves as moral crusades. Looking back, historians dubbed the former the Redemption movement; the latter called itself the religious right.

Both movements read the Bible in strikingly similar ways. Identifying with God's people in the Old Testament, Christian nationalists imagine themselves as an embattled minority, up against the Goliaths of a society dominated by "secular humanism." Biblical narratives of redemption—from the Exodus out of Egypt to Nehemiah's return from exile—are framed as spiritual justification for the crusade to "take back"

America. The myth of America as a chosen nation, founded on Christian principles from which we've strayed, is propagated to support this reading by "teaching ministries" like David Barton's Wallbuilders. If Nehemiah rebuilt the walls of Jerusalem to restore Israel after exile, then Christian nationalists hope a wall at America's Southern border can redeem America from the imagined immorality of liberals who want to let all of "the illegals" in to vote against "godly moral principles." People like Michele Bachmann learned to imagine racist voter suppression as necessary in Bible study, not at Klan rallies.

Because the "Christ" of Christian nationalism often contradicts the teachings of Jesus, who blessed the meek and exhorted his followers to put down their swords, the message of the New Testament is spiritualized in this reading to be primarily about the eternal destiny of individuals. A movement that is obviously invested in political control is thus ironically able to pretend it is apolitical much of the time, focusing the faithful on church planting, evangelism, and other "spiritual" work while teaching that a narrow set of "moral principles" should compel us to vote for conservative politicians.

Over the past four decades of American public life, this way of reading the Bible has done real work for people invested in maintaining a balance of power that was established when the American electorate was overwhelmingly white. By playing to white conservatives' racial fears on cultural issues, the strategy has energized a diminishing electoral base for reactionary political action, delivering the majority of state governments to the Republican Party long before it opened a pathway to the

White House for Donald Trump. But by framing their crusade as a matter of faith, Christian nationalists have also allowed white conservatives to imagine they left racism behind. As they see it, they weren't suppressing Rosanell Eaton's vote because she was black but because every election could be their last chance to stand against the imagined immorality that nonwhite voters would bring upon America.

THE VOICES GOD HEARS

If you read the Bible from Genesis to Revelation, you won't find a single reference to voting rights. But the modern Hebrew word for "vote"—*qol*—is the same as the word for "voice" in the Hebrew Bible. So a kind of voting happens whenever someone speaks in Scripture. In the long struggle for voting rights that Rosanell Eaton embodies, God's attention to the voices of marginalized and oppressed people make a striking biblical case for the expansion of democracy in modern society.

When God speaks to Moses from the burning bush, saying "I have indeed seen the misery of my people. . . . I have heard them crying" (Exodus 3:7), we are reminded of the voices of women in the Exodus story: Shiphrah and Puah, the midwives who engaged in civil disobedience to save Moses and other children when Pharaoh ordered genocide (Exodus 1:15-21); Moses' mother, who hid him in a basket and floated it down the Nile, praying God would make a way out of no way (Exodus 2:1-3); and Miriam, his older sister, who chased the basket down the river and, when Pharaoh's daughter pulled it out of the water, asked, "Shall I go and get one of the

Hebrew women to nurse the baby for you?" (Exodus 2:4-7). These are the voices God hears crying in the Exodus story. They are not the votes of the established authorities but votes that have been suppressed and ignored for generations.

In the New Testament, Jesus tells a parable about a persistent widow—a woman who pled her case to an unjust judge. Even though the judge didn't care about God or people, Jesus said, he eventually gave the woman what she asked to get her to stop bothering him. Luke says Jesus told this story to teach his disciples about the importance of prayer—that is, using your voice to petition God. If even an unjust judge hears the voice of a persistent widow, Jesus asks, "will not God bring about justice for his chosen ones, who cry out to him day and night?" (Luke 18:7). Long before women like Eaton had the opportunity to cast a vote in modern democracies, the Bible makes clear that she had a vote with God, where ultimate power in heaven and earth resides.

God's attention to the voices of women, children, and those who suffer injustice shape an imagination for a new kind of society, which the apostle Paul calls *ekklēsia*—the ones who have been called out. With an imagination soaked in the story of Israel, Paul saw the death and resurrection of Jesus as the creation of a new political reality by which people learn to listen to the voices God hears, even when they are ignored by powerful people in society. Four centuries later, Saint Benedict translated this vision of a community in which people listened to God through one another's voices into a rule for monastic life, which offered a concrete example of radical democracy that ultimately shaped modern political

thought. "Christianity succeeded where the Hellenistic and late classical philosophies had failed," the twentieth-century political philosopher Sheldon Wolin wrote, "because it put forward a new and powerful ideal of community which recalled men to a life of meaningful participation."

If a Christian imagination shaped the ideals of modern democracy, it's equally true that a biblical anthropology compels us to resist the specific action of voter suppression in democratic society. While Christians have and do imagine faithful public witness within other political philosophies, the reality of our current political system is that we equate personhood with citizenship. When politicians who want to hold onto power use tax dollars and legislative power to suppress votes, they aren't just engaging in the messy business of politics. They are implicitly denying the humanity of millions of people. If you are a person born or naturalized in the United States, eighteen or older, you have a right to vote. No one can deny Eaton was born in Franklin County or that she spent over nine decades in the place of her birth. To suppress her vote, then, was to deny her personhood—a reality she understood all too well.

"Many have become my enemies without cause," the psalmist prays, echoing the struggle of women like Rosanell Eaton (Psalm 38:19). But Eaton stood tall well into her nineties, shoulders back and head held high, just as she had when asked to quote the Preamble to the Constitution in the 1940s. She embodied the conviction that God's image is stamped on every person, and she knew in her bones what her church taught her to sing: "This joy I have the world didn't give to me . . . and the world can't take it away."

GIVE US THE BALLOT

While faithful witnesses like Ms. Eaton connect us to the long struggle for voting rights in America, a new generation of activists is working to expand access to the ballot and ensure the democratic principle of one person, one vote through an array of initiatives. In the 2016 election, Donald Trump lost the popular vote by nearly three million votes but won the Electoral College by less than a hundred thousand votes across three different states. With just under sixty-three million votes, Trump became president of the United States with the support of less than 29 percent of eligible voters. The single largest group of voters didn't consist of the people who voted for him or for Hillary Clinton. It was the people who didn't vote at all.

While numbers like these are usually cited to blame or inspire the disproportionately poor citizens who do not vote in most elections, many of the people working hardest for the expansion of voting rights are those who know from experience how many obstacles to the franchise still exist. Census data says there are roughly forty million poor people in America, but a supplemental measure that looks at how many households are one $400 emergency away from not being able to pay their bills suggests there are 140 million poor and low-income people in the United States. That's 43 percent of the population— roughly the same number as those who do not usually vote.

Because time off work is the greatest obstacle to voting for the working poor—especially those with a long commute from the district where they are registered—the NAACP and other voting-rights advocacy groups have introduced proposals for

early voting, same-day registration, automatic registration for eighteen-year-olds, mail-in ballots, and a national holiday for elections. These measures have significantly increased turnout in some states, making politicians of both parties more accountable to the people they represent.

Many of the voter-suppression tactics that have been used since 2010 in the United States have been implemented in response to an expanding and more diverse electorate. So the same groups that have worked to expand access have also fought against restrictive voter-ID laws, voter-roll purges, redrawing district lines to dilute the impact of minority groups, and moving precincts in poor communities to make it more difficult for some people to access them. Many of these people are motivated by their faith and organize through church networks to protect elections and expand voting rights. I met a young African American woman who organized a Righteous Vote initiative in Alabama during the special Senate election in 2017. Though news stories covered Christian nationalists' support for Roy Moore in that race, efforts like hers were also organizing faith communities in Alabama to get out the vote for a moral vision of our common life that includes all people, not just conservative white Christians.

Any movement that wants both to honor the sacrifices of the past and to move forward toward a functioning multiethnic democracy must commit to expanding democracy to include everyone in American society. If we are to stand tall with Rosanell Eaton, defending the image of God in every person, then we who participate in a democratic form of government must commit ourselves not only to make sure that the voice

of every neighbor has the opportunity to be heard but also to ensure that every voice counts the same. That will mean organizing in underresourced communities to make sure everyone who is eligible gets registered, getting churches involved in voter protection, challenging voter suppression in the courts, and voting for politicians who commit to restore the Voting Rights Act and get rid of an Electoral College system that was designed to disproportionately represent slaveholding states. This is a long-term struggle, but we can take courage from people like Rosanell Eaton, who stayed on the battlefield for voting rights her whole life long.

LORD, PREPARE ME TO
BE A SANCTUARY

Pastor José Chicas had lived in the United States for thirty-two years when he went to his annual appointment with Immigration and Customs Enforcement (ICE) in April of 2017. Since ICE was established by the George W. Bush administration in 2003, Chicas had become accustomed to the routine of driving two and half hours from his home in Raleigh to the Charlotte office of ICE, checking in with a caseworker, signing paperwork, getting a new work permit, and going home. But this trip was different. Though Donald Trump had been in the White House for less than three months, his administration had already begun to enforce its "zero tolerance" policy concerning immigration enforcement. "José called me and said he had some bad news," Chicas's wife, Sandra, recalls. "He was being deported."

ICE ordered Chicas to purchase a one-way ticket to El Salvador, the country he had fled during its civil war in 1985. Chicas remembered the bus trip from his hometown to the

city of San Salvador like a veteran reliving the horrors of battle. "There were bodies in the ditch beside the road; I saw bodies hanging from bridges outside the city." Chicas had not been back to El Salvador since he crossed the US border into Texas, seeking asylum in a nation that was at that time sponsoring the Salvadoran government's repression of its people. Because he was initially denied asylum and did not have a lawyer to follow up with appeals on his behalf, Chicas had no legal status in the United States. But employers didn't ask about legal status in the 1980s. Chicas moved to North Carolina, found work, got married, bought a house, and raised four children.

Watching his youngest son move through elementary school as his oldest finished high school, Chicas experienced a new sense of purpose—a call to ministry with a focus on reaching young men with the good news of Jesus. With little chance to process the trauma he had experienced in early adulthood, Chicas knew he had made mistakes, fathering a child he left behind in Texas and struggling with alcoholism in his twenties. But he was equally clear that the grace of God and the persistent love of Sandra and their children had saved him from destroying himself. Chicas wanted to share that good news with the young men he met on the streets of Raleigh. Beginning with one-on-one evangelism to the down and out, he planted a church—Iglesia Evangélica Jesús el Pan de Vida, or Jesus, the Bread of Life, Evangelical Church.

Chicas was mentored in conservative faith communities and embraced the language of family values that he learned there. He experienced the spiritual force of the culture wars

with Pentecostal intensity. Knowing from personal experience
the challenges of life, Chicas resonated with the language of
spiritual warfare he found in Scripture. When TV and radio
personalities told him that liberals were the tools of Satan, he
believed them. And when Donald Trump promised to be a
champion for evangelicals, he told his family and church that •
God sometimes chooses to work through unlikely vessels.
No, Trump wasn't perfect. But neither was Pastor José. The
important thing was to trust God.

Without access to the ballot in the only home he knew,
Chicas could do little more than watch and pray when it came
to politics. Still, he was a religious leader in his community.
The evangelical subculture of Chicas's family and church celebrated President Trump as a gift from God. "I used to be like,
I love God, I'm a Christian, I'm going to support Republicans.
It's the party of God," Sandra recalled a year after the election
of 2016. "But they have shown me that's not true." The Chicas
family learned the hard way how the language of faith can
been co-opted to rally support for the very opposite of what
the Lord requires. In 2017, the politics of family values tore
their family apart.

I met José and Sandra in the summer of 2017, after their
family had exhausted every legal petition to stay together
in North Carolina. When ICE officials refused to hear an
appeal of their decision to deport José, he took sanctuary
at the School for Conversion, where I teach on the property
of St. John's Missionary Baptist Church in Durham, North
Carolina. As a minister in the network of faith communities
who committed to resist the separation of families through

sanctuary, Pastor José became a leader of the twenty-first-century's underground railroad, operating in plain sight. Because School for Conversion was the place where he and Sandra could be together without immediate threat of deportation, our office became a hub for organizing meetings, fellowship, prayer vigils, and education about how Christian faith has been manipulated to turn US citizens against our immigrant neighbors.

"CHRISTIAN NATIONALISM" AND THE BROWNING OF AMERICA

In the summer of 2018, Americans expressed widespread moral outrage when reports emerged that the Trump administration had ordered US Border Patrol to separate thousands of asylum seekers from their children. President Trump's spiritual adviser, Paula White, defended the administration by arguing that Jesus had been a *legal* refugee when the holy family fled to Egypt, and former Attorney General Jeff Sessions quoted Romans 13 to argue "orderly and lawful processes are good in themselves." But most Americans were left wondering how needless cruelty that most conservatives would have condemned a decade earlier had become federal policy in the United States.

It's important to recall how dramatically Republicans have turned against undocumented immigrants in recent history. As the standard bearer of the GOP at the end of the twentieth century, President Ronald Reagan addressed situations like Pastor José's when he said, "Our nation is a nation of immigrants. . . . I believe in the idea of amnesty for those who have put down roots and who have lived here, even though sometime

back they may have entered illegally." As recently as 2010, Richard Land, who served as spokesperson for Southern Baptists on issues of public policy, spoke in favor of outreach to immigrants like José and Sandra, saying, "Hispanics are religious, family-oriented, pro-life, entrepreneurial. They are hard-wired social conservatives, unless they are driven away." Even within the religious and political alliance that used the culture wars to pit Christians against their "secular" and "liberal" neighbors, immigrants were, until recently, often seen as potential allies.

So what changed? An honest look back at the politics of immigration in twentieth-century America reveals that, despite a pro-immigrant consensus among political leaders, a backlash against the browning of America has been building for a long time. Just as the moral outcry against racism in the 1960s led to greater protections for African Americans in the Voting Rights Act of 1965, so too did the political climate of the 1960s produce the Immigration and Nationality Act, which was signed by President Johnson the same year. Since the 1920s, US immigration policy had been based on an explicitly racist quota system, which limited immigrants from many nonwhite countries based on perceived dangers to the "American" gene pool that had been identified by the pseudoscience of eugenics. (This same bad science was used by Aryan nationalists in Nazi Germany to justify the extermination of Jews, Roma people, homosexuals, and disabled people.) White supremacy was written into American immigration codes just as much as it was made law in poll taxes and literacy tests. Many of the same organizations that opposed

Brown v. Board of Education and the Voting Rights Act also began to develop a case against immigration as soon as the 1965 Immigration Act became law.

Founded in 1937 by champions of eugenics, the Pioneer Fund was an avenue through which this backlash against nonwhite immigration was organized. While its resistance to integration was based on a well-documented belief in the inherent inferiority of African Americans, the Pioneer Fund worked hard to distance itself from an explicitly racist past after the 1960s. By the late 1970s, it began investing in the Federation for American Immigration Reform (FAIR), a network founded by retired ophthalmologist John Tanton to preserve American culture via a "European-American majority." While Tanton often met with Ku Klux Klan leaders and avowed white nationalists, he was careful to make his case against immigration in terms of culture, not race. Indeed, Tanton's crusade against immigrants was always about the culture wars.

The terrorist attacks of September 11, 2001, created an opportunity for Tanton's FAIR network—which by then included a think tank, the Center for Immigration Studies, and a lobbying arm, NumbersUSA—to play on the fears of Americans who felt vulnerable. Although the Saudi Arabian members of al-Qaeda who carried out the attacks on the World Trade Center and the Pentagon were clearly driven by an extreme ideology, many Americans who had little experience with Muslims or other immigrants saw in both groups a broader potential threat. When, just seven years later, the fragile pro-immigrant consensus of the post–civil rights era

elected America's first black president—Barack Hussein Obama, whose father was from Kenya—anti-black, anti-Muslim, and anti-immigrant sentiments combined to create a reactionary populism that would turn the Republican Party against immigrants. Two resources proved essential to the extreme-right coalition that formed to take control of the party: one was the anti-immigrant policy agenda that had been created by Tanton's FAIR network. The other was the myth of a "Christian nation" that we encountered in Ms. Rosanell Eaton's lifelong struggle for voting rights.

No single person has been more committed to making the case that America was founded as a Christian nation than political activist David Barton. "For the past thirty years," evangelical historian John Fea writes, "Barton has provided pastors and conservative politicians with inaccurate or mis-interpreted facts used to fuel the Religious Right's nostalgic longings for an American Christian golden age." If nostalgia for the culture of an America controlled by white men was to be socially acceptable, social conservatives since George Wallace have known they had to talk about culture, not race. But Barton offered a way to frame nostalgia for white culture as the longing for an American past that never was.

It's no accident that the LLC (limited liability company) Barton founded to sell his message through conservative religious broadcasters and Christian homeschooling networks is called WallBuilders. Long before the Trump campaign latched onto "the wall" as a symbol of anti-immigrant sen-timent, Barton had baptized the idea as a monument to Christian nationalism. Just as Nehemiah was called to rebuild

the walls of ancient Jerusalem, Christian nationalists imagined a wall on America's Southern border as a concrete act to restore a Christian nation.

If "Make America Great Again" really meant stemming the tide of demographic changes that had begun with the social winds of the civil rights movement and the swell of nonwhite immigrants after 1965, that wasn't how people steeped in the religious right heard it. When they shouted "Build that wall!" they weren't thinking about the electoral future that Republican operatives feared so much as the mythical past Barton and others had taught them to imagine. It wasn't images of kids in cages or families separated by ICE that animated them but the memory of Mayberry, where Andy Griffith sat on the front porch strumming his guitar and singing the hymns we learned growing up in church.

Christian nationalism made xenophobia palatable by making it the necessary condition of standing up for values that were supposedly under threat because of people like José and Sandra. The irony, of course, was that if anyone from Mayberry had ever had the chance to get to know José and Sandra, they would have found they had far more in common with them than they did with political operatives like John Tanton and David Barton, who rarely associated with the "common folk" of small-town America whom they claimed to defend.

THE CHRISTIAN NATIONALIST'S BIBLE

One reason many white evangelicals in the Republican Party's conservative coalition held out so long against the nativism of Tanton's FAIR Network is that the Bible speaks so directly

about God's concern for immigrants. While an issue like abortion or voting rights isn't directly addressed in Scripture, there are literally dozens of texts in the Bible about how we should treat the immigrant, alien, or stranger among us. In fact, after the identity that comes from being people called into covenant with the Creator of the universe, the fact that we are immigrants is probably the second most fundamental identity statement about the people of God in Scripture.

The Bible doesn't exhort us to welcome immigrants simply because it is the ethical or just thing to do. God's people welcome immigrants as a way of remembering that we, too, were once in the same situation. "The foreigner residing among you must be treated as your native-born," the legal code of Leviticus says. "Love them as yourself, for you were foreigners in Egypt" (Leviticus 19:34).

But in American history there is a long tradition of exegesis to explain away the Bible's inconvenient truths. When the revivals of the Second Great Awakening first burned across the American South, many white people who experienced God's saving grace alongside black people—sometimes even from the mouths of black preachers—saw that the same God who brought Israel out of bondage in Egypt had made a new reality possible in Christ. As Paul wrote to the Galatians, "there is neither . . . slave nor free . . . for you are all one in Christ Jesus" (Galatians 3:28). But this plain truth of Scripture, which animated a moral movement for the abolition of slavery in the nineteenth century, also challenged the systems that most people considered normal life in the antebellum South. "If slavery be a sin," a Mississippi preacher

wrote in 1836, "then, verily, three fourths of all the Episcopalians, Methodists, Baptists and Presbyterians, in eleven states of the Union, 'are of the devil.'" Plantation owners paid a host of biblical scholars and preachers to write sermons, pamphlets, and books that assured white Southern slaveholders they were, in fact, the *true* Christians.

Christian nationalism draws on this tradition of slaveholder religion to read the Bible in defense of an anti-immigrant policy agenda. Quoting a song from Deuteronomy about God's faithfulness to Israel after the exodus, David Barton has argued that when God "set up boundaries for the peoples" (Deuteronomy 32:8) in the ancient Near East, a divine blessing was also bestowed upon the borders of the United States and the laws that currently regulate them. Barton doesn't explain why God's will wasn't transgressed when the United States fought a war with Mexico to establish the current boundary or, for that matter, when European settlers first took the land from its indigenous inhabitants. He simply borrows a line from Moses as a prooftext for FAIR's talking points.

But Christian nationalism can never be dismissed as simply the ignorant reading of sloppy exegetes. Like the slaveholder religion that preceded it, the anti-immigrant movement has scholars who have done their homework. Old Testament professor James Hoffmeier, who has taught at both Wheaton College and Trinity Evangelical Divinity School, wrote an entire book on the "immigration crisis," in which he claims to offer a balanced assessment of "both sides." He goes on to make a historical argument that the Hebrew word *ger*, which

is variously translated in English as "stranger," "alien," "so-journer," or "foreigner," cannot mean "illegal immigrant" because, in the ancient world, the *ger* always had permission to dwell in another's land. As long as ICE granted Pastor José a "stay of removal" and permission to work in the United States, we can assume that Professor Hoffmeier would have supported him as a neighbor and brother in Christ. But now that the Trump administration has revoked that permission, the biblical injunction to care for the *ger* no longer applies according to Hoffmeier's reading of the text.

The Christian nationalist's Bible never dismisses Scripture's concern for love and mercy toward the stranger. Instead, like many who defended the institution of slavery, it is ever ready to explain why others misapply those biblical mandates in this particular situation. Many who want to call eleven million of their neighbors "illegal" cite texts like Romans 13:1—"the authorities that exist have been established by God"—as biblical justification for extreme enforcement of America's immigration law. In the name of Jesus, who was executed by the authorities in ancient Rome, they make an unconditional case for obedience to the laws of the land. While they may admit that the issue is complicated, law and order trumps love of neighbor when it comes to neighbors like Pastor José.

Contemporary attacks on immigrants in America cite Scripture and claim the moral high ground precisely because the moral case for someone like Pastor José is so strong. When the Bible offers moral force to a movement that challenges established powers, powerful people know they need

to convince their base that their adversaries are actually God's enemies.

The Christian nationalist's Bible isn't celebrated and lifted up by political operatives in the FAIR network and today's GOP because they are particularly pious people; their "biblical" case against immigrants is necessary to overcome the moral force of simply hearing and understanding a story like Pastor José's. But if the Bible is being used to push back against pro-immigrant appeals, it's all the more important for people of faith to articulate the biblical case for immigrants.

A BIBLICAL CASE FOR IMMIGRANTS

Each morning at 4:30 a.m., Pastor José logs onto Facebook Live to read Scripture and pray with his flock, which has grown during his confinement to include people all over the world. He is often drawn to the exodus story, connecting his experience in sanctuary with both enslaved Hebrews in ancient Egypt and enslaved Africans who heard echoes of their own experience in the exodus story. "The Lord will fight for you," Pastor José reads, imagining Moses up against the Red Sea with Pharaoh's army at his back. Like Moses, José feels stuck with no home to go back to and no legal status with which to move forward in America. But his experience, he tells his flock, is one we all face when we learn from a doctor that we have cancer or when a relationship that has defined us comes to an end. When we know we can't go back and also cannot see a way forward, the Bible's message becomes a promise to cling to: "The LORD will fight for you; you need only to be still" (Exodus 14:14).

In Pastor José's preaching, the Bible's concern for immigrants reveals a basic truth about who we are—people who walk by faith, not sight. As Christian nationalists know, memory is essential to identity formation. The Bible's story begins in an Eden where all is as God meant it to be. But it doesn't teach us to believe we are people who can make creation great again by wresting control of our common life from our enemies. Instead, the biblical story shapes a memory that we are all, in some way, people who cannot go home again. In the place where God intends for us to dwell, we are all *ger* and we are all illegal. The gift of God isn't that we were born in a great nation but that God meets us as aliens and strangers and says, "You will be my people, and I will be your God" (Jeremiah 30:22).

Christian nationalism is a heresy not only because it makes people mean to neighbors we're called to love but also because it reinforces a nativism that lies about who we are. In the Bible's prophetic witness, this idolatry is explicitly connected to public policy that hurts immigrants, widows, and children. God cries out against the political violence that always accompanies the idolatry of nationalism: "You city that brings on herself doom by shedding blood in her midst and defiles herself by making idols, . . . see how each of the princes of Israel who are in you uses his power to shed blood. . . . In you they have oppressed the foreigner and mistreated the fatherless and the widow" (Ezekiel 22:3, 6-7).

In the New Testament, Jesus embodies this prophetic witness when he teaches in Matthew 25 that we welcome him— God in human flesh—when we welcome the stranger. Christian

nationalists often dismiss this text and the broader prophetic witness by claiming that care for immigrants, like works of charity for "those less fortunate than ourselves," are individual responsibilities, not the work of governmental policy. So Matthew 25 doesn't inform their public policy agenda. But Jesus explicitly confronts the idolatry of policy violence in Matthew 25 when he says *nations* will be judged by how we treat the stranger, the hungry, the sick, and the imprisoned.

No, the Bible doesn't speak directly to the complex immigration policy issues in a twenty-first-century democracy. But when we read Scripture with people like Pastor José, it does speak pointedly to how the heart of faith is subverted by nativism. In Luke 4, when Jesus offers his first sermon in his own hometown, the texts says that "all spoke well of him and were amazed at the gracious words that came from his lips" (Luke 4:22). His message, from the prophet Isaiah, had been about the fulfillment of God's promises. But Jesus doesn't bask in the praise of an approving hometown crowd that assumes those promises are for them. Instead, he tells two stories from 1 and 2 Kings about how, in Israel's history, foreigners had received God's blessings when the native-born had been faithless. "All the people in the synagogue were furious when they heard this," Luke 4:28 records. The violence of religious nationalism isn't new. Jesus' neighbors tried to throw him off a cliff when he confronted their nativism with an alternative political memory.

The memory of God blessing outsiders fosters a radical hospitality in Scripture that exhorts followers of Jesus' way to "show hospitality to strangers, for by so doing some

people have shown hospitality to angels without knowing it" (Hebrews 13:2). This welcome is never offered out of paternalistic largess; it flows, rather, from an expectation that God's messengers are people like Pastor José and Sandra. They come to us not because they need our help but because we need to learn together what it means to be a sanctuary—a community in which God's presence can be known in the fellowship of sisters and brothers who know we've been given to one another as gifts.

NO HUMAN BEING IS ILLEGAL

Before I met José and Sandra, I learned to imagine the kind of country the United States might become from young people who were dubbed "Dreamers" when they organized themselves to advocate for the Dream Act in 2007. After a bill that Representative Luis Gutiérrez had first proposed six years earlier finally passed the House, these undocumented college students who had been brought to the United States as children lobbied the Senate for a pathway to citizenship that would allow them to live adult lives alongside their classmates and peers. It was an intense political education for the Dreamers as they saw their hopes crushed when the Senate was unable to reach the sixty votes needed for cloture. In their disappointment, though, some of the young activists realized that their dream had been too small. They had lobbied for an America that would welcome them but criminalize the parents who'd brought them here for a better life.

This realization didn't cause the Dreamers to give up, but to think bigger—to work with communities to imagine anew

the kind of nation we want to be. During the Obama administration, when ICE attempted to execute deportation orders
against mothers and fathers, the Dreamers organized communities to advocate for the people who built the communities' houses, cooked their food, volunteered with their
Parent Teacher Association, and helped with childcare in their
churches. Here in Durham, North Carolina, they helped us
advocate for a youth minister at the local Catholic parish who
was detained because she did not have documentation when
an officer in the next county over stopped her car for driving
with a missing taillight. Three weeks later, when she came
home from the detention center in Georgia that would have
deported her to Mexico, she testified at our Baptist church: "I
prayed to God, and he heard my cry. Glory to God!"

When the new Sanctuary Movement responded to President Trump's zero-tolerance policy by welcoming people
like José into sanctuary, seasoned Dreamer activists helped
people like José and Sandra challenge congressional representatives to take bold action in support of immigrants under
attack. Our response couldn't just be hospitality, they said
to churches, because being welcomed into a church while
the government demonizes you as an "illegal" is just another
form of incarceration. We must challenge politicians who
claim to support immigrants to move beyond words. We
must build a movement that makes just immigration reform
a moral issue.

By organizing and voting toward a pathway to citizenship
for the eleven million undocumented neighbors who are an
integral part of our communities and economy, people of

faith have an opportunity both to remember that we, too, were once strangers and to pray that the heavenly city where every tribe, tongue, and nation will bow together before the throne of God may come here on earth as it is in heaven. Our public engagement with immigration policy cannot perpetuate the second-class citizenship that is a relic of our slaveholding past. Just as abolitionism was a moral movement in the nineteenth century and the civil rights movement was a moral movement in the twentieth century, the movement for undocumented immigrants to win citizenship and the right to vote in America is a moral movement of our time. To join it is to learn both the hope and the struggle of embodying the gospel by working with all our neighbors to become a "more perfect union."

LAW AND ORDER

O n the north side of Saint Louis in the 1950s and 1960s, the Pruitt-Igoe housing complex stood as an eleven-story interruption to the tree-lined streets with low-rise brick homes that marked most midwestern urban communities at the time. A mid-twentieth-century experiment in mass segregated housing, the William L. Igoe Apartments were originally designed as affordable housing for whites while the adjacent Captain W. O. Pruitt Homes offered "separate but equal" accommodations for black residents. When the project was initiated in the early 1950s, demographic trends suggested that both black and white Southerners were coming to find work in Saint Louis's factories. Pruitt-Igoe was designed to house them while accommodating the customs of racial segregation they brought with them from the Deep South.

But the plan didn't work. Like other urban centers, Saint Louis experienced white flight during the 1960s as the federal government slowly enforced the Supreme Court's *Brown v. Board of Education* decision, which had come down the same year Pruitt-Igoe opened. Poor black residents

increasingly struggled to survive in high-rise buildings that lacked basic maintenance, leaving the most vulnerable to fend for themselves in conditions that were often worse than the rural poverty their sharecropping parents had left behind. By the time most public schools in the South were officially desegregated in the early 1970s, Pruitt-Igoe had been condemned. Its 1972 demolition in a televised implosion symbolized the systemic challenge of integration. If a multiethnic democracy was to become reality in America, it would require literal reconstruction.

Ndume Olatushani grew up in Pruitt-Igoe during the 1960s. Though he knew the love of a mother who raised eleven children while also cooking for any kid who was hungry in a high-rise that would soon be condemned, Olatushani felt the injustice his mother faced and her struggle to survive. He decided to try to even the score as a teenager, getting involved in petty crime. Olatushani knew what he was doing was illegal and that, if he was caught, he would go to jail. But like most of the people he grew up with, Olatushani was learning to weigh that risk against the real possibility that he might not survive the conditions that white flight created.

To hear Olatushani tell his story is like listening to tales of Jacob from Genesis. He was an underdog with an indomitable spirit, determined from the start to hang on to life and the people who loved him, even when the means at hand were questionable. But for most of his life, Olatushani didn't get to tell his own story. After he had been labeled "criminal" by Saint Louis police, Olatushani was framed in a shooting that

happened while he was visiting family in California, even though the victim testified in court that "it would be a terrible injustice to convict this man."

While doing time for that conviction in San Quentin, Olatushani got the surprising news that he had been identified as a murder suspect in a hard-to-solve Memphis, Tennessee, case that had been tied to his hometown of Saint Louis by a stolen car. Olatushani had never been to Tennessee, but Saint Louis police saw him as a likely suspect because of his recent conviction in California. He was extradited from San Quentin as a convicted felon and found guilty of murder in a Memphis court. In 1986, Olatushani was sentenced to die in Tennessee's electric chair.

While he was on death row for twenty-seven years, Olatushani's mother died. He nearly lost all hope. But when his mother came to him in a dream and said, "Get up," Olatushani discovered a new imagination through art. "There's a lot of things we should be angry about," Olatushani says. "But you have to learn what to do with your anger. Painting helped me to learn that."

Painting also helped Olatushani find his way to freedom. While still on death row, he met Anne-Marie Moyes, a volunteer who was coordinating an art show for prisoners at the time. Captivated by Olatushani, Moyes began to document the details of how he had been profiled and wrongfully convicted. She eventually went to law school in order to learn how she could work for his release. Though their fight took more than two decades, Olatushani walked out of prison in 2012, married Moyes, and moved into a bungalow not unlike

the homes across from Pruitt-Igoe that had offered such a contrast to the landscape of his youth.

Like the story of Jacob, who became Israel after he received a new imagination while wrestling with God in the night, Olatushani's story is a redemption saga. But his is not the tale of a sinner who wandered far from God only to reach the end of his rope, repent, and return home. That misreading of stories like his, far too common among Christians who have experienced the law on their side, would cast Olatushani as an exception that proves our need for law and order. For Olatushani, redemption has meant learning how some people were for him even when those making decisions in urban planning and law enforcement were against him. As an artist and organizer with the Children's Defense Fund today, Olatushani works to help those who are growing up in the conditions he knew as a child see how they can become an active force in reconstructing the unjust systems they were born into.

FAMILY VALUES AND THE CRIMINALIZATION OF CHILDREN

Olatushani came home from prison and started a family the year before Michael Brown, an unarmed African American teenager, was shot dead by a police officer in Ferguson, Missouri, just miles from where Olatushani had grown up. Though he had been gone for more than three decades, Olatushani knew things hadn't changed much for poor black kids growing up in and around Saint Louis. In her 2010 book, *The New Jim Crow*, Michelle Alexander chronicles how the systemic problems exposed by wrongful convictions and police brutality against young men like Michael Brown grew out of

political resistance to the civil rights movement in the mid-twentieth century. Politicians who appealed to the same racial fear that led white neighbors to move out of Pruitt-Igoe in the 1960s asked residents of the suburbs and the Sun Belt to vote for "law and order" in the 1970s, the War on Drugs in the 1980s, and mandatory minimum sentences for low-level crimes in the 1990s. Alexander's analysis suggests that Michael Brown died in 2014 for much the same reason Olatushani had been condemned to death three decades before him: because both men were born suspect in the criminal caste system that replaced Jim Crow segregation after the civil rights movement.

Jim Crow didn't go away for many poor black people in America; it evolved into a system of mass incarceration that, as Alexander notes, imprisoned more black men in 2010 than it enslaved in 1850. Black Lives Matter resonates so strongly in communities like greater Saint Louis because it is a protest against the lived experience of people like Olatushani and Brown. But if we want to understand why so many white Christians who do not think of themselves as racist push back against this basic assertion of black people's dignity, we have to look more closely at the parallel history of family values in the late twentieth century.

When we remember the racism of Jim Crow, Americans often recall Alabama governor George Wallace's defiant inaugural address, in which he declared "segregation now, segregation tomorrow, segregation forever" nearly a decade after the Supreme Court's *Brown v. Board of Education* decision. Wallace became infamous later that same year for personally

standing in the doorway of the University of Alabama to try to block its integration. But Wallace's political performance for his base in 1963 was based on the political strategy of "interposition," which had sought ways to delay and prevent integration throughout the South for nearly a decade. In 1958, Virginia governor J. Lindsay Almond Jr. shut down public schools in cities with a large African American population rather than implement integration plans. His "massive resistance" campaign, which was supported by the Defenders of State Sovereignty and Individual Liberty, inspired a preacher in Lynchburg, Virginia, to join the organized resistance to integration, which he called the "work of the Devil." The following year, the Reverend Jerry Falwell Sr. volunteered to serve as chaplain for his local Defender's branch.

More than a decade before he would step onto the national stage as the most prominent proponent of family values, Rev. Falwell questioned "the sincerity and nonviolent intentions of some civil rights leaders such as Dr. Martin Luther King, Jr., . . . who are known to have left wing associations." Rather than name his own political associations, Falwell claimed to prefer preaching the "pure saving gospel of Jesus Christ" to any kind of engagement with public issues. But two years later, when Lynchburg finally desegregated its public schools in 1967, Falwell opened the Lynchburg Christian Academy (LCA), which the local paper described as "a private school for white students."

Though private Christian schools like Falwell's LCA eventually made plans for token integration and officially denounced the explicit racism of their past, their emergence as

segregation academies for the children of white Southerners offered a window into the culture that the family-values movement sought to reclaim. Falwell's LCA soon launched a college that would go on to become Liberty University, one of the largest private Christian universities in the world today, boasting as many as 100,000 students in their combined on-campus and online programs. A national network of Christian schools, magazines, radio, and television news networks gave Falwell a base to launch his Moral Majority in 1979, supporting the nation's first "Make America Great Again" campaign—Ronald Reagan's 1980 bid for the White House. To understand the former greatness Falwell and others sought to restore, we need only read the early literature of his Christian academy.

A 1975 ad for Falwell's LCA asserted that "young people are no worse today than 25 years ago. They simply come from worse homes and schools." After Richard Nixon borrowed the language of "law and order" from his opponent, George Wallace, in his 1968 campaign for the Republican presidential nomination, the Southern Strategy had framed advances in civil rights and the War on Poverty as a disruption of the natural order that threatened to send America spiraling into chaos. If the Republican Party promised strong leadership to restore order, Christian schools like the LCA offered a haven from disorder for children. "The school responded to the threat of a culture that questioned authority by underlining both the importance of the family and the lines of authority within it," historian Seth Dowland observes. By instilling faith in authority figures from the home to the White House, the family-values movement taught its followers to trust the

assessment of law enforcement, even when its disparate treatment of black and brown people was recorded on cell phones and broadcast on national television.

As an artist, Olatushani trusts the power of images to transform our imagination. If segregation academies and the cultural world surrounding them taught a generation of Americans to trust the established order of a society shaped by racial inequality, Olatushani wants to help Americans understand the lack of trust he shares with the protesters who stood outside the White House after Michael Brown's murder, chanting, "How many black kids will you kill? Michael Brown, Emmett Till!"

Inside a lecture hall at Vanderbilt University Divinity School, just miles from the Riverbend prison where he spent twenty-seven years on death row, Olatushani walks me through his installation of wooden school desks, each painted with facts about the impact of "law and order" policies on communities of color. On one end of the row, a cradle bears this warning: "One in three black kids born today will go to prison." Across the back of the lecture hall, orange jumpsuits sit in chairs designed for students. One of the jumpsuits is stuffed with cash, flowing out of the hole at the top, where a head should be. Olatushani tells me that the jumpsuit in that chair is the one he wore the day he came home from death row. On the far end of this "cradle to prison pipeline," a final desk sits as a memorial to George Stinney Jr. When he was executed by the state of South Carolina in 1944 at the age of fourteen for allegedly killing two white girls, Stinney walked to the electric chair with a Bible under his arm.

Like Stinney, Olatushani was given a Bible in prison. It sits on one of the desks in the middle of his exhibit, held open by a pair of handcuffs. Yes, Scripture has been open at the center of the established order in America, this installation seems to say. But for anyone who's been caught up in the cradle-to-prison pipeline, it's clear that the Bible's message has been bound, along with their bodies. Maybe none of us can be free until the Bible is set free.

THE BIBLE THAT BLESSES LAW AND ORDER

In 2015, as the Black Lives Matter movement spread from Ferguson to communities across America where unarmed black men and women were killed by police, the Reverend Franklin Graham posted this message to his Facebook page:

> Listen up—Blacks, Whites, Latinos and everyone else. Most police shootings can be avoided. It comes down to respect for authority and obedience. If a police officer tells you to stop, you stop. If a police officer tells you to put your hands in the air, you put your hands in the air. If a police officer tells you to lay down face first with your hands behind your back, you lay down face first with your hands behind your back. It's as simple as that.

As heir of his father's international evangelism ministry, the Billy Graham Evangelistic Association, Franklin Graham leans on biblical authority when he offers practical advice that dismisses the lived experience of black and brown people in America. He is not alone in this. The family-values movement that began in segregation academies like Falwell's

LCA transformed the fight over a state's right to defend segregation into the assertion of parents' right to pass white
culture on to their children as part of a "biblical worldview."
To challenge a white person's family values, then, is to defy
that person's reading of Scripture. We can't understand the
defiance with which Franklin Graham insists that everyone
else "listen up" apart from seeing the way Black Lives Matter
challenges how he sees the world.

In Franklin Graham's personal experience, many outcomes
have come down to "respect for authority and obedience."
Graham described the weight of expectations for the son of
America's most famous preacher in his 1995 memoir, *Rebel with
a Cause*. "Welcome to this sin-sick world and the challenge you
have to walk in your daddy's footsteps," an admirer of his father
wrote to celebrate Graham's birth. The preacher's son rebelled
against expectations, getting himself kicked out of a Christian
college as a young man. But when he chose to repent and submit
to authority, Graham was richly rewarded. In 2015, he was the
highest paid director of an international relief organization in
the world, taking CEO salaries from both Samaritan's Purse and
the Billy Graham Evangelistic Association.

While his personal circumstances are unique, Graham's
way of seeing the world is not. A society that was set up by
white men consistently rewards white men when they submit
to the established authorities within it. In turn, white men
often see the established order in which they succeed as
"natural." I am a white man too. Whenever I thank God for the
successes of my life, I have to grapple with how my gratitude
can easily become a justification for the systems that order

90 REVOLUTION OF VALUES

our shared life, sanctifying a "biblical worldview" in which respect is honored with rewards and adversity is a sign of punishment for disobedience.

For anyone in a privileged position, this way of reading the Bible is tempting. It suggests that sin isn't cooperation with broken systems—"principalities and powers," to use Pauline language—but *willful* disobedience. While Adam and Eve's rejection of God's way in Genesis is the root of humanity's sin on any reading of the story, the Bible that blesses law and order always locates that sin in the rebellious individual rather than the family, community, or political systems that were also compromised by the fall. The gift of God's law, then, isn't an invitation to learn an economy that doesn't demand slavery (Leviticus 25) or a political system that doesn't depend on an exploitative king (1 Samuel 8). It becomes, instead, a ruler to show us how no individual can live up to God's expectations. When that individual confesses the need for a Savior in Jesus Christ, he or she can submit to earthly authorities and reap the benefits of obedience without asking how sin has created the conditions of inequality within the established political and economic systems.

In her book *The Furnace of Affliction*, Jennifer Graber chronicles how this focus on the redemption of individual souls shaped America's prisons through the activism of white Protestants who imagined the personal conversion of inmates as the ultimate solution to criminal behavior. A genuine compassion and concern for incarcerated people drove most nineteenth-century prison reform efforts. But people of faith who began with sympathy for those behind bars increasingly came to see

the systems they had helped to build as confirmation of inmates' rebellious hearts. In the end, Graber notes, "they stressed a Christian faith realized most significantly as moral living and obedience to governmental authority."

"It comes down to respect for authority and obedience," Franklin Graham would proclaim 150 years later. George Stinney, Ndume Olatushani, and millions who went to jail like them would always receive a Bible, but their acceptance of its message would too often be judged by their willingness to submit to the established authorities. In the process, many Christians seemed to forget that the Jesus we worship was a condemned criminal, crucified by the authorities of his day.

READING THE BIBLE WITH THE CONDEMNED

Olatushani's "cradle to prison pipeline" invites us to expand our imagination of what it means to be locked up in an era of mass incarceration. Yes, more than two million people—disproportionately poor, black, and brown—are behind the walls of US jails and prisons on any given day. It's an astounding number: 25 percent of the total number of incarcerated people in the world. But Olatushani's row of desks extends to demonstrate how many more people are damned by the Bible that blesses "law and order." Millions of children have been born suspect in poor neighborhoods, even as more than seventy million people in the United States negotiate the collateral consequences of a criminal conviction on their record. A complex system of state laws, federal policies, implicit bias, and law enforcement practices has succeeded in marking more people in the US today with a record than the total

number of those who voted for any candidate in any presidential election in US history. If there is a true "silent majority" in the United States today, it is the condemned.

But when we read the Bible with those who are born suspect in today's system of mass incarceration, we learn how its message can offer a powerful rebuttal to the dehumanizing judgments of our broken systems of punishment. Humanity's original rebellion is instructive not so much because it reveals the source of criminal behavior but because it demonstrates the consistent theme of God's response to sin— restorative justice.

God makes "garments of skin" to cover Adam and Eve (Genesis 3:21) and puts a mark on Cain, the world's first murderer, to protect him as God's own (Genesis 4:15). The law of God's covenant with Israel is, likewise, a gift to protect and "cover" imperfect people in a broken world, not a reward for the upright or a defense of the established regimes. When Jesus says he has not "come to abolish the Law . . . but to fulfill [it]" (Matthew 5:17), he does not side with secular or religious officers of the law. Instead, he is "numbered with the transgressors" (Luke 22:37), keeping company with sinners and other lawbreakers until he is himself condemned to death for a conspiracy to overthrow the established authorities in Jerusalem.

God's restorative justice consistently meets the twisted human heart and the world's broken systems with a radical love that affirms what is good in creation while disrupting the false order of this world's systems. People who are locked up in today's system of mass incarceration know from experience

that their well-being doesn't simply come down to respect for authority. But many of them find hope in a criminal Christ who took on flesh to be locked up with them, not only to forgive their sins but also to confront the sinful injustice that is so often perpetuated by advocates of "law and order." Reading the Bible with Olatushani, we see what Franklin Graham cannot: that we deny the truth of the gospel when we turn its message of saving grace into an endorsement of the powers that be.

To read the Bible as a defense of broken systems is also to deny the good news it offers those who are the keepers and defenders of unjust systems. In the book of Acts, Paul and Silas are arrested in Philippi, for, as their accusers say, "throwing our city into an uproar by advocating customs unlawful for us Romans to accept or practice" (Acts 16:20-21). When biblical preaching lands the apostles in jail for disorderly conduct, Philippi experiences an earthquake that shakes the jail cells open, setting the captives free. But Paul and Silas do not flee. Instead, they stay to preach to their jailer, who is ready to kill himself when he wakes up to realize that the order he swore to preserve has been disrupted. Notably, the jailer also finds restorative justice in God's mercy. "He was filled with joy," Acts records, "because he had come to believe in God—he and his whole household" (Acts 16:34).

Clearly, this was a deeply personal experience for the jailer, addressing the sin in his heart that had been there all along, even as he dutifully obeyed the authorities in his chain of command. But this biblical story also makes clear that his sin and ours are never only about our individual relationship

with God. The faith of Jesus, which Paul and Silas share, liberates the jailer and his whole household from the lies of a death-dealing system. When the prisoners set their captor free, the broken order of an unjust system is interrupted, helping us all to imagine the future that God's messenger proclaims in Revelation:

> The kingdom of the world has become
> > the kingdom of our Lord and of his Messiah,
> > and he will reign for ever and ever. (Revelation 11:15)

Olatushani's art, in its own way, echoes this message, both for the young person born suspect in a place like Pruitt-Igoe and for the misguided Christian who has been taught to read the Bible as a defense of "law and order." God doesn't bless "law and order," but instead comes to us when we are condemned and offers the hope of a whole new order—a world in which the incarcerated preach good news to their captors and the ones who were condemned help us find our way to freedom.

ABOLISHING MASS INCARCERATION

People like Olatushani know from experience how "law and order" has criminalized whole classes of people and neighborhoods. As they organize against this dehumanizing system, they invite all of us to learn from them and their experience how a vision of restorative justice can heal our communities and nation.

In Chicago, Illinois, Ameena Matthews and her neighbors helped local law enforcement understand gun violence as a public health problem that impacts everyone in their

community. Through their innovative Cure Violence Health Model, they have invested in hiring formerly incarcerated people who have returned to the community as "interrupters" to engage in strategic interventions that stop violence before it happens. Because systemic poverty is itself a root cause of crime in the community, giving people a job is important. (Homeboy Industries, another innovative, faith-rooted program in Los Angeles uses as their tagline: "Nothing stops a bullet like a job.") But "interrupters" aren't doing just any job. They're being compensated for using intimate knowledge of their own communities to serve their neighbors and make these places safer for everyone.

This is the vision at the heart of the movement for abolition of America's retributive justice system. All of Us or None, an activist group led by formerly incarcerated people, is one example of how those who have experienced mass incarceration can help us all advocate for policy changes that turn our criminal justice systems toward a process that heals and restores people who have committed crimes to the community. This can happen at every step of the way along the school-to-prison pipeline. Some communities are replacing uniformed and armed school resource officers (SROs) with restorative justice coordinators in schools. Precharge diversion programs are redirecting low-level offenses away from the courts, where many young people get a record before they get a diploma, to community-based processes where they learn to address both the harms they have done and the systemic violence they were born into. Many of these same groups are also organizing to support district attorneys who

commit to implement restorative justice, end cash bail, and decriminalize drug offenses that have disproportionately impacted poor communities.

In several US states, felony disenfranchisement is still on the books. Another vestige of our Jim Crow past, these laws were instituted in the late nineteenth century to push back against the citizenship African Americans had gained with the Thirteenth Amendment by exploiting the exception clause for those "duly convicted of a crime." In the 2018 midterm elections, organizers from the Florida Rights Restoration Coalition were able to get a ballot measure passed, restoring voting rights to 1.4 million Floridians who had been disenfranchised by convictions for which they had already served their time and paid full restitution. These are the kind of policies that people impacted by "law and order" are advocating for. When we link up to work with them, we have the chance to join the Spirit's work in the world to "proclaim freedom for the prisoners and recovery of sight for the blind" (Luke 4:18), learning all the while how we, too, have been bound and blinded by a system that addresses human evil by trying to distinguish between good and bad guys.

A WOMAN'S WORK IS FOR JUSTICE

In 2015, after graduating from Fuller Theological Seminary in California, Alicia Wilson moved to Indianapolis, Indiana, to take a job with a Christian missions organization. Raised in an evangelical family in California, Wilson attended Christian schools that instilled family values and a pro-life ethic, but her parents also lived the gospel's concern for poor and marginalized people. "If someone asked for money on the street, my dad always invited them to come eat with us," Wilson recalls. "My parents didn't want to protect us from strangers. They wanted us to know them."

The Presbyterian congregation Wilson grew up in had a sister church across the border in Mexico. She started visiting fellow Christians there with her parents when she was five years old. "I loved meeting and learning from people who were different than me—a passion that propelled me forward as I grew older," Wilson says. By her mid-twenties, theological education had shaped her understanding of God's call, and she moved to Indiana to work for a missions organization.

When Wilson arrived in Indiana, Governor Mike Pence, who had risen to political power with strong support from white

evangelicals, had just signed the controversial Religious Freedom Restoration Act (RFRA), which had been widely criticized for using the language of "religious liberty" to undermine the Obama administration's attempts to expand access to healthcare and equal protection under the law. Protestors argued that the RFRA gave conservative Christians license to discriminate against neighbors they disagreed with, and an Indianapolis newspaper's editorial board declared, "Only bold action—action that sends an unmistakable message to the world that our state will not tolerate discrimination against any of its citizens—will be enough to reverse the damage." The Indiana legislature quickly passed an amendment, which Governor Pence signed, to prevent discrimination against LGBTQ people. But the debate about religious freedom in Indiana was far from over.

In 2016, Governor Pence joined his brand of religious liberty with Donald Trump's campaign to "take back" the country from a black president whose citizenship Trump had long questioned. Many white evangelicals squirmed as they listened to Trump's foul language and history with women, but Pence assured them that a President Trump would champion "religious liberty" and appoint conservative judges who would uphold legislation like Indiana's RFRA. Leaders of the religious right were persuaded, and Trump became president with the overwhelming support of white evangelicals' votes. All the while, Wilson was learning from experience how harmful the Trump/Pence brand of religious liberty could be for a woman like her.

Engaged to be married in the spring of 2016, Wilson went to see her doctor about birth control. She and her fiancé, Josh

Baker, wanted to pay off student loans and save money to purchase a home before having kids. After talking with her doctor, Wilson decided that the best form of birth control for her would be a nonhormonal intrauterine device (IUD) that would prevent pregnancy for the next few years but could later be removed when she and Josh were ready to have kids. Through her work, Wilson had health insurance with Guide-Stone Financial Resources, which covered contraceptives under the requirements of the Affordable Care Act. She felt good about her plan and had the IUD inserted a few months ahead of her wedding date.

But just before her big day, as Wilson was rushing to make final preparations with family and friends, she received a letter from her insurance company saying she owed $1,200. "GuideStone does not provide coverage for abortions or abortion-causing drugs, as this violates our biblical convictions on sanctity of life," Wilson read. Despite the fact that she was herself a pro-life evangelical who had pledged abstinence until marriage, Wilson's insurance company was claiming a "religious exemption" to deny coverage for the form of birth control she had chosen.

Wilson became Alicia Wilson Baker amidst a flurry of phone calls and appeals to GuideStone, with her employer attempting to intervene on her behalf. In back-and-forth communication that continued for months after the wedding, GuideStone's lawyers maintained that the religious exemption was their right and threatened to hand the Bakers over to a collection agency if they refused to pay the bill. Ultimately, they decided to pay and move on, even though the

additional debt would add time to the plan the Bakers had made for their family.

Two years later, President Trump and Vice President Pence held a state dinner for evangelicals at the White House. Franklin Graham, Paula White, and Robert Jeffress praised the president for his commitment to "religious liberty." The following week, Trump's second Supreme Court nominee, Brett Kavanaugh, would sit for three days before the Senate Judiciary Committee for confirmation hearings. On the final day, when the committee heard testimony from citizens and expert witnesses, Alicia Wilson Baker shared her story, asking the committee not to confirm Kavanaugh because his record on "religious liberty" suggested he would support the kind of exemption her insurance company had used against her. "As a Christian and a woman," she said, "I urge this Committee and this Senate to weigh heavily the detrimental impact that confirmation of Judge Kavanaugh would have on the health and well-being of ordinary individuals and families, particularly those who already face oppression and discrimination in our society." Though she still identified as a pro-life evangelical, Baker had learned how dangerous the religious liberty of the pro-life/pro-family movement can be, especially when wielded by people in positions of political power.

FAITH AND THE FIGHT FOR WOMEN'S RIGHTS

If the independent Christian schools that Jerry Falwell Sr. and others founded in the South were, in their beginnings at least, segregation academies for white parents who worried that integration would harm their children, the Christian

schools that Baker grew up in had different, though not un-
related, origins. Within the civil rights movement of the
1960s, many black and white women who worked for equal
rights saw that issues of gender justice were often over-
shadowed by calls for racial justice. Their organizing experience taught them what was required to shift public opinion
and build power for systemic change, and they increasingly
spoke out to advocate for women's rights.

At the same time, women who had watched their mothers
work in factories while their fathers left to fight in World
War II were becoming adults themselves. As Betty Friedan
noted in her bestselling book, *The Feminine Mystique*, this
new generation of American women was unwilling to accept
the housewife role that many of their mothers had settled
back into when their fathers returned home after the war.
Young women who had watched their mothers play important roles outside the home while also raising children
questioned the gendered division of public and private roles
as well as the Victorian values that had defined the Industrial Era. Second-wave feminism in the 1960s and 1970s
inspired a generation of American women to take up their
grandmothers' struggle for gender equality.

Looking back, it's striking to note the bipartisan support
for women's rights in the United States during the 1970s. The
Equal Rights Amendment (ERA), which had languished in
Congress since 1923, just after women gained the right to vote,
was buoyed by second-wave feminism to achieve support from
the majority of both Democrats and Republicans, passing the
House in 1971 and the Senate in 1972 with overwhelming

majorities. Pending ratification by thirty-eight states, the United States was poised to amend its Constitution to say "equality of rights under the law shall not be denied or abridged by the United States or by any State on account of sex." When several state legislatures voted for ratification within weeks of Republican president Richard Nixon signing the ERA in the spring of 1972, equal rights for women seemed settled to most political observers.

But to Phyllis Schlafly, a Catholic laywoman and Republican political operative in the suburbs of Saint Louis, Missouri, the ERA became a rallying point for an organized resistance to the expansion of women's rights. "Women's lib is a total assault on the role of the American woman as wife and mother, and on the family as the basic unit of society," Schlafly wrote to women who joined her STOP ERA campaign as the amendment made its way through Congress in 1972. An anti-communist hawk who had spoken for years at the John Birch Society's God and Country rallies, Schlafly was a skilled political organizer with deep connections to extreme right organizations that had been worried about the pace of change in American society since the *Brown v. Board of Education* decision. But STOP ERA opened an avenue for Schlafly to channel conservative anxiety toward a respectable end: defense of traditional family values, not racial segregation.

Schlafly wasn't alone. At the University of Southern California Medical School, a young evangelical professor, Dr. James Dobson, had become concerned during his graduate studies that the parenting advice of the most well-known

child psychologist at the time, Dr. Benjamin Spock, was contributing to the disorder he perceived in America following the social movements of the 1960s. Dobson's 1970 book, *Dare to Discipline*, advocated a version of "law and order" at home to push back against the chaos that Schlafly and others decried as a perversion of natural order in society. "By learning to yield to the loving authority of his parents," Dobson would write in a later book, "a child learns to submit to other forms of authority which will confront him later in his life—his teachers, school principal, police, neighbors and employers." As Dobson churned out parenting advice that would tie the Sun Belt and the suburbs to the Deep South for the next forty years, a pro-life/pro-family coalition emerged to ensure that the ERA would never be ratified.

Through Focus on the Family radio broadcasts, Dobson shared his vision of traditional family values with millions of evangelical Christians like Baker, who did a guided retreat based on one of Dobson's books with her mother when she was in the seventh grade. She has a vivid memory of the Focus on the Family study guide using a piece of paper to symbolize young women. "Sex," the voice on the audio guide told them, "is like glue that sticks you to someone else." After the glue set between two pieces of paper, the sheets couldn't be separated without tearing a layer off of each of them.

To defend the family values he sought to instill through books and radio shows, Dobson launched a political advocacy group, the Family Research Council, in 1981. Through alliances with Schlafly's Eagle Forum, Falwell's Moral Majority, and a host of ministries and religious broadcasts that took

up the pro-life/pro-family message, Dobson sought political power to wage a culture war against efforts to expand the rights of women and equal protection under the law for gay and transgender people. Deep pockets within the Republican Party soon recognized the family-values coalition as a sort of spiritual Super PAC (political action committee) that didn't require the oversight of campaign finance laws. By the late 1990s, when Baker and her mother attended the purity retreat together, Focus on the Family was operating with an annual budget of over $100 million.

At Azusa Pacific University, an evangelical school in Southern California, Baker began to question some of the assumptions that were passed on to her as family values. She saw how the purity culture of the paper-and-glue metaphor left many women who had been harassed or abused with a sense of shame because they had not been able to achieve or defend a gendered order they equated with righteousness. Women seemed to bear overwhelming responsibility for upholding family values while power imbalances in cross-gender relationships were theologically justified.

About the same time, Barack Obama launched his first campaign for president. For the first time in her memory, Baker saw in public life a Christian who talked about politics as a way to serve others rather than a means of defending family values. Maybe faithful politics wasn't primarily about gaining power to defend Christians against their liberal neighbors, Baker thought. Maybe it could be about empowering women to make wise choices and care for all life. As she learned about the work many pro-choice and women's rights

organizations do in poor communities, Baker had a hard time imagining them as the opposite of a "pro-life" position.

But the experience of being denied birth control because of a "religious exemption" made clear to Baker that, in the long fight against women's rights, even she could be seen as the enemy. "I thought I'd done everything right," she told me after her testimony before the Senate in 2018. "I had waited until marriage to have sex. Josh and I wanted the kind of committed family we'd been taught to value." But the "pro-family" politicians who had power in Indiana stood by an insurance company that didn't want to pay for birth control rather than by a woman who had done everything she knew how to be consistently pro-life. None of the pro-family legal firms that raised money from evangelicals to defend religious liberty came to Baker's aid; it was, instead, the National Women's Law Center, founded in 1972 to advocate for the rights that the ERA was to guarantee, that took up her case.

A WORLD ORDERED BY GODLY MEN

The culture wars that pitted women's rights against family values consistently framed objections to family values as a rejection of the Bible. On this reading of Genesis 1 and 2, God created Adam and Eve as male and female with distinct social roles in the family and society. To question those gendered roles was to question God. By 1987, the newly formed Council on Biblical Manhood and Womanhood (CBMW) stated its concern about "widespread uncertainty and confusion in our culture regarding the complementary differences between masculinity and femininity" and went on in its Danvers

Statement to blame an increase in divorce rates, marital infidelity, and spousal abuse on this "confusion." The Danvers Statement did not offer an analysis of gender roles before the Industrial Revolution, when the vast majority of men and women in an agricultural economy shared most responsibilities on family farms. Nor did it offer an analysis of how other factors, like increased mobility and consumer culture, might have impacted family life in mid-twentieth-century America. As a defensive weapon in the culture wars, the Danvers Statement simply offered biblical ammunition for the ongoing crusade against feminism and women's rights.

Like the fundamentalists of the early twentieth century, family-values Christians imagined themselves as an embattled minority that needed to have a handful of irrefutable Scriptures on hand to press back against the "liberal" media, science, and the government. "I do not permit a woman to teach or to assume authority over a man" (1 Timothy 2:12) was not simply a statement of pastoral discernment about a particular situation in a first-century church; it became a universal declaration of the principle of "male headship" that had been threatened by the Equal Rights Amendment. If this doctrine of male headship had not been central to church teaching before, it was only because it had never been questioned, its defenders argued.

Betraying the instincts of men who had used the Bible to justify slavery before them, advocates of male headship deployed the household codes of Ephesians and Colossians to justify submission to men in the twentieth century. When objectors pointed out that "wives, submit yourselves to your

husbands" (Colossians 3:18) was a direct parallel to "slaves, obey your earthly masters" (Colossians 3:22), family values crusaders agreed that it had been wrong to use the Bible to defend slavery, which had been instituted by sinful men. But the family, they insisted, was instituted by God. It did not occur to them that their slaveholding predecessors had also imagined abolitionists as enemies of God and moral order.

Because the family-values movement made the fight against women's rights a battle for the Bible, it presented young women like Baker with a false choice between trusting God and trusting the experience of women who knew that, with unequal power and protections in society, they were often in danger. When the virtuous woman of Proverbs 31 was put up against activists who protested that a woman needs a man like a fish needs a bicycle, many conservative women whose social power depended on their relationship to husbands and fathers were quick to defend femininity, motherhood, and wifely submission. Women who believed it would be wrong to teach a man nevertheless became some of the most passionate advocates for male headship, exhorting their Christian brothers to step up to the role of leadership in the family and in society.

In both public and private life, men are subject to sin, of course. Prominent men in the family-values movement experienced dramatic falls from grace after affairs or abuse was exposed. But after they confessed their sins, televangelists and conservative politicians were often re-presented in the mold of King David, who used political power to steal Uriah's wife, Bathsheba, but was nevertheless remembered as a "man

after [God's] own heart" (1 Samuel 13:14). Men could make mistakes in leadership, but the family-values movement maintained that a woman in leadership was itself a mistake—a confusion of the natural order that would inevitably lead to moral decline and social chaos.

For a quarter-century of American public life, Hillary Rodham Clinton embodied this offense. As a professional working mother, she understood herself to be a co-equal partner with her husband, even after he became president of the United States. For most family-values Christians, it did not matter that Clinton was a committed church member who fought to keep her family together after her husband was caught in a David-like sin before the whole nation. The role she sought to play at home and in public life was unbiblical in their estimation. Clinton was everything the family-values movement had taught them to fight against.

In 2016, when Clinton ran for president against a man who had talked openly about his extramarital affairs and was caught on tape bragging about sexual assault, evangelicals overwhelmingly voted for him. Phyllis Schlafly's last act in her lifelong campaign to STOP ERA was to endorse candidate Trump in the spring of 2016. In her book *The Conservative Case for Trump*, published after her death, Schlafly wrote that "critics can, and will, go on and on about Trump having been married three times, and about how, in the past, he boasted about his indiscretions. But anyone who meets him today will meet an old-fashioned man grounded in his two great priorities—hard work and family—and a man who in other respects has led a remarkably clean life."

James Dobson, his Family Research Council, and their allies in the family-values coalition echoed Schlafly's endorsement of Trump. To outside observers, evangelical support for Trump felt like a farce, with one pro-family advocate after another falling over themselves to praise a man who flouted everything they claimed to believe. But to anyone who'd learned to read the Bible as a rejection of the ERA, the message was clear: even an obviously corrupt man is a better choice than a woman who fights for equal rights.

REBELLIOUS WOMEN AND THE HOPE OF SALVATION

For anyone not enmeshed in the culture wars' debates about gender roles, the Bible is full of stories that reveal how God works through women in all kinds of roles, both in and outside the home. If there's any "headship" in the Genesis account of creation, it is in the ascending order of created beings from land and sea to flora and fauna to Adam and Eve. The fact that Eve, the first woman, is created after Adam in this story doesn't make her a subservient second to her male counterpart; she is the pinnacle of creation—God's final flourish. But the first account Genesis offers of humanity's origin doesn't suggest hierarchy so much as a pairing that reveals the fullness of the creature. With humanity in particular, Genesis claims that something about God's nature is revealed in men and women together: "In the image of God he created them; male and female he created them" (Genesis 1:27). To read Industrial Era gender roles onto Genesis isn't only harmful to women. It also obscures the most visible image Scripture says we have of God here on earth—male and female together.

Nineteenth-century feminist and abolitionist Sojourner Truth highlighted the centrality of women in the biblical story when she asked the 1851 Women's Convention in Akron, Ohio, "Where did your Christ come from? From God and a woman! Man had nothing to do with Him." Not only did Jesus come through a woman to dwell among us; he also entrusted his gospel to women, sending them from the empty tomb to share the good news of his resurrection with male disciples who had gone into hiding after their Messiah was executed. Thankfully, no defender of family values was there in first-century Palestine to tell the women at the tomb that instructing Peter, James, and John about what they had heard and seen would be unbiblical.

Throughout Scripture women play essential roles in God's story, often rebelling against cultural norms to do so. Zipporah, the wife of Moses, plays the role of priest in Exodus 4, circumcising their son and using the blood of that covenant to intercede for her husband, who had angered God. Rahab, a sex worker in ancient Jericho, plays a crucial role in delivering the Promised Land to the Hebrew children as they make their way out of Egypt. In the book of Judges, Deborah leads the people of Israel, exhorting her male general, Barak, to have courage because the Lord had already delivered the enemy commander, Sisera, into their hands. When Sisera escapes the battlefield to hide in a neighboring tent, a woman, Jael, kills him in his sleep.

In the exile stories, when God's people face a holocaust under King Xerxes, it is Queen Esther, a Hebrew among his harem, who steps out of her cultural role as foreign-born

queen to act as an advocate for her people. "I will go to the king, even though it is against the law. And if I perish, I perish," she famously says (Esther 4:16), inspiring generations of women and men who have engaged in civil disobedience to speak truth to power. As priests, prophets, and regents in the biblical narrative, women play every role that the Gospel writers understand Jesus to fulfill—or fully embody—in his ministry on earth. Jesus doesn't only entrust his ministry to women after his resurrection. After Mary of Bethany anoints him as Messiah, he also explicitly says, "Wherever the gospel is preached throughout the world, what she has done will also be told" (Mark 14:9). Whether it is preached by women or men, the gospel of Jesus Christ cannot be proclaimed without reference to the essential role women play in this story.

Despite the best efforts of Schlafly, Dobson, and company, Alicia Wilson Baker got to know the God of the Bible, who works through women who are willing to reject cultural norms in order to stand for justice and serve their neighbors. Within the family-values movement, Baker learned to read Proverbs 31 for instructions on how to be a virtuous woman who brings her husband "good, not harm, all the days of her life." But Baker didn't accept the interpretation of Scripture that was handed to her by a movement that mobilized to deny her equal rights. She read the Bible for herself. And in the very passages that were supposed to shape her into a good housewife, she found the words she would need to testify before the US Senate Judiciary Committee. "My faith dictates that I must speak out on behalf of the millions of

women who stand to lose access to affordable birth control if Judge Kavanaugh is confirmed," Baker said, stepping into a public role that, according to Focus on the Family, a virtuous woman would never embrace. But knowing she was in precisely the place God wanted her to be, Baker quoted Proverbs 31, the very text that was supposed to teach her to defer to her husband and work in the home:

Speak out for those who cannot speak,
 for the rights of all the destitute.
Speak out, judge righteously,
 defend the rights of the poor and needy.
  (Proverbs 31:8-9 NRSV)

"I'm still for life," Baker told me, "but my understanding of what that means has expanded. As Christians, we should work for policies that protect life from the womb to the tomb." For Baker and a growing number of Christians who refuse the categories of the religious right, that means supporting government policies and programs that care for women, families, and children. It looks like maternity leave and childcare, quality public education, access to birth control, affordable health care, and breaking the school-to-prison pipeline that has separated so many poor families over the past generation. Stepping out of the narrow political alliances she inherited, Baker isn't only demonstrating what a virtuous woman looks like. She's showing a new generation of Christians how to defy the legacy of Schlafly and Dobson in order to reclaim the bold public witness of Esther and Mary Magdalene, Sojourner Truth and Fannie Lou Hamer.

These women whose faith compelled them to work for justice in the public square show all of us what faith demands in our own time.

ESTHER IN THE #METOO MOVEMENT

It's no accident that Donald Trump, who was accused of sexual assault by dozens of women and caught bragging about it on tape before his election, found support among the political coalition that formed in opposition to the ERA. Trump's inauguration was immediately followed by the Women's March, which organized the outrage of millions who vowed to challenge the president and hold him accountable. Telling their own individual stories of how they have been abused, women in the #MeToo movement shifted public consciousness around sexual assault and abuse and demanded accountability. Powerful men from Hollywood to corporate boardrooms faced consequences for the ways they manipulated positions of power to abuse both women and men.

Within the faith community, women also shared #ChurchToo stories, demanding accountability for pastors who had abused their positions in the church. Paige Patterson, who had led the prayer at Schlafly's first Pro-Family/Pro-Life Rally in 1977 before going on to lead the charge for "male headship" in the Southern Baptist Church, was forced to resign from leadership at Southwestern Baptist Theological Seminary after women shared publicly how he had silenced rape allegations and discouraged them from reporting crimes committed against them to law enforcement. Within weeks, Bill Hybels, founder of Willow Creek Community Church and the Willow Creek

Association, was forced to resign after accusations of sexual harassment and abuse proved undeniable.

As women in the #MeToo movement demanded accountability, they also organized to run a historically diverse slate of women for congressional seats in the 2018 midterms, inspiring a Rainbow Wave that not only delivered control of the House of Representatives to Democrats but also shifted leadership of several House committees to women of color who have been longtime advocates for policies that would lift up the poor, children, and immigrants.

One new member of Congress elected in 2018 was Lucy McBath, an African American woman who became an advocate for gun reform when her son, Jordan Davis, was shot and killed in 2010 by a white man who objected to the music Jordan was playing on his car stereo at a gas station. Running in Georgia's Sixth Congressional District, a longtime Republican seat once held by Newt Gingrich, McBath was seen as a long shot when she announced her campaign. But she shared her story as a mother and appealed to women and men of faith, offering an agenda to support life and family by passing sensible gun reform, ensuring access to healthcare and education, and mandating living wages for working people. Her victory demonstrated how, even in a red district in a red state, it is possible for women to build new voting coalitions around a different vision of family values.

Across the border to McBath's west, Tabitha Isner lost her bid to represent Alabama's Second Congressional District. But even in defeat, Isner's campaign helped to shift the moral narrative in a state where Roy Moore, an unrepentant sexual

predator and advocate of Christian nationalist extremism, had long been celebrated as a champion of family values. Running on policies like paid family leave and universal access to healthcare, Isner used the hashtag #SeriousFamilyValues to promote her campaign. In her concession speech on election night, she sounded like a revival preacher. "We—all of us—are doing the Lord's work," she proclaimed. And while there will always be some dark Fridays for those who walk the way of Jesus, Isner knows what Esther and Deborah and so many mothers before her learned through faithful struggle— that "weeping may endure for a night, but joy *comes* in the morning" (Psalm 30:5 NKJV). "We are not merely fighting for economic prosperity," Isner told her supporters. "We are not merely fighting for healthcare and the physical well-being of our fellow citizens. We are fighting for the soul of this nation." That is a fight that extends beyond any single campaign or election cycle.

CHAPTER SEVEN

GROANING WITH ALL CREATION

An hour east of Phoenix, in the desert of Arizona, Wendsler Nosie Sr. kneels to pray beside a small stream of water at Oak Flat. Like Moses in the desert of Zin, Nosie's Apache ancestors received water from these rocks and knew it to be a gift from God. "Without water, there is no life," Nosie says. Because San Carlos Apaches have worshiped the Creator while drawing water here for as long as anyone can remember, Oak Flat is holy ground. This place of prayer and sacred ceremony is not unlike the Temple Mount for Muslims, Christians, and Jews. For Nosie, an elder in the San Carlos Apache tribe, the wisdom of his people and their relationship with the Creator is inextricably tied to this place.

But Nosie knows that Oak Flat may not be here for his grandchildren. After years of unsuccessful negotiations and a corruption scandal that landed one Arizona congressman in prison, Senator John McCain added a last-minute rider to the 2014 defense spending bill, giving Resolution Copper rights to dig beneath Oak Flat and mine copper ore located thousands of feet below the surface. Resolution's parent

company, Rio Tinto, has already invested $1.3 billion in the project. The proposed extraction process would use as much water as a small city—6.5 billion gallons annually, which would be polluted with sulfuric acid in order to process the ore. In the end, Resolution acknowledges, a crater two miles wide and a thousand feet deep would replace the holy ground where Nosie's ancestors have come to pray for thousands of years.

In 2015, after the mining rights for Oak Flat were transferred to Resolution Copper, Nosie led a forty-four-mile walk from the Apache reservation where he lives to the national park campground, where Oak Flat is located. "What God has given us as a people, man's greed will bring to an end," he told roughly three hundred walkers, mostly Apache, who set up camp to occupy their holy land. Nosie's granddaughter had come here for her own coming-of-age ceremony a few years earlier. After she ran her people's sacred staff the last leg of the forty-four-mile journey, she joined her grandfather and the circle of San Carlos Apache who have pledged to resist the corporate-government alliance that is determined to destroy their holy land. They pledged to occupy the land in nonviolent civil disobedience.

Nosie is not alone in his conviction that greed will destroy the good gifts the Creator has given us. In 2016, the year after the San Carlos Apache occupied Oak Flat, a coalition of tribes that grew into the largest gathering of indigenous nations in history rallied at Standing Rock, where the Missouri and Cannonball Rivers meet in North Dakota, to resist the construction of the Keystone Corporation's Dakota Access

Pipeline (DAPL). Self-identifying as "water protectors," the allied indigenous communities sought both to protect the sacred lands of the Standing Rock Sioux and to highlight how an unchecked oil-based economy is desecrating all land. They invited supporters to come and learn the wisdom passed down by native elders. Standing Rock was about teaching the world what Wendsler Nosie knows.

My friend Steve Pavey accepted the invitation and joined thousands of others at Standing Rock in late 2016. He quickly realized that he'd been invited into something much more profound than a local land rights struggle. "While we have gathered to stop construction of the 'Black Snake' through the lands of the Standing Rock Sioux Tribe with the immediate goal of protecting the water, we are facing a much greater and important challenge," he wrote. "DAPL is a symptom of a greater 'disease' that native Sioux Sitting Bull called the 'greed' of a white settler colonizing people." As Nosie can see on his own sacred land 1300 miles away, the greed driving our extractive economy threatens to destroy the very basis of our existence. This insight is not new for indigenous people, but it is increasingly confirmed by modern science.

On June 23, 1988, NASA's James Hansen testified to a packed congressional hearing that a "real warming trend" was connected to human activity—a scientific observation that had been discussed in less public settings since the 1950s. But Hansen's testimony that our oil-based economy is permanently altering the climate in irreversible ways launched public debate about what global warming might mean for the future of human civilization. *Time* magazine named "Endangered

Earth" its Man of the Year for 1988, focusing public attention on the same wisdom at the heart of indigenous struggles to save Oak Flat, Standing Rock, and Mother Earth—namely, that the white man's greed, if left unchecked, will ultimately destroy us all.

Writing the cover story for *Time* three decades ago, journalist Thomas Sancton summarized the environmental movement's analysis of how the white settlers' greed is inextricably tied to faith in American public life. "In many pagan societies, the earth was seen as a mother," Sancton wrote, imagining a cosmology in which humans were subordinate to a divine earth and therefore careful to observe its signs and comply with its demands. "The Judeo-Christian tradition introduced a radically different concept," Sancton argued. "The earth was the creation of a monotheistic God, who, after shaping it, ordered its inhabitants, in the words of Genesis: 'Be fruitful and multiply, and replenish the earth and subdue it: and have dominion over the fish of the sea and over the fowl of the air and over every living thing that moveth upon the earth'" (Genesis 1:28 KJV).

Sancton wasn't a biblical scholar; he was a journalist. Reporting on people who called themselves Christian as they permanently altered earth's climate, he observed that indigenous people share a different vision of the created world. If Christians are troubled that Sancton found justification for greed in Genesis, we should be equally eager to reread our Scriptures with indigenous elders who can help us discern their true meaning. Because Sancton was at least right about this: the people who want to dominate earth's

resources for their own personal gain have continued to do so in God's name, using faith to fuel their fight against both native wisdom and climate science.

DOUBTING SCIENCE IN GOD'S NAME

Suspicion of science has deep roots in the fundamentalist subculture that gave rise to the modern religious right. While Christian concern about Darwin's theory of evolution was initially as much about its potential to justify discrimination against the poor through "Social Darwinism" as it was about apparent conflicts with the Bible's account of creation, California businessman Lyman Stewart's campaign to unite fundamentalists around a reactionary definition of traditional doctrine and morality created a movement of people who questioned science in the name of faith. Daniel K. Williams argues in his history of the religious right that the social networks of Christians who would identify their faith with the Republican Party in the late twentieth century began to form in the early-twentieth-century movement we call fundamentalism, after "The Fundamentals" that Stewart championed through a massive publishing project. Fundamentalism's antiestablishment convictions were embodied in William Jennings Bryan's quixotic crusade against evolution at the infamous Scopes Monkey Trial, where the famous preacher tried to prove in court that Darwin was wrong and Genesis was right. Bryan didn't succeed, and fundamentalism's embarrassment was amplified by his unexpected death just after the trial.

If Bryan lost the culture war in the 1920s, he also failed to persuade either major US political party to side with the

fundamentalists. A half century of institution building would be required before movements and organizations like the Moral Majority and the Christian Coalition could persuade the Republican Party that they were able to mobilize a critical electoral base. But long before reactionary faith was identified with a political party, Bryan helped solidify its suspicion of modern science.

While this suspicion has lingered in the fundamentalist and evangelical subcultures, an important piece of the religious right's legitimation in American public life was shedding its backwoods, anti-intellectual image. Science, the handmaiden of economic development and human progress, couldn't be the enemy of Christian nationalism in the late twentieth century. Instead, it had to become its servant. This meant the development of a parallel science that appears to use the same rules of reason, data, and analysis while denying the conclusions of modern science that get in the way of economic progress or the religious right's social agenda.

In her book *Kingdom Coming: The Rise of Christian Nationalism*, Michelle Goldberg reported on the emergence of the "intelligent design" argument in an early-twenty-first-century school board battle in Dover, Pennsylvania, that took up where Bryan's crusade against Darwin had left off eighty years earlier. School board member Bill Buckingham, who chaired the curriculum committee in Dover, objected to the purchase of a standard biology textbook because, he claimed, it was "laced with Darwinism." Buckingham continued, making his political alliances clear: "This country wasn't founded on Muslim beliefs or evolution. This

country was founded on Christianity and our students should be taught as such."

For Buckingham, David Barton's myth of a shared Christian past wasn't enough to guarantee that the next generation of Americans will embrace the values of Christian nationalism. Like Bryan before him, Buckingham argued that public schools needed to challenge the "anti-Christian" science of evolution. But unlike Bryan, Buckingham was able to draw on the work of the Center for Science and Culture (CSC), a public policy think tank funded by many of the same wealthy Christian businessmen who've invested in the broader infrastructure of the religious right. To legitimize their skepticism of mainstream science, the CSC developed a theory of "intelligent design" to counter Darwinian evolution, not on the grounds of faith but as an alternative science. Buckingham quickly took up the language of intelligent design in his objection to the standard biology textbook and soon proposed an alternative textbook, *Of Pandas and People*, which he proposed adding to the curriculum in the name of fairness, even though its polemic against evolution isn't recognized by the overwhelming majority of scientists.

Buckingham's crusade against Darwin was, in many ways, an example of the coming fight that the CSC had outlined in a 1999 fundraising proposal that was later made public online. "The proposition that human beings are created in the image of God is one of the bedrock principles on which Western civilization was built," the document begins. It quickly turns to identifying modern science as antithetical to this conviction, then posits "intelligent design" as the

answer to the contradiction the CSC imagines because it "promises to reverse the stifling dominance of the materialist worldview, and to replace it with a science consonant with Christian and theistic convictions."

Though the CSC's end goal was in line with Buckingham's, they did not end up backing his campaign in Dover, Pennsylvania, because they knew it was not likely to hold up in court. Buckingham was too direct in his frontal attack on Enlightenment norms. "If we view the predominant materialistic science as a giant tree," the CSC told its funders, "our strategy is intended to function as a 'wedge' that, while relatively small, can split the trunk when applied to the weakest points." Rather than propose their alternative pseudoscience as the scientific truth, the CSC proposed using public debates about textbooks to chip away at the accepted norms of modern science. If they could lay a sufficient foundation of doubt in the public consciousness, then they could imagine a future when they would be able to teach intelligent design as the official science of a Christian America.

The religious right's embrace of this alternative science is important because it has sown the seeds of doubt that make it possible for reasonable people in public life to deny climate science. As Bill McKibben chronicled in his 2010 book *Eaarth: Making a Life on a Tough New Planet*, James Hansen's conservative estimates of global warming, which he shared with Congress in 1988, were far outstripped by the measurable realities of climate change over the following two decades. It is an observable reality that we already live on a planet permanently altered by carbon emissions, and more recent

reports from the Intergovernmental Panel on Climate Change (IPCC) suggest that we are merely decades away from a planet where millions will die each year from climate-related catastrophes. Yet the Trump administration pulled the United States out of the Paris Climate Accord and has dismantled the Clean Energy Plan of the Obama administration. These policy decisions, they argue, are good for the economy. But they rely on faith that economic growth can continue despite the evidence of diminishing habitats for human life.

The madness of greed that Sitting Bull diagnosed has become the faith of a political party in the twenty-first century. In spite of the evidence, Republicans have been willing to believe that the US economy can somehow defy the scientific law that what goes up must come down. Indeed, they are willing to bet the planet on this faith. Such fervent belief can only be sustained through regular acts of worship. In concert with their party handlers, leaders of the religious right have written public liturgies to sustain this myth in alternative textbooks and public policies based on a doctrine of "dominion." Struggles like the one in Dover, Pennsylvania, have served to solidify faith-based suspicion of science and the public voices who defend its findings.

REDEEMING AMERICA AND EXERCISING DOMINION

The reading of Genesis that the environmental movement has long scorned and that Thomas Scanton associated with all Judeo-Christian thought in his *Time* article on climate change is not, in fact, how most Jews, Christians, and Muslims have read our shared creation story. It does, however, reflect the

teachings of dominionism, a reading of Genesis and biblical law that was developed in the mid-twentieth century by the Christian Reconstructionist R. J. Rushdoony. In his 1973 book, *The Institutes of Biblical Law*, Rushdoony argued that Christians in America, as the new chosen people of God, are called to do what Adam and Eve failed to do, in his estimation— namely, to create a godly, Christian state that will subdue and rule the world. Rushdoony's Chalcedon Foundation was influential in shaping the vision of many founders of the religious right in the 1970s, but his extreme racism, anti-Semitism, and endorsement of violence muted Rushdoony's voice as the movement sought legitimacy through the Republican Party. But this did not diminish the impact of Rushdoony's teaching. Dominionism was popularized by Pat Robertson and the Christian Broadcasting Network.

The son of a conservative Virginia Senator, Pat Robertson was always at home in the world of politics. But as a young man, the fun-loving, charismatic scion of Virginia horse country had a Pentecostal conversion experience, moved to Harlem, and enrolled in seminary. When he moved back home to southeastern Virginia, Robertson bought a local television station and began building what would become one of the world's largest media empires, which he would sell to Rupert Murdoch in 1997 for $1.9 billion. "God's plan is for His people, ladies and gentlemen, to take dominion," Robertson told viewers of his popular show *The 700 Club*, which had grown by the mid 1980s to reach millions of cable viewers. "What is dominion? Well, dominion is Lordship. He wants His people to reign and rule with Him. . . . And the Lord says, 'I'm going

to let you redeem society. . . . We are not going to stand for those coercive utopians in the Supreme Court and in Washington ruling over us any more. We're not gonna stand for it. We are going to say, "we want freedom in this country, and we want power.""""

After Jerry Falwell's Moral Majority proved unable to build a governing coalition of Christian conservatives during the Reagan administration, Pat Robertson stepped forward to lead the religious right with both the financial and communication resources of his global media empire. He hired a young political operative, Ralph Reed, to develop a grassroots strategy to take control of the Republican Party at the local level, recruiting volunteers in every county to join their Christian Coalition. But the goal was always the same: political power to exercise Christian dominion.

Robertson joined Dobson, Schlafly, Graham, Falwell, and other elders of the religious right to anoint Donald Trump heir of their decades-long organizing efforts in 2016. President Trump, in turn, appointed Oklahoma Attorney General Scott Pruitt to lead the Environmental Protection Agency. Pruitt had made a name for himself by suing the EPA on behalf of oil companies in his state that did not want their profits to be constrained by the regulations of the Clean Power Plan or the carbon emission reductions called for in the Paris Climate Accord. When Director Pruitt sat down for an interview with Robertson's CBN in 2018, he made clear that his faith drove him to fight against regulation. "The biblical world view with respect to these issues is that we have a responsibility to manage and cultivate, harvest the natural

resources that we've been blessed with to truly bless our fellow mankind."

In order to explain how he would apply Rushdoony and Robertson's dominionism, Pruitt deployed a distinction CBN had helped to popularize between a biblical worldview and secular humanism. Unlike native elders and climate scientists who see the earth's resources from a "secular" point of view, Pruitt claimed authority to exercise dominion because his vantage point was "biblical." He and the deregulated corporations he represented would "truly bless" not only themselves but all people.

Pruitt's leadership of the EPA abruptly ended in a public scandal that not even the Trump White House was willing to tolerate, but that didn't diminish in any way Christian nationalists' commitment to dominionism. As with the sex scandals that had shaken Robertson's religious broadcasting empire two decades earlier, true believers were happy to trust that the problem was with Pruitt, not with his reading of the Bible. If he wasn't able to exercise dominion faithfully, God would raise up others to subdue the earth and mine its resources according to their "biblical worldview."

READING THE BIBLE AT OAK FLAT AND STANDING ROCK

The prevalence of dominionism's "biblical worldview" in popular American Christianity is a testament to our need for more compelling ways to imagine the Christian doctrine of creation. *Time* magazine's Thomas Sancton didn't dismiss the Judeo-Christian tradition's creation account after reading biblical scholarship. He was simply reporting on the widespread

observation that Christians have been willing to bless white settler greed, even to the point of denying the science that suggests this greed could destroy the very source of our earthly life. It's no accident that, among the generation that came of age after *Time*'s year of "Endangered Planet Earth," over a third of millennials choose not to affiliate with any religious group.

Young people of faith have been drawn, however, to reread their Bibles alongside the struggle for climate justice at places like Oak Flat and Standing Rock. In these spaces where non-natives have been invited to learn what our world looks like from the perspective of colonized indigenous people, the Bible's concern for the land takes on new meaning. That God calls us to "keep" the earth (Genesis 7:3) with the same Hebrew word that Scripture uses to exhort us to "keep" God's commandments (Exodus 20:6) suggests that creation care is as important as any religious obligation. When we see that this is true, the wisdom of people who've kept the land and protected the water becomes essential to our relationship with the God who created, redeemed, and sustains us.

But as Nosie reminds visitors to Oak Flat, "90 percent of our people were exterminated." The genocide of native people wasn't carried out over the objection of Christian churches but rather by their members and with their blessing. The "Doctrine of Discovery," which originates in a fifteenth-century papal bull that gave Christian missionaries the right to take native lands and proselytize their inhabitants, is still the legal basis for US land titles. Resolution Copper is not departing from this legal tradition as they prepare to blow a hole in the

earth on Apache sacred lands. They are, like the captains of industry and their climate-science-denying enablers, carrying on the hypocritical tradition of ignoring the practical wisdom of the people who've known and kept the land.

"How can we sing the songs of the LORD while in a foreign land?" (Psalm 137:4), we learn to ask in the songbook that sits at the heart of Scripture. When we sing these songs alongside indigenous people on their occupied native lands, we hear in them the cries of colonized people who have been separated from their lands by principalities and powers that are anti-Christ. "Why does the way of the wicked prosper?" (Jeremiah 12:1), we ask with the prophet and the water protectors at Standing Rock. The trees of the field clap their hands (Isaiah 55:12) in praise of the Creator while the corporations defy the Lord's command. If we are to serve God with all our heart, mind, soul, and strength (Mark 12:30), we must decide which side we're on.

When we are drawn into the Psalter's resistance songs, we discover biblical wisdom that resonates with the ways native elders are teaching us to fight back against the violence of our oil economy. We are instructed to

> Trust in the LORD and do good;
>> dwell in the land and enjoy safe pasture.
> Take delight in the LORD,
>> and he will give you the desires of your heart.
>> (Psalm 37:3-4)

As farmers separated from their land, ancient Israelites learned to sing this song in the foreign land of Babylon, where

a narcissistic emperor who erected golden statues to himself claimed divine right to their land and their bodies. The rebellion against this occupation that they wrote into their songs was not a direct insurrection. It was, instead, a determined refusal to live by the exploitative practices of Babylon. God's people would trust the ways and wisdom of their Lord, even as Nebuchadnezzar was on the throne. They would delight in passing that wisdom on to the next generation, trusting their Creator to restore their land after Babylon's greed had run its course.

Because Wendsler Nosie sees how his people's struggle to protect their holy land at Oak Flat is connected to the struggles of other poor and oppressed people who've been harmed by white settlers' greed, he traveled to Washington, DC, in the spring of 2018 to participate in the relaunch of the Poor People's Campaign of 1968. Standing with service workers who want a living wage and mothers who want access to healthcare, Nosie shared with all of us what his people have learned through years of struggle. "Our urgent fight today is for water," he said. "Without water, there is no life."

As I listened to Nosie, I was especially struck by his insight into how we must learn to fight by standing together as one family. "What was family is now being replaced by a corporate mentality," he said, articulating the same family values that drew so many pious Christians into the pro-corporate agenda of the religious right. But just as the psalmist teaches us to "do good" that we might "dwell in the land and enjoy safe pasture," Nosie looked at the diverse gathering of people who

had come from every corner of the nation that occupies his native land and said, "Family cannot be broken."

To reread the Bible at Oak Flat and Standing Rock is sometimes to hear the good news that, even in the midst of our present exile, God has called water protectors and keepers of the land to invite us into a new family where we can learn what it means to dwell peaceably in this place.

THE POLITICS OF WATER PROTECTORS

In the midst of the 2018 midterm elections, I preached at a church in Chapel Hill, North Carolina, that has turned its entire campus into a solar farm. At a churchwide forum between morning services, we talked about the array of issues on people's minds as they prepared to vote—healthcare and immigration, voting rights and equal protection under the law. But as I listened to this particular congregation's concerns, I could tell they were informed by something more than the particular issues that impact them personally or discomfort them with the extreme rhetoric and policies of the Trump administration. "How are we building a movement that will help people recognize we are destroying the earth?" one member asked. It's an essential question for anyone seeking a moral vision for public engagement in our time.

While the wisdom of native elders and the basic facts of climate science can open our eyes to God's enduring concern for all of creation, I don't think it's an accident that congregations and communities where concern for ecological devastation are at the forefront of our minds are ones where people have made institutional commitments to sustainability—like

turning the church campus into a solar farm. For years, organizations like Interfaith Power and Light have encouraged faith communities to make their buildings carbon neutral through efficiency audits and transition to alternative energy sources. Given the incredible amount of carbon emissions from the US military (our single biggest source), power grids, transportation, and industry, the work of transitioning a single building to be carbon neutral can seem futile. But my experience with this particular congregation was a reminder that everything we do together in faith communities is a liturgy shaping our imagination. People who've done the work to go green at church have also learned to think about how their votes will or will not lead to policies that promise a more sustainable future.

When it comes to loving our poorest and most vulnerable neighbors, few issues are more important than ecological devastation. It's long been true that corporations and governments respond to NIMBY (not in my backyard) campaigns by following the path of least resistance to poor communities. Landfills, superfund sites, and extractive industries almost always end up in our poorest neighborhoods, all but guaranteeing that property values will continue to stay low. But as we witness the catastrophic realities of global climate change in real time, it's also increasingly clear that the poor suffer first from the storms and fires that rage at historic levels. When hurricane warnings mandate evacuation, people without reliable transportation or expendable income to stay in a hotel elsewhere are always the last to leave. When the waters rise, their homes in low-lying areas are often the first to be destroyed.

Organizations such as 350.org and Climate Reality are helping to build a movement for ecological justice that puts a face on the real costs of climate change and compels politicians to answer for how they vote on corporate regulations, environmental policy, energy plans, and military spending that directly impacts the health and well-being of the earth that sustains us all. For too long, the "corporate mentality" that Nosie warns against has dominated public thought about what it means for the economy to do well. While some Republicans have flat out denied the warnings of climate science, many Democrats have conceded that short-term economic gains must be prioritized over long-term sustainability. But celebrating the continued rise of the Dow Jones average in an economy addicted to oil is like bragging that your car can run 140 miles per hour while you drive it off a cliff.

Nosie is right: we need a new imagination for what health and well-being mean in our common life. And none of our existing party structures are able to give it to us. Perhaps more than any other single issue, our global ecological crisis makes clear how deeply we need a moral revolution of values to shift public conversation to issues that elders like Nosie have been trying to point to all along.

LIVE BY THE SWORD, DIE BY THE SWORD

Each morning at 6:00 a.m., Basir Bita wakes up to eat breakfast with his wife before he takes a short walk from their apartment to his office. In many ways, his routine is not unlike that of most young professionals in New York City, Chicago, or Durham, North Carolina, where I live—except that Bita is both more religious and more socially conservative than most millennials in urban America. He married young. He has made life choices to prioritize family. Each morning on his walk to work, he tells me that he repeats a simple prayer: "God, please save me today."

The words of Bita's prayer are familiar, even though he says them with a distinct accent over a Skype connection that cuts out intermittently. Bita is at home in Kabul, Afghanistan, trying to explain the only reality he has ever really known in a country that has been a war zone since 2001. "There's always hesitation in my heart whether I'll be able to come home alive," he says matter-of-factly. For Bita, salvation isn't something to consider during the pastor's sermon on a Sunday

morning. "God, please save me" is the prayer of a young man who knows too well the real cost of war.

I was a college student in September of 2001 when a professor knocked on our classroom door to tell us that a plane had flown into the World Trade Center. We walked out of class, stood in front of the TV in the lobby, and watched the second plane fly into the tower. Nine days later, President George W. Bush addressed a joint session of Congress. "Americans should not expect one battle, but a lengthy campaign unlike any other we have ever seen," the president said. The "war on terror" had already begun.

The war that Bita prays to be saved from each morning is the longest and most expensive military campaign in US history. America has been at war since September of 2001— in Afghanistan and Iraq, for sure, but also in dozens of other countries where the US military has carried out drone strikes, supported the military actions of other governments, and undertaken covert operations in the name of stopping terrorism. With bipartisan support, Congress has consistently increased military spending, year after year, approving a $716 billion budget for 2019, which devotes well over half of every discretionary tax dollar to military spending. From the other side of the world, Bita tells me how the war that has impoverished my country has destabilized his. "At first, many Afghans believed the US was coming to help," he says, "but most Afghans increasingly agree that the US invaded." The troops, they have come to realize, are there to stay.

This is an assessment Bita and other Afghans share with Matthew Hoh, a US Army and Foreign Service veteran who

served in both Iraq and Afghanistan before receiving an appointment in 2009 as the Senior Civilian Representative of the US government in Afghanistan's Zabul Province. Five months after he assumed the post, Hoh was the first US official to resign his post in Afghanistan as a protest against the war on terror. "I find specious the reasons we ask for bloodshed and sacrifice from our young men and women in Afghanistan," he wrote to his supervisor, the director general of the Foreign Service. Like Bita, Hoh had come to doubt that the US military's expressed purpose of ridding Afghanistan of the terrorist group al-Qaeda was the real reason for their continued presence there when there were three times as many members of al-Qaeda across the border in Pakistan in 2009. If eight years of military presence hadn't helped stabilize the country, would another two or ten? Hoh couldn't continue to serve in Afghanistan because, like Bita, he had ceased to believe that the US military's strategy included an exit plan.

In his resignation letter, Hoh noted the bloodshed and sacrifice of the American soldiers who also bear the wounds of an unjust war. Hoh knew the statistics—that more US military personnel die from suicide each year than from combat. But he also knew the growing doubts in his own mind, which had driven him to drink too much for years. On his worst days, those thoughts led him to ask whether it might not be better to put a pistol in his mouth and silence the irreconcilable conflict in his mind. Seven years later, after Hoh had resigned, attended to his own healing, and visited Afghanistan as a Veteran for Peace, he told me, "It was taking part in the killing that changed me—that and the lies." When I

replied that he sounded like someone who had experienced a conversion, Hoh recounted the experience of watching an elderly woman on a train apologize to a young man in uniform for not stopping to thank him for his service. She was fifty years his senior and had no doubt served her family, community, and country throughout her life, Hoh noted. But this woman thought she had neglected her duty when she failed to thank a young man in uniform.

Hoh told the story because he wanted to be clear about what he had been saved from. "Our state religion is militarism," he said, "but to me it had come to mean death."

HOW MILITARISM BECAME A FAITH-BASED BUSINESS

In her book *American Evangelicals and the U.S. Military*, historian Anne C. Loveland notes that most evangelicals in the early twentieth century considered the military an immoral institution, rife with temptations for young men and lacking moral leadership among its ranks. Most chaplains in the military were from mainline Protestant denominations and the Roman Catholic Church. In evangelicals' estimation, their ministries had done little to mitigate the debauchery of an unholy institution. After World War II, as Carl Henry, Billy Graham, and the National Association of Evangelicals (NAE) led the charge to legitimize evangelical faith and increase its influence in public life, a number of new ministries formed with the military as their mission field. From Officers Christian Fellowship (OCF) meetings to Navigators Bible studies, evangelicals started investing in a Christianity that would make the military its own.

By the 1970s, when the military was embroiled in the Vietnam War, the number of self-identified evangelical troops had grown considerably. As churches back home were divided by the political backlash against the civil rights movement, the women's rights movement, the War on Poverty, and the war in Vietnam, soldiers in Southeast Asia began to realize that the same dividing lines ran through their ranks. Leaders of mainline churches, which still ordained the majority of military chaplains, were openly critical of the Vietnam War while conservative white evangelicals stood by the troops, insisting that they were heroes in the global struggle against communism. As the young men of the Vietnam generation rose through the ranks of the military, its leadership increasingly identified with the faith that presented as "pro-military." By the beginning of the twenty-first century, two-thirds of all military chaplains self-identified as evangelical or Pentecostal.

Historians like Loveland aren't the only observers who noted this shift in the 1970s and 1980s. Soldiers who served in the military over the past two generations noticed a change as well. A military veteran who was serving in the US Senate in 2009 spoke to a journalist on condition of anonymity, sharing his insight into why the shift to evangelical faith was so compelling to many white men in the military.

Although the military was integrated before much of the United States, he points out, it almost split along racial lines, particularly in the last days of Vietnam. If the military was to rebuild itself, the Southern white

men at the heart of its warrior culture had to come to an understanding of themselves based on something other than skin color. Many, says the senator, turned toward religion, particularly fundamentalist evangelical Christianity—a tradition that, despite its particularly potent legacy of racism, reoriented itself during the post–civil rights era as a religion of "reconciliation" between the races. . . . "They replaced race with religion," says the senator. "The principle remains the same—an identity built on being separate from a society viewed as weak and corrupt."

By the time al-Qaeda had coordinated its terror attacks in 2001, evangelicals who understood themselves to be set apart to promote and defend an exceptional identity had risen to the highest ranks of the US military. When their commander in chief called them into battle against the forces of evil, they heard the battle cry for a modern day crusade. Lt. Gen. William G. "Jerry" Boykin, former commander of the Army's top-secret Delta Force unit, went on a preaching tour in uniform, claiming that terrorists hate America because it is a Christian nation, and that "we in the army of God . . . have been raised up for such a time as this." Testifying about his own experiences with a Somali warlord, Boykin claimed that his confidence and determination to prevail had come from his faith. "I knew my God was bigger than his. I knew that my God was a real God and his was an idol."

Though not the official position of the military, Boykin's public claims were not seen as disqualifying by his superiors.

In the fall of 2003, two years after Bush declared the war on terror a global struggle of good versus evil, Boykin was appointed to serve in the Pentagon as deputy undersecretary of defense for intelligence.

That same year, the US military invaded Iraq. Just before Saddam Hussein's regime fell to US troops in March of 2003, I traveled to Iraq with the Christian Peacemaker Teams (CPT). Our mission was twofold: to tell Iraqis that, as Christians, we didn't want our country to rain fire on them and to witness what was happening on the ground as our nation's military waged a "shock-and-awe" campaign from the sky. As the only Americans on the streets of Baghdad, we also heard the messages that everyday Iraqis hoped we would relay to people back home. I wrote them all down in a little notebook, but one sticks in my memory even now. "Tell Mr. Bush that his cowboy culture will never defeat our civilization," a young man said to me. Even before the troops had made it to his city, he understood what Bita would tell me sixteen years later— the same thing Hoh would come to see after a crisis of conscience: the people quoting their Bible in support of this crusade weren't following the Palestinian rabbi named Jesus but a long tradition of American cowboys.

THE COWBOY'S PROMISE OF FREEDOM

America's cowboy stands in contrast to the Bible's good shepherd. Throughout Scripture, the good shepherd is a metaphor for moral leadership, taken from daily life in Middle Eastern culture. From the promise of economic security for God's people—"He makes me lie down in green pastures"

(Psalm 23:2)—to the image of true authority—"My sheep listen to my voice" (John 10:27), the shepherd offers a model of leadership. Muslims remember that the Prophet Muhammad said, "There was no prophet who was not a shepherd." Good shepherds know the land and are known by their sheep. They are alert to dangers, take care to provide for their flocks, and do it all under God's big sky, ever aware that human freedom is dependent on the green pastures and still waters, which are a gift and not an achievement.

The American cowboy is a contradiction of this image—and not only in the mind of the young man I met on the streets of Baghdad. Fiercely independent, the cowboy embodies the notion that freedom must be achieved by courageous men who subdue the land and fight its native inhabitants. In place of the shepherd's rod and staff, the cowboy has a pistol in his holster. He is the heir of white European settlers who sailed west to find a freedom that entailed violence against native people and enslaved Africans. Their Southern slaveholding representatives demanded a Second Amendment to the US Constitution, guaranteeing them the right to bear arms—a pistol in the holster, a rifle over the door. In the event that enslaved people chose to rebel or join forces with Native Americans, an armed citizenry could form militias to put them down.

But the violence did not end there. Western expansion drove native people on a Trail of Tears. When they encountered other native tribes, adherents to the concept of manifest destiny fought them also. Cowboys and Indians became the stuff of American myth and child's play. If the cowboy

could subdue the West, why not the whole world? Westward expansion did not end at the West Coast but continued to Hawaii and Guam, the Philippines, Japan, and Korea. Today, there are nearly eight hundred US military bases in seventy countries around the world. If the American cowboy could make the world safe for democracy, then those who saw themselves in him believed their notion of freedom might subdue the whole world.

Political leaders from both major US parties asserted that America's notion of freedom—the cowboy's myth—was exceptional. After World War II, as evangelicals were claiming a role in American public life, many religious leaders agreed that American freedom was not only exceptional but godly. "In God We Trust" was stamped on US currency and "under God" was added to the pledge of allegiance to sanctify American democracy over and against "godless communism." The postwar period of the late 1940s and 1950s, when America became a global superpower, is still celebrated as a heyday of American Christianity.

But as congregations were busy building education wings in the new suburbs of America's cities, many church teachers seemed to forget that the Bible tells the story of a people who are exceptional in the history of the world because they survived for thousands of years *without* a standing army. When Abraham was a wandering Aramean, when Israel was in Egypt land, when God's people went into exile under various imperial regimes and were later scattered in diaspora, they did not have a leader with a pistol at his side. Even when, after demanding a king like other nations, God's people did have

soldiers and an army for a brief time, political leaders in ancient Israel were celebrated not for their military prowess but for their devotion to God. David, the shepherd-king who slew Goliath with the same slingshot he used to protect sheep in the field, wrote a victory song that boasted, "Some trust in chariots and some in horses, but we trust in the name of the LORD our God" (Psalm 20:7).

Still, while the good shepherd and the cowboy are contradictory metaphors, this hasn't kept American Christians from using Scripture to justify militarism. Once the "city on a hill" no longer consisted of the disciples who practice the Sermon on the Mount but rather the heirs of American exceptionalism, then each story of God's willingness to stand on the side of a poor and oppressed people in Scripture could be twisted to justify the violence of an empire that believes itself to be God-ordained. Didn't God deliver Jericho into the hands of the Israelites? Then American soldiers, too, can pray for victory at Wounded Knee or in Baghdad. Didn't Jesus tell Peter to make sure he had a sword? Then an individual needs a gun to defend his home, and a nation must defend its borders. Such commonsense realism finds prooftexts to back up its foregone conclusion.

In the Christian tradition, arguments for military action are most often made in terms of the just-war tradition. Over and against the early Christian tradition, which held almost universally that participation in the Roman military was sin, theologians within Christendom, from Saint Augustine to the present, developed language to discern when Christians could justify the limited use of violence for defense of

neighbor and the prevention of some greater harm. The very existence of the just-war tradition suggests that war-making presents a real moral problem to people who follow the teachings of Jesus. Some scholars of the tradition have argued that, in practice, it was almost always deployed in the Middle Ages to restrain the violence of Christian princes who could be persuaded that some people (priests, monks, women, and children) should never fight and some days (holidays, saints' days, every Sunday) should be free of violence. But this is not how the just-war tradition is deployed by Christian nationalists who confuse Jesus with America's cowboy. In their hands, it quickly becomes a justify-any-war tradition.

Case in point: in 2018, when Representative Matt Shea was running for reelection to the Washington state legislature, his four-page pamphlet "Biblical Basis for War" was leaked to the press and reported to the FBI by local law enforcement. Spokane County Sheriff Ozzie Knezovich told the *Seattle Times* that Shea's manifesto, which includes the instructions "if they do not yield—kill all males," is not "a Sunday School project or an academic study. It is a 'how to' manual consistent with the ideology and operating philosophy of the Christian Identity/Aryan Nations movement and the Redoubt movement of the 1990s." Even still, Shea won reelection to his seat in the statehouse.

Though Shea's vision for a "Christian nation" that enforces "biblical law" through military violence is extreme, even among many pro-military Christians, the fact that he felt emboldened to defend his position as chair of the Republican caucus in his state during an election season reflects the

extent to which the just-war tradition has been twisted to justify violence rather than restrain it. In the service of cowboy culture, faith has increasingly become a mallet the religious right uses to beat the drums of war.

SINGING A BETTER SONG

Long before Matthew Hoh's crisis of conscience, another decorated war veteran, President Dwight D. Eisenhower, warned his fellow Americans that "we must guard against the acquisition of unwarranted influence, whether sought or unsought, by the military-industrial complex." To the companies that benefit from war-making, Eisenhower knew that the business of a crusade would be irresistible. "The potential for the disastrous rise of misplaced power exists and will persist," he said in 1961. With a steady beat, those who profit from war have persisted, marching on toward more weapons and new frontiers in a world that feels increasingly less safe. From the national anthem at football games to the games children play on video consoles in their homes, militarism shapes the cadence of daily life in America.

When we sat down to talk in the fall of 2017, Hoh told me that the songs he learned from the movements resisting militarism give him hope. Formed by his military training and academic study, Hoh struck me as a practical guy. He knows how the military-industrial complex works, and he understands from personal experience how hard it is to resist it. Within the daily rhythms of military life, Hoh felt how the senseless violence he was caught up in, the killing and the lies, became normal—routine even.

As a counterrhythm to the drum beat of war, the songs of war resisters offered another imagination—a way of being, both in war zones and at home, in which the default isn't the civil religion of militarism. Like Bita on the streets of Kabul, Hoh realized that he needed to be saved from the inexorable violence of a system that formed and affirmed him as a warrior. He needed a new theme song for his life—a liturgy to tell him who he is and where he is going.

For much of Christian history, people who reflect on war and peace have presented the Christian tradition as a choice between pacifism and the just-war tradition. While those ways of thinking about moral choices in a broken, violent world remain important, a more fundamental claim of Christian faith challenges America's militarism: namely, the conviction at the heart of the church's oldest known song, found in Philippians 2.

And being found in appearance as a man,
   he humbled himself
   by becoming obedient to death—
      even death on a cross!

Therefore God exalted him to the highest place
   and gave him the name that is above every name,
that at the name of Jesus every knee should bow,
   in heaven and on earth and under the earth,
and every tongue acknowledge that Jesus Christ is Lord,
   to the glory of God the Father.
   (Philippians 2:8-11)

Like Hoh in twenty-first-century America, Christians in the early church learned to sing their hope in this Christ

hymn. Echoing biblical songs that had been passed down to them from the psalmists, Hannah, and Miriam, this hymn offered the early church a counterrhythm to the liturgy of the Roman Empire, which proclaimed on its coinage and in its public ceremonies, "Caesar is Lord!" Early Christians could not serve in the Roman army because singing "Jesus Christ is Lord" was a more direct defiance of Rome's civil religion than taking a knee at an NFL football game is in America. Their song put them out of step with Roman militarism.

Once we begin to hear this counterrhythm in Scripture, we can see how much of Scripture is the story of people learning to walk in step with the God who chooses fascination over force. This doesn't make the stories any less violent. Pharaoh's entire army drowns in the Red Sea as Israel comes out of Egypt, just as Goliath drops dead when he's struck by David's smooth stone and the Amalekites kill one another in confusion when Gideon's army surprises them with trumpets, clay jars, and lamps. The Bible's war stories are filled with the tragedy of human struggle. But they do not valorize military might—they mock it. Tales of shepherd boys and tiny armies winning the battle caution against our trust in war-room strategy and military might. They are the stories of the people who sing, "Why do the nations conspire and the peoples plot in vain?" (Psalm 2:1).

Jesus embodies the humility of Scripture's song when he is confronted by a Roman legion in the Garden of Gethsemane. They come to take him before the governing authorities and execute him as an enemy combatant. We sometimes forget that Jesus taught among people living under occupation

whose personal prayers were more like Bita's in Kabul than those of the average Christian in America. "God, save me today," was an existential cry. Peter believed that Jesus was leading the political movement that would save him and his people from Roman occupation. He'd left everything to work for his Messiah's campaign. When occupying forces showed up to arrest Jesus, Peter drew his sword to fight back.

If militarism had any capacity to save us, this would have been its moment. Just days earlier, Jesus' supporters had swamped the capital city to perform a triumphal entry—first-century Palestine's equivalent of an Inauguration Day parade. Everyone knew Jesus had popular appeal. Peter was ready to lead the masses in a revolution that would drive out the enemy and establish biblical law. But Jesus said, "All who draw the sword will die by the sword" (Matthew 26:52). When Jesus had the chance to lead a coup and take control, he opted not to.

THE NECESSITY OF TURNING FROM MILITARISM

As a man living under British occupation, first in South Africa and later in India, Mahatma Gandhi was drawn to the teachings of Jesus. When Jesus told Peter to put his sword away, Gandhi understood that Christ was demonstrating faith in a different kind of power. Experimenting in the political power of truth-force, Gandhi led a nonviolent movement that ultimately liberated India from British rule and inspired African Americans in the South to confront Jim Crow. After a nonviolent bus boycott elevated the Reverend Dr. Martin Luther King Jr. to a national platform for civil rights leadership, King understood

that, as a preacher, his job wasn't only to advocate for the rights of people like him. King spoke out against militarism because he knew it hurt everyone. Our choice today, he taught, is "either nonviolence or nonexistence."

The prophetic call to turn from a spiral of violence that could easily destroy the whole world isn't the same as the age-old debate between just war and pacifism. In practical terms, a moral movement against the idolatry of militarism cannot be for ideological pacifists alone. While the wisdom of peace churches and those who have practiced nonviolence for centuries is important, we also need Veterans for Peace and newer groups like About Face, an organization founded by veterans of the so-called war on terror in Iraq and Afghanistan to turn the United States 180 degrees from militarism toward just-peace building. Without neglecting the real security threats of our world or getting lost in arguments about self-defense, today's moral movement must follow the leadership of people like Hoh and Bita, who know the horrors of war, toward policies that share global power, de-escalate tensions, and challenge imperial abuses.

Multiple nations in our world today have nuclear arsenals that could destroy us all several times over. But in a democratic society we have the capacity to rethink how the nearly unimaginable sums of money we waste on military spending could be reappropriated to ensure "domestic tranquility" and "provide for the common defense," purposes stated in the Preamble to the US Constitution. We could accomplish this by creating green jobs for a new economy; rebuilding America's infrastructure; investing in public education, healthcare, and

affordable housing; and ensuring that working people earn a living wage to support their families. When politicians are pressed on these issues, they usually reply, "But how would we pay for it?" The US government could make significant strides in all these areas without abandoning any military personnel if it reduced the Pentagon's budget by 10 percent and rethought what it means to ensure peace at home and abroad. People who have been deployed know the military's capacity to engage nonmilitaristic missions. It's not resources we lack but an imagination.

I asked Basir Bita, who faces the violence of America's militarism every day on the streets of Kabul, what he would ask of voters in the United States. "The US needs an amendment to make nonviolence part of its Constitution," Bita said. My first thought was that America would have to become a very different country before we could write nonviolence into our Constitution. But then it occurred to me that Bita may see the choice we face more clearly than I do. If he and Hoh—if King and Eisenhower—are right, then the United States may very well cease to exist if we don't become the kind of country that makes nonviolence a fundamental commitment of our social contract. As strange as it sounds to our ears, the Bible's song may offer the cadence that makes it possible to hear Bita's cry and turn from habits that will destroy us all. Those of us who practice this song in lives of worship have an obligation to share it with the world.

If this seems impractical, history may ground us. At the end of April in 1962, at the height of the Cold War between the United States and the USSR, over a thousand Quakers held

a vigil for peace and world order outside the White House and the State Department. In a response that seems unimaginable today, President John F. Kennedy invited a delegation of six protestors into the Oval Office for conversation. He wanted to hear their ideas for de-escalating the war. Appealing to language Kennedy had used in his speech to the United Nations, the Quakers proposed investing in the "peace race" by funding a feeding program for China, citing Jesus' words, "If your enemy is hungry, feed him." They argued for nuclear disarmament, criticizing Kennedy for appointing hawkish conservatives to the advisory board of the Arms Control and Disarmament Agency. Kennedy countered that, while he agreed with the goal of disarmament, he knew he would never be able to bring his military leadership along unless skeptical members of the board became convinced of the need. Then, with a smile, Kennedy asked the moral activists, "You do believe in redemption, don't you?"

After their meeting, the six Quaker activists were impressed by the president's willingness to listen to them. A veteran of World War II, Kennedy had lost close friends, a brother, and a brother-in-law to war. While he was honest about his nation's commitment to militarism, he was also open—eager, even—to find another way. After the near disaster of the Cuban Missile Crisis later that same year, Kennedy secretly reached out to his enemy, Nikita Khrushchev, and began pursuing redemption in practical terms through a relationship of mutual disarmament that would have changed world history. "Without losing sight of our own best hopes in this country," his biographer James Douglass writes, "he began to home in,

with his new partner, Nikita Khrushchev, on the hope of peace
for everyone on this earth—Russians, Americans, Cubans,
Vietnamese, Indonesians, everyone—no exceptions. He made
that commitment to life at the cost of his own."

History is there to remind us that the stakes of turning
from militarism are high. But the costs of not turning are
much higher. If a president of the United States was able to
make an about-face, almost entirely on his own, a moral
movement can hold out hope that we, too, might demonstrate an equal commitment to life in our time. In fact, anything less is a failure to trust that Jesus has saved the world
from the sin that leads to death.

A REVOLUTION OF VALUES

For more than four decades, some of the richest and most powerful people in America invested their political hope in winning the allegiance of people like me. Born on the Saturday after Ronald Reagan was elected president of the United States, I grew up in a Southern Baptist church in North Carolina's tobacco country where "family values" served as a summary statement for all that my people held dear. When we gathered in a brick church house from our small farms on slopes of red clay, we were a people sustained by mothers who worked as public school teachers, fathers who'd taken factory jobs in the city, FHA loans, USDA subsidies, and Bible stories that lifted us up with the reminder that "if God is for us, who can be against us?" (Romans 8:31).

Though we were small players in the American story, my people enjoyed the nostalgic nod to our way of life on reruns of *The Andy Griffith Show*. But Jerry Falwell shared with us a bolder vision in his 1980 manifesto, *Listen, America!* As he toured the country and appeared on television throughout the 1980 campaign season, the preacher who looked and

talked like us called for "a coalition of God-fearing, moral
Americans to represent our convictions to our government."
The same Sunday our pastor announced my birth in the foot-
hills of North Carolina, Falwell stood in the pulpit at Thomas
Road Baptist Church in Lynchburg, Virginia, thanked God for
Reagan's victory, and noted the calls from "important people"
who had also been calling all week to congratulate their pastor.
I grew up in the heyday of the Moral Majority movement,
increasingly learning along with my people how we could put
faith into action and discover our real purpose by standing
up for moral values and backing the Republican Party.

An earnest and ambitious kid, I walked the aisle on a
Sunday morning to accept Jesus Christ as my personal Lord
and Savior when I was seven years old. I memorized Bible
verses in the King James Version and never missed a Sunday
school lesson. I wanted to do all that I could for Jesus so I set
my sights on becoming president of the United States.

I felt empowered as part of a "coalition of God-fearing,
moral Americans" whenever I listened to Christian radio or
read the pamphlets that the burgeoning industry of religious
right ministries provided free of charge. But I didn't actually
know anyone with connections in Washington, DC. The
journey from our little Southern Baptist church to the White
House was a "long row to hoe," as we said in tobacco country.
Still, I was eager to get started by the time I got to junior high
school. I just needed some place to begin.

My grandfather, who drove a Greyhound bus, gave me a
ride to DC when I had a couple of unexpected snow days in
junior high school. Finding our way to the Capitol, we entered

the Senate gallery and I noticed, on the floor below, young people like myself, dressed in blue blazers. I asked a security guard who they were, and he told me about the US Senate page program. I went home and wrote letters until I got myself appointed as a page to Strom Thurmond, president pro tempore of the US Senate.

By the time I got to Capitol Hill, delighted at the thought that I was diving into the righteous work my people had prayed and voted for, Pat Robertson's Christian Coalition had taken up the baton of moral leadership in American public life. Their man in Washington, Ralph Reed, didn't look much older than me. But I had a lot to learn. As I did my homework, I read about Strom Thurmond's campaign as the Dixiecrat candidate for president in 1948 and his record filibuster of the Civil Rights Act of 1957. Sympathetic biographies framed Thurmond as a man who had changed with his times, but I recalled how, at our first meeting, he had looked me in the eye and warned me to take care of myself because Washington was a dangerous town. "Chocolate City," as the African American majority in the District called it, had civil rights veteran Marion Barry as its mayor. The senator from South Carolina wasn't sure he or I was safe in a place like this.

The closer I got to the politics of the religious right, the more its language of moral values began to ring hollow. After I showed up early for my first weekly Bible study at the Senate, I noticed that none of my colleagues from Thurmond's office ever arrived. Back at the office, I learned to sign form responses to the mail-in campaigns organized by groups whose newsletters I'd read. As I watched staff entertain lobbyists

and power brokers, I experienced the disillusionment that is common to any young idealist. Politics was messy. But as I sat in committee meetings and listened to the policies we were working for, I also realized my problem wasn't just with the messiness of our means. I was troubled by the ends we were working toward.

While abstract arguments against big government had made sense to me, the prioritization of military spending over education and healthcare didn't feel pro-life. While so many families in America struggled to make ends meet, including folks I knew back in North Carolina, we were advocating tax breaks and deregulation to boost the bottom line of corporations that rewarded investors rather than workers. When it came to policy, pro-life and pro-family politicians weren't in fact doing much to help families or life flourish. It wasn't just that politics involved complex negotiations; I learned how, in daily practice, the negotiations carried out in the name of family values were actually making it more difficult for many families to get by—especially poor, minority, and immigrant families.

Before I left Washington, DC, in the fall of 1997, I'd come to a vocational dead end. The religious right had offered me a way to be Christian in public life, but its politics didn't reflect what I knew and valued. I didn't know then the long and complicated story of how the John Birch Society and the eugenics movement, the Southern segregationists and the Koch-funded hypercapitalists had worked together to build a coalition that would play on fear and moral indignation to grab and cling to political power. But I knew it didn't feel right. My soul was

hungry for a better way to be Christian in public, but I didn't know where I could find it.

THE POWER OF MORAL NARRATIVES

Two decades after my personal crisis in the religious right, presidential candidate Donald Trump put the moral quandary of the family values movement in stark relief for all to see. An embodiment of materialistic values, the real estate developer and self-promoter did not pretend piety. Trump flouted his wealth, claimed no need for forgiveness, and played to racial fears with a brashness that would have made the Strom Thurmond I knew cringe. Announcing his candidacy in the lobby of Trump Tower, the reality TV star channeled the anger that his birther conspiracy had fueled through eight years of resistance to America's first black president. Trump didn't sound like a politician; he sounded like an aggrieved Fox News commentator.

> The U.S. has become a dumping ground for everybody else's problems. . . .
>
> When Mexico sends its people, they're not sending their best. . . . They're sending people that have lots of problems, and they're bringing those problems with us. They're bringing drugs. They're bringing crime. They're rapists. . . .
>
> It's coming from more than Mexico. It's coming from all over South and Latin America, and it's coming probably—probably—from the Middle East. But we don't know. Because we have no protection and we have

no competence, we don't know what's happening. And it's got to stop and it's got to stop fast.

To most Americans and auditors around the world, candidate Donald Trump sounded like a dangerous demagogue. But not to white evangelicals who had been shaped by forty years of messaging from the religious right. They heard Trump speak with the clarity of a televangelist to denounce the Obama administration. "We have people that are morally corrupt," he said in a cadence reminiscent of the preacher from their church. Over and against black and brown people who are seen as a threat to "our values," Trump offered a path to redemption. Like Reagan before him, he would "Make America Great Again."

In *The Faith of Donald J. Trump*, a self-styled "spiritual biography" of President Trump, CBN correspondent David Brody and Liberty University vice president Scott Lamb explain why their subject, who has often been framed as an unlikely champion of the religious right, was in fact the kind of leader that the pro-life/pro-family coalition built a movement to support. "For those with ears to hear," Brody and Lamb write, "Trump launched his campaign with moral argumentation." To children of the Moral Majority, Trump's brand of authoritarianism met an almost spiritual need. In a world of confusion, it offered a moral narrative to make them feel safe.

However misguided their morality, Brody and Lamb are right about the power of moral narratives. Through the bitter and violent struggle in American public life that climaxed in a bloody Civil War, the nineteenth century's abolitionist

movement claimed the moral narrative in America. Building over the course of three long decades, it ultimately persuaded President Abraham Lincoln and a majority of the Congress that they could not simply preserve the Union; they also had to abolish slavery and lead the nation in an act of public repentance from the sin of allowing people to be owned as chattel property.

Abolitionism's moral narrative sustained Reconstruction in the South for a decade, but it was challenged by a counter-narrative—one that sounds strangely familiar alongside Trump's rhetoric of redemption. Preachers who had defended slavery before the war did not repent of slaveholder religion when they denounced disunion. Instead, they preached against the immorality of corruption and prayed for redemption from "Negro rule." United Methodist minister Linus Parker, who would go one to serve as a bishop for his denomination, contended that "any state that is Africanized is bound to go down." This wasn't a factual claim to be supported by historical or empirical evidence any more than Trump's claim about the United States becoming a "dumping ground." It was, instead, a moral narrative that appealed to the common sense of white men. Parker continued, "No sensible man, not blinded by political prejudice and religious fanaticism, will deny that the political control of the Southern States should be in the hands of the white people." Thus had Linus Parker's God ordained it, and thus would it be if the God-fearing people of the South were willing to fight for righteousness.

Bryan Stevenson, founder of the Equal Justice Initiative and the Legacy Museum in Montgomery, Alabama, often

notes that the North won the Civil War but the South won the narrative war. They won it by claiming the moral narrative and retelling the story of Reconstruction as an era of corruption and immorality from which the godly (white) people of the South had to be redeemed. America endured eight decades of cruel Jim Crow rule before a movement with the moral force of abolitionism, the civil rights movement, amassed enough popular appeal to challenge the false narrative of Redemption. But Rev. Dr. Martin Luther King Jr. wasn't creating a moral narrative out of nothing when he talked about a "revolution of values." He was reaching back to the moral narrative of Frederick Douglass, William Lloyd Garrison, Sojourner Truth, Angelina Grimké, and so many others. Dr. King, along with the broader civil and human rights movements of the 1960s, reclaimed the moral narrative in America. He insisted on nothing less than a Second Reconstruction as the nation looked toward the bicentennial of its experiment in democracy. With the power of this moral narrative, he held out hope that we might yet become the multiethnic democracy we'd never yet been while insisting that we face the reality of the promissory note that had bounced for so many Americans.

But the backlash against a Second Reconstruction—the formation of the religious right that this book has chronicled—also understood the power of moral narratives. Like the Redemption movement of the 1870s, it framed Black Power as lawlessness, women's rights as an assault on families, and government regulation as corruption. Half a decade after the *Roe v. Wade* decision, New Right organizers discovered

in the unborn a nameless victim whose rights they could champion while pushing back on the Warren Court's expansion of Fourteenth Amendment protections. Jerry Falwell's Moral Majority afforded them an opportunity to take the high ground and reclaim the moral narrative.

Given the history of this struggle over the moral narrative in American public life, a president who always hits back is, in many ways, what the religious right has been working toward for four decades. During the 2016 campaign, Rev. Robert Jeffress of First Baptist Church in Dallas, Texas, explained to NPR's Michel Martin why he appreciated Trump's brash demeanor and tough talk. "I don't want some meek and mild leader or somebody who's going to turn the other cheek. I've said I want the meanest, toughest SOB I can find to protect this nation." If the president's language is a little coarse or his personal life a bit messy, so be it, white evangelicals reason. People who've internalized the moral narrative of Redemption through decades of sermons, radio talk shows, magazine articles, and Christian TV see a champion of moral values in Donald Trump. Their faith doesn't chasten their enthusiasm for authoritarian politics. It quickens it.

THE BIBLE TURNED AGAINST ITSELF

Within the imagination of the religious right, the moral narrative of America's redemption from the corruption of its first black president is presented as a "biblical worldview." Any alternative perspective is necessarily evidence of a secular worldview and, quite possibly, atheism. True believers of this mythology cannot be swayed by policy experts, independent

journalism, or the arguments of political opponents. Appeals to facts, history, and reason are in and of themselves an affront to faith in the moral narrative that lifts up Trump and his allies as champions of good while demonizing anyone who challenges them as the enemies of righteousness.

Recall Rev. Robert Dabney's plan for resisting abolitionists in the nineteenth century, described in chapter one of this book. Against a moral argument, he insisted, it is necessary "to push the Bible argument continually, drive abolitionism to the wall, and compel it to assume an anti-Christian position." Christian nationalists do not want to discuss what the Bible actually says about voting rights and immigration, poverty, and peace. Instead, they use their false moral narrative to talk about people who disagree with them as enemies of the Bible. Rather than read Scripture as a story to shape our imagination in ongoing discernment, they deploy it as a defense against moral arguments for love of neighbor through public policy. By endeavoring to "push the Bible argument continually," they effectually turn the Good Book against its expressed purpose and end.

This is not to say that Christians who support the religious right and its institutions do not care about the Bible. They do. They frequent Bible bookstores where an array of multimedia products, greeting cards, and home decor are marketed. They use those products to host Bible studies in their homes, churches, country club dining rooms, and boardrooms at work. They listen to podcasts about a "biblical worldview," attend "Bible-believing" churches, and spend personal time meditating on selections from Scripture. But in all of this,

they are inoculated against the Bible's radical imagination for public engagement rather than immersed in it.

This is no accident. Political operatives who know the power of moral narratives spent decades investing in an infrastructure that would create a cultural world to constantly reinforce the misreadings of Scripture that prop up their politicians. They were not the first to do this. We can still find in the theological libraries of the United States both the scholarly treatises and the popular sermons that promoted slaveholder religion in the nineteenth century. If we go back further, we can read how the Bible was used to justify colonization, crusades, inquisitions, and imperial domination that are widely condemned today.

After I left Strom Thurmond's office and my ambitions to climb the ladder of the religious right, I went to Germany as a "young ambassador" of the United States through an exchange program that the State Department has overseen since World War II. I spent that year learning what we mean when we remember the Holocaust and say, "Never again." As I listened to stories about the rise of the Nazi Party in the 1930s and met people who had been recruited into the *Hitlerjugend* as preteens, I realized how something that seemed so obviously evil in my history classes had been presented as a righteous good by fascist Christians. An elder in the community where I lived broke down in tears as he described to me the pride he felt saluting Hitler and standing up for his nation as a twelve-year-old boy. The swastika at the center of the flag of the *Hitlerjugend* was a Christian cross, he reminded me. When he and his friends marched in nationalist parades,

they thought they were doing their Christian duty. And if they had been old enough, he knew, they would have done their part to deliver Jewish neighbors to the ovens.

"Woe to you, teachers," Jesus says to all who use a "biblical worldview" to cover for systems that exploit the poor, ignore the cries of the oppressed, and reduce the gospel to something that challenges human hearts but not our public life. "On the outside you appear to people as righteous," Jesus says, "but on the inside you are full of hypocrisy and wickedness" (Matthew 23:27-28). Jesus reserves his sharpest rebuke for religious leaders who deploy a false moral narrative to cover for the wickedness of leaders who abuse power and execute policy violence in public life. In this Jesus does not depart from his people's tradition but rather fulfills it. "You who kill the prophets and stone those sent to you," Jesus says, tears in his eyes, "how often I have longed to gather your children together, as a hen gathers her chicks under her wings" (Matthew 23:37).

If we live in a world scarred by wickedness, there's hope that God might gather us in love and change what is into what ought to be. But if the people charged with gathering us around Scripture sell out its message, where will we turn for hope? It's the question that burned like fire in the bones of every biblical prophet. It's the question I found myself asking when I reached the dead end of the way the religious right taught me and found myself crying with a former Nazi.

MORAL-FUSION POLITICS

Turns out I wasn't alone, just ignorant. There was, in fact, another way of reading the Bible and working for love, justice,

and mercy in public life. God hadn't abandoned me. I just needed to find new teachers.

In the Bible's prophetic tradition, when you come to a dead end and feel like you're all alone, God's message is always the same: "Don't lose heart. There is a remnant." After Elijah takes on the king's false teachers and has to run for his life, the prophet prays:

> I have been very zealous for the LORD God Almighty. The Israelites have rejected your covenant, torn down your altars, and put your prophets to death with the sword. I am the only one left, and now they are trying to kill me too. (1 Kings 19:10, 14)

God answers by whispering to Elijah in a "gentle whisper" (1 Kings 19:12) and assuring him that there are, in fact, seven thousand faithful witnesses who have not bowed (1 Kings 20:15). There is a remnant. Elijah learns that he is not alone, but he does need to link up with a new movement.

The remnant I needed wasn't far away. Back home in North Carolina, I met a pastor, the Reverend Dr. William J. Barber II, who had learned from his father and others in the Southern freedom movement that the Bible's message is inseparable from the struggle for justice in public life. "I don't know a way to follow Jesus," Rev. Barber told me, "without engaging in a quarrel with the world." Following his lead into Moral Mondays and the Poor People's Campaign, I met a freedom family that taught me to read the Bible as history, songbook, and practical guide for building up love and justice in society. Marching and singing with them, the Scriptures I had memorized as a kid

came to life. "This is what the whole story was always about," I kept saying to myself. I didn't need to invent a better way to be Christian in public life. I needed to learn it from the people who had been practicing it all along.

In the language of the prophets, there is a remnant in America. It is made up of people like María, Julia, and Ms. Rosanell; José and Sandra; Ndume, Alicia, Wendsler, Basir, and Matthew. And it is sustained in faith communities and organizations like the Mother's Union, the NAACP, sanctuary churches, the Children's Defense Fund, Apache-Stronghold, 350.org, Afghans for Peace, and About Face, among others. There are, indeed, seven thousand and more who have not bowed to the household gods of Christian nationalism. Reading the Bible alongside these people of deep faith and conviction, I've come to know the power of Scripture to reshape our moral narrative and sustain us in the difficult work of building up a new world.

Along the way, Rev. Barber showed me how the Bible offers practical guidance for organizing people around a moral narrative focused on love and justice. Preaching Ezekiel 22, he introduced people who wanted to join the Poor People's Campaign to the moral imagination of the biblical prophet. Ezekiel stood up to politicians who "oppressed the foreigner and mistreated the fatherless and the widow . . . mak[ing] a profit from the poor" (Ezekiel 22:7, 12). Rev. Barber spoke the prophet's words to expose policy violence that has gone on under both Democrats and Republicans as the gap between rich and poor widened in the richest nation in the history of the world. Pointing to policies that separated immigrant children from

their families or proposed taking healthcare from sick children, Rev. Barber lifted a moral critique more searing than anything partisan opponents of those in power might say: "Her officials within her are like wolves tearing their prey" (Ezekiel 22:27). Poor and marginalized people—those who knew the weight of injustice, even if they weren't accustomed to being in church—shouted "Amen."

But the prophet doesn't only challenge politicians, Rev. Barber said. Even worse than wicked political leadership are hypocritical faith leaders who sell out God's good news to cover for political violence. "Her prophets whitewash these deeds for them," Ezekiel declares (Ezekiel 22:28). Up against a false moral narrative that justified the abuse of political power, Ezekiel claimed that God was alone—at a dead end with nowhere to turn. "I looked for someone among them who would build up the wall and stand before me in the gap on behalf of the land so I would not have to destroy it, but I found no one" (Ezekiel 22:30).

After a pause, Rev. Barber said that if we turn over fifteen chapters in the book of Ezekiel, we see how our God can make a way out of no way. In the great tradition of African American revivalists who have preached Ezekiel 37 as their text, Rev. Barber imagined that valley of dry bones strewn with the remnants of people whose flesh was consumed by the ravaging wolves of Ezekiel 22. Here were all the lives snuffed out by genocide and slavery, Jim Crow and internment camps, mass incarceration and deportation, global climate change and income inequality. Here in this valley were the rejected people who'd come to learn about the Poor People's Campaign—

those who had suffered on their own, not knowing how much they had in common with other poor and dejected people whom they had been pitted against because of race, nationality, religion, or sexuality. Wherever we were, from inner-city Detroit to rural Appalachia to the poorest zip code in Texas, Rev. Barber preached Ezekiel to illuminate how we were, all of us, in this valley together. As the Spirit wind blew to connect leg bone to hipbone and hipbone to backbone, we stood to our feet and felt ourselves rising together to new life.

The Poor People's Campaign of 1968 was born again as people pledged to join the nonviolent army God was raising up out of America's valley of dry bones. But this was more than a stirring sermon. From the prophetic text itself, Rev. Barber laid out a plan for how to move forward—a model he called "moral-fusion organizing." He challenged us as a movement to reclaim the moral narrative. We could refuse to let the religious right narrowly define moral issues in public life. We could name the immorality of poverty, injustice, and attacks on immigrants. And we could do it together, in an intersectional coalition made up of everyone who has been harmed by policy violence—whether poverty or systemic racism, ecological devastation or the war economy. Like those bones that had been separated and bleached white in the scorching sun, we can reconnect and rediscover the ties that bind us together in a long-term movement whose aim is not to save a political party but to revive the heart of democracy. This, Rev. Barber said, is the only thing that has ever moved America toward its stated goal of a more perfect union.

REVIVING THE SOUL OF AMERICA

The religious right was not wrong to tell people of faith that the Bible is political. Its critical mistake and enduring sin is not that it challenged Christians to engage in public life but that it invited us to join a reactionary coalition driven by racial fear, male chauvinism, and corporate greed. Decent people with sincere motives joined the Moral Majority and the Christian Coalition to put their faith into practice. But these organizations made fallible people worse than we would have been otherwise. They led us astray.

I know from personal experience how much any attempt to live out my faith in public life must begin with repentance. The sackcloth and ashes of Scripture are appropriate, especially for white evangelicals in our present moment. We have sinned, and our sin has not only stained our souls; it has made life more difficult for millions and threatens to destroy life itself on this planet. The fire this time could just as easily be a nuclear holocaust as a wildfire like the one that is consuming large swaths of California as I write.

But repentance, I have also learned, is more than feeling guilt and saying we were wrong. Repentance is turning around and going in the other direction. It means listening to the people who have suffered most from the false moral narrative I was caught up in and joining with them to offer our neighbors a better story about who we might become. The gift of moral-fusion politics is that it offers us both a history we can learn from and a future we can join—a coalition not led or convened by majority-white faith leaders but one where we can all nevertheless find our place in a moral movement.

Donald Trump's presidency has created a moral crisis, both within the Republican Party and in American public life. It would be irresponsible to ignore this fact, but it would also be naive to pretend that Trumpism somehow emerged apart from the moral narrative that the religious right preached for four decades. The policy violence that presses down on poor people, undocumented people, people of color, and the earth is being executed in God's name. We cannot, as a people, retreat to an apolitical faith that tries not to engage public life any more than an individual can pursue spiritual health without addressing the body's physical needs. While spiritual formation and pastoral care within congregations are essential to Christian discipleship, our public witness is equally important. Now, as ever, we must be prepared, as Saint Peter said, "to give an answer to everyone who asks you to give the reason for the hope that you have" (1 Peter 3:15).

When we point out that faith in American public life has been exploited by the Republican Party, we are neither endorsing the Democratic Party by default nor counting out the possibility of Republicans changing course. A moral movement must push both parties to address issues that impact women, children, the poor, the undocumented, and the environment—the most vulnerable among us whom the prophets will not let us forget. There is nothing partisan about insisting that everybody has a right to live, to learn, to enjoy the fruits of their labor, to have access to healthcare, and to receive equal protection under the law. To call policies that deny our neighbors these basic rights "conservative" is not only an act of violence against our neighbors; it is also a

misrepresentation of conservatism. When we resist extremism within the Republican Party, we do not deny that there are things we should all work to conserve in the American republic. Instead, we insist that those basic values are more important than any party's political power.

Many who, like me, were caught up in the deception of the religious right worry that a religious left could easily mirror the mistakes of the past forty years. It is true that political power will corrupt without regard for party or affiliation. But a moral movement can practice political realism while warning against the dangers of partisanism. When we lift up the voices of people who are hurting and endorse policies that would impact the material circumstances of our lives, we can then use the power of our voices and our votes to support politicians who promise to make those policies law. If they are Democrats in one election, that is no guarantee that they will be a generation from now. I learned from Strom Thurmond that politicians can switch parties without giving up their biases or their grip on power.

Still, we who follow Jesus in the United States of America practice our faith within a two-party system that negotiates a balance of power between Republicans and Democrats. People who are disillusioned by the corruption in either party have at different times in our history tried to imagine a third party. But our electoral systems at both the state and federal levels are not set up to recognize coalition governments like those that a parliamentary system allows for in Canada or Germany. There are good arguments for why such a system would better serve our neighbors, but within the US political

system only the party in power could pass legislation to make those changes (or put them to voters as ballot measures). As our political system is currently set up, a moral movement in America must present the issues that impact us to both Republicans and Democrats and then decide, at each election, which party is more willing to address those issues with policies that promote justice.

If we have read the Bible well, we know that a moral movement will never persuade the powerful to establish God's kingdom here on earth as it is in heaven. History illustrates how those princes and potentates who have been convinced that they were the executors of God's agenda have been some of the most dangerous political leaders. Nevertheless, the prophets exhort us to "cry aloud, spare not" (Isaiah 58:1 KJV). When there is injustice in public life, those who follow Jesus have no choice but to stand with the downtrodden, take up the Bible's prophetic texts, and say aloud for all to hear,

The Spirit of the LORD is on me,
    because he has anointed me
    to proclaim good news to the poor.
    (Luke 4:18)

When we take up this prophetic task today, we must, like Jesus in his own hometown, confront people who read the same Bible and claim to worship the same God we do. Christian nationalism thrives in America today because the political interests that drive extremism within the Republican Party under Donald Trump's leadership are a minority

position without the support of white evangelicals. Without Christian nationalism, there would be no President Trump. However extreme religious nationalists may seem to our neighbors and the watching world, the Republican Party as it is currently constituted cannot exist without them. They are the base that the religious right built.

Within the experiment in multiethnic democracy that we call America, Christian nationalism is the greatest threat to the "more perfect union" that our Constitution calls us to strive toward. In a nation that is increasingly less white and less Christian, the coalition the religious right helped to build clings to power by undermining the democratic principles that sustain America's social contract. In other places and at other times, Christian faith in public life might call us to love our neighbors and build up justice in other ways. But here and now, we must be clear: the task of a moral movement is nothing less than reviving the heart of American democracy.

We must do this for the sake of our near neighbors, and we must do it for the sake of our human family on the other side of the world. But we who claim to follow Jesus must do it alongside people of every race, creed, religion, and culture because the moral crisis of our time continues under the leadership of men and women who claim the blessing of our God.

ACKNOWLEDGMENTS

This book would not have been possible without the coalition of faithful people I have met through the Poor People's Campaign: A National Call for Moral Revival. If you've read this far, you've met several of them. But there are far too many to name. I hope you'll join us.

My writing life is made possible and sustained by partnerships. I thank the School for Conversion for giving me an institutional home, the Rutba House for providing me and my family a physical home, the St. John's Missionary Baptist Church and the Greenleaf Christian Church for being our spiritual home, and InterVarsity Press for offering a publishing home.

Vincent Harding, who was my teacher in the Southern freedom movement, used to point us toward the cloud of witnesses that had preceded us when we sought hope in the struggle for justice. "There is a river whose streams make glad the city of God" (Psalm 46:4). There is a river, indeed. I give thanks for the ancestors who form a great cloud of witnesses that sustain me as I travel along. I call their names as dedication of this work to the common work to which they gave their lives: Frederick and Harriet, Sojourner and Angelina, Ida and W. E. B., Walter and Jane, Mary and Dorothy, Clarence and Florence, Fannie Lou and Septima, Ella and Martin, Rosa and E. D., Ann and C. P., William and Roz, Al and Olinda, Nelson and Joyce, Vincent and Aljosie . . .

FAITH-BASED ORGANIZATIONS WORKING TO SHIFT THE MORAL NARRATIVE

The Poor People's Campaign, which I have introduced in this book, is a coalition made up of many partners. Because *Revolution of Values* is particularly focused on helping people in the Christian tradition to reclaim the moral narrative that has been distorted by the religious right, I have listed below organizations that are helping their constituencies do this work.

Children's Defense Fund's Proctor Institute: www.childrens defense.org/programs/faith-based/samuel-dewitt-proctor -institute/

Evangelicals for Social Action: www.evangelicalsforsocial action.org

Faith in Action: https://faithinaction.org

Faith in Public Life: www.faithinpubliclife.org

Freedom Road: https://freedomroad.us

Kairos Center: www.kairoscenter.org

Red Letter Christians: www.redletterchristians.org

Repairers of the Breach: www.breachrepairers.org

Samuel DeWitt Proctor Conference: sdpconference.info

Sojourners: https://sojo.net

Vote Common Good: www.votecommongood.com

The Witness: https://thewitnessbcc.com

DISCUSSION GUIDE

1. Jonathan writes in the introduction about the need for skills to "scent out the truth" in the fog of the culture wars. What experiences have helped you see the need for this kind of discernment? What background shapes your practice of faith in public life?

2. Jonathan asks in chapter one whether teachers like himself have done enough to equip church members to practice their faith in public life. How have you been taught to think about faith and politics? Where does Dr. King's call for a "revolution of values" challenge you?

3. Defenders of slaveholder religion made it their policy "to push the Bible argument continually, drive abolitionism to the wall, and compel it to assume an anti-Christian position." How have you seen advocates of "biblical values" in public life assume a similar tactic?

4. Chapter two outlines the influence of corporate interests on how many Christians came to think about poverty in America. Where have you seen this influence in your own experience? How does Julia Dinsmore challenge you to read the Bible's message to poor and oppressed people differently? Who is working to build a moral economy in your community?

5. Chapter three introduces the history of the black-led struggle to share political power in the United States. What did you learn about how gerrymandering and voter suppression work today? How does Ms. Eaton's faith challenge or inspire you to live as a Christian in public life?

6. Have you heard of churches practicing sanctuary in your community? What does it mean for you, in your own spiritual formation, to remember that you were once an alien and stranger? How might Pastor José speak to your congregation about immigrants and the policies that impact them?

7. Chapter five describes an image of the Bible bound in handcuffs. What is the artist, Ndume Olatushani, saying about his own experience? How does his story and the history of "law and order" recounted in this chapter challenge or inform your understanding of family values? How might your community support a biblical vision of restorative justice?

8. Alicia Wilson-Baker still considers herself "pro-life," even though she's come to question the origins and political assumptions of the pro-life/pro-family movement. How do you respond to the biblical call to "choose life" in light of this history? How does the experience of women in the Bible and in contemporary society inform your understanding of faith in public life?

9. Can you name ways dominionism has influenced public life in your state? How does Wendsler Nosie's story invite you to reconsider Scripture? What should people of faith who want to "keep" the earth expect of political leaders? What must we expect of ourselves?

10. How have you heard the Bible quoted to support the American cowboy's vision of the world? What does a witness to the good shepherd look like in foreign policy today? What people or movements are helping you learn the counterrhythm of Scripture's song?

11. In what ways does Jonathan confess he was led astray by the religious right? What did repentance entail for him?

12. *Revolution of Values* makes the case that not only conservative Christians, but the American public, need a new moral narrative. What values do you want to see reflected in a public moral narrative? Who do you hear articulating those values in society today?

13. If people who have experienced rejection are leading a revival of democracy, as Rev. Barber preaches from Ezekiel, what does that mean for church people who have not experienced rejection? How does the Spirit that blows across the valley of dry bones stir people whose flesh hasn't been consumed by policy violence?

14. What are you committed to do to bring about a revolution of values? Who will you follow? What communities and partners do you need to practice your faith in public life?

NOTES

Besides providing a reference for the works I've cited and relied upon in this book, these annotated notes are an invitation for you to join the conversations out of which I have written. As many of these conversations are ongoing, I also invite you to follow the organizations and movements within which I most often participate in public conversations: School for Conversion (www.schoolforconversion.org), Repairers of the Breach (www.breachrepairers.org), and the Poor People's Campaign (www.poorpeoplescampaign.org).

INTRODUCTION: MORAL CLARITY IN THE FOG OF WAR

2 *This was not always the case*: This book's argument that Americans need to reimagine public morality draws on critical historical, sociological, and journalistic work over the past two decades. For a good introduction to the history of white religious nationalism, see Randall Balmer's *Politico Magazine* essay from May 27, 2014, "The Real Origins of the Religious Right," www.politico.com/magazine /story/2014/05/religious-right-real-origins-107133. Other historians whose work I have found especially helpful include John Fea, Seth Dowland, Jennifer Graber, Elizabeth Hinton, Daniel K. Williams, Jemar Tisby, and Marjorie Spruill. For ongoing reporting on the influence of white Christian nationalism in American public life, see the work of journalists Sarah Posner, Michelle Goldberg, Chris Hedges, Jeff Sharlet, Eugene Scott, Jack Jenkins, Frances FitzGerald, Katherine Stewart, and Frederick Clarkson. The ongoing sociological work of Robert P. Jones and PRRI (Public Religion Research Institute) and of Andrew Whitehead has been especially helpful. While this book is in no way a scholarly treatment, it draws on the work of these scholars, and I commend their work for further exploration of the history and sociological trends this book outlines.

3   *America is in the midst*: See James Davison Hunter, *Culture Wars: The Struggle to Define America* (New York: Basic Books, 1991), 36. While Hunter's descriptive work has shaped conversations about faith and politics in American public life for two decades, I am drawing on critical historical work that demonstrates how dividing lines have been drawn to privilege white cultural values and the economic interests associated with them. For this critical historical perspective, see Carol Anderson, *White Rage: The Unspoken Truth of Our Racial Divide* (New York: Bloomsbury, 2016); Eddie S. Glaude Jr., *Democracy in Black: How Race Still Enslaves the American Soul* (New York: Crown, 2016); and Kevin M. Kruse, *One Nation Under God: How Corporate America Invented Christian America* (New York: Basic Books, 2015).

4   *Twenty years later*: Jonathan Wilson-Hartgrove, *Reconstructing the Gospel: Finding Freedom from Slaveholder Religion* (Downers Grove, IL: InterVarsity Press, 2018).

7   *Faith in these traditions*: I am drawing here on the Pew Research Center's annual Religious Landscape Study from 2018, www.pewforum .org/religious-landscape-study/. While white Christian nationalism is certainly not embraced by all evangelical Protestants—and some religious nationalists self-identify as Catholic and Jewish—this broad survey shows how the moral narrative of a minority of religious people in America has disproportionately shaped public discourse.

1 WADE IN THE WATER

10   *I met María*: I visited El Paso in October of 2017 and participated in the Border Network for Human Rights "Hugs Not Walls" program as a part of the Poor People's Campaign: A National Call for Moral Revival. I have told the story of BNHR here as it was told to us by multiple women who have been part of the network for over a decade. María, whose full name I have not used to protect her privacy, shared her story publicly at a community forum the day after her reunion with family members in the Rio Grande. A video of her testimony is available here: María, Texas—Immigration, "Testifier Video: Poor People's Campaign Hearing for the Souls of Poor Folk Moral Audit," *Repairers of the Breach*, November 29, 2017, https://youtu.be/WCRDMho6aQo?t=296.

After Donald Trump's 2016: For an example of reporting on Pope Francis's response to President Trump's proposal for a wall between the United States and Mexico, see "Pope on Trump: Person Who Thinks

Only About Building Walls, Not Building Bridges, Is Not Christian," *National Catholic Register*, February 18, 2016, www.ncregister.com /daily-news/pope-person-who-thinks-only-about-building-walls-not -building-bridges-is-no.

12 *Capitalizing on decades of Republican outreach*: In an August 2018 *Washington Post* poll, Trump's approval rating among African Americans was 3 percent. Net nonwhite approval was 19 percent, and overall approval among American adults was only 36 percent. "Q: Do you approve or disapprove . . . ?," *Washington Post*–ABC News Poll, Aug. 26-29, 2018, *Washington Post*, September 4, 2018, www.washingtonpost.com /page/2010-2019/WashingtonPost/2018/08/31/National-Politics /Polling/question_20686.xml.

14 *President Trump defended Nazis*: For Trump's response to the events in Charlottesville, Virginia, see Meghan Keneally, "Trump Lashes Out at 'Alt-left' in Charlottesville, Says 'Fine People on Both Sides,'" *ABC News*, August 15, 2017, https://abcnews.go.com/Politics/trump -lashes-alt-left-charlottesville-fine-people-sides/story?id=49235032.

At a rally in Alabama: For reporting on President Trump's comments about National Football League players at a rally in Huntsville, Alabama, see Aric Jenkins, "Read President Trump's NFL Speech on National Anthem Protests," *Time*, September 23, 2017, http://time .com/4954684/donald-trump-nfl-speech-anthem-protests/.

15 *When I think of you*: For text of Robert Jeffress's sermon presented at President Trump's inauguration ceremony, see "Read the Sermon Donald Trump Heard Before Becoming President," *Time*, January 20, 2017, http://time.com/4641208/donald-trump-robert-jeffress -st-john-episcopal-inauguration/.

Historian John Fea: Evangelical historian John Fea both coins the phrase "court evangelicals" and chronicles the various spokespersons for Christian nationalism in his book *Believe Me: The Evangelical Road to Donald Trump* (Grand Rapids: Eerdmans, 2018); see pp. 115-52 on the "court evangelicals."

16 *Here is our policy then*: For quote from Dabney, see Thomas Cary Johnson, *The Life and Letters of Robert Lewis Dabney* (Richmond, VA: Presbyterian Committee of Publication, 1903), 129.

17 *At the same time*: Frances FitzGerald narrates the data on millennial evangelicals in "The New Evangelicals," which was first published as an article in *The New Yorker* in 2008 and was revised and updated as

a chapter in *The Evangelicals: The Struggle to Shape America* (New York: Simon & Schuster, 2017), 535-84.

21   *Half a century ago*: Dr. King's "revolution of values" phrase and vision come from his speech "Beyond Vietnam," which was delivered at the Riverside Church in New York City on April 4, 1967—one year to the day before King was assassinated in Memphis. A full text of that speech is available in the Stanford University archive of King's papers: https://kinginstitute.stanford.edu/king-papers/documents/beyond-vietnam.

22   *To mark the fiftieth anniversary*: For more on the origins of the Poor People's Campaign: A National Call for Moral Revival, see William J. Barber II with Jonathan Wilson-Hartgrove, *The Third Reconstruction: Moral Mondays, Fusion Politics, and the Rise of a New Justice Movement* (Boston: Beacon Press, 2016). You can also learn more and sign up for regular updates about the campaign at www.poorpeoplescampaign.org.

2 THE WISDOM OF POOR WOMEN

25   *The original Poor People's Campaign*: For historical background on the Poor People's Campaign, the Kerner Commission, and the War on Poverty, see Michael K. Honey, *To the Promised Land: Martin Luther King and the Fight for Economic Justice* (New York: Norton, 2018); and Sylvie Laurent, *King and the Other America: The Poor People's Campaign and the Quest for Economic Equality* (Oakland: University of California Press, 2019). For a critical study of the political reaction against these movements in the 1970s and 1980s, see Elizabeth Hinton, *From the War on Poverty to the War on Crime: The Making of Mass Incarceration in America* (Cambridge, MA: Harvard University Press, 2016).

26   *The rhetoric of Reaganomics*: For more on the use of the myth of the welfare queen to justify trickle-down economics, see Ange-Marie Hancock, *The Politics of Disgust: The Public Identity of the Welfare Queen* (New York: New York University Press, 2004).

Televangelist Robert Tilton: Robert Tilton's ministry is examined alongside others like it in the Word of Faith movement by journalist Sarah Posner in her book *God's Profits: Faith, Fraud, and the Republican Crusade for Values Voters* (Sausalito, CA: PoliPointPress, 2008), 15-17.

27   *Julia Dinsmore spent the 1980s*: Julia K. Dinsmore tells her own story in *My Name Is Child of God . . . Not "Those People"* (Minneapolis: Augsburg Fortress, 2007), 22-28. Further reflections on her experience come

from years of working with Julia and an interview I conducted with her about this book on June 22, 2018.

30   *Their answer that December*: The story of James Fifield's Spiritual Mobilization movement is taken from Kevin M. Kruse, *One Nation Under God: How Corporate America Invented Christian America* (New York: Basic Books, 2015) 3-34. For more on this history, see also Kim Phillips-Fein, *Invisible Hands: The Businessmen's Crusade Against the New Deal* (New York: Norton, 2010).

31   *In his book* The Family: For more on Abraham Vereide's Bible-study network, see Jeff Sharlet, *The Family: The Secret Fundamentalism at the Heart of American Power* (New York: Harper Perennial, 2008). Quote here is from p. 96, emphasis added. The network Vereide helped to launch is behind the National Prayer Breakfast and the Congressional Prayer Caucuses that have become primary organizing tools for Christian nationalist influence on state and federal governments today. Religion News Services (RNS) reporter Jack Jenkins has covered the investigation of Russian influence on the 2016 election through these events.

32   *Serve them Vereide did*: For a history of the Social Gospel among both black and white church leaders in the early twentieth century, see Ralph E. Luker, *The Social Gospel in Black and White: American Racial Reform, 1885–1912* (Chapel Hill: University of North Carolina Press, 1991). More recently, Union Theological Seminary's Gary Dorrien has traced the ministry of the Reverend Dr. Martin Luther King Jr. to the social Christianity that emerged in the late nineteenth century, when black preachers had a public role in American society and the new field of sociology was beginning to influence how people understood their relationship to systems in society. See Gary Dorrien, *The New Abolition: W. E. B. Du Bois and the Black Social Gospel* (New Haven, CT: Yale University Press, 2015); and idem, *Breaking White Supremacy: Martin Luther King Jr. and the Black Social Gospel* (New Haven, CT: Yale University Press, 2018).

33   *While Dinsmore and the Mother's Union*: For detailed reporting on the funding networks that have supported Marvin Olasky's work, see Michelle Goldberg, *Kingdom Coming: The Rise of Christian Nationalism* (New York: Norton, 2007), 111-13.

Throughout the nineteenth century: The Olasky quotes are from his book *The Tragedy of American Compassion* (Washington, DC: Regenery Gateway, 1992), 220, 230.

34   *Olasky in the early 1990s*: Russell H. Conwell's *Acres of Diamonds* (New York: Harper & Brothers, 1915), still in print, remains a touchstone for the Christian business associations that became commonplace in the mid-twentieth century, normalizing a public Christianity that both celebrates capitalism and fosters fear of New Deal–type government programs as "socialism."

35   *If you already know*: Ministries and literature that make the case for Christianity and capitalism are too numerous to cite, but it's important to note that this narrative spans the progressive/traditional divide of the culture wars. While Fifield's pro-capitalist message is reproduced today in ministries that cater to the spiritual but not religious desires of moderate coastal elites, a more populist pro-capitalist gospel is assumed by many evangelical ministries.

36   *When rich men gather*: Biblical scholar and activist Ched Myers has written about the biblical imagination of "Sabbath economics," a theme that runs throughout the Bible. For a scholarly treatment of this reading and the traditions of scriptural interpretation it draws on, see Liz Theoharis, *Always With Us?: What Jesus Really Said About the Poor* (Grand Rapids: Eerdmans, 2017).

42   *The Fight for $15*: The story of the origins of the Fight for $15 and the central role faith leaders have played in it is told by Jonathan Rosenblum in *Beyond $15: Immigrant Workers, Faith Activists, and the Revival of the Labor Movement* (Boston: Beacon Press, 2017). Learn more about the Fight for $15 and how you can get involved at https://fightfor15.org.

      When the Poor People's Campaign: For details from the audit conducted by the Poor People's Campaign, see "The Souls of Poor Folk: Auditing America 50 Years After the Poor People's Campaign Challenged Racism, Poverty, the War Economy/Militarism and Our National Morality," *Poor People's Campaign: A National Call for Moral Revival*, www.poorpeoplescampaign.org/audit/.

3 GIVE US THE BALLOT

46   *When I met Eaton*: I interviewed Ms. Eaton on May 25, 2013, and have reviewed her sworn testimony in the case of *North Carolina NAACP v. McCrory*. I am also relying here on the good reporting of Ari Berman, "The 94-Year-Old Civil-Rights Pioneer Who Is Now Challenging North Carolina's Voter-ID Law," *The Nation*, January 25, 2016, www.thenation.com/article/the-92-year-old-civil-rights-pioneer -who-is-now-challenging-north-carolinas-voter-id-law/.

47 *This is my second time around*: Ari Berman's *Give Us the Ballot: The Modern Struggle for Voting Rights in America* (New York: Farrar, Straus & Giroux, 2015) puts the story of today's struggle for voting rights in the historical context that is sketched here, as does Carol Anderson's *One Person, No Vote: How Voter Suppression Is Destroying Our Democracy* (New York: Bloomsbury, 2018).

In a 1955 book: For Woodward's argument, see C. Vann Woodward, *The Strange Career of Jim Crow*, 3rd rev. ed. (New York: Oxford University Press, 1974).

48 *In North Carolina*: The events of North Carolina's first freedmen's meeting and J. W. Hood's address there are recorded in a report of *The Christian Recorder*, October 28, 1865. Accessible Archives. African American Newspapers: The 19th Century. Reproduced by permission. www.accessible-archives.com. For in-depth history of Reconstruction, see the monumental work of W. E. B. Du Bois in *Black Reconstruction in America: Toward a History of the Part of Which Black Folk Played in the Attempt to Reconstruct Democracy in America, 1860–1880* (New Brunswick: Transaction, 2012) and the more recent scholarship of Eric Foner, *Reconstruction: America's Unfinished Revolution, 1863–1877* (New York: Perennial Classics, 2002).

50 *The John Birch Society*: For more on the John Birch Society's role in resistance to the civil rights movement, see Jean Hardisty, *Mobilizing Resentment: Conservative Resurgence from the John Birch Society to the Promise Keepers* (Boston: Beacon Press, 1999). Nancy MacLean's work, *Democracy in Chains: The Deep History of the Radical Right's Stealth Plan for America* (New York: Viking, 2017), traces the connection between economic theorist James Buchanan and think tanks funded by the Koch network today. For more on those networks and how they have worked to influence state and federal policy, see Jane Mayer, *Dark Money: The Hidden History of the Billionaires Behind the Rise of the Radical Right* (New York: Doubleday, 2016).

51 *By manipulating voter data*: Gerrymanders suppress the votes of African Americans and others by stacking voters that politicians know will not vote for them in a single district so they are more likely to win surrounding districts. Whether the data used to create these gerrymanders are racial or partisan, the effect is the same. Other voter suppression tactics include requiring forms of voter ID that are less common among poor and African American voters, purging

voter rolls, rolling back early voting schedules, and moving or elimi-
nating polling locations.

51 *But gerrymandering is only one instrument*: See "2016 Presidential
    Election results," Politico, December 13, 2016, www.politico.com/2016
    -election/results/map/president/; and Ari Berman, "Rigged: How Voter
    Suppression Threw Wisconsin to Trump," *Mother Jones*, November
    /December 2017, www.motherjones.com/politics/2017/10/voter-
    suppression-wisconsin-election-2016/.

53 *Four days before the election*: For details on the Arkansas voter-
    suppression case, see reporting from Max Brantley, "Arkansas
    Supreme Court Strikes Down Voter ID Law," *Arkansas Times*, October
    15, 2014, www.arktimes.com/ArkansasBlog/archives/2014/10/15
    /arkansas-supreme-court-strikes-down-voter-id-law.

54 *It's a math problem*: For a transcript of Bachmann's interview with
    Brody on CBN, see David Brody, "Exclusive: Michele Bachmann: This
    Will Be 'Last Election' If Hillary Wins Presidency," *Brody File* (blog),
    CBN News, September 1, 2016, www1.cbn.com/thebrodyfile/archive
    /2016/09/01/only-on-the-brody-file-michele-bachmann-says-this
    -will-be-last-election-if-hillary-wins-presidency.

56 *David Barton's Wallbuilders*: To read more about David Barton and
    the work he does to bolster Christian nationalism, see John Fea,
    Believe Me: The Evangelical Road to Donald Trump (Grand Rapids:
    Eerdmans, 2018), 161-65.

58 *Four centuries later, Saint Benedict*: *The Rule of Saint Benedict* is still a
    standard text in introductory Western civilization classes in the
    United States because of the influence of Benedictine communities
    on medieval European society and Western political thought.

59 *Christianity succeeded*: Sheldon S. Wolin, *Politics and Vision: Conti-
    nuity and Innovation in Western Political Thought*, expanded ed.
    (Princeton, NJ: Princeton University Press, 2016), 87.

60 *In the 2016 election*: Data cited here are from "The Souls of Poor Folk:
    Auditing America 50 Years After the Poor People's Campaign Chal-
    lenged Racism, Poverty, the War Economy/Militarism and Our Na-
    tional Morality," *Poor People's Campaign: A National Call for Moral Re-
    vival*, www.poorpeoplescampaign.org/audit/. See also Anderson, *One
    Person, No Vote*. The NAACP Legal Defense and Educational Fund, the
    Advancement Project, and Forward Justice have done important legal
    work to challenge voter suppression in the courts. Grassroots efforts

like the New Georgia Project, which gained national attention when its founder, Stacey Abrams, ran for governor, offer opportunities for volunteers to train in nonpartisan voter protection and advocacy for voting rights. Faith communities can also support Souls to the Polls events and election protection through initiatives like Lawyers and Collars, sponsored by Sojourners and AME Righteous Vote.

4 LORD, PREPARE ME TO BE A SACTUARY

63 *Pastor José Chicas*: I first met José Chicas when his son asked for help with his case at an immigrant-rights rally outside the North Carolina General Assembly in the spring of 2017. St. John's Missionary Baptist Church and the School for Conversion together offered him a place of sanctuary in June 2017; we then connected with the Sanctuary Movement network that is organized by Church World Service. Advocacy groups like the North Carolina Council of Churches, Mijente, the American Friends Service Committee, and Faith in Public Life have been invaluable resources as we have learned what it means to both grow in community with one family and pursue policy change that will impact millions of undocumented people. For background on Chicas's story, see Erica Hellerstein, "For the Last Five Months, Pastor Jose Chicas Has Been Hiding from ICE Inside a Durham Religious Center," *IndyWeek*, November 15, 2017, www.indyweek.com/indyweek/for-the -last-five-months-pastor-jose-chicas-has-been-hiding-from-ice -inside-a-durham-religious-center/Content?oid=9501608. Some quotes here are taken from personal conversations with the Chicas family during the writing of this book. For more information on the School for Conversion, see www.schoolforconversion.org.

66 *In the summer of 2018*: For reporting on family separations at the border from the summer of 2018, see Stephen Collinson and Lauren Fox, "Outrage Grows as Families Are Separated. Will Trump Change His Policy?," *CNN Politics*, June 18, 2018, www.cnn.com/2018/06/18 /politics/immigration-trump-congress-family-separation/index.html.

    President Trump's spiritual adviser: A link to a video of Paula White's commentary on Jesus as a "legal" immigrant on the Christian Broadcasting Network can be found here: Samuel Smith, "Paula White: There's a Difference Between Jesus as a Refugee and Those Who Enter the US Illegally," *Christian Post*, July 10, 2018, www.christianpost .com/news/paula-white-theres-difference-between-jesus-as-refugee -those-who-enter-the-us-illegally-225900/. For former Attorney General Jeff Sessions's defense of child separation policies, see Julie

Zauzmer and Keith McMillan, "Sessions Cites Bible Passage Used to Defend Slavery in Defense of Separating Immigrant Families," *Washington Post*, June 15, 2018, www.washingtonpost.com/news/acts-of -faith/wp/2018/06/14/jeff-sessions-points-to-the-bible-in-defense -of-separating-immigrant-families/.

As the standard bearer of the GOP: For a compelling introduction to the recent history of the US immigration system, see Jose Antonio Vargas, *Dear America: Notes of an Undocumented Citizen* (New York: HarperCollins, 2018). You can read President Ronald Reagan's full "Statement on United States Immigration and Refugee Policy," July 30, 1981, through *The American Presidency Project*, www.presidency. ucsb.edu/node/246714.

67   *As recently as 2010*: Richard Land's quote was reported by Laurie Goodstein, "Obama Wins Unlikely Allies in Immigration," Politics, *New York Times*, July 18, 2010, www.nytimes.com/2010/07/19/us /politics/19evangelicals.html.

68   *Founded in 1937*: On the history of eugenics and its relationship to US immigration policy in the twentieth century, see William H. Tucker, *The Funding of Scientific Racism: Wickliffe Draper and the Pioneer Fund* (Urbana: University of Illinois Press, 2002), especially pp. 131-96 on the Pioneer Fund in the post–civil rights era.

By the late 1970s: For documentation of John Tanton and the FAIR (Federation for American Immigration Reform) network's history, see Heidi Beirich, "The Nativist Lobby: Three Faces of Intolerance," Intelligence Project, *Southern Poverty Law Center*, February 1, 2009, www.splcenter.org/20090131/nativist-lobby-three-faces-intolerance.

69   *No single person*: Though I already introduced David Barton and Christian nationalism, reporting on the role of faith in public issues consistently points to their disproportionate influence across policy areas in American public life. See Julie J. Ingersoll, *Building God's Kingdom: Inside the World of Christian Reconstruction* (New York: Oxford University Press, 2015). John Fea's quote is from *Believe Me: The Evangelical Road to Donald Trump* (Grand Rapids: Eerdmans, 2018), 162. For a more in-depth analysis of Barton's pseudo-historical claims, see John Fea, *Was America Founded as a Christian Nation?: A Historical Introduction* (Louisville, KY: Westminster John Knox, 2011).

71   *If slavery be a sin*: H. Shelton Smith chronicled the debate about Christian faith and slaveholding among nineteenth-century American Christians in his book *In His Image, But . . . : Racism in*

Southern Religion, 1780–1910 (Durham, NC: Duke University Press, 1972). The quote from Rev. James Smylie is found on p. 129. On this history, see also Mark A. Noll, *The Civil War as a Theological Crisis* (Chapel Hill: University of North Carolina Press, 2015); and Jonathan Wilson-Hartgrove, *Reconstructing the Gospel: Finding Freedom from Slaveholder Religion* (Downers Grove, IL: InterVarsity Press, 2018).

72   *Quoting a song from Deuteronomy*: Barton's quote was reported by Julie Ingersoll in "'Professor' David Barton on Immigration: God Drew Our Borders," *Religion Dispatches*, July 27, 2010, http://religiondispatches .org/professor-david-barton-on-immigration-god-drew-our-borders/.

Old Testament professor James Hoffmeier: I have tried to summarize Hoffmeier's argument fairly, though I consider his reading of Scripture both wrong and dangerous. See James K. Hoffmeier, *The Immigration Crisis: Immigrants, Aliens, and the Bible* (Wheaton, IL: Crossway, 2009).

77   *Dream Act in 2007*: For more on the story of how undocumented people have organized to help America reimagine itself in the twenty-first century, see Eileen Truax, *Dreamers: An Immigrant Generation's Fight for Their American Dream* (Boston: Beacon Press, 2015).

78   *Sanctuary Movement*: Learn more and connect with the Sanctuary Movement at Church World Service: https://cwsglobal.org/support -the-sanctuary-movement/. For advocacy opportunities, learn more from Mijente, a national network led by directly impacted people: https://mijente.net/take-action/.

5 LAW AND ORDER

80   *On the north side of Saint Louis*: On the history of Pruitt-Igoe, see Colin Marshall, "Pruitt-Igoe: The Troubled High-rise That Came to Define Urban America," *Guardian*, April 22, 2015, www.theguardian.com /cities/2015/apr/22/pruitt-igoe-high-rise-urban-america-history-cities.

81   *Ndume Olatushani*: I interviewed Olatushani for "Born Suspect," *Sojourners Magazine*, August 2015, https://sojo.net/magazine/august -2015/born-suspect. Some quotes and context for this narrative are also taken from Laura Hutson, "If Not for Love and Art, Ndume Olatushani Would Have Died on Death Row," *Nashville Scene*, May 23, 2013, www.nashvillescene.com/news/article/13048412/if-not-for -love-and-art-ndume-olatushani-would-have-died-on-death-row. You can see an example of Olatushani's powerful art at Ndume Olatushani, *Windows on Death Row: Art from Inside and Outside the Prison Walls*, www.windowsondeathrow.com/ndume-olatushani.

83   *In her 2010 book*: For more on "law and order" backlash against the
      civil rights movement, see Michelle Alexander, *The New Jim Crow:
      Mass Incarceration in the Age of Colorblindness* (New York: New Press,
      2010). Alexander's work describes the policy reality that Ta-Nehisi
      Coates experienced as a young man growing up in Baltimore and
      chronicled in his National Book Award–winning memoir, *Between the
      World and Me* (New York: Random House, 2015). For another per-
      spective by an activist in the Black Lives Matter movement, see Pa-
      trisse Khan-Cullors and Asha Bandele, *When They Call You a Terrorist:
      A Black Lives Matter Memoir* (New York: St. Martin's Press, 2018).

84   *When we remember the racism*: Complete text available at George Wallace,
      "The Inaugural Address of Governor George C. Wallace," Montgomery,
      Alabama, January 14, 1963, *Alabama Department of Archives & History*,
      http://digital.archives.alabama.gov/cdm/ref/collection/voices
      /id/2952.

85   *More than a decade before*: History of Virginia's "massive resistance"
      to desegregation and Jerry Falwell's role in it are described in Frances
      FitzGerald, *The Evangelicals: The Struggle to Shape America* (New York:
      Simon & Schuster, 2017), 284. Falwell's quote is from "Ministers and
      Marchers," a sermon he gave in response to the Selma campaign,
      which was published and distributed as a pamphlet. Later, when
      Falwell started the Moral Majority and became directly engaged in
      politics through the religious right, FitzGerald notes that he tried to
      have copies of "Ministers and Marchers" destroyed.

      Falwell's LCA: On the history of Christian schools and family values,
      see Seth Dowland, *Family Values and the Rise of the Christian Right*
      (Philadelphia: University of Pennsylvania Press, 2015), 23-48.
      Dowland offers a close reading of the origins of Falwell's Lynchburg
      Christian Academy and quotes from the academy's literature are
      taken from archival material published in Dowland's book.

86   *Ronald Reagan's 1980 bid*: Ronald Reagan's 1980 campaign slogan
      was "Let's Make America Great Again," thirty-six years before
      Donald Trump named Paul Manafort, who had worked on Reagan's
      1980 campaign, as his campaign manager and used the same
      slogan. Manafort and other political operatives in the Republican
      Party of the late 1970s and early 1980s practiced the politics of
      nostalgia to build the coalition in the South, the suburbs, and the
      Sun Belt—a coalition that Kevin Phillips had identified as an adviser
      to Richard Nixon's 1968 campaign. See Kevin Phillips, *The Emerging*

Republican Majority, updated ed. (Princeton, NJ: Princeton University Press, 2015).

The school responded: See Dowland, *Family Values*, 28.

87   *If segregation academies*: Timothy B. Tyson explores the powerful connection between the Emmett Till generation of the civil rights movement and today's Michael Brown generation in the epilogue to his powerful book, *The Blood of Emmett Till* (New York: Simon & Schuster, 2017), which quotes the chant from outside the Obama White House in 2014.

One in three black kids: On the disparate likelihood of black boys facing prison time in the United States, see Thomas P. Bonczar, "Prevalence of Imprisonment in the U.S. Population, 1974–2001," *Bureau of Justice Statistics: Special Report*, August 2003, www.bjs.gov /content/pub/pdf/piusp01.pdf.

cradle to prison pipeline: Olatushani does public art and organizing work as part of the Cradle to Prison Pipeline project of the Children's Defense Fund. Learn more at http://cdf.childrensdefense.org/site /MessageViewer?dlv_id=47516&em_id=46568.0.

memorial to George Stinney Jr.: George Stinney's conviction and execution are now understood to be a legal lynching without due process. The Equal Justice Initiative's Legacy Museum in Montgomery, Alabama, is devoted to educating Americans about the long history of our criminal justice system being deployed to control and terrorize black communities. Learn more at "The Legacy Museum: From Enslavement to Mass Incarceration," *EJI*, https://eji.org/legacy -museum. For the original news report on Stinney's execution, see "George Stinney, Who Killed Two Little Girls, Dies Calmly," *Greenville News*, June 16, 1944, www.newspapers.com/newspage/187830594/. In 2014, a South Carolina judge overturned Stinney's conviction, noting that he could not have received due process in the one-day trial during which he was convicted and sentenced to death.

88   *Yes, Scripture has been open*: For a helpful introduction to the way Scripture has been used to justify mass incarceration and to biblical resources for restorative justice, see Dominique DuBois Gilliard, *Rethinking Incarceration: Advocating for Justice That Restores* (Downers Grove, IL: InterVarsity Press, 2018).

Reverend Franklin Graham posted this message: Franklin Graham's Facebook post is quoted from March 12, 2015, www.facebook.com

/FranklinGraham/posts/listen-up-blacks-whites-latinos-and
-everybody-else-most-police-shootings-can-be-/883361438386705/.
Excerpt from telegram is quoted in Franklin Graham, *Rebel with a Cause* (Nashville: Nelson, 1995), 1.

89   *Graham was richly rewarded*: Tim Funk and Ames Alexander reported on Graham's pay in "Franklin Graham Takes Pay He Once Gave Up," *Charlotte Observer*, August 8, 2015, www.charlotteobserver.com/living /religion/article30505932.html.

90   *In her book*: For quote on prison as space for formation in obedience to governing authorities, see Jennifer Graber, *The Furnace of Affliction: Prisons and Religion in Antebellum America* (Chapel Hill: University of North Carolina Press, 2011), 12. Graber's book is an important study for anyone who wants to understand the church's relationship to prisons in American history.

91   *Yes, more than two million people*: Figures on American incarceration statistics quoted in Gary Fields and John R. Emshwiller, "As Arrest Records Rise, Americans Find Consequences Can Last a Lifetime," *Wall Street Journal*, August 18, 2014, www.wsj.com/articles/as-arrest-records-rise -americans-find-consequences-can-last-a-lifetime-1408415402.

92   *But when we read the Bible*: I have studied Scripture alongside incarcerated people for the past decade through Project TURN classes with Duke Divinity School inside North Carolina Prisons. Lauren F. Winner, who also teaches in that program, writes movingly about what she has learned from incarcerated women in her book *Wearing God: Clothing, Laughter, Fire, and Other Overlooked Ways of Meeting God* (New York: HarperCollins, 2015). See also Bob Ekblad, *Reading the Bible with the Damned* (Louisville, KY: Westminster John Knox, 2005).

94   *In Chicago, Illinois*: Learn more about the Cure Violence Health Model at http://cureviolence.org. Father Gregory Boyle has written about Homeboy Industries and the "boundless compassion" he has learned there in *Tattoos on the Heart: The Power of Boundless Compassion* (New York: Free Press, 2010).

95   *All of Us or None*: You can learn more about All of Us or None, a program of Legal Services for Prisoners with Children (LSPC) at www.prisonerswithchildren.org/our-projects/allofus-or-none/.

96   Note: Restorative justice is not only about finding a different way to deal with "bad guys"; it is an effort to take collective responsibility for the historic harms we have inherited and the ways we continue

to harm one another within a system that is supposed to bring about justice. Restorative justice isn't only an alternative to retribution in response to crimes; it is fundamentally about repairing the deeper wounds we all share in our communities.

6 A WOMAN'S WORK IS FOR JUSTICE

97 *Alicia Wilson*: Alicia Wilson Baker testified before the US Senate Judiciary Committee's hearing on the nomination of Judge Brett Kavanaugh to the US Supreme Court on September 7, 2018. Quotes and background for her story are taken from interviews with the author and her written testimony, "Testimony of Alicia Wilson Baker Before the Committee on the Judiciary, United States Senate Hearing on the Nomination of Brett Kavanaugh to Be an Associate Justice of the United States Supreme Court," September 7, 2018, www.judiciary .senate.gov/imo/media/doc/Baker%20Testimony.pdf.

98 *Only bold action*: Quote from an editorial: "Gov. Pence, Fix 'Religious Freedom' Law Now," *IndyStar*, USA Today Network, March 31, 2015, www.indystar.com/story/opinion/2015/03/30/editorial-gov-pence -fix-religious-freedom-law-now/70698802/.

101 *Within the civil rights movement*: For an important history of the role women have played in the civil rights movement and their consciousness of a need for gender equality, both within the movement and in society, see Lynne Olson, *Freedom's Daughters: The Unsung Heroines of the Civil Rights Movement from 1830 to 1970* (New York: Simon & Schuster, 2001).

As Betty Friedan noted: Betty Friedan, *The Feminine Mystique* (New York: Norton, 1963).

Young women who had watched their mothers: For background on second-wave feminism and the political backlash against it, see Marjorie Spruill's history of how the fight for women's rights was countered by the pro-family movement. She frames her telling around events related to the International Women's Year in 1977. Marjorie J. Spruill, *Divided We Stand: The Battle over Women's Rights and Family Values that Polarized American Politics* (New York: Bloomsbury, 2017).

102 *Women's lib*: Schlafly is quoted from Spruill, *Divided We Stand*, 71.

103 *Dobson's 1970 book*: James Dobson, *Dare to Discipline* (Carol Stream, IL: Tyndale House, 1970); now available in a 1992 revised edition: *The New Dare to Discipline*.

By learning to yield: James Dobson, *The Strong-Willed Child: Birth Through Adolescence* (Wheaton, IL: Tyndale House, 1978), 235. Dobson's role in the pro-life/pro-family movement is explained in Seth Dowland, *Family Values and the Rise of the Christian Right* (Philadelphia: University of Pennsylvania Press, 2015), and in Dan Gilgoff, *The Jesus Machine: How James Dobson, Focus on the Family, and Evangelical America Are Winning the Culture War* (New York: St. Martin's Press, 2007).

Through Focus on the Family: For a good overview of recent writing on purity culture's dangers and alternative ways of reading biblical wisdom about human sexuality and relationships, see Sandi Villarreal, "Their Generation Was Shamed by Purity Culture. Here's What They're Building in Its Place," *Sojourners*, March 7, 2019, https://sojo.net/interactive/their-generation-was-shamed-purity -culture-heres-what-theyre-building-its-place.

104   *Focus on the Family was operating*: See Gilgoff, *Jesus Machine*, 27, for financial information on the Focus on the Family organization.

105   *By 1987*: The Council on Biblical Manhood and Womanhood was formed by reactionary conservatives in the mid-1980s to articulate "biblical" definitions of gender in opposition to the gender equality promoted by the women's movement. You can read the full Danvers Statement at the CBMW website: https://cbmw.org/about/danvers -statement/. Formed in response to the misinformation of the pro-family movement, the Center for Biblical Equality (CBE) refutes the reading of Scripture presented in the Danvers Statement. You can learn more about the organization and its literature at www .cbeinternational.org.

108   *Phyllis Schlafly's last act*: For Schlafly's enthusiastic endorsement of Donald Trump, see Phyllis Schlafly with Ed Martin and Brett M. Decker, *The Conservative Case for Trump* (Washington, DC: Regnery, 2016), 12.

110   *Nineteenth-century feminist*: For the text of Sojourner Truth's classic "Ain't I a Woman?" speech, delivered at a Women's Convention in Akron, Ohio, in December 1851, see the *Modern History Sourcebook*, sponsored by Fordham University, https://sourcebooks.fordham .edu/mod/sojtruth-woman.asp.

113   *Women's March*: You can learn about the Women's March, which continues to organize a broad coalition of women for political engagement, at https://womensmarch.com.

#MeToo movement: Tarana Burke, the founder of #MeToo, has a powerful TED Talk, "Me Too Is a Movement, Not a Moment," *TED Women 2018*, which you can watch here: www.ted.com/talks/tarana_burke_me_too_is_a_movement_not_a_moment?language=en. One of the best writers of the #MeToo movement, Lacy M. Johnson, published a collection of essays, *The Reckonings* (New York: Scribner, 2018), that is a must-read for anyone who wants to understand the intersections between #MeToo and almost every other major political issue we face as a society.

114   *Tabitha Isner*: Raw video of Tabitha Isner's concession speech, delivered November 6, 2018, is available from WSFA News in Montgomery, Alabama: www.wsfa.com/video/2018/11/07/raw-video-tabitha-isner-speaks-after-losing-congressional-race-2/.

7 GROANING WITH ALL CREATION

116   *An hour east of Phoenix*: I first met Wendsler Nosie Sr. through the Poor People's Campaign in 2018. For background on the struggle for Oak Flats, see Emily Flitter, "Massive Copper Mine Tests Trump's Push to Slash Regulation," *Reuters*, July 13, 2017, www.reuters.com/article/us-usa-trump-regulation-mining/massive-copper-mine-tests-trumps-push-to-slash-regulation-idUSKBN19Y0D7. MSNBC made a short documentary about the fight to save Oak Flat: "Apache Spring: The Fight for Oak Flat," *MSNBC*, April 12, 2015, www.youtube.com/watch?v=W_mWO1wVmgc.

118   *While we have gathered*: For an account from Standing Rock by an anthropologist who recognized the spiritual implications of the organizing there, see Steve Pavey, "Awaken to the Prophetic Challenge of Standing Rock," *Fig Tree Revolution*, November 21, 2016, www.figtreerevolution.com/blog-1/2016/11/21/awaken-to-the-prophetic-challenge-of-standing-rock.

NASA's James Hansen: For a brief history of the public global warming and climate change debate, see Naomi Klein, *This Changes Everything: Capitalism vs. the Climate* (New York: Simon & Schuster, 2014). Details about Hansen's history are taken from page 73.

119   *In many pagan societies*: See also Thomas A. Sancton, "Planet of the Year: What On EARTH Are We Doing?," *Time*, January 2, 1989.

120   *Daniel K. Williams argues*: On history of fundamentalist attacks against modern science, see Daniel K. William, *God's Own Party: The Making of the Christian Right* (New York: Oxford University Press, 2010), 11-12.

121   *In her book* Kingdom Coming: Quotes and background on the Dover school board controversy are taken from Michelle Goldberg, *Kingdom Coming: The Rise of Christian Nationalism* (New York: Norton, 2006), 80-105. Learn more about the Discovery Institute's Center for Science and Culture at www.discovery.org/id/about/.

122   *Buckingham quickly took up*: Percival Davis and Dean H. Kenyon, *Of Pandas and People: The Central Question of Biological Origins*, 2nd ed. (Richardson, TX: Foundation for Thought and Ethics, 1993).

123   *As Bill McKibben chronicled*: See Bill McKibben, *Eaarth: Making a Life on a Tough New Planet* (New York: Times Books/Holt, 2010). McKibben's 350.org is a global network of grassroots organizations working to end our reliance on carbon and to transition to clean and renewable energy sources. Learn more at https://350.org.

124   *Intergovernmental Panel on Climate Change*: The IPCC is the international community's best effort to compile research from different government agencies around the world on climate change. You can access their most recent reports at www.ipcc.ch/reports/.

125   *Christian Reconstructionist R. J. Rushdoony*: Rousas John Rushdoony, *The Institutes of Biblical Law* (Vallecito, CA: Chalcedon, 1973). For more on the influence of R. J. Rushdoony and Christian dominionism, see Goldberg's *Kingdom Coming* and Chris Hedges, *American Fascists: The Christian Right and the War on America* (New York: Free Press, 2008), 12-15.

      Pat Robertson: If Jerry Falwell's Moral Majority served to offer Southern fundamentalists a political platform, Robertson's media empire and connections in the Pentecostal world served to expand that platform. For more on Pat Robertson's role as leader of the religious right after the decline of the Moral Majority, see Frances FitzGerald, *The Evangelicals: The Struggle to Shape America* (New York: Simon & Schuster, 2017), 365-409. Quote is from a recording of *The 700 Club*, May 1, 1986.

126   *Scott Pruitt*: For a good profile of Scott Pruitt, see Steve Eder and Hiroko Tabuchi, "Scott Pruitt Before the E.P.A.: Fancy Homes, a Shell Company and Friends with Money," *New York Times*, April 21, 2018. Pruitt quote is from David Brody, "Unraveling the 'Weaponization' of the EPA Is Top Priority for Scott Pruitt," *CBN News*, February 26, 2018, www1.cbn.com/cbnnews/us/2018/february/unraveling-the -weaponization-of-the-epa-is-top-priority-for-scott-pruitt.

128   *Young people of faith*: For examples of biblical scholarship and theo-
        logical reflection that highlight the importance of creation care, see
        Ellen F. Davis, *Scripture, Culture, and Agriculture: An Agrarian Reading
        of the Bible* (New York: Cambridge University Press, 2009); and
        Norman Wirzba, *From Nature to Creation: A Christian Vision for
        Understanding and Loving Our World* (Grand Rapids: Baker Academic,
        2015). This is, thankfully, a growing field of scholarship and practice.

132   *Interfaith Power and Light*: Learn more about Interfaith Power and
        Light at www.interfaithpowerandlight.org.

133   *Organizations like 350.org*: See https://350.org and McKibbin, *Eaarth*,
        as noted earlier. The Climate Reality Project is the organization that
        Al Gore started after he narrowly lost the Supreme Court battle for
        the certification of the 2000 US presidential election. He has spent
        the past two decades helping citizen-led groups around the world
        prepare to work democratically for a transition to clean, renewable,
        and sustainable energy systems. Learn more at www.climate
        realityproject.org

8 LIVE BY THE SWORD, DIE BY THE SWORD

134   *Basir Bita*: I interviewed Basir Bita, an organizer with the Afghan Peace
        Volunteers, in the fall of 2017. An edited recording of our conversation
        is available at "The War Economy Is Killing Our Nation's Spirit," *The
        Gathering* (podcast), *Repairers of the Breach*, November 5, 2017,
        https://www.breachrepairers.org/blog/war-economy. For background
        on American foreign policy in Afghanistan and the development
        of the war on terror there, see war correspondent Dexter Filkins,
        The Forever War (New York: Vintage, 2009).

135   *Americans should not expect*: Quote from President George W. Bush is
        from his address to a joint session of Congress and the nation, Sep-
        tember 20, 2001; text available at www.washingtonpost.com/wp-srv
        /nation/specials/attacked/transcripts/bushaddress_092001.html.

        With bipartisan support: Figures on current US military spending are
        from the National Defense Authorization Act for Fiscal Year 2019,
        H.R. 5515, 115th Cong. (2018). Signed into law just after the death
        of Senator John McCain of Arizona, the bill bears his name and was
        a rare bipartisan effort in Congress during the deeply divided 2018
        session. See details of the bill at https://docs.house.gov/billsthis
        week/20180723/CRPT-115hrpt863.pdf. For a brief history of the
        dramatic increase in US military spending since the late 1970s, see

Rachel Maddow, *Drift: The Unmooring of American Military Power* (New York: Broadway, 2013).

This is an assessment: Matthew Hoh resigned from the State Department on the eve of the eighth anniversary of the September 11, 2001, attacks. A copy of his resignation letter was made public via the *Washington Post*: www.washingtonpost.com/wp-srv/hp/ssi/wpc /ResignationLetter.pdf?sid=ST2009102603447. I interviewed Matthew Hoh for the same episode of "The Gathering" that included the recording of my conversation with Basir Bita: "War Economy," www.stitcher.com/podcast/repairers-of-the-breach /the-gathering-2/e/52187864.

137   *In her book* American Evangelicals: Anne C. Loveland, *American Evangelicals and the U.S. Military, 1942–1993* (Baton Rouge: Louisiana State University Press, 1996).

138   *Although the military*: The anonymous US Senator is quoted by journalist Jeff Sharlet, "Jesus Killed Mohammed: The Crusade for a Christian Military," *Harpers Magazine*, May 2009, 42, https://harpers .org/archive/2009/05/jesus-killed-mohammed/.

139   *Lt. Gen. William G. "Jerry" Boykin*: General Boykin story and quotes are taken from Richard T. Cooper, "General Casts War in Religious Terms," *Los Angeles Times*, October 16, 2003, www.latimes.com/archives /la-xpm-2003-oct-16-na-general16-story.html.

141   *There was no prophet*: Hadith of Prophet Muhammad, collected by the scholar Imam Bukhari. Chapter 60, "The Prophets," Hadith 29. Referenced at https://sunnah.com/bukhari/60/79.

       Their Southern slaveholding: For an introduction to the Second Amendment's connection to slaveholding states via James Madison, see Carl T. Bogus, "Was Slavery a Factor in the Second Amendment?," Opinion, *New York Times*, May 24, 2018, www.nytimes.com/2018/05/24 /opinion/second-amendment-slavery-james-madison.html.

142   *Today, there are nearly eight hundred*: To learn more about the eight hundred US military bases in seventy countries around the world, see David Vine, *Base Nation: How U.S. Military Bases Abroad Harm American and the World* (New York: Metropolitan Books/Holt, 2015).

143   *In the Christian tradition*: On the just-war tradition and its commitment to limiting violence, see John Howard Yoder, *When War Is Unjust: Being Honest in Just-War Thinking*, 2nd ed. (Maryknoll, NY: Orbis, 1996), 1-70.

144 *Case in point*: Story about Matt Shea was reported by Chad Sokol, "Washington State Lawmaker Matt Shea Defends Advocacy for 'Holy Army' as Spokane Sheriff Refers His Writings to FBI," *Seattle Times*, November 1, 2018, www.seattletimes.com/seattle-news/politics /state-lawmaker-matt-shea-defends-advocacy-for-holy-army-as -spokane-sheriff-refers-his-writings-to-fbi/.

145 *Long before Matthew Hoh's crisis*: Text of President Eisenhower's farewell address, delivered on television on January 17, 1961, is available at "Military-Industrial Complex Speech, Dwight D. Eisenhower, 1961," *The Avalon Project*, Yale Law School, http://avalon.law .yale.edu/20th_century/eisenhower001.asp.

148 *As a man living under British occupation*: For an introduction to Gandhi as a disciple of the nonviolent way of Jesus, see James W. Douglass, *Gandhi and the Unspeakable: His Final Experiment with Truth* (Maryknoll, NY: Orbis, 2012).

149 *Our choice today*: Quote from Martin Luther King Jr. is from "Pilgrimage to Nonviolence," *Christian Century*, April 13, 1960. Archived with the MLK Institute at https://kinginstitute.stanford.edu/king -papers/documents/pilgrimage-nonviolence.

     Veterans for Peace: You can learn more about Veterans for Peace at www.veteransforpeace.org.

     About Face: Founded in the mid 2000s as Iraq Veterans Against the War, About Face is organizing younger veterans to challenge the militarism of today's war on terror. Learn more at https://aboutface veterans.org.

150 *At the end of April in 1962*: Story about Kennedy's meeting with Quaker peace activists is based on the account of one of the participants, David Hartsough, whom I interviewed in the fall of 2018, and the research of James W. Douglass, who tells this story in his book *JFK and the Unspeakable: Why He Died and Why It Matters* (New York: Simon & Schuster, 2008), 321-24.

151 *Without losing sight*: For Kennedy's quote about Khrushchev, see Douglass, *JFK and the Unspeakable*, 384. The story of Kennedy's turn from Cold War militarism toward peace is the larger theme of Douglass's book, which is essential reading for anyone who wants to follow the way of Jesus in resistance to American militarism.

9 A REVOLUTION OF VALUES

154   *a coalition of God-fearing*: For quote from Jerry Falwell, see his *Listen,*
      America! (Garden City, NY: Doubleday, 1980), 255. For more on
      Falwell and the central role he played in the formation of the religious
      Right, see Frances FitzGerald, *Cities on a Hill: A Journey Through Con-*
      temporary American Cultures (New York: Simon & Schuster, 1986).

157   *The U.S. has become*: See a transcript of Donald Trump's announcement
      of his candidacy for president of the United States: "Trump: Mexico
      Not Sending Us Their Best; Criminals, Drug Dealers and Rapists Are
      Crossing Border," posted by Ian Schwartz, *RealClear Politics*, June 16,
      2015, www.realclearpolitics.com/video/2015/06/16/trump_mexico
      _not_sending_us_their_best_criminals_drug_dealers_and_rapists
      _are_crossing_border.html.

158   *In* The Faith of Donald J. Trump: David Brody and Scott Lamb, *The*
      Faith of Donald J. Trump: A Spiritual Biography (New York: Harper-
      Collins, 2018), 72.

159   *United Methodist minister Linus Parker*: Linus Parker is quoted in
      H. Shelton Smith, *In His Image, But . . . : Racism in Southern Religion,*
      1780–1910 (Durham, NC: Duke University Press, 1972), 253-54.
      Smith's analysis of the primary sources of Redemption-era Southern
      preachers is an important source for anyone who wants to under-
      stand the rhetoric of Trumpvangelicals in America today. For more
      historical context on the backlash against Reconstruction in the
      1870s, see Nicholas Lemann, *Redemption: The Last Battle of the Civil*
      War (New York: Farrar, Straus & Giroux, 2007).

161   *I don't want some meek*: Quote from Robert Jeffress can be found
      here: "Pastor Robert Jeffress Explains His Support for Donald
      Trump," *All Things Considered*, NPR, October 16, 2016, www.npr.org
      /2016/10/16/498171498/pastor-robert-jeffress-explains-his-support
      -for-trump.

162   *Recall Rev. Robert Dabney's plan*: See Thomas Cary Johnson, *The Life*
      and Letters of Robert Lewis Dabney (Richmond, VA: Presbyterian
      Committee of Publication, 1903), 129.

165   *Back home in North Carolina*: For a study of Rev. Dr. Barber's preaching
      in the public square, see Rev. Dr. William J. Barber II, with Rev. Dr. Liz
      Theoharis and Rev. Dr. Rick Lowery, *Revive Us Again: Vision and Action*
      in Moral Organizing (Boston: Beacon Press, 2018). Barber's compelling
      vision for moral-fusion organizing received wide attention after he

preached at the 2016 Democratic National Convention. You can watch a video of the sermon at "Rev. William Barber Full Remarks at Democratic National Convention," C-SPAN, July 28, 2016, www.youtube .com/watch?v=aw3PUghqlAA. My account of his sermon on Ezekiel is based on notes I made at "Moral Revival" services hosted by Repairers of the Breach from 2016 to 2018. You can watch video from many of these services at the Repairers of the Breach YouTube channel: www .youtube.com/channel/UC4q7uQBbo1ipfsflpgprJNw/featured.

ABOUT THE AUTHOR

Jonathan Wilson-Hartgrove is a celebrated spiritual writer and sought-after speaker. A native of North Carolina, he is a graduate of Eastern University and Duke Divinity School.

Jonathan lives with his family at the Rutba House, a Christian community and house of hospitality, in Durham, North Carolina, where he directs School for Conversion (schoolforconversion.org).

You can learn more about Jonathan's writing at jonathanwilsonhartgrove.com.
You can also follow him on Twitter: @wilsonhartgrove and Facebook: @jonathan.wilsonhartgrove.

ALSO BY
JONATHAN WILSON-HARTGROVE

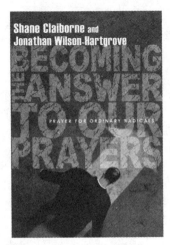

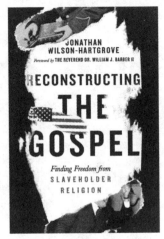

*Becoming the Answer
to Our Prayers*
978-0-8308-3622-2

Reconstructing the Gospel
978-0-8308-4534-7